# THIRTY SEVENTH ILLINOIS
## CIVIL WAR STORIES
## FROM THE BACK OF THE BATTLE

# THIRTY SEVENTH ILLINOIS
## CIVIL WAR STORIES
## FROM THE BACK OF THE BATTLE

### J.H. WILDER

ENGLISH GARDEN PRESS
Teaneck, New Jersey

The Thirty Seventh Illinois at Prairie Grove

Copyright © 1990 and 2012 by Jeremy H. Wilder

Thirty Seventh Illinois – Civil War Stories from the Back of the Battle

Copyright © 2016 and 2017 by J.H. Wilder

All rights reserved. This book or any portion thereof may not be reproduced or used in any manner whatsoever without the expressed written permission of the publisher except for the use of brief quotations in a book review or scholarly journal.

Published by English Garden Press, Teaneck, New Jersey

First Printing: 2016
Second Printing: 2017

ISBN: 978-0-578-18974-1

Library of Congress Control Number 2016934304

J.H. Wilder

Front Cover Photo: L-R – William P Black, Julius White, Elijah A. Clark, Place Unknown, Courtesy Evanston History Center.

Back Cover Photo: John Charles Black, GAR National Commander, National Encampment, Boston, 1904, Courtesy Chicago Public Library Special Collections.

# Dedication

For My Family
And
For My Friends

That's Really All There Is

# Contents

Acknowledgements ..................................................................
Introduction ................................................................... i
1. The First Month ........................................................... 1
2. The Patriarchs ............................................................ 9
3. The Zoo-Zoo's ............................................................ 16
4. Thirty Days at Springfield ............................................... 28
5. The Water March to St. Louis ............................................. 33
6. Boonville ................................................................ 40
7. Death by Mud ............................................................. 48
8. Pea Ridge ................................................................ 54
9. Cassville ................................................................ 60
10. The Election ............................................................ 69
11. Punishment .............................................................. 77
12. The Mutiny .............................................................. 81
13. The Barnes Exit ......................................................... 91
14. The Reluctant Brigadier ................................................. 95
15. Mindless Marching ...................................................... 106
16. Prairie Grove .......................................................... 112
17. The F Word ............................................................. 136
18. The Court of Bad Language .............................................. 146
19. Missouri in the Rearview ............................................... 152
20. Vicksburg .............................................................. 158
21. Microbe War ............................................................ 162
22. Texas .................................................................. 168

| 23. | Reenlistment | 176 |
| --- | --- | --- |
| 24. | The Reenlisted 37th | 184 |
| 25. | The Discharged 37th | 193 |
| 26. | DeVall's Bluff | 205 |
| 27. | Fort Blakeley | 209 |
| 28. | The Last Days of Black and Frisbie | 213 |
| 29. | The Final Pay Call | 219 |
| 30. | The Haymarket Bombing | 228 |
| Epilog | | 235 |
| Appendix 1 – Notes from the War Years | | 239 |
| Appendix 2 – Descriptive Roll | | 342 |
| Notes | | 509 |
| Bibliography | | 525 |
| Index | | 531 |

# Acknowledgements

The author is indebted to many people for indispensable help, cooperation, and good will along the way in the research process; to Michael Winey, David Keough and Richard Sommers of the United States Army Military History Institute; to Michael Musick of the National Archives; to Janice McNeil and Richard Kaplan of the Chicago Historical Society; to Ruth Geffen of the Mercer County Historical Society; to Cynthia Feuner and Roger Bridges of the Illinois State Historical Library; to Judy Belan of the Augustana College Library; to Robert Cox of the Clements Library, University of Michigan; to Pauline Wandschneider of the Downer's Grove Historical Museum; to Nancy Sandleback and Edward Parker of the State Historical Society of Missouri; to Nora G. Frisbie of the Frisbie Family Association; to Albert Scheller of the Vicksburg National Military Park; to Claire Maxwell of the Eugene C. Barker Texas History Center; to Robert Serio of the Prairie Grove State Park; to Dr. Harvey Karlen of Chicago; to Mike Mullins of Wayne, New Jersey; to Amy C. Vedra of the Indiana Historical Society; to Lori Osborne of the Evanston History Center; to Cheryl Schnirring and Roberta Fairburn at the Abraham Lincoln Presidential Library (Springfield, Ill.); to the staff at the Williams Research Center in New Orleans; to Morag Walsh at the Chicago Public Library; and to Robert C. Nash, Sr. of Sioux City, Iowa. And special thanks to the staff at the Newberry Library in Chicago for helping me sift through several cartons of uncatalogued papers from the Lloyd Lewis estate looking for a copy of "The Camp Register."

Lastly I acknowledge the general interest and support of some friends who aided and abetted this quest for historical minutiae; thanks to Bill and Jean Janssen for bed and board in Washington; to Jim Doherty for the same in Chicago; to Bill Janssen for editorial and technical assistance; and to Miki Contrera for her help in preparing the manuscript.

# INTRODUCTION

## Introduction

Sources for this history include standard reference and published narrative, and the written word of the soldiers set down in close proximity to the subject events. The published material consists of the Official Records of the Union and Confederate Armies, papers of the Military Order of Loyal Legion of the United States, published diaries, regimental histories, capsule biographies, local histories, and contemporary newspapers. Unpublished sources include multiple manuscript collections – diaries, journals, and correspondence held in both public archives and in private hands - as well as both unit and individual service records at both federal and state levels.

Of a total 1724 days the regiment was under arms, not more than 50 days (about 3%) were spent under hostile fire in skirmish or battle. While much more than 3% of this work is concerned with live fire days, grand strategy, small unit tactics, battle casualties, etc., the focus here is very much on the other 97% of the time the men spent in camp, on the march, on leave, in hospital, in confinement, or whatever other activity happened to present itself.

Documenting facts sometimes ranged from impossible, in the case of some personal experience, to simply picking out the best of many true versions of the same event. There was no reference in the records of the 2d Illinois volunteers in the Mexican War that Myron Barnes served in that unit as he said he did, or that Edward Anderson was "Porte Crayon," the pseudonym for the author of Virginia Illustrated, a popular 1850's book. He told Will Black that he was, Willy duly reported the tidbit home, and his mother and sisters couldn't wait to meet "Porte Crayon." As a consequence, the Reverend Anderson avoided going to Danville in 1862 probably to avoid admitting he told a fairy story to an impressionable teenager.

Other traps of unverifiable data lurked in post-war recollections, which were subject to some convenient loss of memory, "old soldiering" exaggerations, or just plain fabrication. The account written close to the event was much more reliable in getting a picture of the writer's feeling and the true facts of what occurred. In one instance,

# THIRTY SEVENTH ILLINOIS

Myron Barnes gave a post-war interview to an editor of a biographical sketchbook of Knox County, Illinois, creating a stirring military career for himself in 1863-64, including seeing action at the Battle of Champion Hill, when he had actually been at home as a dismissed colonel running his Rock Island Union newspaper.

In a 1905 speech, Eugene Payne told a story about meeting Confederate General John Marmaduke in front of the Union lines at Prairie Grove, contradicted by at least one colorful version of the same event.

Beyond being more factually credible, the letters and narratives written close to the event have an undiluted power of expression and a vibrancy that the post-war narratives do not have, this due in part to the total absence of any military censorship. The Civil War was the last of our wars in which soldiers' letters were not censored, and reports of unit assignment, location, troop strength and strategic plans riddled the letters home. Some of these were printed, verbatim, in the newspapers, making intelligence gathering easy work.

A devilish failing in the maze of fact and fancy was multiple spellings of the names of the men of the regiment. The European immigrants were the most difficult. The majority were illiterate, and the army clerks would write the best phonetic spelling they could. The mustering clerk may have heard the name differently than the pay clerk, the quartermaster's clerk, or the adjutant's clerk. When the soldier was illiterate, which about a third of the $37^{th}$ was, "his X mark," would appear on the enlistment papers or pay rolls over the clerk's best effort at the spelling of the name. An example of this problem is Henry Heitharands, who was literate, but whose records are spread into twelve separate file jackets in the National Archives, each bearing a different spelling of his name.

Some notes on content are needed here to interpret some of what follows. There will be seemingly unending references to regimental politics. Office seeking was the persistent pastime of the officers and resulted from the Civil War era practice of electing officers by popular vote rather than commissioning based on merit. Many of the candidates for election came from political backgrounds, and had been in politics or intended to go into politics after the war. Some, such as Henry Frisbie and Julius White, learned the rules of the game

# INTRODUCTION

in Chicago. The object of the game was to win, without any particular moral or ethical reservation about how.

The regimental officers who vied with each other for promotion used every dodge, connivance, pressure play, or buy-and-sell tactic at their command to win the office, and nothing that was done was very much different than what would be done in a parallel civilian campaign. The candidates knew the tricks of civilian politics and employed them in army politics.

There will be times when the reader will need to refer to the list below to keep the players straight as to the regimental field grade promotions. This roster lists each officer to hold a field grade commission with date of rank, i.e., who got what and when.

| Name and Rank | Date of Rank |
|---|---|
| *Colonels* | |
| Julius White | July 26, 1861 |
| Myron S. Barnes | June 9, 1862 |
| John C. Black | November 20, 1862 |
| Ransom Kennicott | August 28, 1865 |
| Judson J. Huntley | May 15, 1866 |
| *Lieutenant Colonels* | |
| Myron S. Barnes | August 1, 1861 |
| John C. Black | June 9, 1862 |
| Henry N. Frisbie | November 20, 1862 |
| Eugene B. Payne | October 19, 1863 |
| Ransom Kennicott | September 9, 1864 |
| Judson J. Huntley | October 18, 1865 |
| *Majors* | |
| John C. Black | August 15, 1861 |
| Henry N. Frisbie | June 9, 1862 |
| Eugene B. Payne | November 20, 1862 |
| Ransom Kennicott | October 19, 1863 |
| Herman Wolford | September 9, 1864 |
| Judson S. Huntley | October 4, 1865 |
| John Moran | May 15, 1866 |

# THIRTY SEVENTH ILLINOIS

A note on award inflation. Civil War Brevet General appointments were largely based on politics and not merit resulting in over 1400 war-related awards. Charles Black, Henry Frisbie, Eugene Payne, Julius White (to Brevet Major General), and over 500 others (some already discharged) were appointed Brevet General Officers with the same date of rank (March 13, 1865), a date less than 30 days before war's end in April.

Likewise, Congressional Medals of Honor. Over 1500 were awarded during the war, some later rescinded. In contrast, 472 medals were awarded for acts of bravery in World War II, where many million more men served.

Some parts of what follows are digressions outside the regiment and are here to flesh out either characters or events bearing on the history of the men of the regiment. Elmer Ellsworth created the Zouave system whose influence was shared by the Blacks, by Eugene Payne, and by Ransom Kennicott and Frederick Abbey. General Julius White had a history with the eastern army shared with Captain Henry Curtis and Private Samuel Iches, all members of the 37$^{th}$, particularly and most notably at Harper's Ferry in 1862. The narrative of Will Black's role in the Haymarket bombing affair amplifies the enigmatic character of this very complex, strong willed man. Today, references to Will Black can be found most commonly in Communist Party polemics.

The story of Myron Barnes' editorial set-to with Joseph Danforth in Rock Island, Henry Frisbie's social experiment with the 92d United States Colored Troops, and Josephine Fithian's observations on the Danville, Illinois draft troubles fill out the substance and flavor of the times.

In the 1980's the author requested the microfilming of the Black-Fithian archive in Springfield, Illinois, and the regimental order books in Washington. Since then, there has been an internet information deluge about the 37$^{th}$ Illinois including articles, diaries and journals, reminiscences, pictures and correspondences. Anyone with a further interest in the unit or its members should use their favorite search engine and prepare to be amazed at the results.

Principal research and writing for this work was completed over 25 years ago. An earlier version of Chapter 16 (Prairie Grove) was

INTRODUCTION

published by the Arkansas Historical Society in 1990, reprinted in 2012, and appears here with a few revisions.

This Second Printing contains minor editorial changes and corrects typographical errors, all else unchanged.

## 1. The First Month

In the early morning hours of August 20, 1861, a middle-aged, balding man waited at the depot in Chicago for the night train from Galva, Illinois. A band hired for the occasion stood by. At about 7 A.M., the train arrived. On board was the Lafayette Rifles, an infantry company, Charles V. Dickinson, Commanding. The Lafayette Rifles had answered the call of their greeter and host, 44 year old Julius A. White, soon to be Colonel White, United States Army. White was forming a regiment to go to war, fight the secesh, save the union and free the slaves.

White was originally from Cazenovia, New York. He had come west in 1836 at age 20 and worked at real estate, insurance, and politics in Milwaukee, Waukesha, and Madison, Wisconsin. He represented the Northwestern Fire and Marine Insurance Company in 1850, was President of the Board of Fire Underwriters in Chicago in 1854 and fiscal agent for the Travelers Insurance Company for several years. By the time of the Chicago Fire in 1871, White was assuming the mantle of "the founder of South Evanston," where he was busy subdividing about eighty acres near the Chicago and Northwestern Railway. The Chicago Fire, the building of South Evanston, settling the war between Argentina and Paraguay as U.S. Consul in 1870, all were in the future for White. In 1861, the Civil War lay straight ahead.[1]

In 1861, he held the position of Collector of Customs at Chicago. It was the patronage plum of the west, and was one of the fat jobs that Abraham Lincoln controlled after the 1860 election. White was given the post in 1861, a position of "civic place, power, and large revenue."[2]

On Sunday, July 21, 1861, having had the Customs job about four months, White stood up on his pew in church in Evanston, Illinois and made a speech to the congregation calling on all to stand and declare themselves. With the size of Evanston, it would have taken every man, woman, and child who could walk to fill a regiment. Evanston ultimately claimed four generals and seventy-eight other officers out of a population of 1200, none to the 37th Illinois except Julius White.³

White's power and status came from John C. Fremont and Abraham Lincoln. Fremont, the Pathfinder, was the first Republican Presidential candidate in 1856, and Lincoln its first successful candidate in 1860. White delivered votes for both.

Two days after the patriotic speech in church, White had gotten his authorization from the War Department in Washington to raise a volunteer regiment, and opened a recruiting office in Chicago. The man who gathered the regiment, an amalgam of European and Mexican war veterans, ambitious young attorneys, judges' sons, restless farm boys and uprooted foreign immigrants, had origins outside Illinois.

White's desire for status and a war record which would improve his chances to be a U.S. Senator caused him to resign the Customs job and brought him to the Chicago and Northwestern Railway Depot on that August morning to greet his new charges from Stark County, Illinois. Together with another newly arrived company, the Stark County recruits marched from the Illinois Central Depot to the Sherman House Hotel in Chicago to the cadences of a brass band. After breakfast, both companies marched up North Clark Street to the outskirts of the city, to begin their army career.⁴

The gathering place was Camp Webb, a reception station and, "Camp of Instruction," or boot camp, set up in Wright's Grove, Chicago, an area up North Clark Street at the end of the North Chicago Railway. It had a brief life as Camp White and was quickly renamed Camp Webb after Captain Webb, the regular army mustering officer who came to administer the camp and swear in the men.

One corner of the camp was the assigned space of White's regiment, called the Fremont Rifles, subsequently numbered 37th of over 125 regiments sent from Illinois to the war. The first dinner that evening in Wright's Grove was, "3 potatoes, some bread, meat, and a large tin cup full of grease that they called soup." David Ash, a sergeant in the Lafayette Rifles, confided to his future wife that, "you may bet highly that I did not use much soup," but that his friend, Private George Dudley, "wishes the war would last on account of the grub."⁵

# THE FIRST MONTH

By August 22, four out of a total of ten companies were at Wright's Grove; the Rock Island and Stark County Companies, the Manierre Rifles from Michigan (Capt. John Laimbeer, Commanding), and the Turner Rifles (Capt. Twomey, Commanding, soon to be replaced by Henry Frisbie). Also in the camp was Ransom Kennicott, negotiating with Julius White to raise what would be the Audubon Rifles. Kennicott's and five other companies would arrive in camp over the next ten days.

The Army Table of Organization in 1861 required an infantry regiment to be comprised of ten companies of between 83 and 101 men each. Julius White was able to accept whomever he wanted into the regiment, and he had asked Republican cronies and the sons of his political allies from all over Northern Illinois to raise companies and join him. To fill out the regiment, John Frick came with a company from Rock Island, Eugene Payne and Erwin Messer brought companies from Lake County, Phineas Rust came from Mendota, and Charles Black came in from Danville. These companies, together with Ransom Kennicott's Audubon Rifles, filled out the regiment.

White picked up his headquarters staff in about the same way; a West Point graduate as Adjutant, a preacher and sometime journalist as Chaplain, a Chicago attorney as Quartermaster, and a transplanted Massachusetts physician as Surgeon.

The sum of this accumulation, The Fremont Rifle Regiment, was an intricately sewn patchwork of political alliance. Almost all the officers had influential family or had a company of soldiers to offer someone like Julius White, who couldn't be a colonel unless he had a regiment to be a colonel of. In the beginning, the system was not one of random placement of enlistees into companies. The companies were largely groups of townsmen, friends of the same generation enlisting to serve together. There were cousins and brothers, fathers and sons, and nephews and uncles in these companies. Schoolmates, neighbors and fast friends were complemented by the illiterate immigrants and transient farm laborers and miners who found $13 a month and three squares a day to be the best they could do in 1861.

Some of the common threads through this crossweave of kinship and friendship were Abraham Lincoln, Elmer Ellsworth the Zouave, six greybeard pioneers who built log cabins in the 1830's and 1840's in Illinois, and the prevailing anti-rebellion, anti-slave, anti-south sentiment that sent the men off in a flurry of flags and flowers.

In the heady, torchlight, flag-waving summer of 1861, $13 a month recruits were plentiful. Who would rather stay on Dad's farm in Stark County and shovel cow manure when he could be paid to go on an adventure with friends complete with musket and uniform. For boys who had never worn shoes or drawers before, there was no hard decision to make. Whole neighborhoods of teenagers, friends from childhood on, signed up with Myron Barnes, or Eugene Payne, or Ransom Kennicott and Fred Abbey, or with Charles and Will Black.

Kennicott and Abbey, who recruited the Audubon Rifles, played on their particular Zouave allure and their days spent with the martyred Elmer Ellsworth. They were bona fide Zouave Cadets. Their popularity was widespread, their image grand and dreamy, with braid, plume, and military flash, simply the best recruiting aid available.

All of the companies of the 37th were volunteer. One throwback to the volunteer militia was the designation of officers by election. The first election in the 37th was held on August 31, 1861. The enlisted men voted for the company grade officers (Captain and First and Second Lieutenant), and the officers then chose the field grades (Colonel, Lieutenant Colonel, and Major). In White's regiment, there were no surprises in the top offices. Julius White was elected Colonel and Myron Barnes Lieutenant Colonel on the first ballot. Three ballots were taken for Major. Phineas Rust of the Mendota Company, E.G. Hooke and William Innis, ex-Ellsworth Zouave and ex-Captain of Eugene Payne's Waukegan Zouaves (Company H, Chicago Zouaves), opposed John Charles Black, Captain of the Danville Company. Black won the Majority, and brother William became Captain of the Danville Company. John Jordan took Barnes' place as Captain of the Rock Island Company.[6]

Julius White picked up a chaplain to fill out the regimental staff in a suburb south of Chicago. Edward Anderson, Minister of the Calvary Baptist Church and wartime serial executioner, bid his parishioners farewell, packed his Bible and gun, and went to Wright's Grove.[7]

By September, recruiting was becoming more difficult. The patriotic zealots, the loose-end farm boys and other willing availables

# THE FIRST MONTH

had mostly all been taken by local leaders looking to be officers. Anyone who was able to collect fifty or sixty men was almost always elected Captain.

The Vermilion County Company had arrived at Wright's Grove the most understrength in the regiment. The Black brothers and stepbrother Henry Fithian had come to camp with a hurriedly raised company under the minimum strength for acceptance. Back home in Danville, townsman William Bandy and the Black brothers' stepfather, William Fithian, were having difficulties recruiting. They were competing with two dozen other neighborhood recruiters, some of whom were going house to house looking for privates. The company was filled in the end by borrowing men from other companies that were beyond the maximum.[8]

By mid-September, White had collected nearly 1000 men in the Chicago camp, housed in tents, fifteen to a tent. Bedding consisted of hay and army blankets, the food basic army meat and potatoes. The daily schedule, which was to vary little during the war, was set:[9]

| | |
|---|---|
| Reveille | 5:00 AM |
| Drill | 5:30 |
| Breakfast | 7:00 |
| Sick | 7:30 |
| 1st Sergeant Call | 8:00 |
| Guard Mount | 9:00 |
| Camp & Squad Drill | 10:00 |
| Dinner | 12:00 |
| Drill | 2:00 |
| Dress Parade | 5:00 |
| Supper and Retreat | 6:00 |
| Tattoo | 9:00 |
| Taps | 9:30 |

Liquor was not allowed on the camp grounds, and to get a snootful, the men either had to get a pass or sneak out of camp by running past the camp guard. Drinking and other bad acting was held in check by the certain knowledge that everything would be reported back to the hometown by those that could write about who was in trouble, or

## THIRTY SEVENTH ILLINOIS

homesick, or drunk, or cowardly. This was an effective restraint on personal conduct. Most men would think twice before running away, or crying, or breaking from the strain or hardship of marching or camp life. Their friends and family would know about it by the next mail, and a reputation compromised would be hard to put right.

Army life was new for most men. There were new rules and less freedom; a life of work, pressure, conflict, discomfort and disease, and regimes of unfairness and injustice.

The ten companies of the Fremont Rifles were tentatively lettered A to K (without J, which was too much like I), reflecting Julius White's perception of what would answer the political situation. The arrangement was made permanent later in the month in St. Louis. The flank, or end, positions were the places of honor. On the march, these were the front and rear. In battle line, right and left. Myron Barnes had been elected Lieutenant Colonel, and his company from Rock Island was given the most honorable position (front and right). Charles Black had been elected Major, and his company from Danville was given the other flank. Charles Dickinson was given the next place in line, Company B. Then came Eugene Payne (C), John Laimbeer (D), Phineas Rust (E), Erwin Messer (F), Henry Frisbie (G), John Frick (H), and Ransom Kennicott (I).

White had filled out his headquarters staff and began collecting an eighteen piece band consisting of two principal musicians and sixteen others. The musicians practiced, played at regimental functions, and served as stretcher bearers on battle days. Pay was $12 per month for musicians, $1 less than what a private was paid. Principal musicians did much better at up to $45 per month.

Later in the war, there were also designated "artificiers," who were carpenters, joiners, carriage-makers, blacksmiths, saddlers, and harness-makers. The artificiers were paid extra as were hospital stewards, teamsters, and the wagon master.

Other preparations were carried out in the days to follow. Each man's equipment was numbered and lettered to identify his individual number, the letter of this company, and the number of the regiment.[10] Fairly constant during the war was the daily schedule, varied only as to local circumstance, season of daylight, and whether in field or garrison. Whatever the time, reveille was always too early and work call too frequent.

The fun parts were the uniforms, the pomp of the parades and ceremonies, and the attention of cheering crowds. The daily 5 PM dress parade at Wright's Grove was usually observed by local citizens. This daily opportunity to strut and show off ended after twenty-nine days in the Chicago camp. White got a marching date from the War Department of September 15. After a slight delay and an equipment issue, the 37th broke camp on the 19th and headed for St. Louis.

Two days before the departure, White was given "a splendid black charger" and "a fine sword and sash" at a ceremony organized by his Chicago friends. George Bates presented the horse, accompanied by speeches from Bishop Simpson, U.S. Senator Lyman Trumbull, and Representative Isaac Arnold.[11]

The Wright's Grove Camp of Instruction had taught discipline, etiquette such as saluting, and basic drill. The men left knowing enough to march back down North Clark Street in rank and file formation, keeping an even front, and turning on command. They had also begun their informal training in the survival process of army life; how to get out of a work detail, how to sneak past the guard, how to politic for promotion (for more money and less work), how lazy officers really are, and how to get out of picket duty and guard duty and other nasty little jobs.

About 180 of the 979 men who marched out that day would stay with the regiment for its full term until 1866. The other 799 would leave for various reasons, the most common of which was expiration of term of service after three years. The very first attrition occurred before the muster at Camp Webb, when two boys were snatched back by their fathers. On September 13, John Mason of Payne's company, age 17, was "discharged on demand of father." On the 18th, Isaac Moore of Frisbie's company was "claimed as a minor by his father and disappeared."[12] Moore had given his age as 24. 271 of the original enlisted complement were age 19 or under, 177 were 18 or under, and 17 were ages 14 to 17. Several of these had undoubtedly lied about their age. On the other end of the scale, 71 men were age 36 or over. The oldest were musicians Joseph Edwards, age 60, and Solomon Smith, age 51. Private Stillman Stubbs (Co. D) was 53 and

# THIRTY SEVENTH ILLINOIS

Private Edwin Mears (Co. D) was age 50. Edwards lasted three months and was discharged in December, 1861. Mears died of jaundice in August, 1863, Smith lasted until muster-out of the three year men in August, 1864, and Stubbs went out on disability in June, 1864.[13]

Various other destinies took the others, including promotion, unit transfer, disability or death, and expiration of term of enlistment. A few more were recruited during the war, and in 1865, remnants of three other Illinois regiments were consolidated into the 37th.

The original 979 men that stepped onto North Clark Street that day in September, 1861 served in a very good regiment and by and large did responsible service for up to five years until the 1866 muster-out.

## 2. The Patriarchs

During the 1830's an adventurous crowd of young men came to the lakefront and the flatlands of Illinois. A handful of these adventurers were to have more to do with rank, promotion, and leadership in the 37$^{th}$ over the course of the war than any individual's merit or anyone in the army command structure. Rank and promotion came to their sons and relatives in the 37$^{th}$ with all the political help these patriarchs could lay on to advance their interest. Hiram Kennicott had two sons in the 37$^{th}$, Ransom and George. William Fithian had a son, Henry, and two stepsons, William and John Charles Black, and Tom Payne sent two sons, Eugene and Frederick. Israel Blodgett, who died in 1861, had two sons in the regiment, Wells and Edward. The power broker for Wells and Ed was older brother Henry. Elijah Haines pushed the interests of Tom Payne's son Eugene, who was married to his wife's cousin.

Israel Blodgett was a blacksmith, Dr. Fithian a printer, E.M. Haines a tailor and a teacher, Hiram Kennicott kept a sawmill, and Tom Payne was a farmer when they first arrived among the indians and settled near Lake Michigan. They all worked their way into varying positions of wealth and influence. They had the ability to broker power in Illinois, in the army, and with President Lincoln and wartime Illinois Governor Richard Yates. They were the log cabin crowd in 1830's Illinois. They got there first and got a running jump on the late arrivers in the forests around Chicago.

Hiram Kennicott settled in Illinois by the Aux Plains River near Indian Creek in 1834, and put up a sawmill and kept store. In 1835, he was installed as Justice of the Peace, in part because he had read law with Millard Fillmore in Aurora, New York before moving west.

Kennicott was a squatter on land to which he had no title. The government owned the land, and in 1834 claims were made by Kennicott and others by moving in and building in the absence of civil authority. When he had finished his house, he had the first one with evenly sawed wood in the Henry County neighborhood, proving the blessings of owning a sawmill in the bush.

# THIRTY SEVENTH ILLINOIS

Justice of the Peace Kennicott heard his first case in the fall of 1837, when one Michael Dulanty assaulted one of Kennicott's fellow Justices of the Peace. Kennicott, lecturing Dulanty that it was "a high offense to assault a person representing the dignity of a magistrate of the law," fined Dulanty $5. Dulanty later ran a tavern in Lake County and became a county commissioner, suffering little from appearing as the first misdemeanor on Uncle Hiram's blotter.[1]

The Blacks, Willy and Charles, came to Chicago to join the 37th with the Vermilion Zouaves (Co. K), the company from Danville that Charlie had raised with an assist from his step-father William Fithian and townsman William Bandy. Fithian, a 61 year old physician, had married, as one of his four wives, Charles' and Willy's mother Josephine, after the death of their Presbyterian minister father. Fithian was to be Charlie's anchor, benefactor, healer, advisor, and political protector during the war.

Dr. Fithian was an original western pioneer. He was claimed to be the first white child born in the log-cabin village of Cincinnati in 1799. His father had come from Elizabeth, New Jersey and set up shop in Cincinnati, then Springfield and Urbana, Ohio, where he ran a tavern. The family eventually settled in Danville.

Dr. Fithian's original trade was printing, followed by medicine practiced in Urbana and Mechanicsburg, Ohio, where he doubled as a judge. Fithian came to Danville in 1830. That year, the population of Chicago was fifty souls. Danville, population two hundred, was then an indian trading center. In later years, Fithian's medical practice ranged over Southern Illinois and Indiana, allowing him to form political and commercial alliances. He was in the Home Guard in the War of 1812 at a young age, was a soldier with the Vermilion County Militia in the Black Hawk wars in Illinois, served as a State Senator and State Representative, and was appointed Provost Marshal of the 7th District of Illinois during the Civil War. This appointment was made by old friend Abraham Lincoln. Lincoln had stayed at the Fithian house in Danville while campaigning in 1860, giving a speech from the balcony of the house. Lincoln took a shine to Charles and Willy Black on the visit.[2] Two years later, upon hearing the false report of Charles' and Willy's deaths at Prairie Grove, Lincoln wept in the presence of Danville native Ward Lamon.[3]

# THE PATRIARCHS

Dr. Fithian, "Pa," was a hard man and tight with a buck. On one occasion, he required payment for pistols he purchased for Charles and Willy, making it clear that he did nothing for nothing. In the midst of Charles Black's upset in the summer of 1862, Charles asked for his step-father's influence in Springfield, and in the same sentence offered to pay his expenses to get there, as if a self-financed trip was unlikely.[4] Charles' mother cautioned him in 1862 in no uncertain terms about her husband, saying, "To be plain, Doctor Fithian is not a good advisor in morals, however kindly he may intend. His life is an exemplification of this. He thinks nearly every man is a 'dog....' His advice in business is good, but [not] in morals."[5]

While Hiram Kennicott was cutting trees in Aux Plains and William Fithian was delivering babies in Danville, Elijah Haines, Henry Blodgett, and Tom Payne were earning their pioneer credentials in DuPage, Chicago, and Fremont Centre.

Thomas H. Payne, Eugene's father, who walked most of the way to Illinois in 1836 from Seneca Falls, New York, settled as a squatter before the government land survey, and built a log cabin in what is now Fremont Centre, Illinois. He kept the peace with his indian neighbors, put in a crop in 1837, and then went back to New York for his wife and children. Tom Payne was a county commissioner, farmer, and political ally of U.S. Representative Elihu Washburne, an alliance Eugene Payne traded on in his efforts to gain promotion during the war.[6]

Elijah Haines and Henry Blodgett were the Illinois State Representatives from Lake County at the outbreak of the war. Elijah Haines, or "E.M.," or "Hon. Coz.," as Eugene Payne continually referred to him, was born in 1822 in Onieda County, New York. He was age five when his father died, and his mother moved the family to Michigan. E.M. had a progenitor, John Haines, puritan Governor of Massachusetts and Connecticut in the 1600's. He came to Illinois in 1835 at age twelve with his brother, Long John Haines, who was sixteen at the time. E.M. reminisced about this passage to Illinois on his deathbed in 1889 in Waukegan:

"... open the east window there and let me
see the sun rise up from the lake... Last night
when I heard the robins sing I remembered
when I was a boy 12 years old. My brother
and I walked through the woods from Detroit
to Chicago. That was fifty-four years ago
this spring. One morning up in the Michigan
woods, the robins woke me up, and every
morning all the way on that long tramp to
Chicago the robins would wake me up with
their singing."[7]

After a stint as a tailor in Water Street in Chicago in 1839, then a city of about six thousand, Haines stayed briefly on a farm near Lockport, and then moved with his mother and stepfather to Lake County, Illinois to a claim in what is now Hainesville. At a self-educated age nineteen, Haines became the first schoolmaster in Waukegan in 1841. He was, serially, farmer, land surveyor, School Commissioner, Postmaster, founder of a newspaper (The Lake County Patriot), founder of Hainesville, Illinois (in 1846), attorney (in 1851), author of several books on law and the legal profession, and author of a lifetime project, "The American Indian," an 800-page work that compiled Haines' enormous knowledge gained in several summers spent among the indians, and a lifetime of study and facility with most of the local indian dialects. He was many times elected State Representative (along with Henry Blodgett), and was twice Speaker of the Illinois House.[8]

Haines was a self-made and a crafty master of many trades. No less his brother Long John, who was City Councilman, Water Commissioner, and Mayor of Chicago for two terms during the Civil War.

Elijah Haines married Adelia Wright's cousin Melinda Griswold in 1845. Adelia Wright became Mrs. Eugene Payne in January 1862. Payne was a young lawyer newly graduated from Northwestern University when he met Adelia at the Haines' house in Waukegan. Haines had developed a deep-seated infatuation with his wife's cousin. He was admiring, possessive, and uncomfortably protective. He tried to control Delia's destiny, treating each of her suitors as his rival, and suggesting at every turn that he had the right to approve or disapprove of any of her romantic interests. Payne and his wife used him repeatedly to advance Payne's interests in and out of the army. They regularly called him bad names while depending on him for political protection. Haines' reaction to Eugene Payne's attraction to Delia was sharp and desperate; "To say that I am attached to you would not be a fit expression of my feelings toward you... When I saw you both rushing on without restraint, intoxicating yourselves seemingly beyond control, utterly disregarding my friendly suggestions, I could not but feel hurt..."[9]

Delia's reaction to this anguish and sadness was as warm as a granite slab in a graveyard. Reporting the wrenching pleas to Eugene Payne, she commented, "Let Mr. Haines frown – he is less than nothing to me..."

Payne was less charitable; "I have felt from the first that he wished to break up our union... But no ruthless hand like his shall ever disturb it... His narrow contracted mind imagines perhaps that the cousin of the right Hon. Mr. Haines should...marry some wealthy man of high position! I told you I would seek an early opportunity to force him to an explanation... I will not press it till I return to Waukegan for fear he may throw me out of employment here [in Springfield]... Mr. H. once said that there is no such thing as principle in the world... Is it a reflection of his own narrow and contorted mind?... I detest him..."[10]

This was an odd alliance between Payne and Haines, held together by Delia Wright. Haines did as he was asked throughout the war to further Payne's interests, and promoted his welfare at every opportunity. Axiomatically, what happened to Eugene Payne affected what happened to Company C. After his promotion to Major in 1863, he was able to look after the company in limited fashion, and his promotion made room for Waukeganites Judd Huntley to be Captain and Chauncy Morse First Lieutenant.

Elijah Haines wasn't the only old bear in the Lake County woods. His colleague in the Illinois Legislature, Henry Blodgett, was not as old but just as wise. Henry peddled influence as efficiently on behalf of brothers Wells and Ed as Hiram Kennicott or Elijah Haines or William Fithian for their relatives, and was as close to backwoods Illinois as they were.

# THIRTY SEVENTH ILLINOIS

The two Blodgett brothers who enlisted in the Manierre Rifles (Co. D) of the 37th were younger than Henry. Ed was born in 1835, Wells in 1839, Henry in 1831. Ed Blodgett's education ended at grade school. Wells went to Rock River Seminary (Mount Morris), and Illinois University (Wheaton), and to read the law in his brother's firm in Chicago. An attorney in 1861, he went for the three months service and then enlisted in the 37th and was First Lieutenant of Company D, while brother Ed was Regimental Quartermaster Sergeant.

The Blodgett brothers' father Israel was a Massachusetts smithy up to 1830, when he came to Illinois and built a cabin on a land claim at DuPage. He set up a blacksmith shop, and when the Blackhawk War erupted, deposited his wife and children at Fort Dearborn and went to war against the indians. He came back unscathed, and bought land in Downers Grove. He was a Whig and a rabid abolitionist, and assisted in the escape of slaves throughout the 1840's and 1850's.

Israel Blodgett had seven children before he died in 1861. Son Henry became an attorney in Waukegan, a State Legislator, and an influence on behalf of Charles and Will Black as well as his brothers. Henry was a wire puller extraordinaire, taught at the knee of his log cabin indian-fighter father.[11]

In the 1840's Henry Blodgett began a legal practice in Waukegan, edited the Lake County Visitor, the local newspaper, for six months in 1845, and in 1847 successfully defended the first murder prosecution in Lake County. He defended three men accused of murdering a peddler after a party at Goodale's Tavern in what is now Grant. The prosecutor was William Boardman, whose son Calvin served with the 37th. He competed for law clients at Waukegan against Eugene Payne during the time of Payne's brief legal practice in 1860-61, but most of his daily bread came from his railroad legal practice, representing, variously, the Lake Shore Road, and the Pittsburgh, Fort Wayne, and Chicago Railroad.[12]

Henry Blodgett, in middle age, went to war. This was no isolated urge among forty-plus patriots who went to the battle sites for adventure, or to help sick or wounded relatives. His first trip was to Missouri after the Pea Ridge battle in March 1862, a trip made mostly on horseback through guerilla country. A month later, he went to the Shiloh battlefield with Illinois Governor Yates. By the summer of

# THE PATRIARCHS

1863, he was on the road to Chickamauga where his brother Aziel had been wounded with the 96th Illinois Infantry. Ed Blodgett had by this time resigned from the 37th and taken the Adjutancy of the 96th. Blodgett's party on this trip consisted of himself, a doctor, an ambulance, and four nurses. After a harrowing passage down the Sequatchie Valley road to Chattanooga, getting shot at once, he arrived to get his brother out of a hospital and away in a horse and cart.[13]

One of the comparative latecomers to Illinois was J.S. Messer, who arrived from Vermont in 1857 in the relative modern age of peaceful indians and two-hole outhouses. He was married to a descendant of Mayflower-Plymouth John Alden, one Julia Barker. Among his five children born in Vermont was one who kept the post office in Silver Plume, Colorado, and a set of twins, Erwin and Edwin, who served with the 37th. Erwin was Captain of Company F, and Edwin was Regimental Commissary Sergeant.[14]

These, then, were the civilians that carried the torches, waved the flag, raised the money, and occasionally put themselves in harm's way during the war on behalf of the 37th. In April, 1861, they were putting their efforts into raising and financing Payne's Lake County Zouave Company and Erwin Messer's Rifle Company.

These tribal elders dropped in and out of the affairs of the regiment during the war years as visiting advisors and influence peddlers. They were as involved as if they were the ones wearing the leaves or eagles or stars on their shoulders. Only William Fithian was given military rank at the age of 63, because his Provost Marshal appointment carried the rank of Captain. The others had to be satisfied with making rank for their friends and relatives.

## 3. The Zoo-Zoo's

No other philosophy or credo, other than organized religion, was as prevalent or as influential as the Zouave system in the regiment. It was the most colorful, the most popular, the most moral, and the most widespread regimen among the officers. Those who had not actually worn the goatee and baggy pants had great respect for those who had, and all took great pride that the whole gaudy fad had been created in Chicago, on native ground, by a starving legal copyist, Ephriam Elmer Ellsworth.

Two of Ellsworth's original Cadets, Ransom Kennicott and Frederick Abbey, raised the Audubon Rifles (Company I) of the 37th Illinois. These officers, Kennicott the dentist and Abbey the gunsmith, both came to the 37th at age twenty-four with the distinction of having been members of Ellsworth's Zouave Cadet Company that had earned national fame on a well-publicized and patronized tour of major eastern cities in 1860, showing off their dazzling uniforms and skills at military drill. Ransom Kennicott was a small man, physically adapted to the gymnastic part of the Zouave regimen. He excelled at drill and persevered in the 37th up to 1865, when he got command of the regiment.

The Zouave influence in the 37th did not end with Kennicott and Abbey. Eugene Payne, a brother officer, had a set-to with two other of the original Zouave Cadets, William Innis and Frank Rogers, during the 90-day service at Camp Yates in Springfield in April 1861, and Charles Black had won the election as regimental major of the 37th over Innis at Camp Webb in 1861.

The Black brothers had been members of a Zouave company at Wabash College, had served with Lew Wallace in the 11th Indiana Infantry, and raised a Zouave company for the 37th (Company K). The system influenced Eugene Payne, who helped raise the Waukegan Zouaves for the 90-day service in April 1861, a unit officered by Payne and the two Ellsworth Zouaves.

The grand poo-bah of American Zouave-ism was Elmer Ellsworth. Ellsworth was pure magic and fantasy, and made the

## THE ZOO-ZOO'S

reputation of his Cadet Company by staging a come-one, come-all challenge trip to big city America in 1860.

The Ellsworth Zouaves (the United State Zouave Cadets) was formed by Ellsworth in Chicago in 1859 during the popular rage for local militia companies, hundreds of them across the country. These militia companies were social clubs for young men who met, socialized, and held periodic public drills in outlandish uniforms. Of all these companies in the big cities and tank towns, the Ellsworth Chicago Zouaves became the best, the top, the non-pareil in precision drill.

The difference between this company and all the others lay entirely with its leader, Ephraim Elmer Ellsworth, who was, in life and death, to have more influence on the national enthusiasm for and support of the Civil War in the first year than any other single force save Abraham Lincoln. He was a national hero when Ulysses Grant was an unknown Illinois Colonel, and Sheridan, Sherman, and McClellan had yet to make any mark or assume power or command. Ellsworth's picture was on recruiting posters, stationery, and in newspapers. He was Mr. Lincoln's knight-errant.

Ellsworth's brief life began in the tiny town of Malta, New York in April 1837, as the son of a tailor, poor but proud, etc. Malta is just south of Saratoga, New York, a Revolutionary War battleground where great-grandfather George Ellsworth had fought the British. Ellsworth the small boy had listened to war stories while watching the rich people drive through Malta on the way to Saratoga Springs. He got an early yen to go to West Point, didn't have the educational background, and settled for clerking in a general store, selling oysters, netting pigeons, selling newspapers on the railroad, and forming "The Black Plumed Riflemen" in Mechanicsville, New York, while in his teens.

At age 15, he left home and clerked in a store in Troy, New York, followed by a succession of vagabond jobs in Wisconsin and Michigan, and back to New York where he worked for a time with engineers improving the Hellgate Channel in 1853-4.

He was back in Chicago and Wisconsin and the west at age 17, educating himself in the law and particularly in the art of penmanship.[1] He got into a brief partnership in Chicago with another teenager, Arthur F. Devereux, in the patent soliciting business. They both joined the local militia company, the National Guard Cadets, in 1856, and trained at the armory in Chicago. Ellsworth excelled in gymnastics, organized classes in gymnastics, and later integrated gymnastic exercises in the Zouave Code.

The Zouave concept grew in his head out of a friendship in Chicago with an ex-French Army surgeon and master swordsman, Charles A. DeVilliers. DeVilliers, who was a much better fencer that he was a U.S. Army officer, was later sentenced "to be dismissed from the U.S. service... for habitually insulting and abusing his officers, and for defrauding the government," in 1862. Ellsworth learned the Zouave prototype from DeVilliers, and then fleshed it out to his own standard.[2]

Historically, the Zouaves were Algerian mercenaries whose tactics and uniform were adopted by the French Army in the 1830's, as explained to Ellsworth by DeVilliers. The idea was romantic, exotic, novel, and attractive to a teenager with a latent adolescent interest in military show. The wide trousers, fez, braided jacket, and moustache and goatee were irresistible. Ellsworth sent away to France for books on the Zouave system of drill, and studied it along with U.S. Army General Winfield Scott's book and General Hardee's books on drill. He also became the "the best fencer in Chicago" under Devilliers's instruction.[3]

THE ZOO-ZOO'S

Ephraim Elmer Ellsworth in mufti, ca 1861
Courtesy of New York Historical Society

## THIRTY SEVENTH ILLINOIS

All this reputation building got Ellsworth a job in 1857 as drillmaster of a militia company, the Rockford City Grays. By the end of that year, he had command of the Grays. A newspaper reporter described the 20-year old Ellsworth's appearance at a Grays' banquet in December, 1857 in nearly erotic prose:

> Let me present him as he appeared to me that evening: A boyish figure, not exceeding five feet six inches in height, with well-formed, shapely limbs, clad in undress uniform; a blue fatigue cap, worn slightly tipping toward the right side, giving a jaunty and rakish expression to him; a well-balanced head crowned with a wealth of dark brown hair that fell in careless, clinging curls about his neck, eyes of dark hazel that sparkled and flashed with excitement or melted with tenderness – that looked out beneath straight penciled eyebrows – a large, well-formed nose inclined to be straight but with a slight attempt to 'Romanize,' a broad white forehead, a face as smooth and as fair as a maiden's – the faintest trace of silken down upon the upper lip – mouth broad, lips full and red, half concealing teeth of dazzling whiteness."[4]

Despite this romanticized description, during 1858 and 1859 Ellsworth was living a morose and pathetic personal existence. He was at the time studying law with J.S. Cones in Dearborn Street in Chicago, making small sums as Cones' copyist, sleeping on the floor of the office, eating crackers, reading Blackstone, and suffering depressing bouts of poverty.

Thankfully, the barren personal existence was temporary. Success and recognition were to follow the Spartan suffering. His self-will and hard work during all the dietary deprivation and mental anguish living on Cones' floor had its positive effect on the Zouave Cadets. The pattern of drill took hold, enhanced by the wrestling and gymnastics he added, and with the code of clean living (no gambling,

# THE ZOO-ZOO'S

drinking, or whoring), the company emerged as the best and most skillful of its kind.

The spiritual inspiration for the code of conduct he devised was lifted whole cloth from an Alfred Lord Tennyson passage which Ellsworth often quoted. The company would be:[5]

> "A glorious company, the flower of men, to serve
> as model for the mighty world, and be the fair
> beginning of a time. I made them lay their hands
> in mine and swear to reverence the King, as if he
> were their conscience, and the conscience as their
> King, to break the heathen and uphold the Christ,
> to ride abroad redressing human wrongs, to speak
> no slander, no, nor listen to it, to lead sweet lives
> in purest chastity…"

John Hay, Abraham Lincoln's wartime secretary, and a keen observer and diarist, described Ellsworth as "a Paladin or Cavalier of the dead days of romance and beauty."[6]

The heavy equipment, the tight fitting high collar, uniforms, and heavy hats of the traditional militia companies were out, along with the simplistic traditional maneuvers of the Scott and Hardee drill systems, and also the drinking that made up so much of the social element of the companies.

In their place, Ellsworth put the fez, baggy pants, tiger head badge, gymnastic exercises, and the intricate, complicated, and vastly more entertaining maneuvers of the Zouave system. The end product of this was summarized in the Chicago Sunday Mercury:

> … A fellow with a red bag having sleeves to it for a
> coat; with two red bags without sleeves to them for
> trousers; with an embroidered and braided bag for a
> vest; with a cap like a red woolen saucepan; with
> yellow boots like the fourth robber in a stage play;
> with a moustache like 2 half-pound paint brushes, and
> with a sort of swordgun… for a weapon… that is a
> Zouave.

A fellow who can put up a 110-pound dumbbell, who can climb an 80 foot rope, hand over hand, with a barrel of flour hanging to his heels; who can do giant swings on a horizontal bar with a 56 pound weight tied to each ankle; who can walk up four flights of stairs holding a heavy man in each hand at arm's length, and who can climb a greased pole feet first, carrying a barrel of pork in his teeth – that is a Zouave.

A fellow who can jump 17 feet 4 inches high without a springboard; who can tie his legs in a double bowknot around his neck without previously softening his shinbones in a steambath; who can set a 40 foot ladder on end, balance himself on top of it, shoot wild pigeons on the wing, one at a time, just behind the eye, with a single-barreled minie rifle, 300 yards distance and never miss a shot; who can take a five shooting revolver in each hand and knock the spots out of the ten of diamonds at 80 paces, turning somersaults all the time and firing every shot in the air – that is a Zouave...[7]

Kennicott, Abbey, and the other Cadets were required to sign the Code of Conduct that Ellsworth had devised, or he would not admit them to membership. The code prohibited entering saloons, "houses of ill fame under any circumstance," or any premises for gambling or drinking or playing billiards. Leisure hours were to be spent in a reading room or a chess room, both provided to improve the mind. If the members did not want to toe the mark, they would be dismissed from the company, and several were thrown out for indulging in the prohibited vices.

Kennicott and Abbey joined Ellsworth in 1859, and as that summer wore on into fall, the company was scoring many successes in drill contests, and catching notice of the press and population, leading to a State appointment for Ellsworth which took him to Springfield, Illinois briefly, where he met Abraham Lincoln, John Hay, and Lincoln's law partner Billy Herndon. Lincoln took an instant liking to Ellsworth.

In 1860, preparation began for the national tour of the company which was to begin in the summer, interrupted briefly by falling in to stand as riot police during the Chicago municipal elections in March, as requested by Elijah Haines' brother Long John, then Chicago Mayor, a duty which in the end passed off uneventfully.

The tour was to show off the cadet proficiency in drill and gymnastics. This was to be Ellsworth's grand crusade, a perfect show of the physical excellence produced by virtuous minds and bodies free of drinking and gambling.

The spring was devoted entirely to preparing for the tour, which was planned to answer a joint challenge from the oldest established militia companies in the East. After winning a drill competition in September 1859, Ellsworth wrote a brassy public notice challenging any company to a competition. Several accepted the challenge and in February 1860, a tour was scheduled for the upcoming summer to answer all the challenges.

The exhausting physical training that Ellsworth required of his men in the months from February to June 1860 was born out of the dry crackers and penmanship of Dearborn Street, the disgraced DeVilliers, Mr. Lincoln, Sir Walter Scott, a poor beginning, diminutive stature, and who knows what else. For five months, all things but the members' jobs were foregone. No excuses were accepted for fatigue or other indisposition without some motivational criticism directed at the complainant. Failure to keep uniform, i.e., inability to grow the mandatory goatee and moustache, did not disqualify a man, but placed him in the rear ranks with a chuckle from the other members.

Indoor drill was four hours each day, seven days a week, in addition to outside field and skirmish drill. The indoor drill was always with knapsacks, and the military formations were supplemented with gymnastics using horizontal bars and ladders. Of the original two hundred cadets on the rolls at the founding of the company, 47 stayed the course, including Kennicott and Abbey. Some were unable to stand the physical demands of drill with knapsack and rifle hour on endless hour, and some were swept out by Ellsworth for moral reasons or breaking the strict code he had established. He swept out 12 at one time for drinking. Death took his cadet brother out in June.[8]

The tour itself was a great success. The company gathered praise, cheers, accolades, recognition, and grudging or enthusiastic appreciation from competitors, observers, and critics. The junket began July 3, 1860, moving from Chicago through Detroit, Syracuse, Buffalo, Rochester, Utica, and Albany. At Albany, they were met by the local best, the Burgess Corps.[9]

From Albany, the company went to New York and went through a public drill at City Hall Park shouting their cheer, "1-2-3-4-5-6-7 – T-I-G-E-R – ZOUAVE!" repeated three times in a cadence. The drill commands echoed through the park; "Load in 9 times! Order! Shoulder! Quick Time! In one time and two motions!"

After drilling at the Academy of Music, the company moved to Boston, then back to New York to drill at the armory, and then on to West Point to perform for General Hardee, who pronounced the exercises "showy and not at all practical," whereupon Ellsworth dropped the Zouave evolutions and ordered, "According to Hardee," which was done once with eyes open, once with eyes closed. Hardee pronounced this, "Most wonderful!"[10]

Philadelphia was next, followed by Baltimore and the White House Grounds in Washington. By August 8, the company was in Pittsburgh, and then to Cincinnati and St. Louis. After a stop at Springfield, Illinois, the company returned to Chicago on the 14th of August.[11]

Five days after the return to Chicago, the company drilled in a benefit at the Home of the Friendless. It was Ellsworth's last appearance as leader. Without him, the company puttered around until October and then disbanded preferring to end their history before diminishing the success of the summer, putting Ransom Kennicott back in his dentist's office and Fred Abbey back in his gunshop.

Ellsworth had succeeded in spreading the Zouave system to militia companies nationwide, and had cemented his place at Lincoln's side as trusted retainer. After the first Chicago successes of the Cadets in the summer of 1859, Ellsworth had been given an appointment to reform the state militia, and went to Springfield, met Lincoln, and made a lasting impression on him. Lincoln was eager to use him in

## THE ZOO-ZOO'S

his presidential campaign in 1860 after the Cadet tour was completed, and so Ellsworth took up Lincoln's previous offer of a law reading place. Lincoln had recognized a good thing when he saw it, and so did Ellsworth, who now had designs on reforming the United States Army system of drill and organization.

Lincoln had him on the campaign trail by October, and he drove into the country to give one speech a day. After Lincoln won, Ellsworth passed his bar exam and also managed to get a bill on military reform to the Illinois legislature.

In February, he went to Washington with President-Elect Lincoln, being given the job of head of security for the trip, a plan conceived by Allen Pinkerton. Pinkerton instructed Washington security that,

> The President-Elect will under no circumstances attempt to pass through any crowd until such arrangements are made as will meet the approval of Colonel Ellsworth, who is charged with the responsibility of all matters of this character; and to facilitate this, you will confer a favor by placing Colonel Ellsworth in communication with the chief of your escort, immediately upon the arrival of the train...[12]

Here was a 23 year old to be trusted. Lincoln got him a regular army commission, which he promptly resigned when the war came, and went to New York and raised a regiment, the New York Fire Zouaves.

On the morning of May 24, 1861, about six weeks after Ft. Sumter fell, Ellsworth went to Alexandria, Virginia, and entered a house to take down a rebel flag. On his way out with the flag, he took a point-blank shotgun blast square in the chest from the drunken landlord. Private Francis E. Brownell, the only witness, described it to a narrator;

> "[Jackson, the assassin] discharged one barrel straight to its aim, the slugs or buckshot with which it was

> loaded entering the Colonel's heart, and killing him at the instant... he dropped forward with that heavy, horrible, headlong weight which always comes of sudden death... He had fallen on his face, and the streams of blood that flowed from his wound had literally flooded the way..."[13]

So ended the life of the young friend of Lincoln, in a bloody pool in a strange house, the first Union officer killed in the Civil War. The warrior-hero was martyred and songs and poems were written; goodness cut down in the bloom of youth by evil secesh, and the like.

The man who was living on crackers and water and sleeping on the floor in Dearborn Street less than two years before was now the tragic hero and symbol for the Union cause and war effort. He had stepped straight out of the pages of Sir Walter Scott to lead the most popular drill unit of the 19th century. He fought in Lincoln's service, against powerful enemies, questing for the grail of the Union, armed with a sense of morality and mission. He played the last act out, dying young in service to flag and country, the climax to a passionate medieval performance.

Those early days of the war found two other of Lincoln's young acquaintances, Charles and Willy Black, at Wabash College in Crawfordsville, Indiana. The brothers enlisted from college in the 11th Indiana Infantry with thirty-three other Wabash College students in May 1861.

Charles and Will had worn the uniform of the College Zouave Company; grey, baggy trousers, open-necked shirt, short jacket, and white gaiters and a kepi.

By late June, Charles Black was regimental sergeant major and Willy was a corporal in Colonel Lew Wallace's 11th Indiana Infantry. Wallace was later governor of Indiana and then New Mexico and author of <u>Ben Hur, a Tale of the Christ</u>, among other books.[14]

The climax of the ninety day service with Lew Wallace was a pre-Bull Run raid on Romney, Virginia. The memorable part of this short campaign was the march across the Knobly Mountains of about fifty miles round trip in a space of twenty-four hours. Charles Black's

# THE ZOO-ZOO'S

hallucinations on the return trip (also experienced by others on the march) were a measure of the common fatigue.[15]

The balance of the Blacks' three month service was spent in the Martinsburg-Winchester-Harper's Ferry area. Julius White and the 37th were about a month in the future. Charles and Will Black came home to Danville in August 1861 with a short time to raise what would be Company K and transport it up to Camp Webb where their history with the 37th regiment would begin.

## 4. Thirty Days at Springfield

After the attack on Fort Sumter in April 1861, the government assumed the rebellion would be quickly and sharply put down, and called for a short-term, 90 day length of service from volunteers. This "short war" forecast provided the 90 day window for Eugene Payne, the Black brothers and many more to see service prior to their days with the 37th.

While the Blacks were settling in with the 11th Indiana Infantry in May 1861, several sons of Lake County, Illinois were embarked on a singular and very forgettable army experience in Springfield, Illinois.

The Zouave military system that took hold across the country in 1860 had carried its weight to Waukegan, Illinois in 1861. Eugene Payne, then a young Waukegan attorney, complete with moustache, goatee, and barbells, had a hand in forming a Zouave company which was to have a short, thirty day active life as Company H, Chicago Zouave Regiment.

The townsfolk in Waukegan got the news of the outbreak of war on April 15, 1861 and immediately set up a meeting to discuss finance and enlistment matters in the Waukegan Courthouse and in Dickinson Hall. Henry Blodgett spoke to the crowd on Tuesday, and Eugene Payne and Judd Huntley spoke to a large crowd the day after. The patriotic drum-beating prompted on the spot enlistments into the militia, and a War Finance Committee was formed to raise money to pay the volunteers' food and transportation expenses.

During the week, eighty-five men were recruited into Eugene Payne's company, the Waukegan Zouaves, and among these were the officers of what would be, in August, the Lake County Rifles, Company C of the 37th.[1]

The Zouave enlistees gathered in Waukegan on April 22, marched to the train station, and took the 12:38 PM train to Chicago. The group was mostly all Lake County residents except for the Captain and First Lieutenant, who had been called from Chicago and added by the town fathers because they had been Ellsworth Zouaves. William Innis and B. Frank Rogers came to Waukegan with the larger than life mystique of the Ellsworth Zouave.[2]

# THIRTY DAYS AT SPRINGFIELD

Bringing in Rogers and Innis was not the idea of the company, but of the greybeards of the Waukegan War Finance Committee, who were paying the bills. It took a few days to sort out who would rank whom. Rogers prematurely assumed he would be Captain, without the benefit of an election. Rogers lost the election held when the company reached Chicago. Eugene Payne was elected Second Lieutenant when the company reached Springfield two days later.

When the company arrived in Chicago on April 22$^{nd}$, they were met at the train by the Chicago Zouave Regiment and marched to the Armory to eat. During the meal, Innis mounted a chair and told the men what was expected of them, reciting the Elmer Ellsworth rules of deportment in the same hall where he had heard them the year before as an Ellsworth Zoo-Zoo. Echoing Ellsworth, he said there should be absolutely no drinking in the ranks, drunkenness to be severely punished, as would be gambling, billiards, bar patronage, and other general sins.[3]

On that same evening, scant hours after the train trip down from Waukegan, word came that Springfield was fast filling up with militia companies answering the governor's call for troops, and the early arrivals would have the best chance of getting into a regiment and being accepted into federal service. Otherwise, all the quota would be filled. So, on Monday night, fearful of losing a spot in the temporary army, the company departed in haste, reached Springfield the next day, and were accepted into state service. Because of the unexpected rush to get to Springfield, no provision had been made for food or barracks. Elijah Haines and Henry Blodgett, then Lake County State Representatives, showed up and arranged for these comforts at the Camp Yates rendezvous, and mother-henned their Lake County constituents for the next month, making almost daily visits.

The routine of reveille, drill, mess, parade, and guard at Camp Yates was established early, and from the first week, things started to go bad.

The company had no tents, and was housed in the amphitheater of the old State Fairgrounds, which happened to have a leaky roof. It was damp and rainy at the end of that April and early May, and the rain wet down the straw bedding, eliminating what comfort there was from the single blanket issued as bedclothes, bringing on coughs, colds, and fevers.

The company arrived with eighty men, and ten more came in the first few weeks. The kitchen equipment issued was one knife, two spoons, three plates, and one pan and one kettle for each six men. About a third of this was stolen the first week and was not re-issued[4]

Because of the bad food and general unsanitary conditions, diarrhea spread rapidly through the company, joining the other pestilences which were encouraged by sleeping in the cold on wet straw. In this condition, the men stood guard for several hours at a time in all weather. A half dozen of the sickest, and those physically unfit for service (so certified medically) should have been sent home immediately, but Captain Innis was reluctant to release anyone.

Adding to the demoralizing effects of physical discomfort and despite the political influence of Haines and Blodgett, the company missed getting into the first six Illinois regiments that were formed, and so missed the chance for the ninety days service. None had left Waukegan with the idea of going off for three years, which was the only other option.

The discomfort bred discontent which accelerated rapidly. After about two weeks, between colds and diarrhea, all the men had lost weight (10-20 pounds average). Eugene Payne, as sick or sicker than anyone, wrote two notes to the hometown paper, the Waukegan Daily Gazette. The first one on May 7 was short, mild, and upbeat, and gilded the lily, assigning no blame for the failure to muster into federal service, giving a report of general good health and satisfaction with the surroundings. The officers and men of the company were reported as playing baseball after daily drill amidst beautiful weather, green trees, and blooming flowers.[5]

The second (unsigned) note took a blacker, anguished, accusatory tone. One of its allegations was that Rogers and Innis stole two jugs of brandy that had been purchased for the sick and drank them. Innis was referred to by Payne as "our noble little Captain," who was one of the "little Chicago squirts with red pants," who "couldn't mount a guard without consulting a book."[6]

This love note was printed in the Waukegan Weekly Gazette on May 18. The members of the War Finance committee who had planted Rogers and Innis lost no time in threatening James Cory, editor of the paper, for the name of the author of the letter. Cory buckled and revealed that Eugene Payne had been the author. Despite the fact that the letter had been "unconditionally endorsed by no less than four of the members of that company who were in town and whom we consulted in relation to it before it was allowed to appear in our paper," the committee got their knives out.[7]

They were not interested in facts. They wanted a piece of Eugene Payne for exposing their officer choices as "little Chicago squirts with red pants," and immediately sent a big dog to Springfield to go for his throat.

The attack was vicious enough that Payne had to call on his benefactor Haines. Payne explained it:

"I was lying on my sickbed in Springfield when this agent of this Lake County Committee… came to me & said I must either resign my position as 2d Lieut. or prove the truth of the charges or he would expose me to the Colonel & have me court-martialed. I told him when my Commanding Officer requested me to resign I would & not before & that the committee could go to some bad place & that if they wished to expose me to go ahead, but as I was sick I wished he would wait till the next morning (it was in the afternoon) till Haines could arrive to attend to my case for me. He promised & left me. Before two hours had elapsed, the letter & the report that I was to be court-martialed was all over camp. That night I had a guard of 10 men placed over me. The next morning Haines came down & saw the Governor who examined the charges & said I could not be court-martialed & should not. My company then called a meeting & pledged themselves to rescue me if there was any attempt to court-martial me if they had to shed blood in doing it. The company then disbanded because they would not serve under Capt. Innis, & started for home, carrying me with them…"[8]

Payne was furious with editor Cory for revealing his name. Parts of the community were very unsympathetic toward the company for coming back to town after only one month, but that time at Camp Yates and its adverse conditions would not hold a pale shadow to what many of the same men were to go through a year later in Missouri with the 37th. Even though one man had died at Camp Yates, the early return of ninety unbloodied heads elicited little sympathy at home.

Payne went back to his father's farm at Fremont Centre to recover his health, aggravated in June by underarm boils in addition to diarrhea, fever, and weight loss, and got back on his feet in July. He had just about enough time to reopen his law office when the call came from Julius White to raise a company of three year volunteers.

The Union disaster at Bull Run had happened that July, and the flags and music of the April meetings faded into the past. There was to be no short war. Camp Yates was not quite a closed book though, for Payne and the Waukegan Zouaves were to cross paths once more with William Innis. The thirty days at Camp Yates had been either plain unsavory or disastrous, depending on the man telling the story. In any event, Innis was defeated for the Majority of the 37$^{th}$ at Camp Webb, Chicago. The field grade offices were to be held by a far more interesting group, ultimately including Eugene Payne. The 37$^{th}$ left Camp Webb in September 1861 in the hands of an insurance salesman, a newspaperman, and a college student.

## 5.  The Water March to St. Louis

On September 19, 1861, the order to move out of Wright's Grove had come. The tents were taken down and packed up, along with kitchens, desks, chairs, rations and quartermaster's stores, and the regiment formed and moved out onto North Clark Street. They marched to Chicago, to South Water and LaSalle Streets, to the Board of Trade Building. There they were presented with a regimental flag by the members of the Board of Trade and "numerous insurance agents of the city."[1]

The flag, which cost $200, had on one side a portrait of Major General John C. Fremont, and on the other a scene of Fremont with four followers crossing snowcapped heights in the Rocky Mountains, and another of General Fremont planting the Stars and Stripes on the heights of the Rockies.

Speeches followed the presentation in the flowery, patriotic, inflammatory hyperbole that sprung up out of great moment. J.C. Wright was first, describing "the desperate foe, who with lies and madness strives to destroy... A foe with a halter about his neck, and a traitor's pirate's grave yawning before him..." After a plea to bring back the flag though it may be "torn and tattered... soiled with the smoke of battle... blood-stained and pierced with rebel bullets...," the audience was pumped, and the troops were pumped.[2]

Julius White spoke next and fed the frenzy of the flag loving, rebel hating crowd, declaring September 19, 1861 as the proudest day of his life.

Judge Knox continued the hype: "I tell you, I know Jule White... A truer man never drew a sword...you may follow him...if it be through Hell or Manassas." Knox was then cheered with the Zouave staple, three cheers and a T I G – r r r.[3]

The speeches over, with cheers ringing in their ears, the 37th marched from the Board of Trade Building to the Illinois Central Depot at the foot of Lake Street, and boarded a sixteen car train that chugged out and down the front of the city, on the edge of the lake, destined for the flatlands of southern Illinois and on to Missouri and into the war.

## THIRTY SEVENTH ILLINOIS

It was a trip to the other side of the world. As the lake slid by, the troops saw a number of ladies standing in their doors and windows waving their handkerchiefs at the passing train.

South of Chicago, the country was flat, swampy, desolate, and timberless for about 130 miles. The men ate sea bread and boiled ham for their first meal at about midnight on that clear September evening rolling southward out of Illinois. This was a supplement to the food that was either bought or stolen from saloons at train stops. If the owners wouldn't sell cheap enough, the men just took what they wanted and reboarded the train. Three or four eating spots were cleaned out in this way.

Charitable civilians contributed pies, apples, and other fruit at the train stops as the women waved and cheered. In the midst of the boiled ham and fruit, the men shot livestock for fun from the train. Mike Emery (Co. B) "shot a large hog, and he shot the head off a chicken when the cars were standing still...."[4]

The train reached the Mississippi opposite St. Louis at five the next afternoon, and the men spent the night on the vessel MEMPHIS, which accommodated 960 men by sleeping them about four deep on the deck.

The next morning in St. Louis, with aching joints, the men ate and marched up to meet their commander and namesake, John C. Fremont. After a circuitous march through St. Louis from the dock up Fourth Street to Chateau Avenue amidst cheering crowds, they stopped in front of the stone house where Fremont was staying.[5]

With their $200 flag in the front row, the regiment dressed and covered. Fremont stepped out onto the portico with his staff and his wife Jesse. Standing beside her gray haired, gray bearded husband, Jesse Fremont tied a ribbon on the regimental flagstaff. After a bit more patriotic encouragement, the regiment headed off for nearby Benton Barracks through more cheering crowds.[6]

The arrival at Benton Barracks signaled the beginning of service under General Samuel Curtis, a 54-year old West Pointer and retreaded civil engineer with limited military abilities.[7] "A noble old man, with his grey beard like so many bristles sticking out all over his face...," was Eugene Payne's description on an occasion in April 1862.

## THE WATER MARCH TO ST. LOUIS

The new camp lay on the fairgrounds about four miles northwest of St. Louis. This would be home base for the next five days, enough time for Julius White and his staff to attend to some necessaries such as arming the companies and putting chevrons on the non-commissioned officers.[8]

Final lettering and ordering of the companies was done at Benton Barracks. The final company designation was:[9]

| | COMPANY | CAPTAIN |
|---|---|---|
| A | ROCK ISLAND RIFLES | JOHN JORDAN |
| B | LAFAYETTE RIFLES | CHARLES V. DICKINSON |
| C | LAKE COUNTY RIFLES | EUGENE B. PAYNE |
| D | MANIERRE RIFLES | JOHN LAIMBEER |
| E | MENDOTA RIFLES | PHINEAS B. RUST |
| F | LAKE COUNTY GUARDS | ERWIN B. MESSER |
| G | TURNER RIFLES | HENRY N. FRISBIE |
| H | MOLINE GUARDS | JOHN B. FRICK |
| I | AUDUBON RIFLES | RANSOM KENNICOTT |
| K | VERMILION ZOUAVES | WILLIAM P. BLACK |

The flank companies, A and K, got forty each of the new Colt five shot repeating rifles, which was a Colt revolver with a thirty inch barrel and saber bayonet, and the non-commissioned officers were issued the balance of the two hundred of these ultra-modern weapons allotted to the 37$^{th}$.

Perquisites of rank were magnified when tighter military form and regulation came to bear  As an example, the Army allowed the Commander of an Army or Division twelve quires of writing paper, fifty quills, two ounces of sealing wax and one paper of ink powder. A General had three tents, a Major two. A General was allowed five rooms and five cords of wood per month in the winter. A major struggled along in three rooms and three and one half cords of wood per month.

The pay of a Major General was $220 per month, fifteen rations per day, seven horses, and four servants. A Major's pay was $80 per month with four rations per day, three horses, and two servants.

# THIRTY SEVENTH ILLINOIS

A private, on the bottom rung of the organization, was paid $13 per month, had to steal most of his food in the field, and was generally treated worse than either the horses or the servants and did more work.

The army organizational chart was hierarchical. The Field Army (or Department) was the largest unit, comprised of two or more Corps, which were comprised of two or more Divisions, comprised of two or more Brigades, comprised of two or more Regiments, in which might be two or more Battalions comprised of two or more companies, which were comprised of two or more platoons, comprised of two or more squads, which consisted of private soldiers. Officers were usually assigned as follows:

| | |
|---|---|
| Corporal | Squad |
| Sergeant/Lieutenant | Platoon |
| Captain | Company |
| Major | Battalion (2 companies) |
| Lieutenant Colonel | Battalion (4 companies) |
| Colonel | Regiment (10 companies) |
| Brigadier General | Brigade (20 companies) |
| Major General | Division, Corps, or Army (40 companies) |
| Lieutenant General | Army (80 companies) |

The basic unit of command was the Company, divided into two platoons and four squads of about twenty-one men each at full strength.

The regimental infantry command of ten companies additionally included an Adjutant, Quartermaster, Surgeon, Assistant Surgeon, Chaplain, four staff enlisted, and two principal musicians. The Adjutant and Quartermaster were ranked as Lieutenants.

Along with the Table of Organization came regulations on every aspect of army life, including food, clothing, eating, sleeping, pay, punishment, leave, drill, guard, marching either overland or by boat or rail, and a hundred other things that left very little to anyone's discretion.

## THE WATER MARCH TO ST. LOUIS

The daily nutritional unit was the standard army ration, consisting of ¾ pound of pork or bacon, or 1 ¼ pounds of beef, 18 ounces of bread or flour (or 12 ounces of hard bread), and 1 ¼ pounds of corn meal. With each 100 rations came 8 quarts of beans or 10 pounds of rice, or dessicated potatoes, and 100 ounces of mixed vegetables, 10 pounds of coffee or 1 ½ pounds of tea, and various quantities of sugar, vinegar, candles, soap, and salt. Hospitals got butter, eggs, fruit, pickles, and milk. Occasional issues were molasses and whiskey by the gill.

The same detailed prescription was made for clothing including, "the uniform coat…a single breasted frock of dark blue cloth…," with precise measurements of cut, length, and placement of buttons.

The chevrons of Sergeants and Corporals consisted of worsted tape 5/8 inch wide, green in color. The chevron was to extend from seam to seam on the left arm, midway between the shoulder and elbow. For Sergeants, three chevrons, for corporals two, and for Orderlies (First Sergeants), three chevrons and a diamond.

Conduct was as closely prescribed as food, clothing, and shelter, including (under the Third Article of War) a fine of $1 for the use of "any profane oath or execration," per occasion. Dozens of specific articles followed, down to Article 99, the catch-all covering "all disorders and neglects…to the prejudice of good order and military discipline." This article allowed virtually anything as a court martial offense at a commander's discretion, on whose good side it was smart to stay.[10]

The 37th was one of over 2,000 units of all branches formed on the Union side during the War, and one of the best overall. Largely inexperienced officers and underage privates staffed these units in the beginning, as most of the regular army units were sent intact to Indian Territory or kept around Washington because of the lack of confidence of Congress in the new volunteer army. This provided little chance for regular army officer advancement. Of about 1,100 regular army officers in 1861, only 140 became generals, while volunteers like Julius White and Charles Black took up other general officer appointments. The general officer appointments made of White (to Major General) and Black and of Eugene Payne and Henry Frisbie were political brevets made on March 13, 1865.

# THIRTY SEVENTH ILLINOIS

As for equipment, the men had been marching the flower strewn streets of Chicago and St. Louis as the Fremont Rifle Regiment largely without rifles. Julius White had arranged for 1,000 big bore (.54 caliber) Belgian Rifles from the Washington Arsenal to be sent to him at Chicago, and they were late.

So there the men lay, in St. Louis, weaponless except for the 200 Colt repeaters, in whitewashed barracks on the edge of the trouble in Missouri. White had cast his die for St. Louis and Missouri. Before leaving Chicago, the regiment was scheduled to go to Washington, and White had the orders changed, intending instead to serve with Fremont in Missouri.

On arrival at St. Louis on September 21st, the regiment was supposed to spend one night on the vessel MEMPHIS and go to Jefferson City the next day. This did not suit White, who went to Fremont on the day of the ceremony at his house and begged off Jefferson City, preferring to remain close to and directly under the Pathfinder.

On September 26th, the 37th did march out of Benton Barracks to the river, and boarded three steamers bound for the interior of Missouri on Fremont's rearranged orders. The mission was to face the rebels in the field.

Charles Black was in command on the vessel EWING with Companies F, G, and H. Will Black was on the NORTHERNER with his own company and Kennicott's Zouaves, along with Julius White and General John Pope and his staff. The balance of the regiment – Jordan, Dickinson, Payne, Laimbeer, and Rust – were on the vessel SAM GATY, Myron Barnes in command.[11]

The little fleet sailed up the Mississippi into the Missouri River, passed St. Charles, Missouri, and stopped for the night a few miles above.

On the EWING, Charles Black had a fracas with the Captain on the first night out. The secesh Captain took an immediate dislike to the Union soldiers and had them put out of their cabins, tried to deny them breakfast, and refused to talk to Black who was in command. Black sent Henry Frisbie to threaten the Captain and bring him around.[12]

The pecking order on the EWING was thus clearly established on the first day of the voyage, even though Frisbie may have wanted his breakfast more than he wanted his commander obeyed. These two, Black and Frisbie, would spar and jab at each other for most of the war.

The balance of the trip on the muddy Missouri was largely a monotony, occasionally interrupted by a grounding. The fleet reached Jefferson City on September 28, and after a day and a night there, the men got back on their boats in company with the 9th Missouri (later designated the 59th Illinois), and the steamers WAR EAGLE and one other which swelled the mini-fleet to five vessels for the voyage to Boonville, Missouri.[13]

The regiment disembarked at Boonville, which sat on the south bank of the river surrounded by vineyards and peach and apple orchards, and inhabited largely by a population with Southern sympathies. It was October 1861, and the 37th Regiment was in enemy territory.

## 6. Boonville

The transition from civilian to soldier does not happen automatically or with the cutting of an order or the blowing of a bugle. Before Boonville, army life had been transitory. There were new things to see and do every day. Each man had honors paid him, and had the thrill of parades through cheering crowds, and new friends, new clothes, a life of drill and guard in situations that would change rapidly with a change of station. It was never very far to the next train ride and the new camp. Bad situations were sure to change, perhaps for the worse, but everyone could always hope for and rely on a change, old for new.

This gypsy travel and the emotional rewards of torchlight parades and gifts of food and attention of the envious and the curious stopped at Boonville and at the Lamine River. Boonville and the Lamine Bridge were permanent duty stations in enemy territory, or almost. There was an enemy who would shoot in the right circumstance, and the hardships of hunger and disease were constant. Soldiers began to depend more on their tentmates and messmates than on any hope for tomorrow. As the tomorrows came and went, the war remained. Reveille and tattoo were on schedule, and dysentery and malaria respected no one.

During that autumn in Missouri, the food got worse, the nights got colder, and home with its familiar things faded into a distant past. After a time of discomfort, when the important things are eating enough, staying warm and alive, and answering the work call or the mess call or the sick call or the mail call, civilians cease to be civilians and become soldiers.

The small fleet dropped its passengers at Boonville in early October 1861. Boonville, on the Missouri, was garrisoned by German Missouri Home Guards who occupied the fortifications at the Boonville College Building.

The town itself was a nice spot, built on seven hills overlooking the river. Vineyards and orchards of giant peaches and apples surrounded the town, as well as fields of sweet potatoes and a variety of vegetables.

Camp was near the entrenchments left by the summer's defenders of both battles at Boonville, and the "works" and surrounding trees showed clearly the signs of battle, pockmarked and splintered by minie balls, shotgun and artillery fire.[1]

Charles Black saw the Boonville townfolk as a "quiet, pastoral race, little given to wars or turbulence."[2] He might have had in mind the Ballantine family, formerly from Madison, Indiana. Charles, brother Will, and cousin Henry went to dinner at the Ballantines. They were old friends of his parents, and decidedly southern in sentiment.

The impact and reality of war in Missouri was fixed on the men the first week in October when the wounded of Jim Mulligan's Irish Brigade came down the Missouri River. Chan Morse thought it "one of the most horrible sights I have ever beheld." On the boat was one teenage casualty whose left arm, shoulder, and breast had been shot off by a cannonball.[3]

By the second week, cold weather, driving rain, and bad water were causing widespread sickness. The men had been sheltered ever since leaving Chicago. They had received overcoats at Jefferson City, but were out in the elements at Boonville. Taking a drink of Missouri River water was not much more than gulping a draught of bacteria, sowing the seeds of dysentery.

As fall drew on, the elements and bad water swelled the sick list. The principal complaint was camp diarrhea. The medical staff of Surgeon Luthur Humeston could do little to ease the suffering, and imposed remedies that were universally avoided by the men who "would rather lay down and die than call in the surgeon…" Luthur Humeston was suffering vicious criticism, being accused of "culpable ignorance, criminal neglect," and the like.[4] But what was happening to the 37th was no different than what was happening throughout both armies, and Humeston could do very little to prevent the spread of a variety of pestilence.

Charles Black was one of Humeston's accusers, but Black, aside from focusing the frustration and anger of the men at their physical discomfort, had an ulterior motive. He wanted to make a place as surgeon for his step-father, William Fithian, and started a campaign to do just that.

## THIRTY SEVENTH ILLINOIS

William Fithian's two stepsons, Charles and Willy, and his natural son Henry were all in the 37th, and Dr. Fithian at the age of 61, wanted to be in the war with his sons. By the time he got around to missing his sons, "Hum" (Luthur Humeston) and Assistant Surgeon Elijah Clark were already chosen and mustered. Fithian's wife Josephine was all for the Doctor getting the spot with the 37th, reminding Charles that the Doctor had been one of Fremont's electors in his campaign for the Presidency.[5] When the chance of a brigade surgeon's spot came open, the Doctor told Charles that, "I can get that appointment from President Lincoln if an appointment is not already made... A letter to President Lincoln asking my appointment immediately to that position, I doubt not, with exertions I shall immediately make with the President (through civilians), that the appointment would be made promptly. Once placed in that situation (which is supervisory), I would have my own boys under my own eye and care constantly... I shall write Lincoln today...."[6]

To add urgency to the situation, Willy and Cousin Henry Fithian were both sick and bedridden with chills, fever, vomiting and headache. Neither took medicine or treatment from Doc Humeston.

Eugene Payne was also sick at Boonville with successive bouts of dysentery and fever, and in December, he made the first of what would be constant requests to go home on recruiting duty, on leave, on staff duty, on anything that would get him out of the field. He had good reason to request a recruiting assignment from General John Pope, who was told by Myron Barnes that, "Captain Payne is in very feeble health and a leave of absence for the [30 days] will afford him beneficial relief. He has always been a good officer...."[7]

He got his leave, and however feeble he might have been, he managed to go to Osage, Iowa, a non-railroadized wilderness, to get married in January. He had had a long convalescence after his thirty day service in the spring, was to have another after Vicksburg, and lived with malaria the rest of his life.

While the power play for the surgeon's job was forming midst a worsening sick list, Willy Black was taking treatment from the Chaplain rather than the Surgeon or Assistant Surgeon Doc Clark.

The chaplain was Edward Anderson, self-proclaimed Indian fighter, border raider, and author. He was a man of the cloth, an amateur apothecary, and with Lieutenant Colonel Myron Barnes, was to be the editor of the regimental newspaper, the CAMP REGISTER. Barnes was a newspaperman from Rock Island, and Anderson was the regimental correspondent to the CHICAGO TRIBUNE, and both men could turn a phrase. They set up in a reclaimed printer's shop in Otterville, Missouri, and cranked out a few issues of the REGISTER in the fall of 1861.[8]

At the end of October the REGISTER reported, "There will not average more than ten sick to the company throughout the regiment. In this respect, they have been highly favored."[9] This was notable only in a relative sense, as troops of other regiments were in far worse shape.

The lot of the enlisted men, not having the resources or privilege of influence to get leave, or money, was most miserable. Their sicknesses were not passed in private homes with stoves, featherbeds and quilts, good food and clean water, but for the most part in dirty hospitals, wrapped in smelly, lice ridden blankets.

The first man died on the evening of October 10 at Boonville. German born Andrew Bensinger, a 43 year old gray haired private of Messer's company gave up to the camp diseases. When Bensinger was buried, the whole regiment turned out and marched to the burying ground in platoons at slow time to two tenor drummers and two pipers. Eight men marched behind the coffin, which was draped in the company flag, two guns under the coffin, and a man at each end to carry it.[10]

Sergeant Thomas Newell of Rust's company went next, two days later. He was a 33 year old English born farmer, and died of dysentery at the Boonville Hospital. He was buried near the breastworks in the fairground. Another one of Rust's men went out at 3 AM on the 27th at Otterville. Blue-eyed, blond-haired 18 year old Fred Grosshart died of "inflammation of the bowels." He had come from Bingen, Germany, and was buried next to a farmhouse about ¾ mile south of camp the same afternoon.[11]

In mid-October, the regiment was split between Boonville and Otterville, Missouri, about 25 miles away. Captain Frick (Co. H) and Captain Payne (Co. C) stayed in Boonville as guard and garrison, and the rest of the regiment went to Otterville after foraging enough livestock from the local farmers to haul the regimental wagons cross country. "Foraging" was the semi-official euphemism for stealing. Anything the soldiers wanted in the way of food or fuel or anything else was taken from its owner preemptorily, usually on the justification that the owner was secesh and his property therefore the spoils of war. Occasionally receipts were given for reimbursement purposes.[12]

The stealing supplemented the army rations which were often inadequate and infrequently issued. The Boonville neighborhood had been fought over all summer, and the local farms had been picked over repeatedly. Both sides had long since helped themselves to chickens, hogs, cows and sheep. An occasional overlooked sheep or hog was uncovered and quickly snatched. Honey was another popular staple, along with the fall harvest of ripe fruit and vegetables. All this made up for short or missing army rations, which at its best was meat, bread, and coffee.

Otterville was a gigantic mudhole, a death swamp, and home in that fall and most of the winter for the eight companies of the 37$^{th}$ that left Boonville in the middle of October.

At Boonville, John Frick and Eugene Payne were getting along in varying degrees of health and safety eating grapes, squabbling with the Home Guard, and doing constable duty and guerilla scouting.

There had been two battles at Boonville in the summer and fall of 1861, and the place continued to be a target for raiders and occupation forces until late in the war. The tone of the relationship between the occupying forces and the natives was poisonous. Witness the case of civilian Frank McDearmon who shot a soldier at a dance in the winter of 1861 in East Boonville. McDearmon shot the soldier, the soldier took out his knife and carved up McDearmon, and both died on the spot.[13]

There was trouble with the German Home Guards that went on and on. The Home Guards were a creation of John C. Fremont, were a Missouri state creation, and never served as U.S. troops.

Early on in the occupation by the 37$^{th}$ (November 1861), Lieutenant Joe Eaton of Frick's company was shot at by the Home Guards. Eaton had gone in command of a guard of ten from the 37$^{th}$ to accompany General Pope's quartermaster in efforts to retrieve government property misappropriated by the Home Guard.

The detail went to search Thespian Hall in Boonville for the stores, and the Home Guards drew bayonets to keep Eaton's detail out. Pope's quartermaster, Captain Powell, demanded if mutiny was intended, and fifty Home Guards brandished their bayonets and answered by firing on the detail, wounding three. Powell's holstered pistol stock was hit, throwing him back against a gate. With Joe Eaton at Powell's side, the detail retreated down the street with the Home Guards firing after them.

Local moderates wanted the Home Guards out. They had preyed on the population for weeks by stealing and bullying, but they had to be maintained as the only organized defense against the rebel irregulars should the Union forces be sent elsewhere.

After the incident, Myron Barnes was ordered back from Otterville to take command at Boonville, and he moved the Home Guards out of town to the fairgrounds, put them on guard duty, and asserted himself as commander, which was the limit of what he could do.[14]

The detachment of the 37th at Boonville busied itself that fall in arresting remnants of Confederate General Sterling Price's army who were marauding from the bush and harassing the pro-Union locals. The chaplain led some of these scouts at the head of an armed squad, accompanied on occasion by Myron Barnes and John Laimbeer.[15]

The Confederate irregulars –bushwhackers – were grouped around Boonville, waiting to pick off an unescorted carriage or wagon, or small forces of men. They captured Julius White's new adjutant, Isaac Dodge, with his escort in December. Dodge was carrying orders for a force of about eight hundred cavalry that had stopped at Boonville for horse shoeing.

After Dodge was taken, about forty of the 37th and one hundred of the Iowa 5th Infantry, part of the Boonville Garrison, were summoned off to guard the cavalry camp while the eight hundred cavalry went to clean out the guerilla irregulars. The main force of cavalry met the rebels, who "ran like thunder," and abandoned their camp, horses and wagons. The cavalry burned or destroyed everything except about 200 horses. The lopsided estimate of casualties was Union 3, Rebels 30.[16]

Back at Boonville, the balance of the detachment was, variously, sick, broke, discontented with their camp, their officers, and their lot in general.  Eugene and Fred Payne were both down with measles by the end of November, John Frick was home on leave, and the drilling was left to Myron Barnes, who did well enough at it.  Lieutenant Herman Wolford ran Frick's Company and was liked by the men, most of whom disliked Frick.

One of the other Captains, John Laimbeer, Commander of the Michigan Company (D), was a constant source of trouble.  He had been left at Boonville in October under arrest, and spent most of his fifteen month career with the 37th in arrest.  When he returned to Otterville from Boonville in late November, he had left unpaid debts at Boonville, incurred while in arrest.  Captain John was simply unsuitable as an officer.

His troubles had started in the first days at Camp Webb, where forty-two of his men petitioned for his removal as captain citing, "repeated acts of insubordination, advising and directing his men to sneak past the perimeter guard and leave camp if they felt like it, and otherwise disobey camp regulations."[17]  He frequently did it himself.  He also detailed men from his company to work on his house in Chicago.  He had no military aptitude and had no desire to gain any.  At Camp Webb, his men had been on the edge of mutiny, having been lied to and abused constantly.  Laimbeer once advised two of his men to run the guard, and on that occasion one of them was shot by the officer of the guard.[18]

The Camp Webb petition of Company D to Illinois Governor Yates in September 1861 had the stamp of Laimbeer's Lieutenant, Wells Blodgett, on it, and was transmitted by brother Henry Blodgett, via Julius White, with the endorsement that, "Capt. Laimbeer is not qualified for the position and ought not to be commissioned [recommendation of Julius White], and also that Laimbeer had been that day guilty of an act of insubordination by giving three of his men passes to leave the camp...."[19]

The petition was not successful, Capt. John was commissioned, possibly because Governor Yates knew the Blodgetts, and getting rid of Laimbeer would be a quick way for Wells Blodgett to be promoted to Captain.  It took another year of Blodgett's complaints and Laimbeer's transgressions before Laimbeer was dismissed and Blodgett became Captain.

Blodgett managed the promotion by pulling very little duty with the regiment, getting attached instead to Missouri State Militia General Egbert Brown's staff. Most of this time, Sergeant Jack Moran ran Company D, and didn't get promoted for it until later on.

Gradually through the fall and winter of 1861, civil order in Boonville stabilized under Union protection. A police force was formed, pro-Union civilians returned to town, and commerce revived. A notable exception to this return was the slave economy. After the Missouri slaves learned they were the focus of the banging and crashing they saw around them, discontent spread like a virus. In Boonville, the regiment had its first experience with contrabands, who were to serve as washerwomen, grooms, cooks and servants for the army throughout the war. Slave owners sometimes had a difficult time recovering their property from the army once the troops got used to fobbing off their most menial tasks on this cheap labor that swarmed the camps.

## 7. Death by Mud

The march of the eight companies of the 37th from Boonville to Otterville in October of 1861 was a distance of twenty-five miles and ended in the rain. Recently impressed and unbroken mules tipped over a few wagons in the mud, making a one day trip into three. Most of the men were sick with camp fever, dysentery, and malaria, and so the three day hike was mostly a misery.

The column reached the Lamine River in Missouri on October 15, crossed it on the railroad bridge, passed through Otterville, and camped about two miles beyond, on a hillside on a branch of the Lamine, near Smithtown. Otterville was on the right bank of the Lamine, and was populated by a few hundred mostly southern sympathizers; "a poor little inland Missouri town, remarkable chiefly for its dilapidation and age, and its extreme idleness. Otterville is a little Hole in the Day sort of place two days march from Boonville."[1]

Using the Otterville-Lamine Camp as a base, the regiment was to do some very hard marches requiring unusual physical energy diminished by scanty rations, shoddy clothes, and cheap shoes through some very bad weather.

Sickness continued apace. Rain, cold, and hard marching brought five more men down dead in November, eight in December, and eight more in January. Many more were sick, and the virals were no respecter of rank. Company D Lieutenant William Mazelle was discharged with "consumption" (which could have been anything from chronic bronchitis to tuberculosis or cancer). Julius White's endorsement on the request for discharge of the 30 year old Mazelle read, "I fear [he] will not live long."[2]

Regimental politics and resulting turmoil spawned at Otterville continued throughout the war through fights, flare-ups and backbiting. In less than two months of service, the Michigan Company (D) had its Captain under arrest, its First Lieutenant sniping at him, and its Second Lieutenant discharged, and the Rock Island Company (A) was about to lose its captain, John A. Jordan.

# DEATH BY MUD

Jordan, at age 43, was not up to the marches and camp life, and ultimately went back to Coal Valley, Illinois and kept his hand in at war relief and local politics.

Jordan began acting oddly nearly at the outset in Missouri, a circumstance of opportunity not lost on his lieutenant, Henry Curtis. In mid-November, Jordan had a stroke or similar incident, which ended his military career. He was out and home by January 1862.

The first of many frustrating chases after Sterling Price, Confederate Commander of the Missouri State Guard, came early, when the first hillside camp at the Lamine railroad crossing was broken up on October 29. Orders were to march to Springfield, Missouri. Fremont was there facing Price's force of 30,000 men. The march from the Lamine took four days, over 53 miles of sharp rocks, gullies, and ruts, alternated with dirt roads which made choking dust enjoyed most effectively in the rear ranks.

Rations during the march consisted of a few handfuls of flour unaccompanied by anything to cook it in or by yeast or salt. If there was nothing to steal along the way, the men went hungry. Those who didn't throw their flour away made a paste by adding water, wrapping the glop around their musket ramrods, and cooking it over their campfire.

In November, the regiment met General Fremont enroute to Springfield. Fremont was on the way out, having been relieved by President Lincoln a bit earlier for issuing a premature emancipation proclamation. It was a sad sight for exhausted men to see the man whose face they carried on their regimental flag, dragging out of Springfield relieved of command by President Lincoln.

Fremont was replaced by General David Hunter, Julius White's ally, and the man who would be President of the Board of Inquiry on the surrender at Harper's Ferry in 1862, and the man to whom Julius White would owe his deliverance on that occasion.

After four days in Springfield, having failed to net Sterling Price, the regiment started the walk back to the Lamine, as miserable and sick as when they had left. They were again on half rations of mostly flour. Despite the hardship, the boast was how the $37^{th}$ measured up to the rest of the column. Of the $5^{th}$ Iowa, one hundred dropped out on the march. Of the $9^{th}$ Missouri, two hundred, and of the $37^{th}$, just two. Built up immunity to disease, the twenty mile daily marches, scanty food, a dozen dysenteric bowel movements a day, and worn out shoes and clothing were adversities that were toughening up the men.

After backtracking to Otterville, the regiment reached the old campsite on the Lamine on November 16, and completed the fruitless chase by moving to Syracuse, Missouri on the 18$^{th}$, a town that then boasted six hotels and two saloons.

It was two months into Missouri service, and young Major John Charles Black was cutting his teeth as politician and leader of men. Black was an articulate, intelligent, good looking, ambitious 22 year old with very sharp teeth, as those around and above him were soon to find.

Black had the regimental command in October and early November. Julius White had gone back to Chicago on October 20, and Myron Barnes was at Boonville doing a little bushwhacking, and keeping the Home Guard in check. Black told his family that he was, de facto, head of the regiment, "and, inter vivos, always have been and mean to be,"[3] apparently not having been instructed in the sin of pride by his Presbyterian minister father.

The winter war with the Missouri guerillas went on. Thanksgiving day at Syracuse was interrupted by a fourteen mile march with little meaning except that "...the whole move was to spoil our Thanksgiving dinner...!" according to Henry Curtis.[4] At Co. B., David Ash wolfed his turkey the night before Thanksgiving, a pleasure that might have been denied him on the next day's march.

Hunting was a big hit with most everyone. Deer and wild turkey were plentiful, and easy marks for hunters like Lieutenant Fred Abbey, the best shot in the regiment.

By early December, the food situation was decidedly better as the Lamine railhead assured steady quartermaster supply. The men were also becoming more skillful at buying or stealing food. Butter, eggs, flour and syrup were available from farmers, and the major staples on the midnight market were chickens and honey. "The men confiscate them nights I believe,"[5] was Henry Curtis' innocent explanation of the abundant supply of both commodities.

# DEATH BY MUD

November and December were taken up with scouts, raids, and chases all over the Syracuse vicinity. The houses along the march routes served as restaurants, inns, or hospitals for the men, as whim or circumstance dictated.

The camp at the Lamine Bridge was to be winter quarters, but it was to be a very short winter stay. The men had marched and countermarched in Southwest Missouri since October 29, and had made twenty-eight different camps, stolen most of their food, and left twelve dead buried along the route of march. Almost fifty were sick with all manner of pestilence, so the winter quarters were welcome. Myron Barnes, always the editor-critic, noted that, "Our army seems to be employed principally in marching and counter-marching. Our generals seem to be in no hurry to go out in the cold so long as they have comfortable quarters and are wrapped in warm flannels. It makes a great deal of difference whether a man fares sumptuously every day, or is obliged to lie upon the frozen ground."[6]

The Lamine was chosen for camp because of available water, timber, and means of supply. Permanent camp was made on the bottom land on clay soil in a densely forested low, wet patch of land. Fifteen thousand troops including the $37^{th}$ were posted there. They began at once building huts for the winter.

The best thing that occurred at the Lamine was the first payday since the enlistments at Chicago. The payroll changed hands quickly in true army style in games of chance. The sharp witted took the money from the dim witted. Julius White informed the regiment on December 12 that it was reported that, "gaming was practiced among the private soldiers," and charged sergeants and above to make restoration of the money to the losers and report the names of the winners to him. He went on to declare offending officers unworthy, NCO's to be reduced to privates, and privates, "to be dealt with in the most rigorous manner warranted by the Articles of War."[7] Some of the money lost was to be used for the care of the families the men had left behind in Illinois, until they were double dealt, blackjacked, or euchered out of it.

The same day, Corporal Hugh Shepard of Rust's company was reduced to private by Colonel White with the admonition that "Captain Rust will supply his place by some sober and well behaved soldier."[8] Shepard was a 32 year old carpenter from Mendota. His offense was mild, and by the next fall he was commissioned a 2d Lieutenant in the 8th Missouri Cavalry.

At year's end, most of the men were sleeping in Sibley tents on the ground. The ground remained damp in the river bottom that winter, increasing fever and discomfort. While wood for fuel was plentiful, straw for bedding was not.

The ground in the Lamine camp varied from a sea of mud to a frozen compost of dirt and straw or vegetable matter, frozen into holes and sharp ridges, then transformed once again into a morass by rain or melting snow. The unavoidable sticky, creeping all pervasive mud was a preoccupation of no small moment. Any step outside the tents, to the kitchens, the latrine, to guard duty or parade, put the men in contact with the mud. A step in mud could sink an inch or a foot, and always the boot or shoe came up as if dipped in warm chocolate to be tracked into the tents, onto the bedding or to be spread to the clothing or camp furniture. Every step outside required a mud-cleaning session. Sergeant Major Samuel M. Heartley summed up the camp mudhole in January as, "low and swampy. Ditching does no good... A few days since [January 11] the mud was a foot deep in our camp and all were congratulating themselves on a MUDDY death, when all at once, the cold blasts of the north came down... If Uncle Sam don't take some measures to have us removed from this mudhole before spring, most of our regiment will reach the end...without the aid of secession bullets...."[9]

Continual and chronic malaria, typhoid, dysentery and other varieties of camp fever were, like the mud, everywhere in the cold clammy river bottom.

Small comforts were gained from the completion of a make-work project, building stove fireplaces in one door of each tent. The fireplaces had been a project of Julius White's, who offered a $10 first prize and $5 second prizes to the companies making the best fireplaces. Fireplaces were built for most all the tents and compensated for the flimsiness of the tents and the dampness of the river bottom, restoring warmth and some cheer. Skaters were using the river, conjuring images of home to many, and packages of delights began to arrive from Illinois. Goodies had come in boxes from Danville and

Rock Island; food, mittens, socks, drawers, checkerboards and individual gifts sent by patriotic citizens and families.

Lieutenant Henry Curtis of Company A was employed in his civilian occupation of law at the Lamine by Julius White in drawing courts martial charge sheets, hearing the courts martial, and playing defense attorney. One of his clients in January 1862 was the regimental drum major. Charles Black had him charged, presumably for something more than bad playing, claiming on January 18, "The music has vastly improved in character... I have had the old drum major under arrest & think that is the real cause of the improvement."[10]

By late January 1862, Union General Henry Halleck, commander of the Department of Missouri, decided to resume the chase after Sterling Price. His orders stirred the camp at the Lamine, and at the end of January, the 37th moved off out of the mudhole. On the 22d, the regiment received another pay, and on the 25th the camp was burned and abandoned. There was very little hand-wringing at the move out of the Lamine, going back on the march in the campaign that would culminate in the fierce battle at Elkhorn Tavern near Pea Ridge, Arkansas six weeks later.

## 8. Pea Ridge

In early January 1862, President Lincoln ordered the new Western District Commander, General Henry Halleck, to get up and get moving. Halleck was to collect army units which had been scattered all over Missouri, and search out and destroy Confederate General Sterling Price and his army. Halleck ultimately massed a force of about 12,000 at Lebanon, Missouri. The 37th, a part of the command, was in General Jefferson Davis' Third Division, one of four Divisions making up General Samuel Curtis' Army of the Frontier.

Of the 979 men that had left Camp Webb in Chicago with the 37th, about 960 remained on the regimental strength as of January 1, 1862. Forty-six of those were on the sick list. In January, a few more deaths and a few more desertions subtracted more duty soldiers from the ranks prior to departing the muddy Lamine.[1]

The six weeks from the end of January 1862 to the first of March were spent in bad weather marching from point to point in Southwestern Missouri chasing Sterling Price's army. Payne's and Frick's companies had come down from Boonville, so they would have the misery they missed on the march down in November.

Leaving the sick behind, the regiment marched out of the Lamine River bottom on January 25 to Syracuse, Tipton, Versailles, Springfield, Gravois Bottom, and Linn Creek. Julius White's marching orders were similar to what would precede all the military movements the regiment would make on foot for the balance of the war. No straggling, no entry of houses "on any pretense whatever.... Soldiers who may be detected in robbery of private property will be dealt with in the severest manner. Company officers of this regiment are restricted to the following allowance of camp equipage: One tent to Capt. & 2 Lieuts., 1 stove, pipe, and furniture (20 lbs.) to each officer. Men – one Sibley tent to every 20 men, 2 camp kettles to each tent, 2 frying pans and deep pans to each."[2]

General Samuel Curtis' column went to the Osage River as part of Halleck's plan to run Sterling Price's army to ground. After a three-day march, a camp was made at Gravois Creek. The regiment reached the Osage River on February 3, a waterway with spectacular palisades of several hundred feet in height. Camp was made there on Moore's Plantation.[3]

Crossing the ice-clogged Osage River at Linn Creek was no small feat. All the wagons, animals, and camp equipage had to be transferred on flat barges through the ice floes against the current in the cold February wind.[4]

On February 8th, a sham battle was fought, with Charles Black playing the rebel commander in the make-believe. Orders came to march to Springfield on the 10th, and again the 37th was off in pursuit of Price, who as usual had fled before the arrival of the Union army. The army followed Price south, through Southwestern Missouri and over the state line into Arkansas, nipping at his heels all the way, forcing his army into quick retreats in a headlong flight into Arkansas.

On the 17th of February, the 37th crossed the line into Arkansas to the accompaniment of the regimental band playing "Out of the Wilderness," and "The Arkansas Traveler," to the glee of the yelping, singing, cheering men.[5]

By February 20, 1862, camp was made near Sugar Creek, Arkansas, and then a new camp at Cross Hollows near Bentonville, quickly dubbed Camp Halleck. The men had out-marched their supply wagons, and so food was again in short supply, with few places to buy anything. The diet at Camp Halleck was dried corn and pork. No corn meal, no sugar, no coffee, and clothing and shoes were fast giving out.

The Cross Hollows neighborhood was forbidding, prompting General Philip Sheridan to say, "If I owned Pea Ridge and Sheol, I would rent Pea Ridge and live in Sheol."[6] In this condition of frustration and physical discomfort, the regiment settled into the camp at Sugar Creek and preoccupied themselves with trying to keep warm and stealing enough to eat.

A tragedy occurred on February 21 when Henry Colborn, a 20 year old boatman from Company A accidentally shot and killed himself. Colborn was buried in his clothes and blanket. Total estate, $7.10.[7]

On February 23, Charles Dickinson (Capt. Dick) and Eugene Payne returned, Payne having been on leave and Capt. Dick in Illinois. Mrs. Dick had been acting as an army nurse, and the Captain had taken her home.

February dragged its cold, muddy feet into March, with the elusive Sterling Price staying out of reach. On March 5, a little drama was played out at the Cross Hollow camp. A private in the 59th Illinois resisted being shoved around any further by his officers and refused to get wood for his Captain's fire. When threatened with punishment, he pulled a knife and cut the clothes of his Lieutenant and threatened to kill him.

Measured against his offense, he got off lightly, being sentenced to have his head shaved and drummed out of camp: "...the whole division, 5 regts., 4 cavalry companies and 2 artillery cos [formed] two lines facing inward. The fellow was driven down one line and up the other at the point of a bayonette, the bands following him playing 'The Rogues's March.' It was a sad sight though he stood it bravely, defiantly...."[8]

Although the shaved-head private was not blameless, the responsibility of the offending officers served to mitigate his sentence. Had the situation been different, the young private would have put himself in for a long term in the stockade or for execution, for attacking his officer with a knife.

This tableau must have played in the dreams of some of the witnesses in the division that night, but only until one AM when an alarm was sounded in the Union camps. Price had attacked Federal General Franz Sigel's advance guard, and Siegel was retreating. Everybody got up, packed, cooked three days rations and prepared for battle. There would be no running and chasing on this occasion; the long awaited battle was at hand.

Sterling Price's retreat from Springfield, Missouri on February 12th had led him to the Boston Mountains in Arkansas. In Arkansas, Price had combined with Texas troops and some regiments of indians that had been raised in the Nations, and the formidable rebel army of about thirty thousand took a new commander, General Earl Van Dorn. The Federal forces numbered no more than eleven thousand.

Van Dorn's regular army had been augmented by about three thousand rabble, enlisted for three days in hopes of robbing enough property to make it pay. These men, including Jesse James, were the neighborhood scum, the local bushwhackers, largely without character or military discipline.

In addition, the rebels had raised several thousand indians in the Nations. There were Choctaw, Chickasaw, Pins, Seminoles and Creeks. Their leader was Albert Pike, a poet, a New Hampshireman, who rode for the rebels in a carriage at the head of the straggling indian column, dressed in feathers, beads, and moccasins. Some of the Yankee scalps to be taken in the coming battle by Pike's troops were sent home with great pride by the braves who had removed them from the Union dead.[9]

On the night of the 6th of March, wounded from Sigel's detachment began to arrive in camp. The rebels were in force and they were not running.

On the morning of March 7, battle day, at reveille, every fife and drum in Curtis' army was being tootled or tapped. The music drifted through the trees in the dawn light.

By mid-morning the battle was on. The 37th was part of General Jefferson Davis' 3rd Division, and was shuttled from one point to another from ten in the morning until about two PM when General Davis ordered Colonel Julius White, commanding the second Brigade, to deploy and engage. The rebels were making a stand. All the big brag around the camp fires the night before, all the cheering and all the defiance had come down to this; the 37th was going into the line, and they were going to get shot at.

The regiment was in Leetown, Arkansas in the rebel front. Both sides advanced until at an interval of about seventy yards, they opened fire. The arms of most of the rebel force were shotguns and squirrel guns. The shotguns had to be used at close range to be effective.

The flank companies of the 37th (A and K), and all the regimental corporals and sergeants were armed with five shot Colt repeating rifles, a rare pocket of advanced technology for 1862. The balance of the regiment was armed with large bore Belgian rifled muskets that were effective at long range and made "a horrid hole in the body."[10]

After three incidents of retreating and advancing, being driven back and then rallying, twenty of the 37th lay dead and one hundred fourteen were wounded, including Jim Lee and Albert Hilliard of

Company B. Lee was killed by a stray bullet from Company A and dropped in his tracks.[11]

At the other end of the line the Danville Company lost William Marlatt shot dead with a bullet in the brain. Morris Fitzgerald tried to carry his body off, and he was wounded and died that evening. Eugene Payne's brother Fred was shot and then scalped by some of Albert Pike's Indians. Payne was wounded slightly in the neck.[12] Both Will and Charles Black were wounded, Willie behind the left arm and Charlie in the right arm.

The Rock Island Company (A) was nearest the enemy, and suffered badly. The company went in on the 7$^{th}$ of March with fifty-five men. The next day sixteen answered roll call. Two had been killed and thirty-seven wounded. Among the wounded was Captain Henry Curtis, the Company Commander. He was shot in the ribs and in the shoulder.[13]

Darkness on the eve of the 7$^{th}$ of March suspended the battle, and the men went into bivouac sleeping on their muskets, and moved camp about midnight to reposition for the expected resumption of the battle on the 8$^{th}$.

The dawn light of the 8$^{th}$ filtered through the battle smoke as the sun rose, "Not the bright clear sun ... but a dull, copper-tinted globe, slowly pushing itself up through the murky cloud of cannon smoke that even the long hours of a winter night had not dispelled...."[14]

The end result on the Confederate side was that Van Dorn's rebel army of thirty thousand retreated in the early hours of the 8$^{th}$ after a fifteen hour battle against a Union army of eleven thousand for reasons traceable to poor weapons, poor discipline, poor supply, and the mortality of Confederate Generals McIntosh and McColloch, both killed in the conflict.[15]

The next day, Sunday, March 9$^{th}$, Union General Jefferson Davis organized the burials of the Union dead, ordering mass graves by company in a burial ground near Leetown.

Every house for ten miles around the battle site was a hospital for the wounded. William Fithian, who had come from Danville, Illinois to tend to his stepsons Will and Charles Black, was pressed into service by the medical corps and assigned a district of fourteen miles, all the way to Keitsville, Missouri. Charles Black was still in one such temporary hospital recuperating from his wound at the end of March, and Henry Curtis, twice wounded, was on his way to Rock Island on convalescent leave, noting of the journey that, "I have wasted enough [time in St. Louis] to have gone to New York on any through mule."[16]

The final Federal casualty figures in the battle were 203 killed, 980 wounded, and 201 missing, total 1,384. Of these totals the 37th had 21 killed and 114 wounded, accounting for about 5% of the total force engaged, and 10% of the casualties.[17]

Will Black echoed the thoughts of many after the battle, noting, "I have not learned to love the song of death.... It is not very pleasant to gaze on the faces of 40 or 50 dead faced secessionists, looking up so coldly into the somber light distilled through the treetops...."[18]

The regiment stayed in camp north of the battlefield at Cross Hollows for the rest of March, and in early April, they moved to garrison the post at Cassville, Missouri, while the rest of Curtis' army moved off to campaign in Arkansas and Louisiana.

They were left behind because of the absence or disability of all the field officers. Julius White was in Evanston with a bad leg, Charles Black in a house in Keitsville nursing his wounded arm, and Myron Barnes was in Rock Island with a sore throat.

The night before the march out of Cross Hollows, Rust's Company was "...on a spree generally... Bad whiskey created considerable disturbance in camp."[19] The next day, the army moved off through Cassville, left the 37th there for the next three months as post guard, and went off to chase rebel Generals Price and Van Dorn.

## 9. Cassville

The immediate problems in the Cross Hollows camp (Camp Stephens) at the end of March, before the move to Cassville, were the common ones; food, clothing, and sickness. There was too little of the former and too much of the latter. The responsibilities for regimental supply belonged to Quartermaster John Peck. There was a belief that he was making a personal profit out of short rations, refusing to issue credits for undrawn rations. The food that was issued was foul. At one point, the beef that was issued was buried, and the issue of bread, "would be quite as dangerous if put in a cannon as the stones Price's men used in the late battle." Officers entering Quartermaster Peck's quarters were seen by two visiting Waukegan residents (Messrs. Steele and Herrick, who had sons in the 37th) drinking liquor they alleged Peck refused to issue to the hospital or sick ward.[1] Wagons were also in short supply, and so the men had to carry their own knapsacks.

As for general morale, Colonel White and Major Black were disliked, and the men focused their loyalty on Lieutenant Colonel Myron Barnes, who identified with them and was a loose disciplinarian.

When the time came in April for Federal General Samuel Curtis to chase after Sterling Price and the rebel army, White and Barnes were absent, Black disabled. Julius White had gone home to Evanston with a broken leg he said was sustained at Pea Ridge. Apparently, it was not, and he was perfectly healthy after the battle. The Rock Island, Illinois Argus, a Democratic rag, published the gossip that White was drunk and racing horses with Colonel Chandler of Illinois when he fell off his horse and hurt his leg. The Chicago Republican papers trumpeted that the injury was a battle wound.[2]

Whatever the reason, with Barnes gone to Rock Island, White could not leave for Evanston unless he could dissuade Charles Black from going home to recuperate from his legitimate wound. White talked him out of it on the grounds that there would be another battle and he would be needed. Black consented to stay and then White left.

## CASSVILLE

General Samuel Curtis did not want to take a regiment commanded by a one-winged major on the new campaign, and so the 37th was assigned to garrison duties at Cassville, Missouri.

Cassville was a poor looking town of about forty houses fifty miles south of Springfield in Barry County, Missouri. It had been picked over and fought over for a year, and was a center of secessionist sentiment, guerilla raids, and Union reprisals.

In July of 1861, Sterling Price and his fledgling rebel army had occupied Cassville. The town had been Nathaniel Lyon's destination in August 1861 when he had set off looking for Price. He got no further than Wilson's Creek south of Springfield, where his command was defeated, and he was killed. Three months later, the rebel Missouri legislature met in Cassville for a week to sign the act of secession.

There was a string of killings in the Cassville vicinity in the early part of the war. There were ambush artists on both sides, Home Guards and Militia on both sides, both Union and Confederate regulars, irregular guerila companies, and citizens of varying political leanings. Cassville changed hands several times during the war, and when the rebels occupied the town, Union sympathizers suffered, and then the Union troops would return and southern sympathizers were beaten and murdered. Neutrals were trusted by no one.

Cassville lay on the main route running between Springfield and Fayetteville, Arkansas. The guard on the place in the spring of 1862 was the 37th, two companies of Iowa Cavalry, and a battery of three cannon, along with about one hundred wounded from Pea Ridge. The Mendota Company (E) was sent to nearby Keitsville as garrison and intelligence outpost.

The first regimental casualty at Cassville was William Ring of Messer's Waukegan Company. Ring died of one of the many camp fevers that shadowed both armies.

After the security of the post, a chief concern was for the sick which comprised a great part of the strength. There were over one hundred wounded from Pea Ridge as well as the ongoing complement of men with malaria, dysentery, and varied camp fevers, all laid out in the Court House or in stores and abandoned houses.

## THIRTY SEVENTH ILLINOIS

Three days after Private Ring died, Ransom Kennicott got Doc Humeston to write a certificate that said he, Kennicott, had "chronic diarrhea, produced by long exposure in camp," and Kennicott went home to recover.[3]

One of the small pleasures of the post was the regimental band. It had been fitted out with eight new instruments and a set of cymbals at Cross Hollows. The instruments had been purchased from the 8th Indiana Infantry for $365. The officers paid for the instruments which were to go to the players at discharge, provided they were good players. The band personnel in 1862 were:

> George Smith (Chief Bugler) 1st E Flat Cornet
> O.A. Whitcomb (Bugler) 2d E Flat Cornet
> Lieut C.W. Day (Provost Marshal) 1st B Flat Cornet
> Dr. John Murphy (Hospital Steward) 2d B Flat Cornet
> DeForrest Folsom (Drum Major) 1st E Flat Tenor
> Adolphus Simons 2d E Flat Cornet
> Austin Cruver (Commissary Sergeant) 1st B Flat Bass
> William Patrick 1st E Flat Bass
> Little Charlie Eaton (Drummer Boy) Snare Drum
> Towns Dickinson, Bass Drum
> Levi J. Castle (Private) Cymbals

"Little Charlie Eaton" was Lieutenant Joe Eaton's 14 year old son and the youngest member of the regiment.

Concerts were held every evening. Edward Anderson said they "made even Cassville desirable. A good band is one of the most inspiring aids to an army. If I were in command on the eve of a battle, I would rather trust to a good band for the results of the next day than to any inflammatory speech that could be made...."[4]

Charles Black commanded the regiment during April and kept things in reasonably good order. Myron Barnes returned from his sick leave on May 4 and assumed command of the post. There was little but guard duty to occupy the men, who began to get out of control under Barnes' permissive leadership. General dislike of Charles Black grew among the ill-disciplined set of men. Part of the go-to-hell attitude came from anticipation of the upcoming regimental election.

Lieutenant Colonel Barnes was enjoying himself hugely running the regiment and filling the order books with texts of a disciplinary nature, mostly on drinking and stealing. All the stern orders were read at dress parade to little effect. The admonitions against drinking to excess were strictly on a do as I say, not as I do, footing. Several of Barnes' evenings on the post fell into a pattern. He would drink redeye, remember that he was the commander of all Union forces in Southwestern Missouri, and then act on some spurious bit of intelligence. He convinced himself that all the cutthroat guerillas and red indians in the neighborhood were about to roll over the post raping and pillaging. Sergeant David Ash noted matter-of-factly that, "he takes too much of the sod corn for a man in his position."[5]

In battle dress and in his cups, Barnes would put the entire garrison on alert, cartridges loaded, rifles capped and loaded, for an enemy that never materialized.

On one of these occasions, an accidental discharge shot a man's toes off. On another occasion, he went too far with the post cavalry commander, Major Hubbard. One afternoon, Barnes ordered seven companies armed and ready to march. It was a miserable rainy day, and Hubbard had little patience with the drunken Lieutenant Colonel. He failed to fall in, claiming he could not read the order Barnes had sent him. Barnes had him arrested and took his sword. He returned the sword to Hubbard the next morning, apologizing that he hoped he would not, "take offense at the words or acts of a drunken man."[6] Hubbard did not charge Barnes on that occasion, and Barnes took no lesson from the incident, playing out much the same scene three months later in Springfield.

This type of regime drove Charles Black out of Cassville. Barnes and his friends were in charge, Major Black and his friends were ignored. Ten days after Barnes took command, Charles Black packed his bags and went to St. Louis.

Black's dissatisfaction was largely political. He couldn't be a colonel without winning a regimental election, which he saw he had no hope of doing. He left amidst company officers preoccupied with plotting, intriguing and scheming for position, for the strong suspicion among the ambitious was that Julius White would be gone shortly. He had been nominated as Brigadier General and would be moving to a higher command. His place would be filled and create a vacancy to be filled creating another vacancy, and so on. The logical sequence of succession, by accepted practice and convention, was for the Lieutenant Colonel to be Colonel and the Major to accede to the Lieutenant Colonelcy. That would move Barnes and Black up, and the vacant majority would be filled by one of the ten captains. Of course, if two field grades became vacant, all the better for the captains, as two of them would move up, and there would be vacancies in the companies losing captains. So everyone was involved. Black felt he could not trust Julius White, who was moving as quickly as possible to get out of Missouri. For a man who wanted to be a U.S. Senator, there was little glory to be had in the dirty little guerilla war that was always reported, if reported at all, way under the headlines of the eastern armies and their battles. Beyond this, White felt that infantry should not be wasted fighting mounted guerillas, who could always ride out of the grasp of advancing ground soldiers. He was moving to get his general's star and get out. If he could take the 37$^{th}$ with him when he went, all the better.

White enlisted all the political help he could find to get his name before President Lincoln. He got help from William Fithian, among others, and from Illinois State Adjutant Fuller. He wrote and thanked Fuller from Evanston in April for "the receipt of the papers to Mr. Lincoln."[7]

He also tried to smooth over the exit he made with his broken leg in March, leaving Charles Black to run the regiment with a shot up arm from a sickbed, abandoning him to his fate in the dumpy little guerilla den at Cassville.

White replied to Black's objections by saying, "Now, Major, it won't do for you and I to get excited. You know I never do. Things is working, and will doubtless terminate in some shape."[8]

As for Myron Barnes, he had not been with the regiment much, having been posted as commander at Boonville from November 1861 until the end of January 1862, and had gone on leave after Pea Ridge. In the time he was with the regiment, he became a great favorite with the men. In January, he had joined the ranks in an afternoon battalion drill, and was cheered by the men for doing it.

After Henry Curtis had returned from his convalescence from the Pea Ridge wound, he noticed in camp that "they get up a little scare here once in a while (when Barnes gets drunk, don't tell it!) but it don't amount to much."[9]

Charles Black would not attempt to run the regiment while drunk, but neither would he drop his cape and plumed hats and cut his flowing locks and grab a knapsack and drill with the men in the ranks. Barnes was unstructured, undisciplined, an independent newspaperman who was used to saying what he liked. His leadership style was unmilitary. He was, as David Ash said, "an awful good man," but out of step with the army.

Throughout April and May, the regiment was mostly employed in guard duty, scouting, foraging and drinking. Other time was taken in fortifying a new camp that was chosen in May. It was the military presence that brought stability back to Cassville and revived commerce.

The Blacks, as they usually did, sought out local society. They usually began in a new town by taking a census of pianos. More than two was a four-star town. They also quickly found the ladies of the neighborhood. Cassville did not earn high marks for either.

One of the most successful merchants at Cassville was the post sutler, who had a monopoly vending to a captive clientele. A contributant to the indiscipline at the post was liquor, and the chief supplier was the sutler.

The sutler's store was the modern day Post Exchange. Appointed by the regimental commander, the sutler was the exclusive regimental vendor of groceries, notions, hardware, tobacco, liquor, and anything else he could turn a profit on. The sutler appointed had an exclusive market of up to 1,000 men in one regiment, and the more conniving among them would sell inferior goods at exorbitant prices and earn boxcar profits.

One of the many criticisms leveled at Charles Black at the Cassville camp had his choice (or lack of choice) of sutler at its core. The catch-all policy committee in the regiments was the Council of Administration comprised of officers who would, among other things, recommend or ratify the appointment of the sutler.

The Council of Administration at Cassville that spring consisted of Capt. Dickinson, Capt. Frisbie, Capt. Payne, and Lt. Bandy as Secretary. They passed and sent a resolution to Charles Black referring to Black's choice of retailers as "hucksters and peddlers," as no permanent sutler had been appointed. Further, that if Black was going to allow such men within the camp, he should set the prices they would charge, and not the Council, as Black had requested.[10]

Here is a sampling of a sutler's wares, as contained in a sutler's handbill:[11]

> "Appilles by the barrile, old chese, snuff and Tobackir, Armey and Navey Bread; Sweet Sidur, Pain killer, and Find Comes. _ Pigs feet Pickeld, Lobstur all right, Rock River butter, Sassages, oysters and sardeens, concentrated milk, Lager nice and fresh, Peckles and Sour Krout, Stationery knife and Tobackir boxes for fifty cent, Ground coffee and whool socks and under sherts, Needles and Thred, and pins And butons, &c., Solt Poark and White fish, Armey knives, Yankee Notions, Potatoes by the barrile, Orstothers Bitturs."

Sutlers were an almost universally disapproved of necessary evil, placed to prey on and profit by sales to the soldiers who could purchase up to 50% of their monthly pay on credit No one but the sutler could legally sell anything but newspapers to the regiment.

The sutler's overhead consisted of a horse and wagon, and he paid a levy of 10 cents per man per month to the army to be used by the regiment for purchasing comforts for hospital patients or recreational items for the regiment. His revenue, on average, was about $5 per man per month. This would total $5,000 per month from a full strength regiment. The cost of goods sold could be 50% of the revenue, or about a 100% markup. He could buy cigars 2 for a penny and sell them at 3 cents each. Likewise the markup on paper, pens, combs, or bad whiskey or stale food. Whiskey was the most sought after commodity in the inventory. Most commands forbade the sutler to sell liquor to enlisted men, and some forbade its sale to officers as well, as in Missouri in the spring of 1862.

Because of the restrictions on sales, whiskey smuggling was a popular and profitable occupation. The smuggler might use cans marked "oysters," or pack it in barrels marked meat or bread. The risk of getting caught was usually worth the fine or confiscation compared to the profit to be made. One of the cheaper rotguts was the "Celebrated Schiedam Aromatic Schnapps," billed as, "the cheapest imported gin in the country," imported by one Udolpho Wolfe, 22 Beaver St., New York. Probably imported from The Bronx.

Will Black caught up with a sutler selling liquor in Springfield in July 1862. The penalty was confiscation of the stock (about 7 gallons) and a $25 fine, which amounted to a cost of doing business for the sutler.[12]

The sutler served a purpose, was generally tolerated, and was not the worst problem facing the 37th from the Cassville countryside. There were some larks and some leisure in the Ozark spring, but the deadly dangers were constant outside the limits of the post.

Julius White knew the frustrations of fighting the mounted Missouri guerillas with infantry. Some of the guerillas and bushwhackers were trying to protect the countryside from the rape of the land by Union forces. Union foraging swept up all livestock and property in their path, including fence rails, clapboards, and the contents of cows udders.

The union forage trains became progressively longer and ranged over more distance. The trains of army wagons, twenty or thirty in number, with cavalry escort, would travel up to forty miles in any direction, stripping the land.

Two grisly incidents occurred in June 1862. On the 4th, the regimental scout, Keys, was killed. He left the forage column to get supper at a nearby house, and was shot dead by bushwhackers.[13]

On the 11th, bushwhackers attacked a forage train and killed Sylvester Meisner of the Rock Island Company (A). He was shot twenty-seven times, and was brought back to Cassville "a mass of flesh and bone." Joseph Ring of Frisbie's Chicago Company (G) was shot twice in one leg and the femur of the other was fractured. Ring died that night after Doc Humeston had amputated his legs.

## THIRTY SEVENTH ILLINOIS

Humeston had been detailed as Post Surgeon at Syracuse in March and had missed the Pea Ridge carnage. Ring was his first amputation.[14]

Jacob Hawkins of Payne's Waukegan Company was captured from the same detail. He was moved through several secesh camps past many local rebels who might have shot him in the blink of an eye. He was saved on one occasion by recognizing a man he had known as a stage driver in Wisconsin. Hawkins was moved around Roaring River and Yellville, and was exchanged by rebel General McBride for a Union prisoner he wanted at Alton, Illinois. Hawkins came back to Cassville, took a tour of the guardhouse, and identified one of the bushwhackers who had killed Meisner and shot Ring in the legs.[15]

The war continued in Missouri, day by day, each day much the same. The Union troops would expose themselves to scout for food, and the guerillas with their down-home muskets and shotguns lurked behind the bushes to shoot them when the chance came. This was no Gettysburg or Antietam or Fredericksburg, no glorious daylight charges under waving flags as in the east. The war in Missouri was fought by night-stalking thieves and back-shooters on both sides.

The day Joseph Ring had his legs taken off, the real battle in the 37th was beginning with the campaign for the election of a new field officer to fill newly promoted Julius White's vacated spot. It came to be in the interest of many to rid themselves of Major Charles Black.

# 10. The Election

The volunteer Civil War Union Army elected its officers. The men elected the company grades, and the officers chose the field grades, in the tradition of the 17th and 18th century militia companies. While this was certainly in the spirit of democracy, it was not very good from a long-term military viewpoint. It worked well for a few weeks service hunting bandits or indians, but for a term of years with great armies moving against each other, it was a poor practice.

Ned the cobbler from the old home town might be a wonderful fellow and make a poor officer. On the other hand, Gridley the banker, the hard businessman, might be better suited to the role of leader and disciplinarian among his neighbors, who incidentally, he would have to face after the war, along with friends and relatives.

After the first pre-muster election, where the men who raised the companies usually got to be the officers, any vacancy was usually filled by the men next in line of rank stepping up a grade. When the Rock Island Company (A) went to Chicago to join Julius White, it was Myron Barnes' company, with John Jordan next in line. Barnes became Lieutenant Colonel, and so Jordan was elected Captain, with Henry Curtis 1st Lieutenant, and Charles Hawes 2d Lieutenant. In December 1861, when Jordan resigned, Curtis moved up to the captaincy, Hawes to 1st Lieutenant, and the first sergeant, or orderly sergeant, Lorenzo Morey, got to be 2d Lieutenant, all done by a majority vote of the enlisted men of the company, ratified by the Governor of Illinois. When Henry Curtis resigned in July 1862 to go as staff with Julius White, Lieutenant Charles Hawes got the captaincy, and so on. These elections were usually certified by some informal regimental committee, and the results sent to the state governor, who would rubber stamp the selections and issue commissions in the new rank.

The higher the rank, the higher the pay and influence accrued to the officeholder, and in the normal progression, a captain had to be a major before he could be a colonel, and a colonel before a general. In 1861, a captain's pay was $120.50 per month, and a colonel's $222 per month, broken down as follows:

# THIRTY SEVENTH ILLINOIS

| | |
|---|---|
| Colonel's base pay | $95.00 |
| Plus rations | $54.00 (6 per day allowed) |
| Horses | $24.00 (3 allowed) |
| Servants | $49.00 (2 allowed) |
| | |
| Captain's base pay | $60.00 |
| Plus rations | $36.00 (4 per day allowed) |
| Horses | None |
| Servants | $24.50 (1 allowed) |

The great difference is in horses and servants, as a field grade officer was allowed three horses and two servants, a company grade was allowed no horses and one servant. "Allowed" really meant reimbursable, for in practice, an officer could have as many horses and servants as he could afford.[1]

When the 37th was at the Lamine Bridge in Missouri in January 1862, Julius White was an acting brigadier, Lieutenant Colonel Barnes was at Boonville drinking wine and chasing bushwhackers, and Charles Black, as Major, was commanding the regiment.

All through the spring of 1862, White was pulling every political wire in his control to get promoted to Brigadier General, and by May, the perception was that he would be promoted and leave the 37th to a new colonel. In the traditional line of succession, Barnes would then be Colonel, Black Lieutenant Colonel, and the senior line captain would be the new Major. This was about as fair a system as could be implemented, based on rank and seniority, excepted only by incompetence, cowardice, or other serious debility.

The normal succession was upset in the 37th not by any of the above excepted impediments, but by petulance and disgust on the part of Charles Black, and by less than scrupulously implemented ambition on the part of Captain Henry Frisbie.

Myron Barnes came back to Cassville from his leave in May 1862 and assumed command of the regiment from Charles Black. Shortly afterward, Black walked off, leaving the 37th because he didn't like Myron Barnes or his style of command. Black's plan was to go to St. Louis and wangle a new assignment, one with more of a future.

# THE ELECTION

One of the things that was working against Major Black was that he was not a member of the Masonic Order when being a Freemason was de rigeur. The freemasons, or "ringknockers," who would announce themselves when entering the presence of another officer by banging their masonic ring against the nearest hard surface, were bound by oath to promote each other's interests. Payne, Frisbie, and Barnes, among others, commonly allied with each other against non-masons, albeit temporarily.

Sergeant David Ash was in the hunt for office, as was every other non-commissioned officer in a company with a captain who had any chance of being elected Major. Ash was an orderly sergeant being paid about $20 per month. Officer-enlisted differentials in pay made many interested parties.

June in Cassville was spent in the mostly fulltime occupation of running for office. Everybody was running, everybody with friends who could peddle influence was asking for help.

Aside from being disliked for trying to enforce discipline, Charles Black did himself harm by leaving the regiment to seek another assignment with the army at Corinth, Mississippi. The widespread belief in the regiment was that he would not return. If both White and Black left, there would be two vacancies for two captains to succeed to a field office.

The speculation on who would win, and the cabals and alliances were quick to form. Captain Eugene Payne saw in Charles Black's absence a chance to push his own interests, and allied with frontrunner Henry Frisbie for this purpose. He went straight for the kill, and got up in an officer's meeting in May and said about as follows: "I am an enemy to Major Black, I am an enemy to Major Black's friends and I shall do all I can to defeat them."[2] The politics of the statement was that Payne had Frisbie's support for the Majority if Payne supported Frisbie for the Lieutenant Colonelcy.

In addition to Payne and Frisbie, Captain Charles Dickinson thought he had a chance since he considered himself the senior line captain. Captains Kennicott, Curtis, Rust, and Will Black were also candidates. John Laimbeer was under arrest, no one liked Erwin Messer, and Herman Wolford was the last captain promoted, so they were realistically out of it.

## THIRTY SEVENTH ILLINOIS

Phineas Rust had put his oar in the water, prompting a tongue in cheek letter from Congressman Owen Lovejoy to the Illinois Governor, saying that, "Capt. P.B. Rust ... is willing to take upon himself the duties of a Col. as this I suppose is a thing of rare occurrence, I suppose you will be glad to confer on the him the title. Seriously, if you can I would be glad to have you make him a Col."[3]

Payne's political sensitivity extended to instructing his wife on her travel plans to visit the regiment; "If you come through with [Quartermaster Peck], be careful what you say ... he is an advocate of the opposing interest although he will pretend differently... Look out for Chan. Morse for he is a black-hearted traitor. I cannot stop to enumerate all the things he has done, but enough that he is opposing me for majorship...."[4]

To the surprise of most, Charles Black returned to Cassville in June with Julius White. White had met him in St. Louis and convinced him that running away was not the thing to do. Since White would take command on his return, and his general's star was at that point in some doubt, Charles Black returned to take his chances with his enemies in the regiment.

At the end of June, the regiment moved to Springfield, Missouri and held their election on July 1. Julius White had at last gotten his commission as general, and orders to go to serve with Fremont in Virginia, and he had had the 37th reassigned to Springfield.

Things had been arranged about as follows: Barnes would be unopposed for election to the colonelcy, Frisbie had the support of a majority of the officers for Lieutenant Colonel, passing over Charles Black. Black would most likely be so upset he would again leave the regiment, and Frisbie would use his influence to elect Eugene Payne Major.

The election was held on the morning of July 1. Barnes was quickly elected Colonel unanimously, and Frisbie was elected Lieutenant Colonel by the officers by a 21-9 margin. After the vote was counted, according to Eugene Payne, Black "wept profusely, went to his tent, and before his wail had abated, wrote out his resignation and sent it in."[5] Black's disgrace was in being beaten 21-9. His abandonment of the regiment in May had worked against him, but the game was not over until Illinois Governor Yates issued the commission, and after the election, the pressure and pleas came down on Governor Richard Yates.

The enlisted men rallied to Black's support. Dickinson's company immediately got up a petition to Governor Yates, circulated it, and got eight out of ten companies unanimous in support of Black, recognizing his skills at drill and as a responsible, sober officer. Sergeant Henderson Bleakley gave the petition to General Egbert Brown in Springfield, and asked that it be sent to Governor Yates. The regimental non-commissioned officers paid their respects that July morning by forming up and asking Black to conduct them in the bayonet drill. General Egbert Brown, Brigadier of Militia and Commander at Springfield, supported Black, and worked to have the election overthrown.

Black had powerful allies, and he called in every marker he held and invoked every family and political connection. Wells Blodgett had written to Illinois Adjutant General Fuller in June and July waning of the dangers of "wire-pulling," and "buying and selling," and solicited the efforts of brother Henry Blodgett. He laid the election results to "intrigue and falsehood," and argued that neither men nor officers were pleased with the election of Henry Frisbie.[6]

Julius White was working on Black's behalf, as was Father-in-law William Fithian. Black even wrote to his former Colonel, Lew Wallace, and appealed for help.

His plea to his stepfather was abject. He had to head off Frisbie's commission before it was issued: "Concerning my troubles & their cause & remedy... no time can be lost. Hours are precious to me & a few days will decide whether I remain in the army or return home under a cloud... Brother Will proffered my request for your support. I want it earnestly, more earnestly than I can write. I will defray all expenses of your trip to Springfield or wherever it may be necessary to go...."[7]

Henry Frisbie was also working to ensure that he be commissioned, soliciting all the influence he could bring to bear on the governor. Doc Humeston, with a memory of Charles Black trying to displace him by any means in order to make a place for William Fithian, supported Frisbie, referring to him as a brave man and true soldier, successful business man, etc.

# THIRTY SEVENTH ILLINOIS

Myron Barnes recommended Frisbie in the same general tone, i.e., gentleman, true soldier. Payne even got "Hon. Coz." Elijah Haines to endorse Frisbie, as Payne's fortunes were tightly bound to Frisbie's success. Frisbie's brothers in Chicago pressured to accelerate the commission, as suspicions were rising that the Governor's noticeable delay in issuing it was not working in Frisbie's favor. Frisbie's position as electee was being eroded by the petition of the men of the regiment, and by Charles Black's allies, who were making the case of intrigue and falsehood. They would later make the case of bribed voters.

Julius White was in Chicago in early July and combined with Henry Blodgett to make a plan to get both Charlie and Henry's brother Wells into a better situation. White recognized that even if the Governor reversed the election and commissioned Black over Frisbie, his situation would be very unpleasant with Barnes as Colonel and Frisbie as Major. The plan was to give Black the colonelcy of a new regiment and install Wells Blodgett as Major with him.

The day White and Henry Blodgett had devised this scheme, the Governor had decided on his own compromise. He commissioned Charles Black Lieutenant Colonel and Frisbie Major, and avoided making Lieutenant Wells Blodgett a major. Frisbie had gotten the vote of two thirds of the officers, and Charles Black had the political support and the vote of the men. Black would be promoted in the normal line of succession, and Frisbie would be pushed up one grade, also traditional, and Yates served all political considerations as best he could, except for the Blodgetts, who were being a little pushy in using Black's unfortunate situation to advance the interests of Wells Blodgett.

Frisbie agreed to this, or his allies did, to avoid a struggle with the Black faction, which he might have lost. Making the promotion from Company G (Frisbie's company) also made room for Judge Bell's boy George to advance to the captaincy.

So the deal was cut, and the big loser was Eugene Payne, if in fact he did have votes for Major "by a clear majority," as he believed. He had declared war on the Blacks, had been cut loose to drift on his own by Frisbie, and had ended up with nothing to show for it.

# THE ELECTION

"The Governor was influenced," he said, "by the darned old politicians of Illinois to throw us all overboard and commission Black and Frisbie… I think the governor of the State of Ill. a d—d old fool and his political advisers a set of military commission hucksters bartering to the one who can pay the most. I am ruined completely now unless Frisbie resigns, the old scamp. I will never trust man again. I can see now how Judas came to sell his savior…."[8]

Frisbie wrote to Governor Yates and Adjutant General Fuller, who had the official capacity of administering the Illinois regiments, asking in a roundabout way, why the two to one election majority was overturned and if there were new rules on promotion. He ended with one very oily and overblown bit of exaggeration; "Again, Governor, I thank you for my father's sake, whose sun is almost set, whose head is bare and white from meeting the … winds of near a century. Who bears the scars of war with Algerian pirates, who under our flag crossed African desserts (sic) and maintained our motto, 'Millions for defense, but not one cent for tribute.' Who has upon the ocean with thundering cannon punished British insolence and insult, who has met the savage foes of our own wilderness and help drive back foreign invasion. While the blood flows in me, his spirit animates and for his sake I thank you."[9]

Frisbie's father Fred, who was 73 at the time (a bit short of a century) found time with all this fighting to have fifteen children by four wives before he died in Poughkeepsie, NY in 1869.

Charles Black's stepfather and counsellor, William Fithian, advised him after the election on the matter of friends and enemies. While Mother Black was advising Charles to take the olive branch from Danville townsman Napoleon Hicks, the Doctor was giving some advice from the darker end of the spectrum on White, Barnes, and William Bandy, another Danville townsman; that they were all dangerous enemies and should be so treated. The Doctor was very complimentary to Capt. Dick (Charles Dickinson), who had gone to Springfield with him to secure the commission for Charlie; "I regard Capt. D. as one of God's gentlemen. Say to Capt. D. for me that if I can serve him, he must not hesitate to command me at any and all time."[10]

## THIRTY SEVENTH ILLINOIS

Capt. Dick was unfortunate, because he was part of a long line of office seekers, and probably the one with the best reasons to be disappointed with the election, for of all the claims to seniority in the regiment, his was the strongest. Unfortunately, this was not matched by any useable political influence. For the rest of the war, after losing out on the majority three times, Capt. Dick would set up a mighty caterwaul, punctuated by periodic resignations. He never did advance his rank in the $37^{th}$.

By the end of July, White was long gone, the commissions had been issued and delivered, and things were settling a bit, even though the election had pleased few people. The Danville Lieutenants had opposed the Blacks; Chan Morse (Lieutenant Chauncey Morse of Company C) had opposed Eugene Payne, Captain Dick had come up empty, and Frisbie was denied the office he was elected to by the officers.

A positive result was that the incident caused Governor Yates to make promotion policy for all Illinois regiments. The new rules kept conflicting claims out of the Governor's office and avoided the political damage of disappointing the majority of such claimants. The new General Order 43 was issued in July. The rules were set that company offices be filled from the company with the vacancy, regimental offices from within the regiment, and all by the rule of seniority, except in cases of debility such as incompetence or cowardice, or in cases of exceptional merit. The governor would still want the recommendations of the officers of the unit having the vacancy.

Frisbie, Black, et al., had done a service by promoting these rules. It was one of the few positives to come out of the summer fight for office.

## 11. Punishment

The 37th came to Springfield, Missouri on June 30, 1862, delivered out of the Cassville wasteland into the garden of better looking women and pianos – and into the arms of General Egbert Brown of the Missouri State Militia. Eugene Payne called Springfield, "emphatically one of the loveliest spots I ever saw in (Missouri) not excepting Boonville...."[1]

Satisfaction with Springfield was almost universal. The regimental camp west of town was as attractive as the city. The men got a new issue of uniforms on July 4 and looked, "as nice as a new hat."[2] No matter they were so cheap that many fell apart on the first washing.

The two months at Springfield (July and August 1862) were to be similar to the time at Cassville, but spent in a better location. Other than one man being shot dead by guards while trying to jump the paymaster, the regimental quartermaster attempting a jailbreak with forty armed men from the regiment, and Colonel Myron Barnes attempting to liberate the town from the clutches of the pro-Union State Militia by force, it was a quiet time. Henry Millman of Company D was the man shot by the paymaster's guards, John Peck and Fred Abbey were in on the jailbreak, and Colonel Myron Barnes led the mutiny against the Militia.

One matter that gets looked after in camp that isn't looked after on the march, or in battle, is discipline. Things like drunkenness, stealing, and disrespect to superiors were largely let go in the first weeks in Missouri because of the newness of the war and unfamiliar surroundings. Then the hard marches of the winter came on, and the sickness, and then the February scouts, and then the horrors of Pea Ridge. Nothing much was ever done after the warnings against drinking, straggling, stealing, harassing citizens and other uncouth acts constantly read at evening Dress Parade through the spring of 1862. By the time the 37th was left at Cassville, and later Springfield, there was sufficient time, and sufficiently expanded infractions, to step up the frequency of punishment.

## THIRTY SEVENTH ILLINOIS

The splashiest crime to occur at Cassville was a systematic long-term pilfering of valuables from the mail. The theft continued until Sunday, May 18, when Samuel M. Lemoine, the pet and pride of Fort Lee, New Jersey by way of Lafayette, Illinois, who was the mail clerk, took several letters to the privy and opened them. He had opened several others, leaving the torn-up remnants of the envelopes anywhere and everywhere from the privy to the telegraph office to any convenient vacant house all over town. Several soldiers picked up pieces of letters strewn all over the Cassville post, and Lemoine was collared the next day after selling a pilfered ring to Private Julius Kelsey. During a hearing at the end of the month, Lemoine confessed, laying his dishonesty to the evil influence of Private William Barlow and too much whiskey.[3] Lemoine suffered no permanent damage, and eventually became Regimental Sergeant-Major before the muster-out in 1866.

The casual treatment of Samuel Lemoine for his part in the mail theft was about as far as discipline went in the first year, but regimental punishments gradually increased in severity after that. In May 1862, Private Philip Honlin of the Michigan Company got a traditional army punishment for an unrecorded infraction at a trial before a panel consisting of Capt. Dick, Herman Wolford, and Erwin Messer, Fred Abbey acting as Judge Advocate and Prosecutor. He was tried and convicted of "conduct detrimental to the service." The court sentenced Honlin to stand on a barrel in the front of the regimental guard house from eight to ten o'clock A.M. and from four to six o'clock P.M. on four alternate days in June, to be confined to the guard house for one week on bread and water, and to forfeit a month's pay.[4]

A less embarrassing punishment was given to Private Louis Dubois, a forty-one year old teamster of Kennicott's Company, for using "disrespectful and insulting language towards Lieut. Abbey," while driving a team on a foraging expedition He got five days in the guardhouse, and a $10 fine.[5]

A wide variety of other crimes were adjudicated with varying punishments. On the first day at the new camp at Springfield, regimental election day, Timothy Hickey of Frisbie's Chicago Company did, "in the presence of a large number witnesses, have criminal connection with a woman of the town...." Hickey was sentenced to thirty

# PUNISHMENT

days in the guardhouse and loss of two months' pay. He had to walk every other hour in front of the guard house with a sign suspended from his back with "BLACKGUARD" written on it. He was then to be drummed out of camp; "a man so brutalized is too degraded to be the associate of soldiers of the Army of the Southwest."[6]

Hickey did his punishment but never left the regiment, and was killed at Prairie Grove.

A sampling of other high crimes from the police blotter includes Private Peter Harrison of Wolford's Rock Island Company, who deserted in July 1862, returned in March 1863 under amnesty, and forfeited seven months' pay for the deed.

On August 5, Henry Frisbie set up a police court at Ozark, Missouri, appointing himself, "Regimental Magistrate." Samples of Frisbie's justice included a $2 fine and ten days hard labor to Private Thomas Carman of Payne's Waukegan Company for an absence without leave.[7]

A more serious charge was proved against Private Washington Smith of Payne's Company who pled guilty and said that "he occasionally stole little things." For the theft of a pistol from Private Robert Kellan, he was fined $5, read out at Dress Parade, and then "marched in front of and down the whole length of the Battalion and exhibited as a thief,"[8] and given ten days at hard labor for good measure.

Rank allowed no haven from accusation and arrest. At the end of July, Henry Riggs, sergeant in Frisbie's Company, in writing, threatened Doc Humeston and demanded his removal. Myron Barnes had him stripped of his rank, "in consequence of inciting rebellion in the ranks... that is to say: signing a petition to force an officer to resign, and making threats if said officer did not comply."[9]

As easily as Barnes condemned Riggs, he cleared Sergeant Henry Louis Payne. In July, Egbert Brown had Thomas Henry Louis "By Christ" Payne arrested on a robbery charge. Barnes got him released as there was no proof, and the supposed victim, Citizen Louis Brown of Cassville, could not identify Payne as the villain or pick him out as he went up and down the ranks of the regiment looking into the faces of the soldiers.[10]

# THIRTY SEVENTH ILLINOIS

All this informal, regimental, non-judicial punishment served well for petty crimes of enlisted men. Officers were dealt with in a more formal manner. The usual and frequent officer's punishment was arrest, sometimes at the whim of a superior, other times for genuine felony. Very few officers were exempt. Charles Black was arrested four of five times during the war by various superiors for various reasons.

Serious crimes resulted in court martial, a trial heard by a panel of from five to nine soldiers, most always officers. Captain Henry Curtis sat on these panels in Springfield in the summer of 1862 and complained of it as the hardest work in the service. The duty consisted of endless hot days in uncomfortable straight-backed chairs waiting for every word to be recorded in long hand by the clerk.

The most sensational punishment of the war in the 37th was that given to Myron Barnes by verdict of court martial in September of 1862.

## 12. The Mutiny

In the summer of 1862, Egbert Brown, the General commanding the Missouri Militia and Federal troops in Southwest Missouri, was running his forces all over the district looking for rebels. He reacted to the flimsiest of information, most of it rumor, and dispatched hundreds of men at a moment's notice chasing rebels who were never there, if they were ever there at all, when the Union soldiers arrived. He would send 1000 or 1500 men on forced marches of twenty or thirty miles in the August heat, and back again, with few successes to show for the effort.

Brown became increasingly unpopular with the army because of these wild chases. He was a State Militia officer and not in Federal service. A typical General Brown operation was launched in early August. He sent six companies of the 37th and nine hundred other assorted troops on a march from Springfield to Hartsville, Missouri and back. After a five day excursion over ninety-six miles of dusty road, nothing was found.[1]

At Ozark, and in contrast, Myron Barnes was having some modest success that summer. He sent out one hundred cavalry from Ozark on one occasion, surprised rebel Colonel Lawther's men asleep and sent them running half-dressed into the woods. Three were killed, and Barnes' men captured one prisoner, thirty horses, seventy saddles, fifty guns, their flag, and Colonel Lawther's sword and personal baggage.[2]

On another occasion, Barnes turned out the Ozark Post to go after one of the more notorious Missouri guerillas, Dick Campbell. Barnes, Lieutenant George Bell, and Captain Herman Wolford went and almost caught up with Campbell and about three hundred cavalry below Forsyth, and captured one cannon and eighteen prisoners after a five mile chase.[3]

Compared to what General Brown was achieving, these were very good results. Brown had abandoned much of the countryside to the rebels, having pulled the garrisons at Neosho, Cassville, Mt. Vernon and Newtonia back to Springfield to build forts and wait for an attack that did not come until 1863.

## THIRTY SEVENTH ILLINOIS

This frustration with General Brown, the mutual lack of respect between Brown and Barnes, and Barnes weakness for redeye lead to an ugly incident at the end of August involving Quartermaster John Peck and Lieutenant Fred Abbey.

Some runaway slaves had been caught and put in the Springfield jail by the Militia authorities, who took the southern view of them as property of their owners to be held until their owners could pick them up. Fred Abbey, a rabid abolitionist, a "monomaniac on the subject,"[4] decided to intervene with John Peck's help.

About nine on the evening of August 19, Abbey had succeeded in convincing forty men of the 37th to grab their rifles and accompany him to town to take the contraband runaways out of jail. The jailer would not bend to the threats of the armed force. The jailer was told that if the negroes were not out by the next day, "they should come out, if there was men enough in the 37th Illinois to bring them out." The Post Guard was told just about the same thing.[5]

Peck and Abbey were not successful. Abbey, the British born gunsmith and Ellsworth Zouave, was arrested the next morning as the prime mover in the liberation plot. The next day, Peck was arrested in the square in Springfield while loading his wagon train to go back to Ozark, and was ordered back to the regimental camp.

That was where things stood on Thursday, August 21, when Myron Barnes was sent out with the regiment on a fruitless set of maneuvers, a result of one of Egbert Brown's recurrent panics that Springfield was in imminent danger of attack.

Barnes got back to Springfield on Sunday, the 24th, and in the morning was having a glass or ten of nockum stiff in the Chambers House Hotel on the square. A little after one PM, the Militia Post Commander, Lieutenant John Pound, saw Fred Abbey in the street in violation of the terms of his arrest. He sent the Provost Martial to shoo Abbey back to camp. Abbey showed a pass Barnes had given him permitting him to be in Springfield. The Provost Martial reported this to Pound, who sent over to Barnes to find out by whose authority he had extended Abbey's arrest limits. The Provost Martial, Lieutenant Byrket, found Barnes sauced up in the Chambers House with Herman Wolford. Byrket asked him by what authority, etc.; Barnes

## THE MUTINY

told him, "By God, by authority of my commission! You cannot arrest Lieutenant Abbey. I dare you to interfere with me!"

Byrket came out of the hotel and talked to Fred Abbey and John Peck outside in the street, and then went on his way back to see Col. Pound. He climbed the stairs to Pound's office and reported Barnes' answer. Then there was a shout from the street:

"Pound! Come down here, I want to see you."
Pound went down and found Barnes, Peck, and Abbey.
"Are these men under arrest?" asked Barnes.
"Yes," replied Pound.
"There must be some mistake. I was never notified of it," said Barnes.
"Why have you released them?" asked Pound.
"I have not released them. I only extended Lt. Abbey's limits."
"What authority have you to extend this man's limits?" asked Pound.
John Peck answered, "Who ranks who here? Do you rank [Colonel Barnes], or does [Colonel Barnes] rank you? [Colonel Barnes] gave me the limits of the town, not you!"
"Go to camp, Gentlemen, go to camp. Report to me there." Barnes said, saying he would be responsible for them.

Peck and Abbey walked back to the camp, and Barnes rode over to the Chambers House. There he met Regimental Surgeon Luther Humeston.

There were things about the State Militia that had rankled Barnes and the regiment for months. The militia had peremptorily taken supplies, given the 37$^{th}$ the worst duty, marched and countermarched them to no purpose, punishing the men in the summer heat. Also, Peck and Abbey were not the first officers arrested by General Brown. Captain John Laimbeer, Company D, was under arrest in the Chambers House with a bayonet guard around him, with no charges and no trial. Myron Barnes had just anger at the State Militia, and decided he would take a stand. On this Sunday afternoon, he was drunk enough to take the bull by the horns.

## THIRTY SEVENTH ILLINOIS

He and Doc Humeston went back to Pound's office and walked in as Pound was making out this report to Egbert Brown. Barnes sat down beside him.

"By what authority were my men placed under arrest? Who placed them under arrest?"

"I placed them under arrest. I am Post Commander and they raided a jail on my Post and I arrested them. You know any officer has a right to arrest a man who is committing an offense."

"Who are you? Do you rank me?" asked Barnes.

"I am only doing my duty by order of General Brown."

"Does the Commander of the post command the force here?" asked Barnes.

"No, he does not," replied Pound.

"Who made you Commander of the post?" asked Barnes.

"General Brown," Pound replied.

"Who is General Brown? A Militia General who is a nobody. I don't care a damn for him or his authority or yours! I'll see who is Commander of the post! When I came to this country, I brought something with me that could do something. My regiment came out here to fight and not to submit to the domination of every militia man. I demand you release my men from arrest and I demand they be tried. It is my right!"

"I will not release them from arrest," Pound said. "I cannot do it. The charges have already been sent to Headquarters."

"Yes, you can do it," replied Barnes.

"I will not," Pound said.

"Then I will do it, and I will meet you out in the square. I have been here since last April protecting the citizens of this state in their civil rights and now I and my regiment want our rights! God damn you and the whole lot of you!"

That was the exit line. Barnes and Humeston left and Barnes was in full feather when he hit the street. He got on his horse and rode over to the guard house and paused for a minute. It was regulations that the guard be turned out to salute passing Field Grade and General officers.

# THE MUTINY

After a minute, with no response, he shouted through the window, "Where is the Guard?"

Lt. Byrket was in the guardhouse and came out.

"Who is the Officer of the Guard, and where is the Guard?" shouted Barnes.

The Officer of the Guard came out (Lt. Archie McDonald, 26th Indiana) and faced Barnes.

"Where is your Guard? Why didn't you turn out the Guard?"

"My Guard is on post, and I didn't know who you were," replied McDonald.

Barnes then rode back over and screamed for Pound, who came to his window.

"Where is the Guard?"

"I cannot recognize you, you have no shoulder straps," said Pound.

"My saddle has the trappings," said Barnes. "Pound, you are under arrest. You will send your sword to my quarters."

"I do not recognize your authority and will not obey you," Pound hollered back.

"Well, by God, I'll make you recognize it! I will bring my regiment to arrest you and relieve your guard. We will fight it out in the square!"

Now by this time, the shouting match had attracted the attention of several citizens of Springfield and soldiers who were in the square. Windows opened and neck craned to see from all over the square.

Col. Barnes was furious. He had committed himself to take military control of Springfield. He turned his horse and rode off to camp to get his troops.

When he arrived in camp, he was roaring around out of control. He rode down the color line to his old company, the Rock Island Company (A), and ordered Charles Hawes to form the company. Hawes sized up the situation and refused. Barnes said, "If you do not obey my orders, I will get someone that will. You can go to your quarters under arrest!"

Henry Frisbie came over as he was attempting to order out the men of "B" Company, and got Barnes off his horse and into his tent, ending the attempt to assault Springfield and liberate it from Militia control.

Frisbie related what went on in the tent:

"While in the tent, the Colonel stated he wished to show the men that he was not the cause of all the tom-fool marching the regiment had been doing for some time past.... The first cause of difficulty that day was ... General Brown's denial of sending him to McCullough's Springs. He showed me six orders from General Brown to go to McCullough's and take command of the troops there. He now stated General Brown was amazed to find him at McCullough's, and denied ever having ordered him past Wilson's Creek.

To further show their bad intentions toward him, he instanced the keeping of one of our officers (Laimbeer) under arrest for a good many months without ever furnishing him a copy of the charges.... When they could no longer silence him, they seized him and put him under strict guard surrounded by bayonets, and excluded everyone ... from speaking to him.

...he also mentioned the refusal to sign proper requisitions to get things we needed...

...He said he had enemies and was very mad at them. Parties had told him that I was his enemy. If so, he wanted me to leave his tent. I told him if it was disagreeable to have me there, I would retire. I went out. He followed me and kept saying he was told so. He gesticulated violently and said his was no coward... he said the men were his friends and if the officers were not...."

Frisbie's summary of the conversation was designed to go into the record to make Brown look bad. It also was an incomplete summary, because Barnes literally kicked Frisbie out of his tent. After the heated exchange, Frisbie began retreating from the tent, with Barnes kicking him in the backside and swearing and threatening as Frisbie tried to get away.

A man who saw the incident testified at the court martial called over the incident a week later. He was Private Michael Emery, Company B:

# THE MUTINY

"...all I saw of them was Major Frisbie going away from the Colonel's tent.

COURT: Do you swear upon oath, that that was all you saw pass between them on that day?

EMERY: The Colonel was walking towards Major Frisbie, and the Major was walking a pretty good gait. The Colonel raised his foot toward Major Frisbie, a little higher that he usually did in walking.

COURT: What do you mean by saying that the Colonel raised his foot a little higher than he usually did in walking?

EMERY: I supposed that he meant to kick at Major Frisbie.

COURT: Did Col. Barnes kick Major Frisbie?

EMERY: I could not say. I did not see him kick him...

OBJECTION BY THE ACCUSED: I object to these answers ... the witness is being led by the Government. Also, that the witnesses suppositions are not evidence.

The objection was objected to by the Judge Advocate on the ground of being impertinent ... that the witness was obstinate and would not answer questions...."[6]

General Brown had been insulted and wanted to convict Barnes. John Peck represented Barnes as attorney at the Court Martial. Sixteen witnesses were called, ten of them from the 37th. Barnes afterwards quoted General Brown as saying he would break Col. Barnes, and that he would not have such a troublesome customer in his command.

It became obvious to everyone that Barnes was going to be found guilty, that the resulting dismissal might ruin him, and that he should be dealt with more leniently for his indiscretion.

Before the trial, John Pound tried to withdraw the charges, and General Brown refused to allow it. During the trial, it was apparent that Barnes could not be fairly convicted of the charges, because whatever happened could not be proved. The witnesses from the 37th (including Frisbie) were solidly behind Barnes, and a majority of the court (six to four) was leaning toward acquittal on all charges, which were disobedience of orders, disrespect to superior officers, conduct prejudicial, etc.; beginning, exciting, causing, and joining in a mutiny or sedition, and conduct unbecoming an officer and gentleman.

# THIRTY SEVENTH ILLINOIS

Unfortunately for Barnes, there was too much power against him. Charles Black wanted to be Colonel. Wells Blodgett was Black's firm ally, and through his spot on General Brown's staff, he was able to fill in the unsavory details of all of Barnes' past conduct.

To avoid acquitting Barnes, General Brown found out who favored Barnes on the Court and got General James Totten, Division Commander and well known drunkard, to have these officers "reassigned" in the middle of the trial so that they could not vote in favor of Barnes.

The general sentiment became obvious because of a petition favoring Barnes that was started before the trial was a day old. Among the forty-four signators were twenty-eight officers of the 37th. Charles Black, Wells Blodgett, and Charles Dickinson did not sign. Will Black did sign. Sergeant Major Heartley signed.

Among the other post officers signing were John Pound, the original complainant, Lt. Byrket, Provost Marshal, Majors Hubbard and Banzhaf, commanding the local cavalry, and the Colonel and Chaplain of the 26th Indiana.

The basic plea of the petition was that Barnes was an honorable man, popular, praised his ability as an officer, and stating that the charges brought against him "have resulted in a misapprehension of both purposes and intentions...."[7]

Brown had enough officers on the Court remaining who would vote his way, and no petition would alter that. The petition did make Brown look bad, particularly when read with Frisbie's recital of Barnes' worthy motives, his provocation, and the lack of convincing testimony at the trial. Barnes was found guilty of most of the charges, and immediately ordered to St. Louis by General Totten, who said:

"He is a disorganizer and is guilty of a great deal more that the court found him guilty of. He has been ordered to ... St. Louis ... that the regiment may be relieved of his bad influence."[8]

General James Totten, known as "Uncle Jimmy," or "Bottlenose" by his troops could be charitably described as a strict disciplinarian, and accurately as a sadist. For example, two of the 37th who said to him on one occasion, "Hello, Uncle Jimmy, how are you!" were sentenced to terms on the Dry Tortugas, sentence later reversed.

# THE MUTINY

In the 1870's, when Totten was dismissed from the army for drunkenness, he had the bright idea to appeal to Ulysses Grant, then President, to the effect that: You of all people, should be kind to a fellow drunk and let me stay on.

While in St. Louis, Barnes told Governor Richard Yates of Illinois:

"I am placed under arrest by Brigadier General Brown of the State Militia for words spoken to an inferior officer in the heat of debate over the injustice done to Illinois troops in Missouri....

A Court Martial was called ... three members of the court were withdrawn because they were ... in favor of acquitting me, which left seven members ... three in my favor and four against....

Base and unsoldierlike means have been resorted to break me, simply because I have contended for the rights of my regiment against the State Militia, coupled with the desire of the Lt. Col. of my regiment [Charles Black] to obtain my place....

... I have been driven from post to pillar all summer by the State Militia.

... This whole prosecution against me was [instituted] by another who wanted my place, but who is unfit to command a Battalion...."[9]

Here the finger of the Fourth Estate was pointing straight at John Charles Black.

The appeals were unsuccessful in reversing the conviction. Barnes was formally dismissed from the service on November 20, 1862. Barnes wrote a defense to the Rock Island Argus newspaper, to the people who had sent their sons to war in his company. He didn't leave much out:

"... [General Brown] was the creature of [Missouri] Governor Gamble. He was considered unfit for any responsible position, and withal a notorious coward and drunkard. On his arrival at Springfield, he commenced a series of tyrannies that would have disgraced a Hottentot or Caffree....

## THIRTY SEVENTH ILLINOIS

... there was no feeling of sympathy between the soldiers and the General, who was a tyrant, murderer, and drunkard ... no gentleman and of doubtful courage....

... Had I been inexperienced ... and acquiesced in all that an ignorant general might see fit to impose on me, and continually say great is 'the Missouri State Militia' and freely drink Brown's whiskey, I would have been a great fellow in Brown's eyes and escaped the difficulty I find myself placed in...."[10]

Brown was a drunkard, and the charge of murderer was based on his killing of a German in Tipton, Missouri, for stealing a fence rail from "a notorious and well known rebel of the town." As to cowardice, no evidence.

So Barnes was out, Black was in, Henry Frisbie would be the new Lieutenant Colonel, and the battle began anew for the Major's position.

## 13.  The Barnes Exit

By August 1862, prior to Barnes' exit, changes in the year-old 37th were increasing as officers were moving on, making room for some to move their sign of rank from sleeve to shoulder. Captain Henry Curtis had gone east with Julius White, Henry Frisbie had been promoted to Major, and John Frick and John Jordon had resigned. Captain John Laimbeer was constantly in arrest and not able to influence Company D or any other part of the regiment. The Chaplain, Edward Anderson, had gone in April. Capt. Dick was mustering officer for the 1st Arkansas, a new regiment being recruited from the Arkansas Union refugee ranks, and Dickinson expected, or hoped for, a permanent field office with it. Laimbeer, or so it was reported by Henry Frisbie, was to be Lieutenant Colonel of the 1st Kansas, for which he was recruiting, or was before his close arrest in the Chambers House in Springfield. William Bandy was made Adjutant, replacing Andreas Greve, who resigned. Lieutenants James Day and Warren A. Williams were on the Arkansas regiment project with Dickinson.

Barnes was forced out as regimental commander, and the plotting and posturing for his spot began the day after the incident with Col. Pound and the Militia. All the defeated candidates for field office left over from the July election came to life at this new chance.

One of these was Charles V. Dickinson, Capt. Dick, of Company B. In 1861, Dickinson had been the first to raise his company, first into Camp Webb, and had the misfortune of having his commission date show later than what it should have been. The commission date was important in establishing seniority among the promotable captains. He was not able to accomplish a date change to his advantage before the Cassville campaigning, and had chosen to cast his lot with the new regiment he helped raise, the 1st Arkansas.

The place with the 1st Arkansas did not go to Capt. Dick. The day before Barnes' arrest, Dick had wired Adjutant General Fuller in Illinois to get him something, "in a new regiment, I don't care what it is. It is impossible for me to remain in the thirty-seventh."[1] He was back at Fuller two days later, trying to get his date of rank changed

## THIRTY SEVENTH ILLINOIS

from August 19 to July 26, 1861, making him official as the senior captain. With a changed date of rank and the majority opening up, under the new promotion rules, he would have the place. He told Charles Black that the Governor would not cross Frisbie for the Lieutenant Colonelcy, "he having refused to cross him over before.... I think if you are on one side of [Frisbie] and I can get on the other, we can make him walk pretty straight." Dickinson penned this note to Black from Springfield where he had stayed with his wife to complete construction of one of the forts. He went on to say, "give my regards to Doc Clark, Capt. Black, Blodgett, Jones & Johnson, not forgetting Jingle [Theodore Meeker] & tell the rest they can go to hell."[2]

Charles Black pushed Dickinson for the Lt. Colonelcy, opining that "he was prevented from gaining the position of Major ... by scheming & trickery of the most contemptible character."[3]

Capt. Dick was only one of the candidates for the majority that would open up with Barnes' dismissal, but there was no certainty of Barnes' dismissal while he was appealing.

While most of the officers were waiting for Barnes to be officially dumped, the regiment was building a series of forts around Springfield. Frisbie was in charge of the detail of men who were picking up extra pay for the fatigue duty. Compared to the private's monthly pay of $13, some very considerable sums were paid out in the month of July:[4]

| Edward Rose | $38.80 |
| James Burton | $37.25 |
| Henry Golen | $37.25 |
| William Baney | $37.25 |
| Charles Porter | $48.00 |
| W. Brackett | $60.80 |
| Hugh Miller | $36.25 |
| Louis DuBois | $37.75 |

Most of these men were "artificiers," men skilled as carpenters, blacksmiths, teamsters, etc.

## THE BARNES EXIT

A less fortunate class of laborer were the men sentenced to hard labor as punishment, along with 700 other soldiers and drafted rebel sympathizers from the neighborhood.

The forts were impressive. Fort No. 1 was the largest, at one mile in circumference, surrounded by a wall seven feet high and twenty-two feet thick. Capt. Dick was in charge of construction on one of the other forts. Eugene Payne's view of it was, "Mrs. Dick and husband are building a fort, or in other words, Mrs. Dick is boss of the job...."[5]

The second round of politicking brought about by Barnes' trial was a good deal more vicious than the first one in May and June. The factions again grouped around Black and Frisbie. Black's view was that, as Lieutenant Colonel commanding, he would not allow elections unless positively ordered, that the last election was influenced by bribery, and that elections ruined discipline and fostered drunkenness, disrespect, and mutiny.

Frisbie got busy concocting a charge sheet against Black to try and block his commission as colonel. The charges were to include incapacity, drunkenness, being a citizen of Indiana, and making a false muster. The charges were to be sent to Governor Yates by Myron Barnes, who was to strenuously push Frisbie's claims.

The push was that Yates, Barnes, and Frisbie were Freemasons and sworn to help each other, while Black was not. Eugene Payne, another Mason, solicited E.M. Haines' help with a request to go to the Governor and press Payne's claim as the senior captain. This would give him the majority under the new rules of succession. Black would be Colonel under that same rule with no election.

The wheels were turning at Danville as William Fithian contacted the Honorable Other State Representative from Lake County, Henry Blodgett, (Payne's "Hon. Coz." being THE Representative), about Charles Black's succession. The ever suspicious and cynical Doctor suspected that Payne was playing both sides against the middle, possibly trying to foment the destruction of both sides to his own gain. Here is Henry Blodgett's succinct analysis:

"I cannot imagine why there should be any movement at Waukegan in opposition to Col. Black's promotion, and I don't think there will be any. The only element I can think of from which such opposition could be made in any way effective would be friends of Capt. Payne acting through Mr. E.M. Haines of our county. I had a talk with Haines this morning & find out that all he wants is to get Payne made Major and has promised to cooperate with him in that direction if he & Payne's friends will second Black. I think from what I can learn that Payne can be readily managed in such manner as to easily promote the harmony & efficiency of the regt.

If you are writing to Black I wish you would suggest the matter to him and obtain his views and suggestions.

Payne is a young man of considerable ability and has been a perfectly good soldier. He was deep in the plot to jump Black last summer. But I think his only ambition for the present is to be Major, and that he had rather get that by making up with Black & keeping still than to take his chances of getting it after a fight.

I suppose no time has been lost in the matter as I am told the sentence of the Court Martial has not yet been approved at Headquarters, and Barnes is straining Heaven and earth to keep it from being approved."[6]

At the end of September, with arrival of a new Department Commander, General John M. Schofield, the regiment left Springfield heading south on the 29th. They went with unserviceable tents and no winter clothing with nearly half the regiment suffering from diarrhea, Missus Peck, Day, Smith, and Eaton riding the baggage wagons. The popular belief was that Charles Black had volunteered the regiment for the journey, somehow for his personal gain.

The regiment said its goodbyes in Springfield to girlfriends, bartenders, and washwomen, stepped off on the road with three days cooked rations and headed for Cassville, sixty-five miles south.

In the east General Julius White was in some very deep trouble. He was under arrest in Washington for surrendering the largest amount of men and materiel on the Union side in the war. While Henry Curtis, his Adjutant, and Samuel Iches, his groom, watched from Washington, he went on trial for his part in the surrender at Harper's Ferry.

## 14. The Reluctant Brigadier

Julius White had left the regiment in July 1862 sporting the stars of a Brigadier General on his shoulders. He had gone east to take a command on the front porch of the war – in Virginia. Part of the publicity campaign for his general officer promotion centered around a leg injury supposedly received at Pea Ridge. The medical certificate for the injury was signed in Chicago on May 1 by a Chicago doctor, citing a "fracture of one of the bones of the leg."[1] This fracture was referred to as "the wound received on the battlefield,"[2] by the Republican CHICAGO JOURNAL.

The newspapers – the Republican newspapers – trumpeted this as Colonel White's stepping stone to Brigadier General. It grew into an issue soundly pummeled and kicked by the Democratic press with the obligatory scurrilous story. The Democratic Rock Island ARGUS printed a letter from "a member of the 37th," saying that White was not wounded at Pea Ridge, nor did he have a leg broken there, that the leg was broken at Cassville while White was "on a spree, as some call it,"[3] with Colonel Wyman of the 13th Illinois, and fell or was thrown off his horse, all allegedly confirmed by Colonel Wyman.

White's new adjutant, Henry Curtis, said that White's horse was struck by a ball during the Pea Ridge battle, and his horse had thrown him.[4] Another version had it that White was walking around for several days after the battle without crutches, cane, or lameness, and that "his horse might have jammed his leg against a tree,"[5] and might have become progressively more infected. Whatever the story, there is no evidence that the carping upset Julius White, who might have been glad of the publicity. He left the 37th and by July 1862 was commanding a brigade under General Wool in Virginia.

White had left with his servant, Private Samuel Iches, and with Henry Curtis, Captain of the Rock Island Company, who went as his adjutant. The limited activity of the adjutant's job suited Curtis because of his Pea Ridge wounds.

White had a going-away lawn party at his home in Evanston, Illinois on July 9, 1862. The return of the 37th from Cassville to Springfield had permitted some leaves among the Chicago soldiers, including Peck and Frisbie. After this farewell fete and best wishes of the regiment, White, Curtis, and Iches went to Virginia, and Peck, Frisbie, and the 37th went back under the care of General Egbert Brown of the Missouri State Militia.[6]

By September 1862, White was at Harper's Ferry, Virginia, and then at Martinsburg, Virginia, commanding a brigade of about 2500 men. Martinsburg is on the Maryland state line and about seventy-five miles from Washington. After Second Bull Run, the war had come to Maryland, uncomfortably close to Washington.

Henry Curtis told his mother that, "White is ordered to take command of Martinsburg ... though he is trying to get it fixed some other way."[7] Why he was trying to get it fixed some other way was because he was in the rebel line of supply and communication between Richmond and Robert E. Lee's Maryland invasion forces. The invasion of Maryland culminated in the Battle of Antietam.

One remarkable event occurred while White was in Martinsburg on September 7. He had picketed the Winchester turnpike about three miles south of Martinsburg with men of the 12th Illinois Cavalry, part of his brigade. In the morning, the pickets were driven back by rebel skirmishers, and in a short time, Lt. Col. Hasbrouck Davis of the 12th Illinois found himself with fifty-eight men, confronting the rebels in force at a place called Darkesville, outnumbered five or six to one. At a distance of about one hundred yards, the rebels began firing on Davis. After losing two men, Davis realized he had to either cut and run, change his position, or attack in order to save his command. Any choice but retreat would have resulted in exposure of his men to heavy musket fire and more casualties. Davis reacted instinctively and gave an astonishing order to his command; that they drop their carbines, draw their sabres, and charge the rebel line.[8]

The terror factor of cavalry bearing down with drawn sabres flashing and glistening, ready to slash at heads and limbs of anyone in reach decided the skirmish in favor of Davis and his cavalry.

The encounter turned out to be one little diamond in a bucket of slop as subsequent events unfolded. A few days after Davis' sabre charge, the rebel progress had nearly surrounded Martinsburg. To slip the noose, Julius White evacuated the town. All army property was loaded on to rail cars, and White's Brigade marched out of Martinsburg at about two A.M. on September 12 (about three hours ahead of the rebels), and reached Harper's Ferry, Virginia at about noon.

Tactically, Harper's Ferry was in no better position than Martinsburg. It was in the same southern invasion line, and had to be taken by the rebels to secure their rear. There was very little doubt about the fate of Harper's Ferry on either side. White must have known on the night march down from Martinsburg that he was headed into trouble. He was bringing his 2500 men to join the 11,000 man garrison already at the Ferry, whose fate was all but decided. A good part of the Army of Northern Virginia was set and ready to roll over the post.

The next question was how, and for how long, could the place be defended? The capture of the post was absolutely essential to the rebels, and so a high casualty rate was forecast in the course of an extended defense.

There were three central players in the Federal command structure: General John Wool, District Commander, Col. Dixon Miles, Commander of the Post at Harper's Ferry, and General George B. McClellan, Commander of the Army of the Potomac.

Col. Miles was a career officer of 40 years' experience and an alleged drunk. After First Bull Run in August 1861, one of Miles' commanders charged that he was drunk at the battle. Miles demanded a Court of Inquiry on the charges, alleging that he was given medicinal brandy by the Surgeon on the day of the battle, to which the Court spoke:

"The court considers his illness a very slight extenuation of the guilt attached to his condition.... The court is of the opinion that evidence cannot now be found sufficient to convict Colonel Miles of drunkenness before a Court Martial, that a proper court could only be organized in this Army with the greatest inconvenience at present...."[9]

So Dixon S. Miles walked, and John Wool, another career officer, gave him the command of the extremely critical post at Harper's Ferry in 1862. Wool was 78 years old when he placed this trust in Miles. One old soldier looking after another.

In 1861, the standing army was led mostly by officers who had never had command of more than five hundred men at any one time, and many of these had gone to the rebel army. Then there were men

## THIRTY SEVENTH ILLINOIS

like Dixon Miles and Ulysses Grant, and many others, who had whiled away days of loneliness and depression in Western mud forts by curling up in a bottle. Also, out of Congressional and high command distrust of volunteers, the Regular Army units were maintained intact, and so the leadership positions in the volunteer troops and batteries and regiments went to European immigrants with experience in European armies, to others lightly experienced in the Mexican War, to young zealots like John Charles Black and Francis Jay Herron of Iowa, and to other powerful politicians.

As the war progressed, men like U.S. Grant and William Sherman and Philip Sheridan rose to command positions through merit, but in the 1861-62 period, men such as Miles, Benjamin Butler, John Pope, and others of less than consummate skills were in control.

If there was to be any hope for relief of Harper's Ferry, it would have to come from the Sixth Corps under General Franklin, or the Army of the Potomac under General McClellan relieving and reinforcing the post. Julius White may have anticipated McClellan's likely response as non-response. Little Mac never moved very quickly, never did want to get his army bloody, dirty, or shot up, always overestimated opposing troop strength, and was at the end, reluctant to fight. In the case of Harper's Ferry in September 1862, McClellan relied on General Franklin and the Sixth Corps to fight their way through to relieve Harper's Ferry, a task Franklin was not able to perform.

If the rebel army were to waste its strength assaulting Harper's Ferry without involving the Army of the Potomac, so much the better for McClellan, who would meet a weakened enemy, with better opportunities for enhancing his reputation.

Before the campaign began, McClellan had said Harper's Ferry could not be held, would be captured, and recommended its evacuation. McClellan knew the post was tenuously held, and by implication, he had no particular interest in defending it.

There was the remote possibility that the threatening part of the rebel army would bypass Harper's Ferry on its way into Maryland, join General Lee there, and take it out on the way back, win or lose in the Maryland offensive.

# THE RELUCTANT BRIGADIER

In the black night, dawn, and morning of the 12$^{th}$, Julius White and his brigade were marching into a post commanded by an addled drunk, put there with the blessing of an aging General Wool in dubious judgement, with the main hope of salvation lying with an overcautious McClellan, who had previously pronounced it indefensible.

The orders were clear from Wool and from Henry Halleck, Army Chief of Staff. Wool told Miles on September 5, "You will not abandon Harper's Ferry without defending it to the last extremity," and, "There must be no abandoning of a post, and shoot the first man that thinks of it, whether officer or soldier."[10]

This was a no-win situation for Julius White. He was marching into a military disaster as the senior officer. Wool, Miles, and McClellan were regular army, he was the volunteer. Wool had put Miles in command when he had sent White to Martinsburg with what was much the smaller command. White was now being set up to be the bad guy, the scapegoat in the inevitable surrender. With the craft and guile that had served him well all his life, he solved this dilemma with a solution undoubtedly formulated in his mind during the ten hour march from Martinsburg; upon arrival, he simply declined command.

Command deferral was not without precedent in the army, in situations where the inferior rank actually did have a better understanding of the tactical situation than his senior in executing the mission, whatever it was. But this was probably not the case with Col. Dixon Miles.

By the time of White's arrival at the Ferry, the skirmishing with the rebels had begun. The next day, White gave Col. Miles a note saying that Wool had given the more important command to Miles, and that White took this as a signal that Wool intended Miles to have it and not himself. He also mentioned that Miles was more familiar with the terrain, had set the defenses, and that these factors, "render it improper ... to deprive you of the command for the sole reason of superior rank...." Miles answered that "this act of high-toned chivalric generosity... overwhelms me with the deepest gratitude,"[11] and accepted White's offer to defer command.

# THIRTY SEVENTH ILLINOIS

Julius White must have recognized that Dixon Miles was not in either a healthy or competent mental condition to properly defend Harper's Ferry against siege and assault. Rather than face possible ruin of his Senate hopes, defend the post with an unknown but certainly high casualty rate, and enhance Democrat McClellan in the bargain, White simply stepped aside to let events take their course.

Harper's Ferry is at the confluence of the Potomac and Shenandoah Rivers. The V formed by the rivers pointed east, and Harper's Ferry is in the crotch of the V.

Three significant points of high ground look down on the town. North across the Potomac lies the highest ground, key to the defense, Maryland Heights. Directly opposite and south across the Shenandoah is Loudoun Heights. Behind Harper's Ferry to the west of the town is Bolivar Heights – Camp Hill. Defensively, the rear of the town (Bolivar Heights – Camp Hill) was, river to river, a distance of 1 ½ miles. From Maryland Heights to Bolivar Heights, 2 ½ miles.

The day after White and his brigade arrived (the 13th), Loudoun Heights (to the south) was already occupied by 8,000 rebels, while Stonewall Jackson, with a larger force, lay west of the line at Bolivar Heights. Two divisions of rebels attacked Maryland Heights, and it was abandoned immediately by the defending federal troops.

The next day, 1500 federal cavalry were evacuated from Harper's Ferry, were spared capture, and on the way out captured a rebel ammunition train of ninety-seven wagons and its six hundred man escort. That day and into Monday the 15th, White was in command of the section west of town (Bolivar Heights), successfully defending it against Stonewall Jackson's forces. By eight the next morning, Col. Miles had decided to surrender the town. He told White that the place would fall, and he wanted no more loss of life. White, in true bureaucratic fashion and in accordance with regulations, suggested that this decision be made by committee, so Miles gathered all the Brigade Commanders at White's position on the crest of Bolivar Heights. The rebel cannonade was coming from Loudoun Heights, Maryland Heights, and two other points. Colonel D'Utassy of the 39th New York related the course of the meeting. After he was summoned, and,

# THE RELUCTANT BRIGADIER

"On approaching Col. Miles, he said, 'Good gracious Heaven! get down from your horse; you will draw the enemy's fire on you.'

I smilingly replied, 'Don't mind that; evil grass is never lost,' meaning that there was no danger.

He said, 'Well, if you don't care, I don't want to be shot on your account; get down off your horse and send off your horses.'

General White and Colonel Trimble were present. I dismounted.

Colonel Miles said, 'Well, my boy, we meet again under unpleasant circumstances.'

I said, 'Why?'

He said, 'Well, we don't know what to do.'

I asked, 'In what regard.'

'Well,' said he, 'we must surrender.'

I looked at him a moment, and then said, 'What, surrender?'

'Yes, Sir,' he said. 'What do you want to do?'

I told him, 'Cut our way through.'

'Poh,' he said, 'bosh! nonsense! Today it is too late.'

I said to him, 'Colonel, I offered to do the same yesterday, and I suggested it to Col. Davis, who, as you see, did it.'

'Well,' said he, 'yesterday is not today; what shall we do today?'

I said, 'Is it a council of war or is it a mere private conversation?'

He replied, 'Well, I have half determined what to do, but General White said to call you all together.'

I said to him, 'Then let the junior give his advice.'

Colonel Trimble was the junior, and he said, 'Under actual existing circumstances, nothing else is to be done but to surrender.'

General White stood near us, but did not say one word. Colonel Miles went over to him and said, 'Well, you hear what he says.'

General White said, 'Hear Colonel D'Utassy's opinion.'

I replied, 'You know it; I will never surrender as long as I have a shot.'

Colonel Miles then began to curse, and said, 'How many shots have you?'

I sent for Captain Phillips and Captain Von Sehlen; the one had 3 shots, the other had one, long range ammunition. When I heard that, I said, 'I can do nothing else but surrender particularly as you are averse to cutting our way out, but I will surrender only under honorable conditions.'

General White said, 'What do you mean by honorable conditions? Be sure I will do my best to save our honor.'[12]

After the decision had been made, Julius White went out and negotiated the surrender with General Ambrose P. Hill, CSA. White was fastidiously dressed, Hill looked like a kitchen orderly.[13] Miles' command had suffered 1000 casualties in five days and would have suffered more in an extended defense against a rebel assault or to artillery fire, for which there was no defense. The ammunition was exhausted.

The extra day gained by a further defense might have been important had anyone else but McClellan been in position to take advantage of it, because fully one third of Lee's army was at Harper's Ferry. McClellan knew this on the 13th, as he had seen a copy of General Lee's order to Stonewall Jackson of that date. If he had moved rapidly before the Army of Northern Virginia could join at Antietam, victory would have been easier.

Harper's Ferry fell on the 15th of September, and Stonewall Jackson was able to join Lee in Maryland, and on the 17th, at Antietam, McClellan had to face the united Army of Northern Virginia.

The Harper's Ferry garrison of 12,000 was captured, along with small arms, ammunition, and other ordnance and supplies. The men were thereafter exchanged and several of the officers arrested for agreeing to surrender.

How the events at the Ferry went down with the high command is characterized in General Halleck's order to General Thomas on September 22:

"You will arrest Brig. Gen. Julius White and the other commanders of brigades at Harper's Ferry at the time of the surrender.... Col. Thomas Ford will be arrested, and also any other officers who you may be advised took part in recommending the surrender of Harper's Ferry."[14]

The arrests were made, and a Court of Inquiry was appointed and convened in Washington.

When the court was formed, fortunately for Julius White, its President was General David Hunter, a comrade in arms of White's

# THE RELUCTANT BRIGADIER

from the old Army of the Frontier. The court met for four weeks and took nine hundred pages of testimony, and in the end absolved some and punished others. Julius White came out of it spanky clean. The assessments of the court were: as to Julius White, "...General Julius White merits its approbation. He appears from the evidence to have acted with decided capability and courage."

Of the 126$^{th}$ New York and its officers that prematurely abandoned Maryland Heights: "In this connection, the commission calls attention to the disgraceful behavior of the 126$^{th}$ New York Infantry, and recommends that Major Baird, for his bad conduct ... should be dismissed the service...."

Of Col. Ford, commanding at Maryland Heights: "...Colonel Ford should not have been placed in command on Maryland Heights; that he conducted the defense without ability, and abandoned his position without sufficient cause, and has shown throughout such a lack of military capacity as to disqualify him ... for a command in the service."[15]

Of Col. Dixon S. Miles, alleged inebriate, who died of a wound received on Bolivar Heights: "...what runs through our 900 pages of evidence, [is] strangely unanimous upon the fact that Colonel Miles' incapacity, amounting to almost imbecility, led to the shameful surrender of this important post.... Colonel Miles was unfit to conduct so important a defense as that of Harper's Ferry."

Of 78 year-old John Wool: "the officer who placed this incapable [Miles] in command should share the responsibility.... Major General Wool is guilty to this extent of a grave disaster, and should be censured for his conduct."

Of General McClellan: "...the General-in-Chief [Halleck] has testified that General McClellan, after having received orders to repel the enemy invading the State of Maryland, marched only 6 miles per day on an average when pursuing the invading enemy. The General-in-Chief also testifies that, in his opinion, General McClellan could, and should, have relieved and protected Harper's Ferry, and in this opinion, the Commission fully concur."

Of the elements of the disaster, the Commission concluded: "...1,000 men killed in Harper's Ferry would have made a small loss had the post been secured, and probably save 2,000 at Antietam...

after the surrender... the entire force went off on the double quick to relieve Lee, who was being attacked at Antietam. Had the garrison been slower to surrender, or the Army of the Potomac swifter to march, the enemy would have been forced to raise the siege or have been taken in detail, with the Potomac dividing his forces."[16]

Surprisingly, out of the incident, with senior officers castigated, dead Dixon Miles called an imbecile, and other officers dismissed from the army, the senior, ranking officer at the post, on the scene, comes off clean and with a compliment on his performance. Julius White had covered himself with a crafty bit of maneuvering. Whether relinquishing command was an act of self-protection or not, it saved many lives, and showed up McClellan for what he was.

Alternatively, had White taken command and occupied Maryland Heights, the garrison could have held out longer being in a defensive position, tying up Stonewall Jackson while McClellan took advantage of numbers over Lee at Antietam. The course of the war might have been significantly different. Letting the Regular Army boys screw themselves up was what White chose to do, by relinquishing command of a strategically important post to an "imbecilic" drunk, knowingly and deliberately.

In later years, White's answer to the critics of the surrender was:

"It has often been asserted that Harper's Ferry might have held out a day or two longer, but of those who have claimed that it could have been longer held, no one has yet, so far as the writer is informed, stated HOW a garrison mostly of recruits under fire for the first time could have successfully defended an area of 3 square miles, assailed from all sides by veterans 3 times their number, posted, with artillery, in positions commanding the whole field. The writer, with due deference, expresses the opinion that the force under Jackson could have carried the place by assault within an hour after his arrival ... in spite of any resistance which ... could have been made."[17]

After the war, White returned to Evanston, Illinois, and was not allowed to forget Harper's Ferry because of the taunts of one Billy Norkett, Station Agent for the Chicago & Northwestern Railroad. Every time Norkett saw White on the street, he would comment loud-

## THE RELUCTANT BRIGADIER

ly, "Here comes an old coward." He and White, "nearly came to blows several times" over the gibes.[18]

Julius White moved on to other commands and in 1864, landed square in the middle of another military disaster, the Battle of the Crater, fought before Petersburg. He was there as Ambrose Burnside's Chief of Staff (IX Corps), and got out of town before the Court of Inquiry met, having had very little to do tactically with the battle.

What he was, was a politician first and a soldier second. Maybe he was also unlucky, because after the war he resumed his pre-war vocation as a fire insurance underwriter in Chicago, and was gainfully so employed when Mrs. O'Leary's cow kicked the lamp, or so it was said, in Chicago in 1871.

## 15. Mindless Marching

The 37th left Springfield, Missouri, on the last day of September 1862 on a two month running and chasing episode through Southwest Missouri and Northern Arkansas. The Union army would chase and attack, and the rebels would run, all through the fall of 1862. The Missouri-Arkansas trail led through Little York, Pond Springs, Crane Creek, Newtonia, Cassville, Pea Ridge, Huntsville, Bentonville, Cross Hollows, Fayetteville, Osage, Ford's Springs, Keitsville, Cassville again, Marionville, Finley Creek, back around to Crane Creek and then to Ozark. The marches were done in all kinds of bad weather, made worse by lack of adequate equipment.

Eugene Payne left a forbidding narrative of the October and November marches. He had slipped around most of the hard traveling of the 1861-62 winter by being left at Boonville, and then being sick, and then going home on leave to recruit and get married, and then returning for Pea Ridge. After Pea Ridge came the long spring and summer scouts, but nothing like the fall of 1862, where there was no base camp to return to.

The first days away from Springfield were taken up with exhausting, hard, wet marching and by October 4, the regiment was at Newtonia, Missouri for a "battle," that the newspapers trumpeted as a two hour contest with one hundred rebel casualties. The truth was that the rebel guerillas saw the advancing infantry and retreated. Casualty count was one dead indian.[1]

The months of October and November were filled with cold and drizzle, dirty little guerilla ambushes, depredations on civilians, burned houses, stolen pigs, and hard discipline dictated by the new commanders (army regulars) Generals Schofield and Totten.

The regimental wives in residence had been joined by Missus Messer and Doty. All endured the hardships of the road along with their husbands. In addition to his wife, Lieutenant Joe Eaton had his 14 year old son with the regiment as a drummer boy, and in November, his brother-in-law, "a big fat Dutchman," showed up to open an officers' boardinghouse.[2]

# MINDLESS MARCHING

The October marching took the regiment back to Cassville and to Pea Ridge and scenes of the battle and garrison duty of six months before. The rebels has occupied Cassville in the summer, likewise the Pea Ridge area, and now the ebb and flow of war had put both sites back under Union control.

The regiment was at Ozark, Missouri, again, in mid-November. Willy and Charles Black didn't like being in Ozark enough to stay there long if they could get away and go to Springfield, which they did at the first opportunity, and Bottlenose James Totten had them arrested for it. James Totten, Regular Army West Point, was the new Army commander, and he had gone overboard on discipline. What started out as a regimen to improve obedience and effectiveness degenerated into abuses.

Totten started out blessed with unusual popularity. In September and October, "Iron Face" was thought of as a "true soldier." Charles Black thought the regiment had never served under a general, "as thoroughly to their liking." He endeared himself to the men by sending hot coffee to pickets on a cold night, a cost-free gesture of sensitivity that built his reputation as a good officer. The 37$^{th}$ considered themselves "his pets," a relationship supposedly born out of the affinity of a hard-bitten soldier to a battle-scarred fighting regiment.[3]

The relationship lasted until November when Totten's little cruelties and excessive drinking cost him whatever loyalties he had won from the ranks and from the officers.

After the army went into camp at Ozark, several officers of the division went to Springfield for some eating, drinking, and female company. Will Black, Kennicott, Hawes, and Frisbie were arrested while officers of other regiments were not. Totten took exception to this pleasure spree and seemed to single out the 37$^{th}$ for special punishment.

These forays into the parlors and bars of Springfield and the ensuing arrests sound well worth it. Doc Clarke did the accounting work on one of the bar bills, reporting to Charles Black: "I got $100 from Abbot via Baker, and with the $45 – gave it to Blodgett – all right. Major Anderson says you paid your share of that bill like a gentleman (what a fool he is) and that he will not take the note (which

I return). He says Lt. Marr should have paid for the wine, that you paid more than your fair share. Thus far all good.

Please give this $5 to Capt. Wolford, tell him I will send him the remainder soon...

Saw Clem & Sue last night. Oh, but C. is sweet – and – and – she loves you. True, tis me that envies it, she sends her everlasting love to you....

Good Bye, may the Lord reign in you. Yours in the Gospel, E.A. Clark."[4]

If Totten punished the officers for taking off to enjoy themselves after the trials of October and November, he was no more kind to the men. His pettiness surfaced in the conduct of a court martial over Mrs. Miller's quilt.

The "bed quilt incident" came to trial on November 26 at Spring River, Missouri, Egbert Brown presiding. Private Charles Porter of the Danville Company was charged with "[entering] the premises of Mrs. Miller, a citizen of Missouri, and taking forceable possession of and carrying away one or more bed quilts, the private property of the aforesaid Mrs. Miller, and did keep possession thereof until ordered to return same by Brig. Gen. Totten...." The court found Porter not guilty and acquitted him. Totten would not be overruled, and imposed a sentence, saying that Porter was "at least an accomplice," and ruled that Porter should never be promoted. Samuel Curtis revoked Totten's reversal, saying Totten had no power to meddle with the aqquittal, "nor is it right to deal with a soldier so as to restore him to duty yet deprive him of all incentive to honorable exertion in the future."[5] This notwithstanding, Porter lost his promotion to Corporal in April 1863.

Totten's intervention was the mean charade of a drunkard. General officers are not tasked with being popular with their men, but they are responsible for their welfare.

Drinking itself was not the sin. It was the meanness and useless cruelty that offended. Totten was replaced at the end of November by Iowa General Francis Jay Herron, and at the end of 1862, another General joined the little army who had, like Totten, a regular army background, and like Totten, had never commanded more than a bat-

## MINDLESS MARCHING

talion before the war. General John M. Schofield proved nearly as unpopular as Totten and as ineffective in military matters.

In order to make his newly begotten army more mobile against the mounted rebel irregulars, Schofield cut the number of wagons allowed to each regiment to fifteen. He did this in part by making the men carry their own knapsacks on the march and loading the wagons "to the hoops." This impeded the progress of both wagons and men. He also ordered the soldiers' wives out of camp, most of whom refused to go on the pretext that their husbands had no money to send them home.[6]

The sloppy fall days were spent marching through rain and mud over rough roads ten to twenty miles a day, with rags for clothing, on half rations or none at all, and with cheap shoes and tents with holes and tears, all the while fighting dysentery and malaria. To be loaded down like a mule with an extra thirty pounds of equipment by Schofield's order was an intolerable insanity to most. The upset with Schofield varied proportionately to the amount of rainfall and the food supply.

Carrying the knapsacks was maddening. Charles Black had used a knapsack as punishment in November because it was so distasteful. Robert Welsh of the Danville Company was sentenced to carry a loaded knapsack, "from retreat to reveille, with 2 minutes rest every two hours." Black order the Corporal of the Guard arrested on November 8 because he had allowed some of Welsh's pack weight to be removed. While Black considered this punishment, Schofield considered it normal drill.[7]

The wheels of justice continued to grind. Charles Black reduced three other non-commissioned officers in November; Artemis Judd, "...he having acted the part of a common thief...,"[8] Vernon Hendee of the Waukegan Company, and William Brown of the Michigan Company, for using disrespectful language toward an officer. The Sergeant Major stripped Brown's chevrons in front of the assembled regimental corporals.[9]

Jacob Hawkins of Payne's Company was charged for beating a horse, "in a cruel manner with a large club," and Alden Smith of Messer's Company with a variety of sins. Smith, "while driving the Co. F team, did become so intoxicated as to be totally unfit to manage said team on the march from Ozark to Robinson Mills on November 19 ... and did strike several violent blows with his fist at Elbridge Driscoll, Acting Commissary Sergeant...."[10]

Politics, the officers' favorite game and primary interest, sparked again with the field office vacancy about to be opened by Barnes' dismissal.

There was an incident in early November that raised Black's suspicions that he would again be opposed for promotion. It happened that the company officers got together on their own to discuss the regimental clothing crisis. A committee was appointed consisting of Phineas Rust, Gallio Fairman, Eugene Payne, Herman Wolford, and George Bell. They were to deal with the shoddy, low quality clothing foisted on the army by profiteers and unscrupulous merchants. The committee decided that, "[The clothing] is of the poorest quality, that it is almost entirely worthless, that the pants ... are poor, threadbare and rent in many places, that many of the men have no shoes or coats, and with the exception of a kind of thin blouse, they have nothing to put on for one. That their hats are composed of many colors and many kinds, that they have no flannel overshirts and but very few overshirts of any kind, and that we have made and sent in our requisitions ... but they have failed to bring us the articles...."

The report was given to Charles Black with a request that he sign it and send it forward. Black sent the report back to the committee unsigned; "If your act was intended to be official, you have been mistaken in your authority. If intended to reflect your views & wishes as individuals, it cannot be considered or treated officially.... Your action is inexpedient.... It falls under acts forbidden.... You may not have so intended it, but it does convey censure to some above you ... the unauthorized meeting of two or more officers for discussion of any kind relating to army affairs [is defined] as conspiracy or mutiny.... Your record & this reply will be placed upon the books of the regiment...."[11]

One of the things that had gotten Barnes in trouble was demanding proper clothes and food from Egbert Brown, who gave almost all the supplies to the State Militia and nothing to out-of-state troops. Black was not about to make the same mistake and make demands on Brown, particularly when he needed his political support against Frisbie. Black would do nothing on the subject to risk offending the high command, and so the men spent the winter in rags or worse.

Black's general fears for losing the colonelcy were so great that November that he wrote to Brown, describing the time as, "the crisis in my military history."[12] He also followed Totten out of Springfield for a mile or so down the road, riding with him and relating all of what Barnes had done, and saying that Barnes' appeals to be reinstated should be denied. He also enlisted Dr. Fithian's help to get to General Samuel Curtis, to Congressman Owen Lovejoy, or to anyone who could stop "a ruffian drunkard [from being] restored to a position he disgraces & a commission he cannot fill...."[13]

While the conniving and scheming went on among the officers, the enlisted men, with holes in their pants, did their drill and pulled their guard and stole a chicken once in a while.

The relative mundanities of camp life continued into December. Benjamin Morgan of Capt. Dick's company died. Sergeant Thomas Payne was busted from sergeant to private, Capt. John Laimbeer was still under arrest, and the hunting was good. Little warning came before the abrupt call to the hardest march of the war. Down in Arkansas, after eight months of hide and seek, the rebels were coming at Doctor Blunt with everything they had.

## 16. Prairie Grove

The end of November 1862 found the 37th Illinois Infantry in camp near McCullough's Springs, Missouri, about fourteen miles west of Springfield. They had been there since November 19 resting, according to Eugene Payne, Captain of the Waukegan Company, "to allow our Generals to go to St. Louis to purchase a new supply of liquors."[1]

Payne went on:

"Since we have been here we have had a considerable deal of sport. There are plenty of game here, such as deers, wild turkeys and smaller game of all kinds. Each day a half dozen or more large fine deer are brought to our regt. shot by our boys, and turkeys without number. On Thanksgiving Day, we had a dinner fit for a king, venison and wild turkey cooked in a variety of ways."[2]

Such periods of rest were opportunities for all kinds of mischief, and also afforded time for discipline. Private Charles Porter was charged for stealing a quilt and acquitted. Assistant Surgeon Elijah Clark was reportedly charged by Lt. Col. Black for remaining on hospital detail in Springfield. The report of the charge was false.[3]

In the midst of all this, Captain Will Black wrote home about his time in camp:

"We are in camp at the same place as before with the same valley, the same hills, and rocks, and thickets of scrub-oak surrounding us. Nothing to break the monotony of the scene, and nothing to stir up the sluggish waters of our every day life, which wears on from dawn to dark, from dark to dawn, in the same routine of camp duties, recreations, and pursuits of interest or pleasure."[4]

There was another letter written that day by Doctor Blunt – Federal General James Blunt – to General Samuel Curtis, District Commander. Blunt, who was 125 miles away in Cane Hill, Arkansas with about 5,000 troops, wrote:

"… General [Thomas] Hindman is advancing with a large army. I have sent orders to General [Francis J.] Herron to hurry to my assistance. Before this reaches you, there will have taken place the damndest fight or footrace on record."[5]

Will Black's "sluggish waters" were to turn to raging rapids. The 37th was drawn into both fight and footrace.

The footrace was first. Herron, division commander, had to bring his 8,000 troops from the environs of Springfield over 120 miles to Blunt's aid in Arkansas, before Confederate General Hindman with his 25,000 advanced 60 miles and gobbled up Blunt's command of 5,000. A reasonable judgement, a George B. McClellan, eastern-on-the-Potomac judgement, would have had Blunt running north to avoid capture or annihilation, but he determined to hold fast and wait for Herron.

General Samuel Ryan Curtis received Blunt's message in St. Louis, and wired orders to General Herron in Springfield to reinforce Blunt. Herron's superiors, Generals Schofield and Totten, were absent in St. Louis. Herron received the order on December 3, and at 2 A.M. on the fourth as part of Herron's Division, the 37th began the hike south.[6]

Estimating a non-regulation route-step pace of thirty inches, this march consisted of putting one foot in front of the other about 210,000 times in three and a half days, accomplished with a pack load of from thirty to fifty pounds. The load consisted variously of musket, haversack, knapsack, and overcoat.

The last five miles were paced off to the rumble of the distant artillery duel.[7] Most of the men arrived at Prairie Grove absolutely exhausted, most with blistered and some with bloody feet, shoes in hand, after marching in their bare feet or stocking clad feet through the December Ozark chill.

Hindman's rebels were in not much better shape after their long march, and were less well equipped and less disciplined.

Hindman knew on the evening of Saturday the sixth that Herron was in Fayetteville, and that he would have to revise his strategy of crushing the weaker force under Blunt, as Blunt was about to be joined by Herron. Hindman devised a plan to put on a great show, with a long line of camp fires and pickets in Blunt's front at Cane Hill. He would then pull the main body of the army out and march by night over the Cove Creek Road, and confront Herron to the north before Blunt knew he was gone.[8]

# THIRTY SEVENTH ILLINOIS

Hindman slipped away, and was at Prairie Grove Hill at nine o'clock the next morning, Sunday, December 7. Blunt was at the time still deceived by the one brigade Hindman had left behind to tend the fires.[9]

Had Hindman pressed his advantage early in the morning, he would have caught Herron's exhausted regiments struggling up the Fayetteville Road. Instead, he stopped and fortified Prairie Grove Hill and allowed Herron's troops to form.

Eugene Payne drew this battle map for his wife:[10]

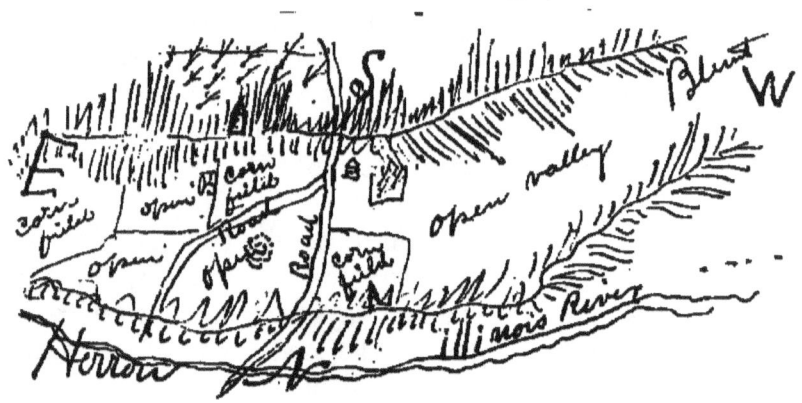

Map of Prairie Grove battlefield, drawn by Eugene Payne for his wife in December, 1862.
(AUTHOR'S COLLECTION)

Herron's troops arrived during the course of that Sunday morning and were marched past whiskey barrels with the heads stove in at a point north of the Illinois River. Each man filled his tin cup as he passed the barrel, and then forded the icy, knee deep water of Illinois Creek.[11]

The 37th went to the cornfield marked "A" by Payne on his map and took position, numbed by exhaustion, cold, and the sedative effect of the liquor. For the first ninety minutes of the fight, the 37th was held in reserve for the defense of the artillery battery, and watched the artillery duel and an unsuccessful charge over the open field up the hill by the 19th Iowa and 20th Wisconsin regiments. These men had briefly captured a battery near the house at the top of the hill, but could not hold it, and came rushing back in great disorder.[12]

# PRAIRIE GROVE

By late afternoon, the 37th was called upon to charge the rebels on the hill. They charged with the 26th Indiana on an angle from the letter "A" on Payne's map, trying to accomplish what the 19th Iowa and 20th Wisconsin had failed to do. These two regiments were beaten back and forced to retreat over their own dead. Eugene Payne told what the 37th found on the hill:

"The rebels were formed in four lines deep up the side of the mountain. The front rank would fire, lay down, then the next, then the next, & so on. The leaden hail came in one continuous stream of fire not unlike a severe hail storm. We marched & fought till we reached the orchard back of the house...."[13]

The 37th got off three rounds from the position in the orchard when the strength of the rebels became apparent. "The orchard was a howling hell," was Eugene Payne's description.[14]

Very quickly, the 26th Indiana to the right of the 37th broke and fled down the hill, and a rebel battery was spotted on the left. The Federal artillery was not in a position to support an advance, the rebel fire was concentrated on the 37th and its 400 men, and enemy artillery was spotted on the right. Colonel Charles Black, "in full uniform, his overcoat lined with red cloth, the cape thrown back on his shoulders his tall plume in the air,"[15] ordered the 37th off the hill, later explaining:

"I gave the order to retreat after the regiment had fired about 3 rounds after gaining cover of the fence on the crest of the hill. The 26th Indiana had advanced on the same line of battle with the 37th, and on our left. At the time I gave the order to retreat, the right of the 26th was steadily and rapidly falling back and had got some distance to my rear. As far in my rear, I judged, as the enemy was in front, and I feared a flank movement from the enemy.

The enemy were in immense force immediately in my front, not more than 15 or 20 paces distant, advancing and firing rapidly as they came. The united fire of the 26th Indiana and the 37th did not seem to check them at all in their advance

The company of skirmishers which I had thrown to the right and front had, a few moments before, reported artillery to the right and under cover of brush and woods, and for these reasons, (1st) because the right of the regiment was enfiladed by artillery, (2nd) its support gone from the left, and (3rd) its being overwhelmed [and] outnumbered in front and no support moving up to our assistance, I gave the order to retreat."[16]

Eugene Payne told his wife:

"[Black] was cool and collected and did not order us back until he saw that if we pushed ahead we were lost forever. You, my Darling, may bless Black for giving that order for it saved your husband's life. I would not be here writing you now in all probability if the 37th Regt. had entered those woods covered as they were with 10,000 secesh and cannon planted so as to rake every inch of ground. I consider Black a hero...."[17]

Fred Abbey and Napoleon Hicks of the 37th were not quick enough getting off the hill and were captured.[18] Charles Black was shot in the left arm above the elbow, shattering the bone into several pieces as he came down the hill. The leftover Pea Ridge wound in the other arm gave him no strength in the saddle, and as he came off the hill he met Col. Dan Huston, his Brigade Commander, who reported it:

"I ordered the Regiments (26th and 37th) up the hill. I should think about 100 yards [up], the enemy opened a terrible fire on the right of the 26th [Indiana]. This part of my command was thrown into confusion, broke, and retreated down the hill. Finding it fruitless to try to rally them then, I started to the 37th Ill., with the intention of halting them on the crest of the hill. While on my way to them, I discovered that they had also broken, and were rushing down the hill in some confusion. I tried to rally them but without success.

As I went up the hill, I met Col. Black coming down. I said to him, 'Great God, Colonel Black, can't you do something to stop this.' He replied, 'Colonel, my arm is broken all to pieces, and I cannot hold my horse.' I then said to him, 'Colonel, go at once to the rear if you are wounded.'"[19]

After falling back some 400 yards, the 37th regrouped near an artillery battery. Will Black described the enemy pursuit:

"We had fallen back some 450 yards and there awaited orders. Meantime, the 26th Indiana had formed under cover of a fence and were already at work again. But in a moment their line was broken, and their forces scattered like chaff before the wind, while the rebels followed like a pack of wolves in the open meadow below. They did not think what a welcome they were to receive.... For the first time ... the enemy stood in an open field ... and we profited by the occasion. Rising up, we poured a volley into their flank. How their ranks went like ripe heavy grain before the mower's scythe ... another volley, another swing of the great scythe of death, and they broke and fled into the woods....[20]

The 37th was armed with Colt revolving rifles and long range big bore Belgian muskets, superior weapons. This firepower had driven the enemy into the woods. As the afternoon wore on, Blunt's command, newly arrived from Cane Hill, took over the bulk of the fighting.[21]

Press puffery and individual drum beating followed the battle. Eugene Payne told his wife:

"You have doubtless seen the description of our battle in the Chicago Daily of the 20th. It was written by a sutler of the 19th Iowa regt. And that is the reason the sneaking scoundrel puffs up the 19th Iowa and 20th Wisconsin and never so much alludes to us. Why, the liar. The 37th and 26th Indiana retook the battery which he admits was taken and lost by both regts. We took it, according to General Herron's report, held it for half an hour, although I don't think it was so long. We are all pretty wrathy and if the lying devil comes among the 37th he may stand a chance of being toasted alive, and thus enjoy his heaven a little before his time.[22]

Years after the war, George Griffith of the 37th read an account of the battle that appeared in a newspaper article written by "Comrade Wilson," an otherwise unidentified soldier from another unit. Griffith wrote the following account of the retreat as an answer to the overproportioned reporting about the 19th Iowa and 20th Wisconsin, who were badly shot up on the hill before the charge of the 26th Indiana and the 37th:

"Comrade Wilson's article ... puts me in mind of the old story, 'How dad and me kotched a bar.' He claims that the 19th Iowa and 20th Wisconsin, after making a march of 115 miles in a little over 3 days, were ordered to get busy, and that they met, charged and whipped a much larger army than ours, that is, with the assistance of a few cavalrymen and small batteries, which assisted in quieting the Johnnies at times during the engagement.

Just 50 years ago, I, as high private in the rear rank of Co. E 37$^{th}$ Ill., had the luck to participate in that little skirmish, and if my memory serves me right, there were other regiments there besides the 20$^{th}$ Wis. and the 19$^{th}$ Iowa. They, too, were made to dance by the Johnnies that day, and they did not wait to 'swing their partners,' either. It must have been right after the 20$^{th}$ Wis. and 19$^{th}$ Iowa had licked the big army of Johnnies that the 26$^{th}$ Indiana and 37$^{th}$ Ill. and (I think) the 94$^{th}$ Ill. received orders to charge that same hill that the 20$^{th}$ Wis. and 19$^{th}$ Iowa had charged before and also retreated from, for there were many of their dead and wounded strewn along the hillside.

When we made that second charge up the hill (and mind you, this was after that large force of Johnnies had been so completely licked by the 20$^{th}$ Wis. and 19$^{th}$ Iowa, according to Wilson) it did not seem to us that they had been very badly licked, by the way they handed their compliments out to us later arrivals.

It was on this charge ... just as we came to the rise of the hill, that there was another rising just across a narrow lane, and in the edge of an old orchard all grown over with weeds and brush, in the shape of two columns of Johnnies, who seemed to know exactly what to do. They proceeded at once, with front ranks kneeling, to pour volley after volley into our ranks, just as though they thought we liked it.

Right at this stage of the game we got orders to retreat, and we all jumped at the chance and were not a bit slow about it either. I honestly believe we made far better time than the 20$^{th}$ Wis. and the 19$^{th}$ Iowa could possibly have made. It was also at the critical time when the order for retreat was given that Gen. John C. Black received a shot in his left arm that put him on the retired list for a time. He had previously been wounded in the right arm at the battle of Pea Ridge....

I do not wish to detract from the glory or honor of the 20$^{th}$ Wis. or the 19$^{th}$ Iowa; they were both good regiments; but there were other regiments that participated in the battle....

The timely arrival of Gen. Blunt from Cane Hill is all that saved our bacon ... the Johnnies had us done up to a frazzle until Blunt showed up....[23]

# PRAIRIE GROVE

The 37th fought no more that Sunday. Of the four hundred members of the 37th, ten were killed and fifty-six were wounded, a casualty rate of about one in six.[24]

Sergeant David Ash described the onset of night:

"Our regt. laid out all night just on the edge of the battlefield and it was awful to hear the wounded men cry for help, as it was quite cold. It was some time before our ambulances got to work getting them off."[25]

Total Union dead and wounded totaled 1251, and the rebel casualties estimated at double that number.[26]

The chaplain of the 20th Iowa was up all night:

"That night I shall never forget ... taking care of wounded and dying. We had about one hundred in and around an old log house.... After midnight, the surgeon and all the nurses gave out from fatigue and loss of sleep. I alone was left to take care of so many...."[27]

The dead were stripped of any property of value, and the field was covered with shoeless coatless dead.[28]

Expecting the battle to be renewed the next day, possibly earlier, orders were that no fires were to be built, and the 37th was the first regiment to violate the order.[29] Blankets and overcoats had been shed on the long three day march from Missouri. Most of the men went to sleep with a Belgian musket for a pillow and with the feeling of the lucky winner, reminded of life and soundness of limb as the wounded suffered, strewn on the field nearby.

Charles Hawes of the Rock Island Company had drawn duty as picket officer that night. He had been one of the day's heroes:

"Capt. Hawes ... led his company in a charge on one of the rebel batteries, and took it, but afterwards was compelled to abandon it.... Capt. Hawes was nearly two rods ahead of his company in the charge, calling the boys to come on.... The boys would have followed him to hell or any other place if he would lead the way."[30]

At about midnight, Hawes was out checking the pickets. He heard a wounded soldier call out for someone from Illinois to bring him water. Hawes went toward the sound of the voice, and heard approaching horses. Before him appeared General John Sappington Marmaduke (CSA), with escort, asking to be taken to Herron's headquarters.[31] What happened next is related by Lieutenant Colonel

# THIRTY SEVENTH ILLINOIS

Henry Frisbie of the 37th in a narrative written in 1889. Its accuracy may be questionable because of the passage of time between the event and the recollection of it, a condition not diminishing its entertainment value. Frisbie was commanding the 37th during Charles Black's incapacity with his wound.

"... It was General Marmaduke, commanding the Rebel Cavalry with a large escort under a flag of truce....

If he came with any bad intent, he must have been convinced, as he rode up in front of our Regiment with their guns protruding through the fence, that it was no time to play ugly tricks.... We then placed the regiment around the entire escort and built that log fire, the first we had felt in many a day.

I rode down to find General Herron and report. He ordered me to bring General Marmaduke to him which I did.... I had quite a talk with Marmaduke about the war and kindred subjects. He would not say why they failed to complete the charge they attempted. Our first talk was quite spicy. I inquired what he had come for; he said, 'to see if we were going to surrender.' I asked him if it looked like it when we were just ready to move to renew the attack. 'It must be that you have come in to surrender for you know that General Blunt has gone around in your rear and you will all be annihilated when we renew the attack.'

General Herron came up for me and we together rode over to see General Blunt. Blunt was very enthusiastic and willing to divide his rations and fight for 30 days. He was sure the battle would be renewed in the morning. I was equally sure that the enemy had retreated and that the flag of truce was a cover for the move I heard them making....

General Herron and myself returned just as the day was breaking and when the sun came up General Marmaduke and his large escort departed. We passed compliments in parting and I remarked, 'General, you will have a long ride to overtake your friends as they have gone a long time before you.' He turned and gave me a look as though he would speak but did not and rode off. I called after him again, 'Well, General, shall we meet on the Arkansas,' giving the broad saw of country. Several turned their heads but none replied.

As soon as they were out of sight and we had investigated, how true it was, that no enemy was to be found when so short a time before the woods were full of them. None but the dead and wounded remained to tell the tale when Rebels had so late met foemen worthy of the union. Our victory was complete but there our labors did not cease. We had to care for the wounded and bury the dead.[32]

Marmaduke had used the truce request as a ploy to buy time to cover the retreat of the rebel army. In a 1905 speech, Eugene Payne told it this way:

"About 1 o'clock that night General Marmaduke, the second ranking General of the Confederate Army, presented himself in front of my regiment with a body-guard of about 30 cavalrymen, under a flag of truce, desiring to see Generals Herron and Blunt. As commanding officer of the regiment present that night, I received him. After I had disarmed and corralled his followers (at which they swore roundly), I blindfolded the General and accompanied him on horseback through our lines to General Herron's tent, where an agreement was effected whereby an armistice to bury the dead was agreed to until 10 o'clock the next morning. This was only a ruse on the part of General Hindman to gain time, as during the night, by his orders, and against the advice of his generals, his army swathed the wheels of their cannon in blankets and like the Arabs silently stole away...."[33]

The reader can choose what is true and what is brag. Hindman's deception in asking for a truce to tend the wounded and bury the dead was successful. His army departed leaving most of his dead and wounded on the field to the care of the Federal surgeons, choosing not to rejoin the battle. His report said, in part:

"Considering the strength of my command as compared with the enemy; considering that my men were destitute of food, their wagons thirty miles in the rear, and not to be brought forward without imminent danger of being lost; that my small supply of ammunition was reduced far below what would be necessary for another day's fighting, and that my battery animals were literally dying of starvation, and could not be foraged in the presence of a superior force of the enemy, I determined to retire and gave the necessary orders for that purpose."[34]

## THIRTY SEVENTH ILLINOIS

The next day the horrors of war came into view with the light of day. Several of the 37$^{th}$ recorded their observations. Lieutenant Joseph Eaton of Wolford's Rock Island Company had the indelicacy to write to the Rock Island, Illinois ARGUS for the families of the dead and wounded to read:

"...when morning came we found the enemy had left us in possession of the field to look after their dead and wounded. Today [Dec 11] we have just got through burying their dead. We found many of them scattered through the woods, half eaten up by the hogs. It was a most horrible sight.

William Little of Co. A received a mortal wound in the abdomen. I found him on the field late at night, with four others. I sent for an ambulance and had him well cared for, but no kindness or care could save him.... It was a cold night and the poor fellow was nearly frozen when I found him.... Peace to his soul.[35]

The smell of burning flesh in the haystacks attracted packs of wild Arkansas hogs, who ate pieces of bodies, heads, arms, and innards. Benjamin McIntyre of the 19$^{th}$ Iowa described the day after the battle:

"...I saw death in its ghostly and most ghastly form.

Our men were scattered over the field for near half a mile, at first singly, but nearing where the rebels had planted their battery, they lay in groups. I might call it heaps. Death was here in almost every variety of form and yet the cause the same. Hundreds of men weltering in their own blood, pools of human gore meeting your sight as you pass along.

On the spot where the charge was made on the rebel battery I noticed a caisson to which were attached six horses, all dead but remaining in harness.

I saw three rebel slaughter pens containing a hundred dead bodies of rebels. Near the house I counted 18 more and several who were mortally wounded.

Our own dead with but few exceptions were rifled of everything worth possessing, while their own have been stripped of their shoes."[36]

Chester Barney of the 20$^{th}$ Iowa observed:

"...we proceeded to perform the melancholy task of burying our dead comrades. A beautiful spot had been selected adjoining the road leading to Cane Hill.... We mournfully deposited the bodies of these martyred heroes in their final resting place, amid the muffled roll of the drums and solemn funeral services...

During the afternoon of the same day we visited the battlefield.... Long trenches were being dug by our men into which the dead were thrown with but little ceremony, and covered with dirt. The fact that our own dead and wounded had been stripped of their clothing by the rebels had much to do with this rough manner of their disposal.

...numbers of the slightly wounded had attempted to follow [Hindman] on this retreat, but after proceeding some distance, became exhausted and secreted themselves in the woods where they perished. They were partly eaten by hogs when their remains were found by us.

In a large farm house standing about 1 mile south from the battlefield ... the floors were strewn with wounded, and the large yard surrounding it was also covered by them. They were lying in the hot sun, moaning piteously, while at a large table in the principal room the surgeons were busily engaged dressing wounds and amputating limbs. After amputation the limbs were thrown out at the back door, and I observed a number of hogs feeding on them. The sight was so disgusting that I hastened away, feeling a still deeper degree of hatred for those villains who had been the instigators or a rebellion which had placed these poor wretches in a position whereby they had become food for hogs."[37]

Doctor William Fithian described a field hospital as it was at the end of December:

"I cannot describe my feelings at some of the scenes which occurred on visiting some of the most seriously wounded. It was painful to witness with what almost frantic joy they would, in the most intense suffering, reach forward and eagerly seize a spoonful of wine or tomatoe, or even a cucumber pickle when presented, yet how very gratifying to know we were adding something, however small, to their comfort."[38]

These men seen by Dr. Fithian were the fortunate ones. Fifty-two percent of the patients who had limbs amputated died as a result.[39]

# THIRTY SEVENTH ILLINOIS

And so Hindman was defeated, his army scattered, his prospects for military success broken and denied. The victory at Prairie Grove came at the darkest most discouraging time of the war for the North. It secured Missouri for the moment and gave Northern morale a boost.

By the end of December, the pursuit of Hindman and what was left of his army had begun, with the 37$^{th}$ among the pursuers.

**JULIUS WHITE - FIRST COLONEL 37TH ILLINOIS**

*Library of Congress.*

**COLONEL CHARLES BLACK, 37TH ILLINOIS, ca. 1863**

*Courtesy Illinois State Historical Library*

**COLONEL MYRON BARNES**

**Colonel Myron Barnes as he appeared to a sketch artist, ca. 1862.**

*From "Biographical Sketches of Illinois Officers Engaged in the War Against the Rebellion of 1861," Chicago, 1862.*

**LIEUTENANT COLONEL EUGENE PAYNE**

*Courtesy Illinois State Historical Library*

**COLONEL HENRY FRISBIE**

Officers and Staff of the 92d U.S. Colored Troops, ca. 1864
Colonel Henry Frisbie, late of the 37th Illinois is the center portrait.
Several members of the 37th Illinois followed Frisbie to this new unit in
1863 and are pictured here.

*from Review of Reviews*

**CHAPLAIN EDWARD ANDERSON**

**Pictured as Colonel of the 12th Indiana Cavalry**

*From Colonels in Blue*

**LT. WILLIAM M. BANDY, CO. K, 37TH ILLINOIS**

*Courtesy Vermilion County Museum*

**CAPTAIN WILLIAM P. BLACK, ca 1861**

*Courtesy Vermilion County Museum*

**HENRY CURTIS, JR., ca 1861**

**Curtis went east with Julius White in 1862**

*Courtesy U.S. Army Military History Institute*

**DOCTOR WILLIAM FITHIAN**

Stepfather to Charles and William Black, who attended a wounded Charles Black after the Battle of Prairie Grove

*From Historical and Biographical Record of Vermilion County*

**LIEUTENANT WELLS MORRILL**

**With his shoulder straps, ca. 1865**

*Courtesy of Illinois State Historical Library*

THIRTY SEVENTH ILLINOIS

## 17.  The F Word

Before the Prairie Grove battle in December 1862, the 37th reported a strength of about eight hundred men. Of these, some were on detached service (staff duty, recruiting, duty as nurses, bakers, etc.), some sick, some in the stockade, and some away without leave, totaling less than one hundred fifty.

The drop-out rate on the march from Springfield to Prairie Grove was high. Of six hundred and fifty or so that started, only about four hundred arrived. Most of the drop-outs were from sickness or exhaustion. Rather than march a formidable distance and speed (forty-two miles in one twenty-four hour period), a soldier could easily sit beside the road until his feet stopped bleeding, or his malarial attack abated, or he got something to eat, or a variety of excuses, when the big payoff at the end of the march to Arkansas was a chance of a bullet in the brain.

Along with the legitimate absent sick and maimed were shirkers. Will Black got after two of his men for it, Frederic Reisser and Edward Robinson, who missed the battle on the plea of physical debility which they did not report and a surgeon's examination did not reveal. They had also missed the skirmish at Newtonia.[1]

In the aftermath of Prairie Grove, the 37th buried its dead, tended its wounded, and resumed the routine of camp life. The monotony was interrupted by a chase after Hindman's army into Van Buren, Arkansas after Christmas. After a two and one half day, fifty mile march through the Boston Mountains, Van Buren, Arkansas was captured without sustaining a casualty. The Federal column killed four, took four hundred prisoners, burned seven steamboats, and captured a quantity of commissary stores. The astonished Van Buren population had believed Hindman's boast that he had won at Prairie Grove, and had to watch the Union column march into town with music playing and flags flying and the soldiers singing "Rally Round the Flag."[2]

After the successful raid, the 37th moved to a new camp at Fayetteville, located about a mile out of town. The Prairie Grove wounded were still scattered in private houses and hospitals around Fayetteville. Charles Black was in a house attended by his stepfather,

# THE F WORD

William Fithian, and by Doc Clark. Black was in pain and his shattered arm was discharging pus continually, the bone having been shattered into fifteen pieces. He was convalescing in the home of Mrs. Washburn and Mrs. Poulson, who were sisters, half Cherokee, bitterly secessionist, whose husbands were off with the Confederate Army. Ten slaves lived behind the house.[3]

Black was a bit of a curiosity, a tourist attraction, visited by many local ladies wanting to see if the Federal soldiers were really demons in human shape.

Doc Clark and Doctor Fithian were determined to save Charlie's arm. Two inches had been taken out of the arm bone. The pieces of bone and the ball that shattered it were sent back to Danville as souvenirs by cousin Henry Fithian.

It would be some time before Charles Black rejoined the regiment. Doctor Fithian would not move him from Fayetteville because of the severity of the wound, so there they stayed all the month of January.

The major fear, which was quite real, was that the army would leave, the rebels move in, and Charles and the Doctor be taken. For some time after Prairie Grove, the town was full of rebel parolees who came in to take the oath of allegiance to the Union.

It was no small thing that Black still had his arm, smashed as it was, and the savior of that limb was Elijah A. Clark, Assistant Regimental Surgeon. Clark was a staunch political ally of the Blacks, and also a man whose medical skills were respected by the regiment. He was in contrast to Surgeon Luthur Humeston, who nobody liked very much. In Black's arm were fifteen shards of bone, a grim condition in an age of primitive surgical technique.

Clark fit right in with the staff of the 37th, getting into his share of hot water. While the regiment was at Springfield in August 1862, Doc Clark set up a limited private practice, allegedly selling certificates of disability to anyone, able-bodied or otherwise, who had the price of 50 cents. He sold one to a Missouri State Militia man, who was glad of the certificate needed to get a discharge or medical leave, but objected to paying 50 cents for it. This patient complained, and Clark was ordered by Egbert Brown to turn over all the fees he had collected to the Provost Marshal, which he did with the defense that the practice was usual, and only done for civilians when it did not interfere with official duty, and that all the money had been spent for delicacies for his hospital patients.[4]

In February, a charge was made against Doc Clark of pilfering a patient's property, one Johnson M. Kelly of the 59th Illinois, who had died almost a year before at Cassville from wounds received at Pea Ridge. Clark answered that it was the job of the hospital steward to gather effects, not his, and that he took no effects, and never saw Kelly after he died. $2.50 of Kelly's money was used to buy a coffin, which were in short supply. Clark went on to say that he frequently had coffins made at his own expense rather than bury men without coffins, and that the effects of about 1000 deceased soldiers lay unclaimed at Springfield. Henry Frisbie's endorsement to Clark's defense stated that he had similar complaints about Clark, "and I have applied to him and he has fixed them up or said he had.... This matter shall be investigated and if he is guilty he shall suffer what is right and just."[5]

Frisbie may have been trying to eliminate by innuendo one of Charles Black's allies in the battle for control of the regiment. Shortly after promising to investigate Doc Clark, Frisbie worked a little more mischief, telling Clark that Charles Black was charging him with absence without leave for his detail at the hospital in Springfield, disobedience of orders, and conduct unbecoming. John Peck confirmed falsely that Charles Black had so charged Clark.

Doctor Fithian intercepted the bitter letter Clark wrote to Charles saying in part, "if it should be so, I would almost doubt the fidelity of Jesus Christ hereafter. Tell me again you never done it, and let me love you as in the days of yore." Fithian told Clark he'd been had by a mischief-maker, and that no charges had been filed. Doc Clark replied, "... our association has always been intimate as brothers. Since [Charles'] recent wound I stood over him with all the anxiety that you could have done, indeed I felt too keen a sympathy in his case to even decide upon the better plan of treatment for his recovery. ... I would not have given credence to the statement of 'F' but Q.M. Peck told me also that he saw the charges and they were as 'F' represented, but I find that the latter gentleman has an equal ability to prevaricate.... I take it all back. Please don't send that letter to the Col."[6]

While this misunderstanding was bubbling along, Doc Clark got an appointment as Surgeon of the 8th Missouri Cavalry, and he left the regiment in March. Charles Black wrote him a short note, curt and cold in tone, to his friend, ally, and the savior of his arm; "Why was your letter so brief and formal?"[7] Clark replied. "I have never heard one word from your arm since you started home. Do you think that I have ceased to care anything for you, and especially the result of so serious a wound as yours was? Col., I think indeed that you have treated me real cool. If I had no professional right to ask you the result of your case, I'm sure I feel that I ought to have a social right...."[7]

So Doc Clark left, and the book closed on another comrade in arms gone out of the 37th to seek his fortune elsewhere. The arm that Clark had saved for Charlie continued a mass of infection and pain for months.

Charles Black's arm was not his only painful difficulty in the early months of 1863. At the regiment, he faced sworn enemy Frisbie as his second in command, while next to him was Eugene Payne, of doubtful personal loyalty, and there was the loss of staunch friends. Brother Will was already planning advancement in anticipation of Charles' permanent absence, Wells Blodgett was keeping as much distance as he could from the regiment, Doc Clark went to the Missouri Cavalry, and Kennicott and Dickinson were upset that Black had allowed Payne to advance as Major.

There was another pot boiling as Black lay on his sick bed in Fayetteville in December 1862, and the lid blew off on New Year's Day 1863.

During Black's convalescence, several officers and men from the regiment, including Henry Frisbie, visited. Francis Jay Herron came to visit on the third, with good tidings of his official report that praised Black for service at Prairie Grove. But at this time, something else arrived, in the form of the January 1 number of the ST. LOUIS DEMOCRAT newspaper, containing a letter about the 37th at Prairie Grove, signed "F."[8]

## THIRTY SEVENTH ILLINOIS

Frisbie had been the correspondent to the CHICAGO TRIBUNE after Edward Anderson had given it up in May 1862. Some of his letters to the Trib were signed, "H.N. Frisbie," or "H.N.F.," but most usually and lately signed simply "F."

There was nothing in the TRIBUNE about Prairie Grove from "F." That letter of the alphabet now appeared in the DEMOCRAT of January 1, 1863, under a letter bearing a date of December 12, 1862. At that time, everyone thought Charles Black would lose his arm, or if not, be in for a long convalescence, leaving Henry Frisbie in command of the 37$^{th}$ as he was on the 12$^{th}$ of December. The letter said in part that Charles Black had no reason to order the retreat off the hill at Prairie Grove, and that the day was saved for the Union only when Charles Black turned command of the 37$^{th}$ over to Frisbie. The gist of it was that Black was a coward and Frisbie a hero.

When the letter was read to Black, he was visibly upset, and guessed who "F" was right away. Will Black said he would kill Frisbie if he ever openly acknowledged the letter, and bought a Colt 5-shot pistol from Fred Abbey for the purpose. "Had the letter appeared above the signature of Major Frisbie, I should have killed him as I would a dog."[9] Will advised brother Charlie to see the editor of the DEMOCRAT on this way home through St. Louis, demand he publish a Jonathan Swift-type letter Will had written about Frisbie, demand that the editor reveal Frisbie as the author and sue for slander or horsewhip him through the streets if he refused.

Charles Black had already taken action before the proddings of his younger brother. On January 12, Charles pronounced the statements false, and demanded a Court of Inquiry on it from the army. Frisbie was after the Colonelcy, and such things were often made in the newspapers. Such a letter as "F" wrote could have cost Charles his colonel's eagles.

This letter-writing was part of the mania among officer-seekers for Barnes' field office vacancy. The news of Barnes' dismissal came to the regiment on December 11, and spurred all the candidates on to greater efforts. Will Black saw his chance if his brother could not return to duty. He asked his stepfather to push Kennicott for Major, thus forcing Payne to resign out of pride, making Will senior captain, ex-Laimbeer.[10] Then Kennicott would support Will for Major. This left the loyal Capt. Dick out in the cold, and Will advised Charlie and Dr. Fithian not to help Dick.

Kennicott put in his claim as senior captain on the point of order of muster – that he was mustered before Payne. Payne was claiming his seniority by the invocation of his letter, C, in the line. These were two of the tie-breakers invented to press seniority claims.

Kennicott had Frisbie's support for the majority, citing among other things his history as an Ellsworth Zouave. He also got John Laimbeer to renounce his seniority.

On Christmas Eve, 1862, Egbert Brown expressed himself on the subject of Henry Frisbie;

> A Major Frisbie ... is represented as being a very troublesome man.... He manages to keep within the law himself while he is getting other men to fight out his difficulties. That he is devoid of honor is unquestioned.
> An officer who will go over a battlefield and rob the dead as it is notorious he did at Pea Ridge is not a man who will raise the moral standard of our army and is a disgrace to the service. The regiment to which he belongs has many good men whose influence is destroyed by the bad effect of a few knaves.
> ...I should inquire into the fitness of the man next in rank before filling the vacant position...[11]

The day after Christmas, Capt. Dick's frustrations came out when he told Black that the claims of Payne and Kennicott to seniority over him were made with the knowledge of both that, "nothing but the blackest lies and villainy gives them the shadow of a claim to that position."[12]

After all this, the biggest gun in the political battle was the one fired by Frisbie when he wrote the letter to the DEMOCRAT and accused Charles Black of cowardice in print for all to see.

Frisbie meant the letter to block Black off the colonelcy, but as things were developing, it might also be the means to knock Frisbie out of the regiment or out of the army. Either Black or Frisbie would have to go, as the animosity and baiting could not be contained. A hearing and a court martial concerning the letter would bring everything to a head in the first months of 1863.

On January 27, before the army inquiry into the "F" letter began, the promotions were announced to adjust the field grades after Barnes' exit. There was no surprise in the top two positions; Black was Colonel and Frisbie was Lieutenant Colonel. The unknown was the majority. The possibilities ranged from Blodgett to Payne to Dickinson to Will Black to Kennicott to Erwin Messer, with Kennicott the favorite, even though Payne had been acting major after Prairie Grove. Payne had been out in a snowbank in the Ozarks from the 9$^{th}$ to the 24$^{th}$ of January with a 200 man detail guarding a commissary train from Huntsville to Carrolton, and was delayed by weather in getting back. Whether Payne was present or absent the regiment in January made no difference; the die was cast. Elijah Haines had prevailed in Springfield, Illinois, and Eugene Beauharnais Payne was the new major of the 37$^{th}$, to date from November 20.

Judd Huntley had told Payne about his promotion before the commissions arrived, and his wife wrote him a letter addressed to "Major Payne," so the surprise of the announcement was not total.[13]

Payne was no one's first choice, but he prevailed principally because of his wife's influence over E.M. Haines who had the ear of the Governor and the Adjutant General in Illinois.

The batch of new commissions included one for Sergeant Jack Moran to be 2$^{nd}$ Lieutenant of the Michigan Company to replace William Johnson, deceased. At the same time, Capt. John Laimbeer's resignation was accepted, and so there was a path up for Wells Blodgett to be Captain. Blodgett was in Springfield, Missouri, on Egbert Brown's staff, and this duty put him in the way of a big scrape in January when Confederate General Marmaduke attacked Springfield with about 8000 men. Both Blodgett and Brown were wounded.[14]

All the promotions sorted out the regimental politics for the moment, and on February 3, 1863, the Court of Inquiry Black had requested over Frisbie's letter began inquiring. Two charges were to

# THE F WORD

be answered; what really happened at Prairie Grove, and who wrote the letter to the ST. LOUIS DEMOCRAT?

Will Black testified that the regiment was ordered up the hill at Prairie Grove from their position defending an artillery battery at about four in the afternoon, left the hill in the face of an overwhelming musket fire, and that brother Charlie, "was with the regiment when it was rallied, and did not leave it until that was done." After that, General Herron came along and ordered an advance by saying, "Come on, boys, General Blunt is at them!" After 20 minutes, the rebels retreated and the regiment fell back and disengaged for the day.

The particulars of Charles Black's presence during the reforming of the regiment was confirmed by Colonel Chandler, Brigade Adjutant, who also testified that the letter stating otherwise was "untrue," but that the double-cannister point-blank firing of two artillery batteries stopped the rebel advance, and not the firing of the 37th.

General Dan Huston, Brigade Commander, supported Black's retreat order as, "the only proper order to give." His opinion of the letter was that "I think [it] almost wholly a tissue of falsehood...."

So much for what happened. As to who "F" was, Lieutenant Marr of the Peoria Battery which was brigaded with the 37th testified that it was Frisbie, and that Frisbie admitted it to Marr and Captain Murphy of the same battery. Murphy approached Frisbie to acknowledge a mistake in the article, which Frisbie did, acknowledging authorship.

If Frisbie wasn't rallying the routed regiment after the retreat, where was he? Charles Black testified that Frisbie had asked him if he could leave the field to report a new rebel battery to Colonel Huston. Black told him to go, and did not see him again until he turned over the command to him 20 or 25 minutes later.

For Frisbie's part, he wrote one version of the events of December 7 three days after the battle and sent it to the editor of the St. Louis Democrat, who published it. He wrote a similar defense in March 1863, and a puffier and more dramatic narrative 27 years later.

The Court of Inquiry finally decided that, "... had he, Lt. Col. Black ... not have ordered a retreat, he would have violated the confidence and trust reposed in him, and been culpable to the highest degree.... The letter of January 1, 1863 ... is almost entirely erroneous, generally false in facts and entirely so in spirit.... Its author is conniving, unscrupulous, and malicious.... The name of the officer guilty of attempting ... to injure the well-earned reputation of a brother officer, is withheld until he shall have an opportunity of acquitting himself before a court martial of the serious offenses with which he is charged. By order of Major General Schofield."[15]

To forestall things, Frisbie decided to ask for his own Court of Inquiry, as Black had done, before he was formally charged and court martialed. He was chiefly offended at being branded as "conniving, unscrupulous, and malicious," and at the imputation of cowardice in leaving the field for 20 minutes in the heat of battle.[16]

The triable, provable violation of regulations was not the events of December 7, but the fact of writing the letter. Article 26 of Army Regulations specifically prohibited such "deliberations or discussions among a class of military men ... whether newspaper, pamphlet, or handbill...."[17]

It took two months to set up Frisbie's Court Martial. He was charged, finally, on April 16 with writing the St. Louis letter and for writing another letter to the Secretary of War without going through the chain of command, and a protracted trial began.

In April, Charles Black and Wells Blodgett came back to the regiment at the Elk Creek camp. Blodgett brought a new piece of ammunition, the gist of which Eugene Payne gleefully reported to his wife: "'F' will soon have his trial the scoundrel. Would you believe it, he has been three times indicted in the courts of Chicago for theft and robbery. It is on record." The charges were assault, horse theft, and fraud in the hay business in Chicago in the 1850's.[18]

The other letter Frisbie wrote went to the Secretary of War in March asking for Charles Black's dismissal on grounds of a 70-day absence due to physical disability. Because the letter did not go through the chain of command properly endorsed, it came back to the regimental commander, who happened to be Eugene Payne. Payne informed both the Blacks, and Willy charged Frisbie with writing the second letter critical of his commanding officer, on the advice of Col. Mc E. Dye, Brigade Commander.[19]

# THE F WORD

As the fires were banking around Frisbie, he planned a defense that would include dozens of civilian and military witnesses to try and save himself.

## 18. The Court of Bad Language

While the Black-Frisbie squabble was dragging along through the early months of 1863, the regiment continued to suffer a death here, a nasty night march there, and a flood of disciplinary problems and desertions constantly moving from place to place all over southwest Missouri, chasing the rebel army, neighborhood guerillas, bushwhackers, or moving for good water, wood, and forage. January saw marches from Fayetteville to Huntsville, Bentonville, Cross Hollows, back to Pea Ridge, then up to Keitsville and Cassville.

In February, they stopped for two weeks at Camp Schofield, twelve miles from Cassville, and then on to Camp Bliss, forty miles south of Springfield near the Three Widows. In March, more moves up to McCullough's Springs and then to Ozark. Then on to Lockport and Camp Bloomington, near Hazlewood, then Hartsville, Elk Creek, and Robideau Creek. Continuing on, packing and unpacking, making and breaking camp, always chasing an enemy that stayed out of reach. After the stop at Robideau Creek, came Piney River, Spring Creek, Little Piney River (Camp Totten), and then to Rolla, out of the muck and mire of southwest Missouri.

One advantage to the constant moving was the unending number of unpolluted, disease-free camp sites. Too long a stay in one location fouled the water and air, and the accumulated waste and garbage of both man and animal bred vermin and insects. In the last six months of 1862, there had been only three deaths from disease in the regiment, partly attributable to immunities against the most prevalent communicable camp fevers, measles, etc., that had devastated the army in the winter of 1861-1862.

Reading a list of estate assets of some of the dead paints a stark picture of their lives. The estate of Thomas Murphy, a farmer of the Rock Island Company, who died in April, shows more than the usual list of possessions that included a portfolio of paper, envelopes, pens & holders, one prayer book, one cigar case, one looking glass, five woolen shirts, one song book, one inkstand, one pair of suspenders, and a pipe.[1]

# THE COURT OF BAD LANGUAGE

As for attrition, after Prairie Grove, there were thirteen disability discharges, and ten dead and fifty-six wounded in battle. Several of the wounded would die or be discharged within the year, including psychiatric profiles, which were rare. Private Henry Upstone, a British born farmer of Kennicott's company, was discharged because of "a paroxysm of insanity last April, caused by an alarm while on picket. He became rational again in some two months, but is still unfit for duty. [He is] incapable of performing the duties of a soldier because of heredity insanity. Last April, he had a parocys of mania, caused from a fright.... Since that time he has been compos mentos, but his constitution is still much impaired, and occasionally threatens with a second attack, when excited from any cause."[2]

The other drain on manpower was confinement as discipline for all manner of offenses including theft, drunkenness, refusing orders, absent without leave, and disrespectful language. A sampling from this time includes John Harman of Messer's Company, who was read out at dress parade for a gunshot within the lines raising a false alarm that an attack on the camp was in progress. Almiran Stillman of Wolford's Company straggled off the line of march and stayed away all night, which cost him $2. On another occasion, he straggled on the way to Bloomington into a house where he took what he wanted and refused to pay. The sentence was harsh; a fine of two month's pay, seven days jail on bread and water, seven days walking a beat eight hours per day (with one hour's rest), with a forty pound pack, and then seven more days in jail. The crime was part of the chronic problem of straggling and citizen complaints of robbery and theft.[3]

In March, on the trip from James River to Bloomington, Andrew Hunter and Oscar Sheldon dropped out enroute. Hunter was fined $13 and Sheldon $5. Sheldon saved $8 because the court conceded he could not keep up after having dropped out.

John Reed of Dickinson's Company was in the stockade in Springfield for larceny when General Marmaduke attacked in January 1863, and was promised release if he would help in the defense. He did, and was released without being charged a month later. Sergeant Benjamin Parkhurst, Co. H, let prisoners out of the stockade under his guard and then Parkhurst and the prisoners all got drunk along with the Commissary Forage guard. The prisoners were in the slam for being drunk and disorderly in the first place. Parkhurst was sentenced to do a private's duty at private's pay for one month.

Andrew Baker of Rust's Company refused to load wood one day which cost him $2.

Disrespectful language was an expensive exercise for a few, however satisfying it may have felt at the moment. Patrick Shields of Frisbie's Company lost three month's pay and four weeks on bread and water for this speech to and about his sergeant, Thomas Murphy: "Murphy is a counterfeit. He takes about an hour to dress the company. Heavens be with McCarthy, he forgot more that he (Murphy) ever learned. Murphy, you are a son of a bitch. You deceive your country and your religion." (McCarthy was Company G First Sergeant Dennis McCarthy).

Before leaving Elk Creek, the same Sergeant Murphy had words with another son of the old sod when he told Private William McAuliffe, "You're a God damned son of a bitch, and, "you're an Irish son of a bitch." In the ensuing court martial, Murphy was fined $15, and the court added this comment: "The court is thus lenient because of the great provocation that the accused had.... The Court considers no cause of provocation, however great, sufficient to justify an officer in using the term, 'You're a son of a bitch,' to any enlisted man."

Patrick Shields had called Murphy a son of a bitch and got fined $39 and 28 days on bread and water, proving that rank has its privileges.

Sergeant John Moran of the Michigan Company had the roughest time with discipline. Of the officers of Co. D, Capt. John Laimbeer was constantly under arrest; First Lieutenant Wells Blodgett, who wanted no part of the company, kept himself on some detail or staff duty away from the regiment as much as possible; and Second Lieutenant William Johnson died of his Prairie Grove wounds. Sergeant Moran, a British born sailor, was left to run the company. Thomas Phillips of Co. D lost a month's pay for telling Moran he would not go out to company drill after he had stood guard the night before for "[Moran] or any other damned man."

## THE COURT OF BAD LANGUAGE

Private Philip Honlin, another of Moran's men told Moran at Elk Creek that he was "a God damned liar, and might go to hell, and might kiss his (Honlin's) ass." Honlin got a ball and chain and hard labor and loss of all pay, sentence afterward reversed in time for him to desert in November 1863.[4]

Myron Barnes' old company from Rock Island had its own set of miscreants. Samuel Lee, Co. A, was arrested at the hospital bakery in Springfield for refusing to return a set of scales and weights, and John Kennedy for not appearing for guard at the proper time for his next tour. Kennedy was sentenced to jail at hard labor for eighteen months with a six pound ball and chain and forfeiture of all pay, an unjust sentence. General Herron reversed the sentence, noting, "a total want of legality and formality in the proceedings.... The Commanding General ... is anxious that the soldiers under his command shall not receive cruel or exorbitant punishments ... the strongest inducement for desertion, a thing already too prevalent in our armies."[5]

Desertions in the spring of 1863 were on the increase army wide, with the 37th no exception. Six men went from Dickinson's Company while on a forage scout to Mount Vernon, taking a horse and David Ash's rubber coat and best mittens. Five went from Company A, three each from Companies C, D, and E, ten from Co. I, and four from Co. K. Will Black asked that the names of the deserters be advertised in the Danville paper: Newton Adams, Theodore Cappock, Albert J. Riley, and Augustus Shaw. These four had left on February 28, taking their muskets with them. Cappock came back two weeks later, Adams returned to Pilot Knob in May, and Riley and Shaw came back shortly after and saw the muster out in May 1866 with the regiment. They took advantage of President Lincoln's 1863 amnesty for deserters who returned promptly.[6]

A large share of this indiscipline was laid to Charles Black's absence for convalescence and then on junkets to Chicago to try and get a new command. The sum of the problem is in a barely literate letter written to Charles Black by Eli Bogue of the Danville Company on March 11, 1863 while he was assigned as the driver of James Totten's mess wagon: "[March 11] Col. the boys are leaveing ever day. Ten of the boys has left Co. I, and foure has left our company; Adams, Bailey, Shaw I for Get the other one. I hop thire ant eny more of them leave for our Reg is so small it don't look like a reg. I hope you will be back to command them in a fue days. I must bring my letter to a close escuse my bed spelling."[7]

Most of the deserters, like Lee Horr and John Nausler of Co. G came back after a few weeks to the charitable judgment that, "They are both young boys and from their youth and inexperience ... they did not fully realize how grave an offense they were committing...."[8]

The regiment clearly was not doing well without its poet-colonel, drillmaster, and disciplinarian Charles Black, who was still absent as February and March 1863 came and went. His arm was, alternately, discharging pus, without strength, then healed, fevered and swollen, then discharging pus again.

The political fever in the regiment was as chronic as Black's arm. Payne was left as regimental commander to spar with Frisbie, who was suspended from duty awaiting trial. Payne describe the relationship as, "Him & I are at sword points."[9]

Since Prairie Grove, the regiment had continued to march in circles around the torn up countryside of southwest Missouri, and the hard marches and bad weather cumulatively had brought Fred Abbey a case of "lung fever," and he was going home on a medical discharge. He had a few things to clear up with his brother officers before he left. He first dealt with Charles Black. Abbey was a sick man in February 1863, and was in no mood to placate anyone. He erupted at a remark Charles Black allegedly made about his capture at Prairie Grove, along the lines that Abbey and Hicks were "taken of their own accord." The remark was supposedly made to Egbert Brown.[10]

Before Abbey left for home, he tried to provide for the vacancy caused by his discharge as First Lieutenant of Company I. By rules of promotion, Second Lieutenant Isaac Dodge was the new First Lieutenant, thus creating the Second Lieutenant vacancy. Abbey got into it with Ransom Kennicott, who thought the spot should go to his brother George, and was in no frame of mind to listen to the idea of the Second Lieutenancy going to George Merrill instead of his brother, even though Merrill had been acting as First Sergeant and had assisted in raising the company in 1861.

# THE COURT OF BAD LANGUAGE

Frisbie endorsed Merrill's claim by the rules of seniority. Unfortunately for Merrill, the commission was issued to George Kennicott as George K, rather than he, showed up on the roll as First Sergeant. Merrill got his promotion two months later as 2d Lieutenant of Wolford's Company.[11]

Ransom Kennicott remained unsatisfied. Payne's promotion had upset him and he still had competition from Capt. Dick and from Will Black for the next one. Hiram Kennicott had at this time gotten the promise of a regular army Second Lieutenancy for his son Ransom, which he finally did take in 1866.

On March 15, 1863, the 37th went into camp on Elk Creek. The politics of the colonelcy overrode all else of consequence. The Black-Frisbie struggle was ripening. Frisbie was to be court martialed for the St. Louis letter, and unless he could do something to Black and make it stick, his prospects were dim. Drawing others into the struggle was inevitable.

Myron Barnes had gotten a reinstatement with the army from Washington and was free to serve again, but not with the 37th. As for Capt. Dick, he had gone to the Philistines for help. He had Frisbie, as regimental commander, write the governor from Bloomington promoting his interests.

These were all little sideshows with Capt. Dick, and Fred Abbey, and Capt. Kennicott and his brother George. The main event was the squawk going on around the regimental throne between its two ranks. Frisbie was taking every advantage of Black's absence from the regiment during February and March. He leaned on Freemasonry, on the Governor through his Chicago-based brothers, and on political bartering in the regiment.

On April 3, the regiment left the Elk Creek camp, southwest Missouri was abandoned, and the 37th never again returned to Cassville or Keitsville or Fayetteville or Dug Springs or any other familiar neighborhood spot on any countermarch or false scout. On that day, the regiment moved east to the huge Union army base at Rolla, then to St. Louis and the Mississippi by month's end.

## 19. Missouri in the Rearview

The march out of Elk Creek in April was as pleasant as such things go. There was good weather, four days over good roads in the direction of civilization. The regiment moved to Little Piney River, to Camp Totten, but with a new army commander, General Francis Jay Herron. The camp was about ten miles southwest of Rolla. The progress out of the strategic defense net of Springfield and southwest Missouri was straight-line and steady.

There were two familiar faces at Rolla. Sam Heartley, former Regimental Sergeant Major, was Captain of a company in the 27th Missouri. He had a second lieutenant who was a Methodist minister and a sergeant who was a Carmolite minister, and Heartley observed, "between their praying and my swearing, we get along bully...."[1]

The other face from the past was John Pound, lately Provost Marshal of the post at Springfield who had stood up to the rampaging Myron Barnes the summer before. He had been discharged for, "incapacity and unfitness," as an officer, and left out in a regimental consolidation, and was in Rolla to try to get another place in the army.[2]

The three weeks at Little Piney – Camp Totten provided the time and opportunity for political games to resume. Sergeant Thomas Payne, Co. E, was promoted to Second Lieutenant. The dust had cleared from his situation, a place was vacant in Company E, Phineas Rust was gone, and Colonel Black and Major Eugene Payne went to bat for him, explaining his prior loss of stripes was done, "for small reasons in an improper manner,"[3] and that he was the choice of all officers and men, that he was placed in the ranks by the whim of Phineas Rust, had fought all the battles, was a good disciplinarian, etc. So, Thomas Henry Louis "By Christ" Payne gained the status to fit his 6'2" stature.

The pleasant days at Little Piney Creek ended in April when the regiment moved the short distance to Rolla, and there took the train to St. Louis, where most everybody went to town.

Everyone had to be collected from various states of carousal and undress in St. Louis when abrupt orders came, at 9 PM on April 23, to get out and get on a riverboat bound for Cape Girardeau, Missouri. About half the men and most of the officers were hurriedly collected, and everybody made it on board the FRANCIS FISHER and left at 3 AM for the Cape.

The rush was that the old antagonist, General John Sappington Marmaduke, was trying to raid the Cape with a good-sized force. By the time the 37$^{th}$ got there on April 27, the fight was over, and Marmaduke had moved off after taking a few shots at a Nebraska infantry company.

The regiment was not able to enjoy Cape Girardeau for more than a day. The evening of the next day, April 28, the chase after Marmaduke began, through a big patch of cypress swamps along a line of march that was forty miles long and done in one night and one day. After a stop at Bloomfield, the men headed for Chalk Bluffs on the St. Francis River, another forty miles spent trying to head off Marmaduke's escape into Arkansas.

The Federal forces caught Marmaduke at the ford of the St. Francis River and had a short skirmish which caused a tragic casualty in the 37$^{th}$. Lieutenant Joe Eaton was killed by a burst of a friendly artillery shell. He took a piece of shrapnel in the right ear and died instantly.

Joseph Eaton had five children, ages four to sixteen. He had the sixteen year-old, Charles, with him in the regiment. Charles had come with the 37$^{th}$ from Chicago as a fourteen year-old drummer boy in 1861. Joe and Charlie were joined for a great part of the Missouri campaigns by Joe's wife Lavinia, making in all an army family circle of three.

The 37$^{th}$ left the Cape on May 9 and backtracked to St. Louis, to Camp Gamble. They had gone one hundred eighty miles in eight days. It had rained every day, and the men were on short rations and were out with no tents on the trip through the "Sunken Ground" between Cape Girardeau and New Madrid, Missouri. Their route was a ridge between the two swamps which had been depressed by the New Madrid earthquake forty years before.

The stay in St. Louis lasted five days, and then the regiment moved to Pilot Knob, Missouri, to a camp on Shepard's Mountain, where the political centerpiece continued to be the Frisbie-Black row.

## THIRTY SEVENTH ILLINOIS

The abrupt moves during April and May had made Henry Frisbie's court martial very difficult to conduct. It had begun April 13 while the regiment was at Little Piney River, and had been suspended entirely during the scout to Cape Girardeau.

Charles Black and Wells Blodgett has returned to the 37th at the beginning of April, and Black lost no time in restoring discipline to officers and men alike. He lifted a few dollars out of the pockets of some of the government's $13 per month help. John Dutcher, Co. F, lost $10 for an overnight out of camp without a pass, and Thomas McAllister, Co. C, lost $13 for escaping from the guard house. John Jones of the Michigan Company requested the watch of Prussian-born Frank Happe by allegedly saying, "You damned Dutch son of a bitch, give me your watch." The court decided that he didn't use the word "damn," nor did he get the watch, and so the whole exercise cost him $10.[4]

Black also fell on two sergeants and a captain. One to suffer was Sergeant David Ash, who got tied up in St. Louis in May on his way back to the regiment, and missed the last train to Pilot Knob. The next morning, he had no pass to leave the city and the Provost Marshall was out. Black told him he would have to go before a military commission and explain his late arrival. Ash felt badly used and told his wife, "I don't think Col. Black did the right thing.... They appear to forget a favor very soon, but I think Col. Black will remember the next one he gets of me ... if he is in a bad humor he can get pleased ...." The reason David Ash felt badly used was that he had done Black a favor by filling in for John Peck as Quartermaster in Peck's absence in April. With the job went responsibility for all the stores, and if anything was missing, Ash could have been held accountable. Black had forgotten the good turn very quickly.[5]

Charles Black's dissatisfaction with David Ash was transitory, but not so with George F. McKay of Bangor, Maine, First Sergeant of Wolford's Company. He reduced McKay to Private because McKay was absent for several days.[6]

Captain George Redfield Bell got off a lot easier, probably because his father was a judge. On the march out of Chalk Bluffs, Bell had left the regiment to get a good dry night's rest in a house, while his men were left out in the rain. Bell's contention was that he was ill. He got off with a slap on the wrist.[7]

Stopping the straggling, swearing, and stealing was given a bit more impetus by Black because he was progressively more edgy and difficult after his return to the regiment. He sensed Frisbie was slipping the noose at his trial. Black was also ignoring several letters written by Julius White, as he was convinced that White had been playing a double game during his trouble with Frisbie. Beyond this, the corruption was draining out of his unhealed arm nearly every day.

Black's animosity toward Julius White came out of his suspicion that White had aided Frisbie, by silence if not overtly, and considered a recommendation solicited of White by Doctor Fithian as faint praise. Generals Brown and Totten were no longer able to help Black, and in fact, the new commander, General Francis Jay Herron, was a declared enemy of Brown, of Totten, and of General Schofield, citing in part their drunken habits in his objections of record.[8]

Henry Blodgett was lobbying fiercely to get brother Wells appointed Judge Advocate. Wells Blodgett's opinion was that, "all Iowa was at work trying to get the position for another man."[9]

Herron was in a spat with Totten and Brown, both Blodgett-ites, which was reason enough to footdrag on the Presidential appointment as Judge Advocate that Henry Blodgett had managed for his brother.

Capt. Dick was still coming up empty – he couldn't resign, he couldn't work a transfer, and he couldn't get promoted. His alliance with Frisbie and his threats to the Governor had come to nothing. His wife had gone home, and he was down to throwing rocks at Charles Black and William Bandy, newly appointed First Lieutenant of Company K, miffed that his sergeant, Oliver Risdon, had written him up for absence at formations. Black came down on Risdon's side, and told Dick, "If you take exception ... prefer charges against the offender."

All these little frictions and punishments were trivia and minutiae rustling around in the shadows of Frisbie's Court Martial, which was the main event, the decisive engagement. With delays and suspensions, his trial dragged on for six weeks. Frisbie called dozens of witnesses, challenged court members, and retained an abrasive attorney to frustrate the court.

## THIRTY SEVENTH ILLINOIS

The concern was rising at the Fithian home in Danville that if Frisbie was not convicted and forced out, "Willie might do something rash, something which would destroy us all," no doubt having in mind a quick snuff-out of Frisbie with the pistol bought from Fred Abbey. Mother Josephine's comment was, "the suggestion distresses me that either of you would touch the contemptible wretch [Frisbie] if the law lets him escape,"[10] having an eye to Charles' personal interest and Willy's violent threats.

Was Willy capable of murder? It is possible that his Mother's opinion was partly influenced by an incident in Missouri summarized in a letter Willy wrote to her in December 1861:

> I was on duty ... as Captain of the Brigade guard.... A little after dark, a train of wagons came into camp, which had been to Otterville for provisions, and one of the pressed teamsters was drunk. Creating some disturbance, or insulting some officer, he was brought down to the guard house under a file of men. He objected considerably to going in, but being compelled to enter, he began to sweare and make a disturbance, when I stepped in to silence him. It was dark and there was no light in the tent except what glimmered through from a fire outside. As I stepped in alone, I said to him, 'See here my friend, you must keep still.' But just as I stepped in and spoke to him, he gave back a little and drew his knife on me, threatening to kill me if I touched him. I could see the blade, some 8 or 10 inches long, gleam in the indistinct light, and knowing he was just drunk enough to be quarrelsome, I own my position somewhat 'ticklish,' to say the least.
>
> Having no notion ... of giving back as I went on talking to him, very quickly I drew my revolver, which was fortunately loaded and capped, and cocked it, placing my finger on the trigger. The fellow recognized me, and in drunken fashion began to appeal to me, and then asked me to drink. This I declined and told him he must empty his canteen. To this he demurred, but telling him I meant just what I said, he con-

cluded there was no help for the matter and proceeded to empty it – down his throat! I took the canteen from his lips and poured the whiskey all out on the ground and then started to leave the tent, when he insisted on following me.

For the first time in my life, I put a loaded capped and cocked revolver to a man's head and told him to stay where he was. He seemed to think this quite a forcible argument, but a moment afterward he was released by Major McGibbon. He was however re-arrested a short time afterword, and drawing his knife on the guard several times. The guard finally struck him in the face with the butt of his gun and knocked him senseless. He will probably be court-martialed and may be shot, more especially as he is not a soldier. I was not scared but kept perfectly cool. At one time, however, I felt much tempted to blow his brains out. I am thankful I got the better of the temptation.[11]

The bad news to the Blacks, to Wells Blodgett, to Eugene Payne, Capt. Dick, and many others came at the beginning of June. Frisbie joined the regiment when he came on board the HANNIBAL tied up opposite Cape Girardeau on June 4, having got out of the judicial vise by getting Captain John Laimbeer to swear that he, and not Frisbie, had written the St. Louis letter, and signed himself "F."[12]

So that was it. Frisbie had escaped justice, and was back with the regiment second in rank to Charles Black. Henry Frisbie would stay with the 37th a few more months before transferring to command the 92d United States Colored Troops as a full colonel.

The 37th made its last march in Missouri on the 3rd of June – from Pilot Knob to Farmington and from there to St. Genevieve. The evening of the 5th of June they left the soil of Missouri. They stepped off the west bank of the Mississippi and onto the Steamer HANNIBAL. The boat turned and steamed south, and their twenty months service in Missouri was history.

## 20. Vicksburg

On June 5, 1863, the regiment boarded the HANNIBAL at St. Genevieve below St. Louis, and left Missouri for good. The first stop was at Cairo, Illinois, across the river. The men were elated with planting their feet on Illinois soil again. When the boat reached the opposite shore, the men jumped over the sides and over the gangway, "shouting, cheering, laughing, running & jumping like wild deer...."[1]

The boat stayed overnight at Cairo to avoid the nighttime guerilla sniping on the river. The HANNIBAL was in a seventeen ship fleet transporting troops to Ulysses Grant at Vicksburg, Mississippi. The days on the water were, as usual, unpleasant for the enlisted men. Not since the ride up the Missouri to Boonville in 1861 had the regiment done any water marching.

The protocol on a transport boat was fixed by practice and by custom, rank, and regulations. The officers got the cabin, shared with the sick men, and the lower deck by the horses and mules. The horses and mules fared better than the men, who were out in the elements on the deck, sleeping two deep in places and having to go ashore to cook.

After five miserable days of boating on the Mississippi River, the fleet reached Vicksburg on June 11th, landed at Yazoo, Mississippi, and marched six miles through a mosquito infested, moss laden swamp to Warrenton, Mississippi, all the while watching the nighttime bombardment of Vicksburg.[2] The bombardment came from about 200 mortars on boats in the river, and land based siege guns, all pumping 200 pound red-hot shells into the town. The hot shells glowed in the dark as they arced through the sultry night air.

The regiment took up a position on the left of the line surrounding Vicksburg in Francis Jay Herron's command. Herron commanded the line from the river's edge for several miles inland.[3]

After three weeks, despite being in the trenches and on scouts around Vicksburg, there were no deaths in the 37th. Among the wounded were Capt. Dick, hit in the lip by a shell fragment, and Michael Cain of Wolford's Company who was shot in the foot near the little toe.[4]

# VICKSBURG

The real killers in Mississippi were the water and the pests, principally the mosquito. As for the agua, the chief source of drinking water was stagnant, scum-covered pools. The bad water spread dysentery to most all who drank it. The men dug holes near the bayous and drank the filtered and slightly purified water that seeped through the earth.[5]

Preventive measures against the dysentery abounded. Will Black's anti-diarrhea diet was milque-toast and chicken broth. Charles Black had ordered some sanitary arrangements in June for the men including prohibiting the consumption of any fried meat or short bread raised with soda, and consumption of any food except in a company mess where officers had inspected what was being served. Bowel or bladder relief anywhere else but the sinks (latrines) was prohibited, i.e., no more wandering out behind a bush. Body clean, blankets clean, clothing clean, etc.[6]

Going into that summer of 1863, the death rate from disease had been slight, but despite all precautions, the months of July and August 1863 on the Mississippi were to be deadly.

One source of food, milk from John Peck's regimental cow, had been lost for a time in mid-June, lost to the foraging activities of the men of General W.W. Orme's Division, who were neighbors in the line. Three days after the theft, Orme sent the cow back to Charles Black with a note; "I am happy in being able to return your cow and hope you may long enjoy her. I can recommend her as a good milch cow from a trial of 3 days. I don't know exactly where my boys found her, but she was left here from a small drove of cows being brought into camp."[7]

On arrival at Vicksburg, summer schedule was established for the regiment, reveille at 4:30 AM, retreat at 6:30 PM, and taps at 9:00 PM. Guard and picket duty were heavy, and the non-duty time was given over by some to a little tourism – going to the forward edge of the trenchline to view Vicksburg. This "dangerous habit" was quickly prohibited to all but officers.[8]

Part of the attraction was to talk to the rebels, so a man could write home and say he did it. There were frequent verbal exchanges in the trenches and forts. Erwin Messer's father, down from Libertyville on a visit to his two sons in the 37th, reported that "the pickets are so near that a conversation is kept up between them. The rebels have been trying to trade our men their jackass officer Pemberton at a low rate."[9] Confederate General John Pemberton was rebel commander at Vicksburg.

The danger on this battlefield came from artillery shelling and not musket fire. Late in the Vicksburg siege, the rebels set up a mortar which fired at a battery in front of the regimental camp. One shell passed over Will Black's head as he sat at dinner and knocked over a tent in the 20th Iowa missing one man's head by about six inches. Ransom Kennicott was sitting near a redoubt while the mortar was shelling it. One shell burst in the air, Kennicott rolled into a trench, and a second later, "my late place was occupied by what looked like about one fourth of an 11-inch shell."[10]

The day before the Vicksburg surrender, on July 3, Will Black, Brigade Picket Officer, had a by-invitation chat with the rebels opposite him the line. An armistice had been declared, and General Ulysses Grant had gone into town. The Federal pickets and rebel defenders met and talked, without arms, and swapped tobacco, coffee, hard tack, and news. Both sides knew the town would surrender, and were friendly to each other, as the rebels' fate was known. Will Black was greeted by Capt. Hill, 42d Georgia, who was assigned to the fort opposite Black's First Brigade rifle pits. After the visit, the men went back to their lines, picked up their muskets, and awaited the next day's surrender.[11]

During their stay at Vicksburg, the men saw a new thing – black soldiers – which was quite startling to many, particularly the Democrat-Copperheads.

For the last ten days of the Vicksburg siege, Eugene Payne had been Division Picket Officer. His pickets had been about three hundred yards from the rebel lines, "plastered right up against the rebel works and forts."[12] The pickets had talked to each other every night, swapping insults. Payne had 1000 men in all, and occasionally had had little engagements, at one point capturing two rifle pits and ten men, killing four. For the first time, Payne had a front line battle command in a major siege, and had Will Black as subordinate Brigade Picket Officer for three days in July. Henry Frisbie, indirectly, had caused Payne's assignment. When Frisbie was acquitted of writing the St. Louis letter about Charles Black, he had been restored to duty a rank above Payne, so Payne went to General Vandever, explained the situation between him and Frisbie, and Vandever promised him a staff position away from the regiment and out of Frisbie's reach.[13] The picket job for Payne lasted from June 24 to the July 4 surrender.

At ten in the morning on July 4, 1863, Lieutenant General John Pemberton, C.S.A., formally surrendered the Vicksburg stronghold along with two major generals, ten brigadiers, and 25,000 men with weapons. The surrender was unconditional, except that all the rebels were to be paroled.[14]

A shortage of food, not ammunition or fortitude, had reduced Vicksburg. The rebel rations at the end of the siege had been mule meat, issued or sold to a disheveled and demoralized garrison dressed in clothing "filthy with dirt, hanging in ragged festoons from their bodies, [feet] bare, or wrapped about...."[15] It was this mob of ragbags that stood and sullenly watched the Union troops march into town on July 4 with bands playing and flags flying.

After the surrender, the glory of being first into Vicksburg went not to the most senior regiment, the 37th Illinois, but to the 20th Iowa. The men of the 37th were furious at this and went into the city all the same, and Charles Black was arrested for permitting it, although he didn't know about it and couldn't have stopped it. This put Frisbie back in command and Eugene Payne, "in a terrible box." Payne would not return to the regiment under Frisbie, and had to cling to his staff position throughout the summer with General Vandever.

The fall of Vicksburg opened the Mississippi, and Ulysses Grant had made enough news to go east and take command of the Union armies there.

## 21. Microbe War

After Vicksburg fell, Eugene Payne got out of town and put some distance between him and Henry Frisbie. He went on leave, saying in his request that he was sick and broke. He hadn't been paid for eight months, mostly because of muster problems as Major, and the double affliction of malaria and dysentery had put him in bad health.[1]

By the end of July 1863, most of the regiment was down with either malaria or diarrhea or both. These diseases were to cause total wartime Union army deaths of 44,000 from diarrhea, and 35,000 from typhoid-malaria. Another 10,000 died from "intermittent fever," or malaria. Pneumonia, mumps, measles, and tuberculosis carried off another 42,000.[2] Despite the widespread sickness, the 37th compared well in general health and mortality with other regiments, having gained assorted immunities in Missouri.

Several men carried the most prevalent disease, malaria, with them into the army. It was a well-known and widespread prewar affliction in southern Ohio, Indiana, Illinois, and Iowa, and in New Jersey and New York.[3] Malaria thrived in warm and wet climates, favorable to its mosquito vector.

As for dysentery, a Wisconsin soldier described the victims of the chronic bowel irritations; "Under its debilitating effects, the vigor and strength soon vanished, men wasted to skeletons, and while most of its victims still clung to duty ... it was in weakness and languor ... the poor victims, with a face like shriveled parchment, lips bloodless, and nearly paralyzed with sheer muscular weakness, was an object pitiful to see"[4]

The medical attrition in some of the regiments on the river that summer was devastating. The 96th Ohio had come to Vicksburg in December 1862. By March 1863, one hundred ninety were dead and buried, the same number sick. The 15th Iowa had arrived in April of 1862, and sixty days later, twenty-five men were fit for duty. Four days later sixteen were fit for duty, and all sixteen had diarrhea; "The dead march can be heard at all times from sun up to sun down in the camps around us.... Not even a coffin is provided."[5] The 38th Iowa had left New Madrid in June, 800 strong. In six weeks, they could muster thirty-one privates and a lieutenant.[6]

The specific for malaria was quinine, and the quinine prolonged and aggravated the dysentery. The malaria, or ague, would come on with regularity. Its symptoms were high fever and chills that shook the body for hours. David Ash was malarial and relied on "Dr. Humeston's man-killer," or "a six mule load of quinine," to cure him, and wished for "as nice water to use as some of the Stark County [Illinois] wells...."[7] The water was a particular problem because of the waste from dozens of boats tied up at the riverbank.

Eugene Payne was home on leave in Waukegan in July with "old Vicksburg running through every pore in my body,"[8] with combined diarrhea and typhoid fever or malaria.

Henry Frisbie was, like Payne, sick and broke. Frisbie had not been paid for a year because of his arrests, suspensions, and promotion to Lieutenant Colonel. He wrote a bitter, critical request for leave, blaming his troubles on, "cowardly, malicious and unscrupulous enemies, acting through Courts of Inquiry and Courts Martial.... I cannot live on faith but must have bread and that will cost money which I have not got.... If this statement will secure for me the absence which other officers take unquestioned for days to the entire neglect of very important duties I shall be thankful for it." Colonel Dye sent Frisbie's request back to Charles Black as it was, "couched in very improper language," and chiding Black for sending it. Frisbie did not get his day in town until the end of the month, and Black was censured for forwarding a letter he knew to be inflammatory, thinking it would work to Frisbie's detriment and not his own.[9]

From the surrender of Vicksburg to the departure of the regiment for Texas at the end of October, time spent in humid, pest infested parts of Mississippi and Louisiana, the 37th suffered its most concentrated non-battle mortality rate of the war. Diseased men who lived out the war were to die later of chronic fevers or dysentery-diarrhea, or a variety of "lung fevers." Among the summer's dead were regimental musician Edwin Mears, a 50 year old lumberman from Michigan. Mears died of jaundice in a hospital in Quincy, Illinois. His daughter was on hand to take his trunk, violin, and $76 cash. Albert Fordham, a painter of Co. G, was taken out by diarrhea in

August. He died in camp. The next day, James Dow of Wolford's Company died of typhoid fever, having to his name a silver watch and $25 in cash. John Carrol, a 37 year old Irish immigrant of the Michigan Company, died in September of "dropsy" (swelling). Total estate - $3.10[10]

At the end of August, civilian J.S. Messer of Libertyville, who was visiting his twin boys Erwin and Edwin in the 37th in July, went home with disease and died in Libertyville, September 1, 1863.[11]

Despite the rampant pestilence in the camps, the neighborhood runaways, the "contraband," continued to crowd in, a good many of them families of the freshly mustered black soldiers who had nowhere else to go.

If a slave with a family joined the Union Army, the whole family was lost to the plantation economy. To prevent confiscation, the owners secreted their slaves, livestock, and property in the swamps and forests. If found, all this property, living and otherwise, was all "contraband," the spoils of war.

The regiment went as part of an expedition to Yazoo City, Mississippi, in mid-July for a small skirmish followed by a celebration of burning and looting of the town during the first night of occupation. The breakdown of discipline and the pillaging that followed was general. An officer of the 94th Illinois in command of a patrol sent out to stop the looting joined in the thievery. Clothing was stolen from the shops and re-sold for 5 cents or 10 cents per garment, or given away or thrown away. Hats were used as footballs, fires blazed in the streets, and vandalism and robbery of citizens were epidemic.[12]

The troops, General W.W. Orme's Division, spent four days at Yazoo City, enough time to push out a few issues of a newspaper called "The Yankee," printed in a captured Yazoo printing plant. Some other enterprising soldiers found a silver-mounted coach and set up the "Lightning Omnibus Accommodation Line," offering 25 cent rides between the river and the city. But after two trips, General Vandever seized the rolling stock and put the fledgling enterprise out of business.[13]

The next move was out of Yazoo City and into the swamps for a five day scout to the Big Black River. No wagons had been brought up on the boats from Vicksburg, and the train that was formed for the move was made up of all the available carts, buggies, wagons, horses, mules, and oxen in the neighborhood. Of course, the oxen hauled the buggies while the mules hauled the large wagons.[14]

The heat was oppressive, and drinking water was in very short supply. Most of the men drank out of stagnant pools or dried up bayous full of warm water coated with a thick green scum.

Hidden cotton bales were everywhere, but little transport was available to seize and return it to Vicksburg. A small amount was confiscated and transported through Vicksburg, seized from stubborn, mean and "disloyal" rebels.[15]

After nine days the regiment returned to Vicksburg, and after two more days, got on the Steamer THOMAS and went upriver to Port Hudson, the other Mississippi River rebel stronghold which had fallen with Vicksburg in July 1863. They stayed there for three weeks, living on the THOMAS and in two camps back of the bluffs, time spent in deteriorating health. The popular sport here was killing alligators, which populated every pond and bayou.[16]

Beyond the heat, alligators and polluted water, there were spiders, rattlers and moccasin snakes, lizards, scorpions, and mosquitoes that bit and buzzed around everyone. The malaria-carrying mosquitoes were so big that, "they could stand flat-footed and drink out of a tin cup," according to one observer. The other vermin, insects and reptilia crept into shoes, packs, food, and bedding.[17]

The pests, bad water, heat, and fever killed dozens a day in the small army. The levees and farms were peppered with fresh graves.

A slight degree of relief came in mid-August, when the 37th went to Carrolton, Louisiana, just above New Orleans, out of the swamps of Mississippi, out of alligator land and nearby to New Orleans, everyone glad of it. The new camp was on the rail line north of the city. Regimental strength was down to 373 at Carrolton, with another 150 at a Brigade Convalescent Camp commanded by Eugene Payne, who was still sick after coming back from his leave.[18]

On September 5, after about three weeks at Carrolton, the regiment went off with the division to the Atchafalaya River, landing at Morgan's Bend, to chase after ex-President Zachary Taylor's boy Dick, a local rebel commander. The principal engagement, at Sterling's Farm, resulted in the capture of two regiments of the division (the 26th Indiana and the 19th Iowa.) The rebels had surrounded their camp and took all the men along with two pieces of artillery.[19]

After the adventure chasing Dick Taylor, the 37th returned to camp on the river at Morganza, Louisiana, finding it burned to the ground. There were ten days more of scouting and capturing contraband and forage near the Atchafalaya, and then everyone went back on board the boats to New Orleans. The orders on the equipment to be taken allowed, "a valise or carpet bag and roll of blankets for each officer. No cots or bedsteads will be taken. Tables and chairs will be left behind ... a mess chest of 150 pounds will be allowed to each mess of from 3 to 5 officers.... General Officers will be allowed one wall tent, staff officers one wall tent to every 2.... The men will be provided with rubber blankets ... all women will be left behind, whether white or black servants or for any other purposes...."[20]

The officers, as usual, were better provided than the men, who were mostly exposed to the late summer elements, and who could not afford to buy extras for their diet. Wartime inflation and shortages pumped prices for staples way up in the mid-1863 occupied south. Milk was 25 cents per pint, potatoes $6 per peck, butter 60 cents per pound, eggs 90 cents per dozen, meat 40 cents per pound. A cow sold for $160.[21]

Missouri prices had been a bit better. Sutler Denison had sold Charles Black some goods at Pilot Knob, including, "2 dozen cans of peaches $18, a brush and comb $1.25, 4 bars of soap 80 cents, 1 bottle pomade 50 cents, 1 pair candle sticks $1, a quart of whiskey $1, and shirts at $3 each."[22]

Staffing was becoming a critical issue. Henry Frisbie had succeeded in getting his commission as colonel of a new black regiment, and left at the end of September, and took with him many of the best officers and non-commissioned officers in the regiment, including Charles Hawes, William Bigelow, Oliver Risdon, William Sands, Henry Riggs, Joseph Gravenhorst, Samuel Gage, Thomas King, Charles Whitney, William Philleo, and Surgeon John Murphy. Charles Black was furious, accusing Frisbie of "trickery" in taking the men.[23] Black had lost men like Doc Clark, Henry Curtis, Edward

Anderson, Sam Heartley, and the others in Missouri. Others had been detached, "temporarily," never to return. The sick list further depleted the regimental strength, and a special detail was levied in all the regiments for men to fill up the artillery batteries.

Black detailed nine men to the artillery temporarily. Balancing this, all enlisted men on duty as officers' servants were ordered back to their companies, and officers were forbidden to employ men in future as servants. This made servants in short supply, and prompted a ploy in mid-October from the camp of the 91st Illinois, when, "... a graceless white man in the garb of a commissioned officer and four negroes dressed as soldiers came into camp and ... feloniously abstracted thirteen colored cooks.... It is a matter of surprise the trick should have been quietly submitted to...."[24]

The regiment did succeed in replacing Edward Anderson as Chaplain with Pleasant W. Bishop in October, while losing recruit James O'Brien. O'Brien had small tumors and abscesses on his neck before leaving Missouri, and had been hospitalized for delirium tremens in St. Louis. By October, he was too far gone to retain for duty, and was sent to the U.S. Insane Hospital.[25]

With the departure of Henry Frisbie to the Corps D'Afrique, the Lieutenant Colonelcy became vacant, and the kicking and clawing for position began anew. Hiram Kennicott pushed his son Ransom, Elijah Haines pushed his constituent Erwin Messer, and Capt. Dick pushed himself, until he became sick in September, and gave it up and tried to resign again. Things were in this status in October when orders arrived sending the 37th off on the fall campaign.

THIRTY SEVENTH ILLINOIS

## 22.  Texas

The summer victories at Vicksburg and Port Hudson put control of the Mississippi River in Union hands and squeezed the borders of the Confederacy. The rebel states west of the Mississippi still had to be returned to Union control, particularly Texas, to block off the Confederate cotton trade with Europe. Strategic military planning was done by the high command during the summer of 1863, and by the first part of October, the direction of the fall offensive was known – it was Texas. Orders were issued to units in the Department of the Gulf on October 11 to be ready to move.

Eugene Payne had come down from the convalescent camp at Carrolton, Louisiana, the cavalry came in from Brashear City, and on October 23, 1863, the 37th loaded onto the Steamer GEORGE PEABODY four miles above New Orleans in a driving rain. The men suffered the usual miseries on the deck, the officers the usual pleasures in the boat's cabin.

While waiting to sail, the officers were comfortably sheltered in the staterooms on the PEABODY, the men were on the deck in a cold drizzle, and the shelter of steerage was reserved for the horses of the First Texas Cavalry. The transports assigned to the Division were the Steamers CRESCENT, BAGLEY, BELVIDERE, EMPIRE CITY, POCAHONTAS, HUSAR, and PEABODY, out of total of thirty ships in the fleet, which included the gunboat escorts MONONGAHELA, VIRGINIA, and KENNEBEC.[1]

On October 27th, the anchors came up and the fleet steamed through Southwest Pass into the Gulf of Mexico. Before dawn of the next day, a furious gale struck. The decks of the transports were awash in the violent storm. Most of the men were seasick and, "many a clever soldier boy issued his rations to the fishes."[2] There were several lake sailors in the regiment, but the boating on Lake Michigan provided no immunity to seasickness during the tempest.

The horses in the holds of some of the vessels were bounced around in the rocky seas and several died or were fatally injured in the pitching and yawing of the ships and had to be thrown overboard.

After two days of fog, rain, and rough seas onboard the PEABODY, the regiment got a sudden wake-up call. In the middle of the night on October 30, the ship's mate hollered, "Get up and out there or we'll go to hell in a minute."[3] The men awoke as rudder chains and rope uncoiled overhead. The rudder chain had snapped and the ship had no steerage. A makeshift line with block and tackle was rigged, and several of the regiment pulling on the line in shifts served to operate the rudder. While making the repairs, the PEABODY lost contact with the fleet for two days, until they met again at the rendezvous at the Padre Islands, off the Texas coast.

The PEABODY reached anchorage off Brazos Santiago and the Padre Islands on October 31, after a seven day voyage, four of them in the storm. After three more days at anchor, mustering the fleet and repairing the storm damage, the regiment came ashore on November 4. As at Yazoo City three months before, the most venerable, battle seasoned and experienced regiment, the 37th, was not given the honor of being the first ashore the conquered land. That honor went to the new Maine regiments, "these upstarts, these $40 last fall men,"[4] as the choice of Union Generals Banks and Dana to carry the Union flags onto Texas soil.

The journey from the PEABODY to the mainland took three days amid perils of salt, sand, and thirst. A sandbar between the anchorage and the island had to be crossed, and a bayou between the island and the mainland had to be forded. To get over the bar, the regiment loaded onto small boats, then to a shallow draft lighter, the EXACT, and spent the night on the EXACT waiting for a rain squall to abate. The last passengers on the lighter had been mules, and the decks offered a memorable odor to the new passengers.[5]

The landing was made the next morning by the 37th and two black regiments, the Second Louisiana Engineers and the Sixteenth Corps D'Afrique. Camp was made on the dunes on the beach on Brazos Santiago for a day and a half, waiting for supplies and equipment to be brought over the bar. Many men passed the time on the beach collecting seashells to pack home to Illinois.[6]

On November 6, leaving all baggage in Quartermaster John Peck's care, the regiment headed for the ford at Boca Chica, Texas. The water was five feet at the deepest, and about one eighth mile wide. The whole force stripped naked and waded across to the mainland, several suffering lacerated feet on the way.[7]

There the land march to Brownsville, Texas began, interrupted by a two-day stop in camp on the Rio Grande River below Palo Alto.[8]

The 37th marched into the dusty streets of Brownsville, Texas on November 9th. Several men had dropped out from thirst and exhaustion during the twenty miles of fast marching through the barren landscape of puckerbush, cactus, and locust trees. Camp was made at nearby Freeport Landing, across the river from Matamoros, Mexico.[9]

The mission of the division was to interdict the European cotton trade that was a staple revenue producer and economic lifeline of the Confederacy. Cotton was sent from Brownsville to Matamoros, Mexico, just across the Rio Grande. The "river" was a little stream in November 1863, "a shallow stream of ten rods in width, and navigable only by boats of very light draft, and so crooked that a man on its banks can hardly tell whether he is in Texas or Mexico."[10]

Impressions of Brownsville – Matamoros and the surroundings and inhabitants were none too flattering, certainly nothing to encourage the tourist trade. The baled Confederate cotton was piled in plain sight across the river in Matamoros, "as effectively out of reach as if twas in Great Britain or France."[11]

Matamoros had in 1863 about 15,000 population, with a garrison of several thousand anti-French Mexican "liberal" troops. Brownsville had a population of about 2,000.[12] Both towns were the scene of some play-for-keeps politics that drew Charles Black and other union army officers into close orbit. The November union army landing at Brazos Santiago had set in motion a disruptive unbalancing chain of events in the area. News of the Union landing reached the rebels in Brownsville, and their response was not to defend, but rather to burn the town, pack up, and move out.

In Matamoros, politics were polarized by the presence of the French, who were attempting some colonial empire building.

Other than the Confederates and the French, the principal players in the local politics, and in the evacuation and burning of Brownsville, were three Mexican Nationals; Jose Cobos (Pro-French), Juan Cortina

(Anti-French Horse Thief and Revolutionary), and Manuel Ruiz (Anti-French Patriot). All had histories.

Juan Maria Cobos was pro-French. He was a native Spaniard and a professional soldier supporting the Mexican Central Government and its despotic French allies. Cobos had come to Mexico from Brownsville in March 1861 as an exile, and was still there at the time of the November landings at Brazos Santiago.

Juan Cortina was a native Mexican who had been a ruthless border raider for years. He was a Mexican patriot, revolutionary, and violently anti-French. He had made border raids into Texas in the 1850's to, "redeem the country [from] the frontiersmen of the north,"[13] propelled over the river by strong anti-American sentiments, and fifty or sixty men squealing, "Mueran los Gringos! (Death to Americans!)." On one such raid in 1860, Cortina had entered Brownsville on a September morning with the avowed purpose of killing Americans. He killed Jailer Johnson, Constable Morris, and a man named Neale in his bed, and chased out the City Marshal before re-crossing the Rio Grande into Mexico. In the months following, he fought American volunteers, Texas Rangers, and the Mexican National Guard, who were out to catch and hang him. But after a dose of two and a half years of Confederate government in Texas, when the Union forces came in November 1863, Cortina's anti-Americanism had moderated.

Cortina, variously a murderer, horse thief, "Robin Hood" patriot, bandit, pillager and destroyer, was the centerpiece of the scene. Strangely, Cortina may have been a U.S. citizen. He spent much of his time on his mother's land, a 40,000 acre ranch near Brownsville. A maternal relative had been the Spanish grantee of the land north of the river where Brownsville stands.[14]

Charles Black visited Cortina in mid-December, 1863; "The celebrated republican general and ex-horse thief.... [I] had to go through a strong guard to reach him. Everything indicates a feeling of insecurity and lack of confidence in [Mexican] institutions...."[15]

A third local politico, Don Manuel Ruiz, the Governor of the Mexican State of Tamaulipas, was a popular and powerful man, pro-American and anti-French.

Cobos, Cortina, and Ruiz were each ready and waiting for an opportunity to seize power when the Union army landed on November 4 at the mouth of the Rio Grande. The Confederate army immediately embarked on their plan of destruction and retreat after hearing news of the size of the Union force. The rebel commander at Fort Brown – General Hamilton Bee – straight away burned the fort and all the cotton held there. The fire spread and burned the block of buildings in front of the river ferry. There happened to be four tons of gunpowder in Fort Brown which exploded during the fire. Burning timbers were hurled in all directions, setting fire to the ferry in the middle of the river among other properties.[16]

Cobos, the pro-French exile, decided to use the fires, the explosion, the crisis and the disorder at Brownsville to reconstitute his political and military power. He took charge of the firefighting, crowd control, civil order, and defense against the vandalism of the fleeing rebels, and used his power to immediately cross the river, occupy Matamoros, and jail Governor Don Manuel Ruiz and his associates. Cobos accomplished this "revolution" with about 500 men and the help of Juan Cortina.

Cobos' revolutionary government lasted one day. After learning that Cobos and his government intended to restore the French in Matamoros, Cortina started the next day's revolution.

In the morning, Governor Cobos was ordering Cortina, who was then the Mayor, to execute a number of men of the Ruiz government who had been made prisoner, including Ruiz. In the selection process, Cobos was naming the prisoners to be executed, and Cortina tapped him on the shoulder and said, "you first."[17]

After a two minute trail, Cobos was marched out of town and publicly executed by a platoon of soldiers, while one of his aides was made to run the gantlet, and was shot dead on the run.

With the execution of Cobos, Ruiz (the former governor) was released, and escaped to Brownsville out of harm's way.

Cortina, now in control of Matamoros, needed a new governor, with one dead and one fled to Texas, and so he installed one Jesus de la Serna, a Juarista. Serna had been the governor of Tamaulipas earlier, and had been forced out of office. Cortina simply got all the influential citizens to sign a petition for his return by threatening to kill them (or intimating this) if they did not sign, and then held them in jail for thirty-six hours until Serna's return and installation so no objection could arise.[18]

Shortly after his flight to safety in Brownsville, Ruiz went up the river to raise a military force of Mexicans and to plan a return to confront Cortina in Matamoros. This was the situation the occupying Union forces came into in November 1863.

The Federal troops had the mission of interdicting the cotton trade, and secondarily capturing or defeating as many rebels as possible, depriving them of the use of the river and its ports. In this they had partial success.

The first direct involvement for the regiment with the locals came about on an expedition 100 miles up the Rio Grande River to Rio Grande City in late November. There was a thriving cotton trade there, and the 37$^{th}$ along with some cavalry, was sent to stop the trade, capture the cotton, and disperse the rebels.

Charles Black took seven companies on the Steamer MUSTANG up the Rio Grande, and Eugene Payne took Companies A, F, and G (about 100 men), by land along with Col. E.J. Davis' Texas Cavalry.[19]

The trip up the river on the MUSTANG was difficult, slow sand bar jumping. The boat was continually running aground, averaging a grounding every half hour, and occasionally for several hours, as at Webber's Ranch. The river was as wide as the boat was long in most places. The slow journey provided time for a nature watch. The river was loaded with geese, ducks, fish and turtles. Shore foraging yielded goats, milk, lamb, honey, and various kinds of fresh meat.

At one point in the expedition, Colonels Payne and Davis waited and waited at the Milstead Ranch and then at Rancho Tabasco and Ringgold for the arrival of the stranded MUSTANG, which was aground more than afloat. At Rancho La Lomita, the boat had to be hauled over a six hundred foot bar, and in several places the water was only a foot or two deep.[20]

By November 25, Davis' cavalry was at Ringgold, Texas waiting for captured cotton and waiting to arrest some American renegades. A week later, Payne met the MUSTANG at Reynosa with $25,000 worth of cotton captured at Rio Grande City. Payne "liberated" the cotton just as it was to follow most of the town's inhabitants across the river into Mexico, and sent it by wagon to Reynosa.[21]

Charles Black's layover wait for the cotton created the opportunity for the local Reynosa military chieftain, Don Florentino, to ingratiate himself with the blue-coated conquerors. He arranged an entertainment, a "fandango," for the soldiers, which was a big hit.[22]

One officer who missed this party was Jack Moran, who was detached to catch marauder John Travinio. Travinio, with a gang of about a dozen men, was crossing from Edinburg, Texas over into Mexico on raids. Don Florentino asked Charles Black to arrest Travinio, as he had always been able to escape back over the river to Texas after the raids. So while Black was dancing with the "sloe-eyed daughters of Montezuma," including Don Florentino's niece, in Reynosa, Jack Moran and the Company D Michigan boys were out searching for Travinio.[23]

They caught up with him and arrested him the next morning, putting the Don in Charles Black's debt.

The regiment came back to Brownsville with the captured cotton in time to watch Don Florentino's friend Juan Cortina oust Ruiz from power in Matamoros a month later.

The day before the regiment returned from Rio Grande City and Reynosa, Ruiz had returned and attacked Matamoros. This forced a settlement between Ruiz and Cortina. Ruiz would have the governorship and Cortina the army. He was to attack the French at Tampico. Cortina delayed marching on Tampico for five days on the plea of paying his troops who would not move without money, and then delayed further on a plea for more ammunition. This standoff dragged into January 1864.

The Tamaulipas governor, Juan de la Serna, stepped aside and gave Ruiz the governorship. Common belief was that Cortina would murder Ruiz and recall Serna, Will Black noting that, "Murder can be hired at a mere song in the land of the Aztec."[24]

On January 12, 1864, Cortina moved on Ruiz and a fight raged in Matamoros endangering the American Consul there, one Leonard Pierce. Pierce had had his hand deep into local politics. In the evening of the 12th, Charles Black with an escort of three full regiments had crossed the river to the Matamoros consulate shortly after the battle had begun to get Pierce, his family, and six safes full of cash (about $1,000,000) out of town.[25]

The Ruiz-Cortina evening fracas was lit by a young moon that glinted off the Rio Grande. The flash of guns was visible from the rooftops in Brownsville, observed by many onlookers.[26] The Mexicans did not engage the well-armed Americans. Ruiz once again fled over to Brownsville in defeat, leaving his supporters to be hunted down and killed by Cortina.[27]

After the Mexican liberal victory, local government stabilized, and a strange fraternity was spawned between Cortina and the Federal commanders at Brownsville, among them a new commander, General John McClernand. McClernand showed off his blue-clad infantry, and Cortina showed off his lancers in multicolored uniforms in two grand reviews. They then had a reception, a dinner, and a ball, and told each other how good they were and how much they liked each other. Then the whole show moved over to Matamoros two days later with Cortina the host of the dining and dancing.[28]

The April-May activity included a Herron-Cortina boat trip down the river to the gulf. All this chummy partying and gladhanding gave some discomfort to the expatriate rebels who had fled to Matamoros. The discomfort turned to panic after Herron handed over a fugitive who had fled to Brownsville seeking protection from Benito Juarez. The rumor spread that there had been a treaty formed between the Mexican and U.S. forces to return each other's fugitives. At this news, the rebels sped out of Matamoros.[29]

While the officers were drinking Cortina's tequila, camp life for the ranks settled into a largely uneventful routine, save for two issues: the unending preoccupation with promotion, and a new issue, reenlistment.

## 23. Reenlistment

The political merry-go-round in the regiment had started up again in New Orleans in September 1863 before the departure for Texas. Henry Frisbie had left to command the 92d U.S. Colored Troops (originally designated 23d Corps d'Afrique) and took a dozen of the 37th with him; officers, sergeants, and the wagonmaster, William Philleo. This move vacated a field office, and renewed the promotion derby. Eugene Payne would take Frisbie's spot as Lieutenant Colonel, vacating the majority to one of the Captains.

There were four contestants for the Major's spot this time; Captains Messer, Black, Dickinson, and Kennicott. Erwin Messer, Captain of Co. F from Lake County started out behind. His date of commission made him junior to the other three, he was unpopular in the regiment, and one field office was already held by a Lake County resident, Eugene Payne. Charles Black, who would be making recommendations, owed Messer nothing.

Next on the list was Ransom Kennicott, who had informally been considered the senior captain. Charles Black had made his own personal case for the Lieutenant Colonelcy over Frisbie on the point of seniority, and Charles Black would morally have to support Kennicott for this reason and because Kennicott had been a supporter in Black's 1862 summer crisis at Cassville, Missouri.

Julius White, who by this time had a command in Tennessee, was again approached to settle the seniority question, and he chose to rank the captains by the order in which they applied to him for authority to raise companies in 1861.[1] Kennicott was senior under this standard, but if the captains were ranked from date of muster, then Dickinson would be senior.

The candidacy of Capt. Dick and brother Will caused Charles Black to make no recommendation, declining to choose between his brother and his "fastest friend," saying "In such a complication of affairs, I've concluded to remain a witness rather than a participant."[2] And so he did, recommending Payne for the Lieutenant Colonelcy and making no recommendation for Major. For Payne's part, despite his assurances to Willy that he would lend his support, he recommended no one for the promotion, and ratified Kennicott as senior captain.[3]

"Hon. Coz." Haines recommended Messer rather than Will Black, Messer being his constituent. Capt. Dick cried foul again; "I learned today that Major E.B. Payne had been promoted.... You are well aware of the claims I have made heretofore.... I have [again] been defrauded out of it by men who could practice villainy better than I can...."[4]

Supporting Dick's claim was the result of an election held in February and sent to the Illinois Adjutant General. The result of the vote was Capt. Dick for Major:[5]

| | |
|---|---|
| William P. Black | 4 |
| Charles V. Dickinson | 10 |
| Herman Wolford | 1 |
| Judson J. Huntley | 1 |
| Henry L. Smith | 1 |
| Ransom Kennicott | 1 |

It made sense for Charles Black to support Kennicott and curry favor with his powerful father Hiram. Messer had no such relatives, neither did Dick, and he would have Willy's help anyway should he need it. Despite the election in Dick's favor, Kennicott got the commission.

While this little bit of business was going on, Charles Black was rolling ahead for his promotion to general. He told his parents, and probably others, that many careers were to be made in the war, and the higher the rank, the better. Charlie's desires were no secret in the company street. Sergeant Henry Ketzle noted that, "Our regiment ... is never allowed to lay at rest for any length of time, the high ambition of a young aspiring leader forbids any such idea...."[6]

The men objected to extra duty and inconvenience and danger, believing they were being volunteered for things that were not to promote the interests of the 500 men of the 37th, but to promote the greater glory of Charles Black.

Keeping the regiment up to strength was essential to Colonel Charles Black. It would permit the field offices to be filled when vacant. If the body count fell too low, field grades would not be filled when vacant, and worse than that, several depleted understrength regiments could be consolidated into one, making many officers excess and unneeded. Enlistments were decreasing as the war wore on, and seasoned officers were detached to recruit and to fill vacancies in their regiments, or the cavalry, or in anyone else's unit. Eugene Payne got an assignment in December 1863 to go to Illinois with a recruiting staff. He left Brownsville on December 30, 1863, and was away from the 37th for nearly four months.[7]

Payne used the recruiter's well-worn cons, dodges, and misrepresentations to get the new men to sign. Payne described Texas as, "formerly the Mecca of the United States," promising "hunting equipments," medical attention, clothing, and $600.[8] The $600 was real, the rest baloney, paying men to enjoy the easy resort life in sunny Texas. Many of his enlistees signed up, took the money, and deserted on the way to the rendezvous at Springfield, and probably went to Michigan, or Indiana, or somewhere else, and did it again for another $200 or more in bounty fee.

As for more operational activity, on December 7, 1863, the men in Brownsville held Prairie Grove anniversary parties. Absent were some of the men of the 37th, gone on the Rio Grande cotton expedition, who were either puddle-jumping down the river on the MUSTANG, or waiting for it to get off the sand bars.[9]

The Rio Grande expedition returned to Brownsville on the 12th of December to a rapidly unraveling political fabric in Matamoros, bags of accumulated mail, and regular rations. Regimental affairs and routine were resumed. Will Black had passed his twenty-first birthday that December, and a personal crisis developed for the former teenage religious zealot when brother Charlie showed him some letters from home. The letters repeated rumors on the Danville, Illinois circuit of Willy's drinking, gambling, swearing, and related dissipation. The letters from Mother Black were well honed sharp objects, shaped to create Puritan guilt. The indictment all but accused Willy of hastening the death of his sister LaRose by drinking liquor and playing cards, i.e., if he hadn't turned into a drunk, LaRose would still be alive, but since she heard that liquor had passed her brother's lips, there was nothing to live for. Will Black's answer, an anguished mea culpa, was directed to a gossip-conscious family; "I drink for medicinal purposes, play cards for fun, and do not swear."[10]

Will was discharged in 1864, went home, and had returned to Christian ways by 1865. He told brother Charlie as much in 1865 while verifying the 1864 Danville gossip; "[I] have wasted my substance in riotous living, wasted my manhood and written a great record of corruption on the page of my life. God helping me, it shall never be re-written. I would I could blot out the memory of it from my life, but this may not be, yet I may correct the evil for the future and mayhap may cover up the past by a more noble, pure, manly, Christian life."[11]

Judging from the depths of Willy's contrition, it must have been some party.

Regimental matters in Texas, beyond the promotion games, were plain, army standard. In November the Regimental Adjutant (or his clerk), the bane of all company clerks, got all over them for their morning reports;

> "Company Commanders will send into these Hd. Qtrs. as soon as possible the usual morning report of their companies. They will assure themselves by a personal examination that the report is correct before it is forwarded.... Mistakes frequent and of a serious character have recently occurred.... It is the duty of all Commanding Officers to satisfy themselves that all reports are correct before they are forwarded, and it is confidently hoped that in the future the mistakes will not be permitted to occur."[12]

While in Texas, the usual potpourri of disciplinary infractions continued to catch the attention of the army judicial system, formal and informal. Almiran Stillman of Wolford's Rock Island Company took a two month holiday in Texas and was in effect pardoned by Francis Jay Herron on the recommendation of Captain Wolford that Stillman fell in with evil companions, that he was repentant, and was the sole support of an aged mother.[13]

## THIRTY SEVENTH ILLINOIS

Lieutenant Martin Leonard was another case, and Charles Black wanted him out of the regiment, stating in January 1864 that, "unless you report for duty with your company tomorrow ... [I] will recommend you for dismissal ... for contracting a loathsome disease rendering you unfit for the duties of your office."[14] Leonard resigned the next month.

Another disciplinary incident, which resulted in victory for the accused and embarrassment for Charles Black, occurred after Black returned from the scout to Rio Grande City.

As Colonel, one of the administrative matters Black dealt with was the promotion of non-commissioned officers. Five of them in Myron Barnes' old company (A) were ready for promotion. The company was short of officers as well as non-coms. Frisbie had taken Charles Hawes and William Bigelow with him to the 92d Colored, and Lorenzo Morey had been on General Staff since before leaving for New Orleans, so Black had put William Wilson in command of the company in September.

Before Christmas, Morey had recommended the men to be promoted to Charles Black, then acting Brigade Commander, who had written out the warrants for promotion and sent them over to the Adjutant to be signed and sent to the company. Among the warrants was one promoting Henry Ketzle from private to First Sergeant.

The promotions (of Henry Ketzle, William Atkinson, Henry Heitharands, Cyrus Earhart, and James Gregg of Company A) were decided on by Lorenzo Morey and Charles Black with Adjutant Bandy's acquiescence. Ketzle was being jumped from private to First Sergeant. Bandy said he "thought Ketzle would make a good Orderly Sergeant ... that he was certainly the best businessman in the company ... and ... believed that he usually made reports instead of the Orderly."[15]

William Wilson got the warrants and was slighted at not being consulted, which is reasonable since he was the company commander, and was particularly irritated that Morey, who had been absent from the company for fourteen of the immediate past seventeen months, should have a say in the decision. Wilson went to Eugene Payne, then commanding the regiment, who likewise had not been consulted in

# REENLISTMENT

the matter, and Payne said that if the case was his, he would hold onto the warrants and not muster the nominees to their new rank. Should Morey return to command the company, he could do as he liked.

On December 29, Charles Black summoned Wilson and asked him why he had not distributed the promotions. Wilson told him they were left in his tent and not given to him personally and that that was improper delivery. He also said it was not doing justice to the men of the company or himself to make the appointments. Black told him to issue the warrants, and Wilson refused to do it.

Black was being told what he could and could not do by a subordinate, and so he made a charge sheet of nine specifications and charges against Wilson, all of which amounted to going against Charles Black's rather despotic wishes.

Wilson was tried by court martial in January 1864. His defense was handled by Chauncey Morse, and Charles Dickinson was on the Court. Wilson's defense was that the order was illegal. Black was not in command of the regiment (Brigade Commander at the time), nor Morey in command of the company (Inspector General duty), and neither had sought the recommendations of the actual commanders Payne and Wilson. Moreover, promoting a private (Ketzle) to First Sergeant was, "clearly in violation of all law and military usage."[16]

The court saw no merit in the defense, were disposed to Black, and found Wilson guilty nine times, and sentenced him to be dismissed. General Herron reviewed the case and saw the error in Charles Black's attempt to make the unorthodox promotions and vacated the sentence, saying that Black had no more power or right to appoint in the 37th than in any other regiment in his command, Morey had no power to recommend, that the order to Wilson to issue the warrants was, "unlawful, [and] the accused might lawfully refuse to obey it," disapproved the sentence, absolved Payne and Wilson of discourtesy, and ordered Wilson to, "resume his sword," and return to duty.[17]

This display of corrupt power by Black reinforced the dislike some of his troops harbored against him. The three year service of the 37th was not to run out until September, but the War Department was pushing reenlistments among the veteran regiments with big bonuses. If reenlistment went badly, the 37th could be mustered out, and the Colonel would no longer be Colonel. In the end, the required number to preserve the regiment did reenlist after a few speeches and the offer of a $600 bonus and a thirty day leave.[18]

To men who had been making $13 per month, $600 in one place was heady stuff, and the way to buy a shop or a farm after the war. For others, it was several nights in the gambling dens and flesh pots of Brownsville or New Orleans or Chicago.

When the veterans sailed for New Orleans on reenlistment leave, and left Will Black and the men who did not reenlist at Brownsville, the 37th was radically sundered for the first time. For the months from February until September, the two sections would walk different roads and have different experiences and serve different masters, the re-ups on the Mississippi and those who did not reenlist in Brownsville.

Of the 240 men that did not reenlist, about 200 continued at Brownsville formed in two companies designated Detachment, 37th Illinois, under command of William Wilson. They had avoided being consolidated into the 38th Iowa (the catch-all regiment), had battalion status, and were attached to the 91st Illinois.[19]

After the veterans (the reenlisted men) left for home, the activity level at Brownsville was summed up in a diary entry of a Wisconsin officer posted there, who said, "February and March passed without anything of importance occurring,"[20] albeit at the edge of the Mexican revolt against the French. The French were rebel trading partners, which made the Juaristas (and Cortina) natural Union allies.

After a spring and summer of guard, drill and drinking at Brownsville, Brazos Island and points in between, the time came for the detachment to be discharged. In September, 1864, 185 men of the 37th Illinois detachment made their last boat trip across the Gulf and up the Mississippi to Cairo and Springfield. The veterans were camped at the mouth of the White River along with 55 non-veterans who had returned from detached service, from leave, and from the hospital. These home-bound troops passed the veterans' camp at the White River on September 14, 1864, and were followed home by Eugene Payne, Will Black, Capt. Dick, and the other men at White River who had chosen civilian life over the $600 bonus and an indefinite term in the army.

## 24. The Reenlisted 37th

On February 10, 1864, in Brownsville, Charles Black and General Edward Otho Cresap Ord made reenlistment speeches to the regiment, and by the next day, "upwards of three fourths" of the 37th had signed up for another three years, a bonus, and a thirty-day leave.[1] The journey out of Texas for the reenlistees, the veterans, began the same day. They marched to Point Isabel, crossed the sand bar on the MUSTANG, and then crossed the Gulf of Mexico, back to New Orleans on the 25th of February. Billets were assigned at the Trader's Cotton Press, and then the Factor's Press near the river for the next three weeks. Muster in and muster out rolls were completed, pay call attended to, partial bounties paid, and property transferred, along with the normal daily regimen of guard and drill.

Ransom Kennicott was to be regimental Mayor, and his successor as Company K Captain had yet to be named. By right of succession, it would be the First Lieutenant, Isaac Dodge. Dodge had been on detail away from the regiment since July 1862, doing duty in the Provost Marshal's Office in Springfield and St. Louis. If he could be denied the Captaincy on account of absence from the regiment, the next in line would be the Second Lieutenant, who was Ransom Kennicott's brother George, so the only course of action for the Kennicott family was to disqualify Dodge.

Dodge, who had married General Egbert Brown's daughter in 1863, and had a good spot in St. Louis as Assistant Provost Marshal General, wrote his claim in 1864, asking to be given, "a brief abstract adverse to my claims in this matter,"[2] and bearing the strong endorsement of General Rosecrans, who volunteered that, "his services here are almost indispensable."[3]

Charles Black and Hiram Kennicott had different opinions. Kennicott pointed out Dodge's oft stated plans never again to return to the regiment, and Black noted that Dodge was unworthy of promotion. He had been in only one battle with the regiment and, "his conduct there will not bear scrutiny."[4] He had been absent since September 1861, save about six weeks.

## THE REENLISTED 37TH

Isaac Dodge did not get the promotion, and George Kennicott did. Right or wrong, the buy and sell system of rewards in the army had operated. This time the decision had gone in favor of Black and his friends the Kennicotts.

After the war, in 1870, Wells Morrill was reporting from St. Louis that, "Dodge. Lt. [is here] ... a hard drinker and worthless fellow. His father-in-law, Genl. Brown (Militia) – broke and has become extinct, don't hear of him anymore."[5]

During the summer and fall of 1864, the regiment lost nine officers through failure to reenlist as veterans or on medical discharges. Edwin Messer and George Bell were discharged in June and July, Pleasant Bishop, Will Black, Charles Dickinson, Isaac Dodge, and Eugene Payne in September, followed by Luther Humeston and William Bandy in October. Of these, Humeston, Payne, and Dodge were on detached service and therefore not with the regiment. Some went home to convalesce, some signed on with other units, and some, like Will Black, wanted to get on with their post-war careers. Black had lined up a spot with Judge Turner in Chicago to study law.

On March 9, 1864, the reenlisted part of the regiment loaded onto the Steamer HOPE, and paddled away up the Mississippi headed for Illinois and thirty days leave. The trip took them again past Carrolton, Red Church, Plaquemine, Baton Rouge, Port Hudson, Bayou Sara, Red River, Fort Adams, Natchez, Grand Gulf, Hard Times, Vicksburg, the Yazoo, Milliken's Bend, Skipwith's Landing, the White River, then to St. Francis, Memphis, Ashport, Eale's Point, New Madrid, Hickman, Columbus, and finally to Cairo, Illinois on March 19. Two more days passing Cape Girardeau, Tower Rock, and St. Genevieve, and the HOPE arrived in St. Louis. The vets took a train from St. Louis to Chicago, where Eugene Payne had arranged for quarters at the Soldier's Rest, and Julius White had a reception planned for his old regiment the next day.[6]

The Chicago reception was elaborate. The regiment was escorted by an honor guard of fourteen Ellsworth Zouaves, Van's & Dean's Light Guard Band and the reception committee including Adjutant General Fuller, Julius White, Eugene Payne, members of the Board of Trade, and a cheering crowd.[7]

## THIRTY SEVENTH ILLINOIS

One noticeable absence was Myron Barnes who was not invited, even though he had a hand in raising the regiment and had spent more time as commander (de facto) than Julius White. According to Hiram Kennicott, "Barnes' attendance would not at all have agreed with White's purpose of absorbing all the honor and glory of [raising] the Regt."[8]

Barnes informed the readers of his newspaper that, "We regret we were unable to be there.... We were absent on business connected with the new regiment [140th Illinois]. We understand that the affair passed off with considerable eclat...."[9]

After the Chicago reception, the men broke off and went home to Rock Island, Mendota, Des Plaines, Pentwater and Manistee, and to Waukegan. A celebration had been laid on at Waukegan for Companies C and F, but fully half the returning soldiers has gotten off the train south of Waukegan. Those that did arrive were met by the Common Council, the Waukegan Band, Henry Blodgett, and assorted citizens at Dickinson Hall. After a meal at the Waukegan House and visiting with old friends, the soldiers left for hearth and home.[10]

The reception in Rock Island for Companies A and H was more subdued, although the body of those returning was greater, numbering over sixty. After arriving, the men went for breakfast and speeches at the Island City Hotel and then home.[11]

To mark and celebrate the thirty days leave, the veterans (i.e., the reenlisted soldiers) at Waukegan, together with the 15th Illinois Regiment men, organized a ball on April 5 at Dickinson Hall, complete with the Great Western Band of Chicago. Likewise, the Rock Island vets held a dinner at the end of their thirty day leave.[12] The leave had marked the first time home for many of the men since August 1861. Drastic changes in the sons, husbands, and brothers who had been cheered out of town two and a half years earlier came right up to the surface. How can little Henry drink so much wine? Dad has a terrible cough and spends too much time in the privy. John is so thin, Fred plays cards, Michael has the shakes every day. George is so quick-tempered, Ralph curses at every turn, Frank has changed so I don't know him, Daniel isn't the man I knew, and on and on.

The thirty days passed off in sleeping, talking, praying, tilling, hoeing, and eating.

At the end of the leave, the Island City Hotel in Rock Island hosted a going-away dinner. Featured speakers included Myron Barnes, followed by a dance. The next week, the veterans left for the rendezvous at their old campsite in Chicago, renamed Camp Fry.

At least two of the participants in the celebration were apprehensive about returning to war. Julius White was, in April, "looking very dull and sad. Complains of his post and evidently sees no light ahead."[13] This was a prophetic observation, because the Battle of the Crater lay four months off in White's future.

Eugene Payne absolutely did not want to return with the regiment. He made a plea to Adjutant General Fuller that he really wanted to go back to the field but was too sick to go and would surely get sicker if he went – probably true. Beyond this he would stay and work to have good friend Fuller elected governor in the fall elections if only he could get some orders to keep him at home, that there were already three field officers for 300 men in the 37th, and that he would return to the field after the election and a summer of acting as Fuller's ally.[14]

The offer to Fuller was not accepted, and so Payne went to the rendezvous and returned south with the regiment to rejoin the non-veterans on the Mississippi to serve out the balance of his three year enlistment. He landed at Memphis on April 30. One of the notables of the Confederacy, Nathan Bedford Forrest, had made an incursion into Memphis the day before, and the 37th was grabbed off the river to chase Forrest.[15]

The regiment chased Forrest by rail and on foot for six days, marching over one hundred miles, never finding him. It was a grand chase a la Missouri, proving once again that it is a fool's errand to send infantry after cavalry. The chase, through Somerville, Bolivar, and the Corinth neighborhood, was done without tents, complete with six nights of sleeping on the ground.[16]

The regiment went back to the boat, made a stop at Nachez, and were back in Vicksburg on May 14 quartered on the Steamer MARINER. After a trip up the Red River to Semmesport, the men marched back to Morganza, Louisiana, to permanent summer camp via the Steamer GREY EAGLE.

Morganza was to be home base for the summer, and the heat, pests and bad water would fill a few shallow graves on the riverbank and aggravate all the men with dysentery or malaria. Sanitary conditions were looked after constantly, water being the priority. The Mississippi supplied the best water for drinking and cooking, and if the regiment upstream was washing, bathing, or emptying the slop buckets, the water was quickly fouled, so rules were made for the use of the water. Washing and bathing were restricted to thirty minutes in the morning, the lunch hour, and thirty minutes in the late afternoon.[17]

Fleas, ticks, lice, mosquitos, spiders and mice were a constant annoyance.

Fleas were the least of Charles Black's worries. Between July 12 and August 6, the regiment was at St. Charles, and bad water had aggravated Black's dysentery badly enough so that the infection caused his bowels to bleed, i.e., bringing on "the bloody flux." By August 20, he had moved out of camp to New Orleans, to 97 Royal Street, into a $10 per week room.[18]

Black had the money and the position to convalesce in his French four-poster bed on Royal Street. Most subalterns and enlisted men had to make do with army surgeons and army hospitals. One of the Lake County soldiers had a common experience with an inexperienced surgeon, one John Mesler. The soldier had for days been complaining of diarrhea, vomiting, and nausea, which became worse as he continued for duty. He went to Assistant Surgeon Mesler, whose RX was, "I don't believe you are a damn bit sick, but I will excuse you today."[19] Mesler was discharged for an unrelated offense within the year.

Personnel morning report and order book entries made at St. Charles were varied and sundry. Sergeant Major Fayette Lacy left in September for a new unit, and probably a good bounty. Black wished him well when he left, a departure from the bitterness surrounding the men Frisbie took for the 92d U.S. Colored.[20]

In June, William Carey's widowed mother tried to get him out of the army. Carey had reenlisted and taken the bonus money. Charles

Black saw no reason for the discharge, which would further deplete the regimental roster, as Carey had sent the money home, and his brother James did not reenlist and would be home. Carey held on until muster-out in 1866.[21]

The game for Charles Black was to stick it out as Colonel long enough for seniority and string pulling to put him on the General's list. He was in his sickbed in the French Quarter in New Orleans in August 1864 plotting the course that he hoped would cure his bleeding bowels and save his rank. He decided to go to Danville and recruit even though he had just returned from there the previous May. He managed to turn the trick, and got orders the last day of August to go home and recruit for one month. If the 37th was to survive and avoid consolidation with another regiment, its strength would have to be increased to replace the non-veterans, the deserters, the dead, and those that went to the 92d U.S. Colored.

Desertion in the 37th was not the problem it was in other units. One of the side effects of the bounty and substitute systems in use to keep the army ranks filled was the creation of a sub-class of habitual deserters and bounty-jumpers. Some of the newly mustered, high-number regiments had to be heavily guarded from enlistment camp to battlefield to prevent wholesale desertion. The police vigilance that stemmed from all the bounty-jumping created nightmares for some soldiers caught in the military justice web who were legitimately absent from their regiments. Other illegitimate absentees wove great alibis for their absence when in jail or to avoid it.

One of the innocent unfortunates was Samuel Bell, who was recruited by George Kennicott in May 1864. After a few days in the army, he was arrested in Chicago, spend 33 days in jail, then was sent to Springfield. The army in Springfield sent him to New Orleans to join the regiment, and he landed in the Marine Hospital with conjunctivitis and no money. Bell finally landed in the Veteran Reserve, or Invalid Corps, in January 1865.[22]

Thomas Cappock of the Danville Company had a similar experience. Arrested in March 1863 for a two week absence, he was left at Cairo for punishment in June 1863. He then was sent to New Orleans in the fall when the regiment had gone to Texas, so he went to Brownsville in 1864. This year-long "desertion" was not desertion except for the two week absence in March 1863 which had begun with a huge drunk on February 25.[23]

Another sad story belongs to George Hosely of Payne's Company C.[24] It was investigated and sworn to by Payne's old office-mate in Waukegan, Francis E. Clarke. It seems Hosely reenlisted in the 37th and was home on the veteran furlough in April 1864. The day the regiment left Camp Fry, he got into a row with Judd Huntley, did not leave with the regiment, and applied to the army in Chicago for transportation to leave the next day. The request was refused, and so he came back to Lake County for money to pay his own passage. He got the money and started back. According to Clarke,

> "... He ... started for his regiment but was arrested for a deserter from some regiment, he thinks a Wisconsin regiment, and taken to Madison, Wisconsin ... and then taken to Winona, Minnesota.... The military authorities ... thought that he belonged to Brackett's Cavalry so called and started him for that Command, which, said George, he never before heard of.... He made his escape and returned to Lake County. He got back ... sometime in July or August, [and] was arrested in Barrington, Ills....
> About the time [he] returned to Lake County ... he received a letter from his Captain Huntley, telling him not to start for the regiment till he heard from him again in regard to transportation or some other thing.... Before he heard from [Huntley] again, Lieut. Col. Payne ... came home.... Hosely applied immediately to him for such papers and statements to enable him to return to his regiment.... As soon as Col. Payne gave him said papers he started for his regiment, but fell in with one [Thomas] Carman, a deserter from [his] company...."

Carman owed Hosely money, so Carman went back to Bureau County, Ill., on promise that Hosely would be paid. After they arrived in early October, Carman was arrested on buggy theft charges.

## THE REENLISTED 37TH

Hosely was arrested along with him, and went to jail in Princeton, Ill., not being able to make bail.

He was released from jail in January 1865. Hosely was the innocent in this, and Carman the villain.

Hosely came back to Lake County for the third time to get money to return to the 37th. This time, Mr. Buell of Waukegan accompanied him to Marengo to the Provost Marshal to make sure he made it out of state should he start for the regiment again. Hosely went home to Crystal Lake, and then Buell took him to Chicago and here delivered Hosely to Camp Douglas.

As to the buggy theft charge, the judge asked Carman if Hosely knew the horse and buggy was stolen, and Carman told the judge that Hosely knew nothing about it. So the judge gave Carman five years in the jug, tacking on two years to the normal sentence for causing so much trouble for George Hosely.

Hosely did return to the regiment and served until his discharge in April 1866.

As for Carman, he had been absent since the summer of 1862. He had gone in August 1862 for three days, which cost him ten days hard labor and a $2 fine. He went for good in October, "on the march from Pea Ridge, Ark. To Huntsville, Ark. Oct. 20, 1862. He is a short thick stout man, quick in his motions. Had on when he left a dirty brown hat, a short jacket, a pair of pantaloons, and shoes."[25]

There were continuing infractions at the regiment subject to discipline. In June, Alpheus Crew, a non-veteran from Rust's old company (E), refused to salute Eugene Payne while on guard. He got docked a month's pay and given ten days hard labor. He also got out of the army on September 24 with many of the others who had not reenlisted. Crew was one of about fifty non-veterans who were with the regiment on the Mississippi rather that with the detachment in Texas.[26]

After being busted down from corporal to private in July, Johnson Thompson, Co. C, got into a fight with Delos Holmes on board the KATE DALE. The court martial set the prize for the fight at $14 - $7 from each fighter.

Thompson and Holmes were among the reenlisted 37th. They were not put off by the disciplinary punishments and took the bounty, the leave and the extra time in the army that followed their reenlistment.

For those who liked card playing, drinking, three square meals a day, no-brain work to do and the comradeship the army offered, reenlisting was the only choice. Many of these men were illiterate, unskilled laborers who needed to be looked after when drunk, punished when wrong, and fed, clothed, and housed. On top of all this, the monthly pay was now $16 for privates, and there was the status of a veteran volunteer in uniform. The alternative would likely have been a twelve hour a day menial laborer's job, no respect, and a shrewish wife in a roach ridden tenement in Chicago. Or possibly a manure-shoveling farmer's helper in the Illinois flatlands. For such men, staying in the army was the right move to make.

Others saw the bounty money as their future and the future of their families, and the thirty day leave as a chance to see the wife and kids for the first time in years. Other frugal, responsible men who had attained rank and extra pay decided to continue their income and the relatively easy army life in Texas or elsewhere in the occupied south.

## 25.   The Discharged 37th

The non-veterans with the regiment at Morganza in the summer of 1864 were counting the days until their enlistment would be up, and they would be paid off and sent home.

That day came in late September. Eugene Payne took the discharged fifty-five men at White River, and Will Black took charge of the Brownsville detachment of one hundred fifty or so, and they all went back to Illinois for muster-out. The muster-out was not a day too early for Eugene Payne. He had had health problems (although professing good health to his wife) dating from the thirty day service with the Waukegan Zouaves at Camp Yates in May of 1861. He would always have the malaria contracted in the army. He had made some of the hard marches and fought in all the battles. He had done his three years, had made some rank, and served well. His was a very good record.

Payne had one other burden, and that was the anxious-wife syndrome. Delia Payne had complained about his service from the earliest days of the war, extracting from him constant apologies and excuses. She began to step up the pressure in the summer of 1864. Payne had promised her constantly and repeatedly to get out of the service, and in the summer of 1864 the time had come. His wife had Hon. Coz. pulling every string in Illinois to get him out of the field and home to Waukegan.

Adelia Payne passed an anguished, tortured summer, and as discharge day drew on, fear that his resignation would not be accepted multiplied the anxiety. Many officers were not being allowed to resign, regardless of expiration of enlistment. Delia Payne had another fear, that Col. Payne would come home and be conscripted again. The draft was due to begin in Illinois in early September, and she feared the draft would net him. She was obsessed with the expiration of the three year enlistment and planned that, "... We will hold that eventful day, the 17$^{th}$ of September, in perpetual remembrance. It shall be one of the sanctified days of our household...." She really wasn't much of an army wife.[1]

## THIRTY SEVENTH ILLINOIS

At White River that summer of 1864, anticipating the possibility of his resignation being turned down, Payne played his big card. He made a major effort to have the regiment destructed by consolidation. If regiments fell way understrength, they were dissolved and the remaining men consolidated with another regiment to serve out their term of enlistment. Payne's motive was simple; he did not want to be extended in the army on field duty. Charles Black's illness gave Payne, as regimental commander, an open field to push the consolidation.

He did not get his way, though, and marked time until Black returned. Payne's initial request to resign was returned disapproved to Charles Black, who endorsed it, "This officer's persistent efforts to resign show that he must have strong reasons for quitting a service honorable to him and he to it. His application made during the temporary absence of the Regimental Commander to have the regt. consolidated shows a disposition to leave no stone unturned to go. Therefore, I earnestly urge that he be honorably discharged the service." The 3$^{rd}$ Division Commander added, "For the sake of peace and harmony in this regiment and for the welfare of the regt. I would earnestly recommend that this officer be honorably discharged...."[2]

Of twenty-one officers of the regiment who submitted resignations, fifteen were disapproved. Eugene Payne's cause for concern at being retained beyond three years was well-founded, but his luck, or persistence, prevailed. He had been muttering about challenging William Bandy to a duel to settle their differences, so frayed were the nerves, and Payne's exit in September avoided any bloodshed on that score.

Payne was a free man as was Capt. Dick, Will Black, the Chaplain, and two hundred others, some of whom went back into the army for more bounty money, but most of whom went back to the farm and glad of it. Half the body of the 37$^{th}$ was no more, dissolved back into the small towns and prairies of Illinois and the Michigan lakefront.

After discharge in the fall of 1864, the war was still the daily fare for some of these soldiers turned back to civilians, and was the social and economic determinant in Eugene Payne's run for office in Lake

## THE DISCHARGED 37TH

County and in Will Black's post in the Danville Provost Marshal's Office.

Julius White was back in Evanston, having resigned after dodging another bullet with Ambrose Burnside at the Battle of the Crater at Petersburg, Virginia. Capt. Dick was back in Stark County, and Fred Abbey had re-opened his gunsmith shop in Chicago.

Eugene Payne arrived home in Waukegan in September 1864, took off his uniform, and began to give political speeches as Colonel Payne, returned war hero, forced home by bad health, running for State Representative from Lake County. His wife had gotten "Hon. Coz." Elijah Haines to take Payne into his Chicago law office to handle pension and bounty claims of returning soldiers, which was to be his civilian career. Political office would improve business in that line.

One accommodation Payne had to make in his pursuit of Republican politics was in his slavery views. The Republican Party was the abolition party, and his racial remarks would not do on the stump in wartime Illinois. His wife was an abolitionist as was Hiram Kennicott, and Haines, and Eugene's father Tom. His father had observed about son Eugene's views that, "... it is that little nasty Judd Huntley that has poisoned his mind if he is in favor of slavery."[3]

Payne's irrational prejudice was akin to Charles Black's prejudice against "the Dutch," and dissipated after the war ended, either philosophically or out of political expediency

Payne had scant time for electioneering between discharge and the November election, and campaigned in Wauconda on October 11. After his speech in the church there, the Waukegan Gazette reported that, "that beautiful town was much purified from the exudence of treason which had flowed only from Copperhead orators who had been infesting the place up to that time."[4] Payne gave speeches all over Lake County on a circuit with Hon. Coz., Henry Blodgett and other local politicians and office-seekers.

In mid-October, a huge celebration was held in Waukegan including, "over 200 feet of tables,"[5] loaded with food for 1000 celebrants. Payne shared the speakers' platform on the occasion with two preachers, and was followed to the rostrum in the evening by Henry Blodgett. The pace picked up the next week, when Payne

## THIRTY SEVENTH ILLINOIS

spoke at Hainesville, Half Day, at Biddlecom's School House in Newport, at Lake Zurich, Milburn, Antioch, and Libertyville, speaking against the Copperheads and slavery. Payne, Henry Blodgett and Elijah Haines and the other locals and candidates pitched the voters in company with the Waukegan Glee club at Dickinson Hall on election eve, November 7. The town rag, the Gazette, touted all the Republican candidates, telling its readers that Payne, "has valiantly served his country, while his opponent has been serving his customers."[6]

Payne won in a landslide against his opponent, Mr. Case, 2,379 to 886. Abraham Lincoln polled 2.403 to 873 for McClellan on the same ballot. All the other major Republican candidates polled over 2.400 votes. Payne settled down with his victory and his bride in his little house on the lake in Waukegan; a combat veteran, attorney, and public servant, delivered out of the Missouri Ozarks and Mississippi bayous, back home on the edge of Lake Michigan.[7]

Across the state, Myron Barnes, lately Colonel of the 37th, had returned to Rock Island in 1862, after his army dismissal in Missouri, to wield the power of the pen in the Abolitionist-Copperhead, Republican-Democrat debates.

The political sentiment in Illinois had changed with the passing of three war years. After the first prideful displays of patriotism and flags and cheering in 1861, home front enthusiasm had waned. Casualties and funerals had become more frequent, revenue stamp taxes for photographs, deeds, wills, bills of lading and other documents of commerce had become more annoying, and a military draft was instituted to feed men to the armies. There was a peace movement afoot, focusing anti-slave, anti-war views.

The Republicans generally favored the abolition of slavery, restoration of the rebel states to the Union, and the prosecution of the war to the defeat of the south. The Democrats were generally the pro-slavery, anti-war party. The Emancipation Proclamation of January 1863 tied the abolition of slavery to the preservation of the Union, or seemed to, and Democrats were less willing to continue the war to the principal end of freeing the slaves.

Newspapers beat the drums on both sides. Rock Island, Illinois had two rival papers; the Republican UNION, and the Democratic

ARGUS. The passions of war raised the level of prose so it spilled over into personal attack, editor on editor. In Rock Island, Myron Barnes' paper, the pro-Republican UNION, was aligned against the Democratic ARGUS, edited by one Joseph B. Danforth, Jr., late of the U.S. Navy.

Danforth had been court martialed in 1858 for irregularities as a Purser and left the Navy.[8] Barnes had been court martialed by the Army in 1862 for attempting the Springfield mutiny, so both were back in the newspaper trade by default of military service.

As editors, both men used vitriol, hyperbole, and personal abuse in quantity. The issues were aired, the newspapers attacked each other, and then the editors attacked each other. The entertaining side of the Barnes-Danforth fracas was in the skill both men had at loading prose with adjectives. Both men could turn a phrase.

After dismissal from the army in 1862, Barnes had spent some months appealing the dismissal in St. Louis and in Washington. Barnes reported his visit to Rock Island in November 1862 as prompted by a death in the family, when he had actually been kicked out of the army.[9]

In those easier, friendlier days, Danforth's ARGUS published a defense of Col. Barnes, stating the case of the railroading done by Militia General Brown in Missouri. Danforth, ARGUS editor, also lent Barnes ink and paper to tide him over when he was short so that the UNION could be published. Danforth mentioned this in a later, less cordial context, referring to Barnes as a "craven, cowardly, lying scoundrel," "dirty dog," and the UNION as a "dirty, lying sheet."[10]

This type of insult sold a lot of papers, a value not lost on either man. The issues did get some attention in the dust kicked up by the name-calling. Items such as the one headed, "The N----- Has Arrived," appeared in the ARGUS in March 1862 while Barnes was still in Missouri, forecasting an inundation of indigent blacks into Illinois if all the soldiers brought their own servants, liberated slaves, back with them at the end of the war.[11] This Letter to the Editor was compatible with the editorial policy of the ARGUS. Illinois had passed laws prohibiting the entry of blacks into the state, a law trumpeted by Democrat Danforth and castigated by Republican Barnes.

# THIRTY SEVENTH ILLINOIS

By the fall of 1863, the two editors filled out their verbal arsenals with derogatory nicknames. Joseph B. Danforth, Jr., was known as "Bub" to the Union readers,[12] and Myron S. Barnes was known as "Buzzard Barnes, the Blanket Thief," to ARGUS readers.[13]

The thrust and parry went on between Bub and Buzzard through 1863 and 1864. Danforth, in Barnes' eye, was "a man who is morally rotten from the crown of his head to the bottom of his feet.... Bub ... is too cowardly to go to war," adding that Stephen A. Douglas, a friend of Danforth's wife, "had been in the habit of using Bub for a bootjack."[14] When Danforth's wife left him, Barnes explained to his readers that, "the fact that the Irish kitchen girl is out of town puts [him] in bad humor."[15]

Various incidents, most of them with a Republican-Democrat, pro-war, anti-war background, were used as contexts for further baiting and hyperbole.

One of these occurred in November 1863. A discharged soldier, one William Jennings, was alleged to have stolen $35 from a store. Although no charges were filed, the matter was dropped into a fertile field for anti-Barnes invective in reprisal for Barnes running the theft story, which he picked up from the GENESEO REPUBLICAN. An ARGUS correspondent wrote that Barnes, "like a poor starved turkey buzzard that had no carrion of his own to feed upon, had some imported from a foreign country by a brother buzzard [the GENESEO REPUBLICAN] so that he might have some of his natural food to stick his nose in." Barnes was also, "a mean sneaking prowling wolf ... pouncing on a poor boy like a hawk upon a chicken ... like a vulture on a kite.... My buzzard has been eating filth all the days of its life so that it has become filth itself...."[16]

The UNION had its own correspondents, not to be outdone on the letter-to-the-editor page. One writer referred to Danforth as, "the cowardly traitorous-hearted scoundrel of a copperhead who mounts the typod of the loathsome sheet [the ARGUS]...."[17]

In late 1863, Danforth wrote an article defending himself against his 1858 arrest and court martial while Purser of the U.S.S. VINCENNES, also repeating a bushel of barbs about Barnes collected by an ex-member of the 37th, David Hick. At first, Danforth had re-

# THE DISCHARGED 37TH

fused to print Hick's piece about Barnes, and so Hick had it printed on handbills in Davenport, Iowa, and circulated it in Rock Island and to the 37th. After Barnes revealed the circumstances of Danforth's discharge from the Navy, Danforth printed Hick's piece. The gist was that Barnes was, "dragged out of the tent of the wife of one of his soldiers in Camp Douglas, where he had gone in the vain hope of gratifying his beastly passions," that he had stolen blankets and muskets from the army, that he was court martialed and discharged from the army, that he was fined for assaulting a woman in Rock Island, and that he was expelled from the camp at Rock Island Barracks.[18]

Hick, "a discharged and worthless drunken soldier"[19] in Barnes' eye, had gotten a medical discharge from the 37th, and had come back to Coal Valley to raise a little hell with both Barnes and Julius White with some made-up stories printed up as "The Regulator." When the circular arrived in Brownsville in December 1863, it was outrageous enough to inspire Henry Ketzle to pen a character sketch of "Gentleman" Dave Hick, painting Hick as a thief, drunk, liar, etc., which Barnes printed.[20]

Hick and his stories thus disposed of at the hands of Company A Private Henry Ketzle, the field was clear for the next skirmish in the editorial wars. In early February 1864, J.B. Danforth made one too many critical anti-union remarks in the ARGUS. He took on the Soldier's Aid Society, which was comprised of the good ladies of Rock Island, good Union ladies. Danforth wrote an editorial asking for a report of their activities, to which Barnes replied, "A man who persistently attacks ladies in his paper, will be set down as a very mean man,"[21] characterizing his general attitude and handling of the ladies.

The "report" requested by Danforth was made to him, in person, on the street in Rock Island in mid-February. Not by one of the ladies collecting food for the sick and wounded, but by an officer of one of the regiments posted at Rock Island guarding the Confederate prisoners there. Major James M. Beardsley of the 13th Illinois, with one arm immobilized by a bullet wound from the Battle of Ringgold, encountered Danforth on the street, took a swing at him and knocked him through a hardware store window, punched him a few more times, and then followed him into the store and got in a few more whacks, all with one arm.

## THIRTY SEVENTH ILLINOIS

The Major's regiment, the 13$^{th}$ Illinois, lost no time in honoring him at an oyster supper the same night at the Island City Hotel, including "toasts, speeches, and a good time." Two of the toasts offered were:

"Major Beardsley: May he always keep that important verse of the Bible before his eyes, viz: 'The seed of the woman shall bruise the serpent's head.'

Copperheads: "May they all be scalped as clean as the Major scalped the Editor of the Argus, leaving their pates as bare as the gable end of a young bird in pokeberry time."

The hat was passed after dinner, and 36 people, including Henry Curtis' law partner (and brother-in-law) Charlie Osborn, contributed $250 to buy the Major a horse.[22]

The telling and re-telling of this flogging was stretched out for some weeks. Major Beardsley had struck blows for the ladies, for the Union, for the army, against traitors, copperhead editors, and Democrats. Barnes milked it for every drop, and Danforth did more than tell his side. One of his friends, former Congressman Isaac N. Morris, sent a copy of the ARGUS, with its account of the proceedings of a Democratic Committee set up on March 12, "to prepare a proper representation of the facts in reference to the attack made upon J.B. Danforth, Jr.," to Secretary of War Stanton. Morris' cover letter said, "… the honor of the general government require [Beardsley's] dismissal from the army…."[23]

The War Department referred the letter to the Union Commander at Rock Island for investigation, which was inconclusive.

With the slow fizzle of the stories about the assault, the stone-throwing tailed off. Neither side was able to find any fresh animal parallels. Asses, adders, carrion buzzards, and skunks had all been used.

Barnes moved on to other things. His army commission was restored by the War Department in May 1864, and he was "authorized and requested" by Adjutant General Fuller, to "immediately recruit and organize volunteers for Government Service of one hundred days."²⁴ So Barnes left his newspaper in June, busy with organizing the 140th Illinois Regiment, but lost the election for the regimental colonelcy. When Myron Barnes left the UNION in the summer of 1864, Danforth said goodbye:

"Barnes has disappeared below the surface, sold out, 'vamoosed the ranch,' and no longer has anything to do with the Union. The principal causes contributing to this result were, want of funds, want of brains, want of discretion and want of confidence on the part of his political friends...

He has published an innumerable number of most villainous lies about us. Well, never mind, we bear him no malice. We forgive him for all the wickedness and injustice he has practiced towards us, and wish him well wherever he may go. Good bye, Barnes."²⁵

The farewell had the ring of the parting of a respected adversary. Barnes and Danforth in later years could share a quart of adult beverage and smile about the kinds of things that are to be done in the newspaper business to boost circulation.

After reporting the 1864 Democratic National Convention from Chicago, Barnes returned to edit the UNION in November, with a vow, "to avoid all controversies with mean, contemptible editors and retailers of street scandal," but went on to say, "a man may be called a buzzard and justly wear the name so far as he meddles with the carrion-carcass of the editor who applies to him the title.... One more word and we have done. Hereafter we aim to avoid personal newspaper controversies...."²⁶

So peace came in the war of insults in Rock Island, just about the time William Fithian and son-in-law Will Black were getting their share of brickbats in Danville.

William Fithian had gotten into the war in 1863 as Captain Fithian, Provost Marshal, 7th Congressional District of Illinois, a position created by the Enrollment Act. The Enrollment Act set up a structure for a military draft. The duties of the district Provost Marshals were to examine and enlist recruits, enroll the eligible male population, arrest deserters, and suppress insurrection.

Danville, Illinois was on the same latitude as Richmond, Virginia, and shared many southern sentiments with the rebel states. Pro-

## THIRTY SEVENTH ILLINOIS

Confederate sentiment was everywhere. In 1862, Governor Yates had described southern Illinois as, "on the precipice of a revolution."[27] The southern districts had voted 6-1 for Democrat Douglas against Lincoln in 1861. In Marion, Illinois, a Confederate company had been raised in 1861, and a pro-Union newspaper editor was forced out of town. This was the climate when William Fithian, at the age of 63, put on his captain's bars and opened the Provost Marshal's office in Danville in mid-1863.

One of the first defined duties was to enroll, or register, all eligible men for the draft, amidst the efforts of Confederate sympathizers to coerce families and threaten death and damage to enrollable citizens.

One of what Eugene Payne and David Ash referred contemptuously to as a "last fall regiment," was the 128th Illinois, raised around Marion, Illinois, which shrunk from 861 men to 161 in five months, because most everybody in the regiment had deserted.[28] This unit had to be disbanded. Many of the officers and men of the 128th who had deserted, went back to Marion and incited riots against the enrollment. Political party lines here were clear. The deserters were Democrats, and the resisters and rioters were largely Democrats.

Lincoln's Emancipation Proclamation of New Year's Day in 1863 had swelled the ranks of the disaffected. Many Democrats would support the war if the objective was to preserve the Union, but when the goal was extended to freedom for the slaves, it was intolerable. There were resisters among the town fathers in Danville, and a number in Company K, the Danville Company of the 37th.

William Fithian and the Black family made no pretenses over where their sentiments lay. Fithian had had a friendship with Abraham Lincoln from years back, and Lincoln had appointed him to the Provost Marshal position.

Union resolve and war spirit was softening in other parts of the north. In the heat of the copperhead rage at the Enrollment Act and the draft, Charles Black had made a speech at the Chicago Board of Trade, inflammatory enough to cause several of the verbally injured to walk out on him in mid-speech.[29]

## THE DISCHARGED 37TH

Lincoln's 1863 Emancipation Proclamation was less than a week old when a public meeting was held in Danville to encourage resisters to the draft which was to occur two months later. Copperhead sentiment in the 37$^{th}$ was strong enough to cause a mutiny plot to hatch among the Democrats in the regiment. In March 1863, Joe Delay of the Danville Company had told Will Black of a plan among the men to desert with weapons and return to Danville to support any revolt against the draft that might break out.[30]

At the same time the plot in the 37$^{th}$ was uncovered, on March 9, 1863, ex-Union Army Colonel Lyman Guiness was walking in Danville with his children. He was returning home with a loaf of bread when Copperhead Doctor Farris shot him. Guiness in turn pistol whipped Farris with Farris' own weapon and, "would probably have killed him had not the Doctor [Fithian] begged for Farris and caught the arm of Guiness."[31] Will Black's comment from Missouri was, "I'm sorry Pa caught his arm. I am one who believes in the extermination of rebels, the more so if they be of the mean, dribbling kind who stay at home, waging war with words, too cowardly to enter the field...."[32]

Later on in the summer of 1863, Guiness got into another brawl with John Payne. Payne was wearing a rebel pin which was torn off by Colonel Hawkins, and then Guiness beat Payne.[33]

Four days later, with both factions armed, a showdown came leaving two dead and two wounded. William Lamon and a Mr. Myers were killed, and John Payne and the sheriff were wounded.[34] The killer, George Barker, had been discharged from the 37$^{th}$ in 1862 after shooting himself at the Lamine. The wound was generally regarded as self-inflicted, and Barker generally regarded as a deserter. Barker was, "an intemperate man and has not the reputation of being either intelligent or honest."[35]

Barker was indicted for murder, tried for manslaughter, and spent almost a year in prison. Fithian called for troops the night of the murders, and their presence discouraged further riot.[36]

By the summer of 1864, Fithian's district had the distinction of paying the highest enlistment bounty in the state, and the second highest in the nation. In July, the bounty reached a high of $1,055.76 per enlistee,[37] taking second place nationwide by about $4. The business of recruiting gave rise to a class of body brokers who would find a substitute or fill a quota if the price was right. At upwards of $1,000 a pop, it made good business for men to enlist, collect, desert, change names, enlist again, collect, desert, etc.

In the fall of 1864, Doctor Fithian had been in office fifteen months, time enough to offend lots of people as the military authority in Danville. Will Black came home in September and went to work in the office with his stepfather, who was under attack from some unhappy citizens, including Colonel Guiness.

The head of the opposition was Townsman Sam Frazier, who organized a petition drive to get rid of Fithian, charging him with doubtful loyalty, tyranny, ungentlemanly behavior, favoring copperheads, and general "inefficiency and unpopularity."[38] Frazier began cursing and abusing Fithian every time the Doctor passed Frazier's house alone. Willy threatened Frazier to lay off the Doctor, and Frazier abused him.

An investigating officer was sent from Springfield, Illinois who reported that the effort at removal was, "an unholy and ungodly conspiracy to remove an able, energetic, and faithful officer,"[39] and so the move to oust Fithian was ultimately quashed.

After the favorable report to the capitol, Charles Black told his stepfather that, "you have at last found your Frisbie in the person of Frazier…. From what I know of his past life he never had held post or drawn pay unless by your influence, and to turn against you now is shameful…. I wrote [Will] not to touch [Frazier] unless he had to…. Will is hot tempered and as fiery as powder…."[40]

By the end of November, the move to dump Fithian had been beaten back temporarily. Upstate in Waukegan, Eugene Payne was snug in the warmth of his little house, his wife's embrace, and his election victory. In Rock Island, Myron Barnes had lost his bid to command the 140th Illinois Infantry, and was angling to get his newspaper back. Henry Frisbie was Colonel of the 92d U.S. Colored Troops at Port Hudson, Edward Anderson was campaigning with 1200 men as Colonel of the 12th Indiana Cavalry, and Lt. Colonel Ransom Kennicott took the 37th into winter quarters in the big army base at DeVall's Bluff, Arkansas.

## 26. DeVall's Bluff

In October 1864, the 37th left the camp at White River Landing and moved to camp at DeVall's Bluff, Arkansas, where they would stay for the next three months, the longest stop since the Cassville posting in 1862.

At the Bluff, specifications were laid out in General Order 41 for the erection of winter quarters. By November 1, thirty-five log huts had been completed, built on cleared land radiating out from the river landing. Huts for 8000 men would be built before the onset of winter. The log huts had fireplaces, and were on the whole spacious and comfortable.[1]

When the construction was completed, frequent details of picket and guard duty occupied the men, who had become unruly and undisciplined under Ransom Kennicott's command at the White River camp. Charles Black's bowels stopped running sufficiently for him to return – late – to the DeVall's Bluff camp at the end of October. Black let Kennicott run the regiment, but took charge when one violent incident occurred on November 22. Three men in Company G were stabbed in a fight, one mortally (William Wood, regimental baker). Black put First Sergeant Thomas Murphy in irons, and arrested the others and put them on bread and water and daily spade drill. He also put the sutler under guard, afterward saying, "Last night at taps this camp lay down and slept and so I mean it shall hereafter, or go on the forts at hard work.... The command ... here is the nearest to a mob I have ever seen save in [Missouri]...."[2] Murphy stayed in jail for a month and then deserted on Christmas Day. The others, Alfonzo Emery, William Doyle, and Lawrence Mahan, were all in their 30's, off the streets of Chicago, and a hard lot. They were let out of the guardhouse after ten weeks so they could go to Mobile with the regiment in February.

This punishment was a departure from Kennicott's more lenient, safer methods of discipline as in the unrelated case of Sergeant Franklin Galbraith of the Michigan Company. Kennicott sentenced Galbraith, a thief, to denial of any passes and given the silent treatment for thirty days.[3]

## THIRTY SEVENTH ILLINOIS

In December, Assistant Surgeon Mesler was dishonorably discharged for conduct unbecoming. The fourteen remaining regimental officers petitioned President Lincoln to review his sentence, and Charles Black, considering him unjustly accused, requested that Mesler's case be heard before a Court Martial. Mesler had been dumped for allegedly using some strong language in October which was apparently uttered by someone else.[4]

On December 14, 1864, the entire DeVall's Bluff post was turned out to witness the execution of a deserter, bounty jumper, and example-setter for anyone else who had desertion in mind.[5]

The days at the Bluff passed off in long swatches of guard, drill, construction labor on the breastwork defenses, and drinking. In early December for some variety, Charles Black took a scout of 180 men up the White River to forage for lumber and to see his Aunt Eleanor.[6]

One soldier in residence summed up the holiday season observing, "Christmas and New Year's on the Bluff were high times for some officers and also men, as bad whiskey made a good many fools, and made duty heavier on the decent part of the crowd."[7]

The relentless pursuit of rank continued as a major focus of activity. Charles Black, although not regimental commander, tried to direct promotions, which meant more money and more power (and usually more comfort and servants) to the successful aspirants. Military pay raises voted by Congress during the summer made the promotions about twenty percent more attractive than before. A private's pay went from $13 to $16 per month, bandleaders to $75, First Class Hospital Stewards to $33, and Sergeants Major to $26.[8] One of the effects of the exodus of over two hundred non-veterans was the higher-rank openings for others to fill. In the case of Messer's Company F, Gallio Fairman became Captain, and he suspected that Charles Black was going to try to deny Second Lieutenant John Cronk, who had right of succession to the First Lieutenancy. Fairman wrote in July, and Erwin Messer applied in person to stop the injustice and head Black off, and they were successful. Someone had lifted copies of Black's critical correspondence about Cronk out of the files in Springfield, and sent copies to Cronk and Fairman.[9]

# DEVALL'S BLUFF

The biggest worry of Black and Kennicott continued to be consolidation. Such a move would cost them both their positions.

In November, Black expected two hundred recruits to come sailing down the river into his arms, filling the regiment up to an allowable strength for the support of three field grade officers, and was recommending Herman Wolford for Major, if and when Kennicott mustered as Lieutenant Colonel.[10]

The recruits never arrived, and by December, Kennicott realized that only Black's friends and influence would keep the 37th from being consolidated. So if Black went, Kennicott went out with him, and so he made a gesture of self-preservation. The mustering officer told Kennicott that if he were mustered as Lieutenant Colonel which could be done at any time, Black would have to go, as the strength of the regiment was below the minimum to have both officer grades. Kennicott declined to be mustered.[11]

During the winter, most of the vacancies were filled, including the Quartermaster spot. Black's heavy hand forced through the appointment of an 18 year old personal friend, Jim Culbertson, at the expense of the logical men, who were Quartermaster Sergeant George Griffith and Commissary Sergeant Austin Cruver. Black pointed out that, "[they] have since my absence been detected in acts that entirely unfit them for promotion."[12] Black's allegations were never proved against the two. Wells Morrill was also a candidate and was disposed of in similar fashion when he and Oscar Sowles were accused of improperly drawing and selling army shoes, also a false accusation.[13]

Through the early winter, the daily grind of drill, guard and picket, eating, drinking, and cards crept unerringly onward from day to week to month. One of the camp priorities, and a priority of Charles Black, was music. The mass mustering out in September had taken many bandsmen, and so ten new musicians were assembled: Horace Pickett, John Plank, Samuel Young, Frank Jacobs, James Polen, Jacob Miller, Fred Davis, John Jennings, and James Kain. Other appointments included Joseph Wechsler as butcher in the beef corral, Jim Day as commander of Company C, and William Wilson as Captain of Company A. Crack shot William Hessey, a new boy recruited in 1863, was made postmaster.[14]

## THIRTY SEVENTH ILLINOIS

What of the lifestyle of a colonel on the Bluffs? A look at Charles Black's sutler bills show purchases of the pleasures of life beyond a barrel of spuds. All the tools of sin were there: cards, tobacco, cigars, wine, beer, and whiskey. He ran up a tab of $132.20 in ninety days, including $49 for tobacco, $25 worth of wine and ale, and $29 on a euphemistic category, "Goods on Order."[15] The balance of the purchases were in the category of bar snacks – cheese & crackers, sardines, pig's feet, assorted fruit, and a $3 knife.

Life amidst the pig's feet, cigars, and warm huts ended with the arrival of New Year's 1865. There was one more offensive wartime campaign for the 37th to help with, and they were soon back on the march to a new battlefield.

## 27.  Fort Blakeley

There are several advantages to living in permanent camp, including better and more regular rations, more comfort, less marching, less exposure to bad weather, steady girlfriends, paid or otherwise, and an altogether better supply of tents, shoes, clothes, etc. On the other hand, as the hardships decrease, discipline becomes more enforceable. There is more pattern, more control, more time to concentrate on regulations. Discipline being a necessary thing in a large group, Charles Black laid out the traditional New Year's list of do's and don't's on January 1, 1865, including the usual provisos against drunkenness and "remissness in the performance of duty."[1]

The 37$^{th}$ had exactly one week on the Bluff to disregard the New Year's warnings. On January 7, 1865, camp was broken and the regiment piled onto the Steamer MEPHAM for a trip to Kennerville, Louisiana, a train depot about fifteen miles above New Orleans that happened, quite logically, to be on Madam Kenner's land.[2]

Camp was made in an old sugar cane field nearby for five weeks until mid-February. Of little account was the reassignment of Lorenzo Morey, who had been absent on staff duty for almost two years. He had been assigned for duty in the Inspector General's Office and had displeased his superior, who had reduced his displeasure to an official request, i.e., "January 8, 1865: The report of Capt. L.B. Morey ... is such a tissue of absurdities and glaring irregularities as far as numbers are concerned that if agreeable ... I will recommend that he be immediately relieved from duty and ordered to his regiment. /s/ John N. Wilson, Lt. Col." Morey went, and although finished as an I.G., he finagled a spot on General Herron's staff and avoided rejoining the regiment.[3]

The Kennerville camp was very handy to New Orleans, where the men took refuge on pass from the wet, rainy, soaking camp surroundings. "It rains 18 hours out of 24, it drizzles, sprinkles, fogs, mists & pours in turn.... Every track is a puddle, every rut a miniature canal. The river, held by artificial banks, is several feet higher than the ground where we are ... and boats go by as if in air."[4]

THIRTY SEVENTH ILLINOIS

The regiment left Kennerville after five uneventful weeks, and went to Mobile Bay by boat, and then to Barrancas, Florida.

After three weeks at Barrancas amid the pines, the regiment moved to Pensacola, and then went on the march through Pollard and Stockton to the rear of Fort Blakeley, Alabama.

By April 1865, the deep-south Confederacy had been pared down to Alabama and parts of Louisiana, Mississippi, Florida, and Georgia. At the end of March, Federal General Steele with 13,000 men, including the 37th, had driven the rebel forces back from Pollard toward Mobile Bay, and finally into the works at Fort Blakeley, Alabama.

Blakeley and Spanish Fort were the two rebel positions on the eastern shore of Mobile Bay. By April 2, both strong and heavily defended rebel positions were surrounded by the Union forces.

For nearly a week, the Federal Army dug trenches, timbered bombproof shelters, and constructed artillery positions all along the line before Blakeley. On April 8, Spanish Fort was taken, and the rebel garrison ran to Fort Blakeley and Mobile. The next day, April 9, the Union army assaulted Fort Blakeley. The late afternoon frontal assault took seventeen minutes. The charge was made over ditches and fallen timber through an artillery barrage.[5]

The charge touched the regiment lightly with one death, Irish-born James Boyd of Kennicott's Company, shot through the neck. The wounded included Horace Disney, Thomas McAllister, John Cline, Milton Keech, Edward Patterson, D.D. Cooper, and Julius Cavier.

Other fallout of the assault concerned John Blanquart, who was charged with cowardice during this last battle by Lt. Chapman of the Danville Company, to wit: " ... [Blanquart laid] down behind a log while his Co. and the Regt. were advancing, and did lay there until the charge was over, thereby failing to take any part with his Co. in the engagement."[6] Belgian-born Blanquart had been enlisted at Danville while the regiment was in Brownsville in November 1863, and had never been in a battle before. He was 40 years old.

The charge at Fort Blakeley on April 9, Palm Sunday, was the regiment's final battle charge of the war. There was a particular tragedy in James Boyd's death because earlier in the day, Lee had

## FORT BLAKELEY

surrendered the Army of Northern Virginia to Grant at Appomattox, constructively ending the war.

The surrender news came to the men at Fort Blakeley the next day while burying their dead and supervising the rebels in unearthing the land mines around the fort. Reaction to the news was somewhat tempered, as there were still rebels to hunt down in the deep south and more campaigning to do, although these would be mop-up actions.

The few short days of bunting and bonfires changed to black crepe and tears on April 14, when Abraham Lincoln was shot in the back of the head and killed by John Wilkes Booth. Lincoln, a Black family friend, who had delivered a campaign speech from the balcony of the Fithian home in Danville in 1860, and taken a special liking to Charles and Willy, and according to Ward Lamon, wept when he heard the false report of Charles' death at Prairie Grove,[7] was suddenly and abruptly removed from the scene in which he had been the centerpiece for four years.

After news of the death reached the army at Mobile, the 37th was put on duty patrolling the streets, so fierce was the sentiment against the rebels. The patrols prevented the deaths of some rebels at the hands of angered Federal soldiers.[8]

The regiment camped in the suburbs of Mobile for a week, and then went off up the Alabama River to Selma liberating a military prison at Cahabin on the way. After two days in Selma, they took an overnight trip to Montgomery at the end of April. While there, Charles Black received orders to join General Frederick Steele's staff as Provost Marshal in Texas. When the regiment left May 1, Black stayed in Montgomery, finally parted from the men he had marched with and led for four years.

After ten days at Selma, the 37th went back to Mobile in time to witness a gigantic explosion on the docks, set off by careless handling of ammunition. Three hundred were killed. Blocks of warehouses, as well as boats and docks, were destroyed. One of the injured was Hosea Young of Company G. Young suffered a fractured skull. The wound was still discharging pus five months later when he was discharged on disability.[9]

The regiment was designated as part of the Provisional Brigade in May and put on duty at Forts Morgan, Gaines, Barrancas, and Pickens

# THIRTY SEVENTH ILLINOIS

around Mobile Bay. The head count was down to one hundred ninety present for duty, most all of whom had good times in the conquered city.[10]

After six weeks in Mobile, the men moved again on their final army detail. They loaded onto the CLYDE, steamed out of Mobile Bay and transferred to the SEDGEWICK and then out into the Gulf of Mexico on June 28, 1865, on their way back to Texas. Charles Black had gone back to Brownsville with General Steele, and the regiment was headed for Galveston. The days on the Mississippi were over, the war was over, and the combat and field history of the 37th was almost over.

## 28. The Last Days of Black and Frisbie

The early summer of 1865 found old adversaries Charles Black and Henry Frisbie both on duty in the conquered south. Frisbie, an occasional brigade commander and full-time Colonel of the 92d U.S. Colored Troops, was at Port Hudson. Charles Black was at Selma and Mobile with the sparsely manned $37^{th}$.

Black left the regiment at Mobile on June 1, presumably to allow it to lapse back into slovenly ways under Ransom Kennicott. Black boarded the Transport CLINTON and steamed across the Gulf of Mexico to a cushy new assignment in Brownsville as General Frederick Steele's Provost Marshal. Black returned to the scene of the 1863-1864 debauch. He was back with old friends on the Mexican Frontier, including Fayette Lacey, former Sergeant Major of the $37^{th}$, and now an Assistant Adjutant General at Brazos Santiago. Addressing his greeting to Black as "My Dear Fellah,"[1] Lacey was full of the idea of fighting the French in Mexico, and updated Black on the renewed political meddling of Steele and the army. Steele was still after Confederate property taken across to Mexico before the Union forces arrived in Texas, and went about pressuring the French-backed Mexicans to return the contraband property.

At the end of June, Charles Black, once more the instrument of political intrigue, received a letter from old anti-French and Juarista party pal Juan Cortina, addressed to "Sr. Coronel ... Don Carlos Black." Charles sent the letter to General Steele and Fayette Lacey in Brazos Santiago for a response. Steele replied through Lacey that, "Cortina must not bring his troops to this side of the river. We will not injure him in any way, but he must not presume too much on our favor"[2]

Steele was echoing the official neutral position of the United States toward Mexico, as it bore directly on relations with England and France.

After stating the official response unofficially, Lacey lent a bit of personal advice in the same letter to Black: "Beware of Mexican clap! It is said to be hell itself – both in quality and duration."[3]

## THIRTY SEVENTH ILLINOIS

In this way did Charles Black settle back into society and intrigue on the border. He had a large room in the house in Brownsville that Generals Herron and Dana had used as a headquarters, did staff duty with no troop responsibilities, and had money in his pocket to enjoy the Brownsville night life.

In August, after deciding that he would rather not join in any military move against the French in Mexico, Charles Black, after considerable thought, decided to resign from the army. He felt that, "as civil law resumes its work, a soldier is most like his sword; of little use and save by constant polishing, of little moment...."[4]

A great deal of this thinking must have been done in Victor's Restaurant in Brownsville. Between July 1 and August 2, Charles Black spent $152 at Victor's mostly on broiled chicken, wine, and champagne.[5]

On August 15, three months after the civil war had ended with the last battle fought outside Brownsville (at Palmito Ranch, May 13), Charles Black gave up any dreams of military adventuring in Mexico, resigned, and went back to Illinois. He was 26 years old.

Meanwhile, at Port Hudson, Henry Frisbie also had life after the army on his mind, and was approaching things on a different plane. Frisbie was post commander at Port Hudson in August 1865. The man who had been accused of horse theft, fraud in the hay business, assault, unofficially of robbing the dead at Pea Ridge, attempting to bribe a military court at St. Louis, and various other heinous deeds by the Black brothers and others, was the military commander of the Mississippi River stronghold. He had been a brigade commander and had led the 92d Colored Troops on the Red River Expedition.

Frisbie had commanded the 92d since the fall of 1863, and before the 37th went to Texas the 92d had been camped near the 37th outside New Orleans. Because Frisbie had taken so many of the best officers and sergeants from the 37th and given them promotions in the 92d, the repartee between the officers of the 92d and the men of the 37th became quite spirited at any sighting of the 92d.[6]

By 1864, the 37th had gone to Texas, and Frisbie and the 92d had gone campaigning up the Red River.

## THE LAST DAYS OF BLACK AND FRISBIE

Frisbie had respect and affection for his command of black troops. They were virtually all illiterate as a result of the laws of the southern states, and each was carried on the descriptive roll of the regiment as "laborer" by occupation.[7] No trades, professions, or education among them, most with homeless families.

The former slave owners, deprived of their capital investment by the war, turned out the families of the departed black soldiers seeing no need to support them further. In September 1865, Port Hudson was surrounded by these homeless, penniless families whose men had joined the Union Army. Henry Frisbie distributed food to them without authority. He had appealed to the Freedmen's Bureau, and took critical issue with their response. The Bureau had been established for just the purpose of providing for former slaves victimized by the destructed southern plantation economy.

In September 1865, Frisbie complained to the Bureau about a plantation owner who had turned out the families of twenty-three of his soldiers. (Forty-three women and children) who had lived above Donaldsville, had worked for two years, "without pay or clothing, and now have been turned out of their cabins without bedding or cooking utensils ... in a starving condition.... Knowing these people as well as I do ... I am every day astonished at [the slave owners'] cruelty and inhumanity."[8]

After receiving an answer to the effect that black soldiers should take care of their own just as white soldiers do, Frisbie pointed out that if blacks were to fend for themselves as whites did, what was the use of having a Freedmen's Bureau, characterizing it as a "useless encumbrance, and the sooner it is shut up and its agents sent home, the better."[9]

Frisbie had described and pointed up the conditions faced by over 3,000,000 former slaves, most of whom had been turned out, at once, on a broken economy, plagued by both homeless civilians and ex-soldiers. He had recognized the social and economic condition of the reconstruction black. The Bureau of Refugees, Freedmen, and Abandoned Lands had been started up at war's end in May 1865, notable thereafter for its corruption. Its first stated objective was, "to supply the immediate necessities of those whose condition was changed by hostilities...."[10]

## THIRTY SEVENTH ILLINOIS

Frisbie got a further answer to his complaint about the Donaldsville planter who had abandoned his former slaves from the Louisiana Freedmen's Bureau Commissioner: "I am not pleased with the tone of your letter, and deeply regret the suffering which you inform me had ensued.... I stated that we could not compel planters to retain these women if their husbands were not on the place, unless contracts had been made with them. This is so. While I am proud of the services which the colored man has rendered to his country, I can see no reason why, with the pay which he received from the government, and the amount which can be earned by an industrious woman, their families cannot be supported and maintained in at least a comfortable manner."[11]

The comment was unrealistic and incompetent, because there were few enough jobs available in the war ravaged southern economy, and those available went to whites by and large.

In June 1865, the 92d had received four months pay at Baton Rouge, about $64 per man for privates, more for sergeants and corporals.[12] After a week, the total sum of about $60,000 was frittered away or cheated away. Frisbie thought that enriching unscrupulous Baton Rouge businessmen, prostitutes, cardsharps, and con artists was a waste of a great deal of capital. The war was won, and the 92d would soon be mustered out, and the men would be without income or property. Henry Frisbie would also be without a job, and he resolved to provide for that eventuality.

After the June payday, Frisbie made a speech to the regiment outlining plans to buy land and form a "colony." The land purchase would be financed by contributions from anyone who wished to participate. The money was to be paid to Frisbie as agent. He told his men that he wanted them all to be "comfortably situated." And that he would pick out the land to purchase and also help the men put in a crop.

Four months later, in October, the regiment received another pay. Frisbie called all the Sergeants to his quarters and made his land offer again. The Sergeants in turn brought all the men who wanted to contribute to Frisbie's quarters, and they paid a total of about $5,000.

## THE LAST DAYS OF BLACK AND FRISBIE

The land was to be allocated proportionate to the amount of the contribution. It would be worked the first year under Frisbie's control with profits distributed to the men. Frisbie's pay was to be, "what the men thought right." Sergeant Hall of the 92d later said that, "We were all keen for it."[13]

What Frisbie was doing was collecting money for the purchase of stock in "The Lincoln Land Association," of which he appointed himself Treasurer. He also collected for the "Lincoln Memorial Fund." What he failed to do was issue either receipts or shares to every man, did not incorporate, had no stockholders meeting, and provided no surety bond as security for the funds collected. It was also against army regulations for officers to have financial transactions with enlisted men.

This activity on behalf of his men brought Frisbie a court martial and an inquiry in October and in December of 1865. Of all the charges (conduct unbecoming, conduct prejudicial, disobedience of orders and other nebulae), the matters triable were handing out food to the starving families of his men, failure to provide for transfer of ordnance at Port Hudson, and having financial transactions with enlisted men. For the ordnance transfer charge and giving away the food, he lost one month's pay. For the land scheme, he was ordered to refund the money collected, which was under $5,000.

There were questionable practices in the land purchase plan. What, "man of means, large business, and established financial reputation," as Frisbie described himself would fail to incorporate or bond his obligation?

The Judge Advocate gave the definitive opinion; "The pure object of the scheme seems to have been not so much to provide homes for his men, but that he might better for his own interest contract their labor... The proper remedy ... combining protection to the enlisted men and condemnation of Col. Frisbie's acts, is to require him to refund the money collected."[14]

So that was the end of the Lincoln Land Association. Or was it? This plan to provide full employment for Frisbie and a home and a future for the discharged men of the 92d was too good to give up. After muster-out in 1866, no court martial could influence the idea, and so 1866 found Frisbie and about 400 of his former soldiers raising cotton and sugar on land he had leased in northern Louisiana in Rapides Parish on the Red River.

Here were 400 black Union Army veterans working land as free men. The locals detested them (and their white officer even more), and things went bad very quickly. The locals harassed and threatened the men, vandalized property, and made death threats against Frisbie. Things finally escalated into lynchings and shots fired at Frisbie in an attempt to kill him.

The noble plan fell apart, and by 1867, Frisbie had sold out and fled to New Orleans, after moving his men by boat to Grand Coupee. The social experiment, if that is what it was, was put on hold, the victim of his unreconstructed southern neighbors.[15]

## 29. The Final Pay Call

Henry Frisbie, Charles Hawes, William Philleo, and the rest who had gone to the 92d Colored Troops heard no more barbs from the 37th after the early summer of 1865, when the 37th, or what was left of it, returned to Texas. Under the command of Ransom Kennicott, the regiment landed at Galveston on July 1, 1865. Quarters were in the Fremont Hotel until a fire destroyed that comfy spot, and camp was moved to a cotton press south of the city.[1]

On July 11, half of the regiment left Galveston on the Steamer FLETCHER for a scout to Sabine, Texas, to seize whatever property there was in the hands of the former rebels, or secreted by the locals. The next day, Ransom Kennicott reported that there were slim pickings at Sabine. Five spiked cannon were found at Fort Griffin, four more cannon five miles out of town, no gunpowder, and one thousand bales of cotton claimed to be private property. Kennicott then put a small force on the Steamer SUNFLOWER to go and police Beaumont, Texas.[2]

The end of the month brought more success with the seizure of twenty guns from Fort Manhaset, a sailboat, and the leader of the local rebel guerillas, or "Regulators."[3]

In August, four companies moved up to Beaumont over Sabine Lake, and camped out in abandoned buildings in the town. War had taken its toll on civilians at Beaumont and Liberty, Texas. Most all were destitute, without property, food, or means of support, the major remaining industry being the smuggling conducted out of Sabine. Kennicott issued rations to the Freedmen at Beaumont, and Gallio Fairman did the same at Liberty, feeding men whose stomachs had been full as slaves and turned empty as free men.[4]

Jack Moran went out to Sabine Pass to stop the contraband cotton shipments and to get together with Major McReynolds, the former rebel commander, to collect all the cattle that had been scattered in the countryside.[5]

In September, Kennicott was made Post Commander at Sabine and Beaumont. Two days before the assignment was made, remnants of three regiments were consolidated into the 37th. As the senior reg-

## THIRTY SEVENTH ILLINOIS

iment, the 37th survived, and the 94th Illinois dissolved into its ranks. Six days later, the 76th Illinois was folded in, followed by the 97th Illinois, bringing the regiment up to a strength of 705.[6]

All three consolidated regiments were August 1862 regiments. Enlistments for most of the troops ran out in August 1865 at the end of three years, and the leftovers, later recruits, were transferred into the 37th to serve out their term of enlistment. The 37th, whose officers had so long feared consolidation, was now host to three other units.

The 76th had been raised in Kankakee, Illinois, and had been at Vicksburg, Jackson, Meridian, Yazoo City, and the capture of Mobile. The 94th had come from Bloomington and McLean County, and had also gone through Missouri and Vicksburg to Galveston. The 97th was a bit more bloodied at Chickasaw Bluffs, Arkansas Post, Port Gibson, Champion Hills, Black River, and Vicksburg.[7]

The new men were apportioned to the line companies of the 37th, some with as little as two months service remaining, and took their discharges over the next eight months. These men, who had been taken from their own battle flags, their own commanders, and their own organizations, reported to Houston and Sabine and Beaumont with the veteran 37th.

After Sabine Pass and Beaumont, the next move for the new agglomeration was by rail to Houston, Texas. After one night camping in the street, the regiment took the train to Alleyton, the terminus of the Austin & Columbus Railroad, and from there to Columbus for more provost-police duty, which included some overseeing chores. Fred Wiffin and George Edwards were ordered to "the Plantation of Mr. Montgomery at Eagle Lake. They will remain there until further orders ... and see that the negroes fulfill all contracts made with their employers...."[8] Soldiers were also sent to the Minter and Suggs Plantations.

And so it went, playing the role of policeman, raider, coercer, crowd controller, and Provost Marshal with some fatigue, guard, and drill mixed in.

In mid-October, the 37th was recalled to Houston after making themselves unpopular with some citizens of Columbus by cutting

## THE FINAL PAY CALL

down and burning fences, trees, and outbuildings, including some pecan trees, when the wood ran out.[9]

The regiment was relieving the 48th Ohio in Houston. Despite deliberate general destruction of the physical plant at Columbus, the repatriated rebel rag THE HOUSTON TELEGRAPH reported that, "The 37th Illinois Regiment, Colonel Kennicott commanding ... has been on duty at Columbus lately, and the paper [there] speaks in high terms of the gentlemanly conduct of the regiment during their stay there."[10]

The regiment was broken up in Houston, and the companies went off to their final duty stations where their army time would be served out; Co. A to Brenham, B to Millican, C back to Columbus, D to Beaumont, F to Richmond, H to Alleyton, and K to Hempstead. Companies E, G, and I stayed at Headquarters Post in Houston. The next seven months passed in these small railhead towns that ringed Houston among unrepentant rebels in the reconstruction south.

Within a week, George Merrill and Company H moved from Alleyton to Columbus, questioning what he was to do to fill the long dusty days of Texas winter in the quiet town of Columbus, Texas.[11]

In Houston, things were not as quiet. In November one of the more avaricious town landlords made an inflated claim on the government for a burned out building, alleging arson by soldiers. The building had been inhabited by negro squatters, and the owner had asked George Kennicott to evict these residents. The next day, the squatters burned the building, and the owner saw the only available source to recoup his loss as the U.S. Government. The claim was denied.[12]

This was one of many incidents off the police blotter to face Houston Post Commander Ransom Kennicott in the days between November 1865 and May 1866. One man's hogs were killed, another's fence and outhouse stolen for firewood, another assaulted and robbed, a freedman beaten, a soldier beaten, a tavern brawl here and a shooting there.[13]

Amid this scene of assault, riot, robbery, arson and murder, Post Commander Kennicott and Regimental Commander Judd Huntley got into a squabble over authority. Kennicott's command of the Post at Houston, to Huntley's mind, gave him no power to arrest men of the

## THIRTY SEVENTH ILLINOIS

37th. Huntley's of record complaints in December sum up the conflict:

> [Dec 16] A guard purporting to act under your orders came into my camp to arrest one of my men. I refused to let them do so. If you want the man arrested, please send an order to that effect and it will be complied with.
>
> [Dec 27] ...a portion of your Post Guard and some prisoners are on the street attacking civilians. Will you please inform me if they are at liberty by your order or not, as I have sent a guard to arrest them.
>
> [Dec 31] ...last night a guard from my command arrested and confined ... a cavalry soldier and a citizen who were raising a disturbance at a dance a short distance from my camp. They drew a revolver on the officer commanding the guard. For further information I would respectfully refer you to Lt. Manzer ... he being the officer making the arrest.[14]

Most of the mayhem was non-fatal, and the regiment suffered limited attrition in Houston.

Death from disease disappeared from the morning report. The water and sanitation in Houston and the surrounding towns, bad as it was, came out a mile ahead of the bayou and canebreak army camps of the war years in Missouri and the deep south. Good potable water made the greatest difference. If anyone did get chronically sick in the months after the shooting war had stopped, they were discharged, expelled to die out of the army to save the government the expense and trouble of hospital care.

Houston in the spring of 1866 was dirty and ill-kempt, not the garden spot of the west. Carcasses of animals and garbage festered in stagnant pools of water in many places. Drains and ditches had been neglected and were plugged or filled creating pools of filth and waste. Dead animals were left lying in gullies and bayous. Carloads of garbage were dumped anywhere convenient, and had accumulated for years near restaurants, hotels, breweries and shops. Privies were simply holes in the ground, with no sink or drain.[15]

## THE FINAL PAY CALL

The regimental hospital books for the stay in Houston show a variety of non-fatal diseases. In October, the Medical Officer admitted a variety of cases, including diagnoses of intermittent fever, diarrhea, "general debility," sore mouth, sore finger, sore hand, poison oak, syphilis, gonorrhea, and "don't know," in the case of William Bishop, who must have been thrilled at such a diagnosis.[16]

Cases like Edward Peterson were disposed of by discharge. Herman Wolford had enlisted the Swedish-born Peterson in 1864 at the age of 16 in Rock Island. By November 1865, he had developed chronic chills, fever, diarrhea, enlarged spleen, had been sick for all his eighteen months in the army, and at 5' 3" in height, weighed under one hundred pounds. Discharging men like Peterson kept the casualty rate down.[17]

Ransom Kennicott had quite enough to manage without writing sympathy letters for men like Edward Peterson, who wasted away in the peacetime army.

In February 1866, Chan Morse lost his clerk to the Galveston Police on a murder charge. The clerk, Charles Postley, was out drinking with Private Hays of the 48th Ohio. Postley started manhandling Hays at his tent, and one Jerry Brown Miller of the 48th Ohio was shot and killed by Postley for trying to protect Hays and stop the noise.[18]

This was a run of the mill incident for the time and place, 1866 reconstruction Texas. A natural resentment between civilian and soldier, rebel and yank, backed up by a plentiful supply of firearms on each side, laid out all the elements so frequently catalyzed by an evening or two with a bottle of bad whiskey. This is what happened with Private Andrew Hunter in Brenham.

The Rock Island Company (A) occupied Brenham in 1866, a town about sixty miles northwest of Houston. Brenham was a trans-shipment point for supplies for General George Custer and his troops in the territories. The railroad ended there, and the stores were off-loaded onto wagons.

The town was part of the unreconstructed south, and in 1866 consisted of three churches, four schools, two newspapers, one photo gallery, five doctors, nine lawyers, two auction houses, four grocery stores, one clothing store, two drug stores, two ladies' shops, two jewelers, three bakeries, three saddleries, a tinsmith shop, a carriage factory, two smithies, seventeen general retailers, and six saloons. The contemporary newspapers noted that, "Brenham continues to exhibit improvement. New businesses ... new buildings erected ... old tenements repaired.[19]

Horses, mules, cotton and other Confederate property was still being rounded up from unrepentant rebels. Company A was doing Provost Marshal duty in Brenham, and the defeated enemy and the Rock Island boys were on less than friendly terms.

On February 11, 1866, Private Andrew Hunter of the 37th and a few messmates were drunk in town. Hunter got into a nasty row on the street, swearing at a cluster of civilians. After verbal characterizations by Hunter as damned sons of bitches, etc., the rebels walked off.

A short while later, after some card playing and bar hopping, Hunter and Privates John Armpriest and Andrew Parks, went into Terry's Saloon, where they saw Hunter's targets of earlier in the evening. After a lot of abuse and baiting, Hunter called out to one of them, "You dirty son of a bitch! Come out here and I will give you what you are wanting!"

The rebels went home and got their pistols. Hunter had armed himself with Sentry Art Kendall's musket by the time the rebels came back, and they faced each other in the street in front of Terry's. Hunter tried to arrest the "traitors," when out of the darkness, someone said, "Pull down on him." Hunter replied, "You will, will you, you Sons of Bitches," attempting to fire Kendall's musket. The rebels fired back and shot Hunter in the left breast. Hunter staggered down the street to Captain William Wilson's Provost Marshal Office, and died there ten minutes later.

In the early part of March 1866, Brenham townsman P.T. Early was tried for killing Hunter. Since no one could positively put him at the scene in the street, or anywhere near Terry's Saloon the night of the killing, Early was acquitted.[20] The real gunmen, apparently two unreconstructed butternuts named Campbell and Rainwater, had left town after the shooting and were never caught or tried.

Andrew Hunter was the last member of the 37th to die by a firearm, but that was not the end of Brenham's troubles with the Yankees. The 37th left in May 1866, and the next unit in, the 17th Infantry, took the measure of the rebels in the fall of 1866 by burning several buildings one night, just to let the locals know who won the war.

In the southwest spring of 1866, most of the 37$^{th}$ were sitting in these small towns around Houston marking time until muster-out.

Everyone's preoccupation was in getting out of the army, or thinking about getting out. Wells Morrill observed that, "I think Col. Kennicott has Plantation on the brain [Kennicott's idea for a post-war vocation], and the men getting out of the service, [make] discipline very slack."[21] What he meant was that discharged soldiers were staying on in town as civilians, associating with their friends who were not yet civilians.

Most of the men who were leaving that spring were from the consolidated regiments. There were a few medicals, and a few like the case of Edward Rose, a 35 year old blacksmith. Gallio Fairman requested his discharge in December 1865, stating that, "he is a ... drunkard and that he indulges in the excess to such an extent that he cannot be trusted in any capacity, and that he must be constantly kept in confinement or be expected to ... associate with negro women and other coarse characters, and that he is a disgrace to the service and to his company and that the company should be relieved of his presence."[22] Edward Rose had been with the regiment since Camp Webb in 1861, and was able to last until muster out in May 1866.

The boredom of those days comes clear in a diary kept by George E. Griffith, a 24 year old 1861 enlistee, who made note of the change in the weather as the most exciting daily occurrence:

### HOUSTON, FEBRUARY 1866

Friday, Feb. 2d: Draw beef and bread. Cloudy, looks like rain. No news on the docket.
Saturday, Feb.3d: Drew and issued 2 days rations. Soft bread today. Got the order transferring me from Co. E. 37$^{th}$ Ills. V.V. Inftry duty to Commy. Sergt. 37$^{th}$ Ills ... going to the dance tonight.
Sunday Feb 4$^{th}$: All quiet. Went to a Dutch ball last night, had a big time. Sold my watch, everything on the square.
Monday 5$^{th}$: Raining all day. A very cold and wet Norther.

## THIRTY SEVENTH ILLINOIS

Tuesday 6th: ...Cold as the Devil.
Sunday 11th: Clear and cold today, nothing new. Here we are yet in Texas.
Monday 12th: Done nothing all day. I played billiards all evening. No news in particular. Got two letters, one from Lundy and from home.
Thursday, 15th: ...Norther still continues. Got some photographs taken this morning.
Saturday 17th: ...Raining like hell, cold as the Devil. Wood wet, stove won't draw worth a Damn. Smoking tobacco now gone, and we don't feel in very good humor.
[Sunday] 18th: Still raining, bad humor not gone yet. Quit raining about 4 PM...
Sunday 25th: Did not draw anything today. Took a long walk this morning and one this afternoon with Manzer.[23]

Orders for discharge came on April 28, 1866. The rendezvous point was Houston, and there, on May 15, the 37th was mustered out of Federal Service after fifty-eight months in the blue cloth coat. The end of army life was too much for one of the Michigan Company, who got drunk and was lost over the side of the transport enroute from Houston to Galveston. A few days later, the incoming Steamer WHITELAW spotted two bodies floating in Buffalo Bayou a few miles below Houston. The Adjutant of the 12th Illinois Cavalry sent the personal effects of John Seabury of Company D, a thirty-six year old Norwegian, back to Springfield. The body of another man was found, but as he was entirely naked, no papers by which he could be identified were found. Both bodies were buried on Dr. Ball's Plantation about two miles from Houston.[24]

At Galveston, the regiment took the Steamer ST. MARY to New Orleans and from there up the Mississippi. Enroute, they stopped at Cairo and held a party at the premises of one John Clancy, who later put in a claim for "items forcibly taken by members of the 37th Ill. Infantry," including two and a half gallons of whiskey, some brandy and ale, glasses, and bitters. A witness to the incident described the visit as, "an outrage committed on the public premises of John Clan-

## THE FINAL PAY CALL

cy." Judd Huntley settled the claim by sending $31 from Camp Butler, "without being able to identify the guilty parties," although Captain John Moran was there and knew exactly who else was in attendance. The men needed to seek involuntary credit for the party because they had not been paid in Texas.[25]

The final payday came on May 31, 1866 at Springfield for the 187 veterans of the 37th. From Springfield, the men drifted off to their civilian pursuits. The central experience of their lives and the life of the nation was behind them.

## 30. The Haymarket Bombing

The regiment had its first reunion at the Palmer House in Chicago on March 6, 1885, the 23$^{rd}$ anniversary of Pea Ridge.

Many of the men had died or drifted away and were absent. But the principals, the majors and colonels, the 5-year men, the Chicago natives, the successful soldiers, were there. Speeches that night included Julius White on "The Fremont Rifles, an Instance of the Self Organizing Power of a Free People," Wells Blodgett on "The Companionship of the Soldier," Eugene Payne on "Our Frontier Service," Henry Curtis on "The Staff, a Good Thing to Lean on," John Reticker on "Rations and Orations," Ed Blodgett on "Twenty Four Years," Charlie Tebbetts on "An Army, Like a Serpent, Moves on its Belly," Francis Jewell and Ransom Kennicott on "Boys of the 37$^{th}$," and Charles Black on "The Presentation of the Colors in 1861."[1]

All the principal players, string-pullers, and top ranks from the past were there that night except Barnes and Frisbie, and Frisbie was not invited or carried on the membership rolls.

Most all had metamorphosed physically and spiritually, and no one of the regiment in attendance that night had changed any more than Will Black. The conversion from his sinning and womanizing in Texas during the war, his terrible temper, his salvation and re-entry into the church, and the conduct of a conservative practice of law in Chicago could not foretell the course of either foolishness, or self-sacrifice, or both on which he would embark a year later in May, 1886.

After his term in the Danville Provost Marshal's Office in 1864-65, Willy joined the bar in Danville in 1866, and spent the next 20 years in a very successful civil law practice in Chicago. By 1886, the practice had grown to yield him a very comfortable income and allowed him to dabble in affairs of social conscience. He developed an honest and deep-seated concern for the downtrodden working man, for the "miserable man whose rags will scarcely shut out from his grinning flesh the splashings of the millionaire's barouche as it dashes by him filled with richly attired people ... the very horse kept in a comfort far surpassing anything he can hope for...."[2]

# THE HAYMARKET BOMBING

On May 4, 1886, the activities of local anarchists were to begin a chain of events that would bring Will Black low and provide the 20$^{th}$ century Communist nations with their common holiday, Mayday.

On that day, the office of the ARBEITER ZEITUNG, a Chicago anarchist newspaper, was a revolutionary armory. Boxes of dynamite were on the floor, the editor's desk was full of ready to use dynamite bombs, and on the compositor's stand was the typeset for a pamphlet that had been distributed earlier in the day calling for the arming of working men who were to rise in revolt. This entreaty ended, "If you are men ... then you will rise in your might, Hercules, and destroy the hideous monster that seeks to destroy you. To arms! We call you to arms!"[3]

This circular was printed a few feet away from the dynamite that had been used to make the bombs that crammed the desk of the Zeitung's editor, one August Spies.

In another nearby bomb factory, 21 year old anarchist Louis Lingg had spent the day in his rooming house building about forty bombs for use in the revolt. Another anarchist, and an out-and-out militarist, Louis Engel, ran another bomb factory in his house nearby.

The worker revolt was to occur in accordance with a standing plan of battle threatened for months in the ARBITER ZEITUNG and in the ALARM, a like-minded anarchist-revolutionary Chicago newspaper. The ALARM, published by Albert Parsons, had in the past counseled specifically in its columns on June 27, 1885: "In filling bombs, use a little wooden stick, and never be careless. Keep the stuff pure! Beware of sand.... It is necessary that the revolutionist should experiment for himself: especially should he practice the knack of throwing bombs. For further information, contact AS, The Alarm, 107 Fifth Ave., Chicago," and "one pound of dynamite is better than a bushel of ballots."[4]

In a similar vein, the ARBITER ZEITUNG, as late as May 1, had advised its readers, "Clean your guns, complete your ammunition. The hired murderers of the capitalists, the police and the militia, are ready to murder. No workingman should leave his house in these days empty-handed."[5]

## THIRTY SEVENTH ILLINOIS

Both papers frequently published the platform of the International Workingman's Association that called for unequivocal and flat out, "destruction of the existing class domination by all means."[6]

"All means" included the tactical urban warfare planning that went on in a meeting held on May 3 at a hall on West Lake Street in Chicago. The meeting was of the "armed" sections of the International, who met periodically for drilling and training in the manufacture of explosives and the use of weapons. These meetings were always called by a code printed in the ARBITER ZEITUNG Letter Box section, which read, "Y. Come [weekday] night." The code duly appeared in the papers, and about fifty men showed up to the meeting on May 3.

Among other things, plans for the coming revolt were discussed. The plan was that when the signal was given, the armed section would attack Chicago police stations with bombs, to prevent reinforcements being sent to the main point of revolt conducted by the massed rank and file. As tactical support, the ARBITER ZEITUNG had published so-called "Charts of Destruction," mapping defensible strong points in the city, and providing diagrams of the city's sewer system and tunnels.

The signal for these bombers to implement their plans against the police was to be given in another code in the ARBITER ZEITUNG. The code word "Ruhe" would appear in the Letter Box column as the signal.

On May 4, the word "Ruhe" appeared in the appointed place, and that night, a bomb was thrown at the police in Desplaines St. near Crane's Alley. Officer Mathias Degan was killed and sixty were wounded.[7]

The editors of the ARBITER ZEITUNG and the ALARM were arrested, as well as Lingg and Engels, the bombmakers, and others. In all, eight men were indicted and tried for Officer Degan's murder. It wasn't surprising that no skilled, reliable, well established attorney could be found to represent the accused. The McCormick's, the Pullman's, and the Marshall Field's, along with the capitalist and newspaper establishment of Chicago arrayed all its power and influence behind the rapid prosecution and execution of the defendants.

## THE HAYMARKET BOMBING

The anarchist defense committee went to Will Black for help. Black trekked all over Chicago trying to enlist the help of an experienced criminal lawyer and found none. Black then decided to lead the defense himself. The decision ruined him. His clients would not sustain him after he voluntarily took the side of those whose avowed purpose was to attack and destroy those same clients. What honest citizen would defend men arrested amid bombs and dynamite stockpiled to accomplish their revolution, and who had conspired to overthrow the government, all these facts undisputed.[8]

Will Black had no skills at criminal law, but it made little difference as the outcome of the trial was not in doubt. The jury was stacked, the judge was prejudiced, the press and the population wanted revenge, and the defendants were bombmakers and violent revolutionaries.

The identity of the actual bomb thrower was never known, and so no direct connection could be or ever was made between the bombing and the eight anarchist defendants who were ultimately convicted. Perhaps the bomb that was thrown at the police was one of the many made by Louis Lingg or Louis Engel, and maybe it wasn't.

Willy's appearance at this point in his life, 25 years after going to Missouri as an 18 year old infantry captain with the 37$^{th}$, was by all reports imposing. He was tall and thin, had a full head of iron gray hair and full beard, and constantly wore a wide brimmed black military slouch hat. The hat was a bit of an affectation, as was his maintenance of military rank, preferring to be called Captain Black over Mr. Black or Counsellor Black.[9] He had honed his skills at oratory and impressed in public and private. One observer noted, "The Captain is an orator in private conversation as he is in public effort – not because he is fond of producing effect by the art of the elocutionist, and the rhetoritician, but because he cannot talk in any other manner. He is an orator whether he wishes to be or not."[10]

It is a fact of life and history that innocent and guilty alike will exercise every protection afforded them under the constitution and by law when put in jeopardy by judicial trial. These invocations are infuriating when the crime alleged is the overthrow of the very system that affords the protection sought by the accused petitioners. This was the case with Will Black's clients. The widespread public perception of guilt made the outrage more pronounced.

Beyond this impediment to successful public relations, Willy's wife, ex-Houston social belle Hortensia MacGreal, did him no service by maintaining and supporting an open friendship with the Mulatto wife of defendant Albert Parsons, the editor of the ALARM, including keeping the defense table in the courtroom supplied with fresh flowers.[11] She wrote a teary letter to the CHICAGO NEWS saying in part that, "When I learned the facts, I became assured in my own mind that the wrong men had been arrested.... During all that trial a soul crucifixion was upon me...."[12]

The trial began in June 1886. The inevitable guilty verdicts were given in July, and sentences in October. Seven of eight defendants were sentenced to hang.

Appeals dragged on until November 1887, when four of the eight were hanged in the Cook County Jail. The pressure to pardon the anarchists had been fierce. Will Black, Elijah Haines, Samuel Gompers and many others had gone to Springfield the day before the execution to plead with the governor. Haines, who had told Eugene Payne in 1860 that, "there is no principle in the world,"[13] apparently had found some. More than objecting to the verdict against the eight defendants, Haines came to speak against capital punishment than argue the merits of the case.

Elsewhere, William Dean Howells and Robert Ingersoll spoke and wrote against the executions. Oscar Wilde circulated petitions and George Bernard Shaw spoke at rallies in England. Public meetings were banned in Germany, and the French Government formally protested the executions to Governor Oglesby of Illinois.[14]

Four executions took place on November 11, 1887. Louis Lingg slipped the noose that day by exploding a dynamite cap in his mouth, blowing his face off. He lived almost six hours after the explosion and died that afternoon.[15]

An observer described the hanging of four of the bomb builders on the 11th:

# THE HAYMARKET BOMBING

"The drop fell.... The light form of Parsons seemed to bound upward as four feet of the drop was accomplished and the end of the rope was reached.... The body of Parsons first settled into almost perfect quiet, and all eyes were directed to that of Spies, which was writhing horribly. The shoulders twisted, the chest heaved, and the legs drew up and straightened out again and again. The man appeared to be strangling to death. The convulsions lasted for a long time, and when they finally became less marked, the body of Fischer began moving also...."[16]

Will Black was particularly sensitive to Parsons' writhing on the gibbet at the end of the white rope. Parsons was clad in a black cutaway coat, blue flannel shirt and slippers. When his cap was removed, "Parsons' face was the most distorted and dreadful of all. The mouth was partly open, and the smoky face was pouched and drawn. A sneer was on his lips."[17]

The horror of the execution was that the hanging did not snap the necks of the four men. The violent, extended death struggles were because the ropes of all four nooses slipped above the tracheas, causing them all to strangle to death while their necks stretched.[18] The rope knots were positioned behind the head instead of to the side guaranteeing slow strangulation rather than a quick broken neck, which may have been deliberate.

Albert Parsons was Will Black's personal tragedy. Parsons had gotten away to Wisconsin after the bombing incident, out of danger. He had grown a beard, and the beard, head, and moustache had grown in white. He was perfectly disguised and unrecognizable. Will Black thought a dramatic courtroom surrender by Parsons would turn public sentiment, and brought Parsons out of hiding so that he could be surrendered in court session which Black would augment with a dramatic speech.

The plan was a failure. When Parsons walked into court, the prosecution pointed him out, and the judge told him to be seated with the other defendants. Will Black's plan was aborted, and so Parsons ended his life slowly strangling to death with his fellow conspirators, trying to breathe through a broken windpipe.[19]

THIRTY SEVENTH ILLINOIS

Five of the eight defendants died on execution day. The other three were pardoned in June 1893 by new Illinois Governor John Peter Altgeld, partly at the insistence of a young associate in his law firm, Clarence Darrow.

The incident put Willy in the history books. He continued to practice law, ultimately in partnership with brother Charlie up to 1915, and became somewhat of a hero in socialist-anarchist circles.

## Epilog

Will Black and the men of the 37th lived out their lives in the post-war years as comrades of hundreds of thousands of other war veterans. Will Black had left the army at the end of his three year enlistment in September 1864, and returned to Danville, Illinois where he worked for his stepfather, William Fithian, who was at the time United States Provost Marshal for the 7th District of Illinois. After the war, he went to law school, joined the bar, and established a lucrative civil law practice in Chicago. As the 19th century wore on, he gradually espoused radical causes, and ultimately ruined his legal practice by assuming the defense of the Haymarket anarchists in 1886. He eventually joined brother Charles and practiced law into the early 20th century, and died in 1916 at age 73.

As for brother Charles, he had left the regiment in June 1865 and left the army in September 1865. He returned to Chicago, studied law, and joined the bar. He became a Congressman, Commissioner of Pensions, United States Attorney, President of the United States Civil Service Commission, and 37th National Commander of the Grand Army of the Republic in 1904. At the Democratic Party convention in 1888, he was nominated as vice presidential candidate to run on a ticket with Grover Cleveland. He was practicing law with brother Will when he dropped dead in a hotel room in Chicago on August 17, 1915, age 76.

Colonel Myron Barnes had been dismissed from the army in November 1862. He returned to Rock Island, Illinois to edit the ROCK ISLAND UNION. In 1864, the War Department permitted him to again command troops, and he helped raise the 140th Illinois, but lost his bid to be its Colonel.

If the Portrait and Biographical Record of Knox County is to be believed, Barnes edited and was a journalist for newspapers in Iowa (The Dubuque Daily Times), Illinois (The Chicago News), and New York after the war, and finally settled in Galesburg, Illinois in 1872 where he edited the Galesburg Press. The source also stated that Barnes was a General, that he had a lifelong active devotion to Temperance work, and the he was forced to retire in 1863 as a result of severe war wounds. He died in 1886.

Henry Frisbie left the regiment in October 1863 to command the 92d United States Colored Troops. He left the army in December 1865 after sustaining a court martial and a Board of Inquiry, and ultimately settled in New Orleans. He died in New Orleans of heat prostration on August 4, 1896, age 66.

Captain John Laimbeer left the army in January 1863 after having spent most of the time with the 37$^{th}$ in arrest. He gave as reasons in his request for discharge, "tyrannical abuse of power and disrespect of law ... by my superior officers.... I have been held in arrest for near ten months. I have been deprived of my pay [and] my family turned out of doors because of inability to support them...."

After the war, Laimbeer took his wife and four children to England where he abandoned them to go to New Zealand. He died there in broken health in the 1880's.

General Julius White left the regiment in June 1862 and went to Virginia. By 1863, he was a Brigadier of Cavalry in the XXIII Corps. He then went back to Springfield, Illinois for six months until June 1864, when he returned to active duty for three months service with the IX Corps in Virginia. He was General Ambrose Burnside's Chief of Staff at the Battle of the Crater, and resigned the army in November 1864.

He returned to Chicago and Evanston, Illinois, and resumed his real estate and insurance business until May 1873 when he went to Buenos Aires as Minister-Resident to the Argentine Republic. In January 1874, when his oldest son died, White returned to Illinois to look after his real estate interests, in the interim having negotiated a treaty with Paraguay. He spent the years after 1874 subdividing South Evanston, and died of heart disease at this home on Judson Avenue in Evanston on May 12, 1890, age 74.

Lieutenant David Ash was discharged in March 1865 after several months of hospitalization, and died at home two months later, age 26.

Major Henry Curtis left the regiment in June 1862 and went to Virginia on Julius White's staff, and then with the Armies of the

# EPILOG

Cumberland and Ohio, and was at the Battle of Campbell's Station and the Siege of Knoxville. He also served on the staff of General James Schofield. After the war he returned to Rock Island, Illinois and practiced law with his brother-in-law. He died in Marblehead, Massachusetts on September 12, 1905, age 72.

Lt. Colonel Eugene B. Payne left the regiment and the army in September 1864 at the end of his three year enlistment, and practiced law in Waukegan and Chicago, specializing in pension and bounty claims. He was an Illinois State Representative in the late 1860's and Postmaster in South Evanston in the 1870's, moving to the United States Pension Bureau in 1887. Payne lived in Cleveland, Ohio for ten years and then after a year in the west moved to Washington, D.C., where he died April 6, 1910, age 75.

Lieutenant Lorenzo B. Morey left the regiment in 1862 and was assigned to Inspector General duty for the last two years of the war. He left the army in June 1865, and went back home to Preemption and Aledo, Illinois and farmed. He died February 20, 1916, age 78.

Lieutenant Frederick J. Abbey left the regiment on a medical discharge in February 1863 with chronic throat and lung infection. He resumed his trade of manufacturing guns with a partner, Christian Oleson, in Chicago. He suffered for fifteen years, "from pain and uneasiness in lungs, weakness of will, shortness of breath, and a cough." One of his treatments at this time consisted of, "the application of needles to puncture the skin, afterwards applying some irritating substance to his chest...." After a long illness, Abbey died on September 22, 1878, age 41.

Colonel Wells H. Blodgett left the regiment in 1862 and thereafter received an appointment as Judge Advocate General of the Army of the Frontier, and then was commissioned Lieutenant Colonel of the 48th Missouri Infantry in August 1864, later promoted to Colonel. After the war, he practiced law in Warrensburg, Missouri and was a State Senator. He became a railroad attorney in 1873 for the Wabash Railway System, and lived into the 20th century.

Major Edward A. Blodgett left the 37th in August 1862 to become Adjutant of the 74th Illinois, and then Adjutant of the 96th Illinois. He was at Chickamauga, Lookout Mountain, and Franklin and Nashville. He settled in Warrensburg, Missouri and was a traveling salesman for ten years, and then was purchasing agent and real estate agent for the Chicago Street Railway Company. He was the prime mover behind the GAR Memorial Hall in the old Chicago Public Library building. He died of heart disease at his home at 2626 Lake View Drive in Chicago on October 27, 1910, age 75.

Chaplain Edward Anderson left the regiment in April 1862 and thereafter was commissioned Colonel of the $12^{th}$ Indiana Cavalry in March 1864 where he served out the balance of the war. In 1865 he was Court Martialed and acquitted of the murder of a prisoner of war and accused of many more murders of guerilla fighters in Alabama. After the war, he resumed his pre-war vocation as protestant minister serving several congregations and was at one time Chaplain-in-Chief of the Grand Army of the Republic. In 1896 he published "Camp Fire Stories," largely based on his wartime experiences. Some of the events that occurred in Missouri with the $37^{th}$ are included as lightly veiled fiction. He died in Quincy, Massachusetts in 1916.

# Appendix 1 – Notes from the War Years

## INTRODUCTION

This section is comprised of excerpts from the writings of members or close observers of the 37th Illinois Regiment. They are included for their narrative value, or their poetic value, or their humor. These vignettes and other ramblings would not be improved by paraphrasing, and, other than a few editorial deletions, appear here verbatim.

Here is the relation of the Notes to the text:

| NOTE YEAR | RELATING TO CHAPTERS |
|---|---|
| 1861 | 1-7 |
| 1862 | 8-16 |
| 1863 | 17-22 |
| 1864 | 23-28 |
| 1865-6 | 29 |

THIRTY SEVENTH ILLINOIS

# 1861 NOTES

# RELATING TO CHAPTERS 1-7

# NOTES FROM THE WAR YEARS

## CHARLES BLACK - ON YOUTH AND AGE

(Summer 1861) I was myself a young man of twenty-two years; my brother, who served with me, was about eighteen. The company in which I enlisted in the Eleventh Indiana regiment, for the three months' service, consisted, among others, of thirty-three college boys from all the classes below senior, who had been, in the main, members of the College Cadets. The company I afterwards enlisted for, the Thirty-seventh Illinois regiment, excluding perhaps eight or ten of its numbers, would hardly have averaged nineteen years; and the regiment itself, recruited in various parts of the State, in July, August, and September of 1861, would scarcely have raised that average to twenty-two years. (Article, by Charles Black, Illinois MOLLUS, Chicago, Illinois, 1892.)

## DAVID ASH - ON THE DEATH OF CHARLES REED

(October 1861) ...This is a lonely time in camp on account of the death of our dear young soldier: I will tell you about his sickness and death.

The day we left camp about 2 miles from here he was unwell and was not able to carry his knapsack but got better and Sunday morning he appeared to be quite well and wrote a letter home and said he was well.... [He] became unwell again Tuesday evening.... I went up and brought Hum down to the tent to see him and George Kirby and another sick man. He looked at them and when he went out I asked what he thought of Reed. He said there was no troubles about him....

Some of the boys come to our tent just about dusk and told me Charley [Reed] was in a good deal of pain. I went down and found him in a good deal of misery. Two of the boys went to the upper part of the camp to see the Doctor. He would not come down, but he sent him some ginger and laudanum.... I gave it to him and he got easier. I thought he was going to get along fine. He got sleepy right away. He was resting in my arm then and Tom made a pillow for him, and says Charlie, let me lay down. I laid him down and covered him over and told the boys as I was not very well myself that I would go to my tent for their tent was full and if they wanted to send for me....

I went to my tent and laid down and in a few minutes the taps were beaten and all lights in the tents were ordered out by Major Black. Our boys told him there was a sick man in that tent. He told them the lights must be put out so they blowed the candle out and as Charley made no fuss at all they laid down and fell asleep.

The Doctor came round about 10 o'clock and went into the tent and found him dying. He woke the boys right away and they sent for me, and [I] went down and found 4 or 5 men by that time rubbing him. I never saw such a sight in my life. He was entirely unconscious and remained so until 2 o'clock and died.

I could not say it made me sick to be in the tent. The last word he said was, 'Lay me down, I am sleepy.' when I was there the first time.... (David Ash, October 1861, DASH.)

### DAVID ASH - ON FORAGING

(October 1861) Our regiment has 96 mules and nearly all of them have never been broken or handled at all. They get them into a small lot and caught them with lasseaus and 6 men or as many as was necessary to hold them caught the rope and tied them to the fence or something, and harnessed them and put 4 to 6 green ones on a wagon all together. I never saw such a time teaming in all my life.

Some would run off, others kick themselves out of the harness. Some would lay down and so went the day muling.

Now I am going to tell you how Uncle Sam got those mules. You know he is a wealthy old fellow and has a great many men employed. He sends a company of men out through the country and tells them to bring a few teams to camp. They go out and when they come across any kind of a team, mule, horse, or anything that suits them, they take whether the owner is willing or not. One company went out and brought in 30 horses and mules. As it happens, our company has not been sent out yet, and I don't want to go on an errand of that kind. (David Ash, October 1861, DASH.)

## CHARLES BLACK – ON FORAGING

(October 1861) The boys were committing depredations on the premesis of a gentleman by the camp and news thereof coming to me, I took a guard consisting of Sergt. Bandy and six men to his place. He proved a gentleman 'possessed of 7 contrabands,' more or less, a doughty ... man, and having a beautiful place, likewise several beautiful daughters, the eldest some 15 years (I mean 15 summers) growth. I made known my errand to him, first leading him to one side, telling him I had business with him. He, seeing the file of armed men behind, thought his day had come.

He was greatly releaved [sic] when he knew I came as a protector not as a foe. The sergeant and guard soon cleared the place of marauders [and] unloaded some of their ill gotten gains right on his back porch, in full sight of the delighted little ladies (who had seen their fathers sustenance destroyed by wholesale), and of the contraband aunties who raised a great yah yah whenever a particularly greedy thief would walk up, led by the stern sergeant, and empty his haversack and then his pockets and then begin to lose his rotundity as the big apples and great peaches were hauled out from his shirt. Some carried at least a peck of grapes away before we reached the spot.

The gentleman ... came from Virginia close to Charlestown, Martinsburg, and the places where we made our spring jaunt. He was good Union and I felt like meeting an old friend. (Charles Black, Letter to his Mother, October 2, 1861, JCBF.)

## WILL BLACK - ON BOONVILLE

(October 1861) Boonville is a very pretty place, lapped and almost hidden among the hills, which all along skirt the Missouri. Buildings mostly are good and it has a beautiful cemetery with the prettiest monument in it I ever saw; a statue of twin sisters in marble, some 4 feet high.... The chaplain ... and I were riding out last evening when we came on this place.... (Will Black to his Mother, October 21, 1861, JCBF.)

## CHARLES BLACK - ON BOONVILLE

(October 1861) I am enchanted with this place.... Again, it has the nameless charms that belong to all Rip Van Winkle towns, which seems to have grown to full stature in bustling times, then sink to sleep and unbeknown to themselves grow gray and old in sleeping, while the thunders of commerce making her 'ten strikes' and the hollow gusty laugh of a busy train of the living have failed to arouse them.

There are a few busy homes, many for the size of the place, and the clangor of war has not wholly hushed the sweet voice of music as the notes of a piano testified to me in passing one of the homes a day ago. Roses, catalpas, oaks, and flowing shrubs of every variety ... beautiful velvet carpets, the quiet air of matron-like dignity, and the presence of shiny-face contrabands, speak the story of a delightful home within.

Main Street is a beautiful arcade after leaving the business part of the town, and the brows of the distant hills have each a white house gleaming through the trees like a Tuscan villa....

I consider the view from ... our camp scarce inferior to that from Maryland Heights at Harper's Ferry although more circumscribed.... (Charles Black to his family, October 2, 1861, JCBF.)

### HENRY CURTIS - ON COMMAND

(Fall 1861) [Oct 10] Our Capt. [John Jordan] is a vain fool and Hawes and myself curse him alternately. He is one of the flustered kind and if he don't get us into some scrape, if we ever smell powder, it'll be a special providence. If he had the good sense to keep his foolishness to himself, it would be a great relief, but he is everlastingly talking about himself. He is just good enough to keep where he is, in my way and never get up. I don't do more than I can help now as he always upsets whatever I do, with some half baked plan of his own... If the Capt had a little more civilized manner of eating it would go along pretty good, but he wanted to eat with the boys, etc.; and have nothing else (being most particularly damned mean) and we had to go ahead without him, when he very naturally took to our fixings....

[Nov 17] Jordan has given out. Had a sort of paralytic stroke the second and says he shall resign.... So if luck holds shall have the company. It suits the boys first rate now. J. having pretty well played out.... J. cannot be trusted out of sight and don't know himself what he will do half the time....

[Dec 1] Jordan isn't here yet (Sunday). Hope he will change his mind and stay at home. He is (or was) crazy and upsets our mess completely....

[Dec 6] Capt. J is back same as ever. They write from home he is crazy and that from physicians. Have been of same opinion some time. He brought two boxes of things for sick from ladies of Rock Island etc. which are going to Devil pretty fast.

[Dec 27] Capt. Jordan has resigned and it has been accepted. Shall be Capt. now in all probability. Hope he will get off soon. His time is out Dec 31 and if no show of pay, he says shall go at once. (Letters, HCJR.)

## WILL BLACK - ON CAMP LIFE

Real winter winds are whistling round us, the frozen ground rings as we tread on it, and fitful snowflakes, the first of the season with us, come dancing through the air occasionally, whispering a tale very winter-like. And amid all this I am without a stove. (Letter to his Mother, November 24, 1861, JCBF.)

# NOTES FROM THE WAR YEARS

(12-1-61)  Last night the sun lay down in a couch of gorgeous rose and gold tinted clouds, and this morning the clouds, they are ashen and sober. (Letter to his Mother, December 2, 1861, JCBF.)

(1-13-62)  ... staying in my out tent [are] Joe Delay & his prospective step-son-in-law, my cook, Corporal Allison. They have invited me to board with them for a time & I guess I will comply.  There were turkeys, chickens, pies, cakes, breads, molasses, etc.; but my enjoyment of these [will be] curtailed, as I am just now enjoying the chills every other day, and so far light, but which are still weakening me somewhat. (Letter to his Mother, January 18, 1862, JCBF.)

## WILL BLACK - AT THE LAMINE

(December 1861)  The Lieuts. and I pitched our tent ... and got everything in apple pie order, our table up, our cot fixed, our stove in full blast.... This morning, orders were given to cut down certain trees (dead) around the camp, and among them, one behind and a little to one side of my tent. The tree was about 3 ½ feet through, and 90 or 100 feet high, and we did not like to way it stood as they chopped. Before it fell, we vacated our tent.... Fair and true a branch 20 inches or two feet through of the mighty monster struck our unfortunate habitation, and in a moment "it was not." Every pole in the tent was crushed into 3 or 4 pieces & in the strong, fine canvas there some half dozen or so unsightly holes.... My cot, our camp stools, were crushed and the wood of the handle of my fine revolver was split off. 'Tis a wonder that all our swords & revolvers, which hung immediately under the limb, were not splintered....

We stood among the ruins, gazing mournfully on, when the sharp wicked report of one of our rifles, followed by the agonizing shrieks, short & few, of a wounded man, called on us for action.  Springing forward, we found Sgt. [George W.] Barker had shot himself through the arm.  The wound was a horrible one, the ball having passed through the fleshy part of the under fore arm grazing ... the radius.  The flesh was not parted but was torn out, and as the arm swelled, a purple angry looking line, sunk in to fill up the vacuum, showed where the ball had gone.  Immediately on reaching him, and baring his arm, I tied a silk handkerchief around his arm below the wound to stop the bleeding....  He is doing very well now and we are in a new tent.  (Letter to his Mother, December 8, 1861, JCBF.)

## CHARLES BLACK - AT OTTERVILLE, MISSOURI

(Fall 1861)  I am happy as a young coon, healthy as a paw-sucking bear, and if the 'secesh' will let me live I promise to improve...

I have a tent 8 ft. square....  In this are two cots for me and my orderly....  I bought at Boonville an elegant little sheet-iron stove weighing some five or six pounds, which glows with a warm fire.  So blow, ye prairie winds, and shake my tent till it flutters and creaks.  I mind you not a straw.

My orderly is a dear nice little fellow, whom I picked up in Chicago, named Theodore Meeker, 17 years old, the son of wealthy and respectable parents, and who cares for me as a child for a father.  I reciprocate as a father for a child, loving and cherishing this beautiful boy.  On the saddle blanket in front of the fire, like Don Ponto, a regimental pet, the prettiest dog I ever saw, nearly, a pointer and graceful as a kitten.  The boys of Co. K. got him between Mattoon and St. Louis and gave him to me.

The aforesaid saddle blanket belongs conjointly to Charlie and Ben. Charlie is the big bay, my battle horse. With him you are acquainted, so I will introduce Mr. Ben. He is a prided iron grey, some fifteen and one half hands high, six years old. When he is simply haltered, he will prick up his ears and snicker at my approach and the sound of my voice, and give his beautiful head to my caresses. Such little ears, such wide nostrils, such a soft loving eye, such a cowling main and long wavy tail, almost sweeping the ground.

But let me mount my Thunderbolt! How he carricols and prances, sometimes standing on three feet, while he paws earth and air with another. His eyes flash, his neck curves high and arching, those little ears play back and forth. His coat shines like steel and the long tail sweeps through the air. Let me shake the reins, he is off like light[ning], and can turn in twice his own length. I ride him hard all day and at night he seems as fresh as when I mounted. He is the finest horse I ever mounted, and rides like a cradle.... He is broadbreasted, slight limbed, and positively the handsomest coat of hair; soft, silky, clean.... When I dismount him and the groom leads him off, every muscle seems lifted into action. He moves like a bird, and is nearer my idea of an Arabian or a picture horse than ever I have seen.

What do I lack to be happy? Shelter, boy, horse, groom, dog, a good supper, warm bread, honey, and coffee gone its way, and one of those cigars in my mouth!

... the desk at which I write. When on the march it is a strong pine box (made originally for rifles), secured by hinges and a padlock.... When we halt, I turn it on its side, put it on a couple of camp stools, swing the lid open, and prop it, put on a blanket for 'Kiver,' and lo! an elegant writing desk, while within is bookcase, pantry and clothes chest. Bookcase? Why, yes...! While at Boonville I received part of my pay and bought a few. Motley's Dutch Republic, Partou's Jackson ... and Burr, Plutarch, and one novel by Mrs. Southworth.  Will has Shakespeare and Doc [Bandy] has Poe.  I never was so hungry for mental foods before I got these.  (Letter to his Mother, October 22, 1861, JCBF.)

# 1862 NOTES

# RELATING TO CHAPTERS 8-16

# THIRTY SEVENTH ILLINOIS

## CHARLES BLACK – ON COMMAND AT OTTERVILLE

(Winter 1862) The command of the Brigade having devolved upon Col. White & Col. Barnes being in command at Boonville leaves me in command of the 37$^{th}$. It is a heavy task for one to assume, care and supervision of the wants & necessities of a thousand men. To restrain them within the bounds of decorum & order, to bend their fancies, feelings, passions, tastes to the rigid lines of military discipline. But although difficult, it is a task eagerly sought for by the ambitious, and the accomplishment of which is a proud triumph.

I have abundance of "friends" such as all men have while the graces of office or power abide with them, but of the true, hearty, earnest sort I have not so many as to wish to forfeit one through neglect or inattention.

The men think it hard, very hard, that they are not allowed to go ad libertum. And so would I if there were not many stern necessities that compel me to pursue the rigid courses. A man needs a face of silver & a heart of steel to conduct properly the affairs of a regiment, where a thousand diverse tastes & sentiments must be made to conform to a standard which was made by men who had lost all of human weaknesses & were, in the fullest sense, soldiers.

My notions with regard to soldiers, ... have been vastly changed. Now I recognize in the true soldiers not the hero of a review or a pageant nor yet only a conqueror; it is one who has heart & passion so under his control he may be ready at any time to forget his own being and simply act the will of others, or if he lives his own life, it is in a separate sphere and when he moves it is in the grooves cut by a higher power....

Mr. Brown said when he was here that I looked somehow different, older.... I feel the fact is working its way into notice on my face, brows, & life. The habit of command is dangerous, but when rightly used, how beautiful!

Well, it is hard for a 'Merican' citizen after reasoning the matter out to his own satisfaction to have discipline. Tell him to shut up it's none of his funeral, and to feel conscious that his destiny is committed irrevocably to others, yet it is so. The Soldier sinks the Citizen, and even now Major Black commands Citizen Black to cease this pleasant gossip for another time. I submit hoping at some future day to regain a lost liberty, which will allow all my neighbors to slap me on the back and say, "how are you old hoss," instead of approaching with the dread formality and etiquette of service, to enquire with lifted hands in the state of the Major's health. (Letter to family, January 5, 11, and 22, 1862, JCBF.)

## CHARLES BLACK – ON CAMP LIFE

(January 1862) My camp is about as handsome as any in the cantonment. It is regularly laid out in main & secondary streets. The one in front of my quarters is called Boulevard le Main; the one in the rear [where] we hold Dress Parade, is handsomely graveled, and called Boulevard La Millie Wear.... The streets are all to be graveled as the mud is ankle deep....

... Miss Millie Wear. She is most graceful ... putting to shame all the splendors of our fair-rings and riding matches. She is very intelligent, well educated, and quite aristocratic. She is quite a favorite for all these reasons among the soldiers. Col. White dubbed our big street as I have written ... to do her honor. (Letter to his Mother, January 18, 1862, JCBF.)

# THIRTY SEVENTH ILLINOIS

## EDWARD ANDERSON – ON SICKNESS AT OTTERVILLE

(January 1862) Letters from camp now are from very sober, sad scenes – sickness, miasma, hardship are the order of the day.... The ankle deep mud outside, oozing into the tent, tracked in by great army boots and shoes, and blended with the straw, with cold raw winds blowing through the flapping tent door, are no romantic affairs. Cold we get along well enough with, but the three inch snow, melting the next day, soaking mud that defies every thickness of sole-leather, and the malaria that stalks almost visibly through the camp, are the horrors of a winter campaign.

Our camp is near the Lamine Bridge, on the Lamine River, one and a quarter miles east of Otterville, and within a pistol shot of the Pacific Railroad....

Generally, the weather is of that sickening, sobbing kind that tells most fearfully on unacclimated soldiers. Our sick list is increasing....

Let me give you a history from real life in camp. A man is on guard, mud two inches deep, formed of a conglomeration of decayed vegetable matter and melting snow. Every third two hours in the twenty four, he paces back and forth in the deepening mud, and at 9 o'clock next morning, when relieved, he endeavors to dry his soaked shoes at the smoking fire in his 'Sibley.' By and by he feels the stretching, aching, horrible sensation of malarius, and by morning he is reported to the surgeon. By night he is in the hospital with well-defined typhoid, and as the wind surges in the forest, drives the smoke down the mud-flue of the hospital fireplace, flaps the folds and fly of the tent, he talks wildly of home, of a dear sister ... talks of the old church and minister and choir,

# NOTES FROM THE WAR YEARS

and by and by, tells of sweet scenes, delightful music, pleasant meals, and celestial companions!

Then the hands are thrown up and the poor boy is dead. We bury him in the lone forest grounds, and kind hearted comrades weep over his grave, as we leave him there, his body's resting place to be forgotten....

All do not die, for we have lost only sixteen men since we left Chicago, but oh! the sickness, the suffering, the lonely hours of pain in the cold, womanless camp. (Letter, January 4, 1862, published January 13, 1862, CTR.)

## DAVID ASH – ON FORAGING

(Winter 1862) Col. White is acting Brig. Genl. and ... Lt. Col. Barnes in command of our regt. He is a good old fellow. He told the boys to go it 2 or 3 times when they come to a secesh store or house. They cleaned out one store at Gravois Creek and one yesterday.

It was fun to see them wearing women's hooped skirts and all kinds of mischief. They went into a hardware store yesterday and took all the pots and kettles they wanted. They will come very handy to bake our bread. (Letter, February 4, 1862, DASH.)

## CHARLES BLACK – ON FORAGING

(January 1862) ... a long string of fence disappeared & the grunting of swine, cackling of geese & chickens became mournfully infrequent. While ... these sounds became less and less frequent, the shouts & laughter of the boys increased, and piles of feathers for which no one could account accumulated behind every stump, log, & and in every hollow. All this country is secesh to the core & I wish it was made so poor by the foraging of our armies as to fail in its support of crime. (Letter to his Mother, February 6, 1862, JCBF)

## EDWARD ANDERSON – ON CROSSING THE OSAGE

(February 1862) Washington crossing the Delaware is being re-enacted in real life before my window. The Osage River, heavy, somber, sluggish, is bearing in surly eddies huge masses of ice, which thump against each other, crush each other, and seem to grow angry in the cold. Yet the sun shines on them, glistening on their edges, laughing at their jostlings, wranglings, and seeming to wink at the General on one side, and the Major on the other side of the river as they look earnestly at the flat, deep scow, in which Quartermaster Peck battles with the quarreling ice flakes. In the boat is a four mule team, with the two extra rats who compose the inevitable 'six-mule' tied behind the wagon. Beside these, are a platoon of men, each armed with gun, knapsack, other accoutrements, and a bundle of hay for their bedding tonight on the snow. Four are pulling at the sweeps, one steering, and four in the bows fending off the masses of ice that stop and endanger the boat. Look at any picture of the scene which is alluded to at the dawn of my letter, and you have the view of the 37$^{th}$ Regiment Illinois Volunteers crossing the Osage at Linn Creek.

But I said I saw these from my window. ... On the bank of the Osage, and some forty rods below the mouth of the Niauga River, stands an ample, but rough looking log house.... It is Mr. Torbert's house, and Mr. T. is a partner of Col. McClurg of the Missouri (Union) Militia. But rough as the external of this house is, the internal economy is wondrous fine. I am sitting on a stuffed hair seat chair, and the Major is just at present sitting in an ample and most luxuriant arm chair, a splendid 'Woodward & Brown' Boston piano stands under a large mirror, and pictures and engraving are hung on the wall. Yet all are side by side with rough logs.... (Letter, February 3, 1862, published February 13, 1862, CTR.)

## EDWARD ANDERSON – ON THE MARCH OUT OF THE LAMINE BOTTOM

(February1862) We have marched from Otterville ... through roads that were perfectly fearful.... A forward movement at this season of the year involves an immense amount of both means, labor, and suffering. The mud, ankle deep to men, becomes hub-deep to the heavy army wagons, and the eight-yoke wagons ('prairie schooners') were almost really schooners, sailing along on a sea of mud....

Our pantaloons, when we drew them on at reveille, were stiff with ice, so also were shirts, coats, boots, everything.... We shivered till our animal heat thawed the ice, and wore wet clothes till they dried on us. This was with the mercury endeavoring to court acquaintance with zero. (Letter, February 3, 1862, published February 13, 1862, CTR.)

## CHARLES BLACK – ON THE MARCH FROM SPRINGFIELD

(February 1862) ... the bird had flown. [Confederate General] Price has run before us and again we occupied the town. The troops almost universally had sworn vengeance on the town and country if the fortunes of war should ever carry us this way again, and before night, a good number of houses had gone to feed the flames. It was a hard yet almost just return for this section.

Next morning began our chase southward after the flying Price. Several skirmishes have marked our way so far, but the fear fledged feet of the rebels have carried them very swiftly.... They have evidently fled in hot haste & terror; broken wagons & disabled horses have strewn the road. We have marched into their camps while the fires still burned & the uncut meat was lying all around. (Letter to home, February 19, 1862, JCBF.)

## HENRY CURTIS – ON HARDSHIPS

(Spring 1862) We are about 12 miles from the camp on Sugar Creek.... We have no stores & many of the men are no better than barefoot. Clothing all in rags too. I don't see how we can go on without shoes, etc.; but can hear of no likelihood of getting any. Our baggage is in Springfield now & I am very nearly out of the single suit I have....

Our tent was burned & we live in a heap in the other.... We might have got Price any day for a week, but for the kindness of somebody in command. We have no ammunition for our rifles except that in the cartridge boxes & nobody who can will try & get any. I'm sick of this service ... so long as we are here, we shall be kicked about as we have been....

Barnes tells me that his wife & three children board at Mrs. Drum's for $6 per week & are satisfied....

This is a tolerable country for a rough one, but back to Springfield is rough as a cats back.... (Letter, February 25, 1862, HCJR.)


## WILL BLACK – ON THE ENTRY INTO ARKANSAS

(March 1862) ... for all the country I have ever seen, for sterility and rockiness, this 'takes the rag off the bush,' as the saying is....

... The hills seems formed of rocks, splintered and riven fine, just as we see them prepared for macadamized roads, and digging through this outer covering ... we come to a burnt looking kind of earth; hard, stony, and dead.... Pole Hicks dryly remarked, "... The Devil must have wheeled his ashes here for the first year.'

... Boys are very ragged and almost shoeless, and also short on rations.... (Letter to his Mother, March 5, 1862, JCBF.)


## JOHN NOBLE – ON ALBERT PIKE AND THE INDIANS AT PEA RIDGE

(March 1862) General Pike ... [was] ... disliked by the Confederates and detested by the Union men; to be known in history as a son of New Hampshire – a poet who sang of flowers and the beauties of sunset skies, the joys of love and the hopes of the soul, and yet one who ... led a merciless, scalping, murdering, uncontrollable horde of half-time savages in the defense of slavery ... against that Union his own native state was then supporting, and against the flag of liberty.... His service was servile and corrupt, his flight was

## THIRTY SEVENTH ILLINOIS

abject, and his reward disgrace. (Noble, John, Pea Ridge, MOLLUS Papers, Missouri Commandery, 1883, p.232.)

### THE INDIANS AT PEA RIDGE

(March 1862) The Cherokee, Choctaw, Creek, and Seminole, of whom some 3000 were engaged in the battle under command of Col. Albert Pike, a Northern man, who deserved and doubtless will receive eternal infamy for his efforts to induce a band of savages to butcher brave men who had taken up arms to prevent the subversion of the Republic....

The Indians in many instances could not refrain from scalping their enemies, and it is said that as many as a hundred of our brave men were thus barbarously treated. They frequently scalped the dead they found on the field, and in 10 or 12 cases so served men who were merely wounded....

So scalping and robbing were, as of yore, their favorite pastimes. They plundered every wounded, dying and dead Unionist they could find, and very frequently murdered those they discovered so badly hurt as to be incapable of offering resistance....

The appearance of some of the besotted savages was fearful. They ... ran with long knives against large odds, and fell pierced by dozens of balls. With bloody hands and garments, with glittering eyes and horrid scowls, they raged about the field with terrible yells....

Friend and foe alike to them: they fired at the nearest mark and used their long knives indiscriminately upon all within their reach. For more than 12 hours they continued this warfare, killing and wounding more of the Missouri and

Arkansas troops, it is believed, than they did of ours. (Article, April 4, 1862, WWG.)

### EDWARD ANDERSON – ON PEA RIDGE

(March 1862) The mortality rate among the rebels was awful to behold. Men shot and mangled in every conceivable way.... A large share of the death seemed to have been caused by shell. To add to the horror, the woods took fire after the battle, and the dead rebels were burned and charred in the flames. (Letter from Edward Anderson, March 11, 1862, published March 19, 1862, CTR.)

### DAVID LATHROP – ON PEA RIDGE

(March 1862) The scene over this field of carnage beggars all description.... Here is a human body, with the mangled remnants of a head, which a cannon ball has torn to fragments. There lies another with both legs shot away. Here is one, the top of whose skull is gone, leaving the brain all exposed to the weather, and see! he is still alive. After 24 hours in this condition, he yet lives. Great is the tenacity of human life! Look yonder, there is one whose light of life has gone out.... Here comes two men with the same numbers on their caps that he has on his, and they are in search of him. How fortunate they are. They are his friends and were his messmates....

What is that fellow doing? That fellow in the dress of a Union soldier.... He is rifling the pockets of the dead.... The dead man was a rebel, and a locket of hair, very fine silky hair.... How mean this Union soldier is.... Why not bury it with him? (Lathrop, David, <u>History of the Fifty-Ninth Regiment</u>, published 1865, p.97.)


## NEWS ARTICLE ON PEA RIDGE

(March 1862) Tree after tree was shattered or perforated by shot and shell, and many were filled with grape and canister balls. One tree was pierced through and through by solid shot, its top slivered by a shell, and the base of its trunk scarred by 17 canister and rifle balls.... Two dead artillerymen were stretched on the earth, each killed by a grapeshot, and by their side was a third, gasping his last, with his side laid open by a fragment of the shell.... 15 wounded rebels lay in one group, and were piteously imploring each passerby for water and relief from their wounds. A few rods from them was another, whose arm had been torn off by a cannon-shot, leaving the severed member on the ground a few feet distant.... Behind a tree ... was a stretched corpse, with two thirds of its head blown away by the explosion of a shell....

The bursting of shells had set fire to the dry leaves on the ground, and the woods were burning in every direction.... Several were found in secluded spots, some of them still alive, but horribly burned and blackened by the conflagration.

The rebels ... removed the shoes from the dead and mortally wounded. Of all the corpses I saw I do not think one twentieth had been left with their shoes untouched. In some cases, pantaloons were taken and occasionally an overcoat or blouse. (Article, New York Herald, March 8, 1862.)

# NOTES FROM THE WAR YEARS

## WILLIAM BAXTER – ON THE CONFEDERATE RETREAT FROM PEA RIDGE

(March 1862) ... The Army was a confused mob ... save two regiments of cavalry ... the rest were a rabble-rout, not four or five abreast, but the whole road about fifty feet wide perfectly filled with men, every one seemingly animated by the same desire to get away.... Very few had guns, knapsacks, or blankets; everything calculated to impede their flight had been abandoned; many were hatless, and the few who had anything to carry were those fortunate enough to pick up a chicken, goose, or pig. If the latter, it was hastily divided so as not to be burdensome and the usual formalities of butchering and taking off the bristles were dispensed with.... Few of them had taken any food for 2 or 3 days.... For hours, the human tide swept by, a broken, drifting disorganized mass.... (Baxter, William, Pea Ridge and Prairie Grove, published 1864, reprinted Van Buren, 1957, pp.98-99.)

## GALLIO FAIRMAN – ON THE DEATH OF W.H. RING AT CASSVILLE

(April 1862) [Ring] found us in Arkansas. When he joined us, health was blooming upon his cheek, and he was rugged and robust as one could wish....

One morning, just as the company was falling in for drill, he came up to our tent and said, "Lieutenant, can I be excused from drill this morning?" I answered, "Ham, what is the matter?"

He said, "I have got the mumps." Said I, "Well, Ham, you had better go down to your tent and keep as quiet as possible...." He went to his tent and lay down. I sent the company to drill under the Sergeant, and then went to see him, and found him with his face slightly swollen, and also an ague chill. I sent him to the Dr. [Murphy] who gave him some medicine that broke the ague and left him quite well, except the swelling in the left cheek, which he called the mumps.

The next day, he said he felt very well, and was about the camp all day, and had not apparent sickness. The next day, we marched to [Cassville], but Ham rode on the wagon. When he arrived at camp, he said he did not feel much sick, and as we expected to march the next morning, I asked him if he had not better stay here at Cassville, in the Hospital, until he was better. He replied that he would not stay behind, but had rather keep with the company. Morning came, and with it came the news that we would not march this morning. Hamilton felt better during the forenoon.

We changed our camp to another place, about ¾ of a mile distant, and he walked one to the other after which he was about camp as usual not claiming to be sick, but that he only had the mumps.... Today his face was swollen still more and he looked curiously especially when he laughed. I saw the Dr. and spoke to him about the case, and he said Erysiplias was showing itself in his face that morning, but thought nothing alarming of it.

In the afternoon, Hamilton sent up and wanted to know if he could take one of our blankets which we immediately gave him. I went again to see him and found his cheek swollen still more. He said he felt a little sick at his stomach, and added that it was because he had just been smoking. He was then sitting by the fire joking with the boys.

After a little they fixed his bed and he lay down [and] went to sleep, slept quietly for a time, but after an hour or two the boys heard a rattling in his throat, on which they attempted to arouse him but could not. They went for the Dr. who came, but could do no better than the boys. He was apparently in a trance and could not be aroused. He breathed and his pulse was good. There was all the signs of life about him. The Erysipilas had struck to the brain.

Capt. Messer went immediately and got Dr. Maynard of the $59^{th}$ Illinois Regiment, who examined him and said his was one of those peculiar cases for which he could do nothing. Dr. Murphy also consulted with the Surgeon of the $6^{th}$ Iowa Cavalry Regiment, who examined him and said there was no help for him. During the time, E.P. Messer tried to relieve his brain by mesmerism, but could not.

We could do nothing for him but hope he might survive the trance and once more become sensitive, but we hoped in vain, for he continued perfectly insensible until half past four o'clock this morning, when he ceased to breathe and his pulse ceased their beating. Thus he expired without even knowing that he was sick or feeling the least pain.

… by his death we all have lost a pleasant and noble companion…. He will be buried tomorrow with all the honors we can give. (Unknown attribution.)

### CHARLES BLACK – AT CASSVILLE

(April 1862) At the time I am writing, this part of the world is quiet. No sounds save the watch dogs bark and an occasional sentry hail. But a good regiment fills the night with eyes to see, ears to hear, & hands to strike a coming foe. Subtle indeed would be the enemy that could reach this camp & not feel the fatal circle that surrounds it with sudden fire, quick lightning and a sudden death.

# THIRTY SEVENTH ILLINOIS

This quiet will reign supreme till the reveille fifes & drums usher in another day....

There is little here indeed to relieve monotony. No society save soldiers. No city or wide-awake institution of any kind. The scenery is tolerably good, high up among the Ozarks. Valleys, hills, woods, fields, brown, yellow, sear, black, green. That's our prophet for amusement.

The most singular feature in the surroundings is the sable cresting of the hills. The Black Jack oak grows along the entire top of a range of hills. At this season of the year they are bare of foliage. Every little twig, the branches and body are black; & the forest, high above you, shaking in the wind & moaning at each gust seems something terrible; the abode of enchanted spirits whose shadows fill their prison house with somber hues of wood. They struck me chill the first time I saw them.... (Letter to his Mother, April 17, 1862, JCBF.)

## SAMUEL LEMOINE – ON HIS MAIL THEFT AT CASSVILLE, MISSOURI

(May 1862) The 18th or 19th of April was the first time I had anything to do with the mail. I had charge of the mail most of the time. When I was not there Barlow and Wilson attended to the business....

I laid up ... letters on Sunday afternoon on the 18th of May on the shelf not having enough for a package. Among them was Capt. Frisbie's letter.... I told him that the man that brot it said it contained a dead man's effects. Says Barlow, "open it for it likely has the man's money and valuables in it." I refused to do it. Says he, "You have done such things before and you must open it – either tonight or tomorrow morning." Barlow then picked up another and said, "there, take those two and the first chance you get open and tell me what is in them."

Well, that night I was sober & would not open them but the next morning I was a little tipsy and opened them.... Says B ... "what was in them." This was after we got Wilson off on the scout that morning. He asked me if I was going to take the contents of Frisbie's letter. I said, "No, I am not going to steal dead men's effects." "Well," says Barlow, "if you are going to be so awful good about it, I will take out the pencil and give it to you." Finally, I did take the pencil when persuaded by Barlow...

On Monday night, May 19$^{th}$, Barlow came into the office and says, "What do you think about this fuss – they can't do anything against us – they have no evidence." I said to Charley Dwyer they will arrest me because I have had the handling of the mail. No, they won't, says he. I said the same to Barlow. Says he aloud, "No, they won't, Sam." Then he whispered to me and says, "You will be arrested, that is sure, but you must not breathe a word against me or you will be a dead man – remember." Then again says Barlow in a whisper, "I have got you fast, I think you will clear me from suspicion. I don't want anything more to do with you."

At one time Barlow showed me a three dollar gold piece after which he had that he had taken it from a letter. He stated to me that he had been a long time in the business, in fact ever since he had come into the office.

[May 29] On the 9$^{th}$ of May, William Barlow gave me two rings. He then gave me an envelope and told me to back it to ---- Reed, Galva, Henry Co., Ill., and to frank it with Col. Barnes' name. I did so. Barlow took the envelope, placed it over a letter and put it into the mail. He also told me to save letters that appeared to be heavy, and never to mention anything which might be going on in the office. Then he

[Barlow] said to me, "I have got you just where I wanted to. The letter which I gave you to back I broke open and the rings I gave you I took from it and if you are accused of robbing the mail I can have that letter produced bearing your writing and the rings in your possession. So you see I have got you...." (Samuel Lemoine, SRNA.)


## WILL BLACK – ON CASSVILLE SOCIETY

(May 1862) Several of the officers ... invited some of the ladies to meet at the house of one of their number. Refreshments were provided from a neighborhood sutler's in the shape of lemons for ade, oysters, pineapple & candy. Lt. Bandy had to make the lemonade & I had to cook the oysters. Those who were not busy were trying to keep up a conversation, the principle part of which, on the ladies side, seemed to be an occasional giggle, followed by a senseless relapse into silence.

The lemonade was ready & on being asked if they would take some, there was a hesitancy which brought on the question, "Don't you like it?" followed generally by the remarkably brilliant reply, "Te Hee, don't know, never tried any, Te Hee!" None relished it though it was very good.

Then came the oysters. "Couldn't some of the ladies cook them?" "Don't know how, Never seed any before."

The oysters were cooked by myself & it does not become me to praise them but they were very good. Of course the demand did not go beyond one course of the delicious bivalves & the greater portion were left to be thrown out to the pigs next morning who I have no doubt, testified their superior civilization by eating them with thankfulness of heart if such sentiments belong to the divine part of pigology.

Such glorious successes having crowned the former part of the evenings entertainment, we prepared to lay before them the remainder of our feast, consisting of pineapple and candy. And though none had ever eaten the former, for a wonder they liked it & pitched in. As for the candy it disappeared in quick metre.

And so, in a short time, we separated. How the natives felt, we know not, but are certain that we were most consummately bored, & as we thought of the good things unappreciated, we remember the scripture passage, "Neither cast ye your pearls before swine," we drew a moral for another day. (Letter to his Mother, May 12, 1862, JCBF.)

## EDWARD ANDERSON – THE DEATH OF KEYS

(June 1862) Our scout and guide, Keys, was taken prisoner during the last march. Poor fellow, he was immediately shot where he was taken. Unfortunately, he had left the main body, in disobedience of orders, and was snapped up. These jayhawks hang about on the flanks and rear of a force, and every straggler meets a sudden and awful fate.

This Keys was a novelty in his way; he was tall and slim, with light hair, and when at rest a calm blue eye…. A roof or a star-lit sky were alike to him for a covering at night, and a handful of parched corn was equal to a rich repast of 'hog and hominy' flanked with corn pone. But when a practiced eye glanced along the heavy rifle barrel all the calm and amiable appearance was gone, and the piercing eye seemed to drink in its object.

Keys, very hungry, went to a house a little from the road for dinner, and while there it was surrounded. Springing to his feet and seizing his trusty rifle, he cried: 'Ye kaint cotch this hunter that it costs ye suthin,' and the thin white smoke as it cleared away showed a dead enemy. But poor Keys fell pierced with a half score of bullets.

I saw young Keys, a son, this forenoon [June 4]. He is picture of his dead father. 'Pap was goin' on 47 years, and cum from old Tennessee, last month 17 years. Ef the old 'uns gone, we boys haint.' This, with a shrug of the shoulders, means very much in borderland. Keys was a brave man, different from ordinary Butternuts, and we all deplore his loss. Our men will avenge it.... (Letter, June 4, 1862, published June 14, 1862, CTR.)

## WILLIAM FITHIAN – ON REGIMENTAL POLITICS

(July 1862) [We learned] that Genl. Julius White was safely on his way to Washington and that you [Charles Black] were left to work out your own promotion against all the hedging and fencing prompted by and done to secure a cushioned seat in Washington City. Political demagogues will sometimes sacrifice even those who have served their cause best....

You have heretofore placed great confidence in Lieut. Bandy and regarded him – to use your own words – "an honorable, high-minded gentleman." Pray what do you think now? Has he done enough yet to wake your unsuspecting nature, to look at him as he is, was and always will be? Is it necessary for me to tell you, he must be regarded as the implacable, uncompromising, dishonorable enemy of Willie and yourself. No kind acts will win him to the side of either of you. Gratitude never had a lodgement in the bosom of a Bandy. The snake you warm and nurse into life, will sting you unless you put it out of your way....

# NOTES FROM THE WAR YEARS

One word volunteered relative to your Colonel [Barnes]. Keep your eyes open steadily for him and his acts. If you can at any time oust him from the regiment by honorable means, I think you should do it. His incompetence and intemperance will always make him your secret enemy.

Sometime since I hired a servant for you and sent you a description: John Ryan, a native of Ireland. Aged 22 years, 5 feet 6 or 8 inches in height, sandy hare, grey eyes a farmer. Engaged 1$^{st}$ of April 1862. (Letter to Charles Black, July 14, 1862, JCBF.)

## LAWN PARTY AT JULIUS WHITE'S HOUSE, EVANSTON, ILLINOIS

(July 1862) An impromptu visit was suggested, and ... they yesterday paid the General a visit. True to their soldierly instincts, the Quartermaster's and Commissary's Departments were bountifully supplied and laden with tents, eatables, and drinkables, [and] a merry car load started for the suburban village of Evanston. Tents were speedily pitched, and flinging the national flag to the breeze, surmounting a secession emblem captured at Pea Ridge, the party fell to and attacked the viands with a zest and will which soldiers can only appreciate....

An evening of enjoyment was experienced, scarcely dampened by the pouring rain which dripped continuously from dark until daylight.

In the morning they were waited upon by the professors of the Biblical Institute, and invited to visit that institution, and were cordially welcomed by Drs. Kidder and Dempster. Gen. White replied in a neat speech, after which Lt. Col. Frisbie and Capt. Peck addressed the students, relating the history of their campaigns in the wilds of Arkansas which was ... greeted with rounds of applause. (News Article, July 10, 1862, CTR.)

### HENRY CURTIS – ON REGIMENTAL POLITICS

(July 1862) ... a few days ago we got word that Black was commissioned Lt. Col. & Frisbie Major. As Frisbie got every vote he had nominating him for Col. by a combined opposition to Black, then to go and sell out to Black was rather a dirty trick. It is a good deal like the man & more are sorry now that they combined on him than there were before and there were enough then.

It is curious, but a fact, that he has got office against the real wishes of the greater part of his own supporters. It was very unlucky for me that Barnes was in my way, or else I would have had the election. I was choice of Major by a large majority, but by the present arrangement, there is no vacancy. So my hopes here for the present are extinct. It is rather provoking to have a good thing slip through your fingers just as you think you have it; which, however, is my usual luck. I shall probably go with Genl. White as Assistant Adjutant General at the present showing, but what may turn up I can't say. I hope for something better before long. (Letter to his Mother, July 15, 1862, HCTR.)

### CHARLES BLACK – ON HIS CAREER

(July 1862) ... I am Lt. Col. of the $37^{th}$, a consummation most devoutly worked for. [How was it effected?] ... Hard work and a great deal of it.

# NOTES FROM THE WAR YEARS

When the result of the election in the 37$^{th}$ was known, I tendered an unconditional resignation, but General Brown refused to accept it or approve it. On the contrary, he at once wrote to Gov. Yates at the same time forwarding the petition from the men....

I want the command of one of the new regiments.... It would be a matter of pride for me to remain with the true men who have stood to me in my trials, but that pride will or may seriously affect my future interests....

The 37$^{th}$ seems at this time irretrievably wedded to the destinies of S.W. Missouri. There is here no grand field for the operation of arms, for the rise of merit, and the test of skill. Courage can be but rashness when it is only exhibited against marauders and skulking ruffians....

With the present organization of my regiment, the feeling of hate & fear, yes, fear, that obtains in its Hd Qtrs for me, I am checked & this progress becomes an impossibility. With my experience & the Colonelcy of a new regiment ... the command of a Brigade or even a Division would be mine & the stepping stone to eminence close & easy.

I feel there is in me some of the elements that make a successful chieftain, and the names that are to make this country luminous are now being produced. Quick action may usher me among them. I hope to God it may.

There is a regiment forming at Chicago known as the "Board of Trade Regiment." Gen. White made endeavors, nearly successful, to obtain the command of it for me. The regiments of Chicago become the pet regiments of the state. The future influence such an organization wields is greater than any other can be. Mr. Blodgett will work to secure this for me, if [Dr. Fithian] will help him obtain the Quartermaster's place for his brother Ed, or maybe a Major's place for [his brother] Wells....

White nearly obtained the place for me & only failed from Yates' issuing the commission of Lt. Col. 37th Ills. instead....

Bandy & Hicks, as I think, feel exceedingly small & mean. I show them only the black side of my face & they will probably regret it. I know [Bandy] now & admit all you say for gospel truth.... (Letter to his stepfather, July 25, 1862, JCBF.)

## ORDER BOOK

(July 1862) Hereafter all privates getting drunk will be promptly be reported to Commander of the Regiment for fine or imprisonment. All non-commissioned officers getting drunk or conniving, aiding, or assisting in getting liquor for privates will be promptly reduced to the ranks and fined or imprisoned.... (Order Book, July 26, 1862, OBNA.)

## DAVID ASH – ON DISCIPLINE

(July 1862) In Springfield there is a good deal of cutting up among the drinking class of men. Whiskey can be got by almost any person but a sober man. The 1st Missouri Cavalry have a hard set of men. I was officer of the guard a few days ago and 3 men got into a quarrel and they had pistols. One shot the other. I went to take one off to the guardhouse. I told him to give me his pistol, he swore I could not have it.

I took hold of him and threw him down and the officer of the day took it from him. I then let him up and he struck at me, and I downed him again and hit him a few and let him up and put him in the guardhouse, and he struck at the sergeant of the guard.

I picked up a gun and hit him and knocked him across the room. He laid there for about 10 hours but is alright now except the track of the gun on his goard.

I suppose you think we are almost savages but I have concluded that I am not going to be jerked around by drunken men if I can help it, and I think I can. (Letter, July 23, 1862, DASH.)

## DAVID ASH – ON CAMP LIFE

(August 1862) ... I must tell you how we get along for grub as we have no cook. I went to a house close by and got 3 meals today. As they have no threshing machines in this country, they make their bread out of straw and when mixed it makes very good bread but somewhat troublesome to eat.

... they have a daughter that suits me very well.... I am going to tell you what kind of lookin' gal she is. I think she would weigh 3 or 4 hundred and 75 pounds. If she was fat, I thought some of getting ten days rations in my haversack and go and try and do some sparking. I think it would take several days to make her acquaintance as I could not get close enough to talk any without sending a dispatch, and I would want to see how good looking she is. I know it would take some time to walk around her.

But to tell the truth about Miss Big Girl, she is a monster....

My paper is almost played out and the blamed fleas are biting me I must close and try to catch them.... (Letter, August 12, 1862, DASH.)

## EDWARD ANDERSON – ON "JINGLE"

(Summer 1862) He [Theodore Meeker] was a bright, plucky little fellow, and gladly took service as the men did. Somewhere he came into possession of a pair of enormous Mexican spurs, with their two inch steel rowels and the danglers, and with broad leathers which covered the whole upper part of his shoe. As he had no horse and always walked, and as he invariably wore his spurs, his approach was heralded by the jingle of his great adornments, and hence the name by which he came to be universally known.... (From Camp Fire Stories by Edward Anderson, pp.52-53.)

## CHARLES BLACK – ON JULIUS WHITE

(August 1862) Julius White has acted the part of an extremely mean man with me through all my troubles. Things have come to my ears that undeceive me more and more. If he and I should ever meet in the future, I trust to make him feel it. A favorite idea of his is that 'things are done by being attended to.' Well, it is so and I will remember it. He will not see more of the Senate than David did of Lazarus in Heaven. His private record I am very conversant with. It had better never been written. If this war lasts, and we live, I hope to see the tables turned between us two. (Letter, Charles Black to William Fithian, August 17, 1862, JCBF.)

# NOTES FROM THE WAR YEARS

## EUGENE PAYNE – ON POLITICS

(September 1862) I did wrong in the case of Barnes, Frisbie & the majorship to listen to my better feelings, to yield because I was fearful it would defeat old Barnes so I sacrificed myself. I was killed because I had a heart. I don't think I will have one any more in my dealings with men, nor with anyone.

Barnes trial is over and the report is that Barnes is cashiered.... Barnes is going to St. Louis to see about the case and if it has gone against him, appeal to higher authority.... He is ruined, gone up, and sooner or later a vacancy will be made. Then comes the tug of war, the old fight all over again.... Will I lose this time? I won't say. There are many a slip, etc.; but I will compete for success. I shall lay aside my heart. I will lay E.B.P up on the shelf and 'go in,' yes I will win, or come home....

Barnes wife came last night. Mrs, Barnes, I pity her, so I do poor Mrs. Peck. She ... has I know suffered unheard of torture. Why, wasn't John Peck drunk when you went away. Hadn't he been drunk for over a week, and hasn't he been beastly drunk to my own knowledge ever since you left? Yesterday Peck told me that Mrs. had not spoken to him for four days. I see nothing of Mrs. Peck now. She does not go out at all. When I see her I will ascertain if I can when she is coming home....

Mrs. Dick is still at Pleasant Retreat I suppose.... Mrs. Humeston, wife of the Doc, is here. She and Mrs. Barnes board at old seceshers Mrs. Weavers where we were....

# THIRTY SEVENTH ILLINOIS

Chauncy [Morse] still stays away. Be a little cautious with his mother. She is a sly old coon.... (Letter, September 12, 1862, EBP.)

### EUGENE PAYNE – ON HARDSHIP

(October 1962) ... night before last [Oct 8] we were at Newtonia, we received orders to pack and march at 4 in the morning. The night set in cold and stormy. 4 o'clock came and the rain was pouring down in torrents ... about 10 o'clock we got started. We marched to [Gadfly], 16 miles.... All through the day, all through that long fearful night following did the rain pour down in torrents and the wind blow perfect gales.... Imagine ... starting out with a gun, forty rounds of cartridge and three days provisions on one's back with rain pouring down in torrents all day long, fording streams, puddles, etc.; and laying down in wet clothes by the side of an open fire with the rain coming down all night, harder and faster and threatening each moment to put out what little fire you had got to blazing. Well, thank God, it is over. Never in all our soldiering have we experienced such a day and night even in camp with a good tent to cover us, and if so hard to us, what must it be to [the] new regiments!

We have two of them with us; the $18^{th}$ and $20^{th}$ Iowa – poor fellows. Day before yesterday, while our sick list numbered 13, that of the $20^{th}$ Iowa numbered 150! 50 of these were sent back to Springfield unable to proceed further. Alas, I fear the poor Iowa boys will drop away.... (Letter, October 10, 1862, EBP.)

### EUGENE PAYNE – ON FAYETTEVILLE, ARKANSAS

(October 1862) [Fayetteville, Oct 29] ... Now we are in Dixie, real genuine Dixie, further south than our army has ever penetrated before.... We have got so lately that we do all of our marching by night. At sundown we were laying at Osage Springs some 20 miles above here.... We traveled 20 miles and arrived ... just at daybreak driving in the enemy's pickets killing one, taking quite a number of prisoners and several wagons, horses, mules, and two wagon loads of n-----s. They had just loaded up the cattle (negroes) to ship south when the sudden entrance of us Feds put a stop to their fun.

This is the most beautiful place I ever saw in Mo. or Ark. ... situated upon a high table ... covered with beautiful groves of live oak with the short grass spreading out like carpet beneath the groves.

To the south and west high hills loom up.... The town has been as large as Waukegan once, but about half of it was destroyed by the secesh.

I have been over the town and find the most bitter feeling everywhere towards the 'plaugey Feds' as they call us. All the men are gone to the secesh army so nothing but the women are left. A large building filled with cook stoves has just been found. I got me a fine one....

I think we go again tonight. Oh, curse this night marching, it is killing the men. We are on half rations now and had not ought to march by night. (Letter, October 22, 1862, EBP.)

## EUGENE PAYNE – ON HIS RETURN TO PEA RIDGE

(October 1862) We are encamped upon the very spot of ground that we occupied the morning before we marched into battle.... My own tent covers the same square feet of earth it did then. But oh, what different pulsations in the hearts of all – with full numbers, with laughing joyous groups around each fire. We only wished to annihilate the secesh and thought that we were bulletproof and invincible. Now how changed, with decimated numbers.... We have not changed to cowards but we are men who know our danger.... No more jokes around the fire circles but instead reminisces and tales of lost ones, the braves that 8 short months ago was chatting and laughing gaily around these same fires.

This morning I went and paid a visit to the grave of poor [brother] Fred and my other brave hero boys. I found them sleeping quietly, not a thing about their graves had been disturbed. The earth was rounded about their graves as nicely as when we left them. The head boards stood out in bold relief as when we left them.... (Letter, October 22, 1862, EBP.)

## CHARLES BLACK – ON HIS RETURN TO CASSVILLE

(October 1862) Here we are again in our old stamping ground. Every scene is familiar, each tree wears a 'welcome back' in its snaps & rustles, 'howdy' from its foliage.... This morning the sun is shining in all the glory of Indian Summer. The great trials of the last week of rain & storm are vanished. The bugles are sounding through the chilly, blue-tinted air.... (Letter, Charles Black to his Mother, October 13, 1862, JCBF.)

## DAVID ASH – ON HIS RETURN TO CASSVILLE

(October 1862) [We] found things changed very much. The rebels has been in since we left and used the buildings for stables, and some of the buildings have been burned. They use the same courthouse that we used but instead of a hospital they have made a stable.

There is not many families living in town and very few of the same that was here when we left. I wish they would burn the infernal rebel town to the ground. There is 1 or 2 men that play off union when our army is here, and are the best kind of rebels when the secesh army is in this place.

About 3 weeks ago the 1$^{st}$ Arkansas, or 40 of them, charged into town and fired into a house that some rebels were staying in and killed ... 14. I was down at the house yesterday evening and the house is shot full of holes. I think there was one woman killed. The floor was all stained with blood. (Letter, October 13, 1862, DASH.)

## HENRY CURTIS – ON WASHINGTON, D.C.

(October 1862) This is a ... mean town. If Congress were running I expect it would be better, but the place has a God-forsaken look now & must all times be poorly built, dirty & slow. All Southern places are slow, that I ever saw. Poor hotels etc.; & big prices to match. Go to a restaurant & order dinner, & if the n----r thinks best & feels lively, you'll get it in the course of a week.

Had a fire this evening [Oct 18] & being a connoisseur in that line, took a look on the avenue. Half the machines (manned by 3 to 6 men each) ran one way & the other half the other. Then after they had gone a mile or so, the steam engine came along at a very moderate pace, with the fires just kindled. Made a note, that I wouldn't give much for the chance of a fire being put out in this town. The steam fire engine stands in the house, with no horses hitched nor visible & I thought it wouldn't get out under ½ hour & was very happy to find my judgement was good. (Letter to his Mother, October 18, 1862, HCJR.)

## EUGENE PAYNE – ON BOOZY GENERALS

(November 1862) We have been hussled about so from pillar to post. Well, well, if I ain't just getting disgusted with soldiering about as fast as a man well can ... such kind of soldiering as we have here is enough to sicken anyone. We have the meanest generals of the Army, from Scofield down. All are drunkards, Totten, Brown, Houston and all just keep soaked with liquor. Then you may imagine how we are treated. Their orders are not the sensible good doing orders of sober earnest men, but the ebuillations of the drunken fancy of beasts and sots. Our men are marched from 25 to 35 miles each day ... and if any of the poor footsore lads drop out & lay down from exhaustion, Old Totten has them tied to the wagons & thus brot along. If he catches any of them away from their commands trying to buy a chicken to keep them from starving, he ties them up & whips them. Oh my God, such tyranny. Every day we see more & more. I have several good men say that if he continued for three months more that he would have no army at all.... We are getting demoralized and from ... this mistaken idea of Old Totten that we should be used in every respect as 'regulars.' (Letter, November 11, 1862, EBP)

## EUGENE PAYNE – ON HARDSHIP

## NOTES FROM THE WAR YEARS

(November 1862) This service here in the west is almost enough to make any man no matter how patriotic he may be, desert this service.... Why, just think for a moment how we are used, worse, far worse, than a farmer would treat his dogs or his hogs. We are half fed, half clothed, and treated worse than a planter's slaves. We are summoned to march by daylight. In the morning, we get ready, pack up our things and get into line and most always are obliged to wait till near noon before we get orders to march. Then we go till 9, 10, or 12 o'clock at night and then we stop not to rest. Our teams are back 10 or 13 miles back. Here we wait till morning and then we go it again, probably 20 or 30 miles and so it goes.

Our last march was like this: Day before yesterday we were ordered to march at daylight ... in consequence of our marching in the rear did not go until 11 o'clock. Then we started in a fine drizzling rain. We traveled about 25 miles. By this time it was 10 o'clock at night, dark as pitch and the rain more than pouring down. Our teams were back 10 miles, and there we were, so we built fires and waited in the rain till morning, then we formed again and without breakfast started. It was very hard marching. It still rained. We went on till night again and had made 10 miles. The mud was ankle deep and the rain still continued to pour down. We halted and camped but like the previous night we had nothing to eat, nothing to sleep on, and rain, rain, still pouring down.... So it continued all night and until noon the next day when our teams came up in charge of Capt. Peck. Some of them had tipped over a time or two, others had broke down in the mud.... But now we are all right. We have got our tents & all ... but the boys do some pretty tall swearing about our incompetent and fool commanders. No wonder, I cannot blame them.... (Letter, November 19, 1862, EBP.)

THIRTY SEVENTH ILLINOIS

# 1863 NOTES

# RELATING TO CHAPTERS 17-22

# NOTES FROM THE WAR YEARS

## DR. WILLIAM FITHIAN – ON REBEL SOLDIERS

(January 1863) ... Since Sunday last hundreds of Hindman's soldiers who were from this part of the state, are deserting him and coming here to take to oath....

Many of them are the most hang-dog set of looking specimens you can conceive of, and I have no doubt, would within an hour after taking the oath of Alliegence, again join the rebel army if they could believe there was a prospect of killing our men and defeating our army. Many of them are really inferior to the stumps of negroes they own in intelligence....

More than half the slaves that I have seen here are mulattoes. Some of them, Jingle thinks, are as white as he is and he thinks he is as white as two thirds of the people in Illinois, and certainly I think he is....

The deserters from Hindman's army are uniformly the most degraded and stupid looking set of men I have ever seen anywhere...

None of those we see here are Missourians. They have sneaked past over the mountains and through the defiles and gone home to join the guerilla bands or to watch and waylay the roads, to murder our men when but 2 or 3 shall be found together.

Just so these Arkansas wretches will do so soon as they shall have taken the oath and passed beyond the lines of our army. Their impudence is almost unbearable. Some of them whose hands are yet red with the butchery of our men at Pea Ridge, Cane Hill, and Prairie Grove.... (Letter, William Fithian to his wife, January 8, 1863, JCBF.)

# THIRTY SEVENTH ILLINOIS

## DR. WILLIAM FITHIAN – ON FREED SLAVES

(January 1863) I am convinced that there is not in all Arkansas ... one genuine reliable union man, except the Negroes. They are reliable, and with few exceptions are, the most intelligent.

Poor creatures, what is to become of them. The first day of January has passed [Lincoln's Emancipation Proclamation], they think they are free, but yet they know not what to do. Four hundred of them started from here a few days since for Kansas, hundreds of them are yet here begging to be taken north. Aunt Katy (our washerwoman), her husband with six children are constantly begging us to ... take them with us when we return home....

We are told the guerilla bands are collecting up their forces, in squads of 6 or 8 hundred within 20 and 30 miles of this place [Fayetteville]. We have here 1000 wounded and unfit for duty. Our men are bushwhacked and murdered within 9 miles of us, and for 60 miles out on the road to Springfield. The secesh who are here are very bitter and vindictive, and would rejoice in an opportunity to cut our throats, sick or well.

Prompted by all the circumstances surrounding us, I shall start just the moment I think Charles able to reach Springfield, Missouri....

... it is known very considerable companies of guerrillas are in the mountains not a days ride from here. It is not unreasonable to think the Confederate forces and guerila bands might make a raid upon Fayetteville and successfully capture all here. Not a single cannon left here [Jan 11].... If the Arkansas River was opened ... I could put Charles on what is here termed 'a stretcher' and have him carried safely to the river on the shoulders of men....

We fear most a raid from Standwaitie and his Indians. No circumstances will avail us an appeal to their mercy. They slaughter indiscriminately, so you see if we should be captured, we would much prefer to fall into other hands.... (Letter, William Fithian to his wife, January 11, 1863, JCBF.)

## HENRY FRISBIE – ON WELLS BLODGETT

(January 1963) Company D of this regiment is a rough unruly set of men and but few men can control or make them submit to discipline. Lt. Blodgett has been in command nearly from its organization and failed to control them satisfactorily either to himself or his regimental commander, and so some six months ago he got detailed as an Assistant Adjutant General in the State Militia leaving his company without a commissioned officer, Lt. Johnson being sick and about that time went home, and his Captain being under arrest more than a year.

By this detail he virtually abandoned his company.... His offense is greater when it is known that he left, being in command, and all that time might have been in command. I do not think Lt. Blodgett was ever in a battle and I think he does not wish to return to this regiment.... (Letter, Henry Frisbie to Adjutant General Allen Fuller, January 25, 1863, RRIA.)

## WILL BLACK – ON POLITICS

(January 1863) Have just been talking with Capt. Messer.... He feels sore about Payne's promotion & speaks & feels bitterly about the letter of the 12$^{th}$ [Frisbie to the Democrat], wants an opportunity to express himself before Frisbie. Even Capt. Bell expressed disgust at the miserable production, joining with me in saying there was not one redeeming note of truth floating through the whole mass of its rottenness. (Letter, Will Black to Charles Black, January 28, 1863, JCBF.)

## DAVID ASH – ON CHARLES DICKENSON

(February 1863) Capt. Dick [Dickenson] is not our Major, Capt. Payne of Co. C of our regt is the man. Dick feels pretty badly plagued about it, and Mrs. Lydia [Dick's wife] feels awful about it. It is fine for me. I am glad of it. For my part, if Cap got to be Major, all of Ills. would not hold him and his wife. I guess that he will find out that there is men besides himself.

Jones, Cap and his wife and I have been messing together for some time. We are living very nice. David Anschutz is our cook.... (Letter, February 3, 1863, DASH.)

## EUGENE PAYNE – ON PROMOTION

(February 1863) ... there is a prospect of old 'F' [Frisbie] going out of the service by being kicked out. If this comes to pass or anything else so I can get to be a Col. or a Lt. Col. I will come home....

Well, about the consternation in the regt. when Payne was announced as the Major!.... Dick & Kennicott & Messer & all were in Frisbie's tent when your letter directed to me as Major arrived. Frisbie picked it up & read it aloud among them. Well, you can imagine how they all felt rather down in the mouth as the saying runs. However, at a little social gathering which I had in my new tent & home, to take a sip of egg nog & smoke a cigar, they all came & we had a fine time. Every commissioned officer in the regt. was in & they treat me well now. I could ask nothing better.... (Letter, February 9, 1863, EBP.)

## EUGENE PAYNE – ON HENRY FRISBIE

(February 1863) Our common enemy has as yet been able to glean nothing ... about the result of the investigation at Springfield. He has tried at least twice to get me to acknowledge myself on his side and for his interest. I told him that I had got disgusted with all intrigues and quarrels in the 37$^{th}$ Ill. and that henceforth I should be neutral. He said that I could not with safety and honor. I told him that I did not care a damn for my safety, that that would take care of itself....

He told me that you and him both could never stay in the regt., that if you did not floor him (which he thot impossible), that he had a sure thing on you.

Now Col, my position is this. I wish to lay low and make the cuss believe I am neutral, because I have some powerful friends who if I came out openly and denounced the cuss as he should be denounced, might turn upon me and do me a great deal of injury. But the man is my enemy, has been ever since he cut my throat in Springfield last summer, and always will be.... (Letter, Eugene Payne to Charles Black, February 13, 1863, JCBF.)

### JOHN PECK – ON CAMP LIFE

(February 1863) The regt is getting saucy. They yelled & hooted at Totten the other day & got into the Guard House & [got] tied to the government wagons, to the number of about 20, so I figured conspicuously as usual....

Holloway is here yet and is a tip top cook. Major Payne is fixed on the regimental line but he & Lt. Col. Frisbie are as cool to each other as a Northwest wind to a Hottentot....

Capt. Bell endeavored to get my cook from me.... Capt. Bell drew up the order for his return, Lt. Col. Frisbie signed it. I told Holloway to keep to work. Bell sent up a Corporal & four men after him. I met them with an order from Headquarters saying that as he had been detailed by Col. White, it would take an order from a Col. to get him away. There I got them.... (Letter, John Peck to Charles Black, February 16, 1863, JCBF.)

### WILL BLACK – ON COPPERHEADS

(February 1863) I am boiling all over at the news from home.... There is the report that Dr. Lamon, the poor pitiable, cowardly sneak, has been going about the streets of Danville carrying a revolver and preaching treason.

Then too comes the report that a man in the streets of Danville trampled on the American Flag....

# NOTES FROM THE WAR YEARS

If such things are so, my brother, do not go on the streets at home ... for your efforts would be unavailing and only get you indicted before some tory court for murder.... Were any miserable traitor to beard me with his treason at home, he or I should take an air line route to eternity. (Letter, Will Black to Charles Black, February 18, 1863, JCBF.)

## WELLS BLODGETT – ON HENRY FRISBIE

(March 1863) [Lt.] Leonard is all right and tells me if 'F' [Frisbie] should become commanding officer ... he will resign, and for that matter, Payne told me when it came to that, he had a few scores of his own to settle & that he & 'F' could not remain in the regiment together. But he is one whom it is dangerous to trust, except where you can watch him....

I am told here in [Chicago] that there is an indictment against Frisbie on file in the Recorder's Court for horse stealing.... I shall have a copy of it before I leave the city....

I am bound ... not to be driven from the regt. by 'F' or any of his co-workers. I find that the same indignation which exists in Springfield, Mo. against 'F' exists here in the mind of every man with whom I have talked, and the universal verdict in his case is that he is a puppy and ought to be kicked out of the Service....

I had a dispatch from [Elihu] Washburne, M.C., last night [March 4] stating that I had been appointed Judge Advocate by the President and that I would be confirmed by the Senate in extra session....

I met Frisbie's brother today and he says that the Lt. Col. has offered to resign and raise a Brigade of Negroes for the service.  Wouldn't that be a good joke, but I will bet 2 to 1 that he gets out of the service upon such a pretense.  He begins to think the day of judgement is approaching.

Frisbie's friends here appear to be posted on the matter contained in the MISSOURI DEMOCRAT, and they say it is absurd to think that he wrote it, for they say if he had written it, that he would not have sent it to the DEMOCRAT for publication when he was a correspondent of the CHICAGO TRIBUNE.  I tell them that kind of argument may do for some, but it is not sufficiently conclusive to do me, and that my opinion is that he did write it, though I did not see him do it.

The fact is, he and his friends begin to smell something, and they are getting very much alarmed about his prospects.

Laimbeer is in town.  I have not seen him, but I have heard of him.  (Letter, Wells Blodgett to Charles Black, March 5, 1863, JCBF.)

## EUGENE PAYNE – ON HENRY FRISBIE

(March 1863)  Day before yesterday (it being Sunday), Gen. Totten sent an order to Lt. Col. 'F' to send up to his HdQtrs a detachment for fatigue.  The Lt. C. wanting to put on style or something else sent word back orally by an orderly, 'That the President's Proclamation exempted all soldiers from labor on the Sabbath Day.'....

Frisbie is now under arrest for insubordination and disrespect.  Poor fool!  He will soon meet the penalty so justly due him by being disgracefully dismissed....

Matters have now assumed the form of an open rupture between him and me. We no longer speak. Well, I am not particular. I have no desire to associate with a man having so much concentrated meanness and hypocrisy in his composition as he has.... 'F' had taken the advantage of Black's absence and had written the Sec. of War urging Black's dismissal. He did, and the letter came back to me (being in command), and thus I was acquainted with his diabolical attempt to undermine a superior officer while that officer was absent by a wound recvd. in action. Such scoundrelism was never heard of....

'F' which stands for fool is still in suspension although relieved from arrest. He is so damnably mean and egotistical that our commander would not return him to duty again. I hope to the Lord he may be tried and justice meted out to him, for if it is he will go up salt river sure. Him & I are at sword's points.

Frisbie is continually working to hurt me among men, but he finds few that he can make believe his lies. (Letter, March 9, 1863, EBP.)

## WILL BLACK – ON RANSOM KENNICOTT

(March 1863) ... I am certain I could get a recommendation from General Totten & Col. Dye for promotion, and will do it if necessary. Nor do I feel such compunction at such a course, as K. [Ransom Kennicott] isn't acting in the manner to suit me now a day, & while Frisbie was in command he was a regular lick-spittle to my notion, while to me he was continually cursing Frisbie.... I believe the fair-weather friend would cling to Frisbie like a leech to the patient if Frisbie once got the upper hand.... (Letter, Will Black to his Mother, March 9, 1863, JCBF.)

# THIRTY SEVENTH ILLINOIS

## EUGENE PAYNE – ON HENRY FRISBIE

(March 1863) The trial of Colonel Frisbie is proceeding. His Counsel ... is doing him harm rather than good & getting the court angry. Still further, the poor fool is getting himself more & more embroiled. You must not say a word of it, but 'F' tried to bribe the Judge Advocate of the Court, a Captain of the 26$^{th}$ Indiana, & a man of high honor. There is some probability, if it be necessary, that the J.A. will prefer charges against him ('F') on that score. Of such a man what is one not tempted to believe. I am not surprised now at the revelation regarding the horse business in Chicago some time since.... (Letter, March 16, 1863, EBP.)

## CHARLES BLACK – ON COPPERHEADS

(March 1863) Your lovely TIMES [newspaper] was bundled, neck and heels, out of the army lines.... Why did not your men of the Board of Trade complete the good work, and bundle the traitor sheet, neck and heels, to the bottom of the lake? Unused to such pollution, the waters might have spewed the filthy carrion Jonah–like upon dry land and given a second Wentworth police newer and dirtier work upon the sands. Nature works to her rules, and might have saved the drowning for the hangman's hands. (Charles Black, speech at the Chicago Board of Trade, quoted in Article, March 14, 1863, CTR.)

## CHARLES BLACK – ON DISEASE

(Summer 1863) The 37$^{th}$ is probably the healthiest regt. in this command, but ah me, I often think with sighs of that happy campaign life in Missouri where the sick of a division were counted by tens, not by hundreds & almost thousands as they are here. The water is bad ... the vast swamps, the earth (itself a charnel house) all conspire against the health of a soldier. I have buried five men since the siege of Vicksburg closed, one more than in the preceding year, & yet we are comparatively healthy.... (Letter, Charles Black to Family, August 6, 1863, JCBF.)

## CHESTER BARNEY – ON WATER MARCHING

(Summer 1863) The condition of troops on board a transport is miserable in the extreme. Huddled together like hogs in a pen – jostled and jammed from side to side – compelled to eat and sleep on the filthy decks – without exercise during the day, and trampled at night while endeavoring to sleep – with rations of half-cooked meat and tasteless pilot bread, and constantly inhaling the impure atmosphere engendered by the dense crowd on board, and arising from mules and horses on the lower deck....

The officers, however, occupied the cabin, with guards stationed at the entrances to prevent intrusion from the soldiers, passing their time in reading, writing letters, and games of cards – Whiskey Poker, California Jack, Old Sledge, Poker, Muggins, and Euchre. A portion of the cabin was assigned to the Surgeons and occupied by our sick men, who were made as comfortable as circumstances would permit. No facilities were afforded for cooking, and we were under the necessity of landing for that purpose. (Barney, C., <u>Recollections of Field Service with the Twentieth Iowa Infantry Volunteers</u>, Davenport, 1865, pp.173-4.)

# THIRTY SEVENTH ILLINOIS

## CHARLES BLACK – ON THE YAZOO CITY RAID

(August 1863) On the 12<sup>th</sup> of July orders were received to get under weigh ... the whistle sounded '1 long and 3 short' & the flagship turned her bow to the current & we were off up the river. The Yazoo empties into the Mississippi some 6 or 8 miles above [Vicksburg].... We turned ... into the sluggish current of the Yazoo – 'River of Death' – as its beautiful Indian name indicates....

For the first 12 miles of the way, the right hand or southern banks were covered with earth works & intrenched camps, the work of our troops after driving the enemy into Vicksburg. Then there was a long space of primeval forest broken only when some sluggish bayou emptied its dark poisons into the river. Then the wall of ... tropical green closed in again & seemed interminable. At 18 miles out, we came suddenly upon our troops at Snyder's Bluff. These are a high line of hills, their fronts all neatly cleaned of the forest growth, their crests crowned with ... works & bristling with cannon.... Then came signs of a more beautiful life. We were entering the most charming country I have ever seen. The river banks on both sides were crowded with plantations, principally sugar.... The negro quarters white, regular, clean & tasty in their outside arrangements.... Groups of wooleys of all sizes & ages & habited in the most grotesque costumes were assembled under them to see the Yankees go by. This was one of the SOUTHERN HEARTS the army had not yet touched.

The river had itself narrowed to a mere canal some 50 yards across but very deep ... the current scarcely perceptible, the water of a dark yellowish hue sickening to the taste & deadly to the drinker. Boiling does not cure it & one can scarce bear to wash the face & hands in its filth....

# NOTES FROM THE WAR YEARS

About noon of the 12$^{th}$ ... the steamer IATAN (so celebrated in the cotton trade) made fast to the right bank & I was ordered ashore with the regiment to advance & reconnoiter with the ill-fated gunboat DEKALB....

Through tangled juniper, beds of weeds, fallen timber, the limbs thickly interlaced all forming an almost impossible jungle, we advanced.

Stumbling, crawling, creeping, pushing, the long line of skirmishers steadily advanced through these obstacles & finally emerged into a cleared ground where the enemy's scouts could be observed.... A detail of men from Co. K ... succeeded completely in outflanking the scouts ... so that they found themselves vis-à-vis to a half-dozen of Colt's Revolving rifles. They yielded....

... the gunboats after exchanging a number of shots with the enemy battery, had fallen back & my orders did not permit me to advance beyond them, I sent for orders. ... down came an order to 'leave 2 cos. as pickets & fall back to the boats.'

Scarcely was my regt. safely on board before ... I saw two regts. from another brigade landed & set out with cheers for the town.... The enemy [was] gone, yet they reaped the laurels of our toil....

... every apology was offered to me that could be by superiors & every amend made [but] ... the bitterest feeling spread sowing itself rather in sad chagrined faces & air of wounded pride than in any spoken words of grief or rage. The officers crowded around me, 'full of strange oaths,' questions of surprise & anger. I had little heart to check them.

About 9:00 P.M. I was once again ordered forward & entered the town to find it filled with roaming soldiery intent

# THIRTY SEVENTH ILLINOIS

on robbing. They were lighted to their work by huge fires built in the principal street & casting their strange lights & shadows on long stacks of arms ... & old buildings whose stone battered fronts showed the hard usage of years....

I started a patrol to put a stop to indiscriminate pillage & to arrest the plunderers, & then sick & weary, laid down upon the side walk & slept till ruddy day kissed the sleep from my eyes & called me from dreams to life & action.... (Letter, Charles Black to Family, August 6, 1863, JCBF.)

## NEW ORLEANS POLICE BLOTTER – 1863

(August 27) John Fagan was tried for furnishing liquor to soldiers. He keeps a small house on Claiborne Street, and was arrested there late at night in company with two soldiers. John was sent to the Workhouse for a month. The two soldiers, countrymen of Fagan's, who were away without a pass from their regiment, the 37$^{th}$ Illinois, who got drunk with Fagan, were sent to their regiment under arrest. (From the Daily Picayune)

(October 23) [Alma] Ellsworth and Richard Lee, of Company B, 37$^{th}$ Illinois, were tried for disturbing the peace, tearing down things from shop-doors, and drawing a revolver on the police. The charge was proved, and the accused were sent back to their regiment with a forfeiture of two months' pay. (From the Daily Picayune)

(October 27) DANGEROUSLY WOUNDED. On Saturday night a difficulty occurred in a dance house on Barrack Street, between two soldiers and the women with whom they were dancing, and during the progress of the difficulty one of the women stabbed a soldier named Frederick Mimms [Frederick Minns, Co. D] very dangerously in his side.

NOTES FROM THE WAR YEARS

Mimms belongs to Company C, 37th Illinois. He was taken to the Charity Hospital. (From the Daily Picayune)

(October 28) ARRESTED. Eliza Beckey, one of the ballet girls of a Barrack Street dance house, was arrested yesterday by Lieut. Miller. She is charged with having, on Saturday night last, dangerously wounded a soldier named Mimms [Frederick Minns, Co. D] who is now confined in the Charity Hospital. Beckey kept herself in concealment until yesterday, but her den was found out, and she was caged. The soldier, we understand, is recovering from the effects of his injuries. (From the Daily Picayune)

## JOSEPHINE FITHIAN – ON THE DANVILLE DRAFT RIOTS AT CASSVILLE, MO.

(August 1863) [Danville, Ill.] We have been passing through the fiery trial of Civil War here.... On last Friday John Payne came out with a butternut breastpin, which a man calling himself Colonel Hawkins tore off, when a fight ensured, with which L. Guiness beat John Payne.

On the next day both were fined for the fight. Both parties were arming until Monday.... At dinner, the Doctor [William Fithian] said there was likely to be a collision, and when he came in sight of Squire Clapp's office, it had occurred.... Payne had aroused a passion among them. Mr. William Lamon, who had just come from his dinner, was shot dead instantly by George Barker. A Dutchman named Myers was killed, and John Payne was shot, as it was thought, mortally, tho he still lingers.

The sheriff was shot through the fore arm.... George Barker is in jail ... others are wounded.

## THIRTY SEVENTH ILLINOIS

Previous to this, the Doctor had sent to Springfield [Ill.] for troops but could not get them unless he or his office were in danger.... About 11 or 12 at night 100 soldiers came from Indiana and at daylight 50 came here from Springfield under a Major Clarke of Chicago, and 2 captains (these latter are still here). The first troops which reached us was a company of 65 from Pilot Township ... before morning there were several hundreds of soldiers all around and eager for the fray.

But the elements had settled down for a time, and all are now gone except the Springfield soldiers who are to guard the office of the Provost Marshal, or rather its contents. They are liable to be called away at any time to other points. There was a terrible panic among the citizens on Monday when it was known that the miners were expected in.

What did we do? Well, we made the house as secure as we could with nails, etc.; got inside a large amount of water (it was thought the house would burn if the miners came before the soldiers could), buried our silverware, then packed in [a] trunk our most necessary and of course most valuable clothing, papers, accounts, etc.; got in all the offensive weapons such as axes, spades, billets of wood to be hurled down on them if they came, and then we watched and waited; that is, myself, Mary, Rose ... for all the rest had gone to the office & took with them everything that would shoot except Rose's little revolver.

About 11 o'clock the Doctor came home for a few minutes and the rest of the night we were alone. I have petitioned for a 'Henry's Revolving Rifle,' 16 shooter, for the use of the house.... (200 men in Mattoon are armed with them.)

The house was kept dark that night. The Doctor slept none from Monday morning to Tuesday eve.

The Iowa troops stationed at Peoria have been ordered to Terre Haute, so another outbreak there may occur at any time....

The Doctor acted with more poise than all the other Union men together. Had he not used every effort to keep down the disturbance, the town may have been but a heap of ruins. The excitement was intense, and all comes from Hawkins taking a pin off the shirt of an imbecile crazy man. He (Hawkins) has sneaked off. The Doctor has won favor ... by his impartiality and lost with the Unionists for not killing copperheads.... (Letter, Josephine Fithian to Charles Black, August 28, 1863, JCBF.)

### MYRON BARNES – ON JOSEPH DANFORTH

(October 1863) 'Bub' [Joseph Danforth, Argus editor] of the Argus, is inconsolable. 'Bub,' do go up to Kaiser's and get a stick of candy and stop your mouth-making. The only thing we are afraid of 'Bub,' we are really your friend, is that people will think that your situation as grass widower and the other fact that the Irish kitchen girl is out of town, puts you in bad humor. (Editorial, October 12, 1863, RIU.)

### MYRON BARNES – ON JOSEPH DANFORTH

(November 1863) We are candid to admit that we touch not only a vile thing, but a nasty thing when we come in contact with 'Bub' and his rag known as the Argus. We are well aware that to touch pitch is to become defiled. 'Bub' you are a pretty subject to talk of vileness, a man who is morally rotten from the crown of his head to the bottom of his feet. Go to.

# THIRTY SEVENTH ILLINOIS

Bub is too cowardly to go to the war – he prefers to stay at home and play the role of traitor.... He was once, as report goes, taken to Washington in irons for his thefts to the government, and only got off by the intercession of Stephen A. Douglas, who was a friend of the editor's wife and had been in the habit of using 'Bub' for a boot jack.

It is unfortunate for the Democratic party that they are obliged to put up with such a scab.... He is viler than copperhead teachings, and there is a green scum which rises to the surface wherever he treads. You might take a dozen skunks and stew their foul scented carcasses down to a thimble full of oil and it would be in sweetness like the oil of roses in comparison to one particle of scent from the man of whom his wife said to one of our citizens, 'Sir, you do not know and never can, what a villain I am obliged to live with,' and who now, as report goes is obliged to live by herself in an eastern city to gain a livelihood.

... the debased creature who edits the Argus ... we should pay no more attention to his ravings than we would to any other insignificant reptile which crawls upon its belly and leaves behind its slimy trail.... 'Bub' has neither character nor manhood to lose, and is believed to be a rascal by everybody in the community. A great many people countenance him just as they would any other plague – the small pox, the yellow fever, the measles, the itch. There is another class of people who will occasionally be seen speaking to him out of fear, for they have a private history which 'Bub' knows, and he stands ready with itching palms to receive the 'blackmail' which he demands of his victim or a paragraph in his black sheet.

We leave this lump of nastiness.... (Editorial, November 4, 1863, RIU.)

# NOTES FROM THE WAR YEARS

## JOSEPH DANFORTH – ON MYRON BARNES

(November 1863) ... Barnes sees a boy by the name of William Jennings that he thinks has already started down hill, so he gathers himself up with all the brute force of an overgrown calf and come down on him like a thousand of brick ... and he, like a poor starved turkey buzzard that had no carrion of his own to feed upon, had some imported from a foreign country by a brother buzzard [Barnes had quoted the Geneseo Republican for the item], so that he might have some of his natural food to stick his nose in.... He has assumed the instinct of a mean sneaking, prowling wolf that has scented up a silly lamb who has strayed from his home.... We find the editor of the Union, pouncing on a poor boy like a hawk upon a chicken ... after he had nearly died in the service of his country....

... There are beings that call themselves men, that delight in torturing ... parents by publishing their children as culprits before there is any evidence of their guilt....

Men that are high in office in the army have filched ... millions of dollars, and yet the editor of the Union will wink at it by his silence. But when it is reported that some poor private is guilty of a misdemeanor he is ready to fly upon him like a vulture on a kite, and devour him at once. (Letter from a Correspondent, November 11, 1863, RIA.)

## JOSEPH DANFORTH – ON MYRON BARNES

(November 1863) ... but what shall I do with the creature now is more than I can tell. If it had been a skunk I might have done something with it by separating it from its filth, but my buzzard has been eating filth all the days of its life so that it has become filth itself, and it is said that he will pollute everything that touches him, and that no chemist can extract anything good from him.

Mr. Buzzard Barnes says: 'A writer in Saturday's Argus commences with a lie in his mouth and winds up his abusive and cowardly tirade with a greater falsehood, by signing himself a Republican.' ... If the writer was a republican, he would have written the editor a gentlemanly note informing him of his error, which would have been instantly corrected.

The sum and substance of it is this: If I had sent Mr. Buzzard Barnes a gentlemanly note ... he would have taken it for granted that I was a republican.... It would have saved me from being called so many naughty names, such as a 'skunk,' a 'coward,' a 'liar,' a 'fool,' an 'ass,' a 'picayune brigand,' a 'conceited scamp,' and 'a Port Byron scavenger.'

If slander and abuse will build up a party, the editor of the Union will take the premium, for there is not much of anything else in his paper.... A jackass would know more than that, and I will not insult that useful animal by calling the editor of the Union an ass. (Letter from 'A Republican,' November 18, 1863, RIA.)

## JOSEPH DANFORTH – ON MYRON BARNES

(December 1863) ... [Barnes] the craven, cowardly, lying scoundrel, after abusing, slandering, and lying about us, has the effrontery to send to us for favors. Twice or three times he could not have published his paper without we had loaned him printing paper which he begged of us for that purpose. And once, he could not have printed it, unless we had supplied the dirty dog with ink....

# NOTES FROM THE WAR YEARS

We sent the poor 'Blanket Thief' the ink, and thus enabled him to get out his dirty, lying sheet, abusing and vilifying us with the very ink we had sold him as a favor, and the paper we had loaned him.

This will suffice for Buzzard Barnes for the present. When we have more leisure we will, if it becomes necessary, give a few chapters of the public and private life of this liar, scoundrel, coward, villain, and 'Blanket Thief' – the leader of the Rock Island Republican Loyal Leagueism. (Editorial, December 2, 1863, RIA.)

## L.W. BURNETT (CITIZEN) – ON JOSEPH DANFORTH

(December 1863) Col. Barnes: In yesterdays Argus is an article in relation to me so basely false.... Whether the article in question was based upon the information of the cowardly traitorous-hearted scoundrel of a copperhead who mounts the typod of that loathesome sheet I am unable to say, neither do I care, for every man, woman, and child in this community is well aware that if J.B. Danforth, Jr. had his just desserts, the major portion of his villainous life would have been spent in the penitentiary, and his own much-abused wife would say Amen .... A more malicious perversion of the facts ... could not have been written had they been penned by the devil himself.... L.W. Burnett (Letter from L.W. Burnett, December 16, 1863, RIU.)

## ALCANDER MORSE – ON THE GULF STORM

(October 1863) About 3 A.M. aboard the PEABODY in a perfect gale. Our rudder chain gave way and for an hour the old ship has rolled as though it were a cradle, with a cross child rocking it....

... A storm at sea is a sight of fearful grandeur. None but those who know by experience can imagine the splendor of those gigantic waves. They come rolling up, chasing each other as though eager to seize their prey, and they break, together or against the ship and roll back to meet the next one.... (October 30, from his journal, RCN.)

## WILL BLACK'S CONFESSION

(November 1863) ... I have never played cards for money, I have played for amusement, but even that very rarely, & never should have done so had it not been the universal pastime, & for the pourpose [sic] of whiling away time, which otherwise would have hung very heavily on my hands. And though I would consider myself as doing wrong to play cards at home, where I have enough to keep me usefully and pleasantly employed, I do not consider it a grievous sin to play here, where time is passed & the mind kept from broodings which would or might otherwise produce a morbid & unhealthy state of feeling & thought....

Evil. Wolsey said, 'Men's evel deeds we write in brass. Their good ones write we in water.'.... I have never yet been under the influence of intoxicating liquors. I have drunk liquor & still do at times. I know this is wrong, and do not attempt to justify it, but I have an excuse. The first drop I ever drank in the army was as a medicine, and during the long months from the Cape Girardeau trip till we went to Morganza, while I was suffering from chronic diarrhea & never knew a well day in near 6 months, I was told by the doctor to drink brandy or good whiskey freely whenever I could get it. To the former, conjointly with careful dieting, I attribute my recovery. Perhaps twas better to have died, but at the time, life had too many attractions, and death too much of fear for me not to wish the one & dread the other, even though the cost were to drink brandy & other liquors & have some busy enemy or careless friend write home that Capt. Black was getting 'to drinking, swearing, and all the vices common in the army.'

Cursing and swearing I am not guilty of, and as for all these charges, please remember that though I am not a Christian, I pretend to be & hope I am an honorable gentleman. Mindful of my own good name & the honor of those whom I love, even while they distrust me, my conduct would not bear inspection at the tribunal of God's justice.... (Letter, Will Black to home, November 11, 1863, JCBF.)

## MARY BLACK – ON DANVILLE POLITICS

(November 1863) ... This week an Inspecting Officer came to investigate.... From him we learn that Frazier has in circulation 15 petitions in this district. On the one belonging to this county, there are 180 names. There are some of them 3 times that number.... The principal charges made against Pa [William Fithian] are disloyalty, inefficiency and unpopularity. The opposing party are moving everything to carry this point and turn Pa out of office. They wished to put Col. Chandler in his place, but yesterday, Mrs. Cain & sister told us that because he, Col. C., had gone into partnership with Donlon & Daniels in the coal business, the Frazier faction have repudiated him and denounced him as a copperhead.... Frazier has abused Pa most outrageously to his face from his own dooryard... Will went to him and told him that if he ever insulted Pa again in his presence on the street he must take the consequences. He then commenced on Will and told him he had not left the army too soon, he was very unpopular, and so forth. One of the men of Company K happened to be by. He sprang up from his seat and denied the statement angrily.

It is very probable that the faction will succeed. John Short is actively engaged in it.... (Letter, Mary Black to Charles Black, November 16, 1863, JCBF.)

## EUGENE PAYNE GOES TO A PARTY

(Texas, November 1863) ... the chief man in the neighborhood, Don Florentino, was marshalling his forces to go to the aid of Cortina. He met me in the Plaza and at length offered if the 'Officers of the Federal Army,' with whom he hoped at all times to remain on the most friendly terms, would come back to Reynosa that evening, he would have a fandango in our special honor and for our benefit....

Evening came, and with it came the stars.... The air was clear and quite cold.

We got the yawl ready & the first load got in & attempted to go ashore but we had been too anxious and loaded our little yawl too heavy, so down we went & the boat filled with water. No one was drowned but we all got a good ducking. But this instead of making us stay at home only made us the more anxious, so going aboard & getting some dry clothes on, we once more embarked, this time with better luck, and soon we were at the fandango.

The hall was a long open shed with a high flat roof, studded thickly with ears of corn pointing downward to symbolize the stalagmites in a cave. Large chandeliers were hung up at each corner. The earth formed the floor leveled down smooth and hard. Chairs were arranged around the whole for seats. Outside of these were the refreshment tables & the game tables, for you must know that gaming forms a part of a Mexican's life....

The night was quite cool, which prevented a very large attendance. There were however about 30 senoritas (Mexican Ladies) present and the evening passed off very pleasantly.

These Mexican women are the best dancers in the world. Although they could not understand a word of English – and we having our own music called the figures in English, yet the danced the figures with as much ease and self possession as if they understood every word. There were several very pretty girls present, but the majority looked like well dressed indians. It was well that the subscriber could not talk Spanish or he might almost have been induced to flirt with some of the fair senoritas. As it was, having to talk through an interpreter, we were obliged to conduct ourselves as sedate as possible.

Owing to the chilliness of the night air, our fandango broke up about 2 o'clock & we adjourned to our boat. As we were going back, we discovered a very fine echo on the bank of the river. It was the plainest most distinct echo that I ever heard. It would articulate five syllables as plain as it would one & give even the intonation of the voice so distinct was it....

I do not think that I was ever better, even in Missouri. I think the rough trip up to Ringgold Barracks has greatly aided in restoring me to my former health. (Letter, November 30, 1863, EBP.)

THIRTY SEVENTH ILLINOIS

## EUGENE PAYNE – ON CHAPLAIN PLEASANT BISHOP

(November 1863) ... It seems that he was an orderly sergeant in the 94$^{th}$ Ills. (a last fall regt.). He soon grew tired of soldiering & going to General Banks prevailed upon him to give him a commission as chaplain in our regt. He is a very ignorant fellow. Knows nothing about his profession outside of a few stereotyped sentences of old fashioned hell-fire and brimstone doctrine. I tried to get him to acknowledge the other day that there was no literal hell; that all the hell there was ... was here & hereafter, but twas no go. I might corner him as many times as I might & he would either go off on a tangent or climb onto his hobby horse [with] some obsolete maxim or sentence.

My officers make so much fun of him now that I am thinking they will force the poor cuss to resign before long. He is in faith a Presbyterian. So much for that piece of 'furniture.'....

(Letter, November 30, 1863, EBP.)

## COPPERHEAD SENTIMENT IN PEORIA

(December 1863) There is a sickly and consumptive sheet published at Peoria called THE MAIL.... This abortion of a newspaper has been forced into existence by the copperhead doctors to blackmail the War Democrats and act as a receptacle of filth from the CHICAGO TIMES.

The individual who edits the MAIL is the same chap who used to live in Wisconsin, and people becoming tired of his presence took and tied him to a post to be used by skunks to ---- operate against, but instead of forcing him to leave the country, as was desired, the skunks all left. They couldn't stand the pressure upon their sense of smelling by the contact. (Article, December 2, 1863, RIU.)

THIRTY SEVENTH ILLINOIS

# 1864 NOTES

# RELATING TO CHAPTERS 23-28

# NOTES FROM THE WAR YEARS

## WILL BLACK – ON HOUSTON WEATHER

(January 1864) Last evening [Jan 4] a norther came up, and this morning there was a thin misty rain falling which froze as it fell, and left a glare of ice on trees & planks, but has scarce served to lay the dust.... The thermometer must be down to about 20 today, and in this climate it makes the wood fire glowing in the court room most decidedly pleasant. The sudden changes ... have had the effect of giving me a cold ... inconvenient chiefly in that it interferes with my singing, which is part of the evening's entertainment whenever I go into company.... (Letter, Will Black to his Mother, January 5, 1864, JCBF.)

## DAVID ASH – ON THE DEATH OF MICHAEL GLEASON

(January 1864) There was a sad occurrence took place in Co. B a few evenings ago. Michael Gleason, an Irishman, got intoxicated and went into a tent where David Anschutz and several other boys were, and began to abuse them. He took hold of several of them and choked them and finally came to Dave and caught him by the throat. Dave begged off and done everything to keep him in a good humor as he supposed Gleason was entirely the best man, but it was of no use, and when he saw it was fight or take a severe whipping he caught hold of a weapon of some kind and knocked him down and struck him several times in the face. Cut him very bad, and he died in about an hour. Dave is not blamed by any person that knows anything of the disposition of Gleason for he was a dangerous man and it was fight or die with Dave. (Letter, January 13, 1864, DASH.)

# THIRTY SEVENTH ILLINOIS

## MYRON BARNES – ON THE REPUBLIC OF MEXICO

(February 1864) ... Goats and people were socially equal, if any difference goats a little ahead, leading one to doubt the truth of Darwin's development theory.... The broad earth was the dining room, kitchen, and table, and the dark-eyed daughters of Montezuma, like the sun, rose and set without changing their toilet....

Texas, at the point where Brownsville is situated, is not at all inviting. At that point Texas borders on Mexico and distraction. It is the dividing line between the United States and the Mount Aetna of nations – between absolute beggary and selling matches, between Wendell Phillips and Wigfall. It is the backyard of the United States and the piazzi of Mexico. The Cleopatra of civilization, and the Mexican lazaroni, the asp upon its bosom.... There Caliban and Ariel are housed upon the island of Prospero. Mexico and America are merged. It is a vast conglomeration of ideas and things, a lottery box of national and worldwide prejudices and peculiarities, a history of the world knocked into pi.

We do not envy the $37^{th}$ in their new quarters. We should prefer to live in the puke state (Missouri) and apply the toe of our boot to some brigadier of State Militia, or in other words, do the thing up BROWN. The most that Southwestern Missouri is celebrated for is its State Militia Generals and wood ticks.... (Editorial, February 3, 1864, by Myron Barnes, RIU.)

## DAVID ASH – ON CHARLES BLACK

(February 1864) ... they won't do much in the regt. as long as Black is our Col. He has been acting so poisonous of late

# NOTES FROM THE WAR YEARS

that he won't take very well. He can use his tyranny for 7 or 8 months, yes, but he can't compel men to re-enlist. Lt. Col. Payne I suppose has arrived in Ills. before this time. If he was our commanding officer, I think the regt. would re-enlist without any trouble. (Letter, February 4, 1864, DASH.)

## HENRY KETZLE – ON CHARLES BLACK

(February 1864) The Colonel's horse, when about half way across, got mired and began to plunge, and at once B. was in danger of getting drowned, and the cheer that went up from his regiment told too plainly the friendly feelings his men have for J.C.B. (Letter, Henry Ketzle, December 13, 1863, published February 10, 1864, RIU.)

## MYRON BARNES – ON THE ASSAULT ON JOSEPH DANFORTH

Our city yesterday was the scene of much excitement, caused by the severe beating of the Editor of the Rock Island ARGUS for an insulting letter which he sent to the officers of the Soldier's Aid Society.

... In front of Harper and Steel's Hardware Store ... Major [J. M. Beardsley] planted a well aimed blow on the end, and under Danforth's smelling organ, knocking him through one of the large windows.... Danforth partially recovered, when the Major followed up the attack by several skillfully planted blows, which brought Danforth to the pavement. Danforth commenced blubbering, and begged like a schoolboy to be let up. This was a pretty position for a man of Danforth's size to be in, and placed there by a one armed man, and un-armed at that, while the baby who lay at his feet was armed

# THIRTY SEVENTH ILLINOIS

with a revolver and a sword cane, in good order; he having just paid Mr. Riggs $3 for putting it in good order. In the fracas Danforth lost his wig, and we learn that he accuses some one of the Grey Beard Regiment of carrying it off.

The Major allowed his adversary to arise when he again aimed several well put blows at Danforth, who bursted in the door of Harper & Steel's store and attempted to gain the further end of the room.... [He] reached the rear end of the store and then ran his head under a box with the rest of him exposed. The Major had not the heart to strike the coward who goes around with revolvers and sword cane after he had his head under a box, so he left him. Thus the affair ended. Danforth went to his office to repair damages, while the people gathered on the sidewalk to talk and laugh the matter over....

... we hope the editor of the Argus will learn by experience and not insult private individuals by a notice in his filthy sheet.

We understand the Major would be willing to make monthly report of the doings of the Ladies Soldier's Aid Society, were he to be at home, and the Copperhead editor should desire it.... (Editorial, February 17, 1864, RIU.)

## MYRON BARNES – ON JOSEPH DANFORTH

(March 1864) We are informed that the Editor of the Argus regales his auditors with a minute detail of the incidents connected with his whipping affair.... His is as much admired now that he is a martyr, by the country copperheads, as the hippopotamus was last summer by the people who visited the show.... Among the wonderful narrations which the martyr impresses upon his auditors is the one that he was attacked by four men in buckram, and that each held in his hands two of Colt's six-shooters, and of course, after his cane was wrenched from him, he had nothing to defend himself with against those four armed men.... (Editorial, March 2, 1864, RIU.)

## COPPERHEAD SENTIMENT IN CHICAGO

(March 1864) The CHICAGO TIMES, a few days ago, published the following slander which is better for the columns of a paper in 'Dixie' than a paper in loyal Illinois, even though it is Jeff. Davis' organ. Comment, however, is unnecessary:

> 'Of the New England school marms who went to Port Royal, sixty four have been obliged to start private nurseries on their own account for the use of little mulattoes. Our abolition contemporaries will undoubtedly designate this a slanderous falsehood; and, we will remark, that we agree with them to the extent of pronouncing it a case of lying-in as far as the school marms are concerned.' (Article, March 16, 1864, RIU.)

## WILL BLACK – ON JOHN WILKES BOOTH

(March 1864) ... I have a good room, board, & gas at $9.50 per week, which for [New Orleans] is very reasonable.... There are seven ladies who play & sing, & in the parlor is a piano, on which we are frequently favored with a noise that you can scarce call music, so much is the instrument out of tune, by the aid of which we are able to get up songs, duets & choruses & pass the evening ... agreeably. Among the la-

# THIRTY SEVENTH ILLINOIS

dies there is one who particularly pleased me, by name Miss Aldrich.... She is from New Hampshire & has come to live with her brother who is master of one of the government plantations....

... the only thing attracting particular interest here at present is the playing of J. Wilkes Booth at the St. Charles theater. I have seen him in the two great characters of Richard 3d and Hamlet & he renders both very well. (Letter, Will Black to home, March 17, 1864, JCBF.)

## CHARLES BLACK – ON SERVANTS

(June 1864) ... I have secured the services of two 'Unbleached Yankees' who promise to be invaluable....

John has already saved our mess from many a pang of hunger & unsatisfied longings. He generally rides a few feet at my rear & will sometimes disappear for 25 or 30 minutes to reappear with a squawking chicken, a bunch of radishes, or some other rather nice gleaning from the line of march. John is honest & pays for what he gets either in fair words or good money as the case demands.

Jeff Davis, the younger & smaller is rather a good looking chap. He came aboard at Memphis & when I asked his name, said, 'Jefferson Davis, sah!' as if quite proud to bear so big a traitor's name, and so small a wooly head. He is only about 4 ft. 8 in. tall & slenderly built....

Bill Barker met with a very sad accident yesterday [June 2]. He was left behind sick when the regt. marched & was cleaning out a tent to secure a good bed when he took hold of a gun by the ramrod to draw it out or move it a little when it exploded, carrying away the three first fingers of his right hand. (Letter, Charles Black to his Mother, June 1, 1864, JCBF.)

## CHARLES BLACK – ON LOUISIANA WILDLIFE

(June 1864) I have had a third visit from mine Ancient, the Ague [malaria] & my head throbbed with the exertion. This morning I have no such trouble, but the meanest set of fleas I ever saw; they bite, they tickle, they are in mouth & eyes & ears & hair on hands & every exposed part. They walk all over this sheet as I write, & while my pen gives the finishing touch to a word, they are wading through its first letters. Persistant! I have fought one of them with my whole energy & routed him three times. To see him come buzzing back to a fresh assault.... (Letter, Charles Black to his sister Mary, June 25, 1864, JCBF.)

## TOBACCO IN CHICAGO – CIRCA 1864

(June 1864) The blackguard practice of smoking in the public streets prevails here to a great extent. It is particularly obnoxious between nine and ten o'clock in the morning. Young men who look as if their mothers might have taught them better, and others who are old enough to know better without teaching, go puffing at their sickly rolls of tobacco, and doing their best to pollute the fresh morning air, and eject their saliva on the sidewalks for the women to wipe up [with their dresses]....

Those who smoke in the street are probably the same class who perform the nazal emuncation with the fingers. (Article, June 25, 1864, WWG.)

# THIRTY SEVENTH ILLINOIS

## MYRON BARNES – ON THE 37$^{TH}$

(July 1864) William Philleo ... called in this morning. We were glad to meet the lieutenant and hear from the troops in Louisiana. He gives us a sad picture of the 37$^{th}$ who are at Morganzie. They are left entirely to themselves. Their colonel has become so dissipated that he is of no account and has no control over the regiment. We believe, however, that there is virtue enough in the regiment to escape the excesses which would degrade them forever if their leader does set them such a bad example.

Lt. Philleo speaks well of the African regiment. This is the regiment of which Col. Frisbie, of Chicago, is commander, and Major Charles W. Hawes of this city, is Major. Most of the line and field officers of this regiment were formerly members of the 37$^{th}$ Illinois Volunteers. (Editorial, July 13, 1864, by Myron Barnes, RIU.)

## ADELIA PAYNE – ON THE ARMY

(August 1864) [Aug 17] ... You stated Col. Black was very sick with dysentery. Your letter came armed to make my soul sing for joy. I was the determination in evidence throughout ... to abandon the hated service of a soldier. That made me doubly happy. These three years of your soldiering I have only existed. I have lived no real life.... We have vegetated along the highways of life taking almost blindly what came to us just as a plant looks up to heaven and dumbly drinks the dew it sends.... Thirty one days more.... We will hold that eventful day, the 17$^{th}$ of September, in perpetual remembrance. It shall be one of the sanctified days in our household.

# NOTES FROM THE WAR YEARS

... I am of the opinion that both Haines and Blodgett are trying for the house of Rep (state). The joke of it is neither of them can get anything higher, and they want a place somewhere to make money by.... Your Father says let a man of common ability step forward at the eleventh hour and both Haines and Blodgett will be cast entirely out. He says the people are sick of both, but particularly of Haines. It is disgusting to hear [Melinda Haines] go on and relate the stories about Mr. Haines that she says, 'Blodgett and his clique have fabricated to injure Mr. Haines,' and when I know every word is truth! and she ought to know it if she don't. All I say is, 'how shameful,' half startled for fear she has discovered the latent sarcasm in my tone....

[Sep 1] ... Father was in last night. He has made arrangements with Haines whereby you can enter his law office immediately on your return to prosecute war claims. It is a great chance for you....

[Sep 4] ... it is a stormy day in Waukegan ... the wind is blowing a gale as I sit here in our little parlor by the window this afternoon looking out on the lake, and carelessly watching the billows rise and heave shoreward.... I said to myself, 'I will write again & will continue writing till he tells me he is ready to come and see me and the dear old lake....' (Letters, August 17, September 1 and 4, Adelia Payne to her husband, EBP.)

## WILL BLACK – ON ENEMIES IN DANVILLE

(October 1864) Pa [William Fithian, Provost Marshal] is in lots of hot water. Voss, assisted by Frasier & Guiness, has got up a petition for his removal, charging doubtful loyalty, tyranny, ungentlemanly behavior & favoring copperheads rather than loyal men. Also, sub-districting the district so as to excuse disloyal districts & tax loyal ones.... Another thing, Frasier had got into the habit of cursing Pa when he passes Frasier's house alone. I proposed to whip him, Pa & Ma both object & my hope now is that Frasier will try something of the kind sometime when I am with Pa, in which case one of us will be terribly whipped in about five minutes. If I do begin on him somebody will be badly hurt. If he continues his abuse when Pa is alone, it's a habit which he must stop sometime soon, or there'll be a 'wumpus.' I think I can whip him handsomely in about 3 ½ minutes. In saying 5, I allow 1 ½ for the contingencies of the case, viz., his whipping me, which would occupy at least that time.

I had a rumpus at home on the subject last night, which was decidedly unpleasant & a very few of which will send me into the army again, or at least away from home. I told Mother that there was a time in every man's life & it behooved us to learn it, when he learned to think for himself & must be guided by his own convictions of right & honor & ruled by no one. Imagine what followed! To do so accurately you probably only have to refer to your past.... (Letter, Will Black to Charles Black, October 25, 1864. JCBF.)

## CHARLES BLACK – ON MUSIC

(November 1864) Last night [Nov 13], when about 10 o'clock there came to my ears from the river, distant some ¾ of a mile, most ravishing strains of music. A bright moon sailed through an unclouded heaven & scintellent stars [I] watched. The steam organ played by a master hand and running through all variations from the blare of trumpet to those soft pianissimo notes that skilled fingers draw from a rich instrument.... Shutting my eyes, I have almost fancied angels feet trod round me ... at last I fell asleep.

About that calliope, they tell a good story in this country. An old French lady, mistress of a large plantation, ... was ... a devout believer in Milleriteism, and of course during her life never quite got the idea removed. A big revival was in progress in the neighborhood, when one night the old lady heard the calliope and instantly she thought of the last day. Her darkeys were soon about her. 'It's Gabriel! It's Gabriel!,' ... and they prayed loud & fast. Presently an old Auntie spoke, 'Mistress, Mistress, Jist hold on. I know it's Gabriel, but he's playin' "Wait for the Wagon," mistress, jist hold on!' (Letter, Charles Black to his Mother, November 4, 1864, JCBF.)

## CHARLES BLACK – AT DEVALLS BLUFF

(November 1864) Thanksgiving Day has come and gone. Would you like to know how we kept it here in camp? One day is like unto another. We slept and wrote and talked and worked....

With us the day was dark and cold and dreary. A dull, leaden sky, a wet earth, and only contented hearts to lighten its gloom....

... our house ... was at last completed. We had patted and smoothed its clay floor, and strewed sawdust thereon, we had hung our banners on its inner walls, and also our old clothes, we built a huge fire in the ample fireplace, then through our window, half glass, half oiled paper, we watched the last faint gleamings of day, lost in the shadows. The door was closed. On the rude logs & boards the fantastic firelight gleamed and faded. The raindrops passed eerily over the roof. Elfin or ghost feet could scarce patter more softly or faries ring sweeter.

# THIRTY SEVENTH ILLINOIS

Bells of silvery tone swirled away more tenderly as their 'good night' sounded on the leaves and died away in the forest and the gloom. There as we sat smoking came the voice of the wind and tenderly it talked to us that Thanksgiving night of the loved and absent.... ...puff, puff, puff, 'Colonel, I say!' speaking the Major. The charm is broken. We fold up our fancies, put away our hearts, talk awhile & go to bed.... (Letter, Charles Black to Will Black, from DeValls Bluff, November 23, 1864, JCBF.)

## LOUISVILLE JOURNAL CORRESPONDENT – ON EDWARD ANDERSON

(1864-1865) ...Pat Davis, a peaceable, quiet, but noble boy, aged 17 years, was one evening bathing in a creek a short distance from home when a squad of soldiers belonging to the 12th Indiana came by and arrested him and took him to camp.... He was carried before Col. Edward (or Edmund) Anderson, who was Colonel of the regiment, and by him asked if he was a bushwhacker? He replied "I am not; I have always been opposed to such a system of warfare, and have had nothing to do with it," which was true. The answer of Anderson was, "you are a damned liar, sir, and if you do not take the oath I will put you in prison until you do." No such threat could intimidate the boy, and he promptly refused. He was confined that night, and the next morning was again carried before Anderson, who told him if he did not take the oath, and give evidence of the bushwhackers supposed to be in the vicinity, he would have him shot. He told him he would take the oath, but knew nothing of the bushwhackers to tell him, which I have every reason to believe was true.

Said Anderson, "I will give you ten minutes to tell me where they are; and if, at the end of that time, you do not tell me all I want to know, you shall be shot." The ten minutes elapsed, and Davis could tell nothing. Anderson, calling to a Tory Lieutenant of his, named John Mayne Lee, told him to take a file of picked men and carry Davis to the woods and shoot him and leave him there. Here the young man told him that he knew nothing of bushwhackers, but that we would take the oath, and stay in his camp as a non-combatant, if he would spare his life. But no attention was paid to his words. He was taken to the woods, a half mile from Anderson's headquarters, tied to a tree and shot. Aye, shot like a dog in a ditch. Some of the privates who were sent out to shoot him, and some of Anderson's picked men, remonstrated with Lee, and even tried to induce him to turn him loose, and report that the boy had escaped.... [Davis] asked them to allow him a few minutes to be devoted to prayer. He was tied with his back to a tree, his hands loose, and then told to say his prayers. With his hands clasped and eyes raised to God, he silently commended his spirit to his savior. While he was yet praying, Lee drew a pistol and shot him through both hands! Again he begged for a few moments, but a second shot passed through another limb! And thus they continued to shoot the poor boy until he was shot sixteen times! Not one shot of them all would have proved mortal! Lee was begged by his men again and again to dispatch him, but he sternly refused. At length a Sergeant, who swore from the first that he would not fire a shot, told Lee that he would stand such barbarity no longer, but fired on the poor boy and shot him through the heart. His body was then left tied to the tree. An eye witness told me that it was three hours from the time Lee fired the first shot until the firing of the final shot by the Sergeant. All of this was in the hearing of Col. Edward (or Edmund) Anderson!

The next day, after this hellish murder, some citizen told Mrs. Davis he had seen the Yankees have Pat under arrest. She became alarmed and went immediately to Col. Anderson, and asked him where her son was. Mark, men of the North, his reply to the widowed mother: "By God, mad-

## THIRTY SEVENTH ILLINOIS

am, he is shot! Why in hell do you come to me about the damned rebel?"

Every man in the regiment was filled with indignation. One Lieutenant alone had the courage to denounce him, and swore that he would never rest until he was court-martialed. Through him charges were preferred against Col. Anderson. He was tried by court-martial, but nothing was ever done.

But the question very naturally arise who was Col. Anderson before the war. And what was he? Some would say "the man must surely have been a robber and murderer." But no such thing. He is today following the same profession that he was engaged in before the war. Every one that reads this will be shocked, when I tell them that he was and is an Episcopal Minister! Today, with every garment stained with blood, he is wrapt in the white robes of an Episcopal Minister, expounding the gospel to Northern men! Beware, Anderson, the sin of hypocrisy is one not easily forgiven, and surely you are the vilest hypocrite that ever disgraced the white robes of the church!

I appeal to every officer and soldier who belonged to the 12th Indiana, at that time, to state whether or not I have narrated the facts as they occurred.

I regret that the name of that noble Lieutenant, who was so active in having Anderson brought to trial, has escaped me. If this should ever reach him, I hope he will come forward and substantiate what I have written.

One deed of the Rev. Col. Edward (or Edmund) Anderson is before the nation.

I am not certain but I think he is in Indianapolis. (From Louisville Journal item, January 25, 1868.)

# NOTES FROM THE WAR YEARS

## EDWARD ANDERSON – ON HIS ALABAMA KILLINGS

(1864-1865) ...I send you herewith the original report of my Court Martial at Nashville for the murder of one Pat Davis, which case was considered the most aggravated, since the boy was shot several times, (this always against my order,) and because the men covered the body with brush, which was explicitly forbidden, since concealment was not part of our duty or policy.

The bringing of this matter before a Court Martial was an act of treachery on the part of a Major (W.H. Calkins) whom I had taken out of a little store in a country town of Indiana, and made – first [Quartermaster] – then Junior Major. Striving by military technicalities to prove himself Senior Major, he hoped through my Court Martial to secure to himself the position of Lt. Colonel and eventually Colonel. This case was the worse because I loved this man tenderly till his treachery was revealed to me through letters which came into my hands....

You will see by this Report of Evidence that I was charged with stealing U.S. horses and mules as well as with murder; and that the only evidence of anything of the sort having been done while I was in command was by the Lt. Col..., who with Calkins, endeavored to get me into this trouble.

This I write in explanation of the Court Martial evidence, by this Court I was fully acquitted.

I would go into details of the guerilla fights in the South, and the various cases of execution of men taken in the act, but such a thing is not perfectly safe, since if papers containing such evidence were to fall into the hands of the friends of the present Administration, they might be used to do harm, if in no other way than for blackmail which I am fully convinced the President is capable of, particularly since some of his own friends ... might be found among the number of guerillas so slain.

These guerillas were citizens of the locality in which they operated; generally poor whites who had little to risk besides their lives, and who were led by men of more or less influence & wealth. They fired from behind logs and trees, shot Union men through the cracks of log barns, or behind their backs, and in a mean, cowardly way.... In Northern Alabama, I arrested some of these men and sent them to the Dist. Prov. Marshal, but soon found they were allowed to take the oath – sometimes the second or third time – and go free, being allowed withal to take their guns! After this I invariably either shot, or ordered executed every man whom I found of the guerilla group, especially if he was found with an oath in his possession, though I do not think I shot a single man without an oath, unless I either shot him in action, or took him in the act of firing upon me or my men, or running away my horses and mules from camp.

In all this I was covered by Gen'l. & Special orders , either written or verbal. Those of the former that I have enclosed you by copy.
Quite a number of these men I shot in Missouri, several enroute from Louisville to Nashville, and some 30 in Northern Alabama, Tennessee, and Mississippi. Every one of these were guerillas, or citizens, taken in actual conflict with me or my command, and several of them had sent bullets in uncomfortable nearness to my head.

On my arrival at Huntsville Ala. with my command I received from Col. Alexander a list of names of men whom I was ordered [to find]. This list I enclose ..., with my endorsement on it made at the time, and which I afterwards recovered as a memorandum. I think all but two or three were shot. The exact number I do not remember.

I send you also copies of orders I received from time to time in regard to the hunting of these men, among them an order from Maj. Gen. Milroy, forwarded me by Brig. Gen. Bob Granger. (Letter to his Father, October 27, 1866, found on the James Julia website.)

Note: The "oath" referred to was an Oath of Alliegance to the United States, and was required of captured combatants as a condition of parole. Many of the southerners who signed did so to gain release from captivity and had no intention of honoring what they had signed.

THIRTY SEVENTH ILLINOIS

# 1865-1866 NOTES

# RELATING TO CHAPTER 29

# NOTES FROM THE WAR YEARS

## CHARLES BLACK – ON THE ARMY

(January 1865) ... to my minds eye is constantly present the drill ground, with its long lines of steady marching blue, lit up & variegated by the lightning flashing bayonet, surmounted by the rainbow hued flags and moving by the voice of the captain ... the shouting is constantly in my ear, the roll of drums, bray of bugles, screech of fifes, and rustling thunder of swift treading feet.... (Letter, Charles Black to Will Black, January 4, 1865, JCBF.)

## CHARLES BLACK – ON CAMP LIFE

(January 1865) December 12, early in the morning. The last notes of the reveille had scarcely died away before I was out of bed and doctoring our fire that through the night had burned to a few smouldering brands and a mass of ashy fire. Then toilette duties, done partly in ice water and a cold back room, then a letter home. It is a fine morning. The sun is out in all glory & pomp.... On the brown walls of our huts, bright beams are laying the fire, gently tinting the curling smoke till its hues are opaline and scattering brilliance from icicles and sleety roofs – Viva Winter.... So much for waking thoughts.

... The presence of women to soldiers is a constant appeal to their finer nature. Mrs. Huston, wife of the Major of the 23$^{rd}$ ... is gladdening her husband & his friends by a sojourn in winter quarters.... We type Mrs. H. in our fireside gossip as the Pet of the Brigade. Night before last, she paid us a visit, and you would have laughed to see us 'slicking up.' Flags unfurled, swords stacked, beds smooth, floor swept, fire rebuilt, rug down, and the room looking really cozy and home-like.

Then about 8 o'clock our string band came in and for a hour regaled us with really delightful music.... (Letter, Charles Black to Will Black, January 4, 1865, JCBF.)

## WILL BLACK – ON EUGENE PAYNE

(January 1865) While in [Springfield] I went into the Senate & House, the most brainless bodies of men, so far as I could judge, that I ever saw. E.B. Payne was in the house, but I did not catch his eye & consequently no signs of recognition passed between us.... (Letter, Will Black to Charles Black, January 21, 1865, JCBF.)

## CHARLES BLACK'S CONFESSION

(January 1865) ... Since leaving home, I have become a vastly altered man. (You need not congratulate me on this ... for that would indicate that you, mon frere, had in times past seen joints in my harness, & friends to friends faults should be blind). I have eschewed the vulgar path of debauchery and claim now to be an artist. Wine I rarely use, never to excess. The natural consequence of this is that my head, heart, & system are cleaner, purer & stronger than ever before since entering the army. Oh, Will, I shudder with horror, disgust & shame when I look back some 15 months in my life [to Brownsville] at what I did and saw in the scarlet portions of this vast Babylon, who crowned with the beauty and splendor of the south, is thick with the blood of thousands of souls, lost to honor, lost to earth, lost to heaven, who have rotted all manliness away in prostitution, and drowned all hopes in fiery drunkenness.

# NOTES FROM THE WAR YEARS

My dear brother, I live out ten years of my life in a short twelvemonth and now if I can, I intend to reclaim the priceless time I so foolishly crowned with bacchanalian grapes & Cyprian bays & sent before me to hell, dark accusers, gloomy scourge-armed nemeses....

[January 17] I was invited to a select little party at Galpin's. I enjoyed myself highly, and must tell you of a little left hand compliment that was paid me.... One of the guests, an officer of eminent position, fine talent, elegant manners asked a friend of mine, 'Is that the same person who used to wear long hair and a red sash about his waist?' 'Yes.' 'Well, I could not induce myself to believe it! He is a perfect gentleman!' I recite this more as a collateral to the opening of my letter than from vanity though it pleased me to know that the change has been legibly written on my outer man. (Letter, Charles Black to Will Black, January 20, 1865, JCBF.)

## HOUSTON TELEGRAPH

(October 27). The 48$^{th}$ Ohio Regiment ... has been ordered to Galveston.... The 37$^{th}$ Ill. Regt., Col. Kennicott Commanding, will take their place. This regiment has been on duty at Columbus lately, and the paper ... speaks in high terms of the gentlemanly conduct of the regiment during their stay there.

(November 8). Several soldiers and colored men got into a difficulty on Monday night at the Market House, and knives and pistols were drawn. The darkies defied the soldiers.... (Houston Telegraph, October 27 and November 8, 1865.)

# THIRTY SEVENTH ILLINOIS

## HENRY FRISBIE – ON THE FREEDMEN'S BUREAU

(October 1865) ... if Colored Soldiers and their families are to be treated like and expected to take care of themselves as white soldiers and their families in the north, then is your Bureau a useless encumbrance, and the sooner it is shut up and its agents sent home the better. It is because the Colored Soldiers' families and their friends are totally unlike in condition to the white soldiers' families and friends that your Bureau is here today, and if you allow Planters to turn off and shut up the cabins of these Soldiers families before provisions are made for them elsewhere, and especially months before anyone else wants to hire them, then has your Bureau utterly failed in its functions contemplated in its establishment.

In regard to the question of food, I am positive that outside of the Parishes around New Orleans and immediately on the river, not one in fifty Planters furnishes food but require labor ... they feed themselves from their little gardens, pigs, chickens, and eggs. In this particular case, no clothing, food, or pay had been furnished for two years. It seems to me proper to require Planters when they have persons on their place not wanted, to request their removal through the Bureau. But to turn them off at their pleasure and keep their pigs and chickens and cooking utensils, and leave them on the levee a week in starving condition, is an injustice towards the families of these soldiers that the Noble Republic, greatful for the services of these men in its hour of peril, will not permit at the hands of any of its agents, and no one knows better than yourself how hard it is to get a boat to take any of these people on board. The boats are run solely in the interests of the white men as controlled by the sentiments of the south ... let a boat show any favor to this class of people and see how much freight they would get after the cry of Abolitionist was raised against it. Why, they had better have the yellow fever on board.

It is the general purpose among Planters to turn off very soon nearly all those upon their places, and already Baton Rouge & Port Hudson are so crowded that there is no room for more, and yet the complaints of cruelty and injustice are so numerous that but a few of them can be attended to. I hear that the same state of things extend elsewhere.

In the north the land is in many hands; little villages everywhere, home and residences already provided, or plenty of friends who have them, and a sentiment favorable to the soldiers, their families, and cause, is scattered everywhere over the north, but here how different. The land is in few hands, few villages where homes are to be had, and these already crowded. The ... people who control these things [are] very hostile to these men, their families, and cause, and yet you say that these men must do as white soldiers of the north do, but how are they to do it? Where are the homes to be had now?

I wish to look at practical measures and discard merely theory or extremes, in such measures as may be taken to make these people wholly self-supporting in the shortest possible time, which I conceive to be the object of your Bureau.... (Letter, Henry N. Frisbie to Thomas W. Conway, October 2, 1865, Record of Court Martial #MM3349, Record Group 153, National Archives.)

## BASEBALL

(April 1866) The formation of Base Ball Clubs seems to be the order of the day among the young men in many cities at the present time. Let us revive the one we had here before the war. After getting the thing a little under way, no doubt us Texans can pick up a multitude of those gloves and fling them back with a vengeance. The fact is, we don't undertake many things which we don't surpass in, particularly in that line. (Article, Houston Telegraph, April 19, 1866.)

## WELLS MORRILL – ON THE WILD WEST

(March and August 1866) Many of the 37$^{th}$ intend to remain in Texas and myself with the rest. I imagine I can do better here than in Ills., and then there happens to be an attraction in the shape of calico, etc.; rendering it a necessity for me to remain.

In regard to personal safety, I think it just as safe for any man here that minds his own business as in any other state.... It is true that laws are not enforced here as in other states. It is nothing strange to hear of a man being shot and killed in a fight and nothing done with the murder. But there is no difficulty of keeping clear of anything of that kind if one is disposed to.

If a man does happen to get in any difficulty, his only hope is to kill first and he will not be molested by the civil authorities. I know at least 15 men in the little town [Hempstead] of 300 inhabitants that have killed their man and some 2 or 3....

# NOTES FROM THE WAR YEARS

Everybody goes armed and all seems to know that if there is any fuss, shooting is going to be done and therefore are very careful....

... the last time I saw Chan [Morse] was in Galveston when I played billiards with him. He had just got a leave of absence for 15 days and did not know where to go.... Col. Kennicott has plantation cotton and free negroes on the brain....

Ed Farnsworth of Co. C was shot a few days ago by a citizen in Houston and probably made a cripple for life. The ball entered his back and it is thought affected the lower part of his body. The man left, and has not been heard of since. A great pity, for he was physically the best man with the regt., on one of the best. (Letter, Wells C. Morrill to Eugene Payne, March 3, 1866, EBP.)

The Kennicott's are here [Galveston] and running a plantation, but the Col., Ransom, is in Kentucky I think, with his regt, a 2d Lieut. Regular Army. Geo. is on the plantation (Brazoria). Brazoria Co. Texas is his address.

I ... am under no fear of being picked off, and in fact have become attached in a measure to Texas. I am steady and go to church regular 3 times Sabbath, sing in the choirs, and am a member of a Harmonic Society and am getting acquainted in the best society in the city....

Sowles is a citizen employee in Quartermaster Dept. at Houston, and doing well, I believe. The silver mine was a complete failure and I understand given up entirely.

In regard to the polical sentiment here, there is plenty of unison, and in fact all are in unison and mighty little Unionism. Yanks are generally below par, but few know that I am a Federal, and I never tell anyone unless I am obliged to. I can stand everything but to hear the Star & Stripes spoken badly of, or Ills. troops. When these two points are spoken of they know who I am.

I had one little adventure that made me a Big Dog with a Brass Colar for a time and with the worst rebs. In a barber shop one night a lot of southern chivalry was collected and all giving the Yanks fits and I said nothing until one fellow that knew me told another that I was a Yank and not to insult me, and he said he did not care if I was. I was a D-n Son of a B-h.

I coolly took a Navy 6 shooter and poked it into the man's face and made him take it back and his own comrades told me to shoot him and told me I should have fair play, and I made him apologize and he left. Every one of them men shook hands and told me if I wanted any friends to call on them. The fellow threatens to knife me but he has got to do it mighty quick or I'll do something for him if he attempts it. It has made him unpopular with his own crowd and made friends to me.

Political matters in general are 5 times as bad as they were when our troops first landed, and people are more bitter.... I would as live jump into the Gulf as say I am a Radical. It makes it disagreeable at times for us that wishes to mingle with society, but there is one thing; we can oblige them to respect us and in time will.... (Letter, Wells C. Morrill to Eugene Payne, August 1, 1866, EBP.)

## THE HOUSTON TELEGRAPH

(January 8). Marshal Lord is determined to break up the outrage of the freedmen being robbed by soldiers in this city.

## NOTES FROM THE WAR YEARS

(January 12). We are glad to learn that the late City Marshal intends to ferret out and bring to punishment all those parties who have imported obscene photographs and clandestinely sold them to boys and young men.

(January 26). A good row took place at the theatre Tuesday night. It seems the soldiers sent a railroad man out of the house [typifying] ... the rude manner in which the guard on duty have shown to the patrons of the city.

(February 16). We hear from passengers lately arrived from Brenham, that a soldier [Andrew Hunter] was killed in that town on Sunday evening last by some unknown person. It seems a party of soldiers got on a drunken spree and came to town, making threats and creating disorder generally. Several shots were fired, but nobody seems to know who did it. One citizen was arrested and brought to this city on Tuesday's train, and he will have an examination in a few days.

(February 18). We have heard of many outrages being committed daily by drunken soldiers in this city. One of them entered a clothing store near Main Street a day or two ago and helped himself to a pair of pants. The owner of the store called officer Herbert, who is a fighting man, and the drunken scoundrel was glad to drop his plunder and to skedaddle in double quick time....

(February 21). A gang of drunken soldiers made a great disturbance on Sunday night on Main Street. Several pistol shots were fired. Cannot something be done to put a stop to such scenes of lawlessness?

(February 22). We hear from passengers who arrived on the Central train yesterday that a party of drunken soldiers raised a disturbance in Millican, and that several shots were fired by the citizens and soldiers....

## THIRTY SEVENTH ILLINOIS

(February 28). We are informed that a number of soldiers both white and black, are scattered throughout the city on detailed duty, with no one to control their coming in or going out. It is said that many carry revolvers.... Every man who sells liquor or firearms to soldiers ought to be arrested and punished. It does not tell very well for the discipline on the troops that the haul of counterfeit money ... was traced through a house of ill fame ... one of the bills had been passed by an officer of considerable rank.

(March 5). There were several bloody noses and black eyes made late Thursday evening, in and around the little grog establishment on the other side of the Bayou, near the lower bridge, in a hot scrimmage between two Irishmen on the one side and a crowd of U.S. Soldiers on the other, most of whom fought under the disadvantage of having many heavy bricks in their hats. No one was seriously hurt, but we understand that one of the Irishmen in the melee had his pocket robbed of sixty dollars.

(March 7). There was some stir on Main Street late Sunday evening, produced by two of Uncle Sam's boys who had been a-smiling rather too frequently. At first when only a few sheets in the wind, they seemed to be in love with all creation, particularly the black portion of it. Finally, they became bellicose, and swore they would wipe out the last African in Houston. One of them ... encountered a big Buck near the "finish," and pitched into him at once. The buck had grit.... The soldiers got the worst of it....

(March 14). Sunday evening, one of Uncle Sam's boys in blue, under the divine influence of a half a gallon of busthead, administered internally, imagined himself metamorphosed into one of the sublimest orators that ever lived under this agreeable hallucination, having collected around him a large crowd of idlers, he resolved himself into a committee of the whole on the state of the Union, and launched forth.

He protested that the Southern People were as good a people as the great gluminary God ever shown upon; that the most of the men were perfect gentlemen, and the ladies were so purty it made his mouth water to look at 'em. He denounced the radicals as a set of damphules.... The [blacks] were nothing but a race of monkeys without tails, that he had a dog at home that was more of a gentleman.... A big buck, not liking this part ... denounced the orator as a Yankee scoundrel and a liar.... Fur flew prodigiously for a while....

(March 23). Private Barney McGunnigle, Co. K, 37$^{th}$ Illinois Volunteers, has been got before a court martial on the charge of assaulting and badly damaging a freedman on the streets of this city. He was sentenced to ... one year at the Dry Tortugas....

(April 4). One of Uncle Sam's boys was heard to explain 'tother morning that he was, "just spiling to get on a regular hell-roaring bust, but that d—d rebel local of the Telegraph would be sure to get hold of it."

(April 13). A crowd of drunken soldiers created a considerable disturbance on Main Street the other evening.... One fellow frequently brandished a pistol in the face of people quietly passing, and one time actually discharged it....

(April 20.) The soldier who was shot the other evening [Edwin Farnsworth] by Officer Herbert of the City Police is doing well. Officer Herbert has vamoosed.... No need of his having done so. He was justifiable.... We understand that some of the soldiers are threatening to shoot Herbert if he should appear on the streets again.

# Appendix 2 – Descriptive Roll

## INTRODUCTION

The data in the following personnel list was taken from the State of Illinois Adjutant General's Reports, regimental records in the Illinois State Archives, and from descriptive rolls, enlistment records, and disability discharge certificates contained in the Individual Compiled Service Records of the 37$^{th}$ Illinois in Record Group 94 in the National Archives.

In cases where information was recorded under several spellings of the same name in Record Group 94, the soldier is alphabetized under the most common spelling of that name, or the spelling most consistently used, or the name in the 1885 Veteran's Association Directory.

In many cases, particularly with illiterate soldiers, spelling depended on the phonetic interpretation of the clerk or officer taking the verbal information. Probably the largest number of variations, over a dozen, occurred with Henry Heitahrands, who was literate. The name Cain would appear variously as Kain, Kane, or Cane. McAuliffe appeared as McOliff, McOlliff, McOllieff, McOLoff, McOlluff, or McOloff. These variations take up Record Jacket numbers 1567 thru 1576 in the Compiled Service Records for the regiment. The bad handwriting of impatient clerks did little to improve the accuracy rate.

Place of enlistment in these records was often listed as place of residence, and enlistment date as muster date. The most probable accurate data has been used in these cases. Enlistment date, unless otherwise noted, can be assumed to be the month of August 1861.

# DESCRIPTIVE ROLL

The information on company assigned, age, occupation and residence is as of the date of enlistment. Individual rank changed several times for some men.

The order of information is:

Name, Assigned Company, Age, Height, Complexion, Color of Eyes, Color of Hair.
Birthplace, Occupation, Residence, Enlistment Date, if recruit.
(Comment on service history, if any.)
Disposition: Mustered Out, Resigned, Discharged Disability, Deserted, Died, Killed, Transferred.

In cases where the records are unclear between birthplace origin and residence, "F." means "From" the place noted. The abbreviation "Res." is for Residence and "Enl." for "Enlisted."

A note on desertion: Many soldiers who were properly transferred, detailed, sick, on leave, promoted or discharged were often carried as deserters even though they were properly absent. Desertion showing on a soldier's records may have been simple absence with permission or orders, and was often a false report.

The inaccuracy of the service records extends beyond spelling. Many times, men were reported as died who had not, and cities, towns, and states (particularly in foreign countries) were so garbled as to make little sense. Add to this the number of 15 and 16 year old boys who reported their age as 18 or older, and the 40 and up men who gave a false age, and a volume of inaccuracies is inevitable.

# THIRTY SEVENTH ILLINOIS

## DESCRIPTIVE ROLL

## A

| Abbey, Frederick | | I | 24 | 5'9" | Dark | Gray | Brn |
|---|---|---|---|---|---|---|---|
| Bedford, England | Gunsmith | Res. Chicago | | | | | |
| Resigned 2-28-63 at Camp Bliss, Mo. on Surgeon's Ctf. | | | | | | | |

| Abernathy, Fielding | | D | 29 | 6'0" | Dark | Brn | Blk |
|---|---|---|---|---|---|---|---|
| B. Indiana | Laborer | Enlisted Manistee, Mich. | | | | | |
| Deserted September 1861 | | | | | | | |

| Ackley, William B. | | K | 28 | 5'9" | Dark | Blue | Brn |
|---|---|---|---|---|---|---|---|
| B. Wayne County, N.Y. | Farmer | Enlisted Danville | | | | | |
| Discharged Disability St. Louis 5-16-62 | | | | | | | |

| Adams, Fayette | | I | 18 | 5'6" | Light | Grey | Brn |
|---|---|---|---|---|---|---|---|
| B. Albany, N.Y. | Farmer | Res. in 1885 Cherry Valley, Enl. Belvidere | | | | | |
| Deserted Camp Bliss 2-25-62 | | | | | | | |

| Adams, Newton | | K | 25 | 5'8" | Dark | Blk | Blk |
|---|---|---|---|---|---|---|---|
| | Farmer | Enlisted Danville | | | | | |
| Mustered out 10-4-64 | | | | | | | |

| Adams, Wilber H. | | I | 20 | 5'10" | Light | Grey | Brn |
|---|---|---|---|---|---|---|---|
| F. Chili, N.Y. | Farmer | Res. in 1885 Cherry Valley | | | | | |
| Re-enlisted in 1st U.S. Artillery 12-31-63 | | | | | | | |

# DESCRIPTIVE ROLL

| Adkins, John T. | | K | 21 | 5'10" | Dark | Blue | Blk |
|---|---|---|---|---|---|---|---|
| B. Fountain Co., Indiana | Farmer | Enlisted Danville | | | | | |
| Discharged Disability 8-28-62 Phithesis | | | | | | | |

| Adkins, Joseph T. | | K | 21 | | | | |
|---|---|---|---|---|---|---|---|
| | | Enlisted Danville | | | | | |
| Discharged Disability 6-19-62 | | | | | | | |

| Adkins, Robert | | K | 23 | 5'8" | Dark | Blue | Blk |
|---|---|---|---|---|---|---|---|
| F. Lodi, Indiana | Farmer | Res. Vermilion | | | | | |
| Died 2-8-64 at Brownsville, Texas | | | | | | | |

| Agler, Charles W. | | E | 23 | 5'7" | Light | Blue | Lgt |
|---|---|---|---|---|---|---|---|
| B. Lycoming Co. Pa. | Farmer | Enlisted Mendota | | | | | |
| Died in Hospital at Vicksburg 7-22-64 | | | | | | | |

| Agler, Henry | | E | 30 | 5'11" | Light | Grey | Lgt |
|---|---|---|---|---|---|---|---|
| B. Lycoming Co. Pa. | Farmer | Enlisted Mendota | | | | | |
| Discharged Disability at Syracuse 8-29-62 Weak Arm. | | | | | | | |

| Agler, Jonathan A. | | E | 24 | 5'7" | Light | Blue | Lgt |
|---|---|---|---|---|---|---|---|
| B. Columbia Co. Tenn. | Black-smith | Enlisted Mendota, Res. 1885 Plano. Ill. | | | | | |
| Mustered Out 5-15-66 | | | | | | | |

| Agler, William | | E | 22 | 5'8" | Light | Blue | Lgt |
|---|---|---|---|---|---|---|---|
| B. Lycoming Co. Pa. | Farmer | Enlisted Mendota | | | | | |
| Discharged 5-3-65 | | | | | | | |

# THIRTY SEVENTH ILLINOIS

| Ahstrom, Axel P.E. | | A | 25 | | | | |
|---|---|---|---|---|---|---|---|
| | | Enlisted Rock Island | | | | | |
| Mustered Out 10-4-64. Wounded at Pea Ridge, slightly in the leg. ||||||||

| Alexander, Benjamin | | D | 44 | 5'10" | Florid | Grey | Drk |
|---|---|---|---|---|---|---|---|
| B. New Castle Isle, Canada | Fisherman | Enlisted Pentwater | | | | | |
| Discharged Disability at St. Louis 5-7-66 Chronic Rheumatism (Illiterate) ||||||||

| Allard, Daniel | | E | 41 | 6' | Light | Blue | Gry |
|---|---|---|---|---|---|---|---|
| B. Genessee, N.Y. | | Enlisted Mendota, Residence in 1885: Cedar Rapids, Iowa. | | | | | |
| Discharged Disability 1-20-62 at Lamine Crossing ||||||||

| Allen, Thomas | | E | 21 | 5'10" | Light | Blue | Lgt |
|---|---|---|---|---|---|---|---|
| B. New York | Farmer | Enlisted at Joliet. Res. 1885 Sandoval, Ill. | | | 3-1-65 | | |
| Mustered Out 2-28-66 ||||||||

| Allison, Frederick | | I | 21 | 5'10" | Light | Blue | Blk |
|---|---|---|---|---|---|---|---|
| B. Vermilion Co. | Clerk – Farmer | | | | | 8-14-62 | |
| Mustered Out 6-9-65 ||||||||

| Allison, Thomas J. | | K | 21 | 5'7" | Fair | Blue | Red |
|---|---|---|---|---|---|---|---|
| B. Vermilion, Ill. | Farmer | Res. Warren Co. | | | | | |
| Mustered Out 9-29-64 ||||||||

| Ames, Levi | | F | 21 | 5'10" | Light | Blue | Lgt |
|---|---|---|---|---|---|---|---|
| B. Sullivan, Pa. | Farmer | Residence Antioch | | | | | |
| Discharged Disability 8-24-62 ||||||||

# DESCRIPTIVE ROLL

| Ames, Walter | | | B | 20 | 5'8" | Dark | Brn | Dark |
|---|---|---|---|---|---|---|---|---|
| B. Lake Co. | | Farmer | Res. Antioch, Res. 1885 St Mary's, Pa | | | | | |
| Mustered Out 4-19-66 | | | | | | | | |

| Anderson, Andrew | | | B | 22 | | Dark | Brown | Brown |
|---|---|---|---|---|---|---|---|---|
| B. Lake Co. | | Farmer | Enlisted Waukegan, Res. 1885 Union, Iowa | | | | | |
| Discharged Wounds 11-24-62. Wounded in the wrist. | | | | | | | | |

| Anderson, Augustus | | | D | 22 | | | | |
|---|---|---|---|---|---|---|---|---|
| B. Sweden | | Lumberman | Res. Hamlin, Mich | | | | | |
| Mustered Out 5-15-66. Wounded at Pea Ridge in the arm. | | | | | | | | |

| Anderson, Charles A. | | | I | 18 | 5'10" | Light | Grey | Brown |
|---|---|---|---|---|---|---|---|---|
| F. Mass. | | Farmer | Res. Marengo, Res. 1885 Bonus, Ill. | | | | | |
| Mustered Out 10-4-64 | | | | | | | | |

| Anderson, Edward (Chaplain) | | | | 27 | | | | |
|---|---|---|---|---|---|---|---|---|
| B. New Hampshire | | Minister | Enlisted Chicago | | | | | |
| Resigned 4-25-62. Later to be Colonel 12th Indiana Cavalry | | | | | | | | |

| Anderson, George | | | I | 18 | 5'10" | Light | Blue | Brown |
|---|---|---|---|---|---|---|---|---|
| F. Leroy, Ill. | | Farmer | Res. Sharon, Wis. Res 1885 Bonus, Ill. | | | | | |
| Mustered Out 10-4-64 | | | | | | | | |

| Anderson, James | | | | 19 | 5'5" | Dark | Hazel | Dark |
|---|---|---|---|---|---|---|---|---|
| B. Canada | | Laborer | Enlisted Chicago | | | 3-28-65 | | |
| | | | | | | | | |

| Anderson, John | | | B | 23 | | Dark | Blue | Brown |
|---|---|---|---|---|---|---|---|---|
| B. Sweden | | Farmer | Enlisted Goshen, Res 1885 West Hills, Neb | | | | | |
| Mustered Out 5-15-65 | | | | | | | | |

# THIRTY SEVENTH ILLINOIS

| Anderson, John | | D | 28 | | | | |
|---|---|---|---|---|---|---|---|
| | | Res. Hamlin, Mich | | | | | |
| Died 2-13-63 Intermittent Fever | | | | | | | |

| Annis, Charles | | C | 22 | | | | |
|---|---|---|---|---|---|---|---|
| | | Res. Wauconda, Res. 1885 Volo, Ill. | | | | | |
| Mustered Out 10-4-64 | | | | | | | |

| Anschutz, Aaron S. | | B | 19 | | | | |
|---|---|---|---|---|---|---|---|
| | | Res. Goshen, Enlisted Lafayette | | | | | |
| Mustered Out 9-29-64 | | | | | | | |

| Anschutz, David | | B | 21 | | Dark | Brown | Black |
|---|---|---|---|---|---|---|---|
| B. Lafayette | Farmer | Res. Goshen | | | | | |
| Mustered Out 5-15-66 | | | | | | | |

| Arbogast, John L. | | G | 18 | 5'8" | Light | Hzle | Brn |
|---|---|---|---|---|---|---|---|
| B. McLean, Ill. | Farmer | Res. Cheney's Grove, Res. In 1885, Saybrook, Ill. | | | | | |
| Mustered Out 10-4-64 | | | | | | | |

| Armpriest, John W. | | A | 28 | 5'11" | Light | Hazle | Sandy |
|---|---|---|---|---|---|---|---|
| B. Berkley Co. West Virginia | Farmer | Enlisted Rock Island | | | | | |
| Mustered Out 5-15-66 | | | | | | | |

| Armstrong, Archibald | | A | 22 | | | | |
|---|---|---|---|---|---|---|---|
| F. Bowling | | | | | | 8-14-61 | |
| Mustered Out 9-29-64 | | | | | | | |

| Armstrong, Christopher | | A | 18 | 5"10" | Fair | Blue | Sandy |
|---|---|---|---|---|---|---|---|
| B. Fermanagh, Ireland | Farmer | Res. Preemption, Res. In 1885, Sutton, Neb. | | | 8-14-62 | | |
| Mustered Out 6-12-65 | | | | | | | |

# DESCRIPTIVE ROLL

| Armstrong, Robert A. | | | A | 25 | 5'9" | Fair | Blue | Sandy |
|---|---|---|---|---|---|---|---|---|
| B. Fermanagh, Ireland | | Farmer | Res. Preemption | | | | 8-14-62 | |
| Died Carrolton, La, 9-22-63 | | | | | | | | |

| Arno, Joseph | | | D | 33 | 5'7" | Dark | Black | Black |
|---|---|---|---|---|---|---|---|---|
| B. Belgium | | Laborer | Enl. Manistee, Res. Hamlin, Mich. | | | | | |
| Deserted from Steamer HANNIBAL enroute to Vicksburg 6-9-63 with arms. | | | | | | | | |

| Arnold, Frederick | | | F | 22 | 5'7" | Dark | Hazel | Dark |
|---|---|---|---|---|---|---|---|---|
| B. France | | Carpenter | Res. Halfday, Res. 1885 Chicago, Ill. | | | | | |
| Discharged at St. Louis 1-4-63, wounds at Pea Ridge. | | | | | | | | |

| Ash, David L. | | | B | 22 | 6'0" | Fair | Blue | Brown |
|---|---|---|---|---|---|---|---|---|
| B. Fayette Co. Pa. | | Farmer | Enlisted Lafayette, Res. Goshen | | | | | |
| Mustered Out 3-14-65 | | | | | | | | |

| Ashley, Robert | | | E | 23 | 5'11" | Dark | Brown | Black |
|---|---|---|---|---|---|---|---|---|
| B. Ottawa, Canada | | Farmer | Enlisted Mendota, Res. 1885 Golden City, Mo. | | | | | |
| Mustered Out 9-29-64 | | | | | | | | |

| Atkins, William W. | | | B | 28 | 5'7" | Fair | Blue | Brown |
|---|---|---|---|---|---|---|---|---|
| B. Warren, Pa. | | Engineer | Enlisted Lafayette | | | | | |
| Discharged Disability 2-1-63, "chronic irritation of spinal cord, pain in the track of spinal cord, which by any exertion excites palpitation of the heart." | | | | | | | | |

| Atkinson, Joseph C. | | | A | 26 | 5'9" | Light | Blue | Brown |
|---|---|---|---|---|---|---|---|---|
| B. Canada West | | Mason | Res. Pleasant Valley, Iowa, Res 1885 Crescent City, Ill. | | | | | |
| Deserted 12-6-62 from Keitsville, took a Colt Revolving Rifle and accoutrements. | | | | | | | | |

# THIRTY SEVENTH ILLINOIS

| Atkinson, Manning | | | G | 24 | 5'5" | Light | Blue | Light |
|---|---|---|---|---|---|---|---|---|
| B. Lake Co. Ohio | | Farmer | Res. Cheney's Grove, Res 1885 Saybrook, Ill. | | | | | |
| Mustered Out 8-14-65 | | | | | | | | |

| Atkinson, William | | | A | 23 | | | | |
|---|---|---|---|---|---|---|---|---|
| F. Fulton | | | Res. 1885 Peoria, Ill. | | | | | |
| Mustered Out 9-29-64 | | | | | | | | |

| Aurand, Robert D. | | | A | 30 | | Dark | Blue | Dark |
|---|---|---|---|---|---|---|---|---|
| B. Union Co. Pa. | | Farmer | Enlisted at Dixon, Ill. | | | 3-16-65 | | |
| | | | | | | | | |

| Austin, Pardon J. | | | E | | 5'9" | Sandy | Blue | Light |
|---|---|---|---|---|---|---|---|---|
| B. New York | | Farmer | Enlisted Mendota, Res. 1885 Mendota, Ill. | | | | | |
| Mustered Out 9-29-64 | | | | | | | | |

| Avery, James | | | F | 18 | 5'6" | Light | Grey | Light |
|---|---|---|---|---|---|---|---|---|
| B. England | | Farmer | Res. Long Grove | | | | | |
| Mustered Out 10-4-64 | | | | | | | | |

| Ayers, Thomas | | | B | 23 | 5'5" | Light | Blue | Red |
|---|---|---|---|---|---|---|---|---|
| B. Essex Co. N.J. | | Farmer | Res. Hopewell | | | 10-1-64 | | |
| Mustered Out 10-9-65 | | | | | | | | |

# B

| Baher, William | | | G | 32 | 5'6" | Light | Grey | Brown |
|---|---|---|---|---|---|---|---|---|
| B. Germany | | Farmer | Enlisted Schaumburg, Ill | | | | | |
| Died 9-1-63 at New Orleans of Disease | | | | | | | | |

# DESCRIPTIVE ROLL

| Bailey, John | | | K | 30 | 6'0" | Dark | Blue | Dark |
|---|---|---|---|---|---|---|---|---|
| F. Vermilion | | Farmer | Enlisted Mendota | | | 9-23-61 | | |
| Mustered Out 10-4-64 | | | | | | | | |

| Baker, Andrew J. | | | E | 22 | 5'6" | Light | Blue | Light |
|---|---|---|---|---|---|---|---|---|
| B. Lycoming Co. Pa. | | Farmer | Res. Mendota, Enlisted at St. Louis | | | 9-20-61 | | |
| Discharged 3-3-66 | | | | | | | | |

| Baker, Asa (Staff) | | | D | 34 | | | | |
|---|---|---|---|---|---|---|---|---|
| | | | Enlisted Chicago, Appt. Brigade Commissary 12-10-61, Res. In 1885 Waterloo, N.Y. | | | | | |
| | | | | | | | | |

| Baker, David | | | F | 20 | 6'0" | Light | Blue | Light |
|---|---|---|---|---|---|---|---|---|
| B. Washington Cty, N.Y. | | Farmer | Res. Halfday | | | | | |
| Died at Otterville Mo. 1-13-62 of disease. | | | | | | | | |

| Baker, Robert W | | | K | 32 | 5'11" | Dark | Blue | Dark |
|---|---|---|---|---|---|---|---|---|
| B. Worcester Co., MD | | Farmer | Res. Catlin Township | | | 6-16-64 | | |
| On Furlough at Muster Out of Regiment | | | | | | | | |

| Balcom, Edward W. | | | E | 44 | 5'9" | Light | Blue | Brown |
|---|---|---|---|---|---|---|---|---|
| B. Vermont | | Carpenter | Enl. Mendota | | | | | |
| Discharge Disability 1-14-64 | | | | | | | | |

| Ballard, John E. | | | F | 20 | 6'0" | Light | Blue | Light |
|---|---|---|---|---|---|---|---|---|
| B. Lake Co. | | Farmer | Res. Halfday, Res. In 1885 Half Day, Ill. | | | | | |
| Mustered Out 3-27-66 | | | | | | | | |

# THIRTY SEVENTH ILLINOIS

| Bandy, George W. | | K | 22 | 5'9" | Fair | Brown | Black |
|---|---|---|---|---|---|---|---|
| B. Danville, Ill. | Lawyer | Res. Danville | | | | | |
| Deserted – Reported on Roll of 12-31-62 | | | | | | | |

| Bandy, Samuel J. | | K | 21 | 5'10" | Dark | Blue | Light |
|---|---|---|---|---|---|---|---|
| B. Danville | Student | Enl. Danville, Res. 1885, Danville, Ill. | | | 3-31-64 | | |
| Discharged Disability 5-12-65, chronic diarrhea with disease of heart. | | | | | | | |

| Bandy, William M. | | K | 22 | 5'10" | Dark | Brown | Black |
|---|---|---|---|---|---|---|---|
| B. Danville | Student | Res. Danville | | | | | |
| Resigned 10-17-64 | | | | | | | |

| Baney, William H. | | B | 26 | 5'7" | Fair | Black | Brown |
|---|---|---|---|---|---|---|---|
| B. Lebanon, Pa. | Farmer | Enl. Lafayette | | | | | |
| Mustered Out 5-1-66 | | | | | | | |

| Bangess, Robert J. | | H | 18 | 5'5" | Dark | Hazel | Brown |
|---|---|---|---|---|---|---|---|
| B. Warren Co. Ill. | Farmer | Res. Millersburg | | | | | |
| Deserted 9-29-62 at Springfield | | | | | | | |

| Baria, Ambrose | | F | 23 | 6'3" | Dark | Brn | Black |
|---|---|---|---|---|---|---|---|
| B. New Orleans | Farmer | Res. Lake County | | | | | |
| Deserted from Bloomington, Mo. 3-9-63 | | | | | | | |

| Barker, George W. | | K | 24 | 5'11" | Dark | Grey | Black |
|---|---|---|---|---|---|---|---|
| B. Danville | Farmer | Res. Danville, Res. 1885 Danville, Ill. | | | | | |
| Discharged Disability 2-28-62 Shot thru the left arm at the Lamine 12-2-61 | | | | | | | |

| Barker, Jesse | | G | 25 | 5'6" | Light | Blue | Brown |
|---|---|---|---|---|---|---|---|
| B. Newport, R.I. | Farmer | Res. East Bend, Res. 1885 Gibson City, Ill. | | | | | |
| Mustered Out 10-4-64 | | | | | | | |

# DESCRIPTIVE ROLL

| Barker, William M. | | | K | 43 | 5'11" | Light | Blue | Light |
|---|---|---|---|---|---|---|---|---|
| B. Powhatton Co. Va. | | Painter | Enlisted Danville, Res. 1885 Danville, Ill. | | | 4-7-64 | | |
| Discharged Disability 7-31-64 | | | | | | | | |

| Barlow, Joseph | | | B | 37 | 5'7" | Dark | Blue | Brown |
|---|---|---|---|---|---|---|---|---|
| B. England | | Farmer | Res. Goshen | | | | | |
| Died New Orleans 5-6-64 of secondary syphilis | | | | | | | | |

| Barnard, Thomas J. | | | K | 23 | | | | |
|---|---|---|---|---|---|---|---|---|
| | | | Res. Vermilion | | | | | |
| Died St. Louis 2-20-64 of typhoid pneumonia at New House of Refuge General Hospital | | | | | | | | |

| Barnes, Francis M. | | | H | 19 | 5'8" | Light | Blue | Light |
|---|---|---|---|---|---|---|---|---|
| B. Howard Co. Md. | | Farmer | Enlisted. Morristown, Res. 1885 Aurora, Neb. | | | 4-20-64 | | |
| Mustered Out 5-15-66 | | | | | | | | |

| Barnes, Myron S. (Staff) | | | | 37 | | | | |
|---|---|---|---|---|---|---|---|---|
| Journalist | | | Res. Rock Island, Res. 1885 Galesburg, Ill. | | | | | |
| Discharged 11-20-62 | | | | | | | | |

| Barrett, Andrew J. | | | E | 20 | 5'8" | Light | Hazel | Light |
|---|---|---|---|---|---|---|---|---|
| B. Edgar Co. Ill | | Laborer | Enlisted Vicksburg | | | 8-8-63 | | |
| Deserted at Houston 2-13-66 | | | | | | | | |

| Barrett, Charles M. | | | E | 20 | 5'10" | Light | Dark | Dark |
|---|---|---|---|---|---|---|---|---|
| B. Wooster Co. Mass. | | | Res. Lasalle Co., Res. 1885 Burr Oak, Kansas | | | | | |
| Discharged Disability 8-29-62, "chronic affection." | | | | | | | | |

# THIRTY SEVENTH ILLINOIS

| Basset, Perris | | | I | 25 | 5'8" | Dark | Black | Black |
|---|---|---|---|---|---|---|---|---|
| F. Pittstown, NY | | Farmer | Res. Belvidere, Res 1885 Rockford, Ill | | | | | |
| Discharge Disability 2-4-63 | | | | | | | | |

| Batcheler, John | | | I | 31 | | Dark | Black | Dark |
|---|---|---|---|---|---|---|---|---|
| B. Switzerland | | Cooper Carpenter | Enlisted at Dunton | | | | | |
| Died 7-23-63 at Hickory St. General Hospital, Phithesis | | | | | | | | |

| Beadleston, Alonzo W. | | | H | 32 | 5'6" | Light | Grey | Brown |
|---|---|---|---|---|---|---|---|---|
| B. Warren Co. NY | | Farmer | Res. Rock Island, Res 1885 Johnsonburg, NY | | | | | |
| Mustered Out 9-29-64 | | | | | | | | |

| Beaumont Charles E. | | | H | 21 | 5'9" | Light | Blue | Brown |
|---|---|---|---|---|---|---|---|---|
| B. Niles, Mich. | | Teamster | Enlisted Rock Island, Res. 1885, Richmond | | | | | |
| Discharged Disability 2-25-64 | | | | | | | | |

| Bell, George R. | | | G | 21 | 5'7" | Light | Blue | Dark |
|---|---|---|---|---|---|---|---|---|
| B. Ada, Mich | | Bookkeeper | Enlisted Chicago | | | | | |
| Resigned 7-7-64. Shot in right arm at Prairie Grove 12-7-62 | | | | | | | | |

| Bell, George | | | E | | | | | |
|---|---|---|---|---|---|---|---|---|
| | | | Enlisted Chicago | | | 5-24-64 | | |
| Transferred Veteran Reserve Corps 1-17-65 | | | | | | | | |

| Bell, Samuel | | | E | 22 | 5'8" | Dark | Hazel | Dark |
|---|---|---|---|---|---|---|---|---|
| B. Leavenworth, Kans. | | Engineer | Enlisted Chicago | | | 5-25-64 | | |
| Transferred Veteran Reserve Corps 1-17-65 | | | | | | | | |

# DESCRIPTIVE ROLL

| Benjamin, Edward W. | | E | 43 | 5'7" | Light | Blue | Dark |
|---|---|---|---|---|---|---|---|
| B. Madison Co. NY | Farmer | Enlisted Mendota | | | | | |
| Discharged Disability 8-29-62 | | | | | | | |

| Bensigner, Andrew | | F | 43 | 5'10" | Dark | Grey | Dark |
|---|---|---|---|---|---|---|---|
| B. Germany | Farmer | Res. Warren | | | | | |
| Died Boonville Mo. 10-10-61 of disease. | | | | | | | |

| Benson, Joseph | | F | 21 | 5'10" | Light | Hazel | Light |
|---|---|---|---|---|---|---|---|
| B. Schoharie, NY | Farmer | Res. Lake Co. | | | | | |
| Died of disease 3-18-62 in Hospital at Cassville | | | | | | | |

| Benwell, Richard | | C | 22 | 5'5" | Fair | Blue | Light |
|---|---|---|---|---|---|---|---|
| B. England | Farmer | Res. Waucanda, Res 1885 Bull City, Kan. | | | | | |
| Mustered Out 5-15-66 | | | | | | | |

| Berdendahl, Augustus G. | | D | 28 | 5'4" | Dark | Brown | Black |
|---|---|---|---|---|---|---|---|
| B. Goteborg, Sweden | Lumberman | Res. Hamlin (Mason Co.) Mich. | | | | | |
| Accidentally killed 5-3-66 by a wagon running over him at Beaumont, TX | | | | | | | |

| Berg, Samuel | | D | 30 | 5'9" | Light | Grey | Light |
|---|---|---|---|---|---|---|---|
| B. Norway | Lumberman | Res. Pentwater, Mich. | | | | | |
| Discharged Disability 3-10-63 of chronic diarrhea | | | | | | | |

| Beverlin, Thomas J. | | K | 21 | 5'6" | Fair | Grey | Black |
|---|---|---|---|---|---|---|---|
| F. Wabash, Ind. | Farmer | Res. Ridge Farm | | | | | |
| Mustered Out 10-4-64 | | | | | | | |

| Bigelow, Opher C. | | H | 18 | 5'6" | Light | Blue | Brown |
|---|---|---|---|---|---|---|---|
| B. St. Lawrence Co. NY | Farmer | Res. Rock Island | | | | | |
| Died of wounds 3-9-62 | | | | | | | |

# THIRTY SEVENTH ILLINOIS

| Bigelow, William G. | | | A | 23 | 5'8" | Light | Blue | Dark |
|---|---|---|---|---|---|---|---|---|
| B. Chesterfield, NY | | Teamster | Enlisted Rock Island, Res. 1885 Thornburgh, IA | | | 7-20-62 | | |
| Resigned 10-19-63 trf to 92d US Colored Volunteers | | | | | | | | |

| Biggs, Jackson | | | A | 27 | 5'9" | Light | Grey | Light |
|---|---|---|---|---|---|---|---|---|
| B. Monmouth, Ill | | | Res. 1885 Columbus Junction, Iowa | | | | | |
| Discharged Disability 10-31-62 Protracted Fever, Inflammatory Rheumatism | | | | | | | | |

| Bilby, John T. | | | F | 24 | 5'10" | Dark | Blue | Dark |
|---|---|---|---|---|---|---|---|---|
| B. Oneida, NY | | Farmer | Res. Lyons | | | | | |
| Mustered Out 9-29-64 | | | | | | | | |

| Bilinski, Henry | | | F | 22 | 5'8" | Dark | Blue | Dark |
|---|---|---|---|---|---|---|---|---|
| B. Troy, NY | | Teamster | Res. Fremont | | | | | |
| Discharged 3-20-63, Wounds at Prairie Grove | | | | | | | | |

| Bishop, John A. | | | E | 21 | 5'8" | Light | Blue | Light |
|---|---|---|---|---|---|---|---|---|
| B. Brown Co. Ohio | | | Res. Minonk, Ill. | | | | | |
| Died at Cassville 6-18-62. Congestion of the Brain, Interred in the Old Burying Ground on top of the hill east of Cassville | | | | | | | | |

| Bishop, Pleasant (Chaplain | | | | 30 | | | | |
|---|---|---|---|---|---|---|---|---|
| | | | Enlisted New Orleans, Res. 1885 Towanda, Ill. | | | 9-7-63 | | |
| Resigned 9-9-64 | | | | | | | | |

| Bishop, Silas | | | E | 26 | 6'1" | Light | Blue | Brown |
|---|---|---|---|---|---|---|---|---|
| B. Brown Co. Ohio | | Farmer | Enlisted Mendota | | | 9-20-61 | | |
| Died 9-12-64 on Steamboat Paragon at Vicksburg. | | | | | | | | |

# DESCRIPTIVE ROLL

| Black, James | | H | 22 | 5'6" | Fair | Grey | Brown |
|---|---|---|---|---|---|---|---|
| B. Roscommon, Ireland | Farmer | Res. Jones, Iowa | | | | | |
| Under arrest at Galveston at Muster Out, attempted rape. | | | | | | | |

| Black, John Charles (Staff) | | | 22 | 5'9" | Fair | Blue | Dark |
|---|---|---|---|---|---|---|---|
| B. Holmes, Miss. | Student | Res. Danville, Res. 1885 Washington, D.C. | | | | | |
| Resigned 8-15-65 | | | | | | | |

| Black, William | | | 21 | 5'5" | Dark | Grey | Dark |
|---|---|---|---|---|---|---|---|
| B. Ohio | Tobacconist | Enlisted Quincy | | | 12-19-64 | | |
| Not on Muster Rolls of Regiment | | | | | | | |

| Black, William P. | | K | 18 | 6'0" | Dark | Hazel | Black |
|---|---|---|---|---|---|---|---|
| B. Woodford, KY | Student | Res. Danville, Res. 1885 Park Ridge, Ill. | | | | | |
| Mustered Out 9-29-64 | | | | | | | |

| Blackstock, David | | H | 18 | 5'5" | Light | Blue | Brown |
|---|---|---|---|---|---|---|---|
| B. Newton Yard, Ireland | Farmer | Res. Pa., Res 1885 Denver, Colorado | | | | | |
| Mustered Out 10-4-64 | | | | | | | |

| Blackstock, John | | H | 18 | 5'5" | Light | Blue | Black |
|---|---|---|---|---|---|---|---|
| B. Newton Yard, Ireland | Farmer | Res. Pa., Res 1885 Plumb Creek, Nebraska or Woodburn, Iowa. | | | | | |
| Mustered Out 10-4-64 | | | | | | | |

| Blair, Joseph F | | H | 26 | 5'11" | Dark | Hazel | Black |
|---|---|---|---|---|---|---|---|
| B. Kingsley, Canada East | Farmer | Res. Moline | | | | | |
| Died 2-5-64 at Brownsville, Texas | | | | | | | |

# THIRTY SEVENTH ILLINOIS

| Blakely, Robert | | A | 20 | | | | |
|---|---|---|---|---|---|---|---|
| Enlisted Rock Island as Musician, Res. Preemption, Res. 1885 Mound Valley, Kansas | | | | | | 8-14-61 | |
| Mustered Out 10-4-64 | | | | | | | |

| Blanquart, John B. | | K | 39 | 5'9" | Dark | Blue | Black |
|---|---|---|---|---|---|---|---|
| B. Belgium | Laborer | Enlisted Danville | | | | 11-23-63 | |
| Mustered Out 5-15-66 | | | | | | | |

| Blass, Phenicia | | K | 24 | 5'7" | Dark | Brown | Black |
|---|---|---|---|---|---|---|---|
| B. Belgium | Laborer | Enlisted Danville | | | | 11-23-63 | |
| Died New Orleans 9-1-64 | | | | | | | |

| Bleakley, Henderson C. | | B | 29 | 5'7" | Dark | Grey | Brown |
|---|---|---|---|---|---|---|---|
| B. Faytte Co. Pa | Farmer | Res. Lynn, Res. 1885 Imogene, Iowa | | | | | |
| Discharged Disability 9-1-62 | | | | | | | |

| Blodgett, Edward A. (Staff) | | | | | | | |
|---|---|---|---|---|---|---|---|
| | | Res. Downer's Grove, Res. 1885 Chicago | | | | | |
| Resigned 8-11-62 to be Adjutant of 74th Ill. Regiment | | | | | | | |

| Blodgett, Wells H. | | D | 24 | 5'7" | Dark | Hazel | Black |
|---|---|---|---|---|---|---|---|
| B. Downer's Grove, Ill. | Lawyer | Enlisted Chicago, Res. 1885 St. Louis, Mo. | | | | | |
| Mustered Out 5-20-63 to be Judge Advocate assigned to 48th Missouri Infantry. Medal of Honor for Newtonia. | | | | | | | |

| Blunt, John W. | | F | 20 | 5'8" | Dark | Hazel | Black |
|---|---|---|---|---|---|---|---|
| B. Rochester, NY | Farmer | Res. Antioch | | | | | |
| Mustered Out 9-29-64 | | | | | | | |

| Boardman, Calvin F. | | C | 21 | 5'8" | Fair | Grey | Brown |
|---|---|---|---|---|---|---|---|
| B. Lasalle, Ill. | Farmer | Res. Waukegan, Res. 1885 Oregon, Ill.. | | | | | |
| Mustered Out 5-15-66 | | | | | | | |

# DESCRIPTIVE ROLL

| Bogue, Eli | | K | 20 | 5'7" | Dark | Hazel | Brown |
|---|---|---|---|---|---|---|---|
| F. Vermilion Co. | Farmer | Res. Ridge Farm | | | | | |
| Mustered Out 10-17-64 | | | | | | | |

| Booker, George J. | | K | 21 | 5'5" | Dark | Blue | Brown |
|---|---|---|---|---|---|---|---|
| | | Enlisted Fairmount | | | | | |
| Mustered Out 10-4-64 | | | | | | | |

| Boorman, Jacob | | H | 23 | 5'5" | | | |
|---|---|---|---|---|---|---|---|
| | Farmer | Enlisted Chicago | | | | | |
| Deserted 9-21-61 at Chicago | | | | | | | |

| Borman, Augustus | | G | 21 | 5'6" | Dark | Brown | Black |
|---|---|---|---|---|---|---|---|
| B. Germany | Farmer | Res. Cheney's Grove, Res. 1885 Chicago | | | | | |
| Discharged, wounds received at Prairie Grove | | | | | | | |

| Boyd, James | | I | 18 | 5'5" | Light | Blue | Brown |
|---|---|---|---|---|---|---|---|
| B. Ireland | Farmer | Res. Boone | | | | | |
| Killed at Ft. Blakely 4-9-65, gunshot in the neck. | | | | | | | |

| Brackett, William H. | | E | 39 | 5'8" | Light | Grey | Grey |
|---|---|---|---|---|---|---|---|
| B. Wolfeborough, NH | Blacksmith | Res. Mendota | | | | | |
| Discharged 3-19-63 by reason of dislocation of hip improperly set, one leg shorter than the other, an injury received in childhood. | | | | | | | |

| Braman, Alonzo | | F | 18 | 5"10" | Dark | Hazel | Dark |
|---|---|---|---|---|---|---|---|
| B. Oneida, NY | Farmer | Res. Half Day | | | | | |
| Died Otterville 1-3-62 | | | | | | | |

| Braunweld, Frederick | | E | 32 | 5'9" | Light | Blue | Brown |
|---|---|---|---|---|---|---|---|
| B. Hannover, Germany | Soldier | Res. Mendota | | | | | |
| Discharge Disability 8-20-62, sore leg. | | | | | | | |

# THIRTY SEVENTH ILLINOIS

| Brewer, Francis M. | | K | 19 | 5'11" | Dark | Brown | Dark |
|---|---|---|---|---|---|---|---|
| B. Vermilion Co. | Farmer | Enlisted at Danville | | | 4-11-64 | | |
| Died 8-8-64, diarrhea and nervous prostration, on board Steamer FREESTONE at White River Landing, Ark. | | | | | | | |

| Briggs, Henry | | C | 21 | 5'11" | Fair | Brown | Light |
|---|---|---|---|---|---|---|---|
| B. Oneida, NY | Farmer | Res. Avon | | | | | |
| Mustered Out 5-15-66 | | | | | | | |

| Briggs, Martin | | K | 28 | 5'10" | Dark | Hazel | Black |
|---|---|---|---|---|---|---|---|
| F. Clark Co. Ohio | Mechanic | Res. Danville | | | | | |
| Mustered Out 10-4-64 | | | | | | | |

| Brink, John | | D | 30 | 5'10" | Light | Grey | Light |
|---|---|---|---|---|---|---|---|
| B. Germany | Lumberman | Res. Manistee, Mich. Res. 1885 Manistee, Mich. | | | | | |
| Mustered Out 5-15-66 | | | | | | | |

| Brown, Albert | | D | 22 | | | | |
|---|---|---|---|---|---|---|---|
| | | Res. Manistee, Mich. | | | | | |
| Died 5-8-62 at Cassville, typhoid fever | | | | | | | |

| Brown, Alva W. | | B | 22 | | | | |
|---|---|---|---|---|---|---|---|
| | | Enlisted Goshen. Res. 1885 Onawa, Iowa | | | | | |
| Mustered Out 9-29-64 | | | | | | | |

| Brown, Henry | | | 18 | 5'3" | Light | Hazel | Red |
|---|---|---|---|---|---|---|---|
| B. Canada | Laborer | Enlisted Chicago | | | 10-31-64 | | |
| (Not on roll) Illiterate. | | | | | | | |

# DESCRIPTIVE ROLL

| Brown, Jeremiah | | C | 23 | 6'0" | Fair | Blue | Dark |
|---|---|---|---|---|---|---|---|
| B. Oswego Co. NY | Farmer | Res. Waukegan | | | | | |
| Killed at Pea Ridge 3-7-62, shot through the heart. ||||||||

| Brown, John | | D | 26 | 5'9" | Dark | Brown | Black |
|---|---|---|---|---|---|---|---|
| B. England | | Enlisted Hamlin, Mich | | | | | |
| Discharged Disability 2-24-63, rupture of capsular ligament of right hip joint cause by dislocation prior to enlistment. ||||||||

| Brown, Morton | | I | 19 | | | | |
|---|---|---|---|---|---|---|---|
| | | Res. Bonus, Res. 1885, Bonus, Ill. | | | | | |
| Mustered Out 10-4-64 ||||||||

| Brown, Thomas R. | | K | 17 | 5'6" | Fair | Blue | Black |
|---|---|---|---|---|---|---|---|
| F. Perrysville, Indiana | Student | Res. Danville, Res. 1885 New Tacoma, Wash. Terr. | | | | | |
| Mustered Out 5-15-66 ||||||||

| Browning, Henry M. | | A | 19 | 5'6" | Fair | Hazel | Sandy |
|---|---|---|---|---|---|---|---|
| B. Steubenville, Ohio | Farmer | Res. Rock Island | | | | | |
| Mustered Out 5-15-66 ||||||||

| Bryan, William M. | | B | 19 | | | | |
|---|---|---|---|---|---|---|---|
| | | Res. Goshen | | | | | |
| Killed at Prairie Grove 12-7-62 shot through the head. ||||||||

| Buffum, Emery S. | | B | 19 | 5'7" | Fair | Grey | Brown |
|---|---|---|---|---|---|---|---|
| B. Galena, Ill. | Farmer | Res. Altona, Res. 1885 Lafayette, Ill. | | | | | |
| Discharged Disability 3-8-63 at Bloomington, Mo., rupture of bowels received in falling over a fence during retreat of his regiment at Prairie Grove. Inguinal hernia of right side. The intestines distend into the scrotum. ||||||||

# THIRTY SEVENTH ILLINOIS

| Buffum, John W. | | B | 20 | 5'7" | Fair | Grey | Brown |
|---|---|---|---|---|---|---|---|
| B. Galena, Ill. | Farmer | Res. 1885 Jewell City, Kansas ||||||
| Mustered Out 3-27-66 |||||||||

| Buhler, Justis | | D | 30 | | | | |
|---|---|---|---|---|---|---|---|
| | | Enlisted Manistee, Mich. Res 1885 Mt. Pleasant, Iowa ||||||
| Mustered Out 9-29-64 |||||||||

| Bunch, Joseph | | D | 24 | 5'9" | Dark | Brown | Black |
|---|---|---|---|---|---|---|---|
| B. New Albany, Ind. | Lumberman | Enl. Manistee, Mich. ||||||
| Deserted 2-28-66 |||||||||

| Burdick, Henry L. | | F | 22 | 5'9" | Dark | Brown | Dark |
|---|---|---|---|---|---|---|---|
| B. Olean, NY | Farmer | Res. Long Grove, Res. 1885 Gilmer, Ill ||||||
| Mustered Out 10-4-64 |||||||||

| Burk, John | | K | 25 | 5'10" | Fair | Grey | Light |
|---|---|---|---|---|---|---|---|
| B. Kildare, Ireland | Miner | Enlisted at Danville | | | 1-20-64 | | |
| Mustered Out 5-15-66 |||||||||

| Burroughs, William H. | | I | 39 | 5'4" | Dark | Grey | Black |
|---|---|---|---|---|---|---|---|
| F. New York | | Res. Boone Co., Enlisted Sheboygan ||||||
| Discharged Disability at St. Louis 1-31-63 |||||||||

| Burton, James H. | | D | 34 | 5'8" | Light | Blue | Light |
|---|---|---|---|---|---|---|---|
| B. Kentucky | Lumberman | Enlisted Manistee, Mich., Res. 1885 Houston, TX ||||||
| Mustered Out 5-15-66 |||||||||

DESCRIPTIVE ROLL

| Butler, David S. | | C | 22 | | | | |
|---|---|---|---|---|---|---|---|
| | | Res. Nunda, Enlisted Waukegan | | | | | |
| Died at Carrolton, La. 8-20-63 | | | | | | | |

| Byerly, Cyrus P | | A | 20 | 5'6" | Dark | Brown | Brown |
|---|---|---|---|---|---|---|---|
| B. Mt. Pleasant, Pa. | Farmer | Enlisted Rock Island, Res. 1885 Raeville, Nebraska | | | | | |
| Mustered Out 5-15-66 | | | | | | | |

| Byers, David | | A | 22 | 5'11" | Light | Blue | Brown |
|---|---|---|---|---|---|---|---|
| B. Montreal, Canada | | Res. Camden, Res. 1885 Columbus Junction, Iowa | | | | | |
| Mustered Out 5-15-66 | | | | | | | |

| Byerrum, Charles C. | | H | 18 | 5'8" | Light | Blue | Light |
|---|---|---|---|---|---|---|---|
| B. Albona (?) Germany | Farmer | Enlisted at Morristown | | | 3-29-64 | | |
| Mustered Out 5-15-66 | | | | | | | |

# C

| Cadwell, Aurelius | | F | 19 | 5'11" | Light | Grey | Light |
|---|---|---|---|---|---|---|---|
| B. Canaan, Vt. | Mason | Res. Lake Co. | | | | | |
| Died of Disease at Carrolton, La. 9-1-63 | | | | | | | |

| Cain, Michael | | H | 35 | 5'10" | Dark | Blue | Black |
|---|---|---|---|---|---|---|---|
| B. Kildare Co., Ireland | Laborer | Res. Wyonett, Ill. | | | | | |
| Mustered Out 5-15-66. Illiterate | | | | | | | |

| Calback, John | | D | 41 | | | | |
|---|---|---|---|---|---|---|---|
| | | Enlisted Chicago | | | | | |
| Mustered Out 9-29-64 | | | | | | | |

# THIRTY SEVENTH ILLINOIS

| Callaghen, Owen M. | | C | 21 | | | | |
|---|---|---|---|---|---|---|---|
| | | Enlisted Waukegan | | | | | |
| Died New Orleans 8-23-63 | | | | | | | |

| Campbell, John | | I | 17 | 5'6" | Light | Blue | Brown |
|---|---|---|---|---|---|---|---|
| F. Oswego, NY | Farmer | Enl. Garden Prairie, Res. 1885 Bay View, Wis. | | | | | |
| Mustered Out 10-4-64 | | | | | | | |

| Campbell, Moses | | H | 26 | 5'6" | Dark | Brown | Black |
|---|---|---|---|---|---|---|---|
| B. Tippecanoe, Ind. | Blacksmith | Enl. Morristown, Res. 1885 Dayton, Ill. | | | | | |
| Discharged Disability 4-21-62. Secondary Syphilis. Disease originated at Chicago on or near 9-15-61. | | | | | | | |

| Campbell, Robert | | A | 19 | | | | |
|---|---|---|---|---|---|---|---|
| | | Enl. Rock Island | | | | | |
| Mustered Out 10-4-64 | | | | | | | |

| Canaday, James W. | | K | 19 | 5'11" | Dark | Hazel | Brown |
|---|---|---|---|---|---|---|---|
| F. Vermilion Co. | Farmer | | | | | | |
| Mustered Out 10-4-64 | | | | | | | |

| Cane, James | | H | 18 | 5'4" | Fair | Hazel | Brown |
|---|---|---|---|---|---|---|---|
| B, New York City | Farmer | Enl. Coal Valley | | | | | |
| Mustered Out 5-15-66 | | | | | | | |

| Cannon, Francis | | A | 28 | 5'7" | Light | Blue | Dark |
|---|---|---|---|---|---|---|---|
| B. Kiall, Ireland | Farmer | Res. Preemption | | | | | |
| Died at Leetown of wounds 4-3-63. Wounded at Pea Ridge, musket ball ranging from left hip to spine. "He was buried in his clothes and left the rest of his effects at Pea Ridge." | | | | | | | |

## DESCRIPTIVE ROLL

| Cappock, Thomas | | K | | 5'5" | Fair | Blue | Brown |
|---|---|---|---|---|---|---|---|
| F. Eugene, Ind. | Farmer | Res. Ridge Farm | | | | | |
| Mustered Out 10-11-64 | | | | | | | |

| Carey, James A. | | E | 19 | 5'11" | Light | Blue | Auburn |
|---|---|---|---|---|---|---|---|
| B. Miami Co. OH | Clerk | Enl. Mendota | | | | | |
| Discharged 1-23-65 | | | | | | | |

| Carey, William | | E | 18 | 5'3" | Light | Grey | Sandy |
|---|---|---|---|---|---|---|---|
| B. Miami Co. OH | Shoe-maker | Enl. Mendota, Res. 1885 Chicago, Ill. | | | | | |
| Mustered Out 5-15-66 | | | | | | | |

| Caries, Henry | | E | 27 | 5'7" | Sandy | Dark | Dark |
|---|---|---|---|---|---|---|---|
| B. Germany | Farmer | Res. Mendota | | | | | |
| Died Springfield 10-17-62 of dysentery. | | | | | | | |

| Carman, Thomas H. | | C | 24 | 5'7" | Fair | Grey | Light |
|---|---|---|---|---|---|---|---|
| B. Ontario, NY | Farmer | Enl. Waukegan | | | | | |
| Deserted on the march from Pea Ridge to Huntsville, Ark. October 20, 1862. He is a short thick stout man quick in his motions. Had on when he left a dirty brown hat, a short jacket, a dark pair of pantaloons and shoes. | | | | | | | |

| Carney, Peter | | C | 22 | 5'8" | Dark | Brown | Dark |
|---|---|---|---|---|---|---|---|
| B. Ireland | Farmer | Res. Fremont | | | | | |
| Died Carrolton 10-20-63 in hospital, chill fever, acute dysentery. | | | | | | | |

| Carpenter, John | | E | 22 | 5'9" | Light | Blue | Light |
|---|---|---|---|---|---|---|---|
| B. Dublin City, Ireland | Farmer | Enl. Mendota | | | | | |
| Discharged Disability 5-7-62 sore leg. | | | | | | | |

# THIRTY SEVENTH ILLINOIS

| Carpenter, Orvin | | C | 21 | 5'6" | Light | Blue | Dark |
|---|---|---|---|---|---|---|---|
| B. Orleans Co. NY | Farmer | Enl. Bonus | | | | 9-10-62 | |
| "Unfit for military duty" on back of enlistment papers. | | | | | | | |

| Carr, John | | G | 34 | | | | |
|---|---|---|---|---|---|---|---|
| B. Ireland | Farmer | Enl. Aurora | | | | | |
| Deserted 9-21-61 in St. Louis | | | | | | | |

| Carr, John | | H | 23 | 5'11" | Light | Blue | Brown |
|---|---|---|---|---|---|---|---|
| B. Rock Island | Farmer | Res. Moline | | | | | |
| Discharged Disability 6-9-62, Rheumatism. | | | | | | | |

| Carroll, John | | D | 35 | 5'4" | Light | Grey | Dark |
|---|---|---|---|---|---|---|---|
| B. Ireland | Laborer | Enl. Chicago | | | | | |
| Died Carrolton, La. 9-17-63 of dropsy (edema). | | | | | | | |

| Carroll, Marcus D. | | K | 33 | 5'8" | Dark | Grey | Brown |
|---|---|---|---|---|---|---|---|
| B. Windham, Conn. | Carpenter | Res. State Line | | | | | |
| Died Cassville, Mo. 5-17-62 | | | | | | | |

| Cartwright, Cornelius E. | | H | 23 | 6'0" | Light | Blue | Brown |
|---|---|---|---|---|---|---|---|
| B. Steuben Co. NY | Farmer | Res. Sharon, Res. 1885 Wabash, Ind. | | | | | |
| Discharged Disability 11-16-62 | | | | | | | |

| Casler, Levi D. | | A | 22 | 5'0" | Sandy | Blue | Red |
|---|---|---|---|---|---|---|---|
| B. Limerick, Ireland | Harness-maker | Enl. Boonville | | | | 10-7-61 | |
| Discharged Disability 7-11-65, chronic diarrhea. | | | | | | | |

# DESCRIPTIVE ROLL

| Cassidy, Peter | | F | 22 | 5'6" | Fair | Brown | Dark |
|---|---|---|---|---|---|---|---|
| B. Scotland | Farmer | Res. Milburn, Enl. Waukegan | | | 2-22-64 | | |
| Mustered Out 5-15-66 | | | | | | | |

| Castle, Asher M. | | F | 23 | 5'9" | Dark | Blue | Dark |
|---|---|---|---|---|---|---|---|
| B. Genessee, MI | Farmer | Res. Halfday, Res. 1885 Oregon, Ill. | | | | | |
| Mustered Out 5-15-66 | | | | | | | |

| Cathcart, John W. | | A | 21 | | | | |
|---|---|---|---|---|---|---|---|
| | | | | | | | |
| Died Syracuse, Mo. 12-11-61 Typhoid Pneumonia | | | | | | | |

| Cathcart, Joseph M. | | H | 19 | 5'7" | Light | Grey | Brown |
|---|---|---|---|---|---|---|---|
| B. Jefferson Co. Pa. | Farmer | Res. Pleasant Ridge, Res. 1885 Spring Creek, Nebraska | | | | | |
| Mustered Out 10-4-64 | | | | | | | |

| Cathcart, William C. | | H | 19 | 5'7" | Fair | Hazel | Auburn |
|---|---|---|---|---|---|---|---|
| B. Jefferson Co. Pa. | Farmer | Enl. Black Hawk, Ill. | | | 10-18-64 | | |
| Mustered Out 10-18-65 | | | | | | | |

| Cavier, Julius | | K | 19 | 5'4" | Dark | Hazel | Dark |
|---|---|---|---|---|---|---|---|
| B. Belgium | Laborer | Enl. Danville | | | 11-23-63 | | |
| Deserted 2-17-66 at Hempstead, Texas. Illiterate | | | | | | | |

| Chadwick, Warren | | C | 19 | 5'6" | Fair | Blue | Light |
|---|---|---|---|---|---|---|---|
| B. Wisconsin | Farmer | Enl. Waukegan | | | | | |
| Killed Morganzia 10-9-63 by guerillas. | | | | | | | |

| Chamberlain, James M. | | C | 21 | | | | |
|---|---|---|---|---|---|---|---|
| | | Res. Warren, Res. 1885 Leroy, Minn. | | | | | |
| Mustered Out 10-4-64 | | | | | | | |

# THIRTY SEVENTH ILLINOIS

| Chamberlain, William | | I | 18 | 5'10" | Light | Blue | Dark |
|---|---|---|---|---|---|---|---|
| F. Boone Co. Ill | Farmer | Enl. Chicago | | | | | |
| Died of disease 7-30-64 at Brownsville, Texas | | | | | | | |

| Chambers, Marion | | H | 18 | 5'7" | Light | Grey | Brown |
|---|---|---|---|---|---|---|---|
| B. Indiana | Farmer | Res. Morristown, Res. 1885 Tecumseh, Nebraska | | | | | |
| Mustered Out 5-15-66 | | | | | | | |

| Chandler, Gustavus | | D | 23 | | | | |
|---|---|---|---|---|---|---|---|
| | | Enl. Manistee, Mich. | | | | | |
| Mustered Out 10-4-64 | | | | | | | |

| Chapman, Thomas | | K | 23 | 5'6" | Fair | Hazel | Brown |
|---|---|---|---|---|---|---|---|
| B. Vermilion Co. | Carpenter | Enl. Ridge Farm | | | | | |
| | | | | | | | |

| Chapman, William | | K | 22 | 5'6" | Fair | Blue | Brown |
|---|---|---|---|---|---|---|---|
| F. Danville, Ill. | Farmer | Res. 1885 Indianola, Ill. | | | | | |
| Mustered Out 10-4-64 | | | | | | | |

| Charleson, John | | B | 43 | 5'4" | Dark | Brown | Brown |
|---|---|---|---|---|---|---|---|
| B. Sweden | Farmer | Enl. Goshen | | | | | |
| Mustered Out 6-23-66. Not mustered out on the day of his expiration of term of service on account of being under arrest and awaiting trial. Deserted from hospital at Rolla, Mo. 15th June 1863. Restored to duty 17th Feb. 1864. | | | | | | | |

| Chellis, Lemon G. | | A | | 6'0" | Fair | Blue | Brown |
|---|---|---|---|---|---|---|---|
| B. Northampton, NY | Farmer | Res. Pleasant Valley, Iowa, Res. 1885 Bridge, Kansas | | | | | |
| Mustered Out 5-15-66, Died 7-6-15 Gypsum, Kansas | | | | | | | |

# DESCRIPTIVE ROLL

| Chesley, Alexander P. | | K | 28 | 5'6" | Dark | Brown | Black |
|---|---|---|---|---|---|---|---|
| B. Virginia | | Enl. Danville | | | | 3-31-64 | |
| Mustered Out 5-15-66 | | | | | | | |

| Christie, Richard | | G | 36 | 5'9" | Dark | Grey | Black |
|---|---|---|---|---|---|---|---|
| B. Ohio | Farmer | | | | | | |
| Discharged Chicago 9-18-61, sickness | | | | | | | |

| Chroninger, Charles B. | | G | 23 | 5'5" | Light | Blue | Light |
|---|---|---|---|---|---|---|---|
| B. Allegeny Co. Pa | Tin-smith | Enl. Chicago | | | | | |
| Resigned 5-15-66 Wounded in right arm at Prairie Grove. | | | | | | | |

| Church, Lucius | | B | 21 | 5'4" | Dark | Brown | Brown |
|---|---|---|---|---|---|---|---|
| B. New York | Farmer | Enl. Goshen | | | | | |
| Discharged 2-14-62 at Syracuse, inflammation of throat. | | | | | | | |

| Clapp, George A. | | K | 19 | 5'7" | Light | Blue | Light |
|---|---|---|---|---|---|---|---|
| F. Vermilion Co. | Farmer | Res. 1885 Danville, Ill | | | | 8-14-62 | |
| Mustered Out 6-9-65 | | | | | | | |

| Clapp, Joseph S. | | K | 20 | 5'4' | Fair | Blue | Light |
|---|---|---|---|---|---|---|---|
| | | Res. Perrysville, Ind. | | | | | |
| Mustered Out 10-4-64 | | | | | | | |

| Clark, Edwin | | F | 19 | 5'10" | Light | Blue | Light |
|---|---|---|---|---|---|---|---|
| B. Middlebury, Vt | Farmer | Res. Antioch | | | | | |
| Died St. Louis 2-1-62 in hospital. | | | | | | | |

| Clark, Elijah A. (Assistant Surgeon) | | | 25 | | | | |
|---|---|---|---|---|---|---|---|
| | | Enl. Chicago | | | | | |
| Resigned 3-13-63 to be Surgeon 8th Missouri Cavalry Regt. | | | | | | | |

# THIRTY SEVENTH ILLINOIS

| Clark, Henry H.B. | | A | 19 | 6'1" | Dark | Brown | Brown |
|---|---|---|---|---|---|---|---|
| B. Preemption | Farmer | Enl. Rock Island | | | 8-14-62 | | |
| Died in camp near New Orleans 8-27-83 chronic diarrhea | | | | | | | |

| Clark, Jackson | | A | 22 | 5'9" | Light | Blue | Light |
|---|---|---|---|---|---|---|---|
| B. Scotland | Farmer | Enl. Rock Island | | | 9-29-62 | | |
| Deserted 5-2-64 | | | | | | | |

| Clark, James B. | | F | 25 | 5'11" | Light | Grey | Light |
|---|---|---|---|---|---|---|---|
| B. Canaan, Vt. | Mason | Res. Libertyville, Res. 1885 Waukegan, Ill. | | | | | |
| Discharged 2-28-62 at Syracuse. Chronic rheumatism. Joints of both feet greatly enlarged, the arch of the foot destroyed. | | | | | | | |

| Clark, Luther B. | | C | 37 | 6'0" | Fair | Blue | Dark |
|---|---|---|---|---|---|---|---|
| B. Ontario, NY | Farmer | Res. Goodale | | | | | |
| Discharged 8-13-62 at Springfield, Mo. An inguinal hernia of several years standing. | | | | | | | |

| Clark, Wilson D. | | K | 18 | | | | |
|---|---|---|---|---|---|---|---|
| B. Ohio Co. Ind. | Farmer | Enl. Danville | | | 3-31-64 | | |
| Mustered Out 5-15-66 | | | | | | | |

| Clarkson, John | | C | 19 | 5'9" | Fair | Grey | Light |
|---|---|---|---|---|---|---|---|
| B. England | Farmer | Res. Goodale | | | | | |
| Died at Carrolton, La. 11-8-63, chronic diarrhea. | | | | | | | |

| Clawson, Timothy | | F | 22 | 5'10" | Dark | Brown | Dark |
|---|---|---|---|---|---|---|---|
| B. Ohio | Farmer | Res. Danville, Res. 1885 White Cross, Colorado | | | | | |
| Mustered Out 10-4-64 | | | | | | | |

# DESCRIPTIVE ROLL

| Clay, Henry | | A | 22 | 6'3" | Fair | Blue | Brown |
|---|---|---|---|---|---|---|---|
| B. Morrison, Ill. | Farmer | | | | | 9-6-62 | |
| Discharged Disability 2-18-65 Chronic Diarrhea ||||||||

| Cleland, James | | A | 20 | 5'7" | Fair | Hazel | Light |
|---|---|---|---|---|---|---|---|
| B. Ireland | Farmer | Enl. Coal Valley ||| 10-4-64 ||
| Mustered Out 10-9-64 ||||||||

| Cleveland, Charles A. | | C | 22 | 5'11" | Fair | Grey | Light |
|---|---|---|---|---|---|---|---|
| B. Columbia, NY | Farmer | Res. Avon, Res. 1885 Andarko, Indian Territory |||||||
| Mustered Out 10-4-64 ||||||||

| Cleveland, James | | C | 23 | 5'11" | Dark | Brown | Dark |
|---|---|---|---|---|---|---|---|
| B. Columbia, NY | Farmer | Res. Avon, Res. 1884 Garnett, Kansas |||||||
| Mustered Out 10-4-64 ||||||||

| Clow, Edward C. | | A | | 5'11" | Light | Blue | Light |
|---|---|---|---|---|---|---|---|
| B. New Castle, Pa | Farmer | Res. Camden, Res. 1885 Milan, Ill. ||||||
| Mustered Out 5-15-66 ||||||||

| Cochran, Oran | | H | 18 | 5'7" | Dark | Brown | Black |
|---|---|---|---|---|---|---|---|
| B. Morgan Co. Ohio | Farmer | Res. Millersburg ||||||
| Died at St. Louis 8-28-63 at Jefferson Barracks. ||||||||

| Cockerton, James W. | | C | 19 | 5'9" | Fair | Grey | Dark |
|---|---|---|---|---|---|---|---|
| B. England | Farmer | | | | | | |
| Died 3-4-62 at Sugar Creek, Typhoid Fever. ||||||||

| Colbert, Patrick | | C | 21 | 5'6" | Fair | Blue | Light |
|---|---|---|---|---|---|---|---|
| B. New York City | Farmer | Res. Wauconda ||||||
| Mustered Out 5-15-66 ||||||||

# THIRTY SEVENTH ILLINOIS

| Colborn, Henry | | A | 20 | 5'8" | Light | Blue | Light |
|---|---|---|---|---|---|---|---|
| B. Cincinnati, OH | Boat-man | | | | | | |
| Accidentally shot and killed himself 2-21-62 at camp near Bentonville, Ark. Death by discharge of a gun in his own hands. Shot in right breast. He was buried in his clothes and blanket – estate $7.10 cash. ||||||||

| Colborn, Laban B. | | H | 21 | 5'8" | Light | Blue | Brown |
|---|---|---|---|---|---|---|---|
| B. Kennebec Co. Me. | Farmer | Enl. Morristown, Ill. ||||||
| Died at Geneseo, Ill 3-5-64 of smallpox, while recruiting. ||||||||

| Cole, Charles B. | | F | 35 | 5'8" | Fair | Grey | Dark |
|---|---|---|---|---|---|---|---|
| B. Greene Co. NY | Farmer | Enl. Long Grove, Res. 1885 Missouri City, MO || 2/22/64 |||
| Mustered Out 4-9-66 ||||||||

| Cole, Elisha | | E | 19 | 5'9" | Light | Blue | Light |
|---|---|---|---|---|---|---|---|
| B. Lawrence, Pa | Farmer | Enl. Vioila, Ill. || 3-28-64 |||
| Died Natchez 6-23-65 Typhoid Fever. Effects to be valued and distributed by [Quartermaster] to the benefit of contrabands. ||||||||

| Collins, William H. | | K | 34 | 6'0" | Light | Blue | Sandy |
|---|---|---|---|---|---|---|---|
| B. Warren Co OH | Farmer | Enl. Danville || 1-1-64 |||
| Died New Orleans 8-2-64, chronic diarrhea. ||||||||

| Comstock, Charles | | K | 25 | 5'5" | Dark | Blue | Brown |
|---|---|---|---|---|---|---|---|
| B. Ohio | Farmer | Res. 1885 Rossville, Ill. |||||
| Discharged at St. Louis. Total loss of vision in right eye & sight imperfect in the left eye. ||||||||

| Conay, John | | K | 23 | 5'3" | Fair | Blue | Dark |
|---|---|---|---|---|---|---|---|
| B. Ireland | Farmer | Enl. Danville || 12-23-63 |||
| Deserted 5-3-65. Illiterate. ||||||||

# DESCRIPTIVE ROLL

| Connolly, Patrick | | I | 21 | 5'7" | Light | Blue | Brown |
|---|---|---|---|---|---|---|---|
| F. Cork, Ireland | Blacksmith | Res. Belvidere, Res. 1885 Belvidere, Ill. | | | | | |
| Mustered Out 5-21-66 | | | | | | | |

| Connor, Francis | | C | 56 | | | | |
|---|---|---|---|---|---|---|---|
| F. Waukegan | | | | | | | |
| Wounded at Pea Ridge – ball entering left side of lower jaw, fracturing bone, passing thru floor of mouth, then entering 1 ½ inches to right of upper end of sternum, and coming out in aseilla. Trf. Invalid Corps. A Mexican Soldier. | | | | | | | |

| Conover, Erasmus M. | | G | 19 | 5'10" | Fair | Brown | Brown |
|---|---|---|---|---|---|---|---|
| F. Franklin, Ind. | Farmer | Res. Covington Ind. | | | | | |
| Absent on leave at Muster Out of Regiment. | | | | | | | |

| Conover, Isaac | | K | 24 | 5'8" | Dark | Grey | Brown |
|---|---|---|---|---|---|---|---|
| B. Fountain, Ind. | Farmer | Res. Covington, Ind., Res 1885 Dexter City, Mo. | | | | | |
| Discharged Disability 7-8-64 Conjunctivitis. | | | | | | | |

| Conover, William M. | | K | 20 | 5'9" | Fair | Blue | Light |
|---|---|---|---|---|---|---|---|
| B. Fountain, Ind. | Farmer | Enl. Danville | | | 3-29-64 | | |
| Died in Hospital at Memphis 7-28-64. | | | | | | | |

| Constant, William | | G | 48 | 5'7" | Light | Blue | Light |
|---|---|---|---|---|---|---|---|
| B. England | Farmer | Res. Cook Co. | | | | | |
| Died Cassville, Mo. 5-21-62 in Hospital. | | | | | | | |

| Cooley, Almon G. | | E | 22 | 5'5" | Light | Dark | Dark |
|---|---|---|---|---|---|---|---|
| B. LaSalle Co. Ill | Farmer | | | | 9-20-61 | | |
| Mustered Out 5-15-66 | | | | | | | |

# THIRTY SEVENTH ILLINOIS

| Cooley, Harvillah | | F | 30 | 6'3" | Dark | Grey | Dark |
|---|---|---|---|---|---|---|---|
| B. Knox Co., OH | Farmer | | | | | | |
| Discharged Disability 12-28-62 Chronic Diarrhea. ||||||||

| Cooper, Daniel D. | | I | 23 | 5'8" | Light | Blue | Light |
|---|---|---|---|---|---|---|---|
| F. Tennessee | Farmer | Res. Belvidere, Res. 1885 Belvidere, Ill. |||||
| Discharged 5-4-65. Left arm amputated, Fort. Blakeley. ||||||||

| Cooper, William | | I | 17 | 6'2" | Light | Blue | Brown |
|---|---|---|---|---|---|---|---|
| B. Burlington, Vt | | Enl. Belvidere |||||
| Mustered Out 5-15-66 ||||||||

| Cox, John | | A | 24 | 5'6" | Fair | Blue | Brown |
|---|---|---|---|---|---|---|---|
| B. Ireland | Laborer | Res. Springpoint, Cumberland Co., Enl. Danville ||| 4-9-66 ||
| Mustered Out 4-9-66 ||||||||

| Crabbs, Francis A. | | A | 26 | 5'9" | Light | Blue | Auburn |
|---|---|---|---|---|---|---|---|
| B. Decatur, Ind. | Farmer | Res. Rural, Ill. |||||
| Discharge 10-5-62 at Newtonia. "General Debility. Has no particular disease, wished to remain in service." ||||||||

| Cragan, Peter | | B | 22 | | | | |
|---|---|---|---|---|---|---|---|
| F. Lynn | | Res. 1885 Colfax, Iowa. |||||
| Mustered Out 10-4-64 ||||||||

| Craig, Edward E. | | C | 28 | 5'8" | Fair | Brown | Dark |
|---|---|---|---|---|---|---|---|
| B. Madison, NY | Painter | Res. Waukegan, Res. 1885 Hainesville, Ill. |||||
| Discharged 3-10-63. Chronic Hepatitis. Vicarious excretion of bile through the kidneys. ||||||||

# DESCRIPTIVE ROLL

| Craig, James A. | | E | 19 | 5'11" | Light | Blue | Sandy |
|---|---|---|---|---|---|---|---|
| B. Miami Co. OH | Clerk | Enl. Mendota | | | | | |
| | | | | | | | |

| Craig, William H. | | B | 19 | 6'0" | Dark | Blue | Brown |
|---|---|---|---|---|---|---|---|
| B. Delhi, Pa. | Farmer | Res. Gosher | | | | | |
| Discharged Disability 1-8-63 at St. Louis. Right elbow useless. | | | | | | | |

| Crandall, Hiram C. | | A | 23 | | | | |
|---|---|---|---|---|---|---|---|
| F. Olean, NY | | | | | | | |
| Transferred to 92d U.S. Colored Volunteers, Died at Port Hudson, 7-21-64 | | | | | | | |

| Crane, Anson | | I | 19 | | | | |
|---|---|---|---|---|---|---|---|
| | | Enl. Marengo | | | | | |
| Mustered Out 10-4-64. | | | | | | | |

| Crane, David C. | | E | 21 | 5'10" | Light | Grey | Light |
|---|---|---|---|---|---|---|---|
| B. Ohio | Farmer | Enl. St. Louis | | | 9-20-61 | | |
| Mustered Out 9-29-64 | | | | | | | |

| Crassalt, Theodore | | D | 28 | | | | |
|---|---|---|---|---|---|---|---|
| F. Michigan | | | | | | | |
| Discharged 3-10-62 at Sugar Creek. | | | | | | | |

| Crew, Alpheus | | E | 20 | 5'5" | Dark | Brown | Dark |
|---|---|---|---|---|---|---|---|
| B. Logan Co. OH | Farmer | Enl. Mendota | | | | | |
| Mustered Out 9-29-64 | | | | | | | |

| Crittenden, Charles | | C | 21 | | | | |
|---|---|---|---|---|---|---|---|
| F. Wauconda | | | | | | | |
| Discharged 9-7-61. Disease of the heart. Never mustered. | | | | | | | |

# THIRTY SEVENTH ILLINOIS

| Cronk, John F. | | F | 25 | 5'9" | Dark | Blue | Dark |
|---|---|---|---|---|---|---|---|
| B. New York | Farmer | Res. Libertyville, Res. 1885 Bristow, Kansas ||||||
| Mustered Out 5-15-66 |||||||||

| Crowder, Andrew J. | | B | 20 | | | | |
|---|---|---|---|---|---|---|---|
| F. Rochester | | Enl. Lafayette, Ill. |||||
| Mustered Out 10-4-64 at Chicago. ||||||||

| Cruver, Austin | | C | 24 | 5'9" | Fair | Blue | Light |
|---|---|---|---|---|---|---|---|
| B. Cook Co. Ill | Carpenter | Res. Wauconda, Res. 1885 Chicago, Ill ||||||
| |||||||

| Cuthbertson, James M. | | K | 18 | 5'9" | Fair | Blue | Brown |
|---|---|---|---|---|---|---|---|
| B. Newport, Ind. | Student | Enl. Chicago | | | 4-20-64 | | |
| Discharged 7-30-65 ||||||||

| Cummings, Elijah | | G | 23 | | | | |
|---|---|---|---|---|---|---|---|
| F. Pine Plains, Minn. | | | | | | |
| Discharged 5-12-62. Wounded in shoulder at Pea Ridge. Enl. Co. L, 4th Michigan Cavalry. ||||||||

| Cummings, William H. | | I | 18 | 5'6" | Light | Grey | Brown |
|---|---|---|---|---|---|---|---|
| F. Marengo, Ill. | Farmer | Res. Belvidere ||||||
| Died 10-18-63 at Memphis, of disease. ||||||||

| Cummins, James M. | | | | | | | |
|---|---|---|---|---|---|---|---|
| F. Danville | | | | | | 11-5-63 | |
| Discharged 12-9-63 ||||||||

## DESCRIPTIVE ROLL

| Cunningham, Janes | | G | 46 | 5'10" | Light | Blue | Brown |
|---|---|---|---|---|---|---|---|
| B. Washington Co. Va. | Farmer | Res. Cheney's Grove | | | | | |
| Died at St. Louis, in hospital. | | | | | | | |

| Curren, Allen B. | | I | 22 | 5'5" | Light | Grey | Brown |
|---|---|---|---|---|---|---|---|
| F. Franklin Co. NY | Farmer | Res. Belvidere, Res. 1885 Grant City, Missouri | | | | | |
| Mustered Out 5-15-66 | | | | | | | |

| Current, Samuel | | K | 18 | 5'5" | Fair | Blue | Light |
|---|---|---|---|---|---|---|---|
| B. Vermilion Co. Ind. | Farmer | Enl. Danville | | | 4-9-64 | | |
| Mustered Out 8-7-65 | | | | | | | |

| Current, William W. | | K | 21 | 5'10" | Dark | Hazel | Black |
|---|---|---|---|---|---|---|---|
| B. Vermilion Co. Ind. | Clerk | Enl. Danville | | | 3-31-64 | | |
| Discharged 9-16-64 | | | | | | | |

| Curtis, Henry Jr. | | A | 28 | | | | |
|---|---|---|---|---|---|---|---|
| F. Rock Island | | Res. 1885 Rock Island, Ill | | | | | |
| Resigned 7-20-62 | | | | | | | |

| Cushman, Joseph B. | | H | 19 | 5'9" | Light | Grey | Brown |
|---|---|---|---|---|---|---|---|
| B. Loran Co. OH | Farmer | Res. Hampton, Res. 1885 Carbon Cliff, Ill. | | | | | |
| Discharged Disability 7-16-62. | | | | | | | |

# D

| Dack, David | | H | 18 | 5'7" | Dark | Hazel | Brown |
|---|---|---|---|---|---|---|---|
| B. Canada West | Farmer | Enl. Camden, Res. 1885 Logan, Kansas | | | 8-15-61 | | |
| Mustered Out 10-4-64 | | | | | | | |

# THIRTY SEVENTH ILLINOIS

| Davis, Frederick | | | F | 25 | 5'3" | Dark | Blue | Dark |
|---|---|---|---|---|---|---|---|---|
| B. Pottville, Pa. | Soldier | Res. Benton | | | | | | |
| Mustered Out 5-15-66 | | | | | | | | |

| Davis, William | | | H | 44 | 5'9" | Sandy | Grey | Brown |
|---|---|---|---|---|---|---|---|---|
| B. Indiana Co. Pa | Teamster | Enl. Moline | | | | 8-15-61 | | |
| Discharged Disability 10-16-62 | | | | | | | | |

| Day, Charles W., 2d Lt. | | | E | 28 | 5'10" | Light | Blue | Light |
|---|---|---|---|---|---|---|---|---|
| B. Catteragus, NY | Farmer | Enl. Mendota | | | | 8-20-61 | | |
| Discharged Disability 11-18-63 on Surgeon's Certificate | | | | | | | | |

| Day, George | | | G | 20 | 5'7" | Light | Grey | Brown |
|---|---|---|---|---|---|---|---|---|
| B. England | Farmer | Enl. Chicago, Res. Cook Co., Res 1885 Wing, Ill | | | | 8-15-61 | | |
| Mustered Out 10-4-64 | | | | | | | | |

| Day, James P. | | | E | 21 | 5'10" | Light | Blue | Dark |
|---|---|---|---|---|---|---|---|---|
| B. Franklin Co. Mass. | Farmer | Enl. Mendota, Res. 1885 San Angelo, Texas | | | | 8-20-61 | | |
| Mustered Out 5-15-66 | | | | | | | | |

| Day, William | | | G | 28 | 5'7" | Light | Blue | Auburn |
|---|---|---|---|---|---|---|---|---|
| B. Kentucky | Farmer | Enl. East Bend | | | | 8-10-61 | | |
| Mustered Out 10-4-64 | | | | | | | | |

| Deamer, Charles | | | C | 20 | 5'5" | Fair | Brown | Dark |
|---|---|---|---|---|---|---|---|---|
| B. Canada | Farmer | Res. Warren, Enl. Waukegan | | | | 5-1-61 | | |
| Died 7-1-63 Vicksburg. | | | | | | | | |

## DESCRIPTIVE ROLL

| DeBesche, Charles F. | | | D | 28 | 5'6" | Light | Blue | Light |
|---|---|---|---|---|---|---|---|---|
| B. Sweden | Lumberman | | Res. 1885 Muskegon, Mich | | | | | |
| Mustered Out 5-15-66 | | | | | | | | |

| Debord, John W. | | | A | 19 | 5'10" | Light | Blue | Sandy |
|---|---|---|---|---|---|---|---|---|
| B. Owen Co. OH | Farmer | | Enl. Millersburg, Res. 1885 Osakis, Minn. | | | 8-14-61 | | |
| Mustered Out 5-15-66 | | | | | | | | |

| Debord, Martin | | | A | 41 | | | | |
|---|---|---|---|---|---|---|---|---|
| | | | Enl. Millersburg, Res. 1885 Alexandria, Minn. | | | 8-14-61 | | |
| Discharged Disability 11-30-61. Protracted illness and absence. | | | | | | | | |

| Deck, Jacob C. | | | K | 23 | 5'10" | Tan | Grey | Brown |
|---|---|---|---|---|---|---|---|---|
| B. Vermilion, Ill | Farmer | | Res. Warren Co. | | | | | |
| | | | | | | | | |

| Decker, Albert E. | | | I | 20 | 5'6" | Light | Blue | Dark |
|---|---|---|---|---|---|---|---|---|
| F. New York | Farmer | | Res. Bonus | | | 8-27-61 | | |
| Discharged Disability at Camp Lamine (Otterville) 1-24-63 | | | | | | | | |

| Deets, John | | | G | 38 | 5'7" | Dark | Brown | Black |
|---|---|---|---|---|---|---|---|---|
| B. Germany | Farmer | | Res. East Bend | | | | | |
| Mustered Out 9-29-64 | | | | | | | | |

| Delavergne, Nelson | | | I | 24 | 5'8" | Light | Grey | Brown |
|---|---|---|---|---|---|---|---|---|
| B. Franklin, Ill. | Farmer | | Res. 1885 Wallace, Ill. | | | 9-9-61 | | |
| Mustered Out 10-4-64 | | | | | | | | |

| Delay, Joseph | | | K | 43 | 5'8" | Dark | Brown | Black |
|---|---|---|---|---|---|---|---|---|
| B. Jackson, OH | Farmer | | Enl. Vermilion Co. | | | 9-7-61 | | |
| Discharged Disability 1-4-65 at Kennerville, La. Chronic Diarrhea. | | | | | | | | |

# THIRTY SEVENTH ILLINOIS

| Delay, William | | | K | 28 | 5'5" | Dark | Brown | Dark |
|---|---|---|---|---|---|---|---|---|
| B. Vermilion Co. | Laborer | Res. Danville | | | | 4-7-64 | | |
| Discharged Disability 12-11-65 at Galveston. Severe sprain of right foot. ||||||||| 

| Delro, Alfred | | | D | 20 | | | | |
|---|---|---|---|---|---|---|---|---|
| B. Hamlin, Mich. | | Enl. Michigan | | | | 8-15-61 | | |
| To Veterans Reserve Corps 9-29-64 |||||||||

| Denny, George P. | | | I | 18 | 5'10" | Dark | Hazel | Dark |
|---|---|---|---|---|---|---|---|---|
| F. New York | Farmer | Res. Bonus | | | | 8-29-61 | | |
| Died 1-1-62 at Camp Lamine – Typhoid. |||||||||

| Desmond, Jeremiah | | | K | 35 | 5'6" | Sandy | Blue | Dark |
|---|---|---|---|---|---|---|---|---|
| B. Cork, Ireland | Miner | Enl. Danville | | | | 1-20-64 | | |
| Deserted 9-9-64 at White River Landing |||||||||

| Dexter, Henry B. | | | B | 27 | 6'1" | Fair | Blue | Brown |
|---|---|---|---|---|---|---|---|---|
| B. Dover, Me. | Farrier | Res. Elmira | | | | | | |
| Mustered Out 5-15-66. |||||||||

| Dickenson, Charles V. | | | B | 26 | 5'11" | Fair | Blue | Brown |
|---|---|---|---|---|---|---|---|---|
| B. Fallsburg, NY | Carpenter | Res. Lafayette, Res. 1885 Galva, Ill. | | | | | | |
| Mustered Out 9-29-64 |||||||||

| Dickinson, William T. | | | B | 22 | 5'10" | Dark | Blue | Brown |
|---|---|---|---|---|---|---|---|---|
| B. Sullivan Co. NY | Carpenter | Res. Goshen, Res. 1885 Lafayette, Ill. | | | | | | |
| Discharged Disability 2-15-63 at Camp Bliss, Mo. Chronic diarrhea, bleeding from the lungs with severe coughing, "phithesis pulmonalis." |||||||||

# DESCRIPTIVE ROLL

| Diller, Adam | | | H | 18 | 5'9" | Fair | Hazel | Brown |
|---|---|---|---|---|---|---|---|---|
| B. Pennsylvania | | Farmer | Enl. Morristown, Res. 1885 Clay Center, KS | | | 8-15-62 | | |
| Mustered Out 6-12-65 | | | | | | | | |

| Diller, Isaac | | | H | 18 | 5'5" | Dark | Hazel | Black |
|---|---|---|---|---|---|---|---|---|
| B. Pennsylvania | | Farmer | | | | | | |
| Mustered Out 5-15-66 | | | | | | | | |

| Dimond, John | | | D | 29 | 5'7" | Light | Grey | Light |
|---|---|---|---|---|---|---|---|---|
| B. Ireland | | Tailor | Enl. Chicago, Res. 1885 Grand Rapids, MI | | | | | |
| Discharged Disability 3-10-63. Wounded at Pea Ridge, compound fracture of the humerus. | | | | | | | | |

| Disney, Barney J. | | | A | 19 | 5'11" | Light | Brown | Dark |
|---|---|---|---|---|---|---|---|---|
| B. Knox Co. OH | | | Enl. Rock Island, Res. 1885 Dixon, Kentucky | | | | | |
| Discharged 7-12-62, wound in left leg below knee | | | | | | | | |

| Disney, Horace W. | | | A | 20 | 5'8" | Light | Blue | Dark |
|---|---|---|---|---|---|---|---|---|
| B. Four Corners, OH | | Farmer | Res. Rock Island, Res. 1885 Springfield, MO | | | | | |
| AWOL at Muster Out. Wounded at Fort Blakeley | | | | | | | | |

| Ditma, John | | | F | 18 | 6'1" | Light | Brown | Light |
|---|---|---|---|---|---|---|---|---|
| B. Germany | | Laborer | Res. Milwaukee, Wis. | | | | | |
| Deserted at Lynn Creek 2-2-62 | | | | | | | | |

| Ditmer, John | | | H | 18 | | | | |
|---|---|---|---|---|---|---|---|---|
| F. Waukegan | | | | | | 8-16-61 | | |
| Deserted 9-19-61 | | | | | | | | |

# THIRTY SEVENTH ILLINOIS

| Dixon, John | | E | 26 | 5'5" | Light | Dark | Dark |
|---|---|---|---|---|---|---|---|
| B. Metz, France | Farmer | Enl. Mendota | | | | 9-20-61 | |
| Mustered Out 10-4-64 ||||||||

| Dobson, Crawford | | G | 28 | 5'8" | Light | Blue | Brown |
|---|---|---|---|---|---|---|---|
| B. Morgan Co. IN | Farmer | | | | | | |
| Deserted 1-25-62. Went to East Bend on furlough. ||||||||

| Dobson, George | | G | 40 | 5'11" | Sandy | Grey | Sandy |
|---|---|---|---|---|---|---|---|
| B. New Brunswick | Farmer | Res. Rockford | | | | | |
| Discharged 7-17-62 at Springfield ||||||||

| Dobson, John M. | | G | 23 | 5'4" | Light | Grey | Auburn |
|---|---|---|---|---|---|---|---|
| B. Champaign, IL | Farmer | Res. East Bend | | | | | |
| Mustered Out 10-4-64 ||||||||

| Dock, Peter | | D | 21 | | | | |
|---|---|---|---|---|---|---|---|
| F. Lincoln, Mich. | | | | | | | |
| Killed at Pea Ridge 3-7-62 ||||||||

| Dodge, Frank B. | | E | 22 | 5'11" | Light | Blue | Dark |
|---|---|---|---|---|---|---|---|
| B. Bureau, Ill. | Farmer | | | | | | |
| ||||||||

| Dodge, Isaac C. | | I | | 5'7" | Light | Blue | Brown |
|---|---|---|---|---|---|---|---|
| F. Syracuse, NY | Bookkeeper | Res. 1885 Lt. Louis, Mo. | | | | | |
| Asst. Provost Marshal at Springfield at 10-64 ||||||||

| Dodge, William | | E | 18 | 5'6" | Light | Grey | Brown |
|---|---|---|---|---|---|---|---|
| B. Bureau Co. IL | Farmer | Enl. Mendota, Ill. | | | | 10-31-61 | |
| Mustered Out 11-26-64 ||||||||

# DESCRIPTIVE ROLL

| Doebler, John | | D | 32 | 5'7" | Light | Grey | Brown |
|---|---|---|---|---|---|---|---|
| B. Bavaria | | Res. Lincoln, Mich. | | | | | |
| Mustered Out 5-15-66 | | | | | | | |

| Donahue, Patrick | | H | 30 | 5'0" | Dark | Blue | Black |
|---|---|---|---|---|---|---|---|
| B. Cork, Ireland | Farmer | Res. Huntley Station | | | | | |
| Mustered Out 10-18-64 | | | | | | | |

| Donnelly, James W. | | B | 19 | | | | |
|---|---|---|---|---|---|---|---|
| F. Galva | | Res. 1885 Washington, DC | | | | | |
| Discharged for promotion to 2d Arkansas Cavalry as 1st/Lt. | | | | | | | |

| Dorrity, John | | A | 19 | | | | |
|---|---|---|---|---|---|---|---|
| F. Preemption | Farmer | Enl. Rock Island | | | | | |
| Discharged Disability 6-25-62. Wound in left ankle, pulmonary abscess, great evacuation, general debility. | | | | | | | |

| Doty, Warren | | F | 23 | 5'8" | Dark | Grey | Dark |
|---|---|---|---|---|---|---|---|
| B. Oneida Co. NY | Salesman | Res. Halfday, Res. 1885 Winona, Minn. | | | | | |
| Mustered Out 5-15-66 | | | | | | | |

| Douglass, Charles | | | 22 | 5'8" | Fair | Blue | Light |
|---|---|---|---|---|---|---|---|
| B. Canada | Farmer | Enl. Waukegan | | | 12-1-62 | | |
| Deserted 6-6-63 at St. Genevieve, Missouri | | | | | | | |

| Dow, James | | H | 25 | 5'3" | Dark | Hazel | Brown |
|---|---|---|---|---|---|---|---|
| B. England | Farmer | Res. Deemington | | | | | |
| Died 8-21-63 at Carrolton, La. Typhoid Fever. | | | | | | | |

| Downey, William | | H | 24 | 5'9" | Dark | Hazel | Black |
|---|---|---|---|---|---|---|---|
| B. Donegal Co., Ireland | Farmer | Res. Millersburg, Res. 1885 Eureka, Kansas | | | | | |
| Discharged Disability 1-31-63 at St. Louis | | | | | | | |

# THIRTY SEVENTH ILLINOIS

| Doyle, Charles | | A | 19 | 5'5" | Light | Blue | Light |
|---|---|---|---|---|---|---|---|
| B. Davenport, IA | Farmer | | | | | | |
| Deserted 9-6-62 at Keitsville. | | | | | | | |

| Doyle, John | | | 22 | 5'3" | Light | Blue | Dark |
|---|---|---|---|---|---|---|---|
| B. Ireland | Machinist | Enl. Chicago | | | 2-24-65 | | |
| | | | | | | | |

| Doyle, William | | G | 28 | 5'7" | Light | Blue | Auburn |
|---|---|---|---|---|---|---|---|
| B. Wexford, Ireland | Farmer | Res. 1885 Vienna, La. | | | | | |
| Mustered Out 5-15-66 | | | | | | | |

| Draper, George Albert | | I | 19 | 5'10" | Light | Blue | Brown |
|---|---|---|---|---|---|---|---|
| F. New York | Farmer | Enl. Belvidere | | | | | |
| Deserted 3-1-63 | | | | | | | |

| Driscoll, Elbridge B. | | B | 19 | 5'8" | Dark | Blue | Brown |
|---|---|---|---|---|---|---|---|
| B. Lafayette, IL | | Res. Goshen | | | | | |
| Died New Orleans 9-5-63 at Carrolton. | | | | | | | |

| Droll, Simon | | F | 25 | 5'6" | Light | Hazel | Light |
|---|---|---|---|---|---|---|---|
| B. Wurttemburg, Germany | Farmer | Res. Long Grove | | | | | |
| Died 1-9-62 at Otterville of disease. | | | | | | | |

| Dubois, Lewis | | I | 40 | 5'10" | Dark | Blue | Black |
|---|---|---|---|---|---|---|---|
| B. Franklin, NY | Teamster | Res. Belvidere, Res. 1885 Belvidere, Ill. | | | | | |
| Deserted 2-25-63 | | | | | | | |

| Duckett, Charles W. | | I | 21 | 5'8" | Dark | Grey | Dark |
|---|---|---|---|---|---|---|---|
| F. Michigan | Farmer | Res. Manitowoc, Wis. | | | | | |
| Mustered Out 3-30-66 | | | | | | | |

# DESCRIPTIVE ROLL

| Dudley, Charles | | B | 27 | | | | |
|---|---|---|---|---|---|---|---|
| F. Lynn | | \multicolumn{6}{l|}{Res. 1885 Galva, Ill.} | | | | | |
| Discharged 8-17-64 | | | | | | | |

| Dudley, Charles | | B | 27 | | | | |
|---|---|---|---|---|---|---|---|
| F. Lynn | | Res. 1885 Galva, Ill. | | | | | |
| Discharged 8-17-64 | | | | | | | |

| Dudley, George W. | | B | 21 | 5'7" | Dark | Grey | Brown |
|---|---|---|---|---|---|---|---|
| B. Goshen, Ohio | Farmer | Res. Lynn, Res. 1885 Garnet, Kansas | | | | | |
| Mustered Out 10-4-64 | | | | | | | |

| Dudley, John S. | | B | 25 | | | | |
|---|---|---|---|---|---|---|---|
| F. Goshen | | | | | | | |
| Discharged 7031062 to accept commission in 1st Arkansas Cavalry | | | | | | | |

| Dudley, William W. | | C | 24 | 6'0" | Fair | Brown | Dark |
|---|---|---|---|---|---|---|---|
| B. Fleming Co Ny | Farmer | Enl. Danville, Res. 1885 Hoopeston, Ill. | | | | | |
| Discharged 3-26-63. Two gunshot wounds, one near the knee & left leg. Ball not extracted. Second, upper part of thigh. The whole leg is colder & smaller than the other. | | | | | | | |

| Dunavan, John M. | | E | 23 | 5'8" | Light | Blue | Light |
|---|---|---|---|---|---|---|---|
| B. Christian Co. Ky. | Farmer | Enl. Keitsville, Res. 1885 Raub, Indiana | | 4-12-62 | | | |
| Mustered Out 5-17-65 | | | | | | | |

| Dunn, Paris B. | | G | 25 | 5'7" | Sandy | Grey | Brown |
|---|---|---|---|---|---|---|---|
| B. Champaign, IL | Farmer | Enl. Chicago | | | | | |
| Died 12-14-64 from wounds received at Prairie Grove. | | | | | | | |

| Dusenberry, James | | F | 21 | 5'9" | Light | Blue | Light |
|---|---|---|---|---|---|---|---|
| B. Tomkins Co. NY | Farmer | Res. Libertyville | | | | | |
| Died 11-19-61 at St. Louis. | | | | | | | |

# THIRTY SEVENTH ILLINOIS

| Dutcher, John | | | F | 20 | 5'8" | Dark | Blue | Light |
|---|---|---|---|---|---|---|---|---|
| B. St. Lawrence Co. NY | | Farmer | Res. Waukegan | | | | | |
| Mustered Out 5-15-66. | | | | | | | | |

| Dwyer, William | | | K | 20 | 5'6" | Light | Grey | Brown |
|---|---|---|---|---|---|---|---|---|
| B. Ireland | | Laborer | Enl. Danville | | | | 3-22-64 | |
| Deserted 1-24-66 from Military Prison at Houston. | | | | | | | | |

| Dykes, John | | | C | 24 | | | | |
|---|---|---|---|---|---|---|---|---|
| F. Fremont | | | Res. 1885 Gages Lakes, Ill. | | | | | |
| Mustered Out 10-4-64 | | | | | | | | |

# E

| Earhart, Cyrus H. | | | A | 23 | 5'8" | Fair | Blue | Sandy |
|---|---|---|---|---|---|---|---|---|
| B. Holdsburgh, Pa | | Farmer | Enl. Rock Island, Res. 1885 Dedham, Iowa | | | | | |
| Mustered Out 5-15-66 | | | | | | | | |

| Eaton, Charles W. | | | H | 14 | 4'11" | Light | Blue | Light |
|---|---|---|---|---|---|---|---|---|
| B. Belmont Co., OH | | Drummer | Enl. Rock Island | | | | | |
| Discharged 2-21-64 | | | | | | | | |

| Eaton, Joseph | | | H | 36 | 6'0" | Light | Grey | Brown |
|---|---|---|---|---|---|---|---|---|
| B. Perry Co. OH | | General Dealer | Enl. Rock Island | | | | | |
| Killed in action Chalk Bluff, Mo. 5-2-63 | | | | | | | | |

| Eberhart, Joseph C. | | | H | 24 | 5'8" | Light | Blue | Brown |
|---|---|---|---|---|---|---|---|---|
| B. Rock Island Co. Ill. | | Farmer | Res. Edgington, Res. 1885 Blue Springs, Neb. | | | | | |
| Mustered Out 5-15-66 | | | | | | | | |

# DESCRIPTIVE ROLL

| Eddy, John A. | | B | 21 | | | | |
|---|---|---|---|---|---|---|---|
| F. Goshen | | Enl. Lafayette, Ill., Res 1885 Augusta, MI ||||||
| Mustered Out 9-24-64 |||||||||

| Edgar, John | | G | 25 | 5'8" | Light | Blue | Brown |
|---|---|---|---|---|---|---|---|
| | | Mustered in 9-18-61 ||||||
| Deserted at Chicago 9-19-61 ||||||||

| Edwards, Albert W. | | E | 24 | 6'1" | Light | Brn | Auburn |
|---|---|---|---|---|---|---|---|
| B. Cumberland, Co. Me. | Farmer | Enl. Mendota |||||
| Discharged Disability 3-27-63 ||||||||

| Edwards, Joseph | | D | 60 | | | | |
|---|---|---|---|---|---|---|---|
| | | Enl. Manitowoc, Wis. as Musician ||||||
| Discharged December 1861 ||||||||

| Eisworth, Frank | | D | 24 | 5'5" | Dark | Brown | Dark |
|---|---|---|---|---|---|---|---|
| B. Pennsylvania | Carpenter | Res. Manistee, Mich., Res. 1885 Erie, Pa. |||||
| Mustered Out 5-15-66 ||||||||

| Eliot, Daniel M. | | G | 39 | 5'8" | Dark | Brown | Dark |
|---|---|---|---|---|---|---|---|
| B. Philadelphia | Clerk | Res. Freeport |||||
| Went to Sister Charity Hospital in St. Louis from Otterville 1-24-62 ||||||||

| Ellsworth, Alma | | B | 23 | 5'8" | Dark | Brown | Black |
|---|---|---|---|---|---|---|---|
| B. Saratoga, Canada | Carpenter | Res. Lynn, Res. 1885 Bigelow, Mo. |||||
| Discharged 1-26-65 ||||||||

# THIRTY SEVENTH ILLINOIS

| Elmer, Parmonas | | I | | 6'0" | Light | Grey | Brown |
|---|---|---|---|---|---|---|---|
| B. Allegheny, NY | | Res. Durham, Enl. Harvard, Res. 1885 Canon City, Colorado ||||||
| Mustered Out 5-15-66 |||||||||

| Elson, Samuel | | B | 26 | | | | |
|---|---|---|---|---|---|---|---|
| F. Rochester | | | | | | | |
| Mustered Out 10-4-64 ||||||||

| Emerson, Harlow | | D | 41 | | | | |
|---|---|---|---|---|---|---|---|
| F. Michigan | | | | | | | |
| Mustered Out 9-29-64 ||||||||

| Emery, Alfonzo | | G | 29 | 5'8" | Light | Blue | Brown |
|---|---|---|---|---|---|---|---|
| B. La Grange, Me | Farmer | Enl. Chicago |||||||
| On Furlough at Muster Out ||||||||

| Emery, Michael N. | | B | 19 | 5'10" | Fair | Blue | Brown |
|---|---|---|---|---|---|---|---|
| B. Stark Co., Ill | Farmer | Enl. Lafayette, Res. 1885 Galva, Ill. ||||||
| Mustered Out 10-4-64 ||||||||

| Emmert, George S. | | H | 21 | 5'11" | Light | Blue | Brown |
|---|---|---|---|---|---|---|---|
| B. Germany | Farmer | Enl. Morristown, Res. 1885 Herkimer, Kansas |||| 9-21-61 ||
| Discharged Disability 3-9-63. Gunshot wound in right knee at Prairie Grove. Amputation at lower third of femur. ||||||||

| Emmerrett, John | | H | 28 | 6'2" | Dark | Grey | Black |
|---|---|---|---|---|---|---|---|
| B. Germany | Farmer | Enl. Morristown, Res. 1885 Colonia, Ill |||| 8-15-62 ||
| Mustered Out 6-12-65 ||||||||

# DESCRIPTIVE ROLL

| Emmert, John P. | | | H | 18 | 5'9" | Fair | Hazel | Brown |
|---|---|---|---|---|---|---|---|---|
| B. Bradford, Co Pa. | | Farmer | Enl. Morristown | | | | 8-15-62 | |
| Mustered Out 6-12-65 | | | | | | | | |

| England, Thomas B. | | | C | 21 | 5'5" | Fair | Grey | Light |
|---|---|---|---|---|---|---|---|---|
| B. England | | Farmer | Enl. Waukegan, Res. 1885 Chicago, Ill. | | | | | |
| Mustered Out 5-15-66 | | | | | | | | |

| English, George | | | K | 19 | 5'9" | Fair | Grey | Auburn |
|---|---|---|---|---|---|---|---|---|
| B. Perrysville, IN | | Student | Enl. Danville | | | | 3-31-64 | |
| Mustered Out 9-29-64 | | | | | | | | |

| Erk, John C. | | | G | 24 | 5'5" | Light | Blue | Brown |
|---|---|---|---|---|---|---|---|---|
| B. Germany | | Farmer | Res. Belle Pear, Res. 1885 Lees, Mo. | | | | | |
| Mustered Out 10-4-64 | | | | | | | | |

| Escott, John | | | E | 18 | 5'2" | Light | Blue | Light |
|---|---|---|---|---|---|---|---|---|
| B. Lincolnshire, England | | Farmer | Enl. Mendota | | | | | |
| Mustered Out 9-29-64 | | | | | | | | |

| Everett, Carlos | | | E | 27 | 5'11" | Brn | Brn | Dark |
|---|---|---|---|---|---|---|---|---|
| B. Hampshire Co. Mass | | Farmer | Res. 1885 New Salem, Kansas | | | | | |
| Absent sick at Muster Out | | | | | | | | |

| Eyerly, Jonas | | | E | 24 | 5'7" | Light | Grey | Brown |
|---|---|---|---|---|---|---|---|---|
| F. Belvedere | | Farmer | | | | | | |
| Died at Leetown of wounds, 4-19-62. From a round in the left leg fired by a six pound cannon ball received at Pea Ridge 3-8-62. | | | | | | | | |

# THIRTY SEVENTH ILLINOIS

# F

| Fairman, Gallio H. | | | F | 22 | 5'8" | Light | Blue | Light |
|---|---|---|---|---|---|---|---|---|
| B. Pennsylvania | | Farmer | Res. Antioch, Res. 1885 Walnut Grove, Ill. | | | | | |
| Mustered Out 5-15-65 | | | | | | | | |

| Fairman, Solon F. | | | F | 20 | 5'7" | Dark | Hazel | Black |
|---|---|---|---|---|---|---|---|---|
| B. Erie Co. Pa. | | | Res. Antioch, Res. 1885 Bushnel, Ill. | | | 8-12-62 | | |
| Discharged Disability 1-8-64 | | | | | | | | |

| Fallen, John W. | | | F | 19 | 5'5" | Fair | Dark | Light |
|---|---|---|---|---|---|---|---|---|
| B. Boston, Mass | | Farmer | Res Libertyville | | | | | |
| Died Keokuk, Iowa 10-9-65 | | | | | | | | |

| Fanness, Francis | | | H | 25 | | Light | Blue | Amber |
|---|---|---|---|---|---|---|---|---|
| B. Clark Co. Ind. | | Farmer | Res. Bloomington | | | | | |
| Deserted 9-19-61 | | | | | | | | |

| Farnsworth, Edwin | | | C | 22 | 5'10" | Fair | Dark | Brown |
|---|---|---|---|---|---|---|---|---|
| B. DuPage, Ill. | | Farmer | Res. Nunda | | | | | |
| Died Centralia 5-25-66 while enroute with the regiment for final payment and disbandment. From gunshot in Houston. | | | | | | | | |

| Farnsworth, Emery F. | | | C | 22 | | | | |
|---|---|---|---|---|---|---|---|---|
| F. Nunda | | | | | | | | |
| Died wounds at Prairie Grove 12-8-62. Wounded in bowels. | | | | | | | | |

| Farrell, Theodore F. | | | D | 22 | 5'6" | Fair | Grey | Brown |
|---|---|---|---|---|---|---|---|---|
| B. Wisconsin | | Laborer | Enl. Manistee, Mich. | | | | | |
| Died Otterville | | | | | | | | |

# DESCRIPTIVE ROLL

| Feeks, Stephen K. | | | G | 43 | 5'9" | Sandy | Blue | Sandy |
|---|---|---|---|---|---|---|---|---|
| B. New York, NY | Farmer | | Res. East Bend | | | | | |
| Mustered Out 9-29-64 | | | | | | | | |

| Felton, Hershal | | | H | 20 | 5'4" | Light | Grey | Brown |
|---|---|---|---|---|---|---|---|---|
| B. Mercer Co. Ill | Farmer | | Res. Millersburg, Res. 1885 Aledo, Ill. | | | | | |
| Discharged Disability 2-25-63, wounded in left foot at Prairie Grove. | | | | | | | | |

| Fenters, John | | | G | 24 | 5'10" | Dark | Blue | Dark |
|---|---|---|---|---|---|---|---|---|
| B. Indiana | Farmer | | Res. East Bend | | | | | |
| Died in Hospital at Syracuse 12-13-61 | | | | | | | | |

| Finney, Marion | | | F | 36 | 6'0" | Light | Blue | Light |
|---|---|---|---|---|---|---|---|---|
| B. Warren Co OH | Farmer | | Enl. Cassville | | | 6-9-62 | | |
| Mustered Out 6-23-65 | | | | | | | | |

| Finnegan, Michael | | | H | 34 | 5'4" | Dark | Grey | Black |
|---|---|---|---|---|---|---|---|---|
| B. Kerry, Ireland | Farmer | | Enl. Rock Island | | | | | |
| Mustered Out 5-15-66 | | | | | | | | |

| Fisher, Henry | | | E | 26 | 5'6" | Light | Blue | Light |
|---|---|---|---|---|---|---|---|---|
| B. Germany | Farmer | | Enl. Mendota | | | | | |
| Mustered Out 5-15-66 | | | | | | | | |

| Fisk, Mark | | | G | 19 | 6'4" | Light | Blue | Light |
|---|---|---|---|---|---|---|---|---|
| B. Oswego, NY | Seaman | | Enl. Chicago | | | | | |
| Mustered Out 10-4-64 | | | | | | | | |

| Fitch, Luthur | | | B | 31 | | | | |
|---|---|---|---|---|---|---|---|---|
| F. West Jersey | | | | | | | | |
| Mustered Out 9-29-64 | | | | | | | | |

# THIRTY SEVENTH ILLINOIS

| Fitch, Martin | | | B | 23 | 5'11" | Fair | Blue | Light |
|---|---|---|---|---|---|---|---|---|
| B. Knox Co. Ill | | | Res. Goshen, Res. 1885 Hustin, Neb. | | | | | |
| Discharged Disability 2-19-63. Chronic bronchitis following an attack of measles, irritation of kidneys with scant and high colored urine. | | | | | | | | |

| Fithian, William (Henry) | | | K | 23 | | | | |
|---|---|---|---|---|---|---|---|---|
| | | | Enl. Danville, Res. 1885 Fithian, Ill. | | | | | |
| Resigned 4-12-62. Ill health & inability to endure camp life. Typhoid Fever. | | | | | | | | |

| Fitzer, Selah H. | | | I | 19 | 5'7" | Dark | Brown | Dark |
|---|---|---|---|---|---|---|---|---|
| F. New York | | Farmer | Res. Chemung | | | | | |
| Died Barrancas, Fla. 5-9-65, chronic diarrhea. | | | | | | | | |

| Fitzgerald, Morris | | | I | 19 | 6'2" | Light | Grey | Brown |
|---|---|---|---|---|---|---|---|---|
| F. Chicago, Ill | | Farmer | Res. Belvidere | | | | | |
| Transferred 1-1-62 to 23d Illinois. | | | | | | | | |

| Fitzgerald, Morris | | | K | 33 | 5'11" | Dark | Blue | Black |
|---|---|---|---|---|---|---|---|---|
| F. Ireland | | Laborer | Res. Danville | | | | | |
| Killed at Pea Ridge 3-7-62 | | | | | | | | |

| Fitzpatrick, Benjamin | | | A | 22 | 5'4" | Fair | Grey | Sandy |
|---|---|---|---|---|---|---|---|---|
| B. Clinton Co. IL | | Farmer | Enl. Rock Island | | | 11-19-62 | | |
| Mustered Out 6-12-65 | | | | | | | | |

| Fitzsimmons, Michael | | | A | 28 | 5'6" | Light | Blue | Sandy |
|---|---|---|---|---|---|---|---|---|
| B. Ireland | | Farmer | Enl. Preemption | | | 8-15-62 | | |
| Mustered Out 6-12-65 | | | | | | | | |

# DESCRIPTIVE ROLL

| Flurer, William F. | | | E | 18 | 5'6" | Light | Grey | Light |
|---|---|---|---|---|---|---|---|---|
| B. Baden, Germany | | Farmer | Res. Mendota, Res. 1885 Norfolk, Virginia | | | | | |
| Discharged 10-4-62 | | | | | | | | |

| Fochtar, Jacob | | | D | 23 | | | | |
|---|---|---|---|---|---|---|---|---|
| | | | Res. Duck Lake, Mich. | | | | | |
| Died 4-4-62, wounds at Pea Ridge. Broke his right leg. | | | | | | | | |

| Foley, Patrick | | | H | 26 | 5'6" | Light | Blue | Brown |
|---|---|---|---|---|---|---|---|---|
| B. Ireland | | Farmer | Res. Edgington | | | | | |
| Discharged Disability 4-16-62, protracted illness. | | | | | | | | |

| Folger, Thomas | | | K | 21 | 5'5" | Dark | Brown | Black |
|---|---|---|---|---|---|---|---|---|
| F. Georgetown, IL | | Farmer | Res. Vermilion Co. | | | | | |
| Mustered Out 10-4-64 | | | | | | | | |

| Folsom, Edgar DeForrest | | | A | | | | | |
|---|---|---|---|---|---|---|---|---|
| F. Rock Island | | Musician Drum Major | Res. 1885 Rock Island, Ill. | | | 2-1-62 | | |
| | | | | | | | | |

| Fones, Daniel | | | J | 20 | 5'9" | Dark | Blue | Black |
|---|---|---|---|---|---|---|---|---|
| B. Erie Co. NY | | Farmer | Res. Geneseo, Res. 1885 Stanberry, MO | | | | | |
| Mustered Out 10-4-64 | | | | | | | | |

| Foranner, Brunot | | | A | | 5'10" | Fair | Blue | Brown |
|---|---|---|---|---|---|---|---|---|
| B. Bossvalle, Belgium | | Farmer | Res. Preemption, Res. 1885 Atkinson, Ill. | | | | | |
| Mustered Out 4-26-66 | | | | | | | | |

| Force, Cummings | | | B | 26 | | | | |
|---|---|---|---|---|---|---|---|---|
| F. Toulon | | | | | | | | |
| Died of disease 7-21-63 Yazoo City, Miss. | | | | | | | | |

# THIRTY SEVENTH ILLINOIS

| Ford, August | | | A | 23 | 5'11" | Dark | Brown | Brown |
|---|---|---|---|---|---|---|---|---|
| B. Hansbeck, Belgium | | Brick-maker | Enl. Rock Island | | | | | |
| Mustered Out 5-15-66 Illiterate | | | | | | | | |

| Fordham, Albert | | | G | 20 | 5'10" | Light | Grey | Light |
|---|---|---|---|---|---|---|---|---|
| B. Chicago | | Painter | | | | | | |
| Died Carrolton, La. 8-20-63. Chronic diarrhea. | | | | | | | | |

| Foss, William W. | | | K | 19 | 5'5" | Fair | Blue | Dark |
|---|---|---|---|---|---|---|---|---|
| B. Amesbury, MA | | Farmer | Enl. Danville | | | 4-20-64 | | |
| Mustered Out 5-15-66 | | | | | | | | |

| Fowler, James | | | H | 31 | 5'9" | Light | Hazel | Brown |
|---|---|---|---|---|---|---|---|---|
| B. Clark Co. Ind | | Farmer | Res. Geneseo | | | | | |
| Discharged Disability 4-3-62 | | | | | | | | |

| Fox, Frank B. | | | A | 23 | 5'8" | Fair | Grey | Sandy |
|---|---|---|---|---|---|---|---|---|
| B. Vermont | | Farmer | | | | | | |
| Mustered Out 5-15-66 | | | | | | | | |

| Franzine, Marshall | | | F | 24 | 5'6" | Light | Blue | Light |
|---|---|---|---|---|---|---|---|---|
| B. Muskegon, MI | | Farmer | Res. Newport | | | | | |
| Mustered Out 5-15-66 | | | | | | | | |

| Fredenburg, Henry | | | E | 21 | 5'8" | Light | Grey | Light |
|---|---|---|---|---|---|---|---|---|
| B. Baden, Germany | | Farmer | Enl. Mendota | | | | | |
| Mustered Out 5-15-66 | | | | | | | | |

| Fredericks, William P. | | | I | 18 | 5'7" | Light | Blue | Brown |
|---|---|---|---|---|---|---|---|---|
| B. Hamburg, Germany | | Farmer | Enl. Belvidere | | | | | |
| Discharged Disability 12-31-65 Chronic diarrhea | | | | | | | | |

# DESCRIPTIVE ROLL

| Freestone, William | | | G | 21 | 5'6" | Light | Blue | Light |
|---|---|---|---|---|---|---|---|---|
| B. Rochester, NY | Gard-ner | | Enl. Chicago, Res. 1885 Ravenswood, Ill. | | | | | |
| Mustered Out 10-4-64 | | | | | | | | |

| Freisenburg, Nelson | | | K | 27 | | | | |
|---|---|---|---|---|---|---|---|---|
| B. Denmark, F. Northfield | | | | | | | 1-25-65 | |
| Mustered Out 1-24-66 | | | | | | | | |

| French, George | | | D | 24 | 6'10" | Dark | Brown | Dark |
|---|---|---|---|---|---|---|---|---|
| B. Illinois | Farmer | | Res. Lena, Res. 1885 Bradshaw, Nebraska | | | | | |
| Discharged Disability 12-1-62. Foot run over by a wagon while attempting to get on for a ride, at Cassville. | | | | | | | | |

| French, William K. | | | D | 22 | | | | |
|---|---|---|---|---|---|---|---|---|
| F. Cook Co. | | | Res. 1885 Peabody, KS | | | | | |
| Mustered Out 10-4-64 | | | | | | | | |

| Frick, John B. | | | H | 36 | 5'6" | Light | Grey | Light |
|---|---|---|---|---|---|---|---|---|
| B. Westmoreland, Pa. | Physi-cian | | Res. Moline | | | | | |
| Resigned 2-8-62, chronic bronchitis. | | | | | | | | |

| Frieben, Otto | | | D | 23 | 5'7" | Fair | Grey | Light |
|---|---|---|---|---|---|---|---|---|
| B. Germany | Show-man | | Res. Lena | | | | | |
| Left from Boonville 10-21-61 | | | | | | | | |

| Frisbie, Henry N. | | | G | 29 | 5'7" | Light | Blue | Light |
|---|---|---|---|---|---|---|---|---|
| B. Oswego Co. NY | Hay Presser | | Res. Chicago | | | | | |
| Discharged 10-17-63 for transfer to 92d U.S. Colored Volunteers. | | | | | | | | |

# THIRTY SEVENTH ILLINOIS

| Frost, Elihu M. | | | E | 19 | 5'7" | Light | Blue | Light |
|---|---|---|---|---|---|---|---|---|
| B. Cass Co., MO | | Farmer | Enl. Cassville | | | | 4-24-62 | |
| Died Cassville 6-2-62 Congestion of the brain. | | | | | | | | |

| Frost, Thomas R. | | | E | 20 | 5'5" | Light | Blue | Light |
|---|---|---|---|---|---|---|---|---|
| B. Cass. Co., MO | | Farmer | Enl. Cassville, Mo. | | | | 4-24-62 | |
| Died New Orleans 2-18-64 | | | | | | | | |

| Fryer, Lewis F. | | | A | 20 | 5'7" | Light | Blue | Red |
|---|---|---|---|---|---|---|---|---|
| B. Dark Co., OH | | Farmer | Res. Pleasant Ridge, Res. 1885 Clay Center, Nebraska | | | | | |
| Mustered Out 5-15-66 | | | | | | | | |

| Furguson, John B. | | | C | 18 | 5'11" | Fair | Grey | Dark |
|---|---|---|---|---|---|---|---|---|
| B. Scotland | | Farmer | Enl. Waukegan | | | | | |
| Died 9-9-63 at Carrolton, La. Chronic diarrhea. | | | | | | | | |

# G

| Gage, Albert E. | | | F | 18 | 5'8" | Light | Grey | Light |
|---|---|---|---|---|---|---|---|---|
| B. Waukegan | | Farmer | Res. 1885 Rockford | | | | | |
| On leave at muster out of regiment. | | | | | | | | |

| Gage, Henry | | | B | 22 | 5'6" | Dark | Grey | Brown |
|---|---|---|---|---|---|---|---|---|
| B. Bradford, Pa. | | Farmer | Res. Galva | | | | | |
| Died at Carrolton, La. 8-23-63 of disease. | | | | | | | | |

| Gage, James M. | | | F | 30 | 5'7" | Dark | Brown | Dark |
|---|---|---|---|---|---|---|---|---|
| B. Oswego, NY | | Farmer | Res. Antioch | | | | | |
| Mustered Out 10-4-64 | | | | | | | | |

# DESCRIPTIVE ROLL

| Gage, Samuel D. | | | G | 24 | 5'11" | Light | Blue | Brown |
|---|---|---|---|---|---|---|---|---|
| B. Lake Co., OH | | Blacksmith | Res. Cheney's Grove | | | | | |
| Transferred to 92d U.S. Colored Volunteers | | | | | | | | |

| Galbraith, Franklin | | | D | 23 | 5'5" | Light | Grey | Light |
|---|---|---|---|---|---|---|---|---|
| B. Ohio | | Farmer | Res. Lena | | | | | |
| Mustered Out 5-15-66 | | | | | | | | |

| Galligher, Hugh | | | K | 18 | 4'10" | Dark | Blue | Black |
|---|---|---|---|---|---|---|---|---|
| F. New York, NY | | Farmer | Res. Vermilion Co. | | | | | |
| Deserted at Natchez 7-14-64, arrested New Orleans 10-3-64 | | | | | | | | |

| Galligher, William H. | | | F | 19 | 5'8" | Light | Blue | Dark |
|---|---|---|---|---|---|---|---|---|
| B. Gardner, Me. | | Farmer | Res. Avon, Res. 1885 Cleopatra, MO | | | | | |
| Mustered Out 10-4-64 | | | | | | | | |

| Ganger, William | | | K | 24 | 5'4" | Fair | Grey | Brown |
|---|---|---|---|---|---|---|---|---|
| B. Germany | | Farmer | Res. Danville | | | | | |
| Mustered Out 6-26-66 | | | | | | | | |

| Gardner, Alpheus | | | I | 20 | 5'8" | Light | Blue | Light |
|---|---|---|---|---|---|---|---|---|
| F. Bonus, Ill. | | Farmer | Res. Bonus | | | | | |
| Died at Memphis 8-3-63 Chronic diarrhea. | | | | | | | | |

| Gardner, Lorenzo D. | | | I | 17 | 5'9" | Light | Blue | Brown |
|---|---|---|---|---|---|---|---|---|
| B. Bonus, Ill. | | Farmer | Res. Bonus | | | | | |
| Mustered Out 5-15-66 | | | | | | | | |

| Garland, Mandy | | | I | 18 | 5'5" | Dark | Brown | Dark |
|---|---|---|---|---|---|---|---|---|
| F. Monroe, NY | | Farmer | Res. N. Kingston | | | | | |
| Mustered Out 10-4-64 | | | | | | | | |

# THIRTY SEVENTH ILLINOIS

| Garton, Stampor | | | A | 24 | 5'8" | Fair | Grey | Brown |
|---|---|---|---|---|---|---|---|---|
| B. Harrison Co. Ky | Laborer | | Enl. Mendota | | | | 10-1-62 | |
| Died Carrolton 10-1-63, lung fever and diarrhea. | | | | | | | | |

| Garton, Thomas N. | | A | 18 | 5'7" | Light | Blue | Light |
|---|---|---|---|---|---|---|---|
| B. Warsaw, Mo. | Farmer | | | | | 10-1-62 | |
| Mustered Out 10-9-65 | | | | | | | |

| Gawley, James | | A | 21 | 5'9" | Light | Blue | Light |
|---|---|---|---|---|---|---|---|
| B. Fermanagh, Ireland | Farmer | Res. Preemption, Res. 1885 Preemption, Ill. | | | | | |
| Mustered Out 10-4-64 | | | | | | | |

| Gerrard, John D. | | K | 23 | 5'5" | Dark | Brown | Dark |
|---|---|---|---|---|---|---|---|
| B. Danville, Ill. | Farmer | Res. Blue Grass | | | | 12-23-64 | |
| Died 8-8-64 on Steamer FREESTONE at White River Landing, diarrhea and nervous prostration. | | | | | | | |

| Gibson, George W. | | K | 18 | 5'7" | Fair | Grey | Black |
|---|---|---|---|---|---|---|---|
| F. Vermilion, Ill | Farmer | Res. Vermilion, Res. 1885 Knoxville, Ill. | | | | | |
| Mustered Out 10-4-64 | | | | | | | |

| Gibson, John | | K | 22 | | | | |
|---|---|---|---|---|---|---|---|
| F. Vermilion Co. | | Res. 1885 Knoxville, Ill. | | | | | |
| Mustered Out 10-4-64 | | | | | | | |

| Gibson, William | | K | 21 | 5'4" | Dark | Grey | Brown |
|---|---|---|---|---|---|---|---|
| F. Vermilion Co. | Farmer | Res. Iroquois Co. | | | | | |
| Mustered Out 10-4-64 | | | | | | | |

# DESCRIPTIVE ROLL

| Giddings, William | | | E | 23 | 5'9" | Light | Blue | Light |
|---|---|---|---|---|---|---|---|---|
| B. Macomb Co. Mich. | | Farmer | Res. Macomb, Enl. St. Louis | | | 9-20-61 | | |
| Discharged 10-4-64 | | | | | | | | |

| Gibert, Stephen | | | G | 29 | 5'9" | Light | Hazel | Auburn |
|---|---|---|---|---|---|---|---|---|
| B. Clay Co., Ky. | | Farmer | Res. Cheney's Grove | | | | | |
| Mustered Out 5-15-66 | | | | | | | | |

| Gill, James | | | C | 31 | 5'9" | Fair | Grey | Dark |
|---|---|---|---|---|---|---|---|---|
| B. Madison Co. NY | | | Res. Fremont | | | | | |
| Discharged Disability 1-16-63 at St. Louis. Partial paralysis. | | | | | | | | |

| Gillis, John P. | | | F | 34 | 5'8" | Dark | Blue | Dark |
|---|---|---|---|---|---|---|---|---|
| B. Prussia | | | Res. Goodale | | | | | |
| Died Lebanon, Mo. March 1862. | | | | | | | | |

| Girlow, Wilson | | | H | 22 | 5'7" | Light | Blue | Brown |
|---|---|---|---|---|---|---|---|---|
| B. Germany | | Farmer | Res. Bloomington | | | | | |
| Mustered Out 10-18-64 or died 8-12-63 Port Hudson. | | | | | | | | |

| Gleason, Michael | | | B | 28 | 5'5" | Fair | Blue | Brown |
|---|---|---|---|---|---|---|---|---|
| B. Limerick, Ireland | | Farmer | Enl. Galva | | | | | |
| Killed by David Anschutz in self-defense at Brownsville 1-9-64. | | | | | | | | |

| Gluss, George | | | E | 30 | 5'6" | Light | Blue | Light |
|---|---|---|---|---|---|---|---|---|
| B. Germany | | Farmer | Res. Mendota | | | | | |
| Killed Pea Ridge 3-7-62. Shot through the body. | | | | | | | | |

| Godfrey, Matthew T. | | | B | 19 | 5'9" | Dark | Black | Brown |
|---|---|---|---|---|---|---|---|---|
| B. New Jersey | | Farmer | Res. Goshen | | | | | |
| Died Brownsville 6-25-64 of dysentery. | | | | | | | | |

# THIRTY SEVENTH ILLINOIS

| Goldsmith, Jacob F. | | I | 43 | 5'7" | Dark | Grey | Brown |
|---|---|---|---|---|---|---|---|
| B. New York | Farmer | Enl. Chicago | | | | 2-22-65 | |
| Mustered Out 10-2-65 ||||||||

| Golen, Henry | | G | 34 | 5'8" | Dark | Blue | Dark |
|---|---|---|---|---|---|---|---|
| B. Canada East | Carpenter | Res. Chicago | | | | | |
| Mustered Out 5-17-66 ||||||||

| Goodnoe, Jonas D. | | H | 27 | 5'11" | Light | Grey | Brown |
|---|---|---|---|---|---|---|---|
| B. Butler Co., OH | Farmer | Enl. Morristown | | | | | |
| Mustered Out 5-15-66 ||||||||

| Goodsell, Hiram | | I | 24 | 5'4" | Light | Blue | Brown |
|---|---|---|---|---|---|---|---|
| B. Pennsylvania | Farmer | Res. Chemung, Res. 1885 DeKalb, Ill. |||||||
| Discharged Disability 1-24-62. Chronic diarrhea, incipient tuberculosis. ||||||||

| Gordon, James B. | | I | 21 | 5'8" | Aubrn | Dark | Aubrn |
|---|---|---|---|---|---|---|---|
| F. Washington Ny | Farmer | Res. Belvidere | | | | | |
| Mustered Out 5-15-66 ||||||||

| Gordon, John | | E | 44 | 5'9" | Dark | Brown | Dark |
|---|---|---|---|---|---|---|---|
| B. Mercer, Pa. | | Res. Mendota, Res. 1885 Oak Hill, Kan. |||||||
| Discharged 8-20-62. Weak Back. ||||||||

| Gordon, John | | I | 25 | 5'7" | Light | Dark | Auburn |
|---|---|---|---|---|---|---|---|
| F. Washington Ny | Farmer | Res. Belvedere | | | | | |
| Mustered Out 5-15-66 ||||||||

| Gorman, Matthew | | F | 30 | 5'6" | Light | Grey | Dark |
|---|---|---|---|---|---|---|---|
| B. London, England | Laborer | Res. Libertyville | | | | | |
| Discharged Wounds 9-29-62 at Springfield ||||||||

# DESCRIPTIVE ROLL

| Gottschalk, Emanuel | | H | 35 | 5'6" | Dark | Hazel | Black |
|---|---|---|---|---|---|---|---|
| B. Prussia | Farmer | Res. Iowa, Res. 1885 Merrill, Iowa ||||||
| Transferred to Veteran Reserve Corps 4-10-64 |||||||||

| Gottstein, George | | I | 33 | 5'4" | Light | Blue | Light |
|---|---|---|---|---|---|---|---|
| F. Germany | Farmer | Res. Belvedere ||||||
| Discharge Disability 1-24-62. Caused from a rupture caused while drilling at camp near Otterville in Nov 1862. ||||||||

| Gough, David | | | 20 | 5'10" | Fair | Blue | Sandy |
|---|---|---|---|---|---|---|---|
| B. Bureau Co. Ill | Gunsmith | Res. LaSalle Co. ||||||
| Died Carrolton, La. 8-27-63. Chronic diarrhea. ||||||||

| Gould, Orlando | | C | 21 | 5'9" | Fair | Grey | Dark |
|---|---|---|---|---|---|---|---|
| B. Oswego, NY | Farmer | Res. Barrington ||||||
| Mustered Out 5-15-66 ||||||||

| Grace, James | | F | 21 | 6'0" | Light | Grey | Sandy |
|---|---|---|---|---|---|---|---|
| B. Lake Co. | Laborer | Res. Lake Co., Res. 1885 Wauconda, Ill. ||||||
| Mustered Out 10-4-64 ||||||||

| Graffin, Isiah | | E | 23 | 6'1" | Light | Brown | Black |
|---|---|---|---|---|---|---|---|
| B. Franklin Co Pa | Farmer | Res. Mendota ||||||
| Killed at Pea Ridge 3-7-62. Shot through the body. ||||||||

| Graham, George | | H | 18 | 5'4" | Dark | Hazel | Brown |
|---|---|---|---|---|---|---|---|
| B. Lawrence Pa. | Brickmaker | Res. Rock Island ||||||
| Died of wounds received at Pea Ridge 12-8-62 ||||||||

# THIRTY SEVENTH ILLINOIS

| Graham, Henry C. | | I | 19 | 5'5" | Dark | Brown | Dark |
|---|---|---|---|---|---|---|---|
| F. Ohio | Sailor | Res. Green Bay, Wis., Res. 1885 Sturgeon Bay, Wis. | | | | | |
| Discharged Disability 2-8-62 | | | | | | | |

| Graham, John W. | | H | 24 | 5'5" | Light | Blue | Auburn |
|---|---|---|---|---|---|---|---|
| B. New Castle Pa | Brick-maker | Res. Rock Island, Res. 1885 Rock Island, Ill. | | | | | |
| Mustered Out 5-15-66 | | | | | | | |

| Grant, Nelson Jr. | | B | 19 | | | | |
|---|---|---|---|---|---|---|---|
| F. Galva | | Res. 1885 Lafayette, Ill. | | | | | |
| Mustered Out 9-29-64 | | | | | | | |

| Gravenhorst, Joseph | | A | 24 | | | | |
|---|---|---|---|---|---|---|---|
| F. Port Byron | | | | | | | |
| Transferred to 92d U.S. Colored Volunteers 9-21-63. | | | | | | | |

| Graves, Theodore | | D | 18 | 5'9" | Light | Grey | Light |
|---|---|---|---|---|---|---|---|
| B. Jo Daviess, Ill. | Farmer | Enl. Chicago | | | 4-24-64 | | |
| Mustered Out 5-15-66 | | | | | | | |

| Gray, Henry L. | | E | 21 | 6'1" | Light | Blue | Brown |
|---|---|---|---|---|---|---|---|
| B. Montpelier, Vt. | Agent | Res. Rockton, Ill. | | | | | |
| Died 12-17-62 from wounds. Shot through the hip at Prairie Grove | | | | | | | |

| Gray, William S. | | A | 25 | 5'10" | Light | Blue | Light |
|---|---|---|---|---|---|---|---|
| F. Richmond City, Mo. | Farmer | Enl. 2d Iowa, Res. 1885 Milan, Ill. | | | | | |
| Discharged Disibility 10-13-62. Wounded in right thigh at Pea Ridge. | | | | | | | |

| Gregg, James | | A | 22 | 5'9" | Dark | Brown | Dark |
|---|---|---|---|---|---|---|---|
| B. Galesburg, Ill. | Farmen | Res. Buffalo | | | | | |
| Died Carrolton, La. 10-6-63. Intermittent fever. | | | | | | | |

# DESCRIPTIVE ROLL

| Gregg, John | | | A | 31 | 5'0" | Dark | Brown | Black |
|---|---|---|---|---|---|---|---|---|
| B. Galesburg, Ill. | Farmer | Res. Buffalo Prairie, Res. 1885 Willis, Kan. | | | | | | |
| Mustered Out 5-15-66 | | | | | | | | |

| Greten, Michael | | | F | 20 | 5'7" | Light | Brown | Dark |
|---|---|---|---|---|---|---|---|---|
| B. Luxemburg | Farmer | Res. Long Grove, Res. 1885 Boone, Iowa | | | | | | |
| Mustered Out 5-15-66 | | | | | | | | |

| Greve, Andreas | | | F | 28 | 5'6" | Light | Hazel | Light |
|---|---|---|---|---|---|---|---|---|
| B. Germany | Soldier | Res. 1885 Collonwood, Ohio | | | | | | |
| Resigned 7-20-62. Ill health. | | | | | | | | |

| Griffin, Robert | | | A | 22 | 5'5" | Fair | Grey | Sandy |
|---|---|---|---|---|---|---|---|---|
| B. Rock Island | Collier | Res. Coaltown | | | | | | |
| Died Mobile 5-28-65. Chronic dysentery. | | | | | | | | |

| Griffith, Benjamin L. | | | E | 22 | 5'8" | Light | Blue | Light |
|---|---|---|---|---|---|---|---|---|
| B. Putnam Co. Ill | Farmer | Res. Mendota, Res. 1885 Des Moines, Iowa | | | | | | |
| Discharged Disability 5-7-62 | | | | | | | | |

| Griffith, George E. | | | E | 19 | 5'8" | Light | Blue | Light |
|---|---|---|---|---|---|---|---|---|
| B. Putnam Co. Ill | Farmer | Res. Mendota, Res. 1885 Des Moines, Iowa | | | | | | |
| Mustered Out 5-15-66 | | | | | | | | |

| Groesbeck, Peter E. | | | D | 21 | 6'1" | Light | Grey | Light |
|---|---|---|---|---|---|---|---|---|
| B. Jefferson, NY | Farmer | Enl. Lena | | | | | | |
| Mustered Out 5-15-66 | | | | | | | | |

| Grosshart, Fred | | | E | 18 | 5'9" | Light | Blue | Light |
|---|---|---|---|---|---|---|---|---|
| B. Bingen, Germany | Farmer | Enl. Mendota | | | | | | |
| Died Smithtown, Ark. 10-27-61. Inflammation of the bowels. Was interred near a farmhouse south of the encampment. | | | | | | | | |

# THIRTY SEVENTH ILLINOIS

| Group, George | | | C | 20 | 5'5" | Fair | Grey | Light |
|---|---|---|---|---|---|---|---|---|
| B. Germany | | Farmer | Res. Fremont, Res. 1885 Kenoma. Mo. | | | | | |
| Discharged 7-9-62. Wounds, ball through thigh, cords of right leg cut by musket ball. | | | | | | | | |

# H

| Hackett, Michael | | | G | 35 | 5'10" | Sandy | Blue | Brown |
|---|---|---|---|---|---|---|---|---|
| B. Waterford, Ireland | | Laborer | Enl. Chicago | | | | | |
| Discharged Disability 7-28-64 | | | | | | | | |

| Hadlow, Calvin | | | F | 21 | 5'10" | Light | Hazel | Light |
|---|---|---|---|---|---|---|---|---|
| B. Camillus, NY | | Farmer | Res. Lake Co. | | | | | |
| Died of wounds received at Prairie Grove 12-8-62 | | | | | | | | |

| Hall, Charles F. | | | F | 21 | 5'9" | Light | Grey | Light |
|---|---|---|---|---|---|---|---|---|
| B. Syracuse, NY | | Farmer | Res. Avon, Res. 1885 Antioch, Ill. | | | | | |
| Mustered Out 9-29-64 | | | | | | | | |

| Halstead, Cass B. | | | H | 28 | 5'9" | Dark | Brown | Black |
|---|---|---|---|---|---|---|---|---|
| B. Ontario Co NY | | Farmer | Res. Hamlet, Ill., Res. 1885 Hamlet, Ill. | | | | | |
| Discharged Disability 2-6-64 | | | | | | | | |

| Halstead, George D. | | | H | 18 | 5'5" | Dark | Grey | Black |
|---|---|---|---|---|---|---|---|---|
| B. Ontario Co NY | | Farmer | Res. Hamlet | | | 8-1-62 | | |
| Mustered Out 6-12-65 | | | | | | | | |

| Halway, Henry L. | | | G | 25 | | | | |
|---|---|---|---|---|---|---|---|---|
| F. Chicago | | | | | | | | |
| Mustered Out 10-4-64 | | | | | | | | |

# DESCRIPTIVE ROLL

| Hamilton, George | | | G | 33 | 5'6" | Sandy | Blue | Red |
|---|---|---|---|---|---|---|---|---|
| B. England | | Seaman | | | | | | |
| Deserted Chicago 9-15-61 | | | | | | | | |

| Hamilton, William | | | D | 19 | 5'7" | Light | Hazel | Light |
|---|---|---|---|---|---|---|---|---|
| B. Canada | | | | Res. Montreal, Canada | | | | |
| Discharged Disability at Springfield. Organic diseases of the heart. | | | | | | | | |

| Hannon, John | | | F | 18 | 5'7" | Light | Blue | Light |
|---|---|---|---|---|---|---|---|---|
| B. England | | Farmer | | Res. Antioch | | | | |
| Mustered Out 10-4-64 | | | | | | | | |

| Happe, Frank | | | D | 29 | 5'9" | Light | Grey | Brown |
|---|---|---|---|---|---|---|---|---|
| B. Prussia | | Lumberman | | Enl. Lincoln, Mich. | | | | |
| Mustered Out 5-15-66 | | | | | | | | |

| Hardy, John H. | | | K | 26 | 5'11" | Light | Blue | Dark |
|---|---|---|---|---|---|---|---|---|
| B. Dark, Co., OH | | Farmer | | Enl. Danville | | | 12-14-63 | |
| Deserted 11-18-65 from Military Prison at Houston | | | | | | | | |

| Harlow, Charles P. | | | E | 26 | 5'6" | Light | Blue | Dark |
|---|---|---|---|---|---|---|---|---|
| B. Suffolk, Mass | | Farmer | | Res. Peoria | | | | |
| Died at Syracuse 13-5-61. Interred in Old Burying Ground. | | | | | | | | |

| Harrington, John | | | D | 24 | 5'9" | Dark | Grey | Brown |
|---|---|---|---|---|---|---|---|---|
| B. Bathurst, Nova Scotia | | Sailor | | Res. Manitowoc, Wis. | | | | |
| Discharged Disability 10-6-62 Chronic diarrhea. | | | | | | | | |

| Harris, Benjamin | | | K | 21 | 5'9" | Dark | Grey | Red |
|---|---|---|---|---|---|---|---|---|
| F. Eugene, Ind. | | Farmer | | Res. Vermilion Co. | | | | |
| Mustered Out 10-4-64 | | | | | | | | |

# THIRTY SEVENTH ILLINOIS

| Harrison, Peter | | H | 31 | 5'6" | Fair | Blue | Brown |
|---|---|---|---|---|---|---|---|
| B. Yorkshire, England | Laborer | Res. Davenport, Iowa | | | | 11-15-61 | |
| Mustered Out 5-15-66 | | | | | | | |

| Harvey, William | | | 20 | 5'9" | Light | Hazel | Black |
|---|---|---|---|---|---|---|---|
| B. Troy, NY | Carpenter | Res. Hampton, Ill., Enl. Quincy | | | | 10-4-64 | |
| | | | | | | | |

| Hatcher, John | | G | 19 | 5'6" | Light | Blue | Light |
|---|---|---|---|---|---|---|---|
| B. Germany | Farmer | Res. Chicago | | | | | |
| Mustered Out 10-4-64 | | | | | | | |

| Hathaway, Chauncey H. | | I | 22 | 5'8" | Dark | Brown | Black |
|---|---|---|---|---|---|---|---|
| F. New York | Farmer | Res. Bonus | | | | | |
| Deserted 12-26-64 | | | | | | | |

| Havens, William H. | | I | 20 | 5'7" | Light | Grey | Brown |
|---|---|---|---|---|---|---|---|
| F. Penn Yan, NY | Farmer | Res. Spring, Res. 1995 Marshall, Mich. | | | | | |
| Discharged Disability 12-10-65 | | | | | | | |

| Hawes, Charles W. | | A | 21 | | | | |
|---|---|---|---|---|---|---|---|
| F. Rock Island | | Res. 1885 Rock Island, Ill. | | | | | |
| Transferred to 92d U.S. Colored Volunteers. | | | | | | | |

| Hawkins, Jacob S. | | C | 20 | 5'10" | Fair | Brown | Light |
|---|---|---|---|---|---|---|---|
| B. Oneida, NY | Farmer | Res. Avon, Res. 1885 Sioux Falls, S. Dakota | | | | | |
| Transferred Battery E 1st Mo. Light Artillery, Jan. 1864. | | | | | | | |

| Haycock, Joseph | | F | 21 | 5'4" | Dark | Blue | Dark |
|---|---|---|---|---|---|---|---|
| B. England | Farmer | Res. 1885 Antioch, Ill. | | | | | |
| Mustered Out 10-4-64 | | | | | | | |

# DESCRIPTIVE ROLL

| Hayden, Samuel S. | | B | 21 | 6'1" | Fair | Blue | Brown |
|---|---|---|---|---|---|---|---|
| B. Ohio | Farmer | Res. Cambridge, Res. 1885 Aurora, Neb. | | | | | |
| Mustered Out 5-14-66 | | | | | | | |

| Hayward, Henry | | C | 23 | | | | |
|---|---|---|---|---|---|---|---|
| F. Fremont | | | | | | | |
| Died at Carrolton, La. 9-12-63 | | | | | | | |

| Heartley, Samuel M. (Staff) | | | 29 | | | | |
|---|---|---|---|---|---|---|---|
| | | | Enl. Rock Island | | | | |
| Transferred 27th Missouri Volunteers | | | | | | | |

| Hedges, Samuel D. | | A | 21 | 6'0" | Light | Brown | Brown |
|---|---|---|---|---|---|---|---|
| B. Pleasant Valley, Iowa | Farmer | | | | | | |
| Died of wounds 10-23-62. Fracture of left thigh by musket ball at Pea Ridge. | | | | | | | |

| Heitharands, Henry | | A | 31 | 5'5" | Light | Blue | Sandy |
|---|---|---|---|---|---|---|---|
| B. Hannover, Germany | Painter | Res. 1885 Rock Island, Ill. | | | | | |
| Mustered Out 5-15-66 | | | | | | | |

| Hendee, Vernon | | C | | | | | |
|---|---|---|---|---|---|---|---|
| F. Avon | | Res. 1885 Hoopeston, Ill | | | | | |
| Mustered Out 10-4-64 | | | | | | | |

| Henderson, Richard | | K | 19 | 5'9" | Light | Brown | Light |
|---|---|---|---|---|---|---|---|
| F. Vermilion, Ill | Farmer | Res. Warren Co. | | | 9-23-61 | | |
| | | | | | | | |

| Henderson, Richard | | K | 21 | 5'9" | Light | Blue | Light |
|---|---|---|---|---|---|---|---|
| B. Vermilion Co. | Farmer | Res. Georgetown | | | 7-10-64 | | |
| Mustered Out 5-15-66 | | | | | | | |

# THIRTY SEVENTH ILLINOIS

| Henderson, Thomas | | G | 25 | 5'8" | Dark | Grey | Dark |
|---|---|---|---|---|---|---|---|
| B. Glasgow, Scotland | Railroader | | | | | 4-8-64 | |
| Deserted 10-21-64 at Morganzia. | | | | | | | |

| Henderson, William M. | | A | 25 | 5'9" | Light | Blue | Light |
|---|---|---|---|---|---|---|---|
| B. Fairfield, Pa. | Schoolteacher | Res. Deamington | | | | | |
| Died in quarters at Carrolton, La. 8-27-63 | | | | | | | |

| Henry, Edward | | I | 19 | 5'8" | Dark | Blue | Dark |
|---|---|---|---|---|---|---|---|
| F. Germany | Fisherman | Res. Sheboygan, Wis. | | | | | |
| Mustered Out 5-15-66 | | | | | | | |

| Herrick, Morris J. | | A | 19 | | | | |
|---|---|---|---|---|---|---|---|
| F. Rock Island | | | | | | | |
| Mustered Out 10-4-64 | | | | | | | |

| Hessey, William E. | | K | 19 | 5'6" | Dark | Blue | Dark |
|---|---|---|---|---|---|---|---|
| B. Vermilion Co IL | Clerk | Enl. Danville | | | | 12-14-63 | |
| Mustered Out 2-27-66 | | | | | | | |

| Hewitt, John S. | | | 45 | 5'7" | Light | Blue | Brown |
|---|---|---|---|---|---|---|---|
| B. Windham, Conn. | Schoolteacher | Res. Lasalle Co., Enl. Mendota | | | | 9-16-62 | |
| Not mustered | | | | | | | |

| Hick, David | | A | 38 | 5'9" | Light | Hazel | Grey |
|---|---|---|---|---|---|---|---|
| B. Yorkshire, England | Gentelman | Res. Coal Valley | | | | | |
| Discharged Disability 10-5-62 | | | | | | | |

# DESCRIPTIVE ROLL

| Hickey, Timothy | | | G | 23 | 5'8" | Dark | Grey | Brown |
|---|---|---|---|---|---|---|---|---|
| B. Ireland | | Laborer | Res. Chicago | | | | | |
| Killed Prairie Grove 12-7-62 | | | | | | | | |

| Hicks, Napoleon B. | | | K | 23 | 5'8" | Fair | Brown | Black |
|---|---|---|---|---|---|---|---|---|
| B. Perryville, Ind. | | Farmer | Res. Perryville, Res. 1885 Catulla, Texas | | | | | |
| Resigned 5-22-63 | | | | | | | | |

| Higgenbotham, Daniel | | | G | 33 | 5'7" | Dark | Grey | Dark |
|---|---|---|---|---|---|---|---|---|
| B. Ohio | | Farmer | Enl. Chicago | | | 4-8-65 | | |
| Mustered Out 4-7-66 | | | | | | | | |

| Higginson, Andrew J. | | | I | 25 | 5'8" | Light | Blue | Brown |
|---|---|---|---|---|---|---|---|---|
| F. New York, NY | | Brake man | Res. Chicago | | | | | |
| Mustered Out 10-4-64 | | | | | | | | |

| Hill, James W. | | | K | 19 | 5'8" | Dark | Grey | Black |
|---|---|---|---|---|---|---|---|---|
| F. Danville | | Student | Res. Pekin, Ill., Res 1885 Ridge Farm, Ill. | | | | | |
| Discharged Disability 6-16-62 | | | | | | | | |

| Hilliard, Albert G. | | | B | 19 | 6'0" | Fair | Grey | Brown |
|---|---|---|---|---|---|---|---|---|
| B. Lafayette, Ill. | | Farmer | Res. Galva, Res. 1885 Osceola, Iowa | | | | | |
| Discharged Disability 10-5-62 at Newtonia. Wounded in the forehead. Ball lodged in head losing right eye. Causes constant pain. | | | | | | | | |

| Hillsberry, David | | | G | 28 | 5'5" | Dark | Brown | Dark |
|---|---|---|---|---|---|---|---|---|
| B. Cumberland Co., Pa. | | Farmer | Res. East Bend | | | | | |
| Mustered Out 10-4-64 | | | | | | | | |

| Himes, Charles F. | | | B | 22 | 5'8" | Dark | Brown | Brown |
|---|---|---|---|---|---|---|---|---|
| B. Stark Co., Ill | | Farmer | Res. 1885 El Dorado, Kansas | | | | | |
| Mustered Out 5-16-66 | | | | | | | | |

# THIRTY SEVENTH ILLINOIS

| Himes, Luman P. | | | B | 25 | 5'10" | Dark | Blue | Brown |
|---|---|---|---|---|---|---|---|---|
| B. Troy, Penn. | | Farmer | Res. Goshen, Res. 1885 Lafayette, Ill. | | | | | |
| Mustered Out 5-15-66 | | | | | | | | |

| Hinkley, Henry | | | H | 23 | 5'9" | Aubrn | Blue | Aubrn |
|---|---|---|---|---|---|---|---|---|
| B. Penobscot, Me. | | Farmer | Res. St. Anthony, Minn., Res. 1885 Old Town, Me. | | | | | |
| Discharged Disability 9-14-62 | | | | | | | | |

| Hohenstein, Henry J. | | | C | 21 | | | | |
|---|---|---|---|---|---|---|---|---|
| F. Goodale | | | | | | | | |
| Died Memphis 10-24-63 | | | | | | | | |

| Holahan, John | | | G | 36 | 5'6" | Light | Blue | Light |
|---|---|---|---|---|---|---|---|---|
| B. Kilkenny, Ireland | | Cooper | Res. Chicago | | | | | |
| Mustered Out 10-4-64 | | | | | | | | |

| Holcomb, Alonzo | | | F | 19 | 5'10" | Dark | Brown | Dark |
|---|---|---|---|---|---|---|---|---|
| B. Vermont | | Farmer | Res. Lake Co. | | | | | |
| Discharged 2-28-62 at Syracuse. | | | | | | | | |

| Holmes, Charles | | | I | 20 | 5'6" | Light | Blue | Brown |
|---|---|---|---|---|---|---|---|---|
| F. Topsfield, MA | | Farmer | Res. Cherry Valley | | | | | |
| Deserted 7-25-63 | | | | | | | | |

| Holmes, Delos | | | C | 21 | 5'9" | Fair | Grey | Dark |
|---|---|---|---|---|---|---|---|---|
| B. Ohio | | Farmer | Res. Ela, Res. 1885 Greenfield, Iowa | | | | | |
| Mustered Out 3-13-66 | | | | | | | | |

| Holmes, John | | | D | 22 | 5'8" | Light | Blue | Light |
|---|---|---|---|---|---|---|---|---|
| B. New York | | Laborer | Enl. Manistee | | | | | |
| Deserted 10-8-62 from Cassville. | | | | | | | | |

# DESCRIPTIVE ROLL

| Holycross, Daniel | | K | 43 | 5'8" | Dark | Blue | Dark |
|---|---|---|---|---|---|---|---|
| B. Champaign | Laborer | Enl. Danville, Res. Danville | | | 1885 4-7-64 | | |
| Mustered Out 8-8-65 | | | | | | | |

| Honlin, Philip | | D | 28 | | | | |
|---|---|---|---|---|---|---|---|
| F. Michigan | | | | | | | |
| Deserted 11-1-63 | | | | | | | |

| Hornbeck, Michael | | E | 32 | 5'10" | Light | Brown | Black |
|---|---|---|---|---|---|---|---|
| B. Germany | Farmer | Enl. Mendota | | | | | |
| Mustered Out 5-15-66 | | | | | | | |

| Hornit, David | | A | 19 | 5'8" | Light | Blue | Brown |
|---|---|---|---|---|---|---|---|
| B. Cork, Ireland | Farmer | Res. Coal Valley | | | | | |
| Mustered Out 5-15-66 | | | | | | | |

| Horr, Lee | | G | 18 | 5'4" | Light | Blue | Light |
|---|---|---|---|---|---|---|---|
| B. Indianapolis | Farmer | Res. Cheney's Grove | | | | | |
| Died at Houston 11-10-65 of disease. | | | | | | | |

| Horton, James | | E | 26 | 5'11" | Light | Blue | Light |
|---|---|---|---|---|---|---|---|
| B. Otsego Co. NY | Farmer | Enl. Mendota | | | | | |
| Mustered Out 5-15-66 | | | | | | | |

| Hosely, George C. | | C | 26 | 5'10" | Fair | Grey | Light |
|---|---|---|---|---|---|---|---|
| B. Madison, NY | Farmer | Res. Avon | | | | | |
| Mustered Out 4-19-66 | | | | | | | |

| Hovey, George H. | | I | 17 | 6'0" | Light | Blue | Brown |
|---|---|---|---|---|---|---|---|
| F. Leroy, Ill. | Farmer | Res. Leroy | | | | | |
| Died 8-4-64 at St. Charles, Ark. Of disease. | | | | | | | |

# THIRTY SEVENTH ILLINOIS

| Howard, Edson C. | | F | 17 | 5'6" | Dark | Hazel | Dark |
|---|---|---|---|---|---|---|---|
| B. Lake Co., Ill | Farmer | Res. 1885 Volo, Ill. | | | | | |
| Mustered Out 9-29-64 | | | | | | | |

| Howe, John | | G | 23 | 5'6" | Light | Blue | Brown |
|---|---|---|---|---|---|---|---|
| B. New York | Farmer | Res. East Bend | | | | | |
| Mustered Out 10-4-64 | | | | | | | |

| Howell, Laurentine H. | | F | 19 | 5'6" | Fair | Blue | Black |
|---|---|---|---|---|---|---|---|
| B. New York | Farmer | Enl. Libertyville, Res. 1885 Chicago, Ill. | 8-15-62 | | | | |
| Mustered Out 6-9-65 | | | | | | | |

| Huff, Thomas B. | | H | 18 | 5'5" | Dark | Hazel | Brown |
|---|---|---|---|---|---|---|---|
| B. Sullivan Co IN | Farmer | Res. Iowa | | | | | |
| Died 2-27-62 at Sugar Creek, Ark. of typhoid fever. | | | | | | | |

| Huffman, Theodore | | I | 19 | 5'9" | Dark | Blue | Dark |
|---|---|---|---|---|---|---|---|
| F. Livingston, NY | Farmer | Res. Bonus | | | | | |
| Mustered Out 5-31-66 | | | | | | | |

| Huffman, William | | B | 20 | 5'10" | Fair | Blue | Light |
|---|---|---|---|---|---|---|---|
| B. Chicago | Farmer | Res. Arlington, Ill. | | | | | |
| Discharged Disability 11-13-65. Chronic diarrhea. | | | | | | | |

| Hughs, Thomas | | B | 21 | 6'1" | Dark | Blue | Brown |
|---|---|---|---|---|---|---|---|
| B. Vermilion | Farmer | Res. West Jersey | | | | | |
| Died 12-19-61 at Otterville – measles. | | | | | | | |

| Humel, Jacob | | D | 19 | 5'8" | Dark | Hazel | Dark |
|---|---|---|---|---|---|---|---|
| B. Switzerland | Painter Chairmaker | Enl. Manistee | 9-19-61 | | | | |
| Died 8-22-63 of congestive chill. | | | | | | | |

# DESCRIPTIVE ROLL

| Humeston, Luthur F. (Surgeon) | | 35 | 5'8" | Fair | Grey | Dark |
|---|---|---|---|---|---|---|
| B. Hampton, MA | Surgeon | Res. Chicago, Res. 1885 Holyoke, Mass. | | | | |
| Mustered Out 10-17-64 | | | | | | |

| Hunter, Andrew | | A | | 5'10" | Dark | Brown | Black |
|---|---|---|---|---|---|---|---|
| B. Masonville, Pa | Farmer | Res. Coal Valley | | | | | |
| Killed 2-11-66 by a mob at Brenham, Texas | | | | | | | |

| Hunter, James B. | | H | 20 | 5'5" | Dark | Hazel | Brown |
|---|---|---|---|---|---|---|---|
| B. Pennsylvania | Farmer | Res. Fairport, Iowa | | | | | |
| Deserted 2-12-62 between Lebanon and Springfield | | | | | | | |

| Hunter, Nathaniel | | A | 22 | 6'0" | Dark | Brown | Black |
|---|---|---|---|---|---|---|---|
| B. Mercer, Ill. | Collier | Res. Hampton, Enl. Quincy | 10-4-64 | | | | |
| Mustered Out 10-9-65 | | | | | | | |

| Huntley, Judson J. | | C | 23 | 5'7" | Fair | Blue | Dark |
|---|---|---|---|---|---|---|---|
| B. Addison, Vt. | Lawyer | Res. Waukegan | | | | | |
| Mustered Out 5-15-66 | | | | | | | |

| Hurd, George H. | | B | 25 | 5'10" | Dark | Blue | Brown |
|---|---|---|---|---|---|---|---|
| F. Galva | Farmer | Res. 1885 Aurora, Neb | | | | | |
| Mustered Out 5-15-66 | | | | | | | |

| Hurd, William H. | | B | 45 | 5'1" | Dark | Blue | Brown |
|---|---|---|---|---|---|---|---|
| F. Galva | | Res. 1885 Lafayette, Ill. | | | | | |
| Discharged Disability 9-7-62 Chronic diarrhea and general disability | | | | | | | |

| Hutchinson, James O. | | F | 18 | 5'4" | Fair | Blue | Dark |
|---|---|---|---|---|---|---|---|
| B. Lake Co., Ill | Farmer | Enl. Libertyville, Res. 1885 Columbus, Wis. | 9-19-62 | | | | |
| Mustered Out 6-9-65 | | | | | | | |

# THIRTY SEVENTH ILLINOIS

| Hyatt, Allen | | | K | 21 | 5'11" | Dark | Blue | Red |
|---|---|---|---|---|---|---|---|---|
| F. Indiana | | Farmer | Res. Warren | | | | | |
| Died Jefferson City | | | | | | | | |

| Hyde, Perry | | | G | 18 | 5'4" | Light | Grey | Light |
|---|---|---|---|---|---|---|---|---|
| B. Switzerland Co., Ind. | | Farmer | Res. East Bend | | | | | |
| Mustered Out 5-15-66 | | | | | | | | |

# I

| Iches, Samuel | | | A | 26 | 5'8" | Light | Brown | Light |
|---|---|---|---|---|---|---|---|---|
| B. Gettysburg, Pa | | Brick-maker | Res. Preemption | | | | | |
| Groom, waiter to Julius White 7-1-62. Discharged Disability 2-10-63. Scrofula. | | | | | | | | |

| Ingelbritsen, Erick | | | D | 25 | 5'10" | Light | Grey | Dark |
|---|---|---|---|---|---|---|---|---|
| B. Norway | | Lumberman | Res. Hamlin | | | | | |
| Mustered Out 5-15-66 | | | | | | | | |

| Ingraham, George | | | A | 26 | 5'9" | Fair | Blue | Sandy |
|---|---|---|---|---|---|---|---|---|
| B. Sandusky, OH | | Laborer | | | | | | |
| Deserted 12-11-61 from camp at Lamine Bridge. | | | | | | | | |

| Ingram, Jonathan B. | | | H | 18 | 5'4" | Dark | Hazel | Black |
|---|---|---|---|---|---|---|---|---|
| B. Chester Co. Pa | | Farmer | Res. Morristown, Res. 1885, Savannah, KS | | | | | |
| Mustered Out 3-14-66 | | | | | | | | |

| Ives, Charles S. | | | B | 23 | 5'11" | Black | Brwn | Brown |
|---|---|---|---|---|---|---|---|---|
| B. Toulon, Ill. | | Farmer | Res. Galva, Res. 1885 Elk City, Kansas | | | | | |
| Discharged 11-15-65 | | | | | | | | |

# DESCRIPTIVE ROLL

| Ives, Isaac Norman | | B | 18 | 5'9" | Fair | Blue | Brown |
|---|---|---|---|---|---|---|---|
| F. Goshen | Farmer | Res. 1885 Bloomington, Ill. | | | | | |
| Discharged wounds 9-21-62. Wounded in the knee. Crippled for life. | | | | | | | |

# J

| Jackson, Andrew | | H | 20 | | | | |
|---|---|---|---|---|---|---|---|
| F. Geneseo | | | | | | | |
| Dropped from rolls. | | | | | | | |

| Jackson, Casimir P. | | B | 27 | | | | |
|---|---|---|---|---|---|---|---|
| | | Enl. Goshen, Res. 1885 Lafayette, Ill. | | | | | |
| | | | | | | | |

| Jackson, Charles | | K | 22 | 5'8" | Dark | Brown | Brown |
|---|---|---|---|---|---|---|---|
| F. Vermilion | | Res. Warren | | | | | |
| Mustered Out 10-4-64 | | | | | | | |

| Jackson, Henry | | H | 18 | 5'8" | Fair | Grey | Brown |
|---|---|---|---|---|---|---|---|
| B. Lake Co. OH | Farmer | Res. Thornton Station | | | | | |
| Died 8-11-63 at Port Hudson, La. | | | | | | | |

| Jacobs, Francis J. | | C | 21 | 5'8" | Fair | Blue | Light |
|---|---|---|---|---|---|---|---|
| B. Onondaigua, NY | Farmer | Res. Avon | | | | | |
| Absent sick at muster out. | | | | | | | |

| Jarvis, Charles | | D | 28 | 5'7" | Light | Hazel | Brown |
|---|---|---|---|---|---|---|---|
| B. Pennsylvania | Carpenter | Enl. Manistee, Mich. | | | | | |
| Deserted 4-19-62 from Cassville. | | | | | | | |

# THIRTY SEVENTH ILLINOIS

| Jennings, John H. | | F | 21 | 5'7" | Dark | Grey | Sandy |
|---|---|---|---|---|---|---|---|
| B. New York, NY | Farmer | Res. Antioch, Res. 1885, Ray, Indiana ||||||
| Mustered Out 5-15-66 |||||||||

| Jerard, Jerome | D | 23 | | | | |
|---|---|---|---|---|---|---|
| F. Pentwater, MI | | | | | | |
| Discharged Springfield |||||||

| Jewell, Francis R. | | E | 35 | 5'11" | Dark | Brown | Black |
|---|---|---|---|---|---|---|---|
| B. Portage Co. OH | Carriage Maker | Res. Mendota, Res. 1885 Chicago, Ill. ||||||
| Absent on furlough at muster out. ||||||||

| Jewell, Henry E. | | E | 33 | 6'2" | Light | Hazel | Brown |
|---|---|---|---|---|---|---|---|
| B. Portage Co OH | Farmer | Res. Mendota ||||||
| Discharged Disability 10-17-62. Chronic disease from exposure of feet. Could not get boots or shoes large enough. Feet 13" long. ||||||||

| Jewell, James L. | | B | 21 | 5'8" | Dark | Blue | Brown |
|---|---|---|---|---|---|---|---|
| B. Washington Co., Pa. | Farmer | Res. Galva ||||||
| Discharged Disability 2-5-63. Chronic irritation of kidneys. ||||||||

| Jewett, John P. | | I | 26 | 6'1" | Sandy | Blue | Brown |
|---|---|---|---|---|---|---|---|
| F. Waldoboro, Me | Farmer | Res. Chemung, Res. 1885 Alexandria, Neb. ||||||
| Discharged Disability 1-31-63 ||||||||

| Johns, George A. | | K | 18 | 5'4" | Dark | Brown | Black |
|---|---|---|---|---|---|---|---|
| B. Coshocton, OH | Laborer | Enl. Danville | | 3-15-64 | | |
| Mustered Out 5-15-66 ||||||||

# DESCRIPTIVE ROLL

| Johnson, John D. | | | A | 25 | 5'10" | Fair | Blue | Brown |
|---|---|---|---|---|---|---|---|---|
| B. Martinsburg Va | | Farmer | Res. Hartford, Ky | | | 9-9-62 | | |
| | | | | | | | | |

| Johnson, Ole | | | I | 25 | 5'8" | Light | Blue | Brown |
|---|---|---|---|---|---|---|---|---|
| F. Norway | | Farmer | Res. Boone, Res 1885 Poplar Grove, Ill. | | | | | |
| Mustered Out 10-4-64 | | | | | | | | |

| Johnson, Wilbert | | | E | 19 | 5'8" | Dark | Brown | Black |
|---|---|---|---|---|---|---|---|---|
| B. Allegheny Co. NY | | Farmer | Res. Mendota | | | | | |
| Discharged 12-5-64 | | | | | | | | |

| Johnson, William | | | D | 22 | | | | |
|---|---|---|---|---|---|---|---|---|
| F. Manistee, Mich | | | | | | | | |
| Died 12-7-62. Wounds received at Prairie Grove. | | | | | | | | |

| Johnson, William V. | | | G | 23 | 5'10" | Dark | Brown | Dark |
|---|---|---|---|---|---|---|---|---|
| B. Madison, Co. NY | | Farmer | Res. Chicago | | | | | |
| Died Bowmansville, Ill. 1-9-62 of dropsy. | | | | | | | | |

| Jones, Daniel H. | | | I | 29 | 6'0" | Light | Blue | Brown |
|---|---|---|---|---|---|---|---|---|
| F. Pike, NY | | Carpenter | Res. Belvedere, Res 1885 Albany, Oregon | | | | | |
| Mustered Out 10-4-64 | | | | | | | | |

| Jones, Francis A. | | | B | 30 | 5'8" | Dark | Blue | Brown |
|---|---|---|---|---|---|---|---|---|
| B. Goshen, Ohio | | Farmer | Res. 1885 Lafayette, Ill. | | | | | |
| | | | | | | | | |

| Jones, John | | | D | 20 | | | | |
|---|---|---|---|---|---|---|---|---|
| F. Michigan | | | Enl. Manistee | | | | | |
| Mustered Out 10-4-64 | | | | | | | | |

# THIRTY SEVENTH ILLINOIS

| Jones, Moses S. | | B | 24 | 5'4" | Dark | Blue | Brown |
|---|---|---|---|---|---|---|---|
| B. Goshen, Ohio | Farmer | Res. Goshen | | | | | |
| Discharged Disability 7-29-65. Chronic Diarrhea, also mucous & blood expectorants. All the symptoms of advanced phithesis. ||||||||

| Jopp, Alphonzo S. | | I | 19 | 5'9" | Dark | Hazel | Brown |
|---|---|---|---|---|---|---|---|
| F. New Hartford, Conn. | Farmer | Res. Excelsior, Wis. Res. 1885 Chetek, Wis. | | | | | |
| Mustered Out 10-4-64 ||||||||

| Jordan, John A. | | A | 43 | | | | |
|---|---|---|---|---|---|---|---|
| F. Coal Valley | | Res. 1885 Orion, Ill. | | | | | |
| Resigned 12-31-61 ||||||||

| Jourdan, Cornelius | | C | 23 | | | | |
|---|---|---|---|---|---|---|---|
| F. Waukegan | | | | | | | |
| Mustered Out 9-29-64 ||||||||

| Judd, Artemas W. | | F | 22 | 5'8" | Light | Hazel | Sandy |
|---|---|---|---|---|---|---|---|
| B. Canada | Farmer | Res. Antioch | | | | | |
| Mustered Out 10-4-64 ||||||||

| Julien, John | | B | 21 | | | | |
|---|---|---|---|---|---|---|---|
| F. Cambridge | | Res. 1885 Arlington, Ill. | | | | | |
| Transferred to Invalid Corps 9-1-63. ||||||||

# K

| Kain, James | | C | 27 | 5'10" | Fair | Blue | Sandy |
|---|---|---|---|---|---|---|---|
| B. Dublin, Ireland | Farmer | Enl. Chicago, Res. 1885 Evanston, Ill. | | | 9-15-61 | | |
| ||||||||

# DESCRIPTIVE ROLL

| Kane, John M. | | | E | 22 | 5'9" | Light | Brwn | Dark |
|---|---|---|---|---|---|---|---|---|
| B. Brown Co. OH | | Farmer | Res. Livingston Co., Nebraska | | | 1-1-62 | | |
| | | | | | | | | |

| Kaufman, Frederick | | D | 25 | | | | |
|---|---|---|---|---|---|---|---|
| F. Hamlin, Mich | | | | | | | |
| Killed at Pea Ridge 3-7-62 | | | | | | | |

| Kay, Walton | | | A | 22 | 5'7" | Fair | Brown | Brown |
|---|---|---|---|---|---|---|---|---|
| B. England | | Coaldigger | Res. Coaltown | | | 3-31-64 | | |
| Mustered Out 5-16-66 | | | | | | | | |

| Keech, Milton | | | E | 23 | 6'0" | Brown | Blue | Black |
|---|---|---|---|---|---|---|---|---|
| B. Jefferson, NY | | Farmer | Res. Mendota, Res. 1885 Gouverneur, NY | | | | | |
| Mustered Out 5-15-66 | | | | | | | | |

| Kees, John C | | | C | 24 | 5'5" | Fair | Grey | Light |
|---|---|---|---|---|---|---|---|---|
| B. Germany | | Farmer | Res. Goodale | | | | | |
| Mustered Out 5-15-66 | | | | | | | | |

| Kein, Edward | | | F | | | | | |
|---|---|---|---|---|---|---|---|---|
| | | | | | | | | |
| Discharged 1-31-64 to enlist in 1st Missouri Artillery | | | | | | | | |

| Kellan, Robert | | | C | 23 | 5'9" | Fair | Blue | Dark |
|---|---|---|---|---|---|---|---|---|
| B. Ireland | | Farmer | Res. Fremont | | | | | |
| Mustered Out 5-15-66 | | | | | | | | |

| Kelleher, Morris | | | H | 18 | 5'8" | Dark | Hazel | Black |
|---|---|---|---|---|---|---|---|---|
| B. Kerry Co., Ireland | | Farmer | Res. Orion, Res. 1885 Burlinghame, Kan. | | | | | |
| Discharged Disability 8-14-65 | | | | | | | | |

# THIRTY SEVENTH ILLINOIS

| Kelley, Edward M. | | E | 20 | 5'3" | Light | Hazel | Brown |
|---|---|---|---|---|---|---|---|
| B. Boston, Mass | Farmer | Res. Mendota, Res. 1885 Chicago, Ill. ||||||
| Mustered Out 5-15-66 ||||||||

| Kelley, Michael | | G | 28 | 5'5" | Light | Blue | Brown |
|---|---|---|---|---|---|---|---|
| B. Ireland | Teamster | Res. Chicago, Res. 1885 Chicago, Ill. ||||||
| Mustered Out 5-15-66 ||||||||

| Kelley, Thomas W. | | A | 22 | 5'6" | Sandy | Grey | Brown |
|---|---|---|---|---|---|---|---|
| B. Genessee, OH | Farmer | Res. Bowling ||||||
| Mustered Out 5-15-66 ||||||||

| Kelsey, Julius | | B | 27 | 5'8" | Fair | Brown | Brown |
|---|---|---|---|---|---|---|---|
| B. Norway | Farmer | Res. Goshen, Res. 1885 Kewaunee, Ill. ||||||
| Mustered Out 5-15-66 ||||||||

| Kemp, William H. | | F | 21 | 5'10" | Dark | Blue | Brown |
|---|---|---|---|---|---|---|---|
| B. Lake Co. | Farmer | Res. Lake Co. ||||||
| Discharged 4-2-62 ||||||||

| Kendall, Arthur R. | | A | | 5'11" | Dark | Brown | Black |
|---|---|---|---|---|---|---|---|
| B. Olena, Ill. | Farmer | Res. Rock Island, Res. 1885 Missouri Valley, Iowa ||||||
| Mustered Out 5-15-66 ||||||||

| Kendall, Edward | | D | 27 | 6'0" | Light | Grey | Light |
|---|---|---|---|---|---|---|---|
| B. Ohio | Lumberman | ||||||
| Mustered Out 5-15-66 ||||||||

| Kennard, Anthony | | B | 27 | 5'8" | Dark | Brown | Brown |
|---|---|---|---|---|---|---|---|
| B. Belmont, OH | Farmer | Res. Goshen ||||||
| Mustered Out 5-15-66 ||||||||

# DESCRIPTIVE ROLL

| Kennedy, John | | | A | 19 | 5'6" | Light | Grey | Brown |
|---|---|---|---|---|---|---|---|---|
| B. Bellville, Ill. | | Farmer | Res. Rock Island | | | | | |
| Died Camp Totten 4-19-63. Typhoid Pneumonia. | | | | | | | | |

| Kennedy, William | | | C | 10 | 5'7" | Fair | Blue | Dark |
|---|---|---|---|---|---|---|---|---|
| B. Dublin, Ireland | | Farmer | Res. Fremont, Res. 1885 Philadelphia, Pa. | | | | | |
| Discharged Disability 6-14-64. Amputation at junction of middle and upper third of left thigh. | | | | | | | | |

| Kennicott, George | | | I | 21 | 5'6" | Dark | Brown | Dark |
|---|---|---|---|---|---|---|---|---|
| F. New Orleans, La. | | Student | Res. Dunton, Res. 1885 Chicago, Ill. | | | | | |
| Mustered Out 5-15-66 | | | | | | | | |

| Kennicott, Ransom | | | I | 24 | 5'3" | Dark | Brown | Dark |
|---|---|---|---|---|---|---|---|---|
| F. Lake Co. | | Dentist | Res. Chicago | | | | | |
| Wounded at Prairie Grove. Mustered Out 5-15-66. | | | | | | | | |

| Kent, James D. | | | G | 19 | 6'0" | Florid | Blue | Red |
|---|---|---|---|---|---|---|---|---|
| B. Litchfield, CT | | Painter | Res. Chicago, Res. 1885 Sacramento, Cal. | | | | | |
| Wounded in left elbow at Prairie Grove 3-7-62. Discharged Disability 2-21-63. | | | | | | | | |

| Ketzle, Henry | | | A | 26 | 5'5" | Light | Hazel | Aubrn |
|---|---|---|---|---|---|---|---|---|
| B. Stuttgart, Wurttemburg, Germany | | Farmer | Res. Preemption, Res. 1885 Reynolds, Ill. | | | | | |
| Mustered Out 5-15-66 | | | | | | | | |

| Kiem, Abram | | | B | 26 | 5'6" | Dark | Brown | Brown |
|---|---|---|---|---|---|---|---|---|
| B. Holmes, Ohio | | Farmer | Enl. Lafayette | | | | | |
| Mustered Out 10-4-64 | | | | | | | | |

# THIRTY SEVENTH ILLINOIS

| Kiem, Daniel | | B | 22 | 5'6" | Dark | Brown | Brown |
|---|---|---|---|---|---|---|---|
| B. Ohio | | Res. Goshen | | | | | |
| Discharged Disability 2-4-63. Chronic Hepatitis. | | | | | | | |

| Kimball, Henry F. | | E | 18 | 5'8" | Light | Blue | Light |
|---|---|---|---|---|---|---|---|
| B. Boston, Mass | Farmer | Res. Mendota | | | | | |
| Discharged Disability 6-6-64 | | | | | | | |

| Kime, Sebastian | | E | 20 | 6'0" | Light | Brown | Black |
|---|---|---|---|---|---|---|---|
| B. Germany | Farmer | Enl. Mendota | | | 9-20-61 | | |
| Deserted while out with forage train near Mt. Vernon, Mo. 2-24-63. | | | | | | | |

| King, Thomas | | A | 24 | 6'1" | Light | Grey | Brown |
|---|---|---|---|---|---|---|---|
| B. Mansfield, NY | Lumberman | Res. 1885 Shamrock, Wis. | | | | | |
| Transferred 92d U.S. Colored Volunteers 9-21-63 | | | | | | | |

| Kirby, George W. | | B | 20 | 5'7" | Dark | Brown | Black |
|---|---|---|---|---|---|---|---|
| B. Fullerton, NY | Farmer | Res. Goshen, Res. 1885 Hastings, Nebraska | | | | | |
| Mustered Out 5-15-66 | | | | | | | |

| Klein, John | | D | 31 | 5'8" | Dark | Grey | Brown |
|---|---|---|---|---|---|---|---|
| B. Prussia | Lumberman | Res. Michigan, Res. 1885 Hamlin, Mich. | | | | | |
| Mustered Out 5-15-66 | | | | | | | |

| Kling, David | | I | 18 | 5'9" | Dark | Brown | Black |
|---|---|---|---|---|---|---|---|
| F. Sharon, Wis. | Farmer | | | | | | |
| Deserted from hospital at Syracuse 2-1-62. | | | | | | | |

| Klosterman, Frederick | | G | 38 | 5'8" | Dark | Blue | Dark |
|---|---|---|---|---|---|---|---|
| B. Germany | Blacksmith | Res. Chicago | | | | | |
| Discharged Disability 1-16-62 | | | | | | | |

# DESCRIPTIVE ROLL

| Knopf, August C. | | F | 20 | 5'9" | Light | Blue | Black |
|---|---|---|---|---|---|---|---|
| B. Louisiana | Farmer | Res. Vernon | | | | | |
| Discharged Disability 11-7-62. Wounds at Pea Ridge. ||||||||

| Koerner, Henry | | D | 32 | 6'2" | Light | Grey | Light |
|---|---|---|---|---|---|---|---|
| B. Germany | Lumberman | Res. Manistee | | | | | |
| Died 7-31-63 at Cape Girardeau, Mo. of gunshot wound of left shoulder received at Chalk Bluffs 5-2-63. Shattered scapula. ||||||||

| Kruger, Otto | | E | 18 | 5'5" | Light | Grey | Dark |
|---|---|---|---|---|---|---|---|
| B. Germany | Laborer | Res. Mendota, Res. 1885, Iola, Kansas | | | | | |
| Discharged Disability 7-17-65. Chronic dysentery. ||||||||

| Kunkle, John | | A | | 6'1" | Light | Blue | Sandy |
|---|---|---|---|---|---|---|---|
| B. Adams, Pa. | Farmer | Res. Rock Island, Res. 1885 Hampton, Ill. | | | | | |
| Mustered Out 5-15-66 ||||||||

# L

| Lacey, Fayette | | B | | | | | |
|---|---|---|---|---|---|---|---|
| F. Goshen | | | | | | | |
| Mustered Out 9-29-64 ||||||||

| Lagore, John | | H | | 5'6" | Dark | Hazel | Black |
|---|---|---|---|---|---|---|---|
| B. Luxembourg | Farmer | Res. Chicago | | | | | |
| Mustered Out 5-15-66 ||||||||

| Laimbeer, John W. | | D | 32 | | | | |
|---|---|---|---|---|---|---|---|
| | | Res. Chicago | | | | | |
| Discharged 1-1-63 Unfitness. ||||||||

# THIRTY SEVENTH ILLINOIS

| Lake, Anson O. | | A | 23 | | | | |
|---|---|---|---|---|---|---|---|
| | | Res. Rock Island | | | | | |
| Discharged 12-3-161. Protracted illness and absence. | | | | | | | |

| Lake, Thomas R. | | B | 25 | 5'9" | Dark | Brown | Brown |
|---|---|---|---|---|---|---|---|
| B. Goshen | Farmer | | | | | | |
| Mustered Out 5-7-66 | | | | | | | |

| Lamm, John M. | | K | 20 | 5'5" | Fair | Grey | Dark |
|---|---|---|---|---|---|---|---|
| B. Vermilion Co. | Lumber Merchant | Res. Danville, Res. 1885 Danville, Ill. | | | | | |
| Mustered Out 9-29-64 | | | | | | | |

| Lamm, Stampor Q. | | K | 18 | 5'6" | Fair | Blue | Light |
|---|---|---|---|---|---|---|---|
| B. Danville, Ill. | Student | Enl. Danville, Res. 1885 Danville, Ill. | | | | 3-31-64 | |
| Mustered Out 4-19-66 | | | | | | | |

| Lamphere, Charles A. | | A | 28 | | | | |
|---|---|---|---|---|---|---|---|
| F. Homerville, NY | | Res. 1885 Arkport, NY | | | | | |
| Mustered Out 10-4-64 | | | | | | | |

| Lamphere, Perry S. | | C | 21 | | | | |
|---|---|---|---|---|---|---|---|
| F. Wauconda | | | | | | | |
| Mustered Out 5-15-66 | | | | | | | |

| Lane, John A. | | E | 22 | 5'9" | Dark | Blue | Dark |
|---|---|---|---|---|---|---|---|
| B. Brown, Ohio | Farmer | | | | | 11-25-61 | |
| Died in camp at Lebanon 2-10-62. | | | | | | | |

| Lane, Thomas | | G | 23 | 5'7" | Fair | Blue | Brown |
|---|---|---|---|---|---|---|---|
| B. England | Farmer | Res. Cheney's Grove | | | | | |
| Died 10-1-63 at New Orleans. Typhoid fever, chronic diarrhea. | | | | | | | |

# DESCRIPTIVE ROLL

| Larch, Franklin | | | D | 29 | 5'7" | Light | Blue | Brown |
|---|---|---|---|---|---|---|---|---|
| B. Belgium | Lumberman | | Res. Michigan, Res. 1885 Houston, Texas ||||||
| Mustered Out 5-15-66 |||||||||

| Lathrop, Joshua | | | C | 23 | 5'6" | Fair | Blue | Light |
|---|---|---|---|---|---|---|---|---|
| B. Wyoming Co. NY | Farmer | | Enl. Waukegan ||||||
| Deserted 3-4-63 on march from Ozark to Bloomington, Mo. |||||||||

| Lawson, Emery | | | A | 20 | | | | |
|---|---|---|---|---|---|---|---|---|
| F. Westmoreland Co. Pa. | | | Enl. Moline ||||||
| Died Cassville 7-8-62 (?) |||||||||

| Lebonta, John | | | D | 26 | 5'7" | Dark | Grey | Dark |
|---|---|---|---|---|---|---|---|---|
| B. Canada | Lumberman | | Res. Pentwater ||||||
| Mustered Out 5-15-66 |||||||||

| Lecander, Charles | | | D | 31 | 5'6" | Light | Grey | Light |
|---|---|---|---|---|---|---|---|---|
| B. Sweden | Lumberman | | Enl. Hamlin ||||||
| Mustered Out 5-15-66 |||||||||

| Lee, Dennis | | | B | 24 | 6'0" | Fair | Grey | Sandy |
|---|---|---|---|---|---|---|---|---|
| F. Goshen | | Farmer | Res. 1885 Peoria, Ill. |||||
| Discharged Wounds 9-21-62. Wounded in the ankle losing foot. Amputated 4" above ankle. Gunshot at Pea Ridge. |||||||||

| Lee, James E. | | | B | 19 | | | | |
|---|---|---|---|---|---|---|---|---|
| F. Goshen | | | |||||||
| Killed at Pea Ridge 3-7-62. Shot through the head. |||||||||

| Lee, Richard M.J. | | | B | 25 | 5'10" | Dark | Grey | Brown |
|---|---|---|---|---|---|---|---|---|
| B. Ohio | | Farmer | Res. Lynn |||||
| Killed by guerillas 4-25-65 while on the way up the Alabama River, by bushwhackers. |||||||||

425

# THIRTY SEVENTH ILLINOIS

| Lee, Samuel G. | | A | 23 | 5'9" | Light | Blue | Auburn |
|---|---|---|---|---|---|---|---|
| B. Middletown, OH | Farmer | Res. Preemption | | | | | |
| Mustered Out 9-29-64 | | | | | | | |

| Leiber, Joseph | | H | 21 | 5'8" | Light | Blue | Auburn |
|---|---|---|---|---|---|---|---|
| B. Buhler Co. OH | Farmer | Enl. Morristown, Res. 1885, Morristown, Ill. | | | 3-29-64 | | |
| Mustered Out 5-15-66 | | | | | | | |

| Lemoine, Samuel M. | | B | 23 | 5'10" | Fair | Blue | Brown |
|---|---|---|---|---|---|---|---|
| B. Fort Lee, NJ | Farmer | Enl. Lafayette, Res. 1885 Augusta, Kansas | | | | | |
| Mustered Out 4-16-66 | | | | | | | |

| Leonard, Frederick | | I | 27 | 5'10" | Dark | Brown | Brown |
|---|---|---|---|---|---|---|---|
| F. New York | Farmer | Res. Chemung | | | | | |
| Discharged Disability | | | | | | | |
| 10-19-62 | | | | | | | |

| Leonard, Martin H. | | K | 24 | 5'8" | Fair | Blue | Light |
|---|---|---|---|---|---|---|---|
| B. Halifax. VT | Farmer | Res. State Line City | | | | | |
| Resigned 2-23-64 | | | | | | | |

| Leroy, Francis | | K | 36 | 5'5" | Dark | Hazel | Black |
|---|---|---|---|---|---|---|---|
| B. Belgium | Laborer | Enl. Danville | | | 11-23-63 | | |
| Mustered Out 5-15-66 Illiterate. | | | | | | | |

| Leslie, William | | G | 18 | 5'5" | Light | Blue | Light |
|---|---|---|---|---|---|---|---|
| B. Washington, DC | Farmer | Res. Chicago | | | | | |
| | | | | | | | |

# DESCRIPTIVE ROLL

| Levene, John J. | | K | 21 | 5'4" | Light | Blue | Light |
|---|---|---|---|---|---|---|---|
| F. State Line | Farmer | | | | 9-20-61 | | |
| Mustered Out 10-4-64 ||||||||

| Lienburg, William N.H. | | H | 29 | 5'1" | Dark | Brown | Black |
|---|---|---|---|---|---|---|---|
| B. Weimar, Germany | Farmer | Res. Moline | | | | | |
| Deserted 4-24-63 at St. Louis, returned 9-17-64. Deserted again at Columbus, Texas 12-25-65. ||||||||

| Liggett, Lawson | | K | 20 | 5'5" | Light | Blue | Brown |
|---|---|---|---|---|---|---|---|
| F. Fountain, Ind. | | Res. Vermilion Co. | | | | | |
| Discharged Disability 21-18-62. Disabled leg. ||||||||

| Liggett, William | | K | 23 | | | | |
|---|---|---|---|---|---|---|---|
| F. Vermilion Co. | | Res. 1885 Thomas Station, Indiana | | | | | |
| Taken prisoner at Prairie Grove. Mustered Out 10-4-64. ||||||||

| Lillie, Calvin H. | | H | 23 | 5'5" | Light | Grey | Brown |
|---|---|---|---|---|---|---|---|
| B. Sullivan Co. NY | Farmer | Res. Edgington | | | | | |
| Mustered Out 10-4-64 ||||||||

| Lindsey, Henry J. | | K | 24 | 5'10" | Dark | Hazel | Dark |
|---|---|---|---|---|---|---|---|
| B. Sinking Springs, Pa. | Farmer | Enl. Danville | | | 3-31-64 | | |
| Mustered Out 5-15-65 ||||||||

| Lippencott, Charles F. | | A | 20 | | | | |
|---|---|---|---|---|---|---|---|
| F. Philadelphia | | Enl. Rock Island | | | | | |
| Mustered Out 10-4-64 ||||||||

| Liscom, Horace F. | | E | 29 | 5'10" | Light | Brown | Dark |
|---|---|---|---|---|---|---|---|
| B. Windham, VT | Farmer | Res. Mendota, Res. 1885 Mendota, Ill. | | | | | |
| Mustered Out 10-4-64 ||||||||

# THIRTY SEVENTH ILLINOIS

| Liscom, Martin F. | | E | 18 | 5'2" | Light | Grey | Brown |
|---|---|---|---|---|---|---|---|
| B. Iowa City, Wis | Farmer | Res. Mendota, Enl. Joliet | | | | | |
| Discharged Disability 11-9-64. General debility, intermittent fever, diarrhea. Never should have been enlisted because of his constitution. ||||||||

| Little, William F. | | A | 23 | 6'0" | Fair | Brown | Brown |
|---|---|---|---|---|---|---|---|
| B. Preemption | Farmer | | | | | 8-14-62 | |
| Died 12-10-62 of wounds at Prairie Grove. Musket ball through both thighs. ||||||||

| Lofinch, Frederick | | C | 18 | | | | |
|---|---|---|---|---|---|---|---|
| F. Belvedere | | Enl. Chicago | | | | | |
| Deserted 3-20-62 on march from Sugar Creek to Camp Stevens in Benton Co. Arkansas. ||||||||

| Logerwick, John | | D | 22 | | | | |
|---|---|---|---|---|---|---|---|
| F. Lincoln, Mich | | | | | | | |
| Mustered Out 10-4-64 ||||||||

| Long, William A. | | K | 20 | | | | |
|---|---|---|---|---|---|---|---|
| F. Vermilion Co. | | | | | | 9-23-61 | |
| Mustered Out 10-4-64 ||||||||

| Lowell, Charles H. | | K | | 5'4" | Fair | Blue | Light |
|---|---|---|---|---|---|---|---|
| F. Kenosha, Wis. | | | | | | | |
| Deserted 11-4-61 at Warsaw, Mo. with musket. ||||||||

| Loyd, William M. | | G | 21 | 5'8" | Light | Blue | Dark |
|---|---|---|---|---|---|---|---|
| B. McLean Co. IL | Farmer | Res. Cheney's Grove, Res. 1885 Saybrook, Ill. | | | | | |
| Deserted 7-3-62 on furlough to Chicago. ||||||||

# DESCRIPTIVE ROLL

| Lucas, Thomas | | K | 20 | 6'0" | Fair | Brown | Black |
|---|---|---|---|---|---|---|---|
| F. Danville | Farmer | | | | | | |
| Deserted, Joined regular service at Newport Barracks 6-30-62. ||||||||

| Lundy, Daniel | | B | 20 | | | | |
|---|---|---|---|---|---|---|---|
| | | Enl. Lafayette, Res. Goshen, Res. 1885 Union, Iowa |||||||
| Mustered Out 9-29-64 ||||||||

| Lundy, James D. | | I | 22 | 5'10" | Fair | Blue | Brown |
|---|---|---|---|---|---|---|---|
| B. Lafayette | Farmer | Res. 1885 Union, Iowa |||||||
| Discharged 2-6-64. Suffering from apoplectic fits since August 1862. Frequent attacks of epilepsy. ||||||||

# M

| Manzer, Gurnsey B. | | C | 22 | 5'8" | Fair | Blue | Dark |
|---|---|---|---|---|---|---|---|
| B. Lake Co. | Farmer | Res. Avon |||||||
| Killed Pea Ridge 3-7-62. Shot through the thigh. ||||||||

| Manzer, Lazell C. | | E | 23 | 5'11" | Fair | Brown | Dark |
|---|---|---|---|---|---|---|---|
| B. Lake Co. | Artist | Res. Waukegan, Res. 1885 Waukegan, Ill. |||||||
| Mustered Out 5-15-66 ||||||||

| Marlatt, William | | K | 20 | 5'7" | Dark | Blue | Dark |
|---|---|---|---|---|---|---|---|
| F. Warren, Ohio | Farmer | Res. Covington, Indiana |||||||
| Killed Pea Ridge 3-7-62 ||||||||

| Marsh, James W. | | F | 19 | 5'8" | Light | Blue | Light |
|---|---|---|---|---|---|---|---|
| B. Lake Co., Ill. | Farmer | Res. Antioch, Res. 1885 Fond Du Lac, Wis. |||||||
| Mustered Out 10-4-64 ||||||||

# THIRTY SEVENTH ILLINOIS

| Martin, James | | | F | 26 | 5'6" | Dark | Grey | Dark |
|---|---|---|---|---|---|---|---|---|
| B. Biddeford, England | | Farmer | Res. Warren | | | | | |
| Mustered Out 9.29-64 | | | | | | | | |

| Martin, Smith | | | C | 25 | 5'11" | Fair | Grey | Dark |
|---|---|---|---|---|---|---|---|---|
| F. Warren | | Mechanic | | | | | | |
| Killed at Boonville 2-12-62. Shot through the heart by a rebel citizen. | | | | | | | | |

| Mason, J. Barney | | | F | 20 | 5'7" | Dark | Grey | Dark |
|---|---|---|---|---|---|---|---|---|
| B. Lake Co. | | | Res. Vernon, Res. 1885 Wheeling, Ill. | | | | | |
| Mustered Out 9-29-64 | | | | | | | | |

| Mason, John | | | C | 17 | | | | |
|---|---|---|---|---|---|---|---|---|
| F. Waukegan | | | | | | | 8-17-61 | |
| Discharged 9-13-61 on demand of father. | | | | | | | | |

| Mather, John | | | F | 37 | | Fair | Grey | Dark |
|---|---|---|---|---|---|---|---|---|
| B. France | | Farmer | Res. 1885 Hastings, Minn. | | | 2-22-64 | | |
| Mustered Out 5-15-66 | | | | | | | | |

| Mathews, Tobias L. | | | F | 25 | 5'9" | Dark | Hazel | Sandy |
|---|---|---|---|---|---|---|---|---|
| B. Warren Co., Indiana | | Farmer | | | | | | |
| Died 12-17-62 at Springfield of phithesis pulmonalis. | | | | | | | | |

| Matthews. Thomas E. | | | | 18 | 5'6" | Light | Blue | Light |
|---|---|---|---|---|---|---|---|---|
| B. Fulton Co. NY | | Farmer | Enl. Rock Island | | | | | |
| Died 7-29-63 on board Steamer THOMAS near Port Hudson of typhoid fever. | | | | | | | | |

| Mattox, Marcellus | | | D | 22 | 5'6" | Dark | Grey | Dark |
|---|---|---|---|---|---|---|---|---|
| B. Montgomery, AL | | | Enl. Manistee | | | | | |
| Deserted 7-5-62 | | | | | | | | |

# DESCRIPTIVE ROLL

| Matzlaff, Valentine | | F | 44 | 5'6" | Light | Grey | Brown |
|---|---|---|---|---|---|---|---|
| B. Strasbourg, France | Baker | Res. Waukegan | | | | | |
| Transferred Invalid Corps 9-30-63 | | | | | | | |

| Maxton, John | | G | 24 | 5'9" | Dark | Blue | Dark |
|---|---|---|---|---|---|---|---|
| B. Perthshire, Scotland | Carpenter | Res. Cheney's Grove | | | | | |
| Mustered Out 10-4-64 | | | | | | | |

| Mazelle, William | | D | 30 | | | | |
|---|---|---|---|---|---|---|---|
| F. Michigan | | | | | | | |
| Resigned 12-9-61 | | | | | | | |

| McAfee, Archibald | | A | 23 | | | | |
|---|---|---|---|---|---|---|---|
| F. Andalusia | | Res. 1885 Taylor Ridge, Ill. | | | | | |
| Mustered Out 10-4-64 | | | | | | | |

| McAllister, James | | C | 18 | 5'8" | Dark | Grey | Brown |
|---|---|---|---|---|---|---|---|
| B. Ohio | Shoemaker | | | | | 8-18-64 | |
| Substitute for Charles F. Kellogg of Chicago. Mustered Out 5-15-66 | | | | | | | |

| McAllister, Thomas | | C | 21 | | | | |
|---|---|---|---|---|---|---|---|
| F. Waukegan | | Res. 1885 Waukegan, Ill. | | | | | |
| Sick at muster out | | | | | | | |

| McAuliffe, Patrick Henry | | E | 23 | 5'10" | Light | Blue | Light |
|---|---|---|---|---|---|---|---|
| B. Canada | Farmer | Res. Minouk, Woodford, Co. | | | | 9-20-61 | |
| Discharged Disability 3-27-63. Spinal irritation, partial paralysis at times of lower extremities. | | | | | | | |

| McAuliffe, William | | G | 18 | 5'8" | Light | Blue | Light |
|---|---|---|---|---|---|---|---|
| B. Ireland | Farmer | | | | | | |
| | | | | | | | |

# THIRTY SEVENTH ILLINOIS

| McCabe, George | | I | 23 | | | | |
|---|---|---|---|---|---|---|---|
| | | Enl. Belvedere | | | | 9-19-61 | |
| Mustered Out 10-24-64 ||||||||

| McCabe, William D. | | I | 19 | 5'8" | Dark | Hazel | Dark |
|---|---|---|---|---|---|---|---|
| F. Scotland | Farmer | Res. Bonus, Res. 1885 Bonus, Ill. ||||||
| Mustered Out 5-15-66 ||||||||

| McCain, John | | H | 21 | 5'9" | Light | Blue | Light |
|---|---|---|---|---|---|---|---|
| B. Henderson-ville, KY | Car-penter | Res. Moline ||||||
| Discharged 12-31-63 at Pass Cavallo, Texas to enlist in U.S. Artillery ||||||||

| McCarthy, Dennis | | G | 28 | 5'10" | Light | Blue | Sandy |
|---|---|---|---|---|---|---|---|
| B. Cork Co., Ireland | Car-penter | Res. Chicago ||||||
| Wounded in leg 3-7-62 ||||||||

| McCarty, Dennis | | I | 24 | 6'0" | Dark | Brown | Brown |
|---|---|---|---|---|---|---|---|
| F. Ireland | Farmer | Res. Cincinnati, Ohio ||||||
| Deserted 2-23-63 ||||||||

| McClelland, Charles | | F | 17 | 6'1" | | | |
|---|---|---|---|---|---|---|---|
| B. Lake Co., Ill. | Farmer | Res. Milbourne | | | Enl. 2-23-64 |||
| Died 9-24-64 of disease at New Orleans ||||||||

| McClellan, Henry W. | | H | 24 | 5'6" | Fair | Blue | Auburn |
|---|---|---|---|---|---|---|---|
| B. Delaware | Farmer | Res. Camden, Res. 1885 Geneseo, Ill. ||||||
| Mustered Out 5-15-66 ||||||||

| McCloud, Collins | | F | 24 | 6'0" | Dark | Blue | Dark |
|---|---|---|---|---|---|---|---|
| B. Lake Co., Ill. | Farmer | Res. Antioch ||||||
| Mustered Out 9-29-64 ||||||||

# DESCRIPTIVE ROLL

| McCord, William D. | | E | 30 | 5'9" | Light | Blue | Light |
|---|---|---|---|---|---|---|---|
| B. Lawrence, Pa. | | Res. Minouk, Woodford Co. | | | | 9-20-61 | |
| Mustered Out 9-29-64 ||||||||

| McCormack, Daniel | | F | 22 | 5'10" | Dark | Grey | Black |
|---|---|---|---|---|---|---|---|
| B. Ireland | Farmer | Res. Antioch, Res. 1885 Libertyville, Ill. |||||||
| Mustered Out 1-4-64 ||||||||

| McCormick, James | | C | 27 | 5'5" | Fair | Grey | Dark |
|---|---|---|---|---|---|---|---|
| F. Avon | Farmer | Res. 1885 Watertown, Ill. |||||||
| Discharged Disability 11-16-62 Phithesis Pulmonalis ||||||||

| McCormick, Ralph | | K | 18 | 5'8" | Dark | Hazel | Light |
|---|---|---|---|---|---|---|---|
| B. Danville | Musician | Enl. Danville, Res. 1885 Abilene, Kansas | | | | 3-31-64 | |
| Mustered Out 5-7-66 ||||||||

| McCrady, Archibald T. | | F | 25 | 5'8" | Dark | Brown | Dark |
|---|---|---|---|---|---|---|---|
| B. Gallowshire, Scotland | Farmer | Res. Antioch |||||||
| Mustered Out 5-16-66 ||||||||

| McCurdy, William | | F | 27 | 5'5" | Red | Blue | Dark |
|---|---|---|---|---|---|---|---|
| B. Belfast, Ireland | Farmer | Res. Fremont, Res. 1885 Ottawa, Canada |||||||
| Mustered Out 5-15-66 ||||||||

| McDaniel, Thomas J. | | B | 25 | | | | |
|---|---|---|---|---|---|---|---|
| F. Goshen | | | | | | | |
| Died 6-9-62 at Cassville, wounds received at Pea Ridge. Wounded in left knee. ||||||||

| McDonald, Michael | | I | 22 | 5'7" | Light | Grey | Brown |
|---|---|---|---|---|---|---|---|
| F. Ireland | Farmer | Res. Sharon, Wis. |||||||
| Died 6-15-62 at Rolla, Mo. Phithesis Pulmonalis. ||||||||

# THIRTY SEVENTH ILLINOIS

| McFadden, Andrew | | F | 19 | 5'10" | Light | Hazel | Sandy |
|---|---|---|---|---|---|---|---|
| B. Montreal, Canada | Farmer | Res. Newport, Res. 1885 Clinton, Mo. | | | | | |
| Deserted 4-26-64 at Chicago. | | | | | | | |

| McGee, Edward | | D | 30 | 5'6" | Fair | Blue | Light |
|---|---|---|---|---|---|---|---|
| B. Ireland | Lumberman | Enl. Lincoln, Mich., Res. 1885 Houston TX | | | | | |
| Mustered Out 5-15-66 | | | | | | | |

| McGinnis, William | | H | 43 | 5'8" | Light | Blue | Auburn |
|---|---|---|---|---|---|---|---|
| B. Philadelphia, Pa. | Papermaker | Res. Davenport, Iowa | | | | | |
| Deserted 1-25-62 at McCullough's Springs. Returned 2-2-63 without penalty. Deserted 6-4-63 at St. Genevieve, Mo. | | | | | | | |

| McGregor, William | | D | 28 | 5'6" | Light | Blue | Light |
|---|---|---|---|---|---|---|---|
| B. Otterville | | | | | | 10-25-61 | |
| Died Cassville 5-6-62. Wounded at Pea Ridge. | | | | | | | |

| McGuire, Charles | | C | 24 | 5'9" | Fair | Brown | Dark |
|---|---|---|---|---|---|---|---|
| B. Saratoga, NY | Wagon Maker | Res. Wauconda | | | | | |
| Deserted 3-4-63 on march from Ozark to Bloomington, Mo. | | | | | | | |

| McGuire, Mathew | | D | 22 | 5'10" | Dark | Grey | Dark |
|---|---|---|---|---|---|---|---|
| B. New York | Fisherman | Res. Lincoln, Mich., Res. 1885 Westport, Wis. | | | | | |
| Wounded at Prairie Grove, ball entering right arm badly fracturing the radius rendering the hand and arm so contracted and deformed as to be wholly unfit for use. | | | | | | | |

| McGuire, Thomas | | I | 17 | 5'10" | Light | Grey | Brown |
|---|---|---|---|---|---|---|---|
| F. Hartford, Ill. | Farmer | | | | | | |
| Reported deserted 4-15-63 | | | | | | | |

# DESCRIPTIVE ROLL

| McGunnigall, Bernard | | K | 19 | 5'9" | Fair | Blue | Light |
|---|---|---|---|---|---|---|---|
| B. Donegal, Ireland | Miner | Enl. Danville | | | | 1-20-64 | |
| Sentence to Dry Tortugas 1865 | | | | | | | |

| McInstry, Hugh | | G | 36 | 5'10" | Light | Blue | Light |
|---|---|---|---|---|---|---|---|
| B. Belfast, Ireland | Carpenter | Res. Chicago | | | | | |
| Discharged 7-17-62, varicose veins of the right leg caused by long & rapid marching. | | | | | | | |

| McKane, John | | K | 24 | 5'9" | Dark | Grey | Brown |
|---|---|---|---|---|---|---|---|
| F. Dayton, Ohio | Farmer | Res. Vermilion Co. Ill | | | | 9-23-61 | |
| Died New Orleans 6-7-64 | | | | | | | |

| McKay, George F. | | H | 20 | 5'8" | Sandy | Blue | Sandy |
|---|---|---|---|---|---|---|---|
| B. Bangor, Me. | Farmer | Res. Moline | | | | | |
| Mustered Out 10-4-64 | | | | | | | |

| McKay, Samuel A. | | H | 18 | 5'10" | Light | Blue | Brown |
|---|---|---|---|---|---|---|---|
| B. Bangor, Me. | Farmer | Res. Moline, Res. 1885 Scandia, Kansas | | | | | |
| Mustered Out 10-4-64 | | | | | | | |

| McKnight, Alexander | | G | 23 | 5'6" | Light | Blue | Brown |
|---|---|---|---|---|---|---|---|
| B. Chenango Co. NY | Farmer | Res. Chicago | | | | | |
| Killed Prairie Grove 12-7-62. Gunshot wound in the breast. | | | | | | | |

| McLane, George | | D | 52 | 5'6" | Dark | Grey | Dark |
|---|---|---|---|---|---|---|---|
| B. Canada | Lumberman | Res. Pere Marquette, Mich. | | | | | |
| Discharged 5-22-62 at St. Louis. Protracted illness. | | | | | | | |

| McLeod, William D. | | E | 30 | 5'9" | Light | Blue | Dark |
|---|---|---|---|---|---|---|---|
| B. Pennsylvania | Farmer | Enl. St. Louis | | | | 9-20-61 | |
| | | | | | | | |

# THIRTY SEVENTH ILLINOIS

| McMeekin, Andrew | | A | 31 | 5'8" | Fair | Blue | Brown |
|---|---|---|---|---|---|---|---|
| B. Ireland | Ship Carpenter | Enl. Rock Island, Res. 1885 Rural, Ill. | | | | 8-30-62 | |
| Mustered Out 6-12-65 | | | | | | | |

| McMillan, Harvey | | K | 18 | 5'4" | Dark | Brown | Dark |
|---|---|---|---|---|---|---|---|
| B. Vermilion Co. | Farmer | Res. Middlefork | | | | 3-8-64 | |
| Mustered Out 5-15-66 | | | | | | | |

| McNally, James | | D | 27 | 5'6" | Fair | Grey | Brown |
|---|---|---|---|---|---|---|---|
| B. Ireland | Laborer | Res. Manistee | | | | | |
| Deserted from Steamer HANNIBAL 6-8-63 enroute to Vicksburg | | | | | | | |

| McNamara, Edward | | E | 19 | 5'5" | Dark | Brown | Dark |
|---|---|---|---|---|---|---|---|
| B. Clare Co., Ireland | Farmer | Res. Mendota | | | | | |
| Died New Orleans 12-6-63 | | | | | | | |

| McNiel, James | | I | 21 | 5'8" | Dark | Blue | Brown |
|---|---|---|---|---|---|---|---|
| F. Ireland | Farmer | Res. Dunton, Res. 1885 Doniphan, Neb. | | | | | |
| Deserted 12-26-64 (left sick). | | | | | | | |

| McWade, William | | G | 36 | 5'6" | Sandy | Blue | Dark |
|---|---|---|---|---|---|---|---|
| B. Belfast, Ireland | Laborer | Res. Chicago | | | | | |
| Discharged 2-4-62 from Hospital. | | | | | | | |

| McWilliams, James | | K | 22 | 5'8" | Dark | Blue | Black |
|---|---|---|---|---|---|---|---|
| B. Madison Co. Ind. | Farmer | Res. Newman | | | | 3-26-64 | |
| Discharged Disability 11-29-64. General debility, intermittent fever. | | | | | | | |

| Mears, Edwin | | D | 50 | 5'5" | Light | Blue | Grey |
|---|---|---|---|---|---|---|---|
| F. Michigan | Lumberman | | | | | 8-15-61 | |
| Died 8-2-63 of jaundice. | | | | | | | |

# DESCRIPTIVE ROLL

| Meeker, Theodore | | K | 17 | 5'6" | Fair | Blue | Dark |
|---|---|---|---|---|---|---|---|
| F. Chicago | Student | Res. 1885 Chicago, Ill. | | | | | |
| Mustered Out 9-29-64 | | | | | | | |

| Melton, Andrew J. | | H | 20 | 5'8" | Light | Blue | Brown |
|---|---|---|---|---|---|---|---|
| B. Madison Co Ill | Farmer | Res. Geneseo | | | 12-1-61 | | |
| Deserted 5-27-63 at Springfield. Not heard from again. | | | | | | | |

| Merriam, Dennis | | F | 23 | 5'5" | Dark | Blue | Dark |
|---|---|---|---|---|---|---|---|
| B. Erie, NY | Laborer | Res. Lyons | | | | | |
| Discharged Disability 7-64. Chronic diarrhea, severe cough, bloody expectorant, symptoms of phithesis. Is extremely emaciated. | | | | | | | |

| Merriam, George | | F | 21 | 5'6" | Dark | Grey | Dark |
|---|---|---|---|---|---|---|---|
| B. Erie, NY | Farmer | Res. Lyons | | | | | |
| Mustered Out 10-4-64 | | | | | | | |

| Merrill, George H. | | I | 23 | 5'9" | Light | Grey | Brown |
|---|---|---|---|---|---|---|---|
| B. North Murkham, England | Farmer | Enl. Belvedere, Res. 1885 Joliet, Ill. | | | | | |
| Mustered Out 5-15-66 | | | | | | | |

| Merwin, Hugh P. | | F | 23 | 5'5" | Dark | Blue | Dark |
|---|---|---|---|---|---|---|---|
| B. Oakland Co., Mich | Farmer | Res. Newport, Res. 1885 Kingsley, Kansas | | | | | |
| Mustered Out 9-29-64 | | | | | | | |

| Mesler, Henry T. (Staff) | | | 33 | 5'6" | Fair | Blue | Brown |
|---|---|---|---|---|---|---|---|
| B. New York | Physician | Res. Chicago, Enl. Cherry Valley | | | | | |
| Mustered on Steamer HANNIBAL at Pilot Knob 5-25-63. Dishonorable Discharge 11-14-64. Reenlisted, duty at Freedman's Bureau 3-29-65 to 4-66. | | | | | | | |

# THIRTY SEVENTH ILLINOIS

| Messer, Erwin P. | | | F | 24 | 5'10" | Dark | Blue | Dark |
|---|---|---|---|---|---|---|---|---|
| B. Addison, VT | | Farmer | Res. Libertyville, Res. 1885 Sutherland, Iowa | | | | | |
| Resigned 1-15-64 | | | | | | | | |

| Messer, Erwin B. | | | F | 24 | 5'11" | Dark | Blue | Dark |
|---|---|---|---|---|---|---|---|---|
| B. Addison, VT | | Farmer | Res. Libertyville, Res. 1885 Chicago | | | | | |
| Resigned 6-25-64. Chronic bronchitis, pulmonary irritation, diarrhea of several months standing. | | | | | | | | |

| Messerline, Frederick | | | D | 36 | 5'7" | Brwn | Brwn | Brown |
|---|---|---|---|---|---|---|---|---|
| B. Bern, Switzerland | | Lumberman | Res. Hamlin, Mich., Res. 1885 Boston Mine, Mich | | | | | |
| Resigned 2-6-64, disability. | | | | | | | | |

| Mewhorter, Richard T. | | | K | 23 | 5'8" | Dark | Grey | Brown |
|---|---|---|---|---|---|---|---|---|
| R. Warren, Ohio | | Farmer | Res. Vermilion Co. | | | | | |
| Left lame at Tipton, Mo. 1-28-62. Died at Syracuse 12-31-62. | | | | | | | | |

| Meyer, Lewis F. | | | A | 19 | 5'10" | Dark | Brown | Brown |
|---|---|---|---|---|---|---|---|---|
| B. Bellville | | Farmer | Res. Davenport, Ia. | | | | | |
| Mustered Out 5-15-66 | | | | | | | | |

| Michner, Joseph | | | A | 19 | 5'11" | Light | Blue | Light |
|---|---|---|---|---|---|---|---|---|
| B. Stark Co., OH | | Farmer | Res. Waukesha, Wis. | | | | | |
| Died 7-20-62 at Springfield. Typhoid Pneumonia. | | | | | | | | |

| Michie, John | | | F | 18 | 5'5" | Light | Blue | Brown |
|---|---|---|---|---|---|---|---|---|
| B. Cook Co., Ill | | Farmer | Res. Lyons, Res. 1885, Sweetwater, Neb. | | | | | |
| Mustered Out 5-15-66 | | | | | | | | |

| Miller, Antoine | | | E | 26 | 5'6" | Light | Blue | Light |
|---|---|---|---|---|---|---|---|---|
| B. Germany | | Farmer | Res. Mendota | | | | | |
| Deserted 4-24-63 at St. Louis | | | | | | | | |

# DESCRIPTIVE ROLL

| Miller, David A. | | H | 23 | | | | |
|---|---|---|---|---|---|---|---|
| F. Geneseo | | | | | | | |
| Died 4-2-63 at Cassville, disease of the heart. | | | | | | | |

| Miller, Frank L. | | I | 18 | 5'11" | Light | Grey | Brown |
|---|---|---|---|---|---|---|---|
| F. Pulaski, Tenn. | Farmer | Res. Belvedere | | | | | |
| Deserted 2-25-63 from Camp Bliss. | | | | | | | |

| Miller, Hugh | | I | 21 | 5'8" | Dark | Brown | Dark |
|---|---|---|---|---|---|---|---|
| F. Pulaski, Tenn. | Farmer | Res. Cherry Valley | | | | | |
| Deserted 1-20-62 | | | | | | | |

| Miller, Jacob E. | | E | 18 | 5'8" | Light | Blue | Dark |
|---|---|---|---|---|---|---|---|
| B. St. Charles, Ill. | Farmer | Res. Viola | | | 3-28-64 | | |
| Mustered Out 5-15-66 | | | | | | | |

| Miller, John | | H | 23 | 5'8" | Dark | Grey | Black |
|---|---|---|---|---|---|---|---|
| B. Wayne Co. OH | Farmer | Res. Geneseo, Res. 1885 Cleveland, Ill. | | | | | |
| Mustered Out 5-25-66 | | | | | | | |

| Miller, Peter S. | | G | 25 | 5'8" | Light | Blue | Dark |
|---|---|---|---|---|---|---|---|
| B. Sandusky Co. Ohio | Farmer | Res. Cheney's Grove | | | | | |
| Wounded in the hip at Pea Ridge 3-8-62. Wounded in the thigh at Prairie Grove 12-7-62. Discharged wounds 4-20-63 at Springfield. | | | | | | | |

| Miller, William | | E | 18 | 5'8" | Light | Blue | Light |
|---|---|---|---|---|---|---|---|
| B. Lee Co., Ill | Farmer | Res. Viola, Res. 1885 Compton, Ill. | | | 3-28-64 | | |
| Mustered Out 5-15-66 | | | | | | | |

| Miller, William F. | | D | 25 | 6'2" | Dark | Brown | Black |
|---|---|---|---|---|---|---|---|
| B. Virginia | Hackman | | | | | | |
| Died 9-25-63 at Carrolton, La. Bilious fever. | | | | | | | |

# THIRTY SEVENTH ILLINOIS

| Millheiser, Peter | | C | 19 | 5'5" | Dark | Brown | Black |
|---|---|---|---|---|---|---|---|
| | Shoemaker | | | | | 1-1-63 | |
| Mustered Out 12-31-65 | | | | | | | |

| Millman, Henry | | D | 22 | | | | |
|---|---|---|---|---|---|---|---|
| F. Chicago | | | | | | | |
| Killed 9-14-62 by the paymaster at Springfield. | | | | | | | |

| Mills, William H. | | A | 19 | 5'9" | Light | Grey | Sandy |
|---|---|---|---|---|---|---|---|
| B. Lancashire, England | Farmer | Enl. Rock Island | | | | | |
| Died 9-9-63 at Carrolton, La. Chronic disease. | | | | | | | |

| Miner, Chauncy R. | | B | 18 | | | | |
|---|---|---|---|---|---|---|---|
| F. Goshen | | Enl. Lafayette, Res. 1885 Lafayette, Ill. | | | | | |
| Discharged 1-26-65 | | | | | | | |

| Miner, Martin V.B. | | B | 20 | 5'8" | Fair | Brown | Brown |
|---|---|---|---|---|---|---|---|
| B. Goshen | Farmer | Res. Lynn, Res. 1885 Grundy Center, IA | | | | | |
| Discharged 1-26-65 | | | | | | | |

| Minns, Frederick | | D | 21 | 5'7" | Light | Grey | Light |
|---|---|---|---|---|---|---|---|
| B. England | Farmer | Res. Lena | | | | | |
| Mustered Out 6-15-66 | | | | | | | |

| Mizner, Sylvester E. | | A | 19 | 5'7" | Light | Blue | Brown |
|---|---|---|---|---|---|---|---|
| B. Maysville, Pa | Farmer | Res. Preemption | | | | | |
| Killed 6-11-62 at Cassville. 29 shots in different parts of his body. Killed by bushwhackers. | | | | | | | |

| Moore, Isaac | | G | 24 | | | | |
|---|---|---|---|---|---|---|---|
| | | | | | | 8-15-61 | |
| Deserted at Chicago 9-16-61. Claimed as a minor by his father & disappeared 9-18-61. | | | | | | | |

# DESCRIPTIVE ROLL

| Moore, James | | | G | 30 | 5'5" | Light | Grey | Red |
|---|---|---|---|---|---|---|---|---|
| B. Ireland | Laborer | | Res. Chicago, Res. 1885 Edgeworthton, Ireland | | | | | |
| Mustered Out 10-4-64 | | | | | | | | |

| Moore, John W. | | | E | 24 | 5'8" | Light | Brown | Dark |
|---|---|---|---|---|---|---|---|---|
| B. Philadelphia | Farmer | | Res. Mendota | | | | | |
| Died 3-10-62 at Leetown of wounds. Shot through the head at Pea Ridge. | | | | | | | | |

| Moore, John W. | | | G | 24 | 5'6" | Light | Blue | Light |
|---|---|---|---|---|---|---|---|---|
| | | | | | | | | |
| Deserted at Chicago 9-17-61 | | | | | | | | |

| Moran, John | | | D | 23 | 5'11" | Light | Grey | Brown |
|---|---|---|---|---|---|---|---|---|
| B. Newcastle-Tyne, England | Sailor | | Res. Manistee | | | | | |
| Mustered Out 5-15-66 | | | | | | | | |

| Morey, Lorenzo B. | | | A | 24 | 5'10" | Fair | Blue | Brown |
|---|---|---|---|---|---|---|---|---|
| B. Fulton, Ill. | Book-keeper | | Res. Geneseo, Res. 1885 Aledo, Ill. | | | | | |
| Resigned 6-3-65 | | | | | | | | |

| Morey, Silas | | | E | 29 | 5'3" | Light | Blue | Brown |
|---|---|---|---|---|---|---|---|---|
| B. Geauga Co OH | Farmer | | Res. Mendota | | | | | |
| Discharged 10-4-64 | | | | | | | | |

| Morgan, Banjamin H. | | | B | 20 | | | | |
|---|---|---|---|---|---|---|---|---|
| F. Goshen | | | | | | | | |
| Died 11-26-62 at Springfield, remittent fever. | | | | | | | | |

| Morgan, William O. | | | K | 18 | 5'5" | Dark | Brown | Black |
|---|---|---|---|---|---|---|---|---|
| F. Danville | | | Res. 1885, Danville, Ill. | | | | | |
| | | | | | | | | |

# THIRTY SEVENTH ILLINOIS

| Moriarty, Thomas | | | G | 22 | 5'10" | Dark | Hazel | Dark |
|---|---|---|---|---|---|---|---|---|
| B. Waterford, Ireland | | Laborer | Res. Chicago | | | | | |
| Discharged Disability 11-17-65. Wounded in the groin, Prairie Grove 12-7-62 | | | | | | | | |

| Morley, Frederick | | G | 18 | 5'4" | Light | Grey | Light |
|---|---|---|---|---|---|---|---|
| B. Scotland | Musician | Res. Chicago | | | | | |
| Discharged 1-16-62 at Hospital in Otterville by reason of youth and inability. | | | | | | | | 

| Morrell, Americus D. | | C | 22 | 6'0" | Fair | Blue | Dark |
|---|---|---|---|---|---|---|---|
| B. Lake Co. | Farmer | Res. Fremont | | | | | |
| Died 5-15-62 at Cassville. Typhoid Fever. | | | | | | | |

| Morrill, Wells C. | | C | 18 | 5'7" | Fair | Grey | Light |
|---|---|---|---|---|---|---|---|
| B. Lake Co. | Farmer | Res. Avon, Res. 1885 San Antonio, Texas | | | | | |
| Mustered Out 5-15-66 | | | | | | | |

| Morris, Jesse | | H | 37 | 5'8" | Light | Grey | Auburn |
|---|---|---|---|---|---|---|---|
| B. Monroe Co Oh | Farmer | Res. Moline | | | | | |
| Mustered Out 10-4-64 | | | | | | | |

| Morrison, Edward W. | | C | 29 | 5'6" | Fair | Grey | Light |
|---|---|---|---|---|---|---|---|
| B. Lockport, NY | Farmer | Res. Waukegan | | | | | |
| Deserted 6-17-63 from Vicksburg. | | | | | | | |

| Morse, Alcander O. | | I | 22 | 5'8" | Light | Grey | Brown |
|---|---|---|---|---|---|---|---|
| F. New York | Farmer | Res. Bonus, Res. 1885 Flora, Dakota | | | | | |
| Mustered Out 10-4-64. Died 9-24-94 at S. Dakota. | | | | | | | |

| Morse, Chauncey C. | | C | 23 | 5'9" | Fair | Brown | Dark |
|---|---|---|---|---|---|---|---|
| B. Lake Co. OH | Lawyer | Res. Waukegan, Res. 1885 Hainesville, Ind. | | | | | |
| Mustered Out 5-15-66 | | | | | | | |

# DESCRIPTIVE ROLL

| Morton, Orville H. | | | 22 | 5'6" | Fair | Brown | Brown |
|---|---|---|---|---|---|---|---|
| B. Richland Co., Ill | Mechanic | | Res. Chicago | | 2-24-64 | | |
| Deserted | | | | | | | |

| Most, John F. | | E | 23 | 5'3" | Dark | Brown | Dark |
|---|---|---|---|---|---|---|---|
| B. Lebanon Co., Pa. | Shoemaker | Res. Medota | | | | | |
| Discharged 10-4-64 | | | | | | | |

| Moulton, J. Arthur | | F | 21 | | | | |
|---|---|---|---|---|---|---|---|
| F. Benton | | Res. 1885 Waukegan, Ill. | | | | | |
| Mustered Out 10-4-64 | | | | | | | |

| Mowers, George | | F | 23 | 5'5" | Light | Blue | Light |
|---|---|---|---|---|---|---|---|
| B. Oneida Co NY | Farmer | Res. Vernon, Res. 1885 Rensselaerville, NY | | | | | |
| Mustered Out 1-23-65 | | | | | | | |

| Mudgett, Charles H. | | C | 29 | 5'9" | Fair | Grey | Dark |
|---|---|---|---|---|---|---|---|
| B. Vermont | Farmer | Res. Nunda | | | | | |
| Died 7-1-63 at Vicksburg, on Hospital Steamer | | | | | | | |

| Mudgett, William H. | | C | 22 | 6'0" | Fair | Grey | Dark |
|---|---|---|---|---|---|---|---|
| F. McHenry Co. | Farmer | Res. Nunda, Res. 1885 McHenry, Ill. | | | | | |
| Mustered Out 5-15-66 | | | | | | | |

| Mulherin, Charles | | H | 37 | 5'7" | Light | Blue | Sandy |
|---|---|---|---|---|---|---|---|
| B. Donegal, Ireland | Laborer | Enl. Rock Island, Res. 1885 Rock Island, Ill. | | | 3-30-64 | | |
| Mustered Out 5-15-64 | | | | | | | |

| Mulligan, Harvey S. | | I | 18 | 5'7" | Dark | Grey | Dark |
|---|---|---|---|---|---|---|---|
| B. Lockport, Ill. | Farmer | | | | | | |
| Discharged Disability 1-6-64 at New Orleans. Chronic diarrhea. | | | | | | | |

# THIRTY SEVENTH ILLINOIS

| Mulvey, Lawrence F. | C | 20 | | | |
|---|---|---|---|---|---|
| F. Shields | | | | | |
| Mustered Out 10-4-64 ||||||

| Murphey, William H. | K | 18 | | | |
|---|---|---|---|---|---|
| | | Enl. State Line | | | |
| Died 8-10-63 at Port Hudson. Disease. ||||||

| Murphy, Daniel | K | 20 | 5'8" | Fair | Grey | Black |
|---|---|---|---|---|---|---|
| B. Warren Co Ind | Farmer | Enl. State Line City | | | | |
| |||||||

| Murphy, Jacob | K | 28 | 5'7" | Fair | Blue | Brown |
|---|---|---|---|---|---|---|
| F. State Line City | | | | | | |
| Mustered Out 10-4-64 |||||||

| Murphy, John | C | 25 | | | |
|---|---|---|---|---|---|
| | | Enl. Libertyville, Res. 1885 Waukegan, Ill. |||||
| Resigned 10-8-63. Appointed Surgeon 92d U.S. Colored Volunteers. ||||||

| Murphy, John | C | 23 | 6'0" | Fair | Grey | Light |
|---|---|---|---|---|---|---|
| B. Lake Co. Ill. | Farmer | Enl. Waukegan | | | | |
| Mustered Out 5-15-66 |||||||

| Murphy, Thomas | G | 28 | 5'7" | Dark | Grey | Black |
|---|---|---|---|---|---|---|
| F. New York, NY | Mason | Res. Chicago | | | | |
| Deserted 12-25-64 at DeVall's Bluff, Ark. while in arrest. |||||||

| Murphy, Thomas J. | A | 20 | 5'11" | Light | Brwn | Brown |
|---|---|---|---|---|---|---|
| B. Montreal, Canada | Farmer | Res. Rock Island | | | | |
| Died Cassville 4-9-62. Some sudden disease. |||||||

# DESCRIPTIVE ROLL

| Murphy, William | | | H | 43 | 6'0" | Dark | Blue | Black |
|---|---|---|---|---|---|---|---|---|
| B. Waterford, Ireland | | Collier | Res. Coal Valley | | | | | |
| | | | | | | | | |

| Myers, Anthony L. | | | A | 21 | 5'7" | Dark | Brown | Black |
|---|---|---|---|---|---|---|---|---|
| B. Bellville, Ill. | | Shoe-maker | Enl. Rock Island. | | | 10-23-62 | | |
| Mustered Out 10-26-65 | | | | | | | | |

| Myers, Hamilton | | | K | 17 | 5'6" | Light | Blue | Brown |
|---|---|---|---|---|---|---|---|---|
| F. Virginia | | Student | Res. Danville | | | | | |
| Re-enlisted as Veteran. | | | | | | | | |

| Myers, Peter | | | E | 32 | 5'8" | Light | Blue | Dark |
|---|---|---|---|---|---|---|---|---|
| B. Coblenz, Germany | | Farmer | Res. Mendota | | | | | |
| Died Houston 11-15-65. Organic disease of the heart. | | | | | | | | |

| Myre, Jacob | | | A | 22 | 5'4" | Dark | Blue | Brown |
|---|---|---|---|---|---|---|---|---|
| B. Romelsbach, Wurttemburg, Germany | | Tailor | Res. Nauvoo | | | | | |
| Deserted 9-10-63 New Orleans. | | | | | | | | |

# N

| Nausler, John | | | G | 20 | 5'6" | Light | Grey | Brown |
|---|---|---|---|---|---|---|---|---|
| B. Ohio | | Farmer | Res. Cheney's Grove | | | | | |
| Mustered Out 10-4-64 | | | | | | | | |

| Neale, George | | | F | 21 | 6'0" | Dark | Brown | Dark |
|---|---|---|---|---|---|---|---|---|
| B. Lake Co. | | Farmer | Res. Waukegan | | | | | |
| Mustered Out 5-15-66 | | | | | | | | |

# THIRTY SEVENTH ILLINOIS

| Nelson, Andrew | | | E | 19 | 5'11" | Light | Grey | Light |
|---|---|---|---|---|---|---|---|---|
| B. Goteborg, Sweden | | Farmer | Res. Mendota | | | | | |
| Mustered Out 9-29-64 | | | | | | | | |

| Nettleton, James A. | | | I | 22 | 5'10" | Dark | Grey | Brown |
|---|---|---|---|---|---|---|---|---|
| B. Watervliet, NY | | Farmer | Res. Leroy, Res. 1885 Burlinghame, Neb. | | | | | |
| Mustered Out 10-4-64 | | | | | | | | |

| Newberry, James | | | G | 18 | 5'4" | Dark | Brown | Dark |
|---|---|---|---|---|---|---|---|---|
| B. Lockport, Ill. | | Laborer | Res. Lockport, Enl. as musician | | | | | |
| Discharged Otterville 12-2-61 | | | | | | | | |

| Newell, Nelson E. | | | I | 19 | 5'11" | Light | Grey | Brown |
|---|---|---|---|---|---|---|---|---|
| F. Tioga Co. NY | | Farmer | Res. Marengo | | | | | |
| Deserted 3-1-63 | | | | | | | | |

| Newell, Thomas | | | E | 33 | 5'9" | Light | Blue | Light |
|---|---|---|---|---|---|---|---|---|
| B. England | | Farmer | Res. Mendota | | | | | |
| Died Boonville 10-12-61, dysentery. | | | | | | | | |

| Newton, Charles H. | | | G | 21 | 5'10" | Light | Blue | Auburn |
|---|---|---|---|---|---|---|---|---|
| B. Kent Co., Mich | | Farmer | Res. East Bend | | | | | |
| Discharged for Promotion 3-19-64 | | | | | | | | |

| Newton, Ira | | | B | 21 | 5'7" | Light | Blue | Light |
|---|---|---|---|---|---|---|---|---|
| B. Lewisburg, Pa. | | Farmer | Res. Goshen | | | | | |
| Mustered Out 3-13-66 | | | | | | | | |

| Newton, Isaac | | | C | 20 | 5'9" | Fair | Blue | Light |
|---|---|---|---|---|---|---|---|---|
| B. Dupage, Ill. | | Farmer | Res. Wheaton | | | | | |
| Mustered Out 5-15-66 | | | | | | | | |

# DESCRIPTIVE ROLL

| Newton, Joseph H. | | B | 18 | 5'8" | Light | Hazel | Dark |
|---|---|---|---|---|---|---|---|
| B. Green Briar Va | Farmer | Res. Goshen | | | 2-6-65 | | |
| Mustered Out 2-6-66 | | | | | | | |

| Nicholson, William | | F | 23 | 5'0" | | | |
|---|---|---|---|---|---|---|---|
| F. Toulon | | | | | | | |
| Died 11-26-61 at St. Louis New House of Refuge. Remittent fever, acute dysentery. | | | | | | | |

| Nieman, Anton (Staff) | | | 30 | | | | |
|---|---|---|---|---|---|---|---|
| | | Enl. Chicago, Res. 1885 Chicago | | | | | |
| Resigned 1862 | | | | | | | |

| Niesten, William H. | | E | 18 | 5'9" | Light | Blue | Light |
|---|---|---|---|---|---|---|---|
| B. Adams, Ind. | Farmer | Res. Adams City, Ind. | | | | | |
| Killed 3-7-62 at Pea Ridge. Shot through the abdomen. | | | | | | | |

| Nolan, John | | D | 15 | 5'1" | Light | Blue | Light |
|---|---|---|---|---|---|---|---|
| B. Bloomington, Ill. | Farmer | Enl. Prairie Grove | | | 12-20-62 | | |
| Deserted 6-27-64 at Chicago. | | | | | | | |

| Noland, David | | B | 19 | | | | |
|---|---|---|---|---|---|---|---|
| F. Goshen | | | | | | | |
| Mustered Out 10-4-64 | | | | | | | |

| Noran, William J. | | B | 21 | 5'6" | Fair | Blue | Brown |
|---|---|---|---|---|---|---|---|
| B. Stockholm, Sweden | Farmer | Res. Goshen | | | | | |
| Mustered Out 10-4-64 | | | | | | | |

# THIRTY SEVENTH ILLINOIS

| Norton, Hiram | | | G | 45 | 5'7" | Dark | Brown | Dark |
|---|---|---|---|---|---|---|---|---|
| B. Edgartown, Mass. | Seaman | Res. Chicago | | | | | | |
| Discharged 2-28-62. Chronic rheumatism of long standing. | | | | | | | | |

| Nunamaker, Eli J. | | | G | 24 | 5'10" | Light | Blue | Brown |
|---|---|---|---|---|---|---|---|---|
| B. Boone Co. Va | Plasterer | Res. Cheney's Grove | | | | | | |
| Died 10-29-62 at Springfield Mo. Chronic dysentery. | | | | | | | | |

| Nunamaker, Solomon | | | G | 25 | 5'10" | Light | Blue | Brown |
|---|---|---|---|---|---|---|---|---|
| B. Boone Co. Va | | Res. Cheney's Grove, Res. 1885 Steubenville, Ohio | | | | | | |
| Mustered Out 10-4-64 | | | | | | | | |

# O

| Oaks, Henry C. | | | I | 20 | 5'10" | Sandy | Grey | Red |
|---|---|---|---|---|---|---|---|---|
| F. Maine | Farmer | Res. Belvidere | | | | | | |
| Died 10-21-63 at Belvidere, Ill. while on sick furlough. | | | | | | | | |

| O'Brien, James | | | K | 30 | | | | |
|---|---|---|---|---|---|---|---|---|
| F. Vermilion Co. | | | | | | 9-23-61 | | |
| Small Tumors in neck 5-11-63. Several abscesses supervened in neck – poulticed 5-12-63. Delerium Tremens at General Hospital, St. Louis 6-21-63. Discharged 7-11-63, admitted to insane asylum, Washington. Discharged 7-11-64. | | | | | | | | |

| O'Brien, Patrick | | | H | 25 | 5'7" | Light | Blue | Brown |
|---|---|---|---|---|---|---|---|---|
| B. Ireland | Laborer | Res. Galesburg, Res. 1885, St. Louis, Mo. | | | | | | |
| Discharged Disability 3-17-63 Wounds. | | | | | | | | |

# DESCRIPTIVE ROLL

| Odell, Lamar G. | | | D | 23 | 5'9" | Dark | Brown | Brown |
|---|---|---|---|---|---|---|---|---|
| B. New York | Lumberman | | Res. Michigan | | | | | |
| Discharged Disability 9-10-63. Consumption. | | | | | | | | |

| Oder, Newton | | K | | | | | |
|---|---|---|---|---|---|---|---|
| F. Vermilion Co. | | | | | | | |
| Deserted | | | | | | | |

| Ogden, Joseph | | | G | 40 | 5'10" | Dark | Grey | Dark |
|---|---|---|---|---|---|---|---|---|
| B. Providence, RI | Farmer | | Res. Chicago | | | | | |
| Discharged Disability 1-16-64 | | | | | | | | |

| O'Leary, William | | | K | 33 | 5'10" | Fair | Blue | Sandy |
|---|---|---|---|---|---|---|---|---|
| B. Dublin, Ireland | Laborer | | Enl. Danville | | | 11-18-63 | | |
| Deserted 12-24-63 between Springfield, Ill. and St. Louis, Mo. | | | | | | | | |

| Oleson, Charles | | | I | 18 | 5'8" | Light | Blue | Brown |
|---|---|---|---|---|---|---|---|---|
| F. Norway | Farmer | | Res. Leroy | | | | | |
| Mustered Out 5-15-66 | | | | | | | | |

| Oliver, Josiah | | | A | 26 | 5'6" | Dark | Blue | Brown |
|---|---|---|---|---|---|---|---|---|
| B. Warren, OH | Engineer | | | | | | | |
| Killed 3-7-62 at Pea Ridge. Musket ball through the abdomen. | | | | | | | | |

| O'Neal, Martin | | | H | 27 | 5'5" | Fair | Blue | Brown |
|---|---|---|---|---|---|---|---|---|
| B. Galway, Ireland | Farmer | | Res. Port Byron | | | | | |
| Deserted 7-31-62 at Springfield. Supposed to be steamboating on the Mississippi River. | | | | | | | | |

| Olson, Ole | | | D | 31 | 5'8" | Light | Grey | Dark |
|---|---|---|---|---|---|---|---|---|
| B. Norway | Lumberman | | Enl. Duck Lake, Mich. | | | | | |
| Mustered Out 5-15-66 | | | | | | | | |

# THIRTY SEVENTH ILLINOIS

| Osborne, Christian | | | G | 25 | 5'6" | Light | Blue | Auburn |
|---|---|---|---|---|---|---|---|---|
| B. Champaign, Ill | | Farmer | Res. East Bend | | | | | |
| Deserted 3-29-62 while on furlough to Ill. Enl. 125th Illinois on 11-11-63 | | | | | | | | |

| Osmer, Charles A. | | | E | 25 | 5'7" | Light | Blue | Light |
|---|---|---|---|---|---|---|---|---|
| B. Wyoming Co. NY | | Farmer | Res. Mendota | | | | | |
| Died 8-6-63 in Hospital at Vicksburg. | | | | | | | | |

| Osmer, Ephriam B. | | | E | 23 | 5'7" | Light | Blue | Sandy |
|---|---|---|---|---|---|---|---|---|
| B. Wyoming Co. NY | | Farmer | | | | | | |
| Mustered Out 9-29-64 | | | | | | | | |

| Osmer, Nathan G. | | | E | 24 | 5'9" | Light | Blue | Sandy |
|---|---|---|---|---|---|---|---|---|
| B. Wyoming Co. NY | | Farmer | Res. Mendota | | | | | |
| Mustered Out 9-29-64 | | | | | | | | |

| Ostrander, George T. | | | I | 18 | 5'5" | Light | Grey | Brown |
|---|---|---|---|---|---|---|---|---|
| F. Franklin Co Ny | | Farmer | Res. Leroy | | | | | |
| Discharged Disability 3-30-62 at St. Louis. Inguinal hernia, left side. | | | | | | | | |

# P

| Packard, Isaac Z. | | | K | 20 | 5'9" | Dark | Blue | Brown |
|---|---|---|---|---|---|---|---|---|
| B. Jefferson Co. Pa. | | Farmer | Res. Vermilion Co., Res. 1885 Fairbury, Neb. | | | | | |
| Discharged Disability 5-9-62. Measles. | | | | | | | | |

| Packard, Lycurgus | | | C | 21 | 5'8" | Fair | Grey | Dark |
|---|---|---|---|---|---|---|---|---|
| B. Illinois | | Farmer | Res. Ela, Res. 1885 Osage City, Kansas | | | | | |
| Absent on furlough at muster out. | | | | | | | | |

# DESCRIPTIVE ROLL

| Paddock, Marshall | | | F | 21 | 5'10" | Dark | Brown | Dark |
|---|---|---|---|---|---|---|---|---|
| B. Milwaukee, Wis. | | Farmer | Res. Antioch, Res. 1885 Lannemier, Ill. | | | | | |
| Discharged Disability 3-4-63. Valvular disease of heart. | | | | | | | | |

| Paff, Frederick | | | I | 21 | 5'5" | Light | Grey | Brown |
|---|---|---|---|---|---|---|---|---|
| F. Sardinia, NY | | Butcher | Res. Belvidere | | | | | |
| Mustered Out 10-4-64 | | | | | | | | |

| Palmer, Isaac R. | | | A | 22 | | | | |
|---|---|---|---|---|---|---|---|---|
| | | | Enl. Rock Island | | | | | |
| Mustered Out 10-4-64 | | | | | | | | |

| Palmer, John H. | | | K | 21 | 5'7" | Dark | Brown | Black |
|---|---|---|---|---|---|---|---|---|
| B. New Town NY | | Clerk | Res. New York City, Res. 1885 Danville, Ill. | | | 2-21-62 | | |
| Mustered Out 2-29-65 | | | | | | | | |

| Parish, Levi | | | E | 30 | 5'3" | Dark | Brown | Black |
|---|---|---|---|---|---|---|---|---|
| B. Mineral Point, Wis. | | Farmer | Res. Mendota | | | | | |
| Deserted 6-3-63 near Pilot Knob. Mo. | | | | | | | | |

| Parkhurst, Benjamin F. | | | H | 24 | 5'11" | Light | Hazel | Brown |
|---|---|---|---|---|---|---|---|---|
| B. Hancock Co., Ind. | | Farmer | Res. Millersburg, Res. 1885 Sweetwater, Neb. | | | | | |
| Mustered Out 5-15-66 | | | | | | | | |

| Parkinson, Richard C. | | | E | 24 | 6'0" | Light | Blue | Light |
|---|---|---|---|---|---|---|---|---|
| B. DeKalb Co., Tenn. | | Farmer | Res. Lynn Creek, Enl. Mendota, Res. 1885 Galena, Mo. | | | 1-1-62 | | |
| Mustered Out 5-15-66. | | | | | | | | |

# THIRTY SEVENTH ILLINOIS

| Parks, Andrew | | | A | 20 | 5'11" | Dark | Blue | Black |
|---|---|---|---|---|---|---|---|---|
| B. Manchester, NH | | Coal Digger | Res. Blassburg, Res. 1885 Bowlesburg, Ill. | | | | | |
| Mustered Out 5-15-66. | | | | | | | | |

| Patrick, William M. | B | 29 | | | |
|---|---|---|---|---|---|
| F. Lynn | | | | | |
| Discharged 1-4-64 | | | | | |

| Patterson, Benjamin F. | | H | 25 | 5'9" | Light | Grey | Brown |
|---|---|---|---|---|---|---|---|
| B. Pennsylvania | Farmer | Res. Moline, Res. 1885 Avoca, Iowa | | | | | |
| Discharged Disability 6-17-62 | | | | | | | |

| Payne, Able W. | | K | 20 | 5'9" | Dark | Brown | Black |
|---|---|---|---|---|---|---|---|
| F. Vandalia, Ill. | Farmer | Res. Danville | | | | | |
| Discharged Disability 3-14-62. Epileptic. | | | | | | | |

| Payne, Eugene B. | | C | 26 | 5'11" | Fair | Brown | Dark |
|---|---|---|---|---|---|---|---|
| B. Seneca Falls, NY | Lawyer | Res. Waukegan, Res. 1885 South Evanston, Ill. | | | | | |
| Discharged 9-9-64 | | | | | | | |

| Payne, Frederick A. | | C | 20 | 5'11" | Dark | Brown | Dark |
|---|---|---|---|---|---|---|---|
| B. Lake Co. | Farmer | Res. Fremont | | | | | |
| Killed 3-7-62 at Pea Ridge. Shot through the brain and leg. | | | | | | | |

| Payne, Thomas Henry Louis | | E | 23 | 6'1" | Light | Blue | Dark |
|---|---|---|---|---|---|---|---|
| B. Middlesex Co. Mass. | Farmer | Res. Mendota, Res. 1885 Philadelphia, Pa. | | | | | |
| Mustered Out 5-15-66 | | | | | | | |

# DESCRIPTIVE ROLL

| Peck, Eugene N. | | | I | 18 | 5'8" | Dark | Hazel | Brown |
|---|---|---|---|---|---|---|---|---|
| F. Lancaster (?) NY | Farmer | | Res Chemung | | | | | |
| Mustered Out 10-4-64 | | | | | | | | |

| Peck, John H. (Quartermaster) | | | | 29 | | | | |
|---|---|---|---|---|---|---|---|---|
| | | | Enl. Chicago | | | | 8-5-61 | |
| Resigned 1-4-64 | | | | | | | | |

| Perkins, Edward | | | B | 21 | 5'8" | Dark | Brown | Black |
|---|---|---|---|---|---|---|---|---|
| B. Litchfield, CT | Farmer | | Res. Goshen | | | | | |
| Discharged 9-29-64 | | | | | | | | |

| Perry, James | | | F | 24 | 5'10" | Dark | Grey | Light |
|---|---|---|---|---|---|---|---|---|
| B. Jefferson Co. NY | Brickmaker | | Res. Waukegan | | | | | |
| Killed 3-7-62 at Prairie Grove | | | | | | | | |

| Perry, John A. | | | B | 21 | | | | |
|---|---|---|---|---|---|---|---|---|
| F. Toulon | | | | | | | | |
| Died 1-13-62 at Otterville. Typhoid pneumonia. | | | | | | | | |

| Perry, William N. | | | B | 19 | | | | |
|---|---|---|---|---|---|---|---|---|
| F. Goshen | | | | | | | | |
| Died 12-1-61. Measles. | | | | | | | | |

| Pesha, Lewis | | | A | 27 | 6'0" | Dark | Grey | Black |
|---|---|---|---|---|---|---|---|---|
| B. Prescott, Canada West | Carpenter | | | | | | | |
| Died 1-11-62 at Otterville. Typhoid Pneumonia. | | | | | | | | |

| Peterson, Charles | | | D | 43 | 5'7" | Fair | Blue | Brown |
|---|---|---|---|---|---|---|---|---|
| B. Sweden | Lumberman | | | | | | | |
| Discharged Disability 2-25-63. Double Hernia. | | | | | | | | |

# THIRTY SEVENTH ILLINOIS

| Peterson, Edward | | | H | 15 | 5'3" | Light | Hazel | Light |
|---|---|---|---|---|---|---|---|---|
| B. Sweden | | Farmer | | | | | 4-20-64 | |
| Discharged Disability 11-17-65. Chronic diarrhea. ||||||||||

| Peterson, Erick | | | D | 24 | | Light | Blue | Light |
|---|---|---|---|---|---|---|---|---|
| B. Wisconsin | | Lumberman | Res. Manitowoc, Wis. ||| | | |
| Discharged Disability 2-3-63 at Syracuse. Disease of the lungs. Phithesis pulmonalis, the disease far advanced. |||||||||

| Peterson, John | | | G | 28 | 5'9" | Light | Grey | Brown |
|---|---|---|---|---|---|---|---|---|
| B. Sweden | | Farmer | Res. Chicago ||| | | |
| Died 8-22-64 at Monganzia, La. Nervous debility and acute diarrhea. |||||||||

| Philleo, William W. | | | A | 22 | | | | |
|---|---|---|---|---|---|---|---|---|
| F. Rock Island | | | | | | | | |
| Transferred to 92d U.S. Colored Volunteers 9-21-63 |||||||||

| Phillips, Danius H. | | | F | 20 | 5'10" | Dark | Brown | Black |
|---|---|---|---|---|---|---|---|---|
| B. Vermont | | Farmer | Res. Benton ||| | | |
| Discharged 7-10-62 |||||||||

| Phillips, James | | | | 35 | 5'9" | Light | Blue | Light |
|---|---|---|---|---|---|---|---|---|
| B. England | | Farmer | Enl. Waukegan ||| | 2-25-64 | |
| |||||||||

| Phillips, Samuel | | | D | 26 | 5'4" | Dark | Blue | Dark |
|---|---|---|---|---|---|---|---|---|
| B. England | | Lumberman | Res. Chicago ||| | | |
| Mustered Out 5-15-66. Illiterate |||||||||

| Phillips, Thomas | | | D | 36 | | | | |
|---|---|---|---|---|---|---|---|---|
| F. Chicago | | | | | | | | |
| Deserted 2-22-63 at Vicksburg. |||||||||

# DESCRIPTIVE ROLL

| Pickard, Albert | | | D | 27 | 5'8" | Sandy | Grey | Sandy |
|---|---|---|---|---|---|---|---|---|
| B. New York | Engineer | | Res. Lena, Ill. | | | | | |
| Discharged Disability 5-28-62 at Rolla. Valvular disease of the heart. | | | | | | | | |

| Pickett, George B. | | | A | 16 | | Light | Blue | Light |
|---|---|---|---|---|---|---|---|---|
| B. Peoria | | Musician | Res. Moline, Res. 1885 Ashland, Nebraska | | | 5-27-62 | | |
| Discharged Disability. Injury from a fall on the march from Fayetteville, Ark. Northward (ca. 1-63). Pickett was at the time doing duty as Regimental Postmaster. Hernia scroti, the intestine nearly filling the scrotum. | | | | | | | | |

| Pickett. Horace G. | | | A | 19 | 5'7" | Fair | Blue | Brown |
|---|---|---|---|---|---|---|---|---|
| B. Peoria, Ill. | | Type Sticker | Res. Rock Island, Res, 1885 Ashland, Nebraska | | | | | |
| Mustered Out 5-15-66 | | | | | | | | |

| Pierce, George | | | G | 18 | 5'5" | Light | Grey | Light |
|---|---|---|---|---|---|---|---|---|
| B. Buffalo, NY | | Drummer | Res. Chicago | | | | | |
| Mustered Out 10-4-64 | | | | | | | | |

| Pike, Daniel W. | | | C | 27 | 5'9" | Fair | Blue | Dark |
|---|---|---|---|---|---|---|---|---|
| B. Hudson City, NY | | Tailor | Res. Waukegan, Res. 1885, Waukegan, Ill. | | | | | |
| Discharged Disability 8-28-62. Stiff leg. | | | | | | | | |

| Pilgrim, George W. | | | A | 55 | 5'5" | Light | Blue | Dark |
|---|---|---|---|---|---|---|---|---|
| B. East Haddam, CT | | Stone Mason | Enl. Rock Island, Res. 1885 Chicago, Ill. | | | | | |
| Discharged Disability 2-17-62. Old age generally. | | | | | | | | |

| Pilgrim, Thomas G. | | | A | 23 | | | | |
|---|---|---|---|---|---|---|---|---|
| F. Chicago | | | Res. 1885 Grinnell, Iowa | | | | | |
| Mustered Out 10-4-64 | | | | | | | | |

# THIRTY SEVENTH ILLINOIS

| Pilgrim, William M. | | B | 21 | 5'11" | Dark | Grey | Brown |
|---|---|---|---|---|---|---|---|
| B. Lincolnshire, England | | Res. Goshen | | | | | |
| Discharged 8-19-64 | | | | | | | |

| Pinkerton, Richard | | D | 21 | 5'9" | Light | Grey | Brown |
|---|---|---|---|---|---|---|---|
| B. Ireland | | Enl. Chicago | | | | | |
| Deserted 7-28-63 while under arrest. | | | | | | | |

| Pitts, John | | G | 24 | 5'6" | Sandy | Blue | Sandy |
|---|---|---|---|---|---|---|---|
| B. Bath Co. KY | Farmer | Res. Cheney's Grove | | | | | |
| Mustered Out 9-29-64 | | | | | | | |

| Plank, John | | A | 30 | 5'8" | Fair | Hazel | Black |
|---|---|---|---|---|---|---|---|
| B. Mifflin, Pa. | School Teacher | Enl. as musician | | | 10-13-62 | | |
| Mustered Out 10-13-65 | | | | | | | |

| Polan, James N. | | E | 19 | 5'7" | Light | Grey | Dark |
|---|---|---|---|---|---|---|---|
| B. Ross Co. OH | Farmer | Res. Clinton, Ill. Res 1885 Lane's Station, Ill. | | | | | |
| Deserted 2-13-66 at Houston | | | | | | | |

| Porter, Charles | | G | 25 | | | | |
|---|---|---|---|---|---|---|---|
| | | Enl. Otterville | | | 11-1-61 | | |
| Discharged 10-4-64 | | | | | | | |

| Porter, Charles R. | | K | | | | | |
|---|---|---|---|---|---|---|---|
| F. Chicago | | | | | 9-19-61 | | |
| | | | | | | | |

| Porter, Jarvis W. | | C | 19 | 6'1" | Fair | Brown | Dark |
|---|---|---|---|---|---|---|---|
| B. Wyoming Co. NY | Musician | Res. Wauconda | | | | | |
| Discharged Disability 8-7-62 Phithesis pulmonalis. | | | | | | | |

# DESCRIPTIVE ROLL

| Potter, Alonzo J. | | C | 19 | | | | |
|---|---|---|---|---|---|---|---|
| F. Avon | | | | | 8-1-61 | | |
| Wounded in leg by Home Guard under Capt. Kysser (Fall 1861). Wounded at Prairie Grove 12-7-62. Died 1-18-63 at Fayetteville, Ark. ||||||||

| Powell, John | | G | 29 | 5'10" | Light | Blue | Brown |
|---|---|---|---|---|---|---|---|
| B. Limerick, Ireland | Laborer | Res. Chicago | | | | | |
| Died 3-12-62 at Little Sugar Creek Bottom, Ark. ||||||||

| Powers, John | | E | 40 | 5'5" | Dark | Brown | Dark |
|---|---|---|---|---|---|---|---|
| B. Limerick, Ireland | Farmer | Res. Mendota, Res. 1885 Milwaukee, Wis. | | | | | |
| Discharged Disability 1-16-64. Chronic rheumatism. ||||||||

| Powers, Orville R. | | E | 24 | 5'10" | Light | Grey | Light |
|---|---|---|---|---|---|---|---|
| B. Chatauqua, NY | Farmer | Res. Ottawa, Ill. | | | | | |
| Died 3-9-62. Shot through the right lung a Pea Ridge. ||||||||

| Powers, Walter W. | | G | 29 | 5'10" | Fair | Hazel | Black |
|---|---|---|---|---|---|---|---|
| B. Fleming Co Ky | Farmer | Res. Cheney's Grove | | | | | |
| Died 9-1-64 at Carrolton, La. Typhoid Fever. ||||||||

| Prentis, James W. | | E | 25 | 5'10" | Light | Grey | Brown |
|---|---|---|---|---|---|---|---|
| B. Rutland Co. Vt | Farmer | Res. Mendota | | | | | |
| Deserted 2-27-63 near Mt. Vernon, Mo. ||||||||

| Priddy, John C. | | E | 45 | 5'10" | Light | Blue | Dark |
|---|---|---|---|---|---|---|---|
| B. Stokes Co. NC | Farmer | Res. Mt. Idem, Ark., Enl. Keitsville | 4-17-62 | | | | |
| Discharged Disability 2-17-63 ||||||||

# THIRTY SEVENTH ILLINOIS

| Proper, Truman | | F | 21 | 5'10" | Light | Blue | Dark |
|---|---|---|---|---|---|---|---|
| B. Livingston, NY | Laborer | Res. Vernon | | | | | |
| Mustered Out 5-15-66 | | | | | | | |

| Pullen, Charles | | F | 23 | 6'0" | Light | Blue | Light |
|---|---|---|---|---|---|---|---|
| B. Kent, England | Farmer | Res. Antioch, Res. 1885, Antioch, Ill. | | | | | |
| Mustered Out 10-4-64 | | | | | | | |

| Purser, David | | K | 21 | | | | |
|---|---|---|---|---|---|---|---|
| F. Vermilion Co. | | Res. 1885, Beaverton, Oregon | | | | | |
| Mustered Out 10-4-64 | | | | | | | |

| Puterbaugh, Abram | | E | 18 | 5'8" | Light | Hazel | Brown |
|---|---|---|---|---|---|---|---|
| B. Windham, Ontario, Canada | Farmer | Res. Mendota, Res. 1885 Compton, Ill. | | | | | |
| Mustered Out 5-15-66 | | | | | | | |

| Puterbaugh, Philip M. | | E | 24 | 5'6" | Light | Hazel | Brown |
|---|---|---|---|---|---|---|---|
| B. Windham, Ontario, Canada | Farmer | Res. Mendota, Res. 1885 Los Angeles, Cal. | | | | | |
| Mustered Out 10-4-64 | | | | | | | |

# Q

| Quest, John | | E | 22 | 5'5" | Light | Grey | Light |
|---|---|---|---|---|---|---|---|
| B. Armstrong, Pa. | Farmer | Res. Mendota, Res. 1885 Spring Hill, Kan. | | | | | |
| Transferred Veteran Reserve Corps 11-11-65 | | | | | | | |

| Quinn, Patrick | | D | 17 | 5'4" | Brwn | Brwn | Brwn |
|---|---|---|---|---|---|---|---|
| B. Ireland | | Res. Manistee | | | | | |
| Deserted 2-8-63 from Camp Schofield, Mo. | | | | | | | |

DESCRIPTIVE ROLL

# R

| Raglan, John | | A | 21 | | | | |
|---|---|---|---|---|---|---|---|
| F. Bluegrass, IA | | Res. 1885 Bellville, Ill. | | | | | |
| Clerk at Gratiot St. Military Prison 9-14-64. Discharged 9-18-64 | | | | | | | |

| Ransom, George | | B | 26 | | | | |
|---|---|---|---|---|---|---|---|
| F. Goshen | Musician | Res. 1885 Valderbilt, Pa. | | | | | |
| Discharged 9-24-64 | | | | | | | |

| Ransom, Madison | | A | 25 | 6'0" | Light | Blue | Auburn |
|---|---|---|---|---|---|---|---|
| B. Bedford, Mich. | Sawyer | Res. Rock Island | | | | | |
| Mustered Out 10-4-64 | | | | | | | |

| Rawson, Thomas | | F | 19 | 5'7" | Dark | Hazel | Dark |
|---|---|---|---|---|---|---|---|
| B. Cleveland, OH | Farmer | Res. Fremont | | | | | |
| Died 12-11-61 in St. Louis in Hospital – disease. | | | | | | | |

| Redfield, Chilion B. | | B | 18 | | | | |
|---|---|---|---|---|---|---|---|
| F. Goshen | | | | | | | |
| Died Cassville 5-3-62. Typhoid pneumonia. | | | | | | | |

| Reed, Edward | | I | 19 | 5'7" | Light | Brwn | Brown |
|---|---|---|---|---|---|---|---|
| B. Buffalo, NY | Farmer | Res. Chemung | | | | | |
| Mustered Out 3-31-66 | | | | | | | |

| Reed, Ira C., Jr. | | B | 22 | 5'7" | Light | Blue | Brown |
|---|---|---|---|---|---|---|---|
| B. Goshen, Ill. | Farmer | Res. Lynn | | | | | |
| Mustered Out 5-15-66 | | | | | | | |

# THIRTY SEVENTH ILLINOIS

| Reed, Isaac W. | | B | 21 | 5'8" | Light | Blue | Brown |
|---|---|---|---|---|---|---|---|
| B. Stark Co., Ill | Farmer | Res. Lynn | | | | | |
| Mustered Out 1-23-66 | | | | | | | |

| Reed, James | | H | 24 | 5'6" | Light | Blue | Brown |
|---|---|---|---|---|---|---|---|
| B. Philadelphia | Farmer | Res. Preemption | | | | | |
| Deserted 2-19-62 at Lebanon, Mo. | | | | | | | |

| Reed, John | | B | 29 | | | | |
|---|---|---|---|---|---|---|---|
| F. Goshen | | Res. 1885 Lafayette, Ill. | | | | | |
| Mustered Out 9-29-64 | | | | | | | |

| Reed, Robert C. | | B | 18 | | | | |
|---|---|---|---|---|---|---|---|
| F. Goshen | | | | | | | |
| Died 10-23-63 at Ottervile. Hemorrhage of lungs. | | | | | | | |

| Reed, William C. | | K | 19 | 5'7" | Fair | Blue | Dark |
|---|---|---|---|---|---|---|---|
| B. Crawford Co. Pa. | Saddler | Enl. Danville | | | 3-31-64 | | |
| Mustered Out 5-15-66 | | | | | | | |

| Reen, Edward | | F | 25 | 5'7" | Dark | Blue | Dark |
|---|---|---|---|---|---|---|---|
| B. Prussia | Farmer | Res. Lyons | | | | | |
| | | | | | | | |

| Reid, George | | G | 18 | 5'7" | Light | Grey | Brown |
|---|---|---|---|---|---|---|---|
| B. England | Farmer | Res. Cheney's Grove | | | | | |
| Mustered Out 5-15-66 | | | | | | | |

| Reisser, Frederick | | K | 22 | 5'8" | Dark | Grey | Red |
|---|---|---|---|---|---|---|---|
| F. Danville | Farmer | | | | | | |
| Died 9-22-64 at Cairo. | | | | | | | |

# DESCRIPTIVE ROLL

| Remington, James H. | | E | 25 | 5'10" | Light | Blue | Sandy |
|---|---|---|---|---|---|---|---|
| B. Windham, CT | Farmer | Res. Mendota, Res. 1885 Ophir, Ill. | | | | | |
| Discharged Disability 1-20-62 | | | | | | | |

| Rencher, John | | E | 33 | 6'3" | Light | Blue | Brown |
|---|---|---|---|---|---|---|---|
| B. Hopkinsville, KY | Laborer | Res. Mendota, Res. 1885 Soldier's Home, Milwaukee, Wis. | | | | | |
| Discharged 3-12-62 at Springfield. | | | | | | | |

| Resser, Charles W. | | H | 18 | 5'7" | Light | Blue | Brown |
|---|---|---|---|---|---|---|---|
| B. Perry Co., Pa. | Farmer | Res. Morristown, Res. 1885 Grinnell, Iowa | | | | | |
| Mustered Out 5-15-66 | | | | | | | |

| Reticker, John M. | | H | 18 | 5'4" | Light | Grey | Sandy |
|---|---|---|---|---|---|---|---|
| B. Baltimore, MD | Clerk | Res. Rock Island, Res. 1885 Rock Island, Il | | | | | |
| Mustered Out 10-4-64 | | | | | | | |

| Reynolds, Jerome S. | | I | 19 | 5'7" | Sandy | Hazel | Red |
|---|---|---|---|---|---|---|---|
| B. Harvard, Ill. | Farmer | | | | | | |
| Died 3-31-66 Columbia, Texas. Disease. | | | | | | | |

| Rich, Peter | | C | 20 | 5'8" | Fair | Grey | Dark |
|---|---|---|---|---|---|---|---|
| B. Lake Co. | | Res. Avon, Res. 1885 O'Brien Co. Iowa | | | | | |
| Mustered Out 5-15-66 | | | | | | | |

| Richards, Rees | | | 41 | 5'8" | Fair | Blue | Grey |
|---|---|---|---|---|---|---|---|
| B. Wales | Tanner Currier | Res. Chicago | | | 8-5-64 | | |
| Substitute for Wirt Dexter. | | | | | | | |

| Richardson, James S. | | I | 21 | 5'8" | Light | Blue | Brown |
|---|---|---|---|---|---|---|---|
| F. Norwalk, NY | Farmer | Res. Marengo | | | | | |
| Died 9-15-62 at Springfield, Mo. in Hospital of disease. | | | | | | | |

# THIRTY SEVENTH ILLINOIS

| Riggs, Henry M. | | | G | 32 | 5'9" | Light | Blue | Dark |
|---|---|---|---|---|---|---|---|---|
| B. Fleming Co Ky | Mason | | Res. 1885 Portland, Oregon | | | | | |
| Transferred to 92d U.S. Colored Volunteers 9-63 | | | | | | | | |

| Riley, Albert J. | | | K | 17 | 5'7" | Dark | Grey | Black |
|---|---|---|---|---|---|---|---|---|
| F. Indiana | | Farmer | Enl. Vermilion Co. | | | | | |
| Reenlisted as Veteran. | | | | | | | | |

| Rinehart, John G. | | | H | 43 | 5'0" | Light | Blue | Light |
|---|---|---|---|---|---|---|---|---|
| B. Gotha, Saxony, Germany | | Carpenter | Res. Chicago | | | | | |
| Discharged Disability 2-12-63. Old age. | | | | | | | | |

| Ring, Joseph | | | G | 24 | 5'6" | Light | Grey | Brown |
|---|---|---|---|---|---|---|---|---|
| B. Ross Co. OH | | Farmer | Res. Cheney's Grove | | | | | |
| Died 6-7-62 at Cassville in hospital. Wounds received from guerillas while on forage guard 6-7-62. | | | | | | | | |

| Ring, William H., Jr. | | | F | 20 | 5'8" | Light | Blue | Light |
|---|---|---|---|---|---|---|---|---|
| B. Lake Co. | | Merchant | Res. Antioch | | | | | |
| Died 4-9-62 of disease in camp at Cassville. | | | | | | | | |

| Rischow, Christian | | | H | 24 | 5'7" | Light | Blue | Auburn |
|---|---|---|---|---|---|---|---|---|
| B. Prussia, Germany | | Farmer | Res. Bloom, Res. 1885 Chicago, Ill. | | | | | |
| Mustered Out 5-15-66 | | | | | | | | |

| Risdon, Oliver F. | | | B | 32 | | | | |
|---|---|---|---|---|---|---|---|---|
| F. Goshen | | | | | | | | |
| Transferred to 92d U.S. Colored Volunteers 9-27-63 | | | | | | | | |

| Rivenburg, Edward D. | | | H | 18 | 5'7" | Light | Blue | Auburn |
|---|---|---|---|---|---|---|---|---|
| B. Susaquehanna, Pa. | | Farmer | Res. Morristown | | | 3-29-64 | | |
| Mustered Out 5-15-66 | | | | | | | | |

# DESCRIPTIVE ROLL

| Roberson, Daniel | | | F | 20 | 5'6" | Light | Brown | Dark |
|---|---|---|---|---|---|---|---|---|
| B. Crawford Co. OH | | Farmer | Res. Lyons | | | | | |
| Deserted 6-19-62 | | | | | | | | |

| Roberts, George W. | | | E | 18 | 5'10" | Light | Blue | Black |
|---|---|---|---|---|---|---|---|---|
| B. New York | | Farmer | Res. Mendota, Res. 1885 Crete, Nebraska | | | | | |
| Mustered Out 5-15-66 | | | | | | | | |

| Roberts, William | | | | 27 | 5'4" | Fair | Brown | Dark |
|---|---|---|---|---|---|---|---|---|
| B. England | | Baker | Res. Chicago, Enl. Waukegan | | | 2-24-64 | | |
| | | | | | | | | |

| Robertson, James | | | K | 20 | 5'5" | Light | Blue | Light |
|---|---|---|---|---|---|---|---|---|
| B. Ross Co., OH | | Farmer | Res. Middlefork | | | 3-8-64 | | |
| Mustered Out 5-15-66 | | | | | | | | |

| Robertson, Robert | | | D | 20 | 5'10" | Light | Grey | Brown |
|---|---|---|---|---|---|---|---|---|
| B. Scotland | | | Res. Chicago | | | | | |
| Mustered Out 10-4-64 | | | | | | | | |

| Robinson, Edward S. | | | K | 17 | 5'5" | Fair | Grey | Light |
|---|---|---|---|---|---|---|---|---|
| F. Newark, Ohio | | Student | | | | | | |
| Mustered Out 10-4-64 | | | | | | | | |

| Rockett, Thomas P. | | | C | 19 | | | | |
|---|---|---|---|---|---|---|---|---|
| F. Waukegan | | | Res. 1885 Jersey City, NJ | | | | | |
| Mustered Out 9-13-64 | | | | | | | | |

| Rodgers, Charles | | | | | | | | |
|---|---|---|---|---|---|---|---|---|
| | | | | | | | | |
| Left sick at Chicago 9-19-61 | | | | | | | | |

# THIRTY SEVENTH ILLINOIS

| Rolph, William | | | 22 | 5'5" | Dark | Brown | Brown |
|---|---|---|---|---|---|---|---|
| B. Canada | Laborer | Res. Lyons, Enl. Chicago | | | 2-8-65 | | |
| | | | | | | | |

| Roof, Samuel | | E | 18 | 5'6" | Fair | Grey | Brown |
|---|---|---|---|---|---|---|---|
| B. Knox Co., OH | Farmer | Res. Osage, Enl. Earlville, Ill. | | | 3-7-64 | | |
| Died 10-24-64 at Memphis. | | | | | | | |

| Roper, Spencer | | I | 19 | 5'11" | Dark | Brown | Brown |
|---|---|---|---|---|---|---|---|
| F. England | Farmer | Res. Garden Prairie | | | | | |
| Discharged Disability. Wounds received at Prairie Grove. | | | | | | | |

| Rose, Edward | | F | 31 | 5'7" | Dark | Blue | Sandy |
|---|---|---|---|---|---|---|---|
| B. Bucks Co. Pa. | Blacksmith | Res. Vernon | | | | | |
| Mustered Out 5-15-66 | | | | | | | |

| Rose, Ira M. | | C | 20 | 5'8" | Brown | Brwn | Black |
|---|---|---|---|---|---|---|---|
| B. Hudson, Mich. | Farmer | Res. Mendota | | | | | |
| Mustered Out 5-15-66 | | | | | | | |

| Rosette, Theodore | | A | 21 | 5'10" | Dark | Brown | Brown |
|---|---|---|---|---|---|---|---|
| B. Pau Pau Ill. | Farmer | Res. Rock Island | | | | | |
| Died 10-23-63 on leave. General debility, chronic diarrhea. | | | | | | | |

| Ross, Vincent C. | | K | 23 | 5'8" | Fair | Grey | Brown |
|---|---|---|---|---|---|---|---|
| B. Belmont Co. Ohio | Laborer | Enl. Danville | | | 10-27-64 | | |
| Deserted 9-23-65 at Columbus, Texas. | | | | | | | |

| Rosson, Joseph W. | | A | 19 | 5'6" | Dark | Brown | Brown |
|---|---|---|---|---|---|---|---|
| B. Frankfort, KY | Farmer | Enl. Boonville | | | 10-14-61 | | |
| Deserted 12-5-62 from Keitsville. | | | | | | | |

# DESCRIPTIVE ROLL

| Rothe, Ernst Henry | | | I | 21 | 5'6" | Light | Blue | Brown |
|---|---|---|---|---|---|---|---|---|
| F. Germany | | Farmer | Res. Cedarville, Wis. | | | | | |
| Mustered Out 5-15-66 | | | | | | | | |

| Rouse, George W. | | | B | 24 | | | | |
|---|---|---|---|---|---|---|---|---|
| F. Goshen | | | | | | | | |
| Reenlisted 1st U.S. Artillery. | | | | | | | | |

| Rowe, Hartford J. | | | B | 22 | 5'8" | Fair | Blue | Brown |
|---|---|---|---|---|---|---|---|---|
| B. Dover, Maine | | Farmer | Res. Toulon | | | | | |
| Mustered Out 5-15-66 | | | | | | | | |

| Rowling Charles J. | | | C | 23 | | | | |
|---|---|---|---|---|---|---|---|---|
| F. Avon | | | Res. 1885 Hainesville, Ill. | | | | | |
| Mustered Out 10-4-64 | | | | | | | | |

| Ruby, Jacob J. | | | | 40 | | | | |
|---|---|---|---|---|---|---|---|---|
| F. Chicago | | Principal Musician | | | | | | |
| | | | | | | | | |

| Runde, John G. | | | | 35 | 5'4" | Fair | Blue | Brown |
|---|---|---|---|---|---|---|---|---|
| B. Germany | | Laborer | Res. Spring Point | | | 4-10-65 | | |
| Mustered Out 5-15-66 | | | | | | | | |

| Rupno. John F. | | | F | 27 | 5'4" | Light | Blue | Dark |
|---|---|---|---|---|---|---|---|---|
| B. Prussia | | Farmer | Res. Marthas | | | | | |
| Mustered Out 10-4-64 | | | | | | | | |

| Russell, Judson | | | G | 41 | 5'10" | Fair | Blue | Light |
|---|---|---|---|---|---|---|---|---|
| B. Rock Co. Wis | | Farmer | Res Magnolia | | | | | |
| Deserted 11-29-61. Went to Middeltown, Ill. on furlough. Discharged Boonville. | | | | | | | | |

# THIRTY SEVENTH ILLINOIS

| Rust, Charles W. | | | E | 18 | 5'8" | Light | Blue | Light |
|---|---|---|---|---|---|---|---|---|
| B. Franklin Co. Ill | | Farmer | Enl. Mendota | | | | 12-10-62 | |
| Died 7-28-63 at Vicksburg. | | | | | | | | |

| Rust, Phineas B. | | | E | 44 | 5'9" | Light | Blue | Dark |
|---|---|---|---|---|---|---|---|---|
| F. Northampton, Mass. | | Farmer | Res. Mendota, Res. 1885 Netawaukee, Kansas | | | | | |
| Resigned 2-23-63 | | | | | | | | |

| Ryan, Daniel | | | H | 28 | 5'11" | Dark | Grey | Black |
|---|---|---|---|---|---|---|---|---|
| B. Limerick, Ireland | | Farmer | Res. Galva | | | | | |
| Died 9-20-63 at New Orleans | | | | | | | | |

# S

| Sackrisson, John | | | B | 22 | 5'7" | Dark | Blue | Light |
|---|---|---|---|---|---|---|---|---|
| B. Sweden | | Farmer | Res. Goshen | | | | | |
| Died 8-25-63. Typhoid Fever. | | | | | | | | |

| Sample, George W. | | | A | 19 | | | | |
|---|---|---|---|---|---|---|---|---|
| F. Preemption | | | Res. 1885 Des Moines, Iowa | | | | | |
| Transferred 1st U.S. Colored Artillery. | | | | | | | | |

| Sample, James | | | A | 30 | 5'8" | Fair | Brown | Blue |
|---|---|---|---|---|---|---|---|---|
| B. Ohio | | Mason | Enl. Preemption | | | | 8-14-62 | |
| Mustered Out 6-12-65 | | | | | | | | |

| Sands, William | | | I | 23 | 5'9" | Light | Grey | Brown |
|---|---|---|---|---|---|---|---|---|
| F. Bonus, Ill. | | Farmer | Res. Bonus, Res. 1885 Pentwater, Mich. | | | | | |
| Transferred to 92d U.S. Colored Volunteers 9-27-63 | | | | | | | | |

## DESCRIPTIVE ROLL

| Sanford, Charles | | | 19 | 5'6" | Fair | Blue | Light |
|---|---|---|---|---|---|---|---|
| b. Whitesides Co. Ill. | Carpenter | Res. Hampton | | | 10-4-64 | | |
| | | | | | | | |

| Savage, Daniel | | | E | 44 | 5'8' | Light | Blue | Dark |
|---|---|---|---|---|---|---|---|---|
| B. Sullivan Co Pa | Farmer | Res. Mendota | | | | | | |
| Killed 12-7-62 at Prairie Grove. Shot through the abdomen. ||||||||| 

| Savage, Ezekiel | | | F | 22 | 5'10" | Dark | Blue | Dark |
|---|---|---|---|---|---|---|---|---|
| B. Clinton, NY | Farmer | Res. Antioch | | | | | | |
| Died 2-18-64 at New Orleans |||||||||

| Savage, James | | | E | 27 | 5'6" | Light | Brown | Dark |
|---|---|---|---|---|---|---|---|---|
| B. Sullivan Co Pa | Farmer | Res. Mendota, Res. 1885, DeWitt, Neb. | | | | | | |
| |||||||||

| Savaugh, Adolph | | | K | 24 | 5'7" | Dark | Blue | Dark |
|---|---|---|---|---|---|---|---|---|
| B. Belgium | Laborer | Enl. Danville | | | | 11-23-63 | | |
| Mustered Out 5-15-66 |||||||||

| Sawyer, Anderson H. | | | B | 19 | | | | |
|---|---|---|---|---|---|---|---|---|
| F. Galva | | | | | | | | |
| Left sick in hospital at Chicago on 9-19-61 |||||||||

| Schwinn, Peter | | | A | 28 | | | | |
|---|---|---|---|---|---|---|---|---|
| F. Rock Island | | Res. 1885 Allegheny, Pa | | | | | | |
| Mustered Out 10-4-64 |||||||||

| Scott, Mathew F. | | | E | 43 | 5'10" | Light | Blue | Dark |
|---|---|---|---|---|---|---|---|---|
| B. Somerset Co. Ohio | Saddler | Res. Mendota, Res. 1885 Colony, Kansas | | | | | | |
| Mustered Out 10-4-64 |||||||||

# THIRTY SEVENTH ILLINOIS

| Scott, Roswell | | | G | 30 | 5'10" | Sandy | Grey | Brown |
|---|---|---|---|---|---|---|---|---|
| B. Genessee, NY | Book-keeper | | Enl. Chicago, Res. 1885 Seattle, Washington Territory | | | | | |
| Discharged Disability 11-16-62. Phithesis pulmonalis. | | | | | | | | |

| Scoville, Lyman B. | | | C | 25 | 5'11" | Fair | Grey | Dark |
|---|---|---|---|---|---|---|---|---|
| B. Allegheny, NY | Farmer | | Res. Goodale | | | 10-2-61 | | |
| Mustered Out 5-15-66. | | | | | | | | |

| Seabury, John | | | D | 32 | 5'8" | Light | Grey | Light |
|---|---|---|---|---|---|---|---|---|
| B. Norway | Lumberman | | Res. Hamlin, Mich. | | | | | |
| Mustered Out 5-15-66. Drowned in Buffalo Bayou after muster out. Fell off ship. | | | | | | | | |

| Selig, George | | | F | 28 | 5'6" | Fair | Grey | Dark |
|---|---|---|---|---|---|---|---|---|
| F. Germany | Farmer | | Res. Vernon | | | 2-13-64 | | |
| Died 11-20-64 at Vicksburg. Chronic diarrhea. | | | | | | | | |

| Sellen, Broda | | | B | 18 | | | | |
|---|---|---|---|---|---|---|---|---|
| F. Lynn | | | | | | | | |
| Mustered Out 10-4-64 | | | | | | | | |

| Senter, Charles E. | | | G | 28 | 5'6" | Light | Grey | Brown |
|---|---|---|---|---|---|---|---|---|
| B. Portsmouth NH | Clerk | | Res. Cheney's Grove | | | | | |
| Deserted 10-4-64 | | | | | | | | |

| Serall, Edward | | | D | 23 | 5'8" | Dark | Brown | Dark |
|---|---|---|---|---|---|---|---|---|
| B. Canada | Laborer | | Res. Manistee | | | | | |
| Deserted 6-8-63 from Steamer HANNIBAL. | | | | | | | | |

| Seymour, Frederick | | | C | 19 | 5'9" | Fair | Blue | Red |
|---|---|---|---|---|---|---|---|---|
| B. Cook Co. Ill. | Farmer | | Res. Goodale | | | | | |
| Died 11-4-61 at Boonville. Typhoid Fever. | | | | | | | | |

# DESCRIPTIVE ROLL

| Shanks, Absalom | | | H | 22 | 5'8" | Light | Blue | Brown |
|---|---|---|---|---|---|---|---|---|
| B. Rock Island, Ill | | Farmer | Res. Moline, Res. 1885 Firth, Nebraska | | | | | |
| Mustered Out 5-15-66 | | | | | | | | |

| Shaw, Augustus | | | K | 18 | 5'6" | Dark | Grey | Brown |
|---|---|---|---|---|---|---|---|---|
| F. New York City, NY | | Farmer | Res. Vermilion Co. | | | | | |
| | | | | | | | | |

| Shawler, Henry | | | K | 22 | | | | |
|---|---|---|---|---|---|---|---|---|
| F. State Line | | | | | | | | |
| Mustered Out 10-4-64 | | | | | | | | |

| Shea, Morris | | | F | 18 | 5'4" | Light | Brwn | Light |
|---|---|---|---|---|---|---|---|---|
| B. Lake Co. | | Farmer | Res. Newport, Res. 1885 Blund, Dakota. | | | | | |
| Mustered Out 5-15-66 | | | | | | | | |

| Shearer, Charles | | | F | 26 | 5'6" | Dark | Brown | Black |
|---|---|---|---|---|---|---|---|---|
| B. Baden, Germany | | Farmer | Res. Vernon | | | | | |
| Mustered Out 9-29-64 | | | | | | | | |

| Sheldon, Lorenzo D. | | | H | 18 | 6'2" | Light | Blue | Brown |
|---|---|---|---|---|---|---|---|---|
| B. Chittenden Co. VT | | Farmer | Res. Moline, Res.1885 Osage City, Kansas | | | | | |
| Mustered Out 5-15-66 | | | | | | | | |

| Sheldon, Oscar F. | | | A | 21 | | | | |
|---|---|---|---|---|---|---|---|---|
| | | | | | | | | |
| Transferred Invalid Corps. | | | | | | | | |

| Shepard, Alonzo B. | | | F | 19 | 5'6" | Dark | Blue | Dark |
|---|---|---|---|---|---|---|---|---|
| B. Lake Co., Ill. | | Clerk | Res. Antioch | | | | | |
| | | | | | | | | |

# THIRTY SEVENTH ILLINOIS

| Shepard, Hugh | | E | 32 | 5'8" | Dark | Brown | Black |
|---|---|---|---|---|---|---|---|
| B. Washington, NY | Carpenter | Res. Mendota | | | | | |
| Promoted 2d Lieutentant Co. K 8th Missouri Cavalry 9-2-62 | | | | | | | |

| Sherwood, Gilbert | | C | 27 | 5'9" | Sandy | Blue | Sandy |
|---|---|---|---|---|---|---|---|
| B. Yates Co., NY | Farmer | Res. Barrington | | | | | |
| Died 3-22-62 at Cassville. General debility or homesickness. | | | | | | | |

| Shields, Patrick | | G | 34 | 5'10" | Dark | Hazel | Brown |
|---|---|---|---|---|---|---|---|
| B. Wexford, Ireland | Track Layer | Res. East Bend | | | | | |
| Discharged Disability 11-17-65. Wounds at Prairie Grove. | | | | | | | |

| Shipps, William P. | | K | 31 | 6'4" | Dark | Blue | Brown |
|---|---|---|---|---|---|---|---|
| B. Coshockton Co. Ohio | Farmer | Enl. Danville | | | 3-31-64 | | |
| Discharged Disability 8-19-64. Anchylosis of right knee joint. Wound at Pea Ridge. | | | | | | | |

| Shuler, William | | F | 26 | 5'5" | Dark | Blue | Dark |
|---|---|---|---|---|---|---|---|
| B. Belgium | Farmer | Res. Antioch, Res. 1885 Aurora, Ill. | | | | | |
| Discharged 2-5-63. Wounds received at Prairie Grove. | | | | | | | |

| Shultz, Charles | | A | 32 | 5'8" | Dark | Blue | Brown |
|---|---|---|---|---|---|---|---|
| B. Magdeburg, Prussia | | Res. St. Joseph, Mo. | | | | | |
| Died 4-11-62 of wounds received at Pea Ridge. Musket ball in left hip. | | | | | | | |

| Side, Paul | | K | 25 | 5'6" | Dark | Brown | Dark |
|---|---|---|---|---|---|---|---|
| B. Canada | Laborer | Res. Denmark, Ill. | | | 12-21-63 | | |
| Discharged 2-17-66 | | | | | | | |

# DESCRIPTIVE ROLL

| Sides, Henry | | | H | 23 | 5'6" | Light | Blue | Brown |
|---|---|---|---|---|---|---|---|---|
| B. Wayne Co. OH | | Farmer | Res. Geneseo, Res. 1885 Altoona, Iowa | | | | | |
| Mustered Out 5-15-66 | | | | | | | | |

| Silvertooth, William M. | | | E | 24 | 5'10" | Dark | Brown | Black |
|---|---|---|---|---|---|---|---|---|
| B. Lauderdale Co. | | Lumberman Farmer | Res. Surrounded Hills, Arkansas | | | 4-12-62 | | |
| Died 7-27-62 at Springfield, Ill. Congestion of the lungs. | | | | | | | | |

| Simons, Adolph | | | C | 29 | 5'11" | Fair | Light | Blue |
|---|---|---|---|---|---|---|---|---|
| B. Rochester, NY | | Farmer | Enl. Waukegan, Res. 1885 Hainesville, Ill. | | | | | |
| Mustered Out 5-15-66 | | | | | | | | |

| Simons, Levi J. | | | F | 20 | 6'2" | Dark | Blue | Dark |
|---|---|---|---|---|---|---|---|---|
| B. Lake Co. Ill | | Farmer | Res. Antioch, Res. 1885 Antioch, Ill. | | | | | |
| Mustered Out 10-4-64 | | | | | | | | |

| Simons, Marcus L. | | | C | 19 | 5'6" | Fair | Brown | Dark |
|---|---|---|---|---|---|---|---|---|
| B. Greensprings, OH | | Farmer | Res. Waukegan, Res. 1885 Rosita, Colorado | | | | | |
| Discharged Disability 11-27-62. Afflicted with the bloody flux and inguinal hernia caused by double quick marching. | | | | | | | | |

| Sims, Henry | | | E | 24 | 5'5" | Brwn | Brwn | Black |
|---|---|---|---|---|---|---|---|---|
| B. England | | | Res. 1885 Dacota, Minn. | | | | | |
| Mustered Out 9-29-64 | | | | | | | | |

| Simson, James | | | A | 27 | 5'7" | Light | Grey | Dark |
|---|---|---|---|---|---|---|---|---|
| B. Seneca, NY | | Bridge-builder | Res. Port Byron | | | | | |
| Killed 3-7-62 at Pea Ridge. Musket ball through left side. | | | | | | | | |

# THIRTY SEVENTH ILLINOIS

| Simpson, Oliver | | 27 | 5'7" | Light | Blue | Light |
|---|---|---|---|---|---|---|
| B. Rock Island | Carriage Painter | Res. Chicago | | | 3-26-64 | |
| | | | | | | |

| Sinclair, James C. | | B | 20 | | | | |
|---|---|---|---|---|---|---|---|
| F. Bishop's Hill | | Res. 1885, East Liberty, Pa. | | | | | |
| Discharged Disability 10-31-62 | | | | | | | |

| Sipe, Henry | | B | 25 | | | | |
|---|---|---|---|---|---|---|---|
| F. Goshen | | | | | | | |
| Mustered Out 10-4-64 | | | | | | | |

| Slocum, Daniel | | G | 35 | 5'9" | Dark | Brown | Black |
|---|---|---|---|---|---|---|---|
| | | | | | | | |
| Deserted at Chicago 9-19-61 | | | | | | | |

| Smiley, Hershel | | E | 22 | 5'7" | Light | Blue | Black |
|---|---|---|---|---|---|---|---|
| B. Fayette Co. TN | Farmer | Res. Minouk, Ill. Res 1885 Stella, Nebraska | | | | | |
| Discharged Disability 6-14-65 at Mobile. Adhesions of pleura. | | | | | | | |

| Smith, Alden | | F | 25 | 5'8" | Dark | Blue | Dark |
|---|---|---|---|---|---|---|---|
| B. No. Haverhill, NH | Pastor | Res. Halfday | | | | | |
| Mustered Out 10-4-64 | | | | | | | |

| Smith, Andrew J. | | K | 22 | 5'5" | Dark | Brown | Black |
|---|---|---|---|---|---|---|---|
| B. Danville | Farmer | Res. Danville | | | | | |
| Discharged Disability 1-12-62. Chronic rheumatism. | | | | | | | |

| Smith, Charles | | E | 19 | 5'8" | Light | Grey | Brown |
|---|---|---|---|---|---|---|---|
| B. Prussia | Laborer | Enl. Chicago | | | 4-8-64 | | |
| Died 3-23-64 at New Orleans in hospital. Chronic diarrhea. | | | | | | | |

# DESCRIPTIVE ROLL

| Smith, Charles C. | | A | 20 | 5'7" | Fair | Blue | Brown |
|---|---|---|---|---|---|---|---|
| B. Lancaster, Pa. | Cigar Maker | Res. Springpoint | | | 4-10-65 | | |
| Mustered Out 4-4-66. Sentenced to Dry Tortugas. | | | | | | | |

| Smith, Charles C. | | F | 20 | 5'8" | Light | Grey | Red |
|---|---|---|---|---|---|---|---|
| B. Norwich, NY | Broom Maker | Res. Freeport, Res. 1885 Loveland, Colorado | | | | | |
| Mustered Out 10-4-64 | | | | | | | |

| Smith, Clarence | | D | 27 | | | | |
|---|---|---|---|---|---|---|---|
| F. Chicago | | | | | | | |
| Resigned 2-14-63 to join 1st Arkansas Cavalry as 1st Lt. | | | | | | | |

| Smith, Edward H. | | E | 18 | 5'4" | Fair | Blue | Sandy |
|---|---|---|---|---|---|---|---|
| B. Schoharie, NY | Farmer | Res. Mendota, Res. 1885 Toledo, Ohio | | | | | |
| Mustered Out 10-4-64. | | | | | | | |

| Smith, George A. | | G | 24 | 5'9" | Sandy | Blue | Res |
|---|---|---|---|---|---|---|---|
| F. Cheney's Grove | | | | | | | |
| Killed at Pea Ridge 3-7-62 | | | | | | | |

| Smith, George W. | | K | 32 | 5'8" | Dark | Brown | Black |
|---|---|---|---|---|---|---|---|
| F. Germany | Mechanic | Res. Vermilion Co. Res. 1885 Rolla, MO | | | | | |
| Discharged Disability 8-31-62. Intermittent fever. | | | | | | | |

| Smith, Harrison | | E | 19 | 5'5" | Fair | Grey | Brown |
|---|---|---|---|---|---|---|---|
| B. Washington Oh | Farmer | Enl. Mendota | | | 9-1-62 | | |
| Mustered Out 6-10-65 | | | | | | | |

| Smith, Henry L. | | E | 36 | 6'0" | Light | Blue | Light |
|---|---|---|---|---|---|---|---|
| B. Litchfield, CT | Farmer | Res. Mendota | | | | | |
| Died 4-10-64 on leave. Smallpox. | | | | | | | |

# THIRTY SEVENTH ILLINOIS

| Smith, Horace W. | | | E | 31 | 5'9" | Dark | Brown | Black |
|---|---|---|---|---|---|---|---|---|
| B. Hampshire MA | | Farmer | Res. Mendota | | | | | |
| Transferred 92d U.S. Colored Volunteers | | | | | | | | |

| Smith, James | | | G | 18 | 5'5" | Fair | Hazel | Brown |
|---|---|---|---|---|---|---|---|---|
| B. Scotland, Iowa | | Farmer | Res. Granby, Mo., Res. 1885 Joplin, Missouri | | | 8-15-62 | | |
| Mustered Out 6-12-65 | | | | | | | | |

| Smith, James | | | A | 19 | 5'7" | Light | Blue | Light |
|---|---|---|---|---|---|---|---|---|
| B. Pleasant Valley, NY | | Farmer | Res. Rock Island | | | | | |
| Died 1-26-62 at St. Louis. Typhoid pneumonia. | | | | | | | | |

| Smith, James E. | | | C | 19 | 5'8" | Fair | Blue | Light |
|---|---|---|---|---|---|---|---|---|
| B. England | | Blacksmith | Res. Wauconda | | | | | |
| Discharged 6-20-62 to 17th Illinois Cavalry. | | | | | | | | |

| Smith, James W. | | | H | 25 | 6'0" | Dark | Grey | Brown |
|---|---|---|---|---|---|---|---|---|
| B. Westmoreland Co. Pa. | | Farmer | Res. Moline | | | | | |
| Mustered Out 10-4-64 | | | | | | | | |

| Smith, John A. | | | F | 23 | 5'8" | Dark | Brown | Black |
|---|---|---|---|---|---|---|---|---|
| B. Haverhill, NH | | Farmer | Res. Halfday | | | | | |
| Discharged Disability 12-28-62 | | | | | | | | |

| Smith, John H. | | | K | 22 | 6'2" | Dark | Brown | Dark |
|---|---|---|---|---|---|---|---|---|
| F. Montgomery Ky | | Farmer | Res. State Line, Res 1885 Cornwall, Ky. | | | | | |
| Discharged 10-25-64 at New Orleans. | | | | | | | | |

# DESCRIPTIVE ROLL

| Smith, John T. | | | K | 26 | 5'8" | Dark | Hazel | Black |
|---|---|---|---|---|---|---|---|---|
| F. Glendale, CT | | Bell Hanger | Res. Danville | | | | | |
| Discharged Disability 4-11-64 at New Orleans. | | | | | | | | |

| Smith, Joseph | | | H | 18 | 5'7" | Dark | Hazel | Brown |
|---|---|---|---|---|---|---|---|---|
| B. Rock Island, Ill | | Farmer | Res. Moline, Res. 1885 Moline, Ill. | | | | | |
| Discharged Disability 7-16-62. Lost an arm at Pea Ridge. | | | | | | | | |

| Smith, Joseph S. | | | E | 23 | 5'9" | Light | Grey | Sandy |
|---|---|---|---|---|---|---|---|---|
| B. Columbia Co. Ohio | | Farmer | Res. Mendota | | | | | |
| Mustered Out 10-4-64 | | | | | | | | |

| Smith, Randall | | | I | 27 | 5'11" | Sandy | Hazel | Brown |
|---|---|---|---|---|---|---|---|---|
| B. New York City, NY | | Farmer | Res. Chemung, Res. 1885 Princeton, Ill. | | | | | |
| | | | | | | | | |

| Smith, Robert | | | A | 27 | 5'5" | Dark | Blue | Brown |
|---|---|---|---|---|---|---|---|---|
| B. Boston, England | | Farmer | Res. Coal Valley, Res. 1885 Milan, Ill. | | | | | |
| Discharged Disability 10-15-62. Gunshot fracture of right humerus. | | | | | | | | |

| Smith, Solomon B. | | | E | 51 | | Dark | Brown | Grey |
|---|---|---|---|---|---|---|---|---|
| B. Delaware Co. NY | | Farmer | Res. Mendota, Res. 1885 Mendota, Ill. | | | | | |
| Discharged 8-18-64 | | | | | | | | |

| Smith, Washington V. | | | C | 19 | 5'8" | Fair | Blue | Light |
|---|---|---|---|---|---|---|---|---|
| B. Wayne, NY | | Shoemaker | Res. Waukegan, Res. 1885 Palatine, Ill. | | | | | |
| Deserted 6-6-63 at St. Genevieve, Mo. | | | | | | | | |

# THIRTY SEVENTH ILLINOIS

| Smith, William | | | K | 32 | 5'6" | Dark | Hazel | Black |
|---|---|---|---|---|---|---|---|---|
| B. Dublin, Ireland | Carpenter | | Res. State Line | | | | | |
| Died 10-4-64. Congestive chills on board Steamer JS PRINGLE. ||||||||||

| Smith, William H. | | | I | 19 | 5'7" | Light | Grey | Brown |
|---|---|---|---|---|---|---|---|---|
| B. On the sea. | Farmer | | Res. Cherry Valley, Res. 1885 Danville, Ill. |||||||
| Discharged 2-18-62. Pneumonia. ||||||||||

| Smith, William H. | | | K | 17 | 5'7" | Dark | Brown | Brown |
|---|---|---|---|---|---|---|---|---|
| F. Wheeling, Va. | Brickmaker | | Res. Danville | | | | | |
| Mustered Out 5-15-66 ||||||||||

| Snell, Burton H. | | | I | 16 | 5'5" | Light | Blue | Light |
|---|---|---|---|---|---|---|---|---|
| F. Madison Co. NY | Farmer | | Res. Belvidere | | | | | |
|  ||||||||||

| Snell, Garrett S. | | | I | 18 | 5'4" | Light | Grey | Dark |
|---|---|---|---|---|---|---|---|---|
| B. Orleans Co NY | Farmer | | Res. Boone Co. | | | 9-15-62 | | |
| Mustered Out 6-10-65 ||||||||||

| Snell, Milton W. | | | I | 17 | 5'8" | Light | Grey | Brown |
|---|---|---|---|---|---|---|---|---|
| F. Madison Co. NY | Farmer | | Res. Bonus | | | | | |
| Mustered Out 5-15-66 ||||||||||

| Snyder, Conrad | | | E | 39 | | | | |
|---|---|---|---|---|---|---|---|---|
| B. Germany | Farmer | | Res. Mendota | | | | | |
| Deserted 9-18-61 at Chicago. ||||||||||

# DESCRIPTIVE ROLL

| Snyder, David W. | | | B | 33 | 5'9" | Dark | Hazel | Brown |
|---|---|---|---|---|---|---|---|---|
| B. Lafayette, Ill. | | Farmer | Res. Goshen, Res. 1885 Lafayette, Ill. | | | 4-24-64 | | |
| Mustered Out 5-15-66 | | | | | | | | |

| Snyder, Frederick | | | G | 21 | 5'10" | Light | Blue | Brown |
|---|---|---|---|---|---|---|---|---|
| B. Fremont, Ill. | | Farmer | Res. Byron, Res. 1885 Gibson City, Ill. | | | | | |
| Mustered Out 10-4-64 | | | | | | | | |

| Snyder, John L. | | | K | 26 | 5'10" | Fair | Brown | Light |
|---|---|---|---|---|---|---|---|---|
| B. Newark, OH | | Sadler | Res. Danville | | | | | |
| Died 4-9-62 at Cassville, Mo. | | | | | | | | |

| Solt, Israel | | | I | | | | | |
|---|---|---|---|---|---|---|---|---|
| | | | | | | | 6-7-65 | |
| Mustered Out 7-12-65 | | | | | | | | |

| Songer, Anderson H. | | | K | 19 | 5'9" | Light | Grey | Brown |
|---|---|---|---|---|---|---|---|---|
| F. Vermilion Co. | | Farmer | Res. Vermilion Co. | | | | | |
| Joined Regular Service. | | | | | | | | |

| Soule, Henry | | | F | 20 | 5'11" | Dark | Blue | Dark |
|---|---|---|---|---|---|---|---|---|
| B. New York | | Farmer | Res. Antioch | | | | | |
| Died 9-23-64 at Springfield, Ill. Chronic dysentery. | | | | | | | | |

| Soules, James D. | | | F | 24 | 5'9" | Dark | Brown | Dark |
|---|---|---|---|---|---|---|---|---|
| B. Onondaigua, NY | | Farmer | Res. Antioch, Res. 1885 Chippewa, Wis. | | | | | |
| Discharged 8-24-62 at Springfield. | | | | | | | | |

| Sowles, Horace G. | | | C | 18 | | | | |
|---|---|---|---|---|---|---|---|---|
| F. Waukegan | | | Res. 1885 Long Pine, Nebraska | | | | | |
| Mustered Out 1-27-65 | | | | | | | | |

# THIRTY SEVENTH ILLINOIS

| Sowles, Oscar | | | C | 22 | 5'11' | Dark | Blue | Dark |
|---|---|---|---|---|---|---|---|---|
| B. New York | | Farmer | Res. Wauconda | | | | | |
| Mustered Out 5-15-66 | | | | | | | | |

| Sprowl, Lendric | | | E | 23 | 5'9" | Light | Blue | Light |
|---|---|---|---|---|---|---|---|---|
| B. Antrim, Ireland | | Farmer | Res. Mendota | | | | | |
| Died 1-9-63. Wounds received at Prairie Grove. | | | | | | | | |

| Squires, Charles S. | | | C | 20 | | | | |
|---|---|---|---|---|---|---|---|---|
| F. Cuba | | | Res. 1885 Chester, Neb. | | | | | |
| Mustered Out 9-29-64 | | | | | | | | |

| Squires, Horace | | | D | 24 | | Light | Grey | Brown |
|---|---|---|---|---|---|---|---|---|
| B. New York | | Farmer | Enl. Manistee | | | | | |
| Deserted 7-20-63 | | | | | | | | |

| Stark, Denton D. | | | H | 21 | 5'5" | Aubrn | Grey | Auburn |
|---|---|---|---|---|---|---|---|---|
| B. Franklin Co Pa | | Clerk | Res. Chicago | | | | | |
| Transferred to 1st Arkansas Cavalry 6-15-62 as officer. | | | | | | | | |

| Stebins, Ludwick H. | | | I | | 5'10" | Fair | Blue | Brown |
|---|---|---|---|---|---|---|---|---|
| F. Germany | | Farmer | Res. Sharon, Wis., Res. 1885 Darien, Wis. | | | | | |
| Mustered Out 10-4-64 | | | | | | | | |

| Stearns, John O. | | | B | 21 | 5'8" | Dark | Brown | Brown |
|---|---|---|---|---|---|---|---|---|
| B. Windham, Vt | | Farmer | Res. Lynn, Res. 1885 Madison, Neb. | | | | | |
| Mustered Out 3-6-66 | | | | | | | | |

| Stearns, Merrill M. | | | E | 23 | 5'10" | Light | Blue | Brown |
|---|---|---|---|---|---|---|---|---|
| B. Worcester Co. Mass. | | Farmer | Res. Clarion | | | | | |
| Discharged Disability 4-18-62. Chronic affection from loss of finger. | | | | | | | | |

# DESCRIPTIVE ROLL

| Steele, Andrew B. | | A | 24 | 5'5" | Light | Blue | Brown |
|---|---|---|---|---|---|---|---|
| B. Chillicothe, Oh | | Res. Rock Island | | | | | |
| Mustered Out 5-15-66 | | | | | | | |

| Stephens, Daniel | | C | 32 | 5'7" | Fair | Blue | Dark |
|---|---|---|---|---|---|---|---|
| B. Philadelphia | Tailor | Res. Rock Island, Enl. Booneville | | | 1-1-62 | | |
| Deserted 6-6-63 at St. Genevieve, Mo. | | | | | | | |

| Stephens, Joseph | C | 22 | | | |
|---|---|---|---|---|---|
| F. Milwaukee | | | | | |
| Deserted 9-7-61 | | | | | |

| Sterrett, Robert | | H | 22 | 5'10" | Dark | Grey | Brown |
|---|---|---|---|---|---|---|---|
| B. Lincoln Co Me | Farmer | Res. Moline | | | | | |
| Mustered Out 10-4-64 | | | | | | | |

| Stevens, Richard | | D | 43 | 5'4" | Light | Grey | Grey |
|---|---|---|---|---|---|---|---|
| B. England | Farmer | Res. Pere Marquette, Mich. | | | | | |
| Mustered Out 9-29-64 | | | | | | | |

| Stevens, Samuel M. | | E | 21 | 5'9" | Light | Blue | Dark |
|---|---|---|---|---|---|---|---|
| B. Berkshire, England | Farmer | Res. Mendota, Res 1885 Mapleton, Iowa | | | | | |
| Discharged Disability 3-19-63 at Springfield. Gunshot wound in heel of left foot. | | | | | | | |

| Stevens, Theodore J. | | A | 24 | 5'8" | Fair | Blue | Brown |
|---|---|---|---|---|---|---|---|
| F. Philadelphia | Brick Maker | Res. Rock Island | | | | | |
| Deserted 6-5-63 at St. Genevieve. | | | | | | | |

# THIRTY SEVENTH ILLINOIS

| Stevenson, Alexander R. | | H | 23 | 5'10" | Light | Blue | Brown |
|---|---|---|---|---|---|---|---|
| B. Mercer Co. Ill. | Farmer | Res. Moline | | | | | |
| Mustered Out 9-29-64 | | | | | | | |

| Stewart, Milton M. | | K | 18 | 5'8" | Fair | Brown | Brown |
|---|---|---|---|---|---|---|---|
| B. Vermilion Co. | Clerk | Enl. Danville, Res. 1885 Saybrook, Ill. | | | 3-31-64 | | |
| Mustered Out 5-16-66 | | | | | | | |

| Stick, John | | D | 21 | 5'10" | Light | Grey | Light |
|---|---|---|---|---|---|---|---|
| F. Germany | Laborer | Res. Manistee | | | | | |
| Deserted 9-61 | | | | | | | |

| Still, Arnold, Jr. | | I | 22 | 5'10" | Light | Grey | Brown |
|---|---|---|---|---|---|---|---|
| F. Bloomfield, Oh | Farmer | Res. Boone | | | | | |
| Died 12-8-62. Shot through the bowels at Prairie Grove. | | | | | | | |

| Stillman, Almiran A. | | H | 18 | 5'5" | Light | Blue | Brown |
|---|---|---|---|---|---|---|---|
| B. Lenawee Co. Mich. | Farmer | Res. Rock Island | | | | | |
| Mustered Out 10-4-64 | | | | | | | |

| Stimpson, Joseph | | C | 35 | 5'6" | Fair | Grey | Dark |
|---|---|---|---|---|---|---|---|
| B. England | Farmer | Res. Wauconda | | | | | |
| Died 8-64 while crossing the Gulf of Mexico. | | | | | | | |

| Stone, Josiah A. | | H | 23 | 5'10" | Light | Blue | Brown |
|---|---|---|---|---|---|---|---|
| B. Greene Co. Ill | Farmer | Res. Wilmer | | | 11-5-61 | | |
| Mustered Out 1-23-65 | | | | | | | |

| Stow, Thomas J. | | I | 19 | 5'8" | Dark | Grey | Dark |
|---|---|---|---|---|---|---|---|
| F. Bonus, Ill. | Farmer | Res. Bonus | | | | | |
| Reenlisted as Veteran. | | | | | | | |

# DESCRIPTIVE ROLL

| Strang, Peter, Jr. | | | F | 20 | 5'4" | Light | Hazel | Light |
|---|---|---|---|---|---|---|---|---|
| B. Lake Co. | | Farmer | Res. Newport, Res. 1885 Milburn, Ill. | | | | | |
| Mustered Out 9-29-64 | | | | | | | | |

| Strang, Sylvanus V. | | | G | 20 | 5'4" | Light | Grey | Brown |
|---|---|---|---|---|---|---|---|---|
| B. Ohio | | Teamster | Res. Byron, Res. 1885 Byron, Ill. | | | | | |
| Wounded in right wrist at Prairie Grove 12-7-62. Mustered Out 5-15-66. | | | | | | | | |

| Stratton, Joseph | | | C | 18 | 5'5" | Dark | Blue | Dark |
|---|---|---|---|---|---|---|---|---|
| B. England | | Farmer | Res. Fremont | | | 9-3-62 | | |
| Died 9-15-63 at Carrolton, La. | | | | | | | | |

| Streeter, Edwin J. | | | I | 28 | 5'8" | Light | Blue | Light |
|---|---|---|---|---|---|---|---|---|
| F. Vernon, Vt. | | Engineer | Res. Two Rivers, Wis. | | | | | |
| Mustered Out 3-23-66 | | | | | | | | |

| Strong, Elisha N. | | | I | 26 | 5'10" | Light | Grey | Light |
|---|---|---|---|---|---|---|---|---|
| F. Allegheny Co. NY | | Farmer | Res. Boone | | | | | |
| Discharged Disability 7-25-62 | | | | | | | | |

| Strouse, James | | | G | 24 | 5'10" | Dark | Blue | Black |
|---|---|---|---|---|---|---|---|---|
| B. Beaver Co. Pa | | Farmer | Res. Chicago | | | | | |
| Mustered Out 10-4-64 | | | | | | | | |

| Strouse, John | | | G | 22 | 5'7" | Dark | Brown | Black |
|---|---|---|---|---|---|---|---|---|
| B. Beaver Co. Pa | | Farmer | Res. East Bend | | | | | |
| Mustered Out 10-4-64 | | | | | | | | |

| Stubbs, Freeman | | | D | 18 | 5'4" | Light | Blue | Brown |
|---|---|---|---|---|---|---|---|---|
| B. Maine | | Lumberman | Res. Chicago, Res. 1885 Manistee, Mich. | | | | | |
| Mustered Out 5-15-66 | | | | | | | | |

# THIRTY SEVENTH ILLINOIS

| Stubbs, Stillman | | D | 53 | 5'8" | Light | Blue | Brown |
|---|---|---|---|---|---|---|---|
| B. Hancock Co. Maine | Farmer | Res. Manistee | | | | | |
| Discharged Disability 6-9-64. Debility and old age. | | | | | | | |

| Stube, John | | K | 19 | 5'7" | Light | Blue | Brown |
|---|---|---|---|---|---|---|---|
| F. Germany | Farmer | Res. Danville | | | | | |
| Discharged Disability 7-23-62. Wounds. | | | | | | | |

| Stutz, John | | D | 29 | 5'5" | Dark | Brown | Dark |
|---|---|---|---|---|---|---|---|
| B. Zurich, Switzerland | Lumberman | Res. Michigan | | | | | |
| Discharged Disability 1-30-64. Chronic diarrhea and fever. Much emaciated. Died 2-10-64 at Cairo. Never made it home. | | | | | | | |

| Sullivan, Francis | | I | 18 | 5'10" | Light | Blue | Light |
|---|---|---|---|---|---|---|---|
| B. Hartland, Ill. | Farmer | Res. Hartland. | | | | | |
| Mustered Out 5-16-66 | | | | | | | |

| Sullivan, John | | D | 26 | 5'7" | Florid | Blue | Red |
|---|---|---|---|---|---|---|---|
| B. Canada | Lumberman | Res. Michigan | | | | | |
| Deserted 5-1-64 at Chicago. | | | | | | | |

| Sunderlin, William W. | C | 21 | 5'8" | Fair | Blue | Dark |
|---|---|---|---|---|---|---|
| B. Waukegan | | | | | 9-8-62 | |
| | | | | | | |

| Swadler, William | | E | 24 | 5'9" | Light | Blue | Light |
|---|---|---|---|---|---|---|---|
| B. Frankfurt, Germany | Farmer | Res. Mendota, Res. 1885 Stewartsville, Neb. | | | | | |
| Mustered Out 10-4-64 | | | | | | | |

| Swap, Andrew L. | | E | 20 | 5'10" | Light | Blue | Light |
|---|---|---|---|---|---|---|---|
| B. Erie Co. Pa. | Farmer | Res. Mendota, Res. 1885 Albion, Pa. | | | | | |
| Mustered Out 5-15-66 | | | | | | | |

# DESCRIPTIVE ROLL

| Swarthout, Samuel B. | | I | 24 | 5'8" | Light | Brown | Dark |
|---|---|---|---|---|---|---|---|
| F. Chemung | Distiller | Res. Belvidere | | | | | |
| Died 10-11-63 | | | | | | | |

| Sweetaple, William H. | | I | 20 | 6'1" | Dark | Brown | Dark |
|---|---|---|---|---|---|---|---|
| F. Spring | Farmer | | | | | | |
| Died 3-9-62 at St. Louis in hospital. Disease. | | | | | | | |

| Swift, Joseph | | G | 24 | 5'8" | Florid | Blue | Sandy |
|---|---|---|---|---|---|---|---|
| B. Philadelphia | Farmer | Res. Chicago | | | 8-15-61 | | |
| Died 4--62 in hospital at Cassville. A minie ball in the thigh. | | | | | | | |

| Swindells, James | | F | 18 | 5'6" | Light | Blue | Light |
|---|---|---|---|---|---|---|---|
| B. Manchester, England | Farmer | Res. Salem, Wis. | | | | | |
| Mustered Out 5-15-66 | | | | | | | |

| Swisher, George W. | | K | 21 | 5'6" | Dark | Blue | Dark |
|---|---|---|---|---|---|---|---|
| B. Vermilion Co. | Farmer | Res. 1885 Danville, Ill. | | | 11-1-61 | | |
| Mustered Out 10-4-64 | | | | | | | |

# T

| Talbot, John | | K | 18 | 5'7" | Dark | Brown | Black |
|---|---|---|---|---|---|---|---|
| F. New York | Farmer | Res. Danville | | | | | |
| Died Syracuse, Mo. | | | | | | | |

| Talladay, William F. | | | 18 | 5'3" | Light | Brwn | Light |
|---|---|---|---|---|---|---|---|
| B. Steuben Co. NY | Laborer | Res. Lasalle Co. | | | | | |
| Never mustered | | | | | | | |

# THIRTY SEVENTH ILLINOIS

| Tabot, Andrew | | G | 22 | 5'6" | Light | Blue | Brown |
|---|---|---|---|---|---|---|---|
| B. Lancaster, Pa | Farmer | Res. Chicago | | | | | |
| Died 6-4-64 at Memphis. Wounds. | | | | | | | |

| Tapel, Diedrick | | G | 27 | 5'10" | Light | Blue | Auburn |
|---|---|---|---|---|---|---|---|
| B. Germany | Farmer | Re. Dunkin's Grove, Res. 1885 Louisville, Neb. | | | | | |
| On furlough at Muster Out. | | | | | | | |

| Taylor, Charles | | H | 24 | 5'5" | Dark | Grey | Brown |
|---|---|---|---|---|---|---|---|
| B. Kings Co. NY | Engineer | | | | | | |
| Discharged Disability 6-9-62 at St. Louis. Wounds. | | | | | | | |

| Taylor, William | | H | 26 | 5'5" | Dark | Blue | Black |
|---|---|---|---|---|---|---|---|
| B. Down Co. Ireland | Farmer | Res. Millersburg, Res. 1885 York, Nebraska | 10-4-61 | | | | |
| Mustered Out 10-18-64 | | | | | | | |

| Tear, James L. | | G | 36 | 5'9" | Fair | Blue | Auburn |
|---|---|---|---|---|---|---|---|
| B. Isle of Man, England | Blacksmith | Res. Cheney's Grove, Res. 1885 Saybrook, Ill. | | | | | |
| Mustered Out 5-15-66 | | | | | | | |

| Tebbetts, Charles H. | | F | 21 | 5'8" | Light | Brwn | Light |
|---|---|---|---|---|---|---|---|
| R. Roxbury, Mass | Farmer | Res. Chicago, Res. 1885 Chicago, Ill. | | | | | |
| Mustered Out 9-29-64 | | | | | | | |

| Thelin, Modest | | D | 33 | | | | |
|---|---|---|---|---|---|---|---|
| | Blacksmith | Enl. Hamlin, Mich. | | | | | |
| Mustered Out 9-29-64 | | | | | | | |

# DESCRIPTIVE ROLL

| Thomas, Cyrus | | | H | 34 | 5'9" | Fair | Blue | Auburn |
|---|---|---|---|---|---|---|---|---|
| B. Dark Co. OH | | Farmer | Res. Edgington, Res. 1885, Winchester, Mo | | | | 10-18-64 | |
| Mustered Out 10-18-65 | | | | | | | | |

| Thomson, Charles | | | H | 23 | 5'9" | Fair | Brown | Dark |
|---|---|---|---|---|---|---|---|---|
| B. New York City, NY | | Telegraph Operator | | | | | 11-15-61 | |
| Put under arrest 12-4-61. Deserted from 1sst Regiment Kansas Volunteers (not 37th Ill. Reference only.) | | | | | | | | |

| Thompson, Francis W. | | | A | 22 | 5'11" | Light | Hazel | Brown |
|---|---|---|---|---|---|---|---|---|
| B. Scott Co. Iowa | | Farmer | Res. Blackhawk | | | | | |
| Died 8-4-63 at Port Hudson, La. Typhoid malarial fever. | | | | | | | | |

| Thompson, Frank | | | I | 22 | 5'7" | Light | Grey | Brown |
|---|---|---|---|---|---|---|---|---|
| B. New York | | Farmer | Res. Leroy | | | | | |
| Discharged Disability 10-5-62 at Newtonia, Mo. | | | | | | | | |

| Thompson, Isaac | | | I | 18 | 5'6" | Light | Grey | Brown |
|---|---|---|---|---|---|---|---|---|
| F. Chicago | | Farmer | | | | | | |
| Killed 1207-62 at Prairie Grove. Shot through the head. | | | | | | | | |

| Thompson, Johnson | | | C | 22 | 5'9" | Fair | Grey | Dark |
|---|---|---|---|---|---|---|---|---|
| B. Canada | | Farmer | Res. Wauconda, Res. 1885 Waukegan, Ill. | | | | | |
| Mustered Out 5-15-66 | | | | | | | | |

| Thompson, Robert | | | G | 19 | 5'9" | Dark | Brown | Black |
|---|---|---|---|---|---|---|---|---|
| B. Ohio | | Farmer | Res. Cheney's Grove | | | | | |
| Died 12-6-61 at Humansville. | | | | | | | | |

# THIRTY SEVENTH ILLINOIS

| Thompson, William M. | C | 22 | 5'8" | Fair | Grey | Dark |
|---|---|---|---|---|---|---|
| F. Canada | Farmer | | Re. Wauconda, Res. 1885 Waukegan, Ill. | | | |
| Discharged Disability 10-5-62. Scrofula, running sores at neck, enlarged lymph glands, possible syphilis. | | | | | | |

| Thornton, William | G | 40 | 5'5" | Florid | Grey | Light |
|---|---|---|---|---|---|---|
| B. England | Spinster | Res. Chicago | | | | |
| Died 10-27-62 in hospital at Springfield, Mo. Debility | | | | | | |

| Thrapp, William B | K | 21 | 5'8" | Dark | Blue | Brown |
|---|---|---|---|---|---|---|
| F. Vermilion Co. | Farmer | Res. Vermilion Co. Res. 1885 Keifersville, OH | | | | |
| Discharged Disability 6-17-64 | | | | | | |

| Titman, John | K | | | | | |
|---|---|---|---|---|---|---|
| F. Portland | | | | | 9-18-61 | |
| Not on muster roll. | | | | | | |

| Todd, Warfield B. | B | 24 | | | | |
|---|---|---|---|---|---|---|
| F. Lyon | | Res. 1885 Lafayette, Ill | | | | |
| Discharged Disability 1-16-62 at Lamine Crossing. Paralysis of right arm and leg. | | | | | | |

| Torkildson, Thomas | I | 14 | 5'4" | Light | Blue | Light |
|---|---|---|---|---|---|---|
| F. Norway | Student Musician | Enl. Chicago | | | | |
| | | | | | | |

| Tousley, Felix W. | G | 19 | 5'6" | Light | Grey | Light |
|---|---|---|---|---|---|---|
| B. Dewitt Co. Ill | Farmer | Res. Cheney's Grove, Res. 1885 Rinard, Ill. | | | | |
| Mustered Out 9-29-64 | | | | | | |

# DESCRIPTIVE ROLL

| Tousley, John V. | | | G | 22 | 5'5" | Light | Grey | Light |
|---|---|---|---|---|---|---|---|---|
| B. Jefferson Co. NY | | Farmer | Res. Cheney's Grove. Res. 1885 Lexington, Ill. | | | | | |
| Wounded 12-7-62 in left leg at Prairie Grove. Mustered Out 10-4-64 | | | | | | | | |

| Tripp, Gardner | | | I | 20 | 6'0" | Light | Grey | Brown |
|---|---|---|---|---|---|---|---|---|
| F. Bonus, Ill. | | Farmer | Res. Bonus | | | | | |
| Transferred 92d U.S. Colored Volunteers 9-27-63. | | | | | | | | |

| Trumbull, Horace | | | F | 22 | 5'9" | Dark | Brown | Black |
|---|---|---|---|---|---|---|---|---|
| B. Burlington, Vt | | Farmer | Res. Newport | | | | | |
| Died 12-8-61 at Syracuse, Mo. | | | | | | | | |

| Truesdale, Robert | | | H | 18 | 5'7" | Light | Blue | Light |
|---|---|---|---|---|---|---|---|---|
| B. Demarest, NJ | | Farmer | Res. Bloom | | | | | |
| Mustered Out 9-29-64 | | | | | | | | |

| Tubbs, Erastus M. | | | C | 25 | 6'0" | Fair | Blue | Dark |
|---|---|---|---|---|---|---|---|---|
| B. Essex Co. NJ | | Carpenter | Res. Springfield, Mo. | | | 7-27-62 | | |
| Deserted 2-23-63 at Camp Bliss, Mo. | | | | | | | | |

| Tupper, Darius | | | F | 20 | 5'6" | Light | Hazel | Light |
|---|---|---|---|---|---|---|---|---|
| B. Vermont | | Farmer | Res. Lyons | | | | | |
| Died 11-27-61 at Otterville. | | | | | | | | |

| Turpin, Richard | | | A | 22 | | | | |
|---|---|---|---|---|---|---|---|---|
| F. Coal Valley | | | | | | | | |
| 3 month volunteer 12th Ill. Regiment. Deserted 12-6-62. Took a Colt's Revolving Rifle. | | | | | | | | |

# U

# THIRTY SEVENTH ILLINOIS

| Upstone, Henry | | | I | 20 | 5'5" | Light | Dark | Brown |
|---|---|---|---|---|---|---|---|---|
| B. England | | Farmer | Res. Cherry Valley | | | | | |
| Discharged 12-31-62 at Springfield. Hereditary insanity. | | | | | | | | |

| Utgrains, Theodore | | | K | 32 | 5'5" | Dark | Blue | Dark |
|---|---|---|---|---|---|---|---|---|
| B. Belgium | | Laborer | Res. Danville | | | 12-24-63 | | |
| Mustered Out 5-15-66 | | | | | | | | |

# V

| Valentine, James | | | A | 28 | 5'9" | Light | Blue | Dark |
|---|---|---|---|---|---|---|---|---|
| B. Quincy, Ill. | | Harness-maker | Res. Camden | | | | | |
| Died 3-9-62. Musket ball in left side at Pea Ridge. | | | | | | | | |

| Vanvetcher, Jacob | | | A | 40 | | | | |
|---|---|---|---|---|---|---|---|---|
| | | | Enl. Rock Island | | | | | |
| Mustered Out 5-15-66 | | | | | | | | |

| Veath, George | | | E | 21 | 5'4" | Fair | Blue | Light |
|---|---|---|---|---|---|---|---|---|
| B. Brance | | Farmer | Res. Mendota | | | 10-1-62 | | |
| Died 8-23-63 at Vicksburg. | | | | | | | | |

| Vogres, Hezekiah | | | H | 18 | 5'5" | Dark | Brown | Brown |
|---|---|---|---|---|---|---|---|---|
| B. Venango, Pa. | | Farmer | Res. Morristown | | | | | |
| Died 8-6-63 at Port Hudson, La. | | | | | | | | |

| Vollmer, Lewis | | | H | 28 | 5'7" | Dark | Blue | Black |
|---|---|---|---|---|---|---|---|---|
| B. Soling, Prussia | | Black-smith | Res. Rock Island | | | | | |
| Discharged Disability 7-3-62. Epilepsy since early youth. | | | | | | | | |

# DESCRIPTIVE ROLL

| Von Hecke, Jacob | | | K | 45 | 5'5" | Dark | Grey | Brown |
|---|---|---|---|---|---|---|---|---|
| F. Bassville, Belgium | | Farmer | Res. Rock Island | | | | 8-14-61 | |
| Mustered Out 5-15-66. | | | | | | | | |

| Von Ullman, John | | | E | 31 | 5'5" | Dark | Brown | Dark |
|---|---|---|---|---|---|---|---|---|
| B. Berne | | Farmer | Res. Mendota | | | | | |
| Transferred Invalid Corps. Discharged Disability 11-19-63 | | | | | | | | |

| Voss, Oliver P. | | | G | 27 | 5'11" | Dark | Brown | Black |
|---|---|---|---|---|---|---|---|---|
| B. Butler Co. OH | | Farmer | Res. Cheney's Grove | | | | | |
| Died 4-14-64 of suicide or smallpox at Noblesville, Ind. | | | | | | | | |

# W

| Wade, James B. | | | G | 21 | 5'8" | Light | Blue | Dark |
|---|---|---|---|---|---|---|---|---|
| B. Harrison Co In | | Farmer | Res. East Bend | | | | | |
| Mustered Out 9-29-64 | | | | | | | | |

| Wadsworth, John | | | A | 22 | 5'5" | Fair | Hazel | Auburn |
|---|---|---|---|---|---|---|---|---|
| B. Ireland | | Farmer | Res. Preemption | | | | 11-9-64 | |
| Mustered Out 10-9-64 | | | | | | | | |

| Wagner, Damien | | | E | 18 | 5'5" | Fair | Hazel | Brown |
|---|---|---|---|---|---|---|---|---|
| B. Waldorf, Germany | | Farmer | Enl. Alton, Ill. | | | | 3-28-62 | |
| Mustered Out 5-15-66 | | | | | | | | |

| Walsh, Peter | | | K | 19 | 5'6" | Dark | Brown | Brown |
|---|---|---|---|---|---|---|---|---|
| F. New York | | Student | Res. Danville | | | | | |
| Mustered Out 10-4-64 | | | | | | | | |

# THIRTY SEVENTH ILLINOIS

| Walton, Robert E. | | C | 23 | | | | |
|---|---|---|---|---|---|---|---|
| | | Enl. Wauconda. Res. 1885 Chicago, Ill. | | | | | |
| Wounded at Pea Ridge. Mustered Out 10-4-64. | | | | | | | |

| Ward, John L. | | E | 18 | 5'9" | Fair | Grey | Grey |
|---|---|---|---|---|---|---|---|
| B. Indiana | Farmer | Enl. Charleston | | | 6-21-64 | | |
| | | | | | | | |

| Ward, John S. | | C | 23 | 6'0" | Fair | Brown | Dark |
|---|---|---|---|---|---|---|---|
| B. Crawford Co. Pa. | Farmer | Res. Avon | | | | | |
| Died 11-18-61 at Boonville. Measles. | | | | | | | |

| Ward, William B. | | E | 20 | 5'8" | Dark | Brown | Dark |
|---|---|---|---|---|---|---|---|
| F. Hendrick Co. Ind. | Farmer | Enl. Olney, Ill. Res. 1885 Rose Hill, Ill. | | | 3-2-65 | | |
| Mustered Out 3-6-66 | | | | | | | |

| Watkins, Francis M. | | G | 24 | 5'9" | Florid | Blue | Sandy |
|---|---|---|---|---|---|---|---|
| B. Montgomery Co. Ind. | Farmer | Res. Yellow Head, Wis. | | | | | |
| Mustered Out 10-4-64 | | | | | | | |

| Watkins, Perry | | A | 22 | | | | |
|---|---|---|---|---|---|---|---|
| F. Sparta, Wis. | | Enl. Rock Island | | | | | |
| Mustered Out 9-29-64 | | | | | | | |

| Weatherly, Edwin A. | | E | 18 | 5'8" | Fair | Blue | Light |
|---|---|---|---|---|---|---|---|
| B. Livingston, Ny | Farmer | Res. Kensoha, Wis. | | | | | |
| Discharged Disability 1-17-63. Gunshot wound in foot. | | | | | | | |

| Weatherly, Elias | | C | 20 | 5'8" | Fair | Grey | Light |
|---|---|---|---|---|---|---|---|
| B. Winnebago, Ill | Farmer | Res. Wauconda | | | | | |
| Mustered Out 3-23-66 | | | | | | | |

# DESCRIPTIVE ROLL

| Weaver, Alexander T. | | C | 21 | 5'11" | Light | Light | Light |
|---|---|---|---|---|---|---|---|
| F. Barrington | Farmer | | | | | | |
| Died 3-19-62 at Springfield. Typhoid fever. | | | | | | | |

| Webb, Austin | | A | 20 | | | | |
|---|---|---|---|---|---|---|---|
| F. Rock Island | | Enl. Rock Island | | | 8-14-61 | | |
| Mustered Out 10-4-64 | | | | | | | |

| Webster, Albert | | K | 19 | 5'8" | Fair | Hazel | Black |
|---|---|---|---|---|---|---|---|
| F. Saline, Mich | Clerk | Res. Danville | | | | | |
| Deserted. Joined regular service. | | | | | | | |

| Weeks, Wesley | | F | 24 | 5'8" | Dark | Grey | Dark |
|---|---|---|---|---|---|---|---|
| B. Cook Co. Ill | Farmer | Res. Lyons | | | | | |
| Died 1-23-64 at Brownsville. Disease. | | | | | | | |

| Welch, Michael | | I | 22 | 5'10" | Light | Grey | Brown |
|---|---|---|---|---|---|---|---|
| B. Ireland | Farmer | Res. Belvedere | | | 8-9-61 | | |
| Mustered Out 10-4-64 | | | | | | | |

| Welch, Robert | | K | 18 | 5'11" | Dark | Blue | Black |
|---|---|---|---|---|---|---|---|
| F. Lenox, Mass. | Farmer | Res. Vermilion Co. | | | | | |
| Mustered Out 10-4-64 | | | | | | | |

| Welch, William | | A | 27 | 5'5" | Light | Blue | Sandy |
|---|---|---|---|---|---|---|---|
| B. Fermanaugh, Ieland | Farmer | Res. Preemption, Res. 1885 Firth, Nebraska | | | 8-14-62 | | |
| Mustered Out 6-12-65 | | | | | | | |

| Wells, Edmond P. | | F | 24 | 5'7" | Dark | Grey | Dark |
|---|---|---|---|---|---|---|---|
| B. Cook Co. | Farmer | Res. Lyons, Res. 1885 Cameron, Missouri | | | | | |
| | | | | | | | |

# THIRTY SEVENTH ILLINOIS

| Wells, Jackson | | | H | 23 | 5'4" | Light | Blue | Auburn |
|---|---|---|---|---|---|---|---|---|
| B. New York | | Farmer | Res. Pippin, Wis. | | | | | |
| Discharged Disability 11-17-65 | | | | | | | | |

| Wells, Wilder E. | | | E | 20 | 5'7" | Light | Grey | Light |
|---|---|---|---|---|---|---|---|---|
| B. Bureau Co. Ill | | Farmer | Res. Mendota, Res. 1885 Oslo, Nebraska | | | | | |
| Mustered Out 10-4-64 | | | | | | | | |

| Welsh, Daniel | | | I | 19 | 5'6" | Light | Grey | Brown |
|---|---|---|---|---|---|---|---|---|
| B. Ireland | | Farmer | Res. Belvidere | | | | 8-30-61 | |
| Deserted 5-14-63 at St. Louis. | | | | | | | | |

| Welsh, James N. | | | C | 34 | | | | |
|---|---|---|---|---|---|---|---|---|
| F. Fremont | | | | | | | | |
| Accidentally shot 10-13-61. Absent sick in Kenosha, Wis. 8-18-62. Not heard from again. | | | | | | | | |

| Wesher, Joseph | | | E | 21 | 5'6" | Light | Brown | Dark |
|---|---|---|---|---|---|---|---|---|
| B. Alsace, France | | Butch-er | Enl. Mendota | | | | 12-10-62 | |
| Mustered Out 1-11-66 | | | | | | | | |

| West, William F. | | | A | 20 | | | | |
|---|---|---|---|---|---|---|---|---|
| F. Rock Island | | | | | | | | |
| Left sick at Ironton 6-3-63. Transferred to Invalid Corps 8-1-63. | | | | | | | | |

| Wetzler, Morris | | | G | 18 | | | | |
|---|---|---|---|---|---|---|---|---|
| F. Rock Island | | | | | | | | |
| Transferred 1-3-64 2d Lieutenant, 5th Infantry Corps D'Afrique. | | | | | | | | |

| Whaples, James | | | F | 20 | 5'3" | Light | Blue | Sandy |
|---|---|---|---|---|---|---|---|---|
| B. Lake Co. OH | | Farmer | Res. Antioch | | | | | |
| Mustered Out 10-4-64 | | | | | | | | |

# DESCRIPTIVE ROLL

| Whitcomb, Orin A. | | H | 24 | 5'10" | Light | Grey | Auburn |
|---|---|---|---|---|---|---|---|
| B. New York | Musician | Res. Moline, Res. 1885 Springfield, MO ||||||
| Discharged 7-2-63 |||||||||

| White, David | | A | 20 | 5'5" | Dark | Brown | Brown |
|---|---|---|---|---|---|---|---|
| B. Philadelphia | Morocco Finisher | Res. Preemption ||||||
| Deserted 3-1-63 from Camp Bliss. |||||||||

| White, Franklin | | A | 23 | | | | |
|---|---|---|---|---|---|---|---|
| F. Richland Grove | | Res. 1885 Cable, Ill. ||||||
| Mustered Out 10-4-64 |||||||||

| White, Julius (Staff) | | | 45 | | | | |
|---|---|---|---|---|---|---|---|
| B. New York | Real Estate, Insurance | Res. Evanston, Res. 1885 Evanston, Ill. ||||||
| Promoted and transferred to Virginia 7-1-62. |||||||||

| Whitehead, Albert | | B | 20 | 5'5" | Dark | Grey | Light |
|---|---|---|---|---|---|---|---|
| B. Kent, England | | Res. Lynn, Res. 1885 Limeston, Kansas ||||||
| Mustered Out 9-29-64 |||||||||

| Whitehead, Harrison | | H | 22 | 5'6" | Sandy | Hazel | Brown |
|---|---|---|---|---|---|---|---|
| B. Indiana | Blacksmith | Res. Geneseo, Res. 1885 Geneseo, Ill. ||||||
| Mustered Out 5-15-66 |||||||||

| Whitney, Arthur | | C | 22 | | | | |
|---|---|---|---|---|---|---|---|
| F. Avon | | | | | | | |
| Died 3-13-63 at Springfield. Wounds. |||||||||

| Whitney, Charles W. | | G | 24 | 5'9" | Light | Grey | Black |
|---|---|---|---|---|---|---|---|
| B. Oswego Co Ny | Farmer | Res. East Bend ||||||
| Transferred to 92d U.S. Colored Volunteers 9-27-63 |||||||||

# THIRTY SEVENTH ILLINOIS

| Whitsell, John C. | | | A | 19 | 5'6" | Light | Blue | Brown |
|---|---|---|---|---|---|---|---|---|
| B. Darlington, Ill | | Farmer | Res. Rock Island | | | | | |
| Killed 3-7-62 at Pea Ridge. Musket ball in the head. | | | | | | | | |

| Widner, John | | | F | 18 | 5'10" | Light | Light | Light |
|---|---|---|---|---|---|---|---|---|
| B. Noble Co. Ind | | Farmer | Res. Moline, Res. 1885, Silver Lake, Kansas | | | 2-20-64 | | |
| Mustered Out 5-15-66. | | | | | | | | |

| Wiffin, Frederick | | | I | 18 | 5'10" | Sallow | Grey | Dark |
|---|---|---|---|---|---|---|---|---|
| B. England | | Farmer | Res. Garden Prairie, Res. 1885 Belvidere, Ill. | | | 9-5-61 | | |
| On furlough at muster out of regiment. | | | | | | | | |

| Wilber, Henry H. | | | B | 19 | 5'8" | Light | Grey | Sandy |
|---|---|---|---|---|---|---|---|---|
| B. Franklin, Vt | | Farmer | Res. Lynn | | | | | |
| Discharged Disability 10-14-63 at Carrolton. Wounds. | | | | | | | | |

| Wilcox, George J.A. | | | I | 19 | 5'6" | Light | Blue | Brown |
|---|---|---|---|---|---|---|---|---|
| B. Tioga, Pa. | | Farmer | Res. Boone, Enl. Chemung, Res. 1885 Capron, Ill. | | | 9-8-61 | | |
| Mustered Out 10-4-64 | | | | | | | | |

| Wilcox, James | | | E | 20 | 5'9" | Fair | Grey | Black |
|---|---|---|---|---|---|---|---|---|
| B. Steuben Co Ny | | Farmer | Res. Osage | | | 3-7-64 | | |
| Mustered Out 5-15-66 | | | | | | | | |

| Wilcox, Martin | | | B | 26 | 5'8" | Dark | Blue | Black |
|---|---|---|---|---|---|---|---|---|
| B. Ledyard, CT | | Farmer | Res. Goshen | | | | | |
| Mustered Out 5-15-66 | | | | | | | | |

# DESCRIPTIVE ROLL

| Wilkinson, Alexander | | E | 26 | 5'10" | Dark | Brown | Black |
|---|---|---|---|---|---|---|---|
| B. Green Co. Ill | Farmer | | | | | 9-20-61 | |
| Deserted 2-15-62 on march between Springfield and Cassville. ||||||||

| Wilkinson, Temple | B | 28 | | | | |
|---|---|---|---|---|---|---|
| F. Lynn | | | | | | |
| Mustered Out 10-4-64 |||||||

| Wilks, George | | H | 36 | 5'5" | Dark | Hazel | Brown |
|---|---|---|---|---|---|---|---|
| B. Warwickshire, Enland | Black-smith | Res. Rock Island | | | | | |
| Mustered Out 10-4-64 ||||||||

| Williams, Charles G. | | D | 19 | | | |
|---|---|---|---|---|---|---|
| F. Cook Co. | | Res. 1885 Tecumseh, Nebraska ||||||
| |||||||

| Williams, Herman S. | | H | 22 | 5'5" | Light | Blue | Light |
|---|---|---|---|---|---|---|---|
| B. Pennsylvania | Farmer | Res. Deamington | | | | | |
| Mustered Out 5-15-66 ||||||||

| Williams, Isaac K. | | A | 21 | 5'8" | Light | Blue | Dark |
|---|---|---|---|---|---|---|---|
| B. Greenville, Pa. | Farmer | Res. Rock Island | | | | | |
| Died 3-20-62 at Cassville. Wounded in left side by musket ball at Pea Ridge. ||||||||

| Williams, John | | K | 21 | 5'7" | Dark | Blue | Dark |
|---|---|---|---|---|---|---|---|
| F. Libertyville | | | | | | | |
| Deserted 3-2-62 from Cross Timbers, Arkansas. ||||||||

| Williams Lewis D. | | F | 23 | 6'3" | Dark | Hazel | Sandy |
|---|---|---|---|---|---|---|---|
| B. Madison, NY | Farmer | Res. Libertyville, Res. 1885 Beliot, Kansas |||||||
| Discharged 7-10-62 ||||||||

# THIRTY SEVENTH ILLINOIS

| Williams, Thomas J. | A | 21 | 6'2" | Fair | Blue | Brown |
|---|---|---|---|---|---|---|
| B. Jerseyville, NJ | Farmer | | | | 8-27-62 | |
| Mustered Out 6-12-65 ||||||||

| Williams, Warren | F | 26 | 5'10" | Dark | Grey | Dark |
|---|---|---|---|---|---|---|
| B. Fairfield, Conn | Farmer | Res. Antioch, Res. 1885 Antioch, Ill. ||||
| Resigned 2-29-64 |||||||

| Williamson, Thomas | A | 25 | 5'6" | Dark | Brown | Black |
|---|---|---|---|---|---|---|
| B. South Mahoning, Iowa | Farmer | Res. Deamington ||||
| Killed 3-7-62 at Pea Ridege by musket ball in breast. |||||||

| Willis, Kendall | H | 28 | 5'4" | Dark | Hazel | Brown |
|---|---|---|---|---|---|---|
| B. Maryland | Farmer | Res. Moline ||||
| Killed 3-7-62 at Pea Ridge. |||||||

| Wilson, Andrew | A | 25 | 5'6" | Light | Brwn | Brown |
|---|---|---|---|---|---|---|
| B. Donegal, Ireland | Laborer | Res. Preemption ||||
| Died 2-24-64 at home |||||||

| Wilson, James H. | H | 27 | 5'10" | Light | Blue | Auburn |
|---|---|---|---|---|---|---|
| B. Bradford Co Pa | Clerk | Res. Rock Island ||||
| Discharged Disability 4-16-62 |||||||

| Wilson, John M. | E | 49 | 5'11" | Light | Blue | Light |
|---|---|---|---|---|---|---|
| | | Enl. Jasper Co. Ill. ||| 8-20-62 | |
| Discharged 11-20-65 from confinement at Springfield, Ill. |||||||

| Wilson, William C. | H | 22 | 5'11" | Light | Grey | Brown |
|---|---|---|---|---|---|---|
| B. Christiana, Norway | Farmer | Res. Morristown, Res. 1885 Wellington, Kansas ||||
| Mustered Out 5-15-66 |||||||

DESCRIPTIVE ROLL

| Wilson, William R. | | C | 20 | | | | |
|---|---|---|---|---|---|---|---|
| F. Antioch | | | | | | | |
| Transferred to 92d U.S. Colored Volunteers 10-19-63 | | | | | | | |

| Winehamer, John A. | | E | 22 | 5'8" | Light | Blue | Auburn |
|---|---|---|---|---|---|---|---|
| B. Germany | Farmer | Res. Mendota, Res. 1885 Panola Station Ill. | | | | | |
| Mustered Out 3-23-66. | | | | | | | |

| Winn, Irvin | | G | 33 | 5'7" | Light | Blue | Auburn |
|---|---|---|---|---|---|---|---|
| B. Sullivan Co. Tenn | Painter | Res. Cheney's Grove | | | | | |
| Deserted 5-8-62 | | | | | | | |

| Wire, Nehemiah | | D | 21 | | | | |
|---|---|---|---|---|---|---|---|
| F. Lena, Ill. | | | | | | | |
| Killed 3-7-62 at Pea Ridge. | | | | | | | |

| Witt, John B. | | F | 21 | 5'9" | Light | Brwn | Light |
|---|---|---|---|---|---|---|---|
| B. Will Co. Ill | Farmer | Res. Lyons | | | | | |
| Died 5-13-63 of wounds. | | | | | | | |

| Witzerman, John | | E | 35 | 5'10" | Light | Blue | Light |
|---|---|---|---|---|---|---|---|
| B. Germany | Farmer | Enl. Alton, Ill., Res. 1885 Manville, Ill. | | | 1-18-64 | | |
| Discharged Disability 11-13-65. Gunshot wounds. | | | | | | | |

| Wolford, Herman | | H | 30 | 5'11" | Light | Brwn | Brown |
|---|---|---|---|---|---|---|---|
| B. Soligen, Prussia | Butcher | Res. Rock Island | | | | | |
| Discharged 7-13-65 | | | | | | | |

| Wood, Alonzo C. | | C | 18 | 5'6" | Fair | Light | Grey |
|---|---|---|---|---|---|---|---|
| B. Canada | Mason | Res. Waukegan, Res. 1885 Chicago | | | 12-8-61 | | |
| | | | | | | | |

# THIRTY SEVENTH ILLINOIS

| Wood, William H. | | H | 24 | 5'6" | Dark | Brown | Black |
|---|---|---|---|---|---|---|---|
| B. France | Baker | Res. Edgington | | | 11-15-61 | | |
| Put under arrest as deserter from 1st Regiment Kansas Volunteers. | | | | | | | |

| Woodring, Peter | | H | 18 | 5'7" | Dark | Grey | Black |
|---|---|---|---|---|---|---|---|
| B. Northumber-land Co. Pa. | Farmer | Res. Durand | | | | | |
| Mustered Out 5-15-66 | | | | | | | |

| Woodruff, Edward | | A | 24 | | | | |
|---|---|---|---|---|---|---|---|
| F. Neelysville | | | | | | | |
| Mustered Out 10-4-64 | | | | | | | |

| Woods, Zera M. | | G | 29 | 5'8" | Light | Grey | Light |
|---|---|---|---|---|---|---|---|
| B. St. Clair, Mich | Baker | Res. Chicago | | | | | |
| Died 12-26-64 at Devall's Bluff. Wounds. | | | | | | | |

| Wooley, Eugene | | D | 22 | 5'4" | Light | Grey | Light |
|---|---|---|---|---|---|---|---|
| B. Ohio | Farmer | Res. Lena | | | | | |
| Killed 11-12-65 while attempting to force the Provost Guards while in confinement at Beaumont, Texas. | | | | | | | |

| Woolsy, Henry C. | | E | 20 | 5'11" | Light | Grey | Red |
|---|---|---|---|---|---|---|---|
| B. Knox Co. Ill | Farmer | Enl. New Orleans | | | 1-21-64 | | |
| Deserted at Houston 2-13-66 | | | | | | | |

| Wooster, James Clark | | I | 22 | 5'8" | Light | Blue | Brown |
|---|---|---|---|---|---|---|---|
| B. McHenry Co. Ill | Farmer | Res. Chemung, Res. 1885 Sheboygan, Mich. | | | 9-8-61 | | |
| Discharged Disability 7-28-62 at St. Louis. | | | | | | | |

| Work, William W. | | E | 18 | 5'9" | Fair | Brown | Black |
|---|---|---|---|---|---|---|---|
| B. Marshall Co Ill | Farmer | Res. Osage | | | 3-7-64 | | |
| Mustered Out 3-9-66 | | | | | | | |

# DESCRIPTIVE ROLL

| Worman, Thomas J. | | E | 35 | 5'8" | Light | Hazel | Dark |
|---|---|---|---|---|---|---|---|
| B. Virginia | Carpenter | Res. Mendota, Res. 1885 Rock Falls, Ill. | | | | | |
| Discharged Disability 8-29-62. Venereal Disease causing rheumatism, etc. | | | | | | | |

| Wright, U. | | K | 34 | 5'8" | Dark | Brown | Dark |
|---|---|---|---|---|---|---|---|
| B. Montgomery, Ohio | Laborer | Enl. Danville | | | 4-7-64 | | |
| Deserted from Hospital at New Orleans after June 1865. | | | | | | | |

| Wyman, James S. | | B | 25 | 5'8" | Light | Hazel | Sandy |
|---|---|---|---|---|---|---|---|
| B. Berwick, Me. | Farmer | Res. Lynn | | | 1-13-65 | | |
| Mustered Out 1-13-66. | | | | | | | |

| Wyman, James | | B | 20 | 5'6" | Dark | Brown | Sandy |
|---|---|---|---|---|---|---|---|
| B. Berwick, Me. | Farmer | Res. Lynn | | | | | |
| Discharged Disability 10-14-62. Severely wounded in the groin. | | | | | | | |

# Y

| Yates, Ferdinand | | C | 20 | 5'7" | Fair | Blue | Light |
|---|---|---|---|---|---|---|---|
| B. Germany | Farmer | Res. Warren | | | | | |
| Discharged Disability 8-28-62. Idiotic by reason of mental incapacity. | | | | | | | |

| Yates, Uziel | | H | 21 | 5'5" | Fair | Hazel | Brown |
|---|---|---|---|---|---|---|---|
| B. Lake Co. Ill | Farmer | Res. Warren | | | | | |
| Died 11-30-63 at New Orleans. | | | | | | | |

| Yeager, John | | H | | | | | |
|---|---|---|---|---|---|---|---|
| F. Morristown | | Res. 1885 Hastings, Neb. | | | | | |
| Taken prisoner 9-29-63 at Morganzia. Mustered Out 9-29-64. | | | | | | | |

# THIRTY SEVENTH ILLINOIS

| Yeager, Peter | | | H | 20 | 5'4" | Light | Blue | Auburn |
|---|---|---|---|---|---|---|---|---|
| B. Pennsylvania | | Farmer | Res. Morristown, Res. 1885 Moline, Ill. | | | | | |
| Discharged Disability 10-5-62 at Newtonia. Gunshot wounds in leg. | | | | | | | | |

| Young, George W. | | | E | 18 | 5'4" | Fair | Blue | Light |
|---|---|---|---|---|---|---|---|---|
| F. Jasper Co. Ill | | Farmer | Enl. Charleston | | | 1-20-64 | | |
| Mustered Out 5-15-66 | | | | | | | | |

| Young, Hosea H. | | | G | 18 | 5'7" | Dark | Brown | Dark |
|---|---|---|---|---|---|---|---|---|
| B. Pike Hollow, NY | | Farmer | Res. Plato, Res. 1885 Unionville, Michigan | | | | | |
| Absent sick at Muster Out of Regiment. | | | | | | | | |

| Young, Orlando | | | C | 18 | | | | |
|---|---|---|---|---|---|---|---|---|
| F. Fremont | | | | | | | | |
| Died 5-18-62 at Cassville. Typhoid fever. | | | | | | | | |

| Young, Samuel W. | | | B | 20 | 5'8" | Dark | Grey | Light |
|---|---|---|---|---|---|---|---|---|
| B. Marion, Pa. | | Farmer | Res. Toulon, Res. 1885 Houston, Texas | | | | | |
| Mustered Out 5-15-66 | | | | | | | | |

DESCRIPTIVE ROLL

## CONSOLIDATION

In late 1865, three understrength Illinois Regiments (76th, 94th, and 97th Illinois Infantry) were phased out of service. Men of those units were consolidated into the 37th to serve out their remaining enlistment time. Time spent with the 37th varied from several weeks to seven months. Names of these men who served briefly in the 37th are listed below with the number of their original regiment. More complete personnel data may be found in National Archives Record Group 94 filed under their original regimental commands.

# THIRTY SEVENTH ILLINOIS

## A

Addington, Randolph 94
Aikens, George W 97
Albert, Henry 94
Alott, Benjamin 76
Anderson, John 97
Arnold, George 76
Arnold, Stephen W. 97
Arpin, Edward 76
Altes, Henry 94
Andrews, William 97

## B

Ball, Clinton 97
Ball, Jesse 97
Barnes, John F. 94
Barrett, Andrew J. 97
Barthelow, Emery C. 94
Barthelow, James N. 94
Barthlow, Jacob 97
Barthlow, Samuel 97
Bean, Francis 76
Beaumont, Charles E. 76
Beekman, Henry 76
Bell, Jessie 97
Bellren, James 94
Benefiel, Francis 97
Bennett, Charles 94
Bennett, Harry 94
Bennett, Joseph 94
Benson, Sylvester 94
Bishop, John E. 76
Bishop, William 94
Blair, Alexander C. 94

Blakely, Seth W. 94
Boner, Jeremiah 76
Boots, William E. 76
Boyd, William T. 76
Brannon, Charles W. 97
Brash, David E. 76
Breese, John 97
Brennan, John 97
Bridges, John 97
Briggerman, Henry 97
Brooks, Elias 97
Brown, Abraham 94
Brown, Denny W. 76
Brown, Joseph 94
Brown, Thomas 76
Brown, William 94
Buckmaster, Charles W 97
Burton, George W. 97

## C

Calahan, John 97
Campbell, James 94
Campbell, William M. 97
Caravan, Lewis 76
Carkoff, John 97
Carothers, Alexander 76
Carroll, Charles 97
Carter, Thomas 97
Carter, William 97
Carther, William 97
Case, James 97
Caslick, Nicholas 97
Cassell, Benjamin 76
Caven, Stephen D. 76
Chambers, John 97

u
Chapman, Joseph 76
Chartie, Joseph 76
Christy, Patrick 94
Clark, John 97
Clark, Joseph 97
Clayton, William 97
Cloyd, Henry F. 76
Cole, David 97
Conger, Robert M. 94
Conger, Samuel O. 94
Constantine, Alfred 76
Coons, Fred A.M. 97
Corbin, Andrew J. 76
Cox, Andrew J. 76
Craig, Leander 94
Crookshanks, John 94
Crose, Truman 94
Curran, John 94
Cutler, John 94

**D**

Daniels, William 94
David, Jacob P. 97
Davidson, James 94
Davis, Cyrus W. 97
Davis, Joseph 97
Day, Philander R. 94
Denman, William 94
Dennis, Thomas 94
Devine, Bernard 97
Deyer, Andrew 97
Dickinson, Merritt 94
Ditters, Charles 76
Dodson, Emerzick 97
Doyle, Thomas 97

Doyle, Henry 97
Dugan, John 97
Dunbar, Jasper 97
Dunn, James 97
Dwiggins, David 97

**E**

Edwards, George 97
Eisle, Gottlieb 76
Eldridge, John 97
Elkins, Joel 97
Endsley, James C. 76
English, Philip 97
Enslow, George M. 97
Epperson, John 94
Etter, Sebastine 97
Evans, Eli T. 94
Evans, John D. 94
Evering, John H. 97
Evland, Joseph 97
Evland, William B. 97
Ewing, George 97

**F**

Fairman, Foster N. 76
Falley, Patrick 97
Finn, Patrick 97
Finully, Alexander 94
Fitts, Andrew 97
Ford, William 97
Forest, Bayles 97
Forsyth, Nelson 94
Frame, Jeremiah 97
Fuller, Samuel D. 76

# THIRTY SEVENTH ILLINOIS

Funk, Peter 97

## G

Garrick, Harrison 97
Gates, David A. 76
Gates, Thomas G. 76
Gaugron, Gilbert 76
Gaugron, Lewis 76
Gay, Christopher 94
Giles, Jacob 97
Glassmaker, Warren 97
Goodard, Francis 94
Gorden, William 97
Graham, Robert 76
Grant, John 76
Grary, William A. 97
Graves, John H. 97
Gray, Eleaser 76
Greenwood, Zaiarn 76
Greeson, David C. 97
Greeson, Henry O. 97
Gilliland, William 76
Grice, Daniel G. 76
Griggs, Henry 76
Griggs, Lawson P. 76
Grojean, Francis 97

## H

Haith, Gabriel 76
Haley, James 97
Hall, Charles 97
Hall, Obediah 94
Hamilton, John B. 97

Hand, Joseph 76
Handy, James 97
Handwick, William 76
Haney, John A. 76
Hanna, Thomas J. 97
Harper, Hiram C. 97
Harris, Louis 97
Hart, Miles 76
Harting, Isiah 76
Hays, James K. 97
Hayes, Samuel 94
Hazel, John B. 94
Heath, Jeremiah 97
Hefner, George M. 94
Heller, Joshua 76
Herring, John S. 94
Hines, Hervey B. 94
Hodgdon, George 97
Holland, John 76
Holland, William 97
Hoop, Joseph 76
Hooton, Milton 94
Hughes, William 76
Hunter, William 94
Hutton, Isaac 97
Hyndes, Lawrence 76

## I

Ives, Isaac N. 94

## J

Jackson, William 97
James, Robert 97
James, Samuel L. 97

DESCRIPTIVE ROLL

Jennings, Darius E. 76
Johnson, Charles W. 94
Johnson, Edward 97
Johnson, James 97
Jones, Allen S. 97
Jones, Ephriam M. 97
Jones, George H. 94
Jones, George W. 94
Jones, Isaac 76
Jones, James 97
Jones, John W. 94

**K**

Kaith, Gabriel 76
Kamp, John 94
Kamp, Peter 94
Kelley, John M. 94
Kelsey, Orison 76
Kemp, James W. 97
Kennan, Joseph 76
Kerman, Edward 94
Kerr, Thomasa P. 94
Kerr, William 94
Kimber, Thomas 94
Kinney, Joseph M. 76
Kirby, John 76
Kraimer, Augustus 97
Kraimer, Henry 97

**L**

Labrie, Joseph E. 76
Laflain, Frank 76
Lafleur, Charles S. 76
Langler, Moses 76

Leach, George W. 97
Lee, James 97
Lesage, Desire 76
Letter, John 94
Linderman, Frederick 97
Lisle, George 94
Loiselle, Frank 76
Long, Daniel W. 76
Lordermilk, Anderson 76
Lyman, Jackson 76

**M**

Maberry, David 94
Mahan, George L. 94
Marcott, Joseph 76
Martin, Joseph 97
Martin, Meador 76
Masher, Joseph 94
Mathie, William 97
McBride, Thomas 97
McCabe, Charles E. 97
McComus, Oliver 94
McCulloch, Thomas 94
McGraw, James 97
McGuire, James 97
McLaine, Charles 94
McStaunton, John B. 97
Menard Maxime 76
Merrifield, John 94
Meyers, Eli 76
Meyers, Louis 76
Mickels, William H. 76
Miller, Erastus 94
Miller, Samuel 94
Miller, William J. 76

# THIRTY SEVENTH ILLINOIS

Montgomery, Henry E. 76
Moore, William 94
Moore, William A. 76
Moran, Thomas 76
Morgan, William H. 94
Morris, David 97
Morrison, Edward 97
Milot, William R. 76
Morphy, John 97
Myers, William 94

## N

Neffrigger, Valentine 94
Nutt, Daniel D. 97

## O

O'Donnell, Patrick 94
Orr, John H. 97
Osborn, Charles 76
Osborn, Jacob 97
Otis, George 76
Otis, Joseph 76
Ostrander, Charles 76

## P

Paddock, Henry C. 76
Palmiton, Charles A. 97
Parmely, William P. 76
Parmentier, Leander 76
Parmentier, Pierre 76
Paudent, Prudent 76
Pope, Richard 97
Parrish, Isaac 97

Pearson, Joseph 94
Perry, Oliver H. 97
Perryman, Joseph 97
Petrie, Louis 76
Pierson, Willis S. 94
Powers, David 97
Powers, Edward B. 94
Powers, William 97
Pratt, Robert N. 94

## R

Racine, Louis 97
Racine, Joseph 97
Ramsay, Samuel 97
Randall, Ancil B. 76
Rees, Ebenezer 76
Reeves, Alfred C. 97
Reeves, James R 97
Regnier, Joseph 76
Regnier, Moize 76
Renkal, John 94
Reynolds, William 94
Rhodes, Waifield 94
Richmond, Milton 97
Ricketts, James 94
Rike, William 94
Robb, Wallace 76
Roberts, William 94
Robidon, John 97
Robisho, Jacob 76
Rockey, Christian 94
Rockhold, William 94
Rodd, Timothy 76
Roush, Jacob 76
Rohu, Charles 97

DESCRIPTIVE ROLL

Rosette, Lewis 76
Rudolph, Jacob 97
Ryburn, David G. 94
Ryburn, Samuel J. 94

**S**

St. Pierre, Lewis 76
Sandy, Phillip 97
Sapp, David 76
Schrier, John 97
Seeger, Louis 76
Selsea Francis W. 76
Shaw, William J. 94
Sicard, John 76
Sindes, Jacob A.J. 76
Single, John 94
Smith, Henry W. 94
Smith Jeremiah W. 97
Snow, Barney 76
Sparks, Otto 97
Spears, John B. 76
Spivey, Daniel 76
Spron, Jacob O. 97
Steed, James 97
Steed, Thomas 97
Stewart, Duncan 94
Stringfield, Charles 94
Stahl, Lewis P. 94
Stephen, William 97
Stone, John 94
Stroup, John 94
Sullivan, John 94
Swain, Aza 97
Sweetland, Henry 97

**T**

Tatro, James 76
Tevis, Lemoine 97
Thomas, Asa B. 76
Todd, Isiah 76
Todd, Joseph 76
Torbett, James W. 97
Townsend, Eli 97
Trimmer, John F. 94
Turner, James 94
Turnipseed, Thomas 94
Turpin, Daniel 94

**U**

Unbanhower, William 76

**V**

Vance, Tayler 94
Vancurien, Henry 76
Vandever, Jacob 94
Vankirk, Thomas M. 76
Vanscayal, Stephen 76

**W**

Wadkins, William 94
Wagner, Damon 97
Wagner, George M. 76
Wagner, Theodore 97
Walker, John 97
Walters, Martin 76
Ward, John L. 97
Ward, William B. 97

# THIRTY SEVENTH ILLINOIS

Warren, James T. 97

Webb, Jesse 97
White, David 94
White, Silas B. 76
Wicker, John L. 97
Wiley, Henry 97
Wilkinson, John 94
Williams, Albert 94
Williams, Albyn 97
Williams, Charles 94
Williams, Charles G. 76
Williams, John M. 97
Williams, Joseph 97
Williams, Simeon 97
Williamson, James K.P 76
Willis, Peter W. 76
Wilson, Alexander 76
Wilson, John M. 97
Wilson, William 97
Witzerman, John 97
Wood, Albert M. 76
Wood, William 97
Woolsey, Henry 97
Wood, Allen 94
Worthy, Benjamin 97
Wright, Sanford M. 76

## Y

Young, George M. 97[1]
Young, John M. 94
Young, Joseph 76

## Z

Zisk, George W. 97

# Notes

## ABBREVIATION KEY TO NOTES

**JCBF**
The John Charles Black Family manuscript collection in the Manuscript Division of the Illinois State Historical Library, Springfield, Illinois

**EBP**
Letters of Eugene B. Payne to his fiancée/wife, Adelia, in the author's collection.

**HCJR**
Letters of Henry Curtis to his wife or mother, in the collection of the United States Army Military History Institute, Carlisle Barracks, Pennsylvania.

**DASH**
Letters of David Ash to his finance/wife, Eliza, in the collection of the United States Army Military History Institute, Carlisle Barracks, Pennsylvania.

**RCN**
Journal of Alcander Morse, courtesy of Robert C. Nash, Sr.

**OBNA**
Order, Endorsement, Hospital Books or miscellaneous papers of the 37th Illinois Volunteer Infantry Regiment, Record Group 94, National Archives, Washington, D.C.

**SRNA**
Individual Compiled Service Records, 37th Illinois Infantry Regiment, Record Group 94, National Archives, Washington, D.C.

# THIRTY SEVENTH ILLINOIS

**RRIA**
Records, 37th Illinois Infantry Regiment, Illinois State Archives, Springfield, Illinois.

**WWG**
Extract, Waukegan Weekly Gazette Newspaper, published at Waukegan, Illinois.

**RIU**
Extract, Rock Island Union newspaper, published at Rock Island, Illinois.

**RIA**
Extract, Rock Island Argus newspaper, published at Rock Island, Illinois.

**CTR**
Extract, Chicago Tribune newspaper, published at Chicago, Illinois.

**HTEL**
Extract, Houston Telegraph newspaper, published at Houston, Texas.

**MOLLUS**
Papers of the Military Order of the Loyal Legion of the United States, a postwar officers' association.

# NOTES

CHAPTER 1. THE FIRST MONTH
[1] Obituary of Julius White from the Evanston Press, published at Evanston, Illinois, May 17, 1890.
[2] MEMORIALS, Illinois Commandery, MOLLUS, Chicago, 1891.
[3] Reeling, Viola C., Evanston, Evanston, 1928.
[4] Journal of Henry Ketzle, no date, in the Mercer County Historical Society Collection, Aledo, Illinois.
[5] From Camp Webb, Chicago, August 21, 1861, DASH.
[6] August 23, 1861, CTR.
[7] September 4, 1861, CTR.
[8] Letter of William Fithian in Danville, Illinois, to Charles Black, September 7, 1861, JCBF.
[9] Journal of Henry Ketzle, no date, in the Mercer County Historical Society Collection, Aledo, Illinois.
[10] Revised Regulations for the Army of the United States, Philadelphia, 1861.
[11] September 20, 1861, CTR.
[12] From the Compiled Service Records of John Mason and Isaac Moore, SNRA.
[13] Statistics compiled from information, SRNA.

CHAPTER 2. THE PATRIARCHS
[1] Past and Present of Lake County, Illinois, Chicago, 1886.
[2] Letter, Josephine Fithian to Charles Black, March 6, 1861, JCBF.
[3] Sandburg, Carl, The War Years, New York, 1926.
[4] Letter, Charles Black to William Fithian, July 3, 1862, JCBF.
[5] Josephine Fithian, from Danville, Illinois, to Charles Black, September 28, 1862, JCBF.
[6] Past and Present of Lake County, Illinois, Chicago, 1886.
[7] Obituary, Elijah M. Haines, ca. 1886, CTR.
[8] Obituary, Elijah M. Haines, ca. 1886, CTR.
[9] Letter, Elijah Haines, from Waukegan, to Adelia Wright, December 19, 1860, EBP.
[10] Letter, January 12, 1891, EBP.
[11] Portrait and Biographical Album, Dupage County, Illinois, Chicago, 1894.
[12] Portrait and Biographical Album of Lake County, Illinois, Chicago, 1891.
[13] Blodgett, Henry, Autobiography, Waukegan, ca. 1888.
[14] Portrait and Biographical Album of Lake County, Illinois, Chicago, 1891.

CHAPTER 3. THE ZOO-ZOO'S
[1] Randall, Ruth P., Colonel Elmer Ellsworth, Boston, 1947, p.33.
[2] Article, May 5, 1862, CTR.
[3] Randall, p. 33.
[4] Ingraham, Charles A., Elmer E. Ellsworth and the Zouave Cadets of 1861, publication of the Chicago Historical Society.
[5] Ibid., p.33.
[6] Quoted in Randall, pp.136-7.
[7] Quoted in Ingraham, p.36.
[8] Reminiscence of Truman Cleveland, November 5, 1912, CTR.
[9] Miller, Henry, H., Ellsworth's Zouaves, Paper read at a meeting of the Survivors of the United States Zouave Cadets at the residence of Colonel Edwin L. Brand, 1918

# THIRTY SEVENTH ILLINOIS

Michigan Avenue, Chicago, Illinois. Published in McIlvaine Mable, Reminiscences of Chicago during the Civil War, Citadel Press, New York, 1967.
[10] Newspaper Article, May 25, 1881, found in the Ellsworth Scrapbook, Chicago Historical Society
[11] Article, Chicago Press Tribune newspaper, August 14, 1860.
[12] Ingraham, op. cit., p.40.
[13] Article, The Taking of Alexandria, Chicago Evening Journal newspaper, ca. May 26, 1861, found in the Ellsworth Scrapbook, Chicago Historical Society.
[14] Letter, Charles Black to his Mother, May 14, 1861, JCBF.
[15] Letter, Charles Black to his Mother, June 16, 1861, JCBF.

CHAPTER 4. THIRTY DAYS AT SPRINGFIELD
[1] Partridge, Charles, Lake County War History and Record, Chicago, 1881, p.461-71.
[2] Article, April 27, 1861, WWG.
[3] Letter, B. Frank Rogers to S.H. Gilbert of the Waukegan War Finance Committee, April 26, 1861, printed May 4, 1861, WWG.
[4] Letter, Eugene Payne, May 10, 1861, WWG.
[5] Letter, Eugene Payne, May 7, 1861, WWG.
[6] Letter, Eugene Payne, May 10, 1861, WWG.
[7] Editorial, James Y. Cory, May 7, 1861, WWG.
[8] July 30, 1861, EBP.

CHAPTER 5. THE WATER MARCH TO ST. LOUIS
[1] Article, September 19, 1861, CTR.
[2] Article, September 20, 1861, CTR.
[3] Article, September 20, 1861, CTR.
[4] Letter, September 21, 1861, DASH.
[5] Letter, Charles Black to his Mother, September 27, 1861, JCBF.
[6] Article, September 26, 1861, CTR.
[7] Letter, Charles Black to William Fithian, September 28, 1861, JCBF.
[8] Letter from Edward Anderson, September 25, 1861, published September 30, 1861, CTR.
[9] General Order 6., September 24, 1861, OBNA.
[10] Revised Regulations for the Army of the United States, Philadelphia, 1861.
[11] Letter, Will Black to his Mother, September 29, 1861, JCBF.
[12] Letter, Charles Black to his sister Mary, October 19, 1861, JCBF.
[13] Letter, Charles Black to William Fithian, September 28, 1861.

CHAPTER 6. BOONVILLE
[1] Letter from Chauncey Morse, October 7, 1861, published October 26, 1861, WWG.
[2] Letter, Charles Black to his sister Mary, October 10, 1861 JCBF.
[3] Letter from Chauncey Morse, October 7, 1861, published October 26, 1861, WWG.
[4] Letter, Charles Black to his Mother, October 22, 1861, JCBF.
[5] Letter, Josephine Fithian to her son Charles Black, October 6, 1861, JCBF.
[6] Letter, William Fithian to Charles Black, October 30, 1861, JCBF.
[7] Eugene Payne, SRNA.
[8] Catton, Bruce, Grant Moves South, Boston, 1960, p.62.
[9] Letter, ca. October 1861, DASH.

# NOTES

[10] Letter, October 13, 1861, DASH.
[11] Frederick Grosshart, SRNA, and entry of October 27, 1861, OBNA.
[12] Letter, Charles Black to his Mother, October 2, 1861, JCBF.
[13] Melton, E.J., History of Cooper County, Missouri, Columbia, 1937, p.91.
[14] Letter, Charles Black to family, October 2, 1861, JCBF.
[15] Letter, "QUOD" to St. Louis Democrat newspaper, November 7, 1861 reprinted November 12, 1861, CTR.
[16] Letter, "XYZ," January 10, 1862, RIA.
[17] Petition to Richard Yates, Governor of Illinois, September 20, 1861, and Letter, September 20, 1861, to Illinois Adjutant General Fuller, RRIA.
[18] Letter, Will Black to William Fithian, December 4, 1861, JCBF.
[19] Petition to Gov. Yates, op. cit.

CHAPTER 7. DEATH BY MUD
[1] Letter, Charles Black to his Mother, October 22, 1861, JCBF.
[2] William Mazelle, SRNA.
[3] Letter, Charles Black to William Fithian, November 22, 1861, JCBF.
[4] Letter, Henry Curtis, to his mother, December 1, 1861, HCJR.
[5] Letter, Henry Curtis, to his Mother, December 1, 1861, HCJR.
[6] Letter, Myron Barnes, January 4, 1862, published January 15, 1861, RIA.
[7] Order Book, December 12, 1861, OBNA.
[8] Order Book, December 12, 1861, OBNA.
[9] Letter, Samuel Hartley, January 4, 1862, published January 15, 1862, RIA.
[10] Letter, Charles Black to his Mother, January 18, 1862, JCBF.

CHAPTER 8. PEA RIDGE
[1] Interview, Asa D. Baker, January 7, 1861, CTR.
[2] Order Book, Special Order 19, January 28, 1862, OBNA.
[3] Letter, Will Black to his sister Rose, February 3, 1862, JCBF.
[4] Letter, Edward Anderson, February 3, 1862, published February 13, 1862, CTR.
[5] Letter, Samuel Heartley, February 19, 1862, published March 12, 1862, WWG.
[6] Article, Eugene Payne, The 37th Illinois at the Battle of Pea Ridge, District of Columbia Commandery, MOLLUS, Washington, 1887.
[7] Henry Colborn, SRNA.
[8] Letter, Will Black to his Mother, March 5, 1862, JCBF.
[9] Monaghan, Jay, Civil War on the Western Border, Boston, 1955, p.231.
[10] Letter, Edward Anderson, published March 24, 1862, CTR.
[11] Letter, March 11, 1862, DASH.
[12] Article, Eugene Payne, op. cit.
[13] Letter, Henry Curtis, March 9, 1862, HCJR.
[14] Moore, Frank, Rebellion Record, New York, 1863, Vol.4, p.249, Narrative from the New York Herald newpaper.
[15]. Baxter, William, Pea Ridge and Prairie Grove, pub. 1864, reprinted, Van Buren, 1957.
[16] Letter, Henry Curtis to his Mother, March 28, 1862, HCJR.
[17] Miller, Francis T. (editor) The Photographic History of the Civil War, reprinted New York, 1957, Vol. X., p.142.
[18] Letter, Will Black to his Mother, March 26, 1862, JCBF.

[19] Order Book, Company E. Diary apparently kept by George Griffith, OBNA.

CHAPTER 9. CASSVILLE
[1] Letter, Messrs. Herrick & Steele, April 1, 1862, WWG.
[2] Article, April 11, 1862, RIA.
[3] Entry, SRNA.
[4] Letter, Edward Anderson, June 4, 1862, CTR.
[5] Letter, March 17, 1862, DASH.
[6] Letter, Will Black to Charles Black, May 22, 1862, JCBF.
[7] Letter, Julius White to Adjutant General Fuller, April 21, 1862, RRIA.
[8] Letter, Julius White to Charles Black, April 21, 1862, JCBF.
[9] Letter, Henry Curtis to his Wife, May 22, 1862, HCJR.
[10] Letter to Charles Black from Regimental Council of Administration, April 20, 1862, JCBF.
[11] Advertisement, January 13, 1864, CTR.
[12] Letter, Will Black to his Mother, July 10, 1862, JCBF.
[13] Letter, Edward Anderson, June 4, 1862, published June 14, 1862, CTR.
[14] Letter, Henry Frisbie, June 25, 1862, published June 14, 1862, CTR.
[15] Ibid.

CHAPTER 10. THE ELECTION
[1] Revised Regulations for the Army of the United States, Philadelphia, 1861.
[2] Letter, Will Black to Charles Black, May 22, 1862, JCBF.
[3] Letter, Owen Lovejoy to Richard Yates, July 14, 1862, RRIA.
[4] Letter, June 25, 1862, EBP.
[5] Letter, July 1, 1862, EBP.
[6] Letter, Wells H. Blodgett to Richard Yates, June 18, 1862, RRIA.
[7] Letter, Charles Black to William Fithian, July 2, 1862, JCBF.
[8] Letter, July 17, 1862, EBP.
[9] Letter, Henry Frisbie to Adjutant General Fuller, July 4, 1862, RRIA.
[10] Letter, William Fithian to Charles Black, July 14, 1862, JCBF.

CHAPTER 11. PUNISHMENT
[1] Letter, July 1, 1862, EBP.
[2] Letter from "W," July 6, 1862, RIA.
[3] Samuel Lemoine, SRNA.
[4] Philip Honlin, SRNA.
[5] Louis Dubois, SRNA.
[6] Timothy Hickey, SRNA, and G.O. 36, July 30, 1862, OBNA.
[7] Miscellaneous Papers, 37th Illinois Infantry, OBNA.
[8] Washington Smith, SRNA.
[9] Special Order 46, July 30, 1862, OBNA.
[10] Letter, Myron Barnes to Wells Blodgett, July 10, 1862, found in Miscellaneous Papers, 37th Illinois Regiment, OBNA.

CHAPTER 12. THE MUTINY
[1] Letter, Will Black to his Mother, August 3, 1862, JCBF.
[2] Letter, David Hick, August 6, 1862, published August 13, 1862, RIA.

# NOTES

³ Letter, August 18, 1862, published August 13, 1862, RIA.
⁴ Letter, September 6, 1862, EBP.
⁵ Frederick Abbey, Record of General Court Martial, August 31, 1862, SRNA.
⁶ Myron S. Barnes, Record of General Court Martial, August 31, 1862, Record Group #153, National Archives, Washington, D.C.
⁷ Letter to Myron S. Barnes, September 2, 1862, signed by forty-four officers of the Post at Springfield, Missouri, SRNA.
⁸ Letter from General James Totten to Lieutenant Colonel C.W. Marsh, September 10, 1862, SRNA.
⁹ Letter, Myron S. Barnes to Richard J. Yates, Governor of Illinois, October 24, 1862, SRNA.
¹⁰ Letter, Myron S. Barnes, January 14, 1863, RIA.

CHAPTER 13. THE BARNES EXIT
¹ Telegram, Charles V. Dickenson to Adjutant General Fuller, August 23, 1862, RRIA.
² Letter, Charles Dickinson to Charles Black, October 28, 1862, JCBF.
³ Letter, Charles Black to Governor Yates, October 28, 1862, RRIA.
⁴ Order Book, ca. July 1862, OBNA.
⁵ Letter, September 21, 1862, EBP.
⁶ Letter, Henry Blodgett to William Fithian, September 25, 1862, JCBF.

CHAPTER 14. THE RELUCTANT BRIGADIER
¹ Julius White, SRNA.
² Article, Chicago Journal newspaper, quoted April 16, 1862, RIA.
³ Article, May 21, 1862, RIA.
⁴ Article, April 16, 1862, RIA.
⁵ Article, April 9, 1862, RIA.
⁶ Article, An Improptu Affair at Evanston, July10, 1862, CTR.
⁷ Letter to his Mother, September 4, 1862, HCJR.
⁸ Article, Julius White, The First Sabre Charge of the War, read January 12, 1888, MOLLUS Papers, Illinois Commandery, pp.25-35.
⁹ Boatner, Mark, Civil War Dictionary, New York, 1959, p.550.
¹⁰ Official Records of the Union and Confederate Armies, published by the War Department, 1880-1901, Vol. XIX, Part I, p.525.
¹¹ Ibid.
¹² Ibid., pp.598-9.
¹³ Robertson, James I., General A.P. Hill, New York, 1987, p.138.
¹⁴ Official Records, op. cit. p.980.
¹⁵ Ibid., p.798.
¹⁶ Ibid., pp.799-800.
¹⁷ Article, The Capitulation of Harper's Ferry, by Julius White, in Battles and Leaders of the Civil War, Vol. II, p.615.
¹⁸ Manuscript, subject Julius White, author unknown, p.11, in the collection of the Evanston Historical Society.

CHAPTER 15. MINDLESS MARCHING
¹ Letter, October 13, 1852, DASH.
² Letter, November 16, 1862, EBP.

# THIRTY SEVENTH ILLINOIS

[3] Letter, Will Black to his Mother, October 13.1862, JCBF.
[4] Letter, E.A. Clark to Charles Black, November 24, 1862, JCBF.
[5] Charles Porter, SRNA.
[6] Letter, November 19, 1862, EBP.
[7] Entry, November 8, 1862, OBNA.
[8] Entry, November 23, 1862, OBNA.
[9] Ibid.
[10] Entry, December 2, 1862, OBNA.
[11] Entry, November 8, 1862, OBNA.
[12] Letter, Charles Black to Egbert Brown, November 26, 1862, RRIA.
[13] Letter, Charles Black to William Fithian, November 26, 1862, JCBF.

CHAPTER 16. PRAIRIE GROVE
[1] Letter, November 19, 1862, EBP.
[2] Ibid.
[3] Private Charles Porter, SRNA, and S.O. 100, OBNA.
[4] Letter, Will Black to his Mother, December 1, 1862, JCBF.
[5] Barney, Chester, Recollections of Field Service with the 20$^{th}$ Iowa, Davenport, Iowa, 1865, p.116.
[6] Letter, Henry Frisbie to Charles Hawes, November 4, 1889, in the collection of the Prairie Grove State Park, Arkansas.
[7] Ibid.
[8] Report of the Confederate General Thomas Hindman on the Battle of Prairie Grove, December 25, 1862, manuscript copy in the Francis Jay Herron Papers, in the collection at the New York Historical Society, New York, N.Y.
[9] Payne, Prairie Grove, p.7.
[10] Letter, December 9, 1862, EBP.
[11] Payne, Prairie Grove, p.7.
[12] Report of Henry Bertram, Lieutenant Colonel (USA) on the Battle of Prairie Grove, in The Rebellion Record, ed. Frank Moore, New York, 1863, Vol. 6, pp.67-68.
[13] Letter, December 9, 1862, EBP.
[14] Payne, Prairie Grove, p.7.
[15] Letter (unpublished), Will Black to the Editor of the St. Louis, Missouri Democrat newspaper, January 4, 1863, JCBF.
[16] John C. Black, unpublished testimony, Record of Court of Inquiry requested by John. C. Black, into his conduct at the Battle of Prairie Grove, SRNA.
[17] Letter, December 11, 1862, EBP.
[18] Letter, December 9, 1862, EBP.
[19] Testimony of Dan Huston, Colonel (USA), Charles Black Inquiry, SRNA.
[20] Letter, Will Black, December 10, 1862, published December 25, 1862, CTR.
[21] Payne, Prairie Grove, p.15.
[22] Letter, January 2, 1863, EBP.
[23] Letter, George E. Griffith, to the National Tribune newspaper, ca. 1914, JCBF.
[24] Letter, Joseph Eaton to the Rock Island Argus, December 11, 1862, published January 7, 1863, RIA.
[25] Letter, December 10, 1862, DASH.
[26] Payne, Prairie Grove, p.15.
[27] Uriah Eberhart, History of the Eberharts, Des Moines, Iowa, 1891, p.236.

# NOTES

[28] Benjamin F. McIntyre, 19th Iowa Infantry Regiment, his diary, published as Federals on the Frontier, ed. N.M. Tilley, Austin, Texas, 1967, p.62.
[29] Letter, Will Black to his Mother, December 9, 1862, JCBF.
[30] Article, quoting a letter from William F. West, Co. A. 37th Illinois, January 7, 1863, RIA.
[31] Addendum to letter of Henry Frisbie to Charles Hawes, November 4, 1889, in the collection at Prairie Grove State Park, Arkansas.
[32] Ibid.
[33] Payne, Prairie Grove, p.14.
[34] Report, Thomas Hindman, op. cit.
[35] Letter, Joseph Eaton, op. cit.
[36] McIntype, op. cit., pp.62-63.
[37] Barney, op. cit., pp.129-31.
[38] Letter, William Fithian to his Wife, December 27, 1862, JCBF.
[39] Dammann, Gordon, Pictorial Encyclopedia of Civil War Medical Instruments and Equipment, Missoula, Montana, 1983, p.1.

CHAPTER 17. THE F WORD
[1] Letter, Will Black to Henry Frisbie, December 14, 1862, found in Frederick Reisser, SRNA.
[2] Letter, January 2, 1863, EBP.
[3] Letters, William Fithian to his Wife, January 1, January 2, and January 17, 1863, JCBF.
[4] Letter, E.A. Clark to F.A. Switzer, Major, Provost Marshal, August 19, 1862, SRNA.
[5] Letter, E.A. Clark to Adjutant General Fuller, February 20, 1863, RRIA.
[6] Letter, E.A. Clark to William Fithian, March 11, 1863, JCBF.
[7] Letter, E.A. Clark to Charles Black, April 8, 1863, JCBF.
[8] Article, January 1, 1863, Daily Missouri Democrat, Record of Inquiry, Charles Black, SRNA.
[9] Letter, Will Black to Charles Black, January 13, 1863, JCBF.
[10] Letter, Will Black to William Fithian, December 10, 1862, JCBF.
[11] Letter, Egbert Brown to Adjutant General Fuller, December 24, 1862, JCBF.
[12] Letter, Charles Dickinson to Charles Black, December 26, 1862, JCBF.
[13] Letter, February 9, 1863. EBP.
[14] Wells Blodgett, SRNA.
[15] Record of Inquiry, Charles Black, SRNA.
[16] Letter, Henry Frisbie to Col. Marsh, A.A.G., March 8, 1863, Henry Frisbie, SRNA.
[17] Revised Regulations for the Army of the United States, Philadelphia, 1861, p.38.
[18] Records, 37th Illinois Infantry, RRIA.
[19] Letter, March 16, 1863, EBP.

CHAPTER 18. THE COURT OF BAD LANGUAGE
[1] Thomas Murphy, SRNA.
[2] Henry Upstone, SRNA.
[3] Almiran Stillman, SRNA.
[4] Infractions of Andrew Hunter, Oscar Sheldon, John Reed, Benjamin Parkhurst, Andrew Baker, Patrick Shields, Thomas Murphy, Thomas Phillips and Phillip Moran are found in OBNA, various dates.

# THIRTY SEVENTH ILLINOIS

[5] Samuel Lee, OBNA.
[6] Letter, Will Black to Charles Black, March 6, 1863, JCBF.
[7] Letter, Eli Bogue to Charles Black, March 11, 1863, JCBF.
[8] Letter, George Bell to Col. Marsh, AAG, March 27, 1863, Miscellaneous Papers, OBNA.
[9] Letter, March 19, 1863, EBP.
[10] Letter, Will Black to Charles Black, March 11, 1863, JCBF.
[11] George Kennicott, SRNA.

CHAPTER 19  MISSOURI IN THE REARVIEW
[1] Letter, Samuel Heartley to Charles Black, February 3, 1863, JCBF.
[2] Letter, John Pound to Charles Black, April 13, 1863, JCBF.
[3] Letter, Charles Black to Richard Yates, April 2, 1863, JCBF.
[4] Letter, Charles Hawes to his Mother, May 7, 1863, published May 21, 1863, RIA.
[5] Miscellaneous Papers, 37th Illinois, OBNA.
[6] Letter, May 22, 1863, DASH.
[7] Order Book, May 18, 1863. OBNA.
[8] Manuscript, found in the Francis J. Herron Papers, New York Historical Society.
[9] Letter, Henry Blodgett to Charles Black, May 2, 1863, JCBF.
[10] Letter, Charles Black to Charles Dickinson, May 25, 1863, JCBF.
[11] Letter, Will Black to his Mother, December 2, 1861, JCBF.
[12] Letter, Josephine Fithian to Charles Black, April 24, 1863. JCBF.

CHAPTER 20. VICKSBURG
[1] Letter, Charles Black to his Mother, June 8, 1863, JCBF.
[2] Eberhart, Uriah, History of the Eberharts, Chicago, 1891, p.240.
[3] Letter, Ransom Kennicott to the Vicksburg Commission, October 28, 1901, in the collection of the Vicksburg National Military Park.
[4] Letter, Charles Black to his Mother, June 19, 1863, JCBF, and Michael Cain, SRNA.
[5] Letter, Will Black to his Mother, June 22, 1863, JCBF.
[6] Order, Charles Black, June 26, 1863, OBNA.
[7] Letter, General W.W. Orme to Charles Black, June 24, 1863, JCBF.
[8] General Order 2., June 8, 1863, OBNA.
[9] Letter, J.S. Messer to the Waukegan Weekly Gazette, June 15, 1863, published July 4, 1863, WWG.
[10] Letter, Ransom Kennicott to Vicksburg Commission, August 24, 1903, in the collection of the Vicksburg National Military Park.
[11] Letter, Will Black to his Mother, July 3, 1863, JCBF.
[12] Letter, June 24, 1863, EBP.
[13] Letter, June 24, 1863, EBP.
[14] Letter, July 4, 1863. EBP.
[15] Letter, July 4, 1863. EBP.

CHAPTER 21. MICROBE WAR
[1] Letter, Benjamin S. Cory, Surgeon, to General John A. Rawlins, found in Eugene B. Payne, SRNA, and letter, Eugene Payne to Charles Black, July 24, 1863, JCBF.
[2] Steiner, Paul E., Disease in the Civil War, Springfield, Ill., 1968, p.10.
[3] Ibid., p.21.

# NOTES

[4] Ibid., p.20.
[5] Ibid., p.169.
[6] Letter, August 7, 1863, DASH.
[7] Letter, July 29, 1863, DASH.
[8] Letter, Eugene Payne to Charles Black, July 24, 1863, JCBF.
[9] Letter, Henry Frisbie to C.S. Lake, Assistant Adjutant General, August 18, 1863, with endorsements, Henry Frisbie, SRNA.
[10] Edwin Mears, Albert Fordham, James Dow, John Carroll, SRNA.
[11] Article, September 12, 1863, WWG.
[12] Letter, Charles Black to Home, August 8, 1863.
[13] Barney, Chester, Recollections of Field Service with the Twentieth Iowa, Davenport, 1865, p.214.
[14] Ibid., p.215.
[15] Ibid.
[16] Letter, August 3, 1863, DASH.
[17] Barney, Chester, op. cit., p.225.
[18] Returns, 37th Illinois, August 1863, RRIA.
[19] Official Records of the Union and Confederate Armies, pub. United States War Department, Washington, D.C., 1880-1901, Vol. XXVI, Part I, pp.321-25, 329-32.
[20] General Field Orders #2 (2d Division), September 23, 1863, OBNA.
[21] Letter, September 18, 1963, EBP.
[22] Bill of H.S. Denison, Sutler, August 29, 1863, JCBF.
[23] Letter, Charles Black to Assistant Adjutant General Leiber, October 13, 1863, Letter Book, OBNA.
[24] General Order #31 (2d Division), October 19, 1863, OBNA.
[25] James O'Brien, SRNA.

CHAPTER 22. INVASION OF TEXAS
[1] General Order #37 (2d Division), October 22, 1863, OBNA.
[2] Tilley, Nannie M. ed., Federals on the Frontier, Austin, 1963 p.242.
[3] Letter, Henry Ketzle, November 20, 1863, published December 16, 1863, RIU.
[4] Letter, November 14, 1863, EBP.
[5] Letter, Charles Black to his Mother, November 12, 1863, JCBF.
[6] Letter, November 12, 1863, EBP.
[7] Ibid.
[8] Ibid.
[9] Letter, Charles Black to his Mother, November 12, 1863, JCBF.
[10] Letter, Erwin Messer, November 10, 1863, published November 16, 1863, WWG.
[11] Letter, November 10, 1863, EBP.
[12] Chatfield, W.H., The Twin Cities: Brownsville, Texas, and Matamoros, Mexico, New Orleans, 1893, p.15.
[13] Ibid., p.13.
[14] Ibid., p.2.
[15] Letter, Charles Black to Home, December 21, 1863, JCBF.
[16] Official Records of the Union and Confederate Armies, pub. United States War Department, Washington, D.C., 1880-1901, Vol. XXVI, p.435, Report of Confederate General Hamilton Bee.
[17] Chatfield, op. cit., p.13.

# THIRTY SEVENTH ILLINOIS

[18] Ibid.
[19] Official Records, Vol. XXXVIII, pp.423-4.
[20] Letter, Charles Black to William Fithian, November 24, 1863, JCBF.
[21] Letter, November 30, 1863, EBP.
[22] Letter, Charles Black to Mary, his sister, November 29, 1863, JCBF, and letter, November 30, 1863, EBP.
[23] Letter, Charles Black to John Moran, December 1, 1863, and Moran's reply, December 2, 1863, OBNA.
[24] Letter, Will Black to Home, December 11, 1863.
[25] Letter, Colonel Henry Bertram to General Francis Jay Herron, January 12, 1864, in the Francis Jay Herron Collection, New York Historical Society.
[26] Lemke, W.J., ed. Captain Edward Gee Miller of the 20th Wisconsin, His War, Fayetteville, 1960, p.21.
[27] Official Records, Vol. XXXIV, Part 1, p.84.
[28] Tilley, Nannie, M., ed. Federals on the Frontier, Austin, 1963, pp.301, 322-3, 326.
[29] Letter, Will Black to Home, May 1, 1864, JCBF.

CHAPTER 23. REENLISTMENT
[1] Letter, Julius White to Adjutant General Allen Fuller, February 5, 1864, RRIA.
[2] Letter, Charles Black to William Fithian, November 24, 1863.
[3] Letter, Eugene Payne to Adjutant General Allen Fuller, February 5, 1864, RRIA.
[4] Letter, Charles Dickinson to Adjutant General Allen Fuller, January 26, 1864, RRIA.
[5] Proceedings of a Meeting of the Line Officers, etc., February 2, 1864. RRIA.
[6] Letter, Henry Ketzle to Rock Island Union, November 20, 1863, published December 16, 1863, RIU.
[7] Eugene Payne, SRNA.
[8] Advertisement, February 13, 1864, WWG.
[9] Letter, Charles Black to William Fithian, November 24, 1863, JCBF.
[10] Letter, Will Black to Home, December 17, 1863, JCBF.
[11] Letter, Will Black to Charles Black, March 8, 1865, JCBF.
[12] Circular, /s/ William Bandy, Adjutant, November 13, 1863, OBNA.
[13] Almiran Stillman, SRNA.
[14] Circular, /s/ William Bandy, Adjutant, November 13, 1863, OBNA.
[15] Court Martial Proceeding, William Wilson, MM1314, Record Group 153, National Archives, Washington, D.C.
[16] Ibid.
[17] Ibid.
[18] Letter, Will Black to Home, February 18, 1864, JCBF.
[19] Letter, Lyman Scoville to Waukegan Weekly Gazette, February 25, 1864, published April 2, 1864, WWG.
[20] Lemke, W.J., ed. Captain Edward Gee Miller of the 20th Wisconsin, His War, Fayetteville, 1960, p.21.

CHAPTER 24. THE REENLISTED 37TH
[1] Special Order #37, Extract #4, February 11, 1864, OBNA.
[2] Letter, Isaac Dodge to C.W. Marsh, AAG, with endorsements, February 20, 1864, Dodge SRNA.

# NOTES

[3] Ibid.
[4] Letter, Charles Black, to Adjutant General Allen Fuller, May 19, 1864, RRIA.
[5] Letter, Wells Morrill to Eugene Payne, December 6, 1870, author's collection.
[6] Article, March 26, 1864, WWG.
[7] Ibid.
[8] Letter, Hiram Kennicott to Charles Black, March 28, 1864, JCBF.
[9] Article, March 30, 1864, RIU.
[10] Article, March 26, 1864, WWG.
[11] Article, March 30, 1864, RIU.
[12] Article, April 2, 1864, WWG.
[13] Letter, Charles Black to William Fithian, April 5, 1864, JCBF.
[14] Letter, Eugene Payne to Adjutant General Allen Fuller, April 20, 1864, RRIA.
[15] Letter, May 12, 1864, DASH.
[16] Letter, Charles Black to his Mother, May 13, 1864, JCBF.
[17] Special Order #33, June 16, 1864, OBNA.
[18] Letter, Charles Black to his Mother, August 24, 1864, JCBF.
[19] Henry Mesler, SRNA.
[20] Letter, Charles Black to Fayette Lacey, June 13, 1864, Letter Book, p.93, OBNA.
[21] Letter, Charles Black to War Department, June 13, 1864, OBNA.
[22] Charge Sheet, Samuel Bell, Miscellaneous Papers, ca. June 1864, OBNA.
[23] Ibid., Thomas Cappock.
[24] Ibid., George Hosely.
[25] Ibid., Thomas Carman.
[26] General Order #4, July 24, 1864, Alpheus Crew, OBNA.

CHAPTER 25. THE DISCHARGED 37TH
[1] Letter, Adelia Payne to Eugene Payne, August 17, 1864, author's collection.
[2] Letter, Eugene Payne to Frederick Speed, Assistant Adjutant General, September 3, 1864, with endorsement of General G.F. McGinnis, SRNA.
[3] Letter, Adelia Payne to Eugene Payne, August 13, 1864, in the author's collection.
[4] Article, October 15, 1864, WWG.
[5] Article, October 23, 1864, WWG.
[6] Article, November 5, 1864, WWG.
[7] Article, November 12, 1864. WWG.
[8] Article, Danforth Defends Himself, January 13, 1864, RIA.
[9] Article, November 12, 1862, RIA.
[10] Article, January 13, 1864, RIA.
[11] Article, March 12, 1862, RIA.
[12] Article, October 12, 1863, RIU.
[13] Article, November 11, 1863, RIA.
[14] Article, November 4, 1863, RIU.
[15] Article, October 12, 1863, RIU.
[16] Letter, November 11, 1863, RIA.
[17] Letter, L.W. Burnett to Rock Island Union, December 16, 1863, RIU.
[18] Letter, Henry Ketzle to Myron Barnes, February 10, 1864, RIU.
[19] Article, November 4, 1863, RIU.
[20] Letter, Henry Ketzle to Myron Barnes, February 10, 1864, RIU.
[21] Article, February 17, 1864, RIU.

# THIRTY SEVENTH ILLINOIS

[22] Article, February 17, 1864, RIU.
[23] Article, May 25, 1864, RIA.
[24] Editorial, May 21, 1864, RIU.
[25] Editorial, August 24, 1864, RIA.
[26] Editorial, November 30, 1864, RIU.
[27] Dayton, Aretas, A., Article, Raising Union Forces in Illinois, 1861-1865, Journal of the Illinois State Historical Society, March 1961, pp.410-35.
[28] Ibid.
[29] Article, Chicago Tribune, March 14, 1863.
[30] Letter, Will Black to his Mother, March 19, 1863, JCBF.
[31] Letter, Josephine Fithian to Charles Black, March 9, 1863, JCBF.
[32] Letter, Will Black to Josephine Fithian, his Mother, March 29, 1863, JCBF.
[33] Letter, Josephine Fithian to Charles Black, July 31, 1863, JCBF.
[34] Letter, Josephine Fithian to Charles Black, August 28, 1863, JCBF.
[35] George W. Barker, SRNA.
[36] Dayton, op. cit., p.430.
[37] Dayton, op. cit., p.432.
[38] Letter, Mary Black to Charles Black, November 16, 1863, JCBF.
[39] Letter, Will Black to Charles Black, November 30, 1863, JCBF.
[40] Letter, Charles Black to William Fithian, December 1, 1863, JCBF.

CHAPTER 26. DEVALL'S BLUFF
[1] General Order 41, October 14, 1864, OBNA.
[2] Letter, Charles Black to Will Black, November 23, 1864, JCBF.
[3] Special Order #68, October 14, 1864, OBNA.
[4] Ibid.
[5] Letter, Charles Black to his Mother, December 16, 1864, JCBF.
[6] Letter, Charles Black to his Mother, December 5, 1864, JCBF.
[7] Ketzle, Henry, Military History, Manuscript Collection, Mercer County Historical Society, Illinois.
[8] Article, July 16, 1864, WWG.
[9] Letter, Charles Black to Adjutant General Allen Fuller, December 24, 1864, RRIA.
[10] Letter, Charles Black to his sister Mary, November 26, 1864, JCBF.
[11] Letter, Charles Black to his Mother, November 14, 1864, JCBF.
[12] Letter, Charles Black to Adjutant General Allen Fuller, November 1, 1864, RRIA.
[13] Letter, Erwin Messer to Charles Black, January 5, 1865, JCBF.
[14] Letter, Charles Black to his Mother, November 27, 1864, JCBF, and Special Order #66, October 22, 1864, OBNA.
[15] Sutler Bill from Spearing and Cutler, Sutlers to 20th Iowa, to Charles Black, JCBF.

CHAPTER 27. FORT BLAKELEY
[1] Circular No 1, January 1, 1865, OBNA.
[2] Letter, Charles Black to his Mother, January 8, 1865, JCBF.
[3] Letter, from Lt. Col. John N. Wilson, Assistant Inspector General, Department of the Gulf, January 9, 1865, Miscellaneous Papers, Record Group 159, National Archives, Washington, D.C.
[4] Letter, Charles Black to his Mother, February 6, 1865, JCBF.

# NOTES

⁵ Hills, Charles S., The Last Battle of the War, MOLLUS Papers, Missouri Commandery, St. Louis, 1892, p.181.
⁶ Statement ca. April 9, 1865, re: John Blanquart, found in collection, JCBF.
⁷ Sandburg, Carl, The War Years, New York, 1939, Volume I., p.214.
⁸ Letter, Ransom Kennicott to Charles Black, May 9, 1865, JCBF.
⁹ Hosea Young, SRNA.
¹⁰ Letter, Wells Morrill to Eugene Payne, June 26, 1865, in the author's collection.

CHAPTER 28. THE LAST DAYS OF BLACK AND FRISBIE
¹ Letter, Fayette Lacey to Charles Black, June 22, 1865, JCBF.
² Letter, Fayette Lacey to Charles Black, June 29, 1865, JCBF.
³ Ibid.
⁴ Letter, Charles Black to his Mother, August 1, 1865, JCBF.
⁵ Restaurant Bill from Victor's Restaurant, Brownsville, Texas, August 2, 1865, JCBF.
⁶ Article, November 4, 1864, RIU.
⁷ Compiled Service Records, 92d United States Colored Troops, Record Group 94, National Archives, Washington, D.C.
⁸ Letter, Henry Frisbie to Thomas W. Conway, October 2, 1865, Court Martial Record of Colonel Henry Frisbie, MM3349, Record Group 153, National Archives, Washington, D.C.
⁹ Ibid.
¹⁰ Stanton, E.M., Annual Report of the Secretary of War, Washington, D.C., 1865.
¹¹ Letter, Thomas W. Conway to Henry Frisbie, October 5, 1865, M3349.
¹² Statement of Henry N. Frisbie, December 2, 1865, Record of the Board of Inquiry, SRNA.
¹³ Ibid., Testimony of Sergeant Richard Johnson and Sergeant William Hall.
¹⁴ Judgement of Judge Advocate, MM3349.
¹⁵ Report of the Select Committee on the New Orleans Riots, pp. 411-14, U.S. Gov't Printing Office, 1867.

CHAPTER 29. THE FINAL PAY CALL
¹ Ketzle, Henry, Military History.
² Letter, Ransom Kennicott to Major Emery, July 12, 1865, OBNA.
³ Ibid.
⁴ Letter, Ransom Kennicott to Colonel Perkins, August 11, 1865, OBNA.
⁵ Ibid.
⁶ Special Order #82, 13$^{th}$ Army Corps, July 13, 1865, and Special Order #84, July 19, 1865, OBNA.
⁷ Historical Encyclopedia of Illinois, Chicago, 1900, pp.562-3.
⁸ Special Order #7, August 28, 1865, OBNA.
⁹ General Order #4, October 18, 1865, OBNA.
¹⁰ Article, ca. October 1865, HTEL.
¹¹ Ketzle, Henry, Military History.
¹² Letter, Ransom Kennicott, November 2, 1865, OBNA.
¹³ Letter, Ransom Kennicott, December 4, 1865, Letter Book, OBNA.
¹⁴ Letters, Judson Huntley to Ransom Kennicott, Letter Book, December 16, December 27, December 31, 1865, OBNA.
¹⁵ Letter, A.W. Morgan, March 23, 1866, Letter Book, OBNA.

[16] Hospital Books, 37th Illinois Veteran Volunteer Infantry, Record Group 94, National Archives, Washington, D.C.
[17] Edward Peterson, SRNA.
[18] Article, February 22, 1865, HTEL.
[19] Article, April 11, 1866, HTEL.
[20] P.T. Early, Record of General Court Martial, March 10, 1866, MM3586, Record Group 153, National Archives, Washington, D.C.
[21] Letter, Wells Morrill to Charles Black, March 28, 1866, JCBF.
[22] Edward Rose, Endorsement Book, December 8, 1865, OBNA.
[23] George E. Griffith, Diary, February-March 1866, Letter Book, OBNA.
[24] Letter, Adjutant of the 12th Illinois Cavalry to Adjutant General Allen Fuller, May 19, 1866, re: John Seabury, RRIA, and Item, May 20, 1966. HTEL.
[25] Letter, Judson Huntley to General Oakes, May 30, 1866, Miscellaneous Papers, 37th Illinois, RRIA.

## CHAPTER 30. THE HAYMARKET BOMBING

[1] Constitution, Proceedings and Roster of the 37th Illinois Volunteer Infantry Veteran Association, Chicago, 1885, p.4-5.
[2] Black, William P., Introduction to the Story of the Anarchists as Told by Themselves, originally published in October 1886 in the Journal Knights of Labor, reprinted as The Autobiographies of the Haymarket Martyrs, ed. Philip Foner, American Institute for Marxist Studies, New York, 1969.
[3] Zeisler, Sigmund, Reminiscences of the Anarchist Case, Chicago, 1926, p.7.
[4] Pierce, Bessie Louise, A History of Chicago, Chicago, 1957, p.268 and Note 72.
[5] Barnard, Harry, Eagle Forgotten, The Life of John Peter Altgeld, New York, 1938, p.97.
[6] Zeisler, op. cit., p.31.
[7] Barnard, op. cit., p.101.
[8] Article, "Black's Great Fight," ca. 1890, unidentified newspaper clipping, JCBF.
[9] Article, "Pen Picture of Captain Black," ca. 1890, unidentified newspaper clipping, JCBF.
[10] Ibid.
[11] Article, "A Texas Romance," August 27, 1886, Houston Daily Post, JCBF.
[12] David, Henry, The History of the Haymarket Affair, New York, 1936, p.239.
[13] Letter, Eugene Payne to Adelia Wright, December 4, 1860, EBP.
[14] Aldeman, William, Haymarket Revisited, Chicago, 1957, p.22.
[15] Barnard, op. cit., p.113.
[16] Article, "Violated Law Vindicated," November 12, 1887, New York Times.
[17] Ibid.
[18] Ibid.
[19] David, op. cit., p.237.

# Bibliography

### 1. NEWSPAPERS

Chicago Times

Chicago Tribune

Houston, Texas Daily Telegraph

New Orleans Daily Picayune

New York Times

Rock Island Weekly Argus

Rock Island Weekly Union

Waukegan Weekly Gazette

### 2. ARTICLES

Black, John Charles, "Our Boys in the War," MOLLUS, Illinois Commandery, originally read June 9, 1892, Vol II. pp 443-56. Chicago 1891.

Blodgett, Edward A., "The Army of the Southwest and the Battle of Pea Ridge," MOLLUS, Illinois Commandery,.

Blodgett, Wells H., "Address on the Occasion of the Dedication of the Monument Erected at Bellefontaine Cemetery...", May 30, 1894, ST. Louis, 1894.

Constitution, Proceedings and Roster of the 37th Illinois Volunteer Infantry Veteran Association, Chicago, 1885.

Crabtree, John D., "Recollections of the Pea Ridge Campaign," MOLLUS, Illinois Commandery, Chicago, 1897.

Emery, William H., and Jack Hilbing, "Exploits of the 37th Illinois Regiment and John Charles Black," Illinois Postal Historian, May 1985.

Frye, Dennis E., "The Siege of Harpers Ferry," Blue & Gray Magazine, September 187, pp. 8-27, 47-54.

Haselberger, Fritz, "Wallace's Raid on Romney in 1861," West Virginia History, Vol. XXVII #2, January 1966, pp. 97-110.

Hills, Charles S., "The Last Battle of the War – Recollections of the Mobile Campaign," MOLLUS, Missouri Commandery, St. Louis, 1892.

# THIRTY SEVENTH ILLINOIS

Leake, Joseph B., "Campaigns of the Army of the Frontier," MOLLUS, Illinois Commandery, Vol. II, Chicago, 1892.

Noble, John W., "Battle of Pea Ridge or Elkhorn Tavern," MOLLUS, Missouri Commandery, St. Louis, 1892, pp. 211-42.

Payne, Eugene B., "The 37th Illinois Veteran Volunteer Infantry at the Battle of Pea Ridge, Arkansas," MOLLUS, District of Columbia Commandery, Washington, D.C., 1892.

Payne, Eugene B., "Prairie Grove," MOLLUS, District of Columbia Commandery, Washington, D.C. 1892, pp. 3-22.

White, Julius, "The First Sabre Charge of the War, September 3, 1862," MOLLUS, Illinois Commandery, Chicago, 1895, Vol iii, pp. 25-35.

### 3. MANUSCRIPTS

Records of the Adjutant General, State of Illinois, Illinois State Archives, Springfield, Illinois. (37th Illinois).

Ash, David, collection of letters from the field to his fiancée/wife, Eliza Messenger, in the Collection of the Army Military History Institute, Carlisle Barracks, Pennsylvania.

John Charles Black and Family Collection, Illinois State Historical Library, Springfield, Illinois. This collection includes letters to and from John Charles Black, William Perkins Black, Mary Black, Josephine Fithian, and William Fithian.

Curtis, Henry, collection of letters to his Wife and his Mother, United States Army Military History Institute, Carlisle Barracks, Pennsylvania.

Frisbie, Henry N., letter to Charles Hawes, in the collection at Prairie Grove State Park, Prairie Grove, Arkansas.

Herron, Francis J., Miscellaneous Papers, in the collection of the New York Historical Society.

Individual Compiled Service Records, 37th Illinois Veteran Volunteer Infantry, Record Group 94, National Archives, Washington, D.C.

Ketzle, Henry, Military History of the 37th Illinois Volunteer Infantry, in the collection of the Mercer County Historical Society, Aledo, Illinois.

Morse, Alcander O., A Journal, Recording his Daily Experiences while a Member of Company I, 37th Illinois, September 1862 – September 1864, Courtesy of Robert C. Nash, Sr.

# BIBLIOGRAPHY

Payne, Eugene B., collection of letters to and from Eugene B. Payne, his wife Adelia Wright Payne, his brother-in-law George Frederick Wright, his cousin-in-law Elijah M. Haines, and others, in the author's collection.

White, Julius, miscellaneous collection of recollections of Julius White and Evanston, news clippings, and pictures, Evanston Historical Society, Evanston, Illinois.

### 4. BOOKS

Anderson, Edward, "Camp Fire Stories," Chicago, 1900.

Barney, Chester, "Recollections of Field Service with the Twentieth Iowa," Davenport, 1865.

Barnard, Harry, "Eagle Forgotten, The Life of John Peter Altgeld," New York, 1938.

Blodgett, Henry W., "Autobiography," Waukegan, 1906.

Boatner, Mark, "Civil War Dictionary," New York, 1959.

Botkin, B.A. ed., "A Civil War Treasury of Tales, Legends, and Folklore," New York 1947.

Browne, Junius Henri, "Four Years in Secessia," Chicago, 1865.

Catton, Bruce, "Grant Moves South," Boston 1960.

Catton, Bruce, "Reflections on the Civil War," ed. John Leekley, New York, 1981.

Charfield, W.H., "The Twin Cities: Brownsville, Texas and Matamoros, Mexico," New Orleans, 1893.

Dammann, Dr. Gordon, "Pictorial Encyclopedia of Civil War Medical Instruments and Equipment," 2 Vols., Missoula, 1983 and 1988.

Daddysman, James W., "The Matamoros Trade," Newark, Delaware, 1984.

David, Henry, "The History of the Haymarket Affair," New York, 1936.

Davis, William C., ed., "The Image of War: 1861-1865," Six Volumes, Garden City New York, 1983

Eberhart, Uriah, "History of the Eberharts," Chicago, 1891.

Escott, George S., "History and Directory of Springfield," Springfield, Missouri, 1878.

Foner, Philip S., ed., "The Autobiographies of the Haymarket Martyrs," New York, 1969.

# THIRTY SEVENTH ILLINOIS

Foster, Clyde D., "Evanston's Yesterdays," Evanston, 1956.

Frisbee, Olin E., "The Frisbee – Frisbie Family Genealogy," 1964, available at the New York Public Library.

Haskew, Corrie P., "Historical Records of Austin and Waller Counties [Texas]," Houston, 1969.

Herr, George W., "Episodes of the Civil War," San Francisco, 1890.

"History of Barry County [Missouri]," Chicago, 1888. Goodspeed Bros.

"History of Cooper County, Missouri," ed.H. Levens and N. Drake, St. Louis, 1876.

"History of Greene County, Missouri," St. Louis, 1883.

"History of Newton, Lawrence, Barry, and McDonald Counties, Missouri," Chicago, 1888, Goodspeed Bros.

Ingraham, Charles A., "Elmer Ellsworth and the Zouaves of '61," Chicago, 1937.

Hyde and Conard, eds., "Encyclopedia of the History of St. Louis, Missouri," St. Louis, 1899, Vol. III.

"Illinois at Vicksburg," prepared by the Vicksburg Military Parks Commission, Chicago, 1907.

Johnson, Robert V., and Clarence Buel, eds., "Battles and Leaders of the Civil War," New York, 1887, Vol. II.

Kirkland, Frazar, "The Pictorial Book of Anecdotes and Incidents of the War of the Rebellion," Hartford, 1866.

Lathrop, David, "The History of the Fifty Ninth Regiment Illinois Volunteers," Indianapolis, 1865.

Lemke, W.J., ed., "Captain Edward Gee Miller of the Twentieth Wisconsin, His War," Fayetteville, 1960.

Melton, E.J., "History of Cooper County, Missouri," Columbia, 1937.

"Military Service Records, a Select Catalog of National Archives Microfilm Publications," Washington, D.C., 1985.

Miller, Francis T., ed., "The Photographic History of the Civil War," reprint New York, 1957, Vol. X.

Monaghan, Jay, "Civil War on the Western Border 1854-1865," Boston, 1955.

Moore, Frank, ed., "Rebellion Record," New York 1863.

# BIBLIOGRAPHY

Mullins, Michael, "The Fremont Rifles, A History of the 37th Illinois Veteran Volunteer Infantry," Wilmington, North Carolina, 1990.

Munden, Kenneth W., and Henry Putney Beers, "The Union, A Guide to Federal Archives Relating to the Civil War," Washington, D.C., 1986.

"Our War Songs North and South," pub. S. Brainard's Sons, Cleveland, 1887.

Payne, Eugene B., ed., "United States Interior Department, Digest of Decisions of the Department of the Interior in Appealed Pension and Bounty Land Claims," Washington, D.C., 1905.

Partridge, Charles A., "Lake County War History and Record," Chicago, 1884.

Pearson, G.C., "The Past and Present of Vermilion County," Chicago, 1903.

Perry, Albert J., "History of Knox County, Illinois," Chicago, 1912, Vol. I.

Pierce, Bessie L., "A History of Chicago," Chicago, 1957, Vol. III.

"Portrait and Biographical Record of Cook & Dupage Counties, Illinois," Chicago, 1884.

"Portrait and Biographical Record of Knox County, Illinois," Chicago, 1884.

Randall, Ruth P., "Colonel Elmer Ellsworth," Boston 1947.

Reeling, Viola, C., "Evanston, Its Land and People," Evanston, 1928.

"Reminiscences of Chicago During the Civil War," intro. Mabel McIlvaine, New York, 1967.

"Report of the Joint Committee on the Conduct of the War, in Three Parts," Washington, 1863.

Roberts, Bobby, and Carl Moneyhon, "Portraits of Conflict," Fayetteville, 1987.

Sandburg, Carl, "Abraham Lincoln: The War Years," New York, 1939.

Shalhope, Robert E., "Sterling Price," Columbia, Missouri, 1971.

Snetsinger, Robert J., ed., "Kiss Clara for Me, The Story of Joseph Whitney and His Family, early days in the Midwest, and soldiering in the American Civil War [96th Illinois]," State College, Pennsylvania, 1969.

Steiner, Paul E., "Disease in the Civil War, Natural Biological Warfare in 1861-1865," Springfield, Illinois, 1968.

Tilley, Nannie M., ed., "Federals on the Frontier: The Diary of Benjamin F. McIntyre [19th Iowa]," Austin, Texas, 1963.

"Revised Regulations for the Army of the United States," pub. By Authority of the War Department, Philadelphia, 1861.

# THIRTY SEVENTH ILLINOIS

Vance, J.W., "Report of the Adjutant General of the State of Illinois," Springfield, 1886.

Webb, W.L., "Battles and Biographies of Missourians," Kansas City, Missouri, 1900.

Willard Frances E., "A Classic Town: The Story of Evanston," Chicago, Woman's Temperance Publishing Association, 1891.

Wharton, Clarence R., "History of Fort Bend County, Texas," San Antonio, 1939.

Zeisler, Sigismund, "Reminiscences of the Anarchist Case," Chicago, 1926.

# Index

Abbey, Frederick, iv, 4, 16, 22, 23, 24, 50, 77, 78, 82, 83, 116, 140, 150, 151, 156, 195, 237
Abolition, 14, 82, 195, 196, 317
Academy of Music, 24
Adams, Newton, 149
Alabama River, 211
Alden, John, 15
Aledo, Illinois, 237
Alexander, Col., 328
Alexandria, Virginia, 25
Alleyton, Texas, 220, 221
Altgeld, Gov. John, 234
Anarchist, 229, 231, 234
Anderson, Edward, i, 4, 42, 43, 62, 91, 107, 140, 167, 204, 238, 254-7, 261, 269, 276, 324-7
Anschutz, David, 288, 313
Antietam, Maryland, 68, 96, 102-4
Antioch, Illinois, 196
Arbiter Zeitung, 229, 230
Armpriest, John, 224
Army of Northern Virginia, 97, 102, 211
Army of the Frontier, 54, 103, 237
Army of the Southwest, 79
Arnold, Isaac, 7

Artificiers, 6, 92
Ash, David, 2, 50, 63, 65, 71, 119, 149, 154, 163, 202, 236, 241-3, 255, 274-5, 280, 288, 313-4
Atkinson, William, 180
Audubon Rifles, 3, 4, 16
Baird, Major, 103
Baker, Andrew, 148
Ballantine Family, 41
Band, 1, 2, 6, 55, 56, 62, 161, 185-6, 332
Bandy, William, 5, 10, 66, 75, 91, 155, 180, 185, 194, 243, 250, 268, 270, 274
Baney, William, 92
Banks, Gen. Nathaniel, 169, 310
Banzhaf, Major, 88
Barker, George, 203, 248, 299
Barker, Julia, 15
Barker, William, 318
Barlow, William, 78, 266-8
Barnes, Myron, i-ii, iv, 4, 6, 38, 42-6, 50-1, 59-62, 64, 69-70, 74, 77, 79-83, 93, 127, 151-152, 180, 186-7, 196-7, 201, 204, 235, 314, 320
Barney, Chester, 295
Barrancas, Florida, 210-11
Barrington, Illinois, 190

# THIRTY SEVENTH ILLINOIS

Baseball, 30, 336
Bates, George, 7
Baton Rouge, Louisiana, 185, 216, 335
Baxter, William, 263
Beardsley, Maj. J.M., 199-200, 315
Beaumont, Texas, 219-21
Bee, Gen. Hamilton, 172
Belgian Rifles, 38
Bell, George, 74, 81, 110, 154-5, 185, 288, 290
Bell, Samuel, 189
Benton Barracks, 34, 35, 38
Bentonville, Arkansas, 55, 106, 146
Big Black River, 164
Bigelow, William, 166, 180
Bishop, Pleasant W. (Chaplain), 167, 185, 310
Bishop, William, 223
Black Hawk Wars, 10
Black, John Charles, iv, 3-4, 6, 9, 11, 16, 26-7, 37-8, 41, 50, 53, 55, 58-75, 80, 88-9, 92-4, 98, 107, 109-10, 115-16, 120, 134-44, 149-50, 154-5, 157, 159, 161, 163, 166, 170-77, 180-1, 184, 188-9, 194-5, 202-14, 228, 241, 244-5, 270-71, 276, 280, 288-95, 298, 301, 308, 319, 322-4, 331-3
Black, William P. (Will), i, iv, 4, 14, 27, 38, 59, 67, 71, 88, 107, 112-13, 116, 136, 140-3, 149, 151, 159-60, 174, 177-9, 182, 185, 193-5, 201, 203-4, 228-35, 244, 288, 291, 293, 307, 313, 318, 322, 324, 331-3
Black, LaRose, 178
Black, Mary, 307
Blanquart, John, 210
Bleakley, Henderson, 73
Blodgett, Aziel, 15
Blodgett, Edward, 14, 15, 228, 237
Blodgett, Henry, 11-14, 28-30, 46, 73-4, 93, 155, 186, 195-6, 273, 321
Blodgett, Israel, 9, 14
Blodgett, Wells, 46-7, 73-4, 88, 92, 107, 139, 142, 144, 148, 154-7, 228, 287, 291-2
Bloomfield, Missouri, 153
Blunt, Gen. James (Doctor), 111-14, 117-18, 120-1, 143
Board of Trade, 33, 185, 202, 273, 294
Boardman, Calvin, 14
Boardman, William, 14
Boca Chica, Texas, 169
Bogue, Eli, 149
Bolivar Heights, 100, 103
Booneville, Missouri, 39-50, 54, 64, 70, 77, 106, 158, 244, 248-9, 252
Booth, John Wilkes, 211, 317, 318
Boston Mountains, Arkansas, 56, 136

# INDEX

Bounty-jumping, 189
Boyd, James, 210
Brackett, William, 92
Brazoria County, Texas, 337
Brazos Santiago, Texas, 169, 170, 171, 213
Brenham, Texas, 221, 223, 224, 339
Brevet Appointments, 37
Brown, General Egbert, 47, 73, 77-89, 96, 108, 110, 137, 141-2, 150, 155, 184, 197, 273
Brown, Louis, 79
Brown, William, 109
Brownell, Francis E., 25
Brownsville, Texas, 170-5, 178, 182, 184, 189, 193, 199, 210, 212-14, 314, 332
Buenos Aires, Argentina, 236
Burgess Corps, 24
Burnett, L.W., 305
Burnside, Gen. Ambrose, 105, 195, 236
Burton, James, 92
Butler, Gen. Benjamin, 98
Cahabin, Alabama (prison), 211
Cain, Michael, 158
Cairo, Illinois, 158, 182, 185, 189, 226
Calkins, Maj. W.H., 327
Camp Bliss, 146
Camp Bloomington, Missouri, 146
Camp Douglas, 191, 199
Camp Fry, 187, 190

Camp Register, 43
Camp Schofield, 146
Camp Stephens, 60
Camp Webb, 2, 7, 16, 27, 32, 46, 54, 91, 225
Camp Yates, 16, 29-32, 193
Campbell, Dick, 81
Campbell's Station, Battle of, 237
Cane Hill, Arkansas, 112-18, 123, 285
Cape Girardeau, Missouri, 153-4, 157, 185, 306
Cappock, Theodore, 149
Cappock, Thomas, 189
Carey, James, 189
Carey, William, 188-9,
Carman, Thomas, 79, 190-1
Carrol, John, 164
Cassville, Missouri, 59-72, 77-9, 81, 91, 94-5, 106-7, 138, 146, 151, 176, 205, 263-5, 268, 280
Castle, Levi, 62
Cavier, Julius, 210
Chalk Bluffs, Missouri, 153-4
Chandler, Colonel, 60, 143, 307
Chapman, Lt. Thomas, 210
Charity Hospital, 299
Chicago, Illinois, i, iii, 1-5, 7, 9-12, 14, 16-18, 20, 23-4, 28, 29-34, 38, 41, 46, 50-1, 54, 60, 67, 69, 74, 78, 95, 104-5, 117, 127, 144, 149, 151, 153, 182, 185-92, 195, 201-2, 205, 228-31, 235-8,

241, 248, 255, 273, 291, 294, 300, 317, 319-20
Chicago Journal, 95
Chicago News, 232
Chicago Sunday Mercury, 21
Chicago Times Newspaper, 310, 317
Chicago Tribune, 43, 140, 292
Chickamauga, 15, 237
Clancy, John, 226, 227
Clapp, Squire, 299
Clark, Asst. Surgeon Elijah, 42, 112
Clarke, Francis E., 190
Clarke, Major, 300
Cleveland, Pres. Grover, 235
Cline, John, 210
Coal Valley, Illinois, 49, 199
Cobos, Jose, 170, 171, 172
Colborn, Henry, 55, 372
Colorado, Silver Plume, 15
Colt Revolving Rifle, 35, 38, 57, 117, 297, 317
Columbus, Texas, 185, 220-1, 333
Cones, J.S., 20
Consolidation, 152, 189, 194, 207, 220
Conway, Thomas W., 335
Cooper, D.D., 210
Copperhead, 160, 196-204, 290, 294, 301-2, 305, 307, 310, 316-17, 321
Corinth, Mississippi, 71, 187
Cortina, Juan, 170-75, 182, 213, 308
Cory, James, 31
Cotton, 165, 168-74, 178, 218-19, 224, 297, 337
Council of Administration, 66
Crane Creek, Missouri, 106
Crane's Alley, Chicago, Illinois, 230
Crater, Battle of the, 105, 187, 195
Crew, Alpheus, 191
Cronk, John, 206
Cross Hollows, Arkansas, 55, 59, 60, 62, 106, 146
Cruver, Austin, 62
Culbertson, James, 207
Curtis, Gen. Samuel, 34, 54, 57-61, 108, 111-12
Curtis, Henry, iv, 49, 50, 53, 58-9, 65, 69, 71, 80, 91, 94, 95-6, 166, 200, 228, 236, 245, 258, 272, 281
Custer, Gen. George, 223
D'Utassy, Colonel, 100, 101
Dana, Gen., 169, 214
Danforth, Joseph, iv, 197-201, 301-5, 315-16
Danville, Illinois, i, iv, 3-10, 11, 27, 52, 58, 75, 76, 93, 108-9, 137, 149, 156, 178-9, 189, 195, 201-4, 210-11, 228, 235, 290, 299, 307, 321
Darkesville, Virginia, 96
Davenport, Iowa, 199, 295
Davis, Col. E.J., 173
Davis, Fred, 207

# INDEX

Davis, Gen. Jefferson, 54, 57, 58, 317
Davis, Jeff, 318
Davis, Lt. Col. Hasbrouck, 96, 101, 173
Davis, Pat, 324, 325, 327
Day, C.W., 62
Day, James, 207
Day, Lt. James, 91
Day, Mrs., 94
Degan, Mathias, 230
Delay, Joseph, 203, 247
Des Plaines, Illinois, 186
Desertion, 54, 79, 146, 149, 178. 189, 202, 205, 206
Detroit, Michigan, 12, 24
DeValls Bluff, Arkansas, 323
Devereux, Arthur F., 18
DeVilliers, Charles A., 18, 23
Diarrhea, 30, 32, 41, 62, 94, 159, 162, 163, 188, 223, 306
Dickinson Hall, 28, 186, 196
Dickinson, Charles, 1, 6, 35, 38, 55, 66, 71, 73, 75-8, 88, 91-3, 111, 139-42, 147, 149, 151, 155, 157-8, 167, 176-7, 181-2, 185, 194-5, 288
Dickinson, Mrs. Charles, 56, 93, 277
Dickinson, Towns, 62
Disease, 6, 40, 50, 146, 159, 162, 164, 180, 222, 236, 238, 294
    Diarrhea, 30, 32, 41, 62, 94, 159, 162-3, 188, 223, 306
    Dropsy, 164
    Dysentery, 40-3, 48, 52, 61, 109, 159, 162-3, 188, 320
    Malaria, 40, 42, 48, 52, 61, 109, 158, 162-3, 165, 188, 193, 254, 319
Disney, Horace, 210
Dodge, Isaac, 45, 150, 184-5
Donaldsville, Louisiana, 215-6
Doty, Mrs., 106
Douglas, Stephen A., 198, 202, 302
Dow, James, 164
Downer's Grove, Illinois, i, 14
Doyle, William, 205
Dr. Ball's Plantation, 226
Driscoll, Elbridge, 110
Dry Tortugas, 88, 341
DuBois, Louis, 92
Dudley, George, 2, 385
Dug Springs, Missouri, 151
Dulanty, Michael, 10
DuPage, Illinois, 11, 14
Dutcher, John, 154
Dwyer, Charles, 267
Earhart, Cyrus, 180
Early, P.T., 224
Eaton, Joseph, 44-5, 62, 106, 122, 153
Eaton, Lavinia, 153
Eaton, Little Charlie, 62
Eaton, Mrs. Joseph, 94
Edinburg, Texas, 174
Edwards, George, 220
Edwards, Joseph, 7
Eighth Indiana Infantry, 62

# THIRTY SEVENTH ILLINOIS

Eighth Missouri Cavalry, 52, 139
Election, ii, 1, 4, 16, 29, 63, 68-78, 91, 93, 177, 187, 195-6, 201, 204, 272-3
Eleventh Indiana, 241
Eleventh Indiana Infantry, 16, 26, 28
Elk Creek, Missouri, 144, 146, 148-152
Elkhorn Tavern, 53
Ellsworth, Alma, 298
Ellsworth, Ephriam Elmer, iv, 3, 4, 16-29, 82, 141, 185
Emancipation Proclamation, 196, 202, 203, 286
Emery, Alfonso, 205
Emery, Alfonzo, 205
Emery, Michael, 34, 86, 87
Engel, Louis, 229, 231
Enlistment Bounty, 203
Enrollment Act, 201, 202
Evanston, Illinois, iv, i, 1, 59, 60, 64, 95, 104, 195, 236, 237, 271
Fairman, Gallio, 110, 206, 219, 225, 263
Farmington, Missouri, 157
Farnsworth, Edward, 337
Farris, Doctor, 203
Fayetteville, Arkansas, 61, 106, 113-14, 136, 137, 139, 146, 151, 278, 286
Fifteenth Iowa, 162
Fifty-Ninth Illinois, 39, 56, 138, 265

Fillmore, Millard, 9
Finley Creek, Missouri, 106
First Arkansas, 91, 281
First Missouri Cavalry, 274
Fithian, Henry, 5, 42, 137
Fithian, Josephine, iv, 156, 299, 301
Fithian, William, 5, 9-15, 41-2, 58, 64, 73, 75, 93, 123, 137, 201-2, 235, 276, 285-7, 299, 307, 321
Fitzgerald, Morris, 58
Florentino, Don, 174, 308
Folsom, DeForrest, 62
Foraging, 43, 65, 67, 78, 159, 173, 242-3 255-6
Ford, Col. Thomas, 102
Ford's Springs, Missouri, 106
Fordham, Albert, 163
Forrest, Gen. Nathan B., 187
Fort Blakeley, 209-11,
Fort Brown, 172
Fort Dearborn, Illinois, 14
Fort Griffin, 219
Fort Lee, New Jersey, 78
Fort Manhaset, 219
Forty-Eighth Missouri, 237
Forty-Eighth Ohio, 221, 223, 333
France, 18, 170, 213
Franklin, General, 98
Frazier, Sam, 204, 307
Freedmen's Bureau, 215-16, 334
Freeport Landing, Texas, 170
Fremont Hotel, 219

# INDEX

Fremont Rifles, 2, 6, 228, 515
Fremont, Gen. John C., 2, 33-4, 38, 42, 44, 49, 72
Frick, John, 3, 6, 35, 43-4, 46, 54, 91
Frisbie, Henry N., ii, iv, 3, 6, 37-8, 70-73, 79, 85, 90-91, 120, 129, 138, 139-41, 154, 157, 160-63, 166-7, 176, 204, 213-216, 219, 236, 287
Fuller, Illinois Adjutant General, 64, 73, 75, 91, 185, 187, 200, 287
Gage, Samuel, 166
Galbraith, Franklin, 205
Galesburg, Illinois, 235
Galva, Illinois, 1, 267
Galveston, Texas, 212, 219-20, 223, 226, 333, 337
Geneseo Republican, 198
Gleason, Michael, 313
Golen, Henry, 92
Gomphers, Samuel, 232
Goodale's Tavern, 14
Grand Coupee, Louisiana, 218
Granger, Gen. Robert, 329
Grant, Gen. Ulysses, 17, 89, 98, 158, 160-1, 211
Grant, Illinois, 14
Gravenhorst, Joseph, 166
Gravois Bottom, Missouri, 54
Gravois Creek, Missouri, 54, 255
Gregg, James, 180
Greve, Andreas, 91
Grey Beard Regiment, 316
Griffith, George, 117, 225

Griswold, Melinda, 12
Grosshart, Fred, 43
Guerillas, 14, 44-5, 61, 64, 106, 158, 238, 285-6, 327, 328
Guiness, Lyman, 203, 204, 299, 321
Gulf of Mexico, 168, 184, 212-13
Haines, "Long John," Mayor, 11
Haines, Elijah, 9, 11-13, 23, 29-31, 74, 93-4, 142, 167, 177, 195-6, 232, 321
Haines, John, 11
Haines, Melinda, 321
Hainesville, Illinois, 12, 196
Half Day, Illinois, 196
Hall, Sgt., 217
Halleck, General Henry, 53-5, 99, 102-3
Happe, Frank, 154
Harman, John, 147
Harper's Ferry, iv, 27, 49, 94-104, 245
Harrison, Peter, 79
Hartsville, Missouri, 81, 146
Hawes, Charles, 69, 85, 107, 119, 166, 180, 219, 245, 320
Hawkins, Colonel, 203, 299
Hawkins, Jacob, 68, 109
Hay, John, 21, 22
Haymarket Bombing, iv, 229-34
Hays, Private, 223
Hazlewood, Missouri, 146

# THIRTY SEVENTH ILLINOIS

Heartley, Samuel M., 52, 88,152
Heitharands, Henry, ii, 180
Hempstead, Texas, 221
Hendee, Vernon, 109
Henry County, Illinois, 9
Henry Revolving Rifle, 300
Herndon, Billy, 23
Herron, Gen. Francis J., 98, 108, 112-14, 117, 119-21, 139, 143, 149, 152, 155, 158, 175, 179, 181, 209, 214
Hessey, William, 207
Hick, David, 198, 199
Hickey, Timothy, 78, 79, 409
Hicks, Napoleon, 75, 116, 150, 259, 274
Hill, Gen. Ambrose P., 102
Hilliard, Albert, 57
Hindman, Gen. Thomas, 112-14, 121, 123-4, 136, 285
Holmes, Delos, 191
Honlin, Philip, 78, 149
Hooke, E.G., 4
Horr, Lee, 150
Hosely, George, 190-1
Houston Telegraph, 221, 333, 338
Houston, Texas, 220-226, 232, 282, 313, 336-7, 340
Howells, William D., 232
Hubbard, Major, 63, 88
Humeston, Surgeon Luthur, 41-2, 62, 67-8, 73, 79, 83-4, 137, 163, 185, 277

Hunter, Andrew, 147, 223-4, 339
Hunter, General David, 49, 102
Huntley, Judson J., iii, 13, 28, 142, 177, 190, 195, 221-2, 227
Huntsville, Arkansas, 106, 142, 146, 191, 328
Huston, Col. Dan, 116, 143, 331
Iches, Samuel, iv, 94-6
Illinois University (Wheaton), 14
Indian Creek, Illinois, 9
Indians, 9, 12, 14-15, 56, 57, 63, 69, 259, 260, 309
Ingersoll, Robert, 232
Innis, William, 4, 16, 28-32
International Workingman's Association, 230
Iowa Fifth Infantry, 45
Iowa, Osage, 42
Island City Hotel, 186, 187, 200
Jackson, Gen. Thomas J., 100-102, 104
Jacobs, Frank, 207
James, Jesse, 56
Jefferson City, Missouri, 38, 39, 41
Jennings, John, 207
Jennings, William, 198, 303
Jewell, Francis, 228
Johnson, William, 142, 148
Jones, John, 154

# INDEX

Jordan, John, 4, 38, 48, 49, 69, 245-6
Juarez, Benito, 175
Judd, Artemis, 109
Kain, James, 207
Kankakee, Illinois, 220
Keech, Milton, 210
Keitsville, Missouri, 58, 59, 61, 106, 146, 151
Kellan, Robert, 79
Kelly, Johnson M., 138
Kelsey, Julius, 78
Kendall, Art, 224
Kennedy, John, 149
Kennerville, Louisiana, 209-10
Kennicott, George, 151, 184, 185, 189, 221
Kennicott, Hiram, 9, 10, 11, 13, 151, 167, 184, 185, 186, 195
Kennicott, Ransom, iii, iv, 3-4, 6, 16, 22-24, 35, 38, 62, 71, 78, 107, 139, 140-2, 147, 150-1, 160, 176-7, 184, 204-5, 207, 210, 213, 219, 221, 223, 225, 228, 289, 293, 333, 337
Ketzle, Henry, 177, 180-1, 199, 315
Keys, Scout, 67, 269, 270
King, Thomas, 166
Kirby, George, 241
Knobly Mountains, 26
Knox, Judge, 33
Knoxville, Tennessee (Siege of), 237
Lacy, Fayette, 188

Lafayette Rifles, 1, 2
Lafayette, Illinois, 78
Laimbeer, Capt. John, 3, 6, 38, 45-6, 71, 83, 86, 91, 111, 141-2, 148, 157, 236, 292
Lake County, Illinois, 3, 10-15, 28-9, 31, 93, 176, 188, 190-1, 195
Lake County Patriot, 12
Lake County Visitor, The, 14
Lake Shore Railroad, 14
Lake Zurich, Illinois, 196
Lamine River, Missouri, 40, 48-54, 70, 203, 247, 254, 257
Lamon, Ward, 10, 211
Lamon, William, 203, 290, 299
Lathrop, David, 261
Lawther, Colonel, 81
Lebanon, Missouri, 54
Lee, Gen. Robert E., 96
Lee, Jim, 57, 58
Lee, John Mayne, 325
Lee, Richard, 298
Lee, Samuel, 149
Leetown, Arkansas, 57, 58
Lemoine, Samuel, 78, 266, 268
Leonard, Martin, 180
Liberty, Texas, 219
Libertyville, Illinois, 159, 164, 196
Lincoln Land Association, 217
Lincoln, Pres. Abraham, i, 1, 2-3, 9-10, 17, 21-26, 42, 49, 54, 64, 149, 196, 202-3, 206, 211, 217, 286

# THIRTY SEVENTH ILLINOIS

Lingg, Louis, 229-32
Linn Creek, Missouri, 54-5, 256
Liquor, 60, 65, 67, 114, 178, 274, 282, 298, 306, 340
Little Piney Creek, Missouri, 152
Little York, Missouri, 106
Little, William, 122
Lockport, Illinois, 12, 146
Lookout Mountain, Battle of, 237
Loudoun Heights, 100
Lovejoy, Owen (Congressman), 72, 111
Lyon, Nathaniel, 61
MacGreal, Hortensia, 232
Madison, Indiana, 41
Mahan, Lawrence, 205
Malaria, 40, 42, 48, 52, 61, 109, 158, 162, 163, 165, 188, 193, 254, 319
Malta, New York, 17
Manierre Rifles, 3, 14
Manistee, Michigan, 186
Manzer, Lazell, 222, 226, 429
Marblehead, Massachusetts, 237
Marion, Illinois, 202
Marlatt, William, 58
Marmaduke, Gen. John, ii, 119-21, 142, 147, 153
Marr, Lt., 108, 143
Martinsburg, Virginia, 27, 96, 97, 99, 244

Maryland Heights, 100, 103-4, 245
Mason, 93
Mason, John, 7
Masonic Order, 71
Matamoros, Mexico, 170, 172-5, 178
Mattoon, Illinois, 248, 300
Mazelle, Lt. William, 48
Mc. E Dye, Colonel, 144, 163, 293
McAllister, Thomas, 154, 210
McAuliffe, William, 148, 342
McBride, General, 68
McCarthy, Dennis, 148, 432
McClellan, Gen. George, 17, 97-104, 113, 196
McClernand, Gen. John, 175
McColloch, Gen., 58
McCullough's Springs, Missouri, 86, 112, 146
McDearmon, Frank, 44
McDonald, Archie, 85
McGibbon, Major, 157
McGunnigle, Bernard, 341
McIntosh, Gen., 58
McKay, George F., 154
Mears, Edwin, 7
Mechanicsburg, Ohio, 10
Mechanicsville, New York, 17
Meeker, Theodore, 92, 248, 276, 285
Mendota, Illinois, 3, 4, 52, 61, 186
Meisner, Sylvester, 67, 68

# INDEX

Memphis, Tennessee, 185, 187, 318
Merrill, George, 150-1, 221
Mesler, John, 188, 206, 437
Messer, Edwin, 185
Messer, Erwin, 3, 6, 15, 35, 43, 61, 71, 78, 109, 142, 147, 159, 167, 176, 177, 206, 265, 288, 289
Messer, J.S., 15, 164
Messer, Mrs. Erwin, 106
Mexican National Guard, 171
Mexican War, i, 98
Mexico, 314
Milburn, Illinois, 196
Miles, Col. Dixon, 97-104
Militia, Vermilion County, 10
Miller, Hugh, 92
Miller, Jacob, 207
Miller, Jerry Brown, 223
Milroy, Maj. Gen., 329
Milstead Ranch, Texas, 173
Minns, Frederick, 298-9
Minter Plantation, 220
Missouri Democrat Newspaper, 292
Missouri Ninth Infantry, 39, 49
Missouri State Militia, 47, 77, 90, 96, 137
Missouri, German Home Guard, 44
Mobile, Alabama, 205, 210-13, 220
Montgomery, Alabama, 211
Moore, Isaac, 7
Moore's Plantation, 55

Moran, John, iii, 47, 142, 148, 149, 174, 219, 227
Morey, Lorenzo, 69, 180-1, 209, 237
Morgan, Benjamin, 111
Morganza, Louisiana, 166, 188, 193, 306
Morning Report, 179, 188, 222
Morrill, Wells, 185, 207, 225, 336-8
Morris, Congressman Isaac N., 200
Morse, Alcander, 305
Morse, Chauncey, 13, 41, 72, 76, 181, 223, 277, 337
Mt. Vernon, Missouri, 81
Mulligan's Irish Brigade, 41
Murphy, Captain, 143
Murphy, John (Surgeon), 62, 166, 264-5
Murphy, Thomas, 148, 205
Music, 32, 53, 57, 136, 207, 245, 255, 309, 317, 322, 332
Musicians, 6, 7, 36, 207
Natchez, Mississippi, 185
National Guard Cadets, 18
Nausler, John, 150
Neosho, Missouri, 81
New Madrid, Missouri, 153, 163, 185
New Orleans, Louisiana, i, 165-6, 168, 176, 180, 182, 184, 188-9, 209, 214, 218, 226, 236, 298, 317, 334
Newell, Thomas, 43
Newport, Illinois, 196

## THIRTY SEVENTH ILLINOIS

Newtonia, Missouri, 81, 106, 136, 278
Niauga River, Missouri, 256
Nineteenth Iowa Infantry, 114-118, 122, 166
Ninety Sixth Illinois Infantry, 15, 237
Ninety-First Illinois, 167
Ninety-Fourth Illinois, 164, 220
Ninety-Second U.S. Colored Troops, 176, 188-9, 204, 213
Ninety-Seventh Illinois, 220
Ninety-Sixth Ohio, 162
Ninth Corps, 105, 236
Noble, John, 259
Norkett, Billy, 104, 105
Northwestern University, 12
O'Brian, James, 167
O'Leary, Mrs., 105, 449
Oath of Allegiance, 137
Oath of Alliegence, 285
Oglesby, Gov., 232
One Hundred Fortieth Illinois, 186, 201, 204, 235
One Hundred Twenty-Eighth Illinois, 202
One Hundred Twenty-sixth New York Infantry, 103
Ord, Gen. E.O.C., 184
Orme, Gen. W.W., 159, 164
Osage River, Missouri, 54, 55, 256
Osage, Missouri, 106
Osborn, Charles, 200

Otterville, Missouri, 43-50, 156, 248, 252, 254, 257
Ozark, Missouri, 67, 79, 81-2, 106-7, 110, 113, 146
Padre Islands, Texas, 169
Palmer House, 228
Palmito Ranch, 214
Palo Alto, Texas, 170
Parkhurst, Benjamin, 147, 148
Parks, Andrew, 224
Parsons, Albert, 229, 232-3
Patrick, William, 62
Patterson, Edward, 210
Payne, Adelia, 193, 320, 321
Payne, Eugene ii, iv, 3-4, 6, 11-16, 28-34, 37, 42, 44, 55, 58, 71-4, 76-7, 93, 106, 110, 112, 114-17, 121, 139, 144, 152, 157, 160-5, 168, 173, 176, 178, 180, 182, 185, 187, 191, 193-5, 202, 204, 228, 232, 290, 337-8
Payne, John, 203, 299
Payne, Thomas H.L., 9, 11, 79, 111
Pea Ridge, 14, 53-55, 60-1, 64-5, 68, 77, 95, 106-7, 116, 118, 138, 141, 146, 191, 214, 228, 259-63, 271, 279, 285
Peck, John, 60, 72, 77, 82-3, 87, 96, 138, 154, 159, 169, 256, 271, 277, 283, 290
Peck, Mrs. John, 94
Pemberton, Gen. John, 160, 161

# INDEX

Pentwater, Michigan, 186
Peoria, Illinois, 310
Petersburg, Virginia, 105, 195
Peterson, Edward, 223
Philleo, William, 166, 176, 219, 320
Phillips, Thomas, 148
Pickett, Horace, 207
Pierce, Consul Leonard, 174, 175
Pike, Albert, 57, 58, 259, 260
Pilot Knob, Missouri, 149, 153-4, 157, 166
Pilot Township, Illinois, 300
Piney River, Missouri, 146, 152, 154
Pinkerton, Allen, 25
Pittsburgh, Fort Wayne, and Chicago Railroad, 14
Plank, John, 207
Point Isabel, 184
Polen, James, 207
Pond Springs, Missouri, 106
Pope, General John, 38, 42, 44-5, 98
Port Hudson, 165, 168, 185, 204, 213-17, 335
Port Royal, 317
Porter, Charles, 92, 108, 112
Post Exchange, 65
Postley, Charles, 223
Potomac River, 100, 104, 113
Pound, John, 82-88, 91, 152
Prairie Grove, iv, i, ii, iv, 10, 79, 112-14, 114, 124, 134, 136-143, 147-8, 150, 178, 211, 263, 285

Preemption, Illinois, 237
Price, General Sterling, 45, 49, 53-56, 59-61, 257-8
Princeton, Illinois, 191
Quincy, Massachusetts, 238
Rancho La Lomita, Texas, 173
Rancho Tabasco, Texas, 173
Rapides Parish, Louisiana, 218
Recruiting, 2, 4-5, 17, 42, 91, 136, 178, 204
Red River, 185, 187, 214, 218
Reed, Charles, 241
Reed, John, 147
Reenlistment, 175, 181-2, 184, 192
Regulations, 3, 36, 46, 84, 100, 144, 158, 209, 217
Reisser, Frederick, 136
Reticker, John, 228
Reynosa, Texas, 173, 174, 308
Richmond, Texas, 221
Richmond, Virginia, 96, 201
Riggs, Henry, 79, 166
Riley, Albert, 149
Ring, Joseph, 67-8
Ring, William, 61-2, 263
Rio Grande City, 173-4, 180
Rio Grande River, 170, 173
Risdon, Oliver, 155, 166
Roaring River, Missouri, 68
Robideau Creek, Missouri, 146
Robinson Mills, Missouri, 110
Robinson, Edward, 136
Rock Island Argus, 95, 122, 197-200, 315
Rock Island, Illinois, ii, iv, 3-4, 6, 43, 48, 53, 58-60, 67, 69,

543

79, 85, 89, 95, 119, 122, 146, 149, 179, 186-7, 196-204, 223-4, 235, 237, 246, 305, 315
Rock Island Union, 196-8, 201, 235
Rock River Seminary, 14
Rockford City Grays, 20
Rogers, B. Frank, 16, 28-31
Romney, Virginia, 26
Rose, Edward, 92, 225
Rosecrans, Gen., 184
Ruiz, Manuel, 171-175
Rust, Phineas, 3-4, 6, 35, 38, 43, 51, 59, 71-2, 110, 148, 152, 191
Ryan, John, 271
Sabine Pass, Texas, 219-20
Sabine, Texas, 219-20
Sands, William, 166
Saratoga, New York, 17
Scalps, 57, 58, 200, 259-60
Schofield, Gen. John M., 94, 106, 109, 113, 144, 155, 237
Scott, Gen. Winfield, 18, 21
Scott, Sir Walter, 23, 26
Seabury, John, 226
Second Louisiana Engineers, 169
Selma, Alabama, 211, 213
Seneca Falls, New York, 11
Serna, Jesus de la, 172-4
Seventy-Sixth Illinois, 220
Shaw, Augustus, 149
Shaw, George B., 232
Sheldon, Oscar, 147

Shenandoah River, 100
Shepard, Cpl. Hugh, 51, 52
Sheridan, Gen. Philip, 17, 55, 98
Sherman House Hotel, 2
Sherman, Gen. William, 17, 98
Shields, Patrick, 148
Shiloh, 14
Short, John, 308
Sigel, Gen. Franz, 56, 57
Simons, Adolphus, 62
Simpson, Bishop, 7
Sixteenth Corps D'Afrique, 169
Sixth Corps, 98
Slaves, 1, 14, 47, 82, 137, 160, 164, 196-7, 202, 215-16, 219, 283, 285
Smith, Alden, 109
Smith, George, 62
Smith, Henry L., 177
Smith, Mrs., 94
Smith, Solomon, 7
Smith, Washington, 79
Smithtown, Missouri, 48
Snyder's Bluff, Mississippi, 296
Soldier's Aid Society, 199, 315, 316
Sowles, Oscar, 207, 337
Spanish Fort, 210
Spies, August, 229, 233
Spring Creek, Missouri, 146
Springfield, Illinois, iv, 22, 24, 28, 142, 204, 232, 236, 300, 332

# INDEX

Springfield, Missouri, 49, 54-6, 61, 63, 67, 72-3, 77-82, 85-6, 89, 91-95, 106-7, 111-13, 136-8, 142, 146-9, 152, 178, 184, 197, 257, 258, 259, 274, 278, 286, 291

St. Charles, Louisiana, 188, 318

St. Charles, Missouri, 38

St. Francis River, 153

St. Louis Democrat, 139, 143

St. Louis, Missouri, 6, 7, 24, 33-5, 38, 59, 63, 70, 72, 88, 89, 112-13, 140, 143-4, 151-54, 157-8, 161, 167, 184-5, 197, 214, 248, 277

Steele, Gen. Frederick, 60, 210, 211, 212, 213

Sterling's Farm, 166

Stillman, Almiran, 147, 179

Stubbs, Stillman, 7, 8

Sugar Creek, Arkansas, 55, 258

Suggs Plantation, 220

Sutlers, 65-7, 117, 205, 208, 268

Syracuse, Missouri, 50-1, 54, 68

Syracuse, New York, 24

Tamaulipas, Mexico, 171-2, 174

Tampico, Mexico, 174

Taylor, Dick, 165-6

Taylor, Pres. Zachary, 165

Tebbetts, Charles, 228

Tennyson, Alfred, 21

Terry's Saloon, 224

Texas, i, 56, 163-179, 184, 189, 191-2, 211-214, 219-223, 226-8, 308, 314, 336-7

Texas Rangers, 171

Thespian Hall, 45

Thirty-Eighth Iowa, 162, 182

Thompson, Johnson, 191

Three Widows, The, 146

Tipton, Missouri, 54, 90, 438

Totten, Gen. James, 88-9, 106-13, 146, 149, 152, 155, 282, 290, 292-3

Travinio, John, 174

Trimble, Colonel, 101

Troy, New York, 17

Trumbull, Lyman, 7

Twelfth Illinois Cavalry, 96, 226

Twentieth Iowa Infantry, 119, 122, 160-1, 278

Twentieth Wisconsin Infantry, 114-15, 117

Twenty-Seventh Missouri Volunteers, 152

Twenty-sixth Indiana Infantry, 85, 88, 115-18, 166, 294

Twenty-Third Corps d'Afrique, 176

U.S. Insane Hospital, 167

Upstone, Henry, 147

Urbana, Ohio, 10

Van Buren, Arkansas, 136, 263

Van Dorn, Gen. Earl, 56

Vandever, General, 161, 164

Versailles, Missouri, 54

# THIRTY SEVENTH ILLINOIS

Vicksburg, Mississippi, i, 42, 158-165, 168, 185-7, 220, 295-6
Von Sehlen, Captain, 101
Wabash College, 16, 26
Wallace, Lew, 16, 26, 73
Warrensburg, Missouri, 237
Warrenton, Mississippi, 158
Washburne, Elihu, 11, 291
Washington, D.C., 237, 281
Wauconda, Illinois, 195
Waukegan, Illinois, 4, 11-16, 28-32, 60-1, 68, 79, 93, 109, 112, 163, 186, 190-1, 193, 195-6, 204, 237, 279, 321
Wear, Millie, 253
Webber's Ranch, Texas, 173
Wechsler, Joseph, 207
Welsh, Robert, 109
West Point, 3, 17, 24, 107
Whig Party, 14
Whiskey, 37, 59, 66, 67, 78, 90, 114, 157, 166, 206, 208, 223, 226, 306
Whitcomb, O.A., 62
White River, 182
White, Julius A., ii-iv, 1-7, 24, 27, 32-3, 35, 37-8, 45-54, 57, 59-60, 64-76, 91, 94-105, 133, 155, 176, 182, 185-7,193-5, 199, 205-6, 228, 236, 252-3, 255, 270-4, 276, 290
Whitney, Charles, 166
Wiffin, Fred, 220
Wilde, Oscar, 232
Williams, Lt. Warren A., 91
Wilson, Lt. Col. John N., 209
Wilson, William, 180-182, 207, 224
Wilson's Creek, Missouri, 61, 86
Winchester, Virginia, 27, 96
Wolfe, Udolpho, 67
Wolford, Herman, iii, 46, 71, 78-82, 108, 110, 122, 147, 151, 154, 158, 164, 177, 179, 207, 223
Women, 34, 77, 166, 215-16, 225, 255, 279, 298, 309, 319, 331
Wood, William, 205
Wool, Gen. John, 95, 97, 99, 103
Wright, Adelia, 12, 513, 539
Wright, J.C., 33
Wright's Grove, 2-5, 7, 33
Yates, Governor Richard, 9, 14, 46, 72-76, 89, 93, 202, 273, 274
Yazoo, Mississippi, 158, 164, 169, 185, 220, 296
Yellville, Missouri, 68
Young, Hosea, 211
Young, Samuel, 207
Zouave, iv, 3-4, 15-22, 24, 26, 28-9, 33, 82, 141, 185
Zouaves, Vermilion, 10

www.ingramcontent.com/pod-product-compliance
Lightning Source LLC
Chambersburg PA
CBHW030328240426
43661CB00052B/1566